A MENCKEN CHRESTOMATHY

T0204449

H. L. MENCKEN

A Mencken Chrestomathy

EDITED AND ANNOTATED
BY THE AUTHOR

VINTAGE BOOKS
A Division of Random House
New York

First Vintage Books Edition, May 1982
Copyright © 1916, 1918, 1919, 1920, 1921, 1922, 1924, 1926, 1927
1932, 1934, 1942, 1949 by Alfred A. Knopf, Inc.
All rights reserved under International and Pan-American
Copyright Conventions. Published in the United States by
Random House, Inc., New York, and simultaneously in Canada
by Random House of Canada Limited, Toronto. Originally
published by Alfred A. Knopf, Inc., New York, in June 1949.

Library of Congress Cataloging in Publication Data
Mencken, H. L. (Henry Louis), 1880-1956.
A Mencken chrestomathy.
Reprint. Originally published: New York: Knopf, 1949.
I. Title.
[PS3525.E43A6 1982]   818'.5209   81-52593
ISBN 0-394-75209-0   AACR2

Manufactured in the United States of America
Cover photograph courtesy of Wide World Photos
3 5 7 9 C 8 6 4 2

PREFACE

IN my title I revive the word *chrestomathy* in its true sense of "a collection of choice passages from an author or authors," and ignore the late addition of "especially one compiled to assist in the acquirement of a language." In the latter significance the term is often used by linguists, and some of the chrestomathies issued by them in recent years — for example, Dr. Edgar H. Sturtevant's "Hittite Chrestomathy" of 1935 — are works of capital importance. But I see no reason why they should have a monopoly on what is not, after all, their invention. Nor do I see why I should be deterred by the fact that, when this book was announced, a few newspaper smarties protested that the word would be unfamiliar to many readers, as it was to them. Thousands of excellent nouns, verbs and adjectives that have stood in every decent dictionary for years are still unfamiliar to such ignoramuses, and I do not solicit their patronage. Let them continue to recreate themselves with whodunits, and leave my vocabulary and me to my own customers, who have all been to school. *Chrestomathy* is actually more than a century old in English, which makes it quite as ancient as *scientist*, which was invented by William Whewell in 1840, or *anesthetic*, which was proposed by Oliver Wendell Holmes I in 1846. In Greek, where it was contrived by joining *chrestos*, meaning useful, and *mathein*, meaning to learn, it goes back to Proclus Disdochos, who used it in Athens in the year 450.

Whether anyone will find anything useful in what follows, or learn from it otherwise, is not for me to guess, but at all events I like the word better than the *omnibus*, *reader*, *treasury*, *miscellany*, *panorama* and *portable* that have been so horribly overworked of late. The aim of the volume is simply to present a selection from my out-of-print writings, many of them now al-

v

most unobtainable. They come mostly from books, but others are magazine or newspaper pieces that never got between covers, and a few of them are notes never previously published at all. I have an enormous collection of such notes, mainly accumulated for books that, after long struggles, failed to get themselves written, and some day I may gather them into a couple of volumes. The books levied on here are the six of the "Prejudices" series, "A Book of Burlesques," "Damn: a Book of Calumny," "In Defense of Women," "Making a President," "Notes on Democracy" and "Treatise on Right and Wrong." All save two of these had fair successes in their day, and I still receive frequent correspondence about them, but they are so full of the discussion of matters now of only historical interest that I have hesitated to let them be reprinted in toto. It seemed to be much more rational to dig out of them the material that continues to be of more or less current interest, and to print all of it in one volume, at a price substantially less than the cost of a dozen. I have done my own editing, and the judicious may observe some evidence that I have occasionally allowed partiality to corrupt judgment, but I assume that any other editor would have been guilty of a similar softness. Some of the lesser pieces following — for example, "The Sahara of the Bozart," my bathtub hoax and my translation of "The Declaration of Independence" into the American vulgate — have carried on a vigorous life for years, and I have therefore thought it worth while to give them one more embalming before consigning them to statistics and the devil.

In general, I have made few changes in the original texts, and in consequence several thumpingly false prophecies and other howlers are preserved. But when it seemed to make for clarity I have not hesitated to change the present tense into the past, and to omit repetitive and otherwise unnecessary passages. In all cases where I could determine it I have given the date and place of original publication. My later books — for example, "The American Language" and its Supplements and the three "Days" books — are not represented, for all of them are still in print.

For the same reason I have passed over "The Artist," "Christmas Story" and "Treatise on the Gods," the last of which came out in a revised edition so recently as 1946. What the total of my published writings comes to I don't know precisely, but certainly it must run well beyond 5,000,000 words. A good deal of it, of course, was journalism pure and simple — dead almost before the ink which printed it was dry. But I certainly do not regret that I gave so much of my time and energy, especially in my earlier years, to this journalism, for I had a swell time concocting it, and in its day it got some attention. Even in my later years, with wisdom radiating from me like heat from a stove, I have occasionally gone back to it, to my complete satisfaction and the apparent approval (or horror) of the customers. There is something delightful about getting an idea on paper while it is still hot and charming, and seeing it in print before it begins to pale and stale. My happiest days have been spent in crowded press-stands, recording and belaboring events that were portentous in their day, but are now forgotten. These recordings usually died with the events, but I am well aware, as an old book reviewer, that multitudes of books have died too, including many once gloated over as masterpieces.

Those who explore the ensuing pages will find them marked by a certain ribaldry, even when they discuss topics commonly regarded as grave. I do not apologize for this, for life in the Republic has always seemed to me to be far more comic than serious. We live in a land of abounding quackeries, and if we do not learn how to laugh we succumb to the melancholy disease which afflicts the race of viewers-with-alarm. I have had too good a time of it in this world to go down that chute. I have witnessed, in my day, the discovery, enthronement and subsequent collapse of a vast army of uplifters and world-savers, and am firmly convinced that all of them were mountebanks. We produce such mountebanks in greater number than any other country, and they climb to heights seldom equalled elsewhere. Nevertheless, we survive, and not only survive but also flourish. In no other country known to me is life as safe and agreeable,

taking one day with another, as it is in These States. Even in a
great Depression few if any starve, and even in a great war the
number who suffer by it is vastly surpassed by the number who
fatten on it and enjoy it. Thus my view of my country is predominantly tolerant and amiable. I do not believe in democracy, but I am perfectly willing to admit that it provides the
only really amusing form of government ever endured by mankind.

Baltimore   H. L. MENCKEN

TABLE OF CONTENTS

I. *Homo Sapiens*

	PAGE
The Life of Man	3
Man's Place in Nature	4
Meditation on Meditation	6
Coda	9

II. *Types of Men*

The Romantic	10
The Skeptic	10
The Believer	11
The Toiler	11
The Physician	12
The Scientist	12
The Business Man	13
The King	13
The Metaphysician	13
The Average Man	14
The Truth-Seeker	15
The Relative	15
The Relative-in-Law	15
The Friend	16
The Philosopher	16
The Altruist	17
The Iconoclast	17
The Family Man	18
The Bachelor	18
The Good Man	19
The Eternal Male	19
The Slave	20

III. *Women*

The Feminine Mind	21
Women as Outlaws	28
The Cold Woman	30
Intermezzo on Monogamy	32
The Libertine	34
The Lure of Beauty	36

	PAGE	
The Incomparable Buzz-Saw		40
The War Between Man and Woman		41
The Nature of Love		44
The Eternal Farce		46
The Helpmate		47
The Sex Uproar		48
Women as Christians		50
The Lady of Joy		54
A Loss to Romance		57
The Balance Sheet		58
Compulsory Marriage		58
Cavia Cobaya		60
Art and Sex		61
Offspring		61
Sex Hygiene		62
Eugenics		62
The Double Standard		63
The Supreme Comedy		63
Woman as Realpolitiker		64
After-Thoughts		64
Romantic Interlude		65
Apologia		66

IV. *Religion*

The Cosmic Secretariat	67
The Nature of Faith	69
The Restoration of Beauty	73
Holy Clerks	73
The Collapse of Protestantism	76
Immune	80
A New Use for Churches	81
Free Will	82
Sabbath Meditation	84
The Immortality of the Soul	86
Miracles	88
Quod est Veritas?	89
The Doubter's Reward	89
Holy Writ	90
The Powers of the Air	92
Memorial Service	95

V. *Morals*

The Origin of Morality   **PAGE**   99
The Good Citizen   103
Free Will Again   108
An Ethical Dilemma   110
Honor   111

VI. *Crime and Punishment*

The Criminal Law   112
The Penalty of Death   118
On Hanging a Man   121
Cops and Their Ways   126

VII. *Death*

On Suicide   129
Under the Elms   132
Exeunt Omnes   134
Clarion Call to Poets   139

VIII. *Government*

Its Inner Nature   145
More of the Same   146
The Politician   148
Governmental Theories   152
Note on a Cuff   153

IX. *Democracy*

Its Origins   154
A Glance Ahead   157
The Democratic Citizen   159
A Blind Spot   162
Rivals to Democracy   164
Last Words   166

X. *Americans*

The Anglo-Saxon   169
American Culture   178

XI. *The South*

The Sahara of the Bozart	**PAGE**	184
The Confederate Mind		195
The Calamity of Appomattox		196
A Class A Blunder		200

XII. *History*

Historians	201
Forgotten Men	202
Revolution	206
New England	207
New Deal No. 1	209
The Greeks	213
War	216
A Bad Guess	218
Undying Glories	219

XIII. *Statesmen*

Pater Patriæ	220
Abraham Lincoln	221
Portrait of an Immortal	223
A Good Man in a Bad Trade	226
Roosevelt I	229
In Memoriam: W. J. B.	243
The Archangel Woodrow	248
Coolidge	251
Imperial Purple	254

XIV. *American Immortals*

Mr. Justice Holmes	258
Professor Veblen	265
John D.	276

XV. *Odd Fish*

A Good Man Gone Wrong	279
Valentino	281
An American Bonaparte	285
Sister Aimée	289

XVI. *Economics*

To Him That Hath   PAGE 293
Capitalism 294
On Getting a Living 297
Personal Note 300

XVII. *Pedagogy*

The Educational Process 301
Travail 307
Classical Learning 311
The Boon of Culture 313
Bearers of the Torch 315

XVIII. *Psychology*

Psychologists in a Fog 317
The Mind of the Slave 319
The Crowd 323
The Art Eternal 325

XIX. *Science*

Hypothesis 329
Darwin 329
Caveat Against Science 330
The Eternal Conundrum 333
The Universe 337
The Boons of Civilization 339

XX. *Quackery*

Christian Science 343
Chiropractic 346
The Fruits of Comstockery 351
The Foundations of Quackery 353
Hooey from the Orient 355
The Executive Secretary 357
The Husbandman 360
Zoos 365

XXI. *The Human Body*

Pathological Note 368
The Striated Muscle Fetish 370
Moral Tale 372

Comfort for the Ailing   PAGE   374
Eugenic Note   376

XXII. *Utopian Flights*

A Purge for Legislatures   378
A Chance for Millionaires   380
The Malevolent Jobholder   384
Portrait of an Ideal World   388

XXIII. *Souvenirs of a Journalist*

The Hills of Zion   392
Dempsey vs. Carpentier   399
How Legends are Made   403
Lodge   408
The Perihelion of Prohibition   411
The End of Prohibition   416
The New Deal   424

XXIV. *Criticism*

The Critical Process   429
Examination for Critics   440

XXV. *Literature*

The Divine Afflatus   442
The Poet and His Art   449
The New Poetry   459
On Style   460
Authorship as a Trade   463
The Author at Work   465
Foreign Poisons   467
The Blue-Nose   470
Folk-Literature   471
The Literary Amenities   473
The Author's League   475

XXVI. *Literati*

The Moonstruck Pastor   477
Aristotelian Obsequies   478
Poe   479
Whitman   482

PAGE

Memorial Service   484
Footnote   484
Credo   485
The Man Within   485
The Dean   489
Ambrose Bierce   492
Stephen Crane   496
Hamlin Garland   498
Henry James   500
Dreiser   501
Ring Lardner   506
Huneker: a Memory   510
Joseph Conrad   518

XXVII. *Music*

Beethoven   523
Schubert   527
Brahms   532
Wagner   536
More of the Same   537
Johann Strauss   538
Tempo di Valse   541
Richard Strauss   542
Bach at Bethlehem   543
Opera   545
Music as a Trade   547
The Music-Lover   548
The Reward of the Artist   549
Masters of Tone   550

XXVIII. *The Lesser Arts*

Hand-Painted Oil Paintings   551
Art Critics   554
The New Architecture   557
Art Galleries   559
Art and Nature   562
The Artist   562
The Greenwich Village Complex   564
Reflection on the Drama   564
Actors   567
The Comedian   569

Contents

Arrière-pensée   PAGE 570
Oratory   572
The Libido for the Ugly   573

XXIX. *Buffooneries*

Death: a Philosophical Discussion   577
The Declaration of Independence in American   583
The Visionary   587
A Neglected Anniversary   592
Star-Spangled Men   597
The Incomparable Physician   606
A *Smart Set* Circular   608
Suite Américaine   610
People and Things   612

XXX. *Sententiæ*

The Mind of Man   616
Masculum et Feminam Creavit Eos   619
The Citizen and the State   621
Arcana Cœlestia   624
This and That   625

XXXI. *Appendix*

Catechism   627
Epitaph   627

A MENCKEN CHRESTOMATHY

THE COPTIC CHRESTOMATHY

I. HOMO SAPIENS

The Life of Man

From Prejudices: Third Series, 1922, pp. 120–32.
First printed in the Smart Set, Oct., 1918, pp. 80–81

THE OLD anthropomorphic notion that the life of the whole
universe centers in the life of man — that human existence is
the supreme expression of the cosmic process — this notion
seems to be happily on its way toward the Sheol of exploded
delusions. The fact is that the life of man, as it is more and
more studied in the light of general biology, appears to be
more and more empty of significance. Once apparently the
chief concern and masterpiece of the gods, the human race
now begins to bear the aspect of an accidental by-product of
their vast, inscrutable and probably nonsensical operations. A
blacksmith making a horse-shoe produces something almost as
brilliant and mysterious — the shower of sparks. But his eye
and thought, as we know, are not on the sparks, but on the
horse-shoe. The sparks, indeed, constitute a sort of disease of
the horse-shoe; their existence depends upon a wasting of its
tissue. In the same way, perhaps, man is a local disease of the
cosmos — a kind of pestiferous eczema or urethritis. There are,
of course, different grades of eczema, and so are there different
grades of men. No doubt a cosmos afflicted with nothing worse
than an infection of Beethovens would not think it worth
while to send for the doctor. But a cosmos infested by Socialists, Scotsmen and stockbrokers must suffer damnably. No
wonder the sun is so hot and the moon is so diabetically green.

Man's Place in Nature

From the same. First printed in the *Smart Set*, Aug., 1919, pp. 61–62

As I say, the anthropomorphic theory of the world is made absurd by modern biology — but that is not saying, of course, that it will ever be abandoned by the generality of men. To the contrary, they will cherish it in proportion as it becomes more and more dubious. Today, indeed, it is cherished as it was never cherished in the Ages of Faith, when the doctrine that man was god-like was at least ameliorated by the doctrine that woman was vile. What else is behind charity, philanthropy, pacifism, the uplift, all the rest of the current sentimentalities? One and all, these sentimentalities are based upon the notion that man is a glorious and ineffable animal, and that his continued existence in the world ought to be facilitated and insured. But this notion is obviously full of fatuity. As animals go, even in so limited a space as our world, man is botched and ridiculous. Few other brutes are so stupid or so cowardly. The commonest yellow dog has far sharper senses and is infinitely more courageous, not to say more honest and dependable. The ants and the bees are, in many ways, far more intelligent and ingenious; they manage their government with vastly less quarreling, wastefulness and imbecility. The lion is more beautiful, more dignified, more majestic. The antelope is swifter and more graceful. The ordinary house-cat is cleaner. The horse, foamed by labor, has a better smell. The gorilla is kinder to his children and more faithful to his wife. The ox and the ass are more industrious and serene. But most of all, man is deficient in courage, perhaps the noblest quality of them all. He is not only mortally afraid of all other animals of his own weight or half his weight — save a few that he has debased by artificial inbreeding —; he is even mortally afraid of his own kind — and not only of their fists and hooves, but even of their sniggers.

No other animal is so defectively adapted to its environment. The human infant, as it comes into the world, is so puny that if it were neglected for two days running it would infallibly perish, and this congenital infirmity, though more or less concealed later on, persists until death. Man is ill far more than any other animal, both in his savage state and under civilization. He has more different diseases and he suffers from them oftener. He is easier exhausted and injured. He dies more horribly and usually sooner. Practically all the other higher vertebrates, at least in their wild state, live longer and retain their faculties to a greater age. Here even the anthropoid apes are far beyond their human cousins. An orang-outang marries at the age of seven or eight, raises a family of seventy or eighty children, and is still as hale and hearty at eighty as a European at forty-five.

All the errors and incompetencies of the Creator reach their climax in man. As a piece of mechanism he is the worst of them all; put beside him, even a salmon or a staphylococcus is a sound and efficient machine. He has the worst kidneys known to comparative zoölogy, and the worst lungs, and the worst heart. His eye, considering the work it is called upon to do, is less efficient than the eye of an earthworm; an optical instrument maker who made an instrument so clumsy would be mobbed by his customers. Alone of all animals, terrestrial, celestial or marine, man is unfit by nature to go abroad in the world he inhabits. He must clothe himself, protect himself, swathe himself, armor himself. He is eternally in the position of a turtle born without a shell, a dog without hair, a fish without fins. Lacking his heavy and cumbersome trappings, he is defenseless even against flies. As God made him he hasn't even a tail to switch them off.

I now come to man's one point of unquestionable natural superiority: he has a soul. This is what sets him off from all other animals, and makes him, in a way, their master. The exact nature of that soul has been in dispute for thousands of years, but regarding its function it is possible to speak with some authority. That function is to bring man into direct contact with God, to make him aware of God, above all, to make him resemble God. Well, consider the colossal failure of the device. If we assume that man actually does resemble God, then we are forced into the impossible theory that God is a coward, an idiot and a bounder. And if we assume that man, after all these years, does *not* resemble God, then it appears at once that the human soul is as inefficient a machine as the human liver or tonsil, and that man would probably be better off, as the chimpanzee undoubtedly *is* better off, without it.

Such, indeed, is the case. The only practical effort of having a soul is that it fills man with anthropomorphic and anthropocentric vanities — in brief, with cocky and preposterous superstitions. He struts and plumes himself because he has this soul — and overlooks the fact that it doesn't work. Thus he is the supreme clown of creation, the *reductio ad absurdum* of animated nature. He is like a cow who believed that she could jump over the moon, and ordered her whole life upon that theory. He is like a bullfrog boasting eternally of fighting lions, of flying over the Matterhorn, of swimming the Hellespont. And yet this is the poor brute we are asked to venerate as a gem in the forehead of the cosmos. This is the worm we are asked to defend as God's favorite on earth, with all its millions of braver, nobler, decenter quadrupeds — its superb lions, its lithe and gallant leopards, its imperial elephants, its honest dogs, its courageous rats. This is the insect we are besought, at infinite trouble, labor and expense, to reproduce.

Meditation on Meditation

From the same. First printed in the *Smart Set*, June, 1920, pp. 45–46

MAN'S capacity for abstract thought, which most other mammals seem to lack, has undoubtedly given him his present mastery of the land surface of the earth — a mastery disputed only by several hundred thousand species of insects and microscopic organisms. It is responsible for his feeling of superiority, and under that feeling there is undoubtedly a certain measure of reality, at least within narrow limits. But what is too often overlooked is that the capacity to perform an act is by no means synonymous with its salubrious exercise. The simple fact is that most of man's thinking is stupid, pointless and injurious to him. Of all animals, indeed, he seems the least capable of arriving at accurate judgments in the matters that most desperately affect his welfare. Try to imagine a rat, in the realm of rat ideas, arriving at a notion as violently in contempt of plausibility as the notion, say, of Swedenborgianism, or that of homeopathy, or that of infant damnation, or that of mental telepathy. Man's natural instinct, in fact, is never toward what is sound and true; it is toward what is specious and false. Let any great nation of modern times be confronted by two conflicting propositions, the one grounded upon the utmost probability and reasonableness and the other upon the most glaring error, and it will almost invariably embrace the latter. It is so in politics, which consists wholly of a succession of unintelligent crazes, many of them so idiotic that they exist only as battle-cries and shibboleths and are not reducible to logical statement at all. It is so in religion, which, like poetry, is simply a concerted effort to deny the most obvious realities. It is so in nearly every field of thought. The ideas that conquer the race most rapidly and arouse the wildest enthusiasm and are held most tenaciously are precisely the ideas that are most insane. This has been true since the first "advanced" gorilla put on underwear, cultivated a frown and began his first lecture tour, and it will be so until the high gods, tired of the farce at last, obliterate the race with one great, final blast of fire, mustard gas and streptococci.

No doubt the imagination of man is to blame for this singular weakness. That imagination, I daresay, is what gave him his first lift above his fellow primates. It enabled him to visualize a condition of existence better than that he was experiencing, and bit by bit he was able to give the picture a certain crude reality. Even today he keeps on going ahead in the same manner. That is, he thinks of something that he would like to be or to get, something appreciably better than what he is or has, and then, by the laborious, costly method of trial and error, he gradually moves toward it. In the process he is often severely punished for his discontent with God's holy ordinances. He mashes his thumb, he skins his shin; he stumbles and falls; the prize he reaches out for blows up in his hands. But bit by bit he moves on, or, at all events, his heirs and assigns move on.

Bit by bit he smooths the path beneath his remaining leg, and achieves pretty toys for his remaining hand to play with, and accumulates delights for his remaining ear and eye.

Alas, he is not content with his slow and sanguinary progress. Always he looks further and further ahead. Always he imagines things just over the sky-line. This body of imaginings constitutes his stock of sweet beliefs, his corpus of high faiths and confidences — in brief, his burden of errors. And that burden of errors is what distinguishes man, even above his capacity for tears, his talents as a liar, his excessive hypocrisy and poltroonery, from all the other orders of mammalia. Man is the yokel *par excellence*, the booby unmatchable, the king dupe of the cosmos. He is chronically and unescapably deceived, not only by the other animals and by the delusive face of nature herself, but also and more particularly by himself — by his incomparable talent for searching out and embracing what is false, and for overlooking and denying what is true.

The capacity for discerning the essential truth, in fact, is as rare among men as it is common among crows, bullfrogs and mackerel. The man who shows it is a man of quite extraordinary quality — perhaps even a man downright diseased. Exhibit a new truth of any natural plausibility before the great masses of men, and not one in ten thousand will suspect its existence, and not one in a hundred thousand will embrace it without a ferocious resistance. All the durable truths that have come into the world within historic times have been opposed as bitterly as if they were so many waves of smallpox, and every individual who has welcomed and advocated them, absolutely without exception, has been denounced and punished as an enemy of the race. Perhaps "absolutely without exception" goes too far. I substitute "with five or six exceptions." But who were the five or six exceptions? I leave you to think of them; myself, I can't.

But if truth thus has hard sledding, error is given a loving welcome. The man who invents a new imbecility is hailed gladly, and bidden to make himself at home; he is, to the great masses of men, the *beau ideal* of mankind. Go back through the history of the past thousand years and you will find that nine-tenths of the popular idols of the world — not the heroes of small sects, but the heroes of mankind in the mass — have been hawkers of palpable nonsense. It has been so in politics, it has been so in religion, and it has been so in every other department of human thought. Every such hawker has been opposed, in his time, by critics who denounced and refuted him; his contention has been disposed of immediately it was uttered. But on the side of every one there has been the titanic force of human credulity, and it has sufficed in every case to destroy his foes and establish his immortality.

Coda

First printed in the *Smart Set*, Dec., 1920, p. 45

To sum up:

1. The cosmos is a gigantic fly-wheel making 10,000 revolutions a minute.

2. Man is a sick fly taking a dizzy ride on it.

3. Religion is the theory that the wheel was designed and set spinning to give him the ride.

II. TYPES OF MEN

The Romantic

From PREJUDICES: THIRD SERIES, 1922, p. 266.
First printed in the New York *Evening Mail*, March 25, 1918

THERE is a variety of man whose eye inevitably exaggerates, whose ear inevitably hears more than the band plays, whose imagination inevitably doubles and triples the news brought in by his five senses. He is the enthusiast, the believer, the romantic. He is the sort of fellow who, if he were a bacteriologist, would report the streptococcus pyogenes to be as large as a St. Bernard dog, as intelligent as Socrates, as beautiful as Beauvais Cathedral and as respectable as a Yale professor.

The Skeptic

From the same, pp. 266–67. First printed in the *Smart Set*,
May, 1919, pp. 49–50

No man ever quite believes in any other man. One may believe in an idea absolutely, but not in a man. In the highest confidence there is always a flavor of doubt — a feeling, half instinctive and half logical, that, after all, the scoundrel *may* have something up his sleeve. This doubt, it must be obvious, is always more than justified, for no man is worthy of unlimited reliance — his treason, at best, only waits for sufficient temptation. The trouble with the world is not that men are too suspicious in this direction, but that they tend to be too confiding — that they still trust themselves too far to other men, even after bitter experience. Women, I believe, are measurably less sentimental, in this as in other things. No married woman ever trusts her husband absolutely, nor does she ever act as if she *did* trust him. Her utmost confidence is as wary as an American pickpocket's confidence that the policeman on the beat will stay bought.

The Believer

From the same, pp. 267–68

FAITH may be defined briefly as an illogical belief in the occurrence of the improbable. There is thus a flavor of the pathological in it; it goes beyond the normal intellectual process and passes into the murky domain of transcendental metaphysics. A man full of faith is simply one who has lost (or never had) the capacity for clear and realistic thought. He is not a mere ass: he is actually ill. Worse, he is incurable, for disappointment, being essentially an objective phenomenon, cannot permanently affect his subjective infirmity. His faith takes on the virulence of a chronic infection. What he says, in substance, is this: "Let us trust in God, *Who has always fooled us in the past.*"

The Toiler

From the same, pp. 268–69

ALL democratic theories, whether Socialistic or bourgeois, necessarily take in some concept of the dignity of labor. If the have-not were deprived of this delusion that his sufferings on the assembly-line are somehow laudable and agreeable to God, there would be little left in his ego save a belly-ache. Nevertheless, a delusion is a delusion, and this is one of the worst. It arises out of confusing the pride of workmanship of the artist with the dogged, painful docility of the machine. The difference is important and enormous. If he got no reward whatever, the artist would go on working just the same; his actual reward, in fact, is often so little that he almost starves. But suppose a garment-worker got nothing for his labor: would he go on working just the same? Can one imagine his submitting voluntarily to hardship and sore want that he might express his soul in 200 more pairs of ladies' pants?

The Physician

From the same, p. 269

HYGIENE is the corruption of medicine by morality. It is impossible to find a hygienist who does not debase his theory of the healthful with a theory of the virtuous. The whole hygienic art, indeed, resolves itself into an ethical exhortation. This brings it, at the end, into diametrical conflict with medicine proper. The true aim of medicine is not to make men virtuous; it is to safeguard and rescue them from the consequences of their vices. The physician does not preach repentance; he offers absolution.

The Scientist

From the same, pp. 269–70. First printed in the *Smart Set*, Aug., 1919, pp. 60–61

THE VALUE the world sets upon motives is often grossly unjust and inaccurate. Consider, for example, two of them: mere insatiable curiosity and the desire to do good. The latter is put high above the former, and yet it is the former that moves one of the most useful men the human race has yet produced: the scientific investigator. What actually urges him on is not some brummagem idea of Service, but a boundless, almost pathological thirst to penetrate the unknown, to uncover the secret, to find out what has not been found out before. His prototype is not the liberator releasing slaves, the good Samaritan lifting up the fallen, but a dog sniffing tremendously at an infinite series of rat-holes.

The Business Man

From the same, pp. 270–71. First printed in the *Smart Set*,
Feb., 1921, p. 36

IT is, after all, a sound instinct which puts business below the professions, and burdens the business man with a social inferiority that he can never quite shake off, even in America. The business man, in fact, acquiesces in this assumption of his inferiority, even when he protests against it. He is the only man above the hangman and the scavenger who is forever apologizing for his occupation. He is the only one who always seeks to make it appear, when he attains the object of his labors, *i.e.*, the making of a great deal of money, that it was not the object of his labors.

The King

From the same, p. 271

PERHAPS the most valuable asset that any man can have in this world is a naturally superior air, a talent for sniffishness and reserve. The generality of men are always greatly impressed by it, and accept it freely as a proof of genuine merit. One need but disdain them to gain their respect. Their congenital stupidity and timorousness make them turn to any leader who offers, and the sign of leadership that they recognize most readily is that which shows itself in external manner. This is the true explanation of the survival of monarchism, which always lives through its perennial deaths.

The Metaphysician

A hitherto unpublished note

A METAPHYSICIAN is one who, when you remark that twice two makes four, demands to know what you mean by twice, what by two, what by makes, and what by four. For asking such questions metaphysicians are supported in oriental luxury in the universities, and respected as educated and intelligent men.

The Average Man

FROM PREJUDICES: THIRD SERIES, 1922, pp. 273-74

IT is often urged against the Marxian brethren, with their materialistic conception of history, that they overlook certain spiritual qualities that are independent of wage scales and metabolism. These qualities, it is argued, color the aspirations and activities of civilized man quite as much as they are colored by his material condition, and so make it impossible to consider him simply as an economic machine. As examples, the anti-Marxians cite patriotism, pity, the esthetic sense and the yearning to know God. Unluckily, the examples are ill-chosen. Millions of men are quite devoid of patriotism, pity and the esthetic sense, and have no very active desire to know God. Why don't the anti-Marxians cite a spiritual quality that is genuinely universal? There is one readily at hand. I allude to cowardice. It is, in one form or other, visible in every human being; it almost serves to mark off the human race from all the other higher animals. Cowardice, I believe, is at the bottom of the whole caste system, the foundation of every organized society, including the most democratic. In order to escape going to war himself, the peasant was willing to give the warrior certain privileges — and out of those privileges has grown the whole structure of civilization. Go back still further. Property arose out of the fact that a few relatively courageous men were able to accumulate more possessions than whole hordes of cowardly men, and, what is more, to retain them after accumulating them.

The Truth-Seeker

From the same, p. 274

THE MAN who boasts that he habitually tells the truth is simply a man with no respect for it. It is not a thing to be thrown about loosely, like small change; it is something to be cherished and hoarded and disbursed only when absolutely necessary. The smallest atom of truth represents some man's bitter toil and agony; for every ponderable chunk of it there is a brave truth-seeker's grave upon some lonely ash-dump and a soul roasting in Hell.

The Relative

From the same, pp. 275–76. First printed in the *Smart Set*, Aug., 1919, p. 63

THE NORMAL man's antipathy to his relatives, particularly of the second degree, is explained by psychologists in various tortured and improbable ways. The true explanation, I venture, is a good deal simpler. It lies in the plain fact that every man sees in his relatives, and especially in his cousins, a series of grotesque caricatures of himself. They exhibit his qualities in disconcerting augmentation or diminution; they fill him with a disquieting feeling that this, perhaps, is the way he appears to the world, and so they wound his *amour propre* and give him intense discomfort.

The Relative-in-Law

From the *Smart Set*, March, 1920, p. 50

A MAN dislikes his wife's relatives for the same reason that he dislikes his own, to wit, because they appear to him as disgusting caricatures of one he holds in respect and affection, to wit.

his wife. Of them all, his mother-in-law is obviously the most offensive, for she not only burlesques his wife; she also foreshadows what his wife will probably become. The vision naturally sickens him. Sometimes, perhaps, the thing is more subtle. That is to say, his wife herself may be the caricature — say of a younger and prettier sister. In this case, being tied to his wife, he may come to detest the sister — as one always detests a person who symbolizes one's failure and one's slavery.

The Friend

From PREJUDICES: THIRD SERIES, 1922, pp. 276–77.
First printed in the *Smart Set*, July, 1919, p. 67

A MAN of active and resilient mind outwears his friendships just as certainly as he outwears his love affairs, his politics and his epistemology. They become threadbare, shabby, pumped-up, irritating, depressing. They convert themselves from living realities into moribund artificialities, and stand in sinister opposition to freedom, self-respect and truth. It is as corrupting to preserve them after they have grown fly-blown and hollow as it is to keep up the forms of passion after passion itself is a corpse. A prudent man, remembering that life is short, gives an hour or two, now and then, to a critical examination of his friendships. He weighs them, edits them, tests the metal of them. A few he retains, perhaps with radical changes in their terms. But the majority he expunges from his minutes and tries to forget, as he tries to forget the cold and clammy loves of year before last.

The Philosopher

From THE HUMAN MIND, PREJUDICES: SIXTH SERIES, 1927, p. 85

THERE is no record in human history of a happy philosopher: they exist only in romantic legend. Many of them have committed suicide; many others have turned their children out of doors and beaten their wives. And no wonder. If you want to find out how a philosopher feels when he is engaged in the practise of his profession, go to the nearest zoo and watch a chimpanzee at the wearying and hopeless job of chasing fleas. Both suffer damnably, and neither can win.

The Altruist

From PREJUDICES: FOURTH SERIES, 1924, pp. 205–06.
First printed in the *Smart Set*, March, 1920, p. 51

A LARGE part of altruism, even when it is perfectly honest, is grounded upon the fact that it is uncomfortable to have unhappy people about one. This is especially true in family life. A man makes sacrifices to his wife's desires, not because he greatly enjoys giving up what he wants himself, but because he would enjoy it even less to see her cutting a sour face across the dinner table.

The Iconoclast

From the same, pp. 139–40. First printed in the *American Mercury*,
Jan., 1924, p. 75

THE ICONOCLAST proves enough when he proves by his blasphemy that this or that idol is defectively convincing — that at least *one* visitor to the shrine is left full of doubts. The liberation of the human mind has been best furthered by gay fellows who heaved dead cats into sanctuaries and then went roistering down the highways of the world, proving to all men that doubt, after all, was safe — that the god in the sanctuary was a fraud. One horse-laugh is worth ten thousand syllogisms.

The Family Man

From the same, pp. 140–41

AGAIN, there is the bad author who defends his manufacture of magazine serials and movie scenarios on the ground that he has a wife, and is in honor bound to support her. I have seen a few such wives. I dispute the obligation. . . . As for the biological by-products of this fidelity, I rate them even lower. Show me 100 head of ordinary children who are worth one "Heart of Darkness," and I'll subside. As for "Lord Jim," I would not swap it for all the brats born in Trenton, N. J., since the Spanish War.

The Bachelor

From the same, pp. 118–19. First printed in the *Smart Set*,
Sept., 1922, p. 43

AROUND every bachelor of more than thirty-five legends tend to congregate, chiefly about the causes of his celibacy. If it is not whispered that he is damaged goods, and hence debarred from marriage by a lofty concept of Service to the unborn, it is told under the breath that he was insanely in love at the age of twenty-six with a beautiful creature who jilted him for an insurance underwriter and so broke his heart beyond repair. Such tales are nearly always moonshine. The reason why the average bachelor of thirty-five remains a bachelor is really very simple. It is, in brief, that no ordinarily attractive and intelligent woman has ever made a serious and undivided effort to marry him.

The Good Man

From the same, pp. 199–200. First printed in the *Smart Set*,
July, 1923, p. 47

MAN, at his best, remains a sort of one-lunged animal, never completely rounded and perfect, as a cockroach, say, is perfect. If he shows one valuable quality, it is almost unheard of for him to show any other. Give him a head, and he lacks a heart. Give him a heart of a gallon capacity, and his head holds scarcely a pint. The artist, nine times out of ten, is a dead-beat and given to the debauching of virgins, so-called. The patriot is a bigot, and, more often than not, a bounder and a poltroon. The man of physical bravery is often on a level, intellectually, with a Baptist clergyman. The intellectual giant has bad kidneys and cannot thread a needle. In all my years of search in this world, from the Golden Gate in the West to the Vistula in the East, and from the Orkney Islands in the North to the Spanish Main in the South, I have never met a thoroughly moral man who was honorable.

The Eternal Male

In part from IN DEFENSE OF WOMEN, 1918; revised, 1922, pp. 77–78,
and in part from the *Smart Set*, Nov., 1919, p. 71

LISTEN to two or three boys talking among themselves; their gabble is almost wholly made up of boasting — about their prowess at games, their successes in school, the wealth and animal vigor of their fathers, the elegance of their homes. And as with males of tender years, so with males of greater growth. Man is, of all quadrupeds, at once the most vain and the most idiotic. A genuine popinjay, whatever that may be, is as a shrinking violet compared to him. He cannot imagine himself save as at the center of situations. He never opens his mouth without talking of himself. He never undertakes the most trivial act without attitudinizing and hocus-pocusing it. However banal the position in which he finds himself, he tries to make something singular and glorious of it. If, in one of his obscure and sordid combats with another imbecile, he chances to get the better of it, the fact fills him with such pride that he is like to bust. And if, instead of getting the better of it, he is floored by an adept blow with a length of gas-pipe, he takes almost the same lofty joy in his defeat and ignominy. Thus we have, on the one hand, the hero, and on the other hand, the martyr. Both are puerile and preposterous fellows. Both are frauds.

The Slave

From PREJUDICES: FOURTH SERIES, 1924, p. 200.
First printed in the *Smart Set*, Nov., 1922, p. 52

DON'T tell me what delusion he entertains regarding God, or what mountebank he follows in politics, or what he springs from, or what he submits to from his wife. Simply tell me how he makes his living. It is the safest and surest of all known tests. A man who gets his board and lodging on this ball in an ignominious way is inevitably an ignominious man.

III. WOMEN

The Feminine Mind

From In Defense of Women, 1918; revised, 1922, pp. 3–22

A man's women folk, whatever their outward show of respect for his merit and authority, always regard him secretly as an ass, and with something akin to pity. His most gaudy sayings and doings seldom deceive them; they see the actual man within, and know him for a shallow and pathetic fellow. In this fact, perhaps, lies one of the best proofs of feminine intelligence, or, as the common phrase makes it, feminine intuition. The marks of that so-called intuition are simply a sharp and accurate perception of reality, a habitual immunity to emotional enchantment, a relentless capacity for distinguishing clearly between the appearance and the substance. The appearance, in the normal family circle, is a hero, a magnifico, a demigod. The substance is a poor mountebank.

A man's wife, true enough, may envy her husband certain of his more soothing prerogatives and sentimentalities. She may envy him his masculine liberty of movement and occupation, his impenetrable complacency, his peasant-like delight in petty vices, his capacity for hiding the harsh face of reality behind the cloak of romanticism, his general innocence and childishness. But she never envies him his shoddy and preposterous soul.

This shrewd perception of masculine bombast and make-believe, this acute understanding of man as the eternal tragic comedian, is at the bottom of that compassionate irony which passes under the name of the maternal instinct. A woman wishes to mother a man simply because she sees into his helplessness, his need of an amiable environment, his touching self-delusion. That ironical note is not only daily apparent in real life; it sets the whole tone of feminine fiction. The woman novelist, if she be skillful enough to be taken seriously, never takes her heroes

21

so. From the day of Jane Austen to the day of Selma Lagerlöf she has always got into her character study a touch of superior aloofness, of ill-concealed derision. I can't recall a single masculine figure created by a woman who is not, at bottom, a booby.

That it should be necessary, at this late stage in the senility of the human race, to argue that women have a fine and fluent intelligence is surely an eloquent proof of the defective observation, incurable prejudice, and general imbecility of their lords and masters. Women, in fact, are not only intelligent; they have almost a monopoly of certain of the subtler and more utile forms of intelligence. The thing itself, indeed, might be reasonably described as a special feminine character; there is in it, in more than one of its manifestations, a femaleness as palpable as the femaleness of cruelty, masochism or rouge. Men are strong. Men are brave in physical combat. Men are romantic, and love what they conceive to be virtue and beauty. Men incline to faith, hope and charity. Men know how to sweat and endure. Men are amiable and fond. But in so far as they show the true fundamentals of intelligence — in so far as they reveal a capacity for discovering the kernel of eternal verity in the husk of delusion and hallucination and a passion for bringing it forth — to that extent, at least, they are feminine, and still nourished by the milk of their mothers. The essential traits and qualities of the male, the hall-marks of the unpolluted masculine, are at the same time the hall-marks of the numskull. The caveman is all muscles and mush. Without a woman to rule him and think for him, he is a truly lamentable spectacle: a baby with whiskers, a rabbit with the frame of an aurochs, a feeble and preposterous caricature of God.

Here, of course, I do not mean to say that masculinity contributes nothing whatsoever to the complex of chemico-physiological reactions which produces what we call superior ability; all I mean to say is that this complex is impossible without the feminine contribution — that it is a product of the interplay of the two elements. In women of talent we see the opposite picture. They are commonly somewhat mannish, and shave as well as shine. Think of George Sand, Catherine the Great, Elizabeth of England, Rosa Bonheur, Teresa Carreño or Cosima Wagner. Neither sex, without some fertilization of the complementary characters of the other, is capable of the highest reaches of human endeavor. Man, without a saving touch of woman in him, is too doltish, too naïve and romantic, too easily deluded and lulled to sleep by his imagination to be anything above a cavalryman, a theologian or a corporation director. And woman, without some trace of that divine innocence which is masculine, is too harshly the realist for those vast projections of the fancy which lie at the heart of what we call genius. The wholly manly man lacks the wit necessary to give objective form to his soaring and secret dreams, and the wholly womanly woman is apt to be too cynical a creature to dream at all.

What men, in their egoism, constantly mistake for a deficiency of intelligence in woman is merely an incapacity for mastering that mass of small intellectual tricks, that complex of petty knowledges, that collection of cerebral rubber-stamps, which constitute the chief mental equipment of the average male. A man thinks that he is more intelligent than his wife because he can add up a column of figures more accurately, or because he is able to distinguish between the ideas of rival politicians, or because he is privy to the minutiæ of some sordid and degrading business or profession. But these empty talents, of course, are not really signs of intelligence; they are, in fact, merely a congeries of petty tricks and antics, and their acquirement puts little more strain on the mental powers than a chimpanzee suffers in learning how to catch a penny or scratch a match.

The whole mental baggage of the average business man, or even the average professional man, is inordinately childish. It takes no more actual sagacity to carry on the everyday hawking and haggling of the world, or to ladle out its normal doses of bad medicine and worse law, than it takes to operate a taxicab or fry a pan of fish. No observant person, indeed, can come into close contact with the general run of business and professional men — I confine myself to those who seem to get on in the world, and exclude the admitted failures — without marveling at their intellectual lethargy, their incurable ingenuousness, their appalling lack of ordinary sense. The late Charles Francis Adams, a grandson of one American President and a great-grandson of another, after a long lifetime in intimate associa-

tion with some of the chief business "geniuses" of the United
States, reported in his old age that he had never heard a single
one of them say anything worth hearing. These were vigorous
and masculine men, and in a man's world they were successful
men, but intellectually they were all blank cartridges.

There is, indeed, fair ground for arguing that, if men of that
kidney were genuinely intelligent, they would never succeed at
their gross and driveling concerns — that their very capacity to
master and retain such balderdash as constitutes their stock in
trade is proof of their inferior mentality. The notion is certainly
supported by the familiar incompetency of admittedly first-rate
men for what are called practical concerns. One could not think
of Aristotle multiplying 3,472,701 by 99,999 without making a
mistake, nor could one think of him remembering the range of
this or that railway share for two years, or the number of ten-
penny nails in a hundredweight, or the freight on lard from Gal-
veston to Rotterdam. And by the same token one could not
imagine him expert at bridge, or at golf, or at any other of the
idiotic games at which what are called successful men commonly divert themselves. In his great study of British genius,
Havelock Ellis found that an incapacity for such shabby expertness is visible in almost all first-rate men. They are bad at
tying cravats. They are puzzled by bookkeeping. They know
nothing of party politics. In brief, they are inert and impotent
in the very fields of endeavor that see the average men's highest performances, and are easily surpassed by men who, in actual
intelligence, are about as far below them as the *Simidæ*.

This lack of skill at manual and mental tricks of a trivial character — which must inevitably appear to a barber as stupidity,
and to a successful haberdasher as downright imbecility — is a
character that men of the first class share with women of the
first, second and even third classes. One seldom hears of women
succeeding in the occupations which bring out such expertness
most lavishly — for example, tuning pianos, practising law, or
writing editorials for newspapers — despite the circumstance
that the great majority of such occupations are well within their
physical powers, and that few of them offer any very formidable
social barriers to female entrance. There is no external reason
why they should not prosper at the bar, or as editors of maga-

zines, or as managers of factories, or in the wholesale trade, or as hotel-keepers. The taboos that stand in the way are of very small force; various adventurous women have defied them with impunity, and once the door is entered there remains no special handicap within. But, as everyone knows, the number of women actually practising these trades and professions is very small, and few of them have attained to any distinction in competition with men.

The cause thereof, as I say, is not external, but internal. It lies in the same disconcerting apprehension of the larger realities, the same impatience with the paltry and meretricious, the same disqualification for mechanical routine and empty technic which one finds in the higher varieties of men. Even in the pursuits which, by the custom of Christendom, are especially their own, women seldom show any of that elaborately conventionalized and half automatic proficiency which is the pride and boast of most men. It is a commonplace of observation that a housewife who actually knows how to cook, or who can make her own clothes with enough skill to conceal the fact from the most casual glance, or who is competent to instruct her children in the elements of morals, learning and hygiene — it is a platitude that such a woman is very rare indeed, and that when she is encountered she is not usually esteemed for her general intelligence.

This is particularly true in the United States, where the position of women is higher than in any other civilized or semi-civilized country, and the old assumption of their intellectual inferiority has been most successfully challenged. The American bourgeois dinner-table becomes a monument to the defective technic of the American housewife. The guest who respects his esophagus, invited to feed upon its discordant and ill-prepared victuals, evades the experience as long and as often as he can, and resigns himself to it as he might resign himself to being shaved by a paralytic. Nowhere else in the world have women more leisure and freedom to improve their minds, and nowhere else do they show a higher level of intelligence, but nowhere else is there worse cooking in the home, or a more inept handling of the whole domestic economy, or a larger dependence upon the aid of external substitutes, by men provided, for the skill that is wanting where it theoretically exists. It is surely no mere coincidence that the land of the emancipated and enthroned woman is also the land of canned soup, of canned pork and beans, of whole meals in cans, and of everything else ready-made. And nowhere else is there a more striking tendency to throw the whole business of training the minds of children upon professional pedagogues, mostly idiots, and the whole business of developing and caring for their bodies upon pediatricians, playground "experts," sex hygienists and other such professionals, mostly frauds.

In brief, women rebel — often unconsciously, sometimes even submitting all the while — against the dull, mechanical tricks of the trade that the present organization of society compels so many of them to practise for a living, and that rebellion testifies to their intelligence. If they enjoyed and took pride in those tricks, and showed it by diligence and skill, they would be on all fours with such men as are head waiters, accountants, schoolmasters or carpetbeaters, and proud of it. The inherent tendency of any woman above the most stupid is to evade the whole obligation, and, if she cannot actually evade it, to reduce its demands to the minimum. And when some accident purges her, either temporarily or permanently, of the inclination to marriage, and she enters into competition with men in the general business of the world, the sort of career that she commonly carves out offers additional evidence of her mental superiority. In whatever calls for no more than an invariable technic and a feeble chicanery she usually fails; in whatever calls for independent thought and resourcefulness she usually succeeds. Thus she is almost always a failure as a lawyer, for the law requires only an armament of hollow phrases and stereotyped formulæ, and a mental habit which puts these phantasms above sense, truth and justice; and she is almost always a failure in business, for business, in the main, is so foul a compound of trivialities and rogueries that her sense of intellectual integrity revolts against it. But she is usually a success as a sick-nurse, for that profession requires ingenuity, quick comprehension, courage in the face of novel and disconcerting situations, and above all, a capacity for penetrating and dominating character; and whenever she comes into competition with men in the arts, particularly on

those secondary planes where simple nimbleness of mind is unaided by the master strokes of genius, she holds her own invariably. In the *demi-monde* one will find enough acumen and
daring, and enough resilience in the face of special difficulties,
to put the equipment of any exclusively male profession to
shame. If the work of the average man required half the mental
agility and readiness of resource of the work of the average
brothel-keeper, the average man would be constantly on the
verge of starvation.

Men, as everyone knows, are disposed to question this superior intelligence of women; their egoism demands the denial,
and they are seldom reflective enough to dispose of it by logical
and evidential analysis. Moreover, there is a certain specious
appearance of soundness in their position; they have forced
upon women an artificial character which well conceals their
real character, and women have found it profitable to encourage
the deception. But though every normal man thus cherishes the
soothing unction that he is the intellectual superior of all
women, and particularly of his wife, he constantly gives the lie
to his pretension by consulting and deferring to what he calls
her intuition. That is to say, he knows by experience that her
judgment in many matters of capital concern is more subtle
and searching than his own, and, being disinclined to accredit
this greater sagacity to a more competent intelligence, he takes
refuge behind the doctrine that it is due to some impenetrable
and intangible talent for guessing correctly, some half mystical
supersense, some vague (and, in essence, infra-human) instinct.

The true nature of this alleged instinct, however, is revealed
by an examination of the situations which inspire a man to call
it to his aid. These situations do not arise out of the purely
technical problems that are his daily concern, but out of the
rarer and more fundamental, and hence enormously more difficult problems which beset him only at long and irregular intervals, and so offer a test, not of his mere capacity for being
drilled, but of his capacity for genuine ratiocination. No man, I
take it, save one consciously inferior and hen-pecked, would consult his wife about hiring a clerk, or about extending credit to
some paltry customer, or about some routine piece of tawdry
swindling; but not even the most egoistic man would fail to

sound the sentiment of his wife about taking a partner into his business, or about standing for public office, or about marrying off their daughter. Such things are of massive importance; they lie at the foundation of well-being; they call for the best thought that the man confronted by them can muster; the perils hidden in a wrong decision overcome even the clamors of vanity. It is in such situations that the superior mental grasp of women is of obvious utility, and has to be admitted. It is here that they rise above the insignificant sentimentalities, superstitions and formulæ of men, and apply to the business their singular talent for separating the appearance from the substance, and so exercise what is called their intuition.

Intuition? Bosh! Women, in fact, are the supreme realists of the race. Apparently illogical, they are the possessors of a rare and subtle super-logic. Apparently whimsical, they hang to the truth with a tenacity which carries them through every phase of its incessant, jelly-like shifting of form. Apparently unobservant and easily deceived, they see with bright and horrible eyes. . . . In men, too, the same merciless perspicacity sometimes shows itself — men recognized to be more aloof and uninflammable than the general — men of special talent for the logical — sardonic men, cynics. Men, too, sometimes have brains. But that is a rare, rare man, I venture, who is as steadily intelligent, as constantly sound in judgment, as little put off by appearances, as the average multipara of forty-eight.

Women as Outlaws

From the same, pp. 51–54. First printed, in part, in the *Smart Set*, Dec., 1921, pp. 28–29

PERHAPS one of the chief charms of women, as figures in human society, lies in the fact that they are relatively uncivilized. In the midst of all the puerile repressions and inhibitions that hedge them round, they continue to show a gipsy and outlaw spirit. No normal woman ever gives a hoot for law if law happens to stand in the way of her private interest. The boons of civilization are so noisily cried up by sentimentalists that we are all apt to overlook its disadvantages. Intrinsically, it is a mere device for regimenting men. Its perfect symbol is the goose-step. The most civilized man, in the conventional sense, is simply that man who has been most successful in caging and harnessing his honest and natural instincts — that is, the man who has done most cruel violence to his own ego in the interest of the commonweal. The value of this commonweal is always overestimated. What is its purpose at bottom? Simply the greatest good to the greatest number — of petty rogues, ignoramuses and chicken-hearts.

The capacity for submitting to and prospering comfortably under this cheese-monger's civilization is far more marked in men than in women, and far more in inferior men than in men of the higher categories. It must be obvious to even so pathetic an ass as a college professor of history that very few of the genuinely first-rate men of the race have been wholly civilized, in the meaning given to the term in newspapers. Think of Cæsar, Bonaparte, Luther, Frederick the Great, Cromwell, Barbarossa, Innocent III, Bolivar, Hannibal, Alexander, and to come down to our own time, Grant, Stonewall Jackson, Bismarck, Wagner and Cecil Rhodes.

The fact that women have a greater capacity than men for controlling and concealing their emotions is not an indication that they are *more* civilized, but a proof that they are *less* civilized. This capacity is a characteristic of savages, not of civilized men, and its loss is one of the penalties that the race has paid for the tawdry boon of civilization. Your true savage, reserved, dignified, and courteous, knows how to mask his feelings, even in the face of the most desperate assault upon them; your civilized man is forever yielding to them. Civilization, in fact, grows more and more maudlin and hysterical, and especially under democracy it tends to degenerate into a mere combat of crazes. The whole aim of practical politics is to keep the populace alarmed (and hence clamorous to be led to safety) by menacing it with an endless series of hobgoblins, all of them imaginary.

Wars are no longer waged by the will of superior men, capable of judging dispassionately and intelligently the causes behind

them and the effects flowing out of them. They are now begun
by first throwing a mob into a panic; they are ended only when
it has spent its ferine fury. Here the effect of civilization has
been to reduce an art that was once the repository of an exalted
etiquette and the chosen avocation of some of the best men of
the race, to the level of a raid on a fancy-house or a fight in a
waterfront saloon. All the wars of Christendom are now disgusting and degrading; the conduct of them has passed out of
the hands of nobles and knights and into the hands of demagogues, money-lenders and atrocity-mongers. To recreate one's
self with war in the grand manner, as Prince Eugene, Marl-
borough and the Old Dessauer knew it, one must now go among
barbarian peoples.

The Cold Woman

From the same, pp. 55–58

THE FEMININE talent for concealing emotion is probably mainly
responsible for the belief of so many American men that women
are devoid of passion, and contemplate its manifestations in the
male with something akin to horror. Here the talent itself is
helped out by the fact that very few masculine observers, on the
occasions when they give attention to the matter, are in a state
of mind conducive to scientific observation. The truth is, of
course, that there is absolutely no reason to believe that the
normal woman is frigid, or that the minority of women who unquestionably *are* is of appreciable dimensions. To be sure, the
vanity of men makes them place a high value upon the virginal
type of woman, and so this type tends to grow more common by
sexual selection, but despite that fact, it has by no means super-
seded the normal type, so realistically described by the theologians and publicists of the Middle Ages. It would, however, be
rash to assert that this long-continued selection has not made itself felt, even in the normal type. Its chief effect, perhaps, is to
make it measurably easier for a woman to conquer and conceal
emotion than it is for a man. But this is a mere reinforcement of

a native quality or, at all events, a quality long antedating the rise of the curious preference just mentioned.

That preference obviously owes its origin to the concept of private property and is most evident in those countries in which the largest proportion of males are property owners, *i.e.*, in which the property-owning caste reaches down into the lowest conceivable strata of bounders and ignoramuses. The low-caste man is never quite sure of his wife unless he is convinced that she is entirely devoid of amorous susceptibility. Thus he grows uneasy whenever she shows any sign of responding in kind to his own elephantine operations, and is apt to be suspicious of even so trivial a thing as a hearty response to a connubial kiss. If he could manage to rid himself of such suspicions, there would be less public gabble about anesthetic wives, and fewer books written by quacks with sure cures for them, and a good deal less cold mutton formalism and boredom at the domestic hearth.

I have a feeling that the husband of this sort does himself a serious disservice, and that he is uneasily conscious of it. Having got himself a wife to his austere taste, he finds that she is rather depressing — that his vanity is almost as painfully damaged by her emotional inertness as it would have been by a too provocative and hedonistic spirit. For the thing that chiefly delights a man, when some woman has gone through the solemn buffoonery of yielding to the aphrodisiac potency of his great love, is the sharp and flattering contrast between her reserve in the presence of other men and her enchanting complaisance in the presence of himself. Here his vanity is enormously tickled. To the world in general she seems remote and unapproachable; to him she is docile, fluttering, gurgling, even a bit abandoned. The greater the contrast between the lady's two fronts, the greater his satisfaction — up to the point where his oafish suspicions are aroused. Let her diminish that contrast ever so little on the public side — by smiling at a handsome actor, by saying a word too many to an attentive head waiter, by holding the hand of the rector of the parish, by winking amiably at his brother or at her sister's husband — and at once the poor fellow begins to look for clandestine notes, to employ private inquiry agents, and to scrutinize the eyes, ears, noses

and hair of his children with shameful doubts. This explains
many domestic catastrophes.

Intermezzo on Monogamy

From the same, pp. 97–100

THE PREVALENCE of monogamous marriage in Christendom is
commonly ascribed to ethical considerations. This is quite as
absurd as ascribing wars to ethical consideration — which is, of
course, frequently done. The simple truth is that such considerations are no more than deductions from experience, and
that they are quickly abandoned whenever experience turns
against them. In the present case experience is still overwhelmingly on the side of monogamy; civilized men are in favor of it
because they find that it works. And why does it work? Because it is the most effective of all available antidotes to the
alarms and terrors of passion. Monogamy, in brief, kills passion
— and passion is the most dangerous of all the surviving enemies to what we call civilization, which is based upon order,
decorum, restraint, formality, industry, regimentation.

The civilized man — the ideal civilized man — is simply one
who never sacrifices the common security to his private passions.
He reaches perfection when he even ceases to love passionately
— when he reduces the most profound of all his instinctive experiences from the level of an ecstasy to the level of a mere device for replenishing the armies and workshops of the world,
keeping clothes in repair, reducing the infant death-rate, pro-
viding enough tenants for every landlord, and making it possible
for the police to know where every citizen is at any hour of the
day or night. Monogamy accomplishes this by destroying appetite. It forces the high contracting parties into an intimacy that
is too persistent and unmitigated; they are in contact at too
many points, and too steadily. By and by all the mystery of the
relation is gone, and they stand in the unsexed position of
brother and sister. Thus that "maximum of temptation" of
which George Bernard Shaw speaks has within itself the seeds

of its own decay. A husband begins by kissing a pretty girl, his wife; it is pleasant to have her so handy and so willing. He ends by making machiavellian efforts to avoid kissing the everyday sharer of his meals, books, bath towels, pocketbook, relatives, ambitions, secrets, malaises and business: a proceeding about as romantic as having his shoes shined. Not all the native sentimentalism of man can overcome the distaste and boredom that get into it. Not all the histrionic capacity of woman can attach any appearance of gusto and spontaneity to it.

The advocates of monogamy, deceived by its moral overtones, fail to get all the advantage out of it that is in it. Consider, for example, the important moral business of safeguarding the virtue of the unmarried — that is, of the still passionate. The present plan in dealing, say, with a young man of twenty is to surround him with scarecrows and prohibitions — to try to convince him logically that passion is dangerous. This is both supererogation and imbecility — supererogation because he already knows that it is dangerous, and imbecility because it is quite impossible to kill a passion by arguing against it. The way to kill it is to give it rein under unfavorable and dispiriting conditions — to bring it down, by slow stages, to the estate of an absurdity and a horror. How much more, then, could be accomplished if the wild young men were forbidden polygamy, before marriage, but permitted monogamy. The prohibition in this case would be relatively easy to enforce, instead of impossible, as in the other. Curiosity would be satisfied; nature would get out of her cage; even romance would get an inning. Ninety-nine young men out of a hundred would submit, if only because it would be much easier to submit than to resist.

And the result? Obviously, it would be laudable — that is, accepting current definition of the laudable. The product, after six months, would be a well-harnessed and disillusioned young man, as devoid of disquieting and demoralizing passion as an ancient of eighty — in brief, the ideal citizen of Christendom.

The Libertine

From the same, pp. 144–51

THE AVERAGE man of our time and race is far more virtuous than
his wife's imaginings make him out — far less schooled in sin,
far less enterprising in amour. I do not say, of course, that he is
pure in heart, for the chances are that he isn't; what I do say is
that, in the overwhelming majority of cases, he is pure in act,
even in the face of temptation. And why? For several main reasons, not to go into minor ones. One is that he lacks the courage. Another is that he lacks the money. Another is that he is
fundamentally moral, and has a conscience. It takes more sinful initiative than he has to plunge into any affair save the most
casual and sordid; it takes more ingenuity and intrepidity than
he has to carry it off; it takes more money than he can conceal
from his consort to finance it. A man may force his actual wife
to share the direst poverty, but even the least vampirish woman
of the third part demands to be courted in what, considering
his station in life, is the grand manner, and the expenses of that
grand manner scare off all save a small minority of specialists in
deception. So long, indeed, as a wife knows her husband's income accurately, she has a sure means of holding him to his
oaths.

Even more effective than the fiscal barrier is the barrier of
poltroonery. The one character that distinguishes man from the
other higher vertebrata is his excessive timorousness, his easy
yielding to alarms, his incapacity for adventure without a crowd
behind him. In his normal incarnation he is no more capable
of initiating an extra-legal affair — at all events, above the mawkish harmlessness of a flirting match with a cigar girl in a café —
than he is of scaling the battlements of Hell. He likes to think
of himself doing it, just as he likes to think of himself leading a
cavalry charge or climbing the Matterhorn. Often, indeed, his
vanity leads him to imagine the thing done, and he admits by
winks and blushes that he is a bad one. But at the bottom of all
that tawdry pretense there is usually nothing more material
than a scraping of shins under the table. Let any woman who is

disquieted by reports of her husband's derelictions figure to herself how long it would have taken him to propose to her if left to his own enterprise, and then let her ask herself if so pusillanimous a creature could be imagined in the rôle of Don Giovanni.

Finally, there is his conscience — the accumulated sediment of ancestral faint-heartedness in countless generations, with vague religious fears and superstitions to leaven and mellow it. What! a conscience? Yes, dear friends, a conscience. That conscience may be imperfect, inept, unintelligent, brummagen. It may be indistinguishable, at times, from the mere fear that someone may be looking. It may be shot through with hypocrisy, stupidity, play-acting. But nevertheless, as consciences go in Christendom, it is genuinely entitled to the name — and it is always in action. A man, remember, is not a being *in vacuo*; he is the fruit and slave of the environment that bathes him. One cannot enter a State Legislature or a prison for felons without becoming, in some measure, a dubious character. One cannot fall overboard without shipping water. And by the same token one cannot live and have one's being in a modern democratic state, year in and year out, without falling, to some extent at least, under that moral obsession which is the hallmark of the mob-man set free.

The moment a concrete Temptress rises before him, her nose talced, her lips scarlet, her eyelashes dropping provokingly — the moment such an abandoned wench has at him, and his lack of ready funds begins to conspire with his lack of courage to assault and wobble him — at that precise moment his conscience flares into function, and so finishes his business. First he sees difficulty, then he sees danger, then he sees wrong. The result? The result is that he slinks off in trepidation, and another vampire is baffled of her prey. It is, indeed, the secret scandal of Christendom, at least in the Protestant regions, that most men are faithful to their wives. You will travel a long way before you find a married man who will admit that *he* is, but the facts are the facts. For one American husband who maintains a chorus girl in levantine luxury around the corner, there are hundreds who are as true to their oaths, year in and year out, as so many convicts in the death-house, and would be no more capable of any such loathsome malpractice, even in the face of free opportunity, than they would be of cutting off the ears of their young.[1]

The Lure of Beauty

From the same, pp. 34–40

SAVE on the stage, the handsome fellow has no appreciable advantage in amour over his more Gothic brother. In real life, indeed, he is viewed with the utmost suspicion by all women save the most stupid. A ten-cent store girl, perhaps, may plausibly fall in love with a movie actor, and a half-idiotic old widow may succumb to a gigolo with shoulders like the Parthenon, but no woman of poise and self-respect, even supposing her to be transiently flustered by a lovely buck, would yield to that madness for an instant, or confess it to her dearest friend.

This disdain of the pretty fellow is often accounted for by amateur psychologists on the ground that women are anesthetic to beauty — that they lack the quick and delicate responsiveness of man. Nothing could be more absurd. Women, in point of fact, commonly have a far keener esthetic sense than men. Beauty is more important to them; they give more thought to it; they crave more of it in their immediate surroundings. The average man, at least in England and America, takes a bovine pride in his indifference to the arts; he can think of them only as sources of somewhat discreditable amusement; one seldom hears of him showing half the enthusiasm for any beautiful thing that his wife displays in the presence of a fine fabric, an effective color, or a graceful form. Women are resistant to so-called beauty in men for the simple and sufficient reason that such beauty is chiefly imaginary. A truly beautiful man, indeed, is as rare as a truly beautiful piece of jewelry.

---

[1] I see nothing in the Kinsey Report to change my conclusions here. All that humorless document really proves is (*a*) that all men lie when they are asked about their adventures in amour, and (*b*) that pedagogues are singularly naïve and credulous creatures.

What men mistake for beauty in themselves is usually nothing save a certain hollow gaudiness, a revolting flashiness, the superficial splendor of a prancing animal. The most lovely movie actor, considered in the light of genuine esthetic values, is no more than a study in vulgarity; his like is to be found, not in the Uffizi gallery or among the harmonies of Brahms, but among the plush sofas, rococo clocks and hand-painted oil-paintings of a third-rate auction-room. All women, save the least intelligent, penetrate this imposture with sharp eyes. They know that the human body, except for a brief time in childhood, is not a beautiful thing, but a hideous thing. Their own bodies give them no delight; it is their constant effort to disguise and conceal them; they never expose them esthetically, but only as an act of the grossest sexual provocation. If it were advertised that a troupe of men of easy virtue were to do a strip-tease act upon a public stage, the only women who would go to the entertainment would be a few delayed adolescents, a psychopathic old maid or two, and a guard of indignant members of the parish Ladies Aid Society.

Men show no such sagacious apprehension of the relatively feeble loveliness of the human frame. The most effective lure that a woman can hold out to a man is the lure of what he fatuously conceives to be her beauty. This so-called beauty, of course, is almost always a pure illusion. The female body, even at its best, is very defective in form; it has harsh curves and very clumsily distributed masses; compared to it the average milk-jug, or even cuspidor, is a thing of intelligent and gratifying design — in brief, an *objet d'art*. Below the neck by the bow and below the waist astern there are two masses that simply refuse to fit into a balanced composition. Viewed from the side, a woman presents an exaggerated S bisected by an imperfect straight line, and so she inevitably suggests a drunken dollar-mark.

Moreover, it is extremely rare to find a woman who shows even the modest sightliness that her sex is theoretically capable of; it is only the rare beauty who is even tolerable. The average woman, until art comes to her aid, is ungraceful, misshapen, badly calved and crudely articulated, even for a woman. If she has a good torso, she is almost sure to be bow-legged. If she has good legs, she is almost sure to have bad hair. If she has good hair, she is almost sure to have scrawny hands, or muddy eyes, or no chin. A woman who meets fair tests all round is so uncommon that she becomes a sort of marvel, and usually gains a livelihood by exhibiting herself as such, either on the stage, in the half-world, or as the private jewel of some wealthy connoisseur.

But this lack of genuine beauty in women lays on them no practical disadvantage in the primary business of their sex, for its effects are more than overborne by the emotional suggestibility, the herculean capacity for illusion, the almost total absence of critical sense in men. Men do not demand genuine beauty, even in the most modest doses; they are quite content with the mere appearance of beauty. That is to say, they show no talent whatever for differentiating between the artificial and the real. A film of face powder, skillfully applied, is as satisfying to them as an epidermis of damask. The hair of a dead Chinaman, artfully dressed and dyed, gives them as much delight as the authentic tresses of Venus. False bosoms intrigue them as effectively as the soundest of living fascia. A pretty frock fetches them quite as surely and securely as lovely legs, shoulders, hands or eyes.

In brief, they estimate women, and hence acquire their wives, by reckoning up purely superficial aspects, which is just as intelligent as estimating an egg by purely superficial aspects. They never go behind the returns; it never occurs to them to analyze the impressions they receive. The result is that many a man, deceived by such paltry sophistications, never really sees his wife — that is, as our Heavenly Father is supposed to see her, and as the embalmer will see her — until they have been married for years. All the tricks may be infantile and obvious, but in the face of so naïve a spectator the temptation to continue practising them is irresistible. A trained nurse tells me that even when undergoing the extreme discomfort of parturition the great majority of women continue to modify their complexions with pulverized magnesium silicate, and to give thought to the arrangement of their hair. Such transparent devices reduce the psychologist to a sour sort of mirth, yet it must be plain that

they suffice to entrap and make fools of men, even the most
discreet.

And what esthetic deafness, dumbness and blindness thus
open the way for, vanity instantly reinforces. That is to say,
once a normal man has succumbed to the meretricious charms
of a definite fair one (or, more accurately, once a definite fair
one has marked him out and grabbed him by the nose), he defends his choice with all the heat and steadfastness appertaining
to the defense of a point of honor. To tell a man flatly that his
wife is not beautiful is so harsh and intolerable an insult that
even an enemy seldom ventures upon it. One would offend him
far less by arguing that his wife is an idiot. One would, relatively speaking, almost caress him by spitting into his eye. The
ego of the male is simply unable to stomach such an affront. It
is a weapon as discreditable as the poison of the Borgias.

Thus, on humane grounds, a conspiracy of silence surrounds
the delusion of female beauty, and its victim is permitted to get
quite as much delight out of it as if it were sound. The baits
he swallows most are not edible and nourishing ones, but simply
bright and gaudy ones. He succumbs to a pair of well-managed
eyes, a graceful twist of the body, a synthetic complexion or a
skillful display of legs without giving the slightest thought to the
fact that a whole woman is there, and that within the cranial
cavity of the woman lies a brain, and that the idiosyncrasies of
that brain are of vastly more importance than all imaginable
physical stigmata combined. But not many men, lost in the
emotional maze preceding, are capable of any very clear examination of such facts. They dodge those facts, even when they
are favorable, and lay all stress upon the surrounding and concealing superficialities. The average stupid and sentimental
man, if he has a noticeably sensible wife, is almost apologetic
about it. The ideal of his sex is always a pretty wife, and the
vanity and coquetry that so often go with prettiness are erected
into charms.

The Incomparable Buzz-Saw

From APPENDIX ON A TENDER THEME, PREJUDICES: SECOND SERIES,
1920, pp. 236–37.
First printed in the *Smart Set*, May, 1919, p. 54

THE ALLUREMENT that women hold out to men is precisely the allurement that Cape Hatteras holds out to sailors: they are enormously dangerous and hence enormously fascinating. To the average man, doomed to some banal drudgery all his life long, they offer the only grand hazard that he ever encounters. Take them away and his existence would be as flat and secure as that of a moo-cow. Even to the unusual man, the adventurous man, the imaginative and romantic man, they offer the adventure of adventures. Civilization tends to dilute and cheapen all other hazards. Even war has been largely reduced to caution and calculation; already, indeed, it employs almost as many press-agents, letter-openers and generals as soldiers. But the duel of sex continues to be fought in the Berserker manner. Whoso approaches women still faces the immemorial dangers. Civilization has not made them a bit more safe than they were in Solomon's time; they are still inordinately menacing, and hence inordinately provocative, and hence inordinately charming.

The most disgusting cad in the world is the man who, on grounds of decorum and morality, avoids the game of love. He is one who puts his own ease and security above the most laudable of philanthropies. Women have a hard time of it in this world. They are oppressed by man-made laws, man-made social customs, masculine egoism, the delusion of masculine superiority. Their one comfort is the assurance that, even though it may be impossible to prevail against man, it is always possible to enslave and torture a man. This feeling is fostered when one makes love to them. One need not be a great beau, a seductive catch, to do it effectively. Any man is better than none. To shrink from giving so much happiness at such small expense, to evade the business on the ground that it has hazards — this is the act of a puling and tacky fellow.

The War between Man and Woman

From In Defense of Women, 1918; revised, 1922, pp. 26–33

Not many men, worthy of the name, gain anything of net value by marriage, at least as the institution is now met with in Christendom. Even assessing its benefits at their most inflated worth, they are plainly overborne by crushing disadvantages. When a man marries it is no more than a sign that the feminine talent for persuasion and intimidation — *i.e.*, the feminine talent for survival in a world of clashing concepts and desires, the feminine competence and intelligence — has forced him into a more or less abhorrent compromise with his own honest inclinations and best interests. Whether that compromise be a sign of his relative stupidity or of his relative cowardice it is all one: the two things, in their symptoms and effects, are almost identical. In the first case he marries because he has been clearly bowled over in a combat of wits; in the second he resigns himself to marriage as the safest form of liaison. In both cases his inherent sentimentality is the chief weapon in the hand of his opponent. It makes him cherish the fiction of his enterprise, and even of his daring, in the midst of the most crude and obvious operations against him. It makes him accept as real the bold playacting that women always excel at, and at no time more than when stalking a man. It makes him, above all, see a glamor of romance in a transaction which, even at its best, contains almost as much gross trafficking, at bottom, as the sale of a mule.

A man in full possession of the modest faculties that nature commonly apportions to him is at least far enough above idiocy to realize that marriage is a bargain in which he seldom wants *all* that taking a wife offers and implies. He wants, at most, no more than certain parts. He may desire, let us say, a housekeeper to protect his goods and entertain his friends — but he may shrink from the thought of sharing his bathtub with anyone, and home cooking may be downright poisonous to him. He may yearn for a son to pray at his tomb — and yet suffer acutely at the mere approach of relatives-in-law. He may dream of a beautiful and complaisant mistress, less exigent and mercurial than any bachelor may hope to discover — and stand aghast at admitting her to his bank-book, his family-tree and his secret ambitions. He may want company and not intimacy, or intimacy and not company. He may want a cook and not a partner in his business, or a partner in his business and not a cook.

But in order to get the precise thing or things that he wants, he has to take a lot of other things that he doesn't want — that no sane man, in truth, could imaginably want — and it is to the enterprise of forcing him into this almost Armenian bargain that the woman of his "choice" addresses herself. Once the game is fairly set, she searches out his weaknesses with the utmost delicacy and accuracy, and plays upon them with all her superior resources. He carries a handicap from the start. His sentimental and unintelligent belief in theories that she knows quite well are not true — *e.g.*, the theory that she shrinks from him, and is modestly appalled by the banal carnalities of marriage itself — gives her a weapon against him which she drives home with instinctive and compelling art. The moment she discerns this sentimentality bubbling within him — that is, the moment his oafish smirks and eye-rollings signify that he has achieved the intellectual disaster that is called falling in love — he is hers to do with as she listeth. Save for acts of God, he is forthwith as good as married.

Men usually get their mates by this process of falling in love; save among the aristocracies of the North and Latin men, the marriage of convenience is relatively rare; a hundred men marry "beneath" them to every woman who perpetrates the same folly. And what is meant by falling in love? What is meant by it is a procedure whereby a man accounts for the fact of his marriage, after feminine initiative and generalship have made it inevitable, by enshrouding it in a purple maze of romance — in brief, by setting up the doctrine that an obviously self-possessed and mammalian woman, engaged deliberately in the most important adventure of her life, and with the keenest understanding of its utmost implications, is a naïve, tender, moony and almost disembodied creature, enchanted and made perfect by emotions that have stolen upon her unawares, and which she could not acknowledge, even to herself, without blushing to death. By this preposterous doctrine, the defeat and enslavement of the man is made glorious, and even gifted with a touch of flattering naughtiness. The sheer horsepower of his wooing has assailed and overcome her maiden modesty; she trembles in his arms; he has been granted a free franchise to work his wicked will upon her. Thus do the ambulant images of God cloak their shackles proudly, and divert the judicious with their boastful shouts.

Women are much more cautious about embracing the conventional hocus-pocus of the situation. They seldom acknowledge that they have fallen in love, as the phrase is, until the man has revealed his delusion, and so cut off his retreat; to do otherwise would be to bring down upon their heads the mocking and contumely of all their sisters. With them, falling in love thus appears in the light of an afterthought, or, perhaps more accurately, in the light of a contagion. The theory, it would seem, is that the love of the man, laboriously avowed, has inspired it instantly, and by some unintelligible magic; that it was non-existent until the heat of his own flames set it off. This theory, it must be acknowledged, has a certain element of fact in it. A woman seldom allows herself to be swayed by emotion while the principal business is yet afoot and its issue still in doubt; to do so would be to expose a degree of imbecility that is confined only to the half-wits of the sex. But once the man is definitely committed, she frequently unbends a bit, if only as a relief from the strain of a fixed purpose, and so, throwing off her customary inhibitions, indulges in the luxury of a more or less forced and mawkish sentiment. It is, however, almost unheard of for her to permit herself this relaxation before the sentimental intoxication of the man is assured. To do otherwise — that is, to confess, even *post facto*, to an anterior descent — would expose her to the scorn of all other women. Such a confession would be an admission that emotion had got the better of her at a critical intellectual moment, and in the eyes of women, as in the eyes of the small minority of genuinely intelligent men, no treason to the higher cerebral centers could be more disgraceful.

The Nature of Love

From Appendix on a Tender Theme, Prejudices: Second Series,
1920, pp. 229–36.
First printed in the *Smart Set*, July, 1920, pp. 59–60

Whatever the origin (in the soul, the ductless glands or the convolutions of the cerebrum) of the thing called romantic love, its mere phenomenal nature may be very simply described. It is, in brief, a wholesale diminishing of disgusts, primarily based on observation, but often, in its later stages, taking on a hallucinatory and pathological character. Friendship has precisely the same constitution, but the pathological factor is usually absent. When we are attracted to a person and find his or her proximity agreeable, it means that he or she disgusts us less than the average human being disgusts us — which, if we have delicate sensibilities, is a good deal more than is comfortable.

Because human contacts are chiefly superficial, most of the disgusts that we are conscious of are physical. We are never honestly friendly with a man who is appreciably dirtier than we are ourselves, or who has table manners that are more baroque than our own (or merely noticeably different), or who laughs in a way that strikes us as hyenical. But there are also psychical disgusts. Our friends, in the main, must be persons who think substantially as we do, at least about all things that actively concern us, and who have the same general tastes. It is impossible to imagine a Brahmsianer being honestly fond of a man who enjoys jazz, and by the same token, it is impossible to imagine a woman of genuine refinement falling for a Knight of Pythias, a Methodist or even a chauffeur; when such a wonder actually occurs either the chauffeur is a Harvard athlete in disguise or the lady herself is a charwoman in disguise. Here, however, the force of aversion may be greatly diminished by contrary physical attractions; the body, as usual, is enormously more potent than the so-called mind. In the midst of the bitterest wars, with every man of the enemy held to be a fiend in human form, women constantly fall in love with enemy soldiers who are of pleasant person and wear showy uniforms. And many a fair agnostic, as everyone knows, is on good terms with a handsome priest.

Once the threshold is crossed emotion comes to the aid of perception. That is to say, the blind, almost irresistible mating impulse, now relieved from the contrary pressure of active disgusts, fortifies itself by manufacturing illusions. The lover sees with an eye that is both opaque and out of focus, and begins the familiar process of editing and improving his girl. Features and characteristics that, observed in cold blood, might have quickly aroused his most active disgust are now seen through a rose-tinted fog, like drabs in a musical comedy. The lover ends by being almost anesthetic to disgust. While the spell lasts his lady could shave her head, or take to rubbing snuff, or scratch her leg in public, and yet not disgust him. Here the paralysis of the faculties is again chiefly physical — a matter of obscure secretions, of shifting pressures, of metabolism. Nature is at her tricks. The fever of love is upon its victim. His guard down, he is little more than an automaton. The shrewd observer of gaucheries, the sensitive sniffer, the erstwhile cynic, has become a mere potential papa.

This spell, of course, doesn't last forever. Marriage cools the fever and lowers the threshold of disgust. The husband begins to observe what the lover was blind to, and often his discoveries affect him most unpleasantly. And not only is the fever cooled; the opportunities for exact observation are enormously increased. It is a commonplace of juridical science that the great majority of divorces have their origin in the connubial chamber. Here intimacy is so extreme that it is highly dangerous to illusion. Both parties, thrown into the closest human contact that either has suffered since their unconscious days *in utero*, find their old capacity for disgust reviving, and then suddenly flaming. The girl who was perfect in her wedding gown becomes a caricature in her *robe de nuit*; the man who was a Chevalier Bayard as a wooer in his best suit becomes a snuffling, shambling, driveling nuisance as a husband in ill-fitting pajamas — a fellow offensive to eyes, ears, nose, touch and immortal soul.

The day is saved, as everyone knows, by the powerful effects of habit. The acquisition of habit is the process whereby disgust is overcome in daily life — the process whereby one may cease to be offended by a persistent noise or odor. One suffers horribly at first, but after a bit one suffers less, and in the course of time one scarcely suffers at all. Thus a man, when his marriage enters upon the stage of regularity and safety, gets used to his wife as he might get used to a tannery down the street, and *vice versa*. I think that women, in this direction, have the harder row to hoe, for they are more observant than men, and vastly more sensitive in small ways. But even women succumb to habit with humane rapidity, else every marriage would end in divorce. Disgusts pale into mere dislikes, disrelishes, distastes. They cease to gag and torture. But though they thus shrink into the shadow, they are by no means disposed of. Deep down in the subconscious they continue to lurk, and some accident may cause them to flare up at any time, and work havoc. This flaring up accounts for a familiar and yet usually very mystifying phenomenon — the sudden collapse of a marriage or a friendship after years of apparent prosperity.

The Eternal Farce

From REFLECTIONS ON HUMAN MONOGAMY, PREJUDICES:
FOURTH SERIES, 1924, pp. 104–05

IN Shakespeare love is always depicted as comedy — sometimes light and charming, as in "Twelfth Night," but usually rough and buffoonish, as in "The Taming of the Shrew." This attitude is plainly visible even in such sombre plays as "Hamlet" and "Romeo and Juliet." In its main outlines, I suppose, "Hamlet" is reasonably to be taken for a tragedy, but if you believe that the love passages are intended to be tragic then all I ask is that you give a close reading to the colloquies between Hamlet and Ophelia. They are not only farcical; they are downright obscene; Shakespeare, through the mouth of Hamlet, derides the whole business with almost intolerable ribaldry. As for "Romeo and Juliet," what is it but a penetrating burlesque upon the love guff that was fashionable in the poet's time? True enough, his head buzzed with such loveliness that he could not write even burlesque without making it beautiful — compare "Much Ado About Nothing" and "Othello" — but nevertheless it is quite absurd to say that he was serious when he wrote this tale of calf-love. Imagine such a man taking seriously the spasms and hallucinations of a *Backfisch* of fourteen, the tinpot heroics of a boy of eighteen. Shakespeare remembered very well the nature of his own amorous fancies at eighteen. It was the year of his seduction by Ann Hathaway, whose brother later made him marry her, much to his damage and dismay. He wrote the play at forty-five. Tell it to the Marines!

The Helpmate

From the same, pp. 114–15

EVERY intelligent woman knows instinctively that the highest aspirations of her husband are fundamentally inimical to her, and that their realization is apt to cost her her possession of him. What she dreams of is not an infinitely brilliant husband, but an infinitely "solid" one, which is to say, one bound to her irretrievably by the chains of normalcy. It would delight her to see him get to the White House, for a man in the White House is policed as relentlessly as an archbishop. But it would give her a great deal of disquiet to see him develop into a Goethe or a Wagner.

I have known in my time a good many men of the first talent, as talent is reckoned in America, and most of them have been married. I can't recall one whose wife appeared to view his achievements with perfect ease of mind. In every case the lady was full of palpable fear — the product of feminine intuition, *i.e.*, of hard realism and common sense — that his rise shook her hold upon him, that he became a worse husband in proportion as he became a better man. In the logic I can discern no flaw. The ideal husband is surely not a man of active and daring mind; he is the man of placid and conforming mind. Here the good business man obviously beats the artist and adventurer.

His rewards are all easily translated into domestic comfort and happiness. He is not wobbled by the admiration of other women, none of whom, however much they may esteem his virtues as a husband, are under any illusion as to his virtues as a lover. Above all, his mind is not analytical, and hence he is not likely to attempt any anatomizing of his marriage — the starting point for the worst sort of domestic infelicity. No man, examining his marriage intelligently, can fail to observe that it is compounded, at least in part, of slavery, and that he is the slave. Happy the woman whose husband is so stupid that he never launches into that coroner's inquest.

The Sex Uproar

From RONDO ON AN ANCIENT THEME, PREJUDICES: FIFTH SERIES,
1926, pp. 100–03

I DOUBT that the lives of normal men, taking one with another, are much colored or conditioned, either directly or indirectly, by purely sexual considerations. I believe that nine-tenths of them would carry on all the activities which now engage them, and with precisely the same humorless diligence, if there were not a woman in the world. The notion that man would not work if he lacked an audience, and that the audience must be a woman, is a hollow sentimentality. Men work because they want to eat, because they want to feel secure, because they long to shine among their fellows, because they are urged by a blind lust for function, and for no other reason. A man may crave his wife's approbation, or some other woman's approbation, of his social graces, of his taste, of his generosity and courage, of his general dignity in the world, but long before he ever gives thought to such things and long after he has forgotten them he craves the approbation of his fellow men. Above all, he craves the approbation of his fellow craftsmen — the men who understand exactly what he is trying to do in his narrow world, and are expertly competent to judge his doing of it. Can you imagine a surgeon putting the good opinion of his wife above that of other surgeons? If you can, then you can do something that I cannot.

Here, of course, I do not argue absurdly that the good opinion of his wife is nothing to him. Obviously, it is a lot, for if it does not constitute the principal reward of his work, then it at least constitutes the principal joy of his hours of ease, when his work is done. He wants his wife to respect and admire him; to be able to make her do it in the face of her sharper perception is also a talent. But if he is intelligent himself he must discover very early that her respect and admiration do not necessarily run in ratio to his intrinsic worth, that the qualities and acts that please her are not always the qualities and acts that are most satisfactory to the censor within him — in brief, that the relation between man and woman, however intimate they may seem, must always remain a bit casual and superficial — that sex, at bottom, belongs to comedy and the cool of the evening and not to the sober business that goes on in the heat of the day. That sober business, as I have said, would still go on if woman were abolished and heirs and assigns were manufactured in rolling-mills. Men would not only work as hard as they do to-day; they would also get almost as much satisfaction out of their work. Of all the men that I know on this earth, ranging from poets to ambassadors and from bishops to statisticians, I know none who labors primarily because he wants to please a woman. They are all hard at it because they want to impress other men and so please themselves.

Women, plainly enough, are in a far different case. Their emancipation has not yet gone to the length of making them genuinely free. They have rid themselves, very largely, of the absolute need to please men, but they have not yet rid themselves of the impulse to please men. Perhaps they never will: one might easily devise a plausible argument to that effect on biological grounds. But sufficient unto the day is the phenomenon before us: they have got rid of the old taboo which forbade them to think and talk about sex, but they still labor under the old superstition that sex is a matter of paramount importance. The result, in my judgment, is an absurd emission of piffle. In every division there is vast and often ludicrous exaggeration. The campaign for birth control, as it is carried on by female propagandists, takes on the proportions of a holy war. The venereal diseases are represented to be widespread, at least in men, as colds in the head, and as lethal as apoplexy or cancer. Hordes of viragoes patrol the country, instructing school-girls in the mechanics of reproduction and their mothers in obstetrics. The light-hearted monogamy which produced all of us is denounced as an infamy comparable to cannibalism. Laws are passed regulating the mating of human beings as if they were horned cattle and converting marriage into a sort of coroner's inquest. Over all sounds the battle-cry of quacks and zealots at all times and everywhere: *Veritas liberabit vos!*

The truth? How much of this new gospel is actually truth? Perhaps two per cent. The rest is idle theorizing, doctrinaire nonsense, mere scandalous rubbish. All that is worth knowing about sex — all, that is, that is solidly established and of sound utility — can be taught to any intelligent boy of sixteen in two hours. Is it taught in the current books? Certainly not. Absolutely without exception these books admonish the poor apprentice to renounce sex altogether — to sublimate it, as the favorite phrase is, into a passion for free verse, Rotary or international coöperation. This admonition is silly, and, I believe, dangerous. It is as much a folly to lock up sex in the hold as it is to put it in command on the bridge. Its proper place is in the social hall. As a substitute for all such nonsense I drop a pearl of wisdom, and pass on. To wit: the strict monogamist never gets into trouble.

Women as Christians

From IN DEFENSE OF WOMEN, 1918; revised, 1922, pp. 162–65

THE GLAD tidings preached by Christ were obviously highly favorable to women. He lifted them to equality before the Lord when their very possession of souls was still doubted by the majority of rival theologians. Moreover, He esteemed them socially and set value upon their sagacity, and one of the most disdained of their sex, a lady formerly in public life, was among

His regular advisers. Mariolatry is thus by no means the invention of the medieval popes, as Protestant theologians would have us believe. On the contrary, it is plainly discernible in the Four Gospels. What the medieval popes actually invented (or, to be precise, reinvented, for they simply borrowed the elements of it from St. Paul) was the doctrine of women's inferiority, the precise opposite of the thing credited to them. Committed, for sound reasons of discipline, to the celibacy of the clergy, they had to support it by depicting all traffic with women in the light of a hazardous and ignominious business.

The result was the deliberate organization and development of the theory of female triviality, lack of responsibility and general looseness of mind. Woman became a sort of devil, but without the admired intelligence of the regular demons. The appearance of women saints, however, offered a constant and embarrassing criticism of this idiotic doctrine. If occasional women were fit to sit upon the right hand of God — and they were often proving it, and forcing the church to acknowledge it — then surely *all* women could not be as bad as the theologians made them out. There thus arose the concept of the angelic woman, the natural vestal; we see her at full length in the romances of medieval chivalry. What emerged in the end was a double doctrine, first that women were devils and secondly that they were angels. This preposterous dualism has merged into a compromise dogma in modern times. By that dogma it is held, on the one hand, that women are unintelligent and immoral, and on the other hand, that they are free from all those weaknesses of the flesh which distinguish men. This, roughly speaking, is the notion of the average male numskull today.

Christianity has thus both libelled women and flattered them, but with the weight always on the side of the libel. It is therefore, at bottom, their enemy, as the religion of Christ, now wholly extinct, was their friend. And as they gradually throw off the shackles that have bound them for a thousand years they show appreciation of the fact. Women, indeed, are not naturally religious, and they are growing less and less religious as year chases year. Their ordinary devotion has little if any pious exaltation in it; it is a routine practise, forced on them by the masculine notion that an appearance of holiness is proper to their lowly station, and a masculine feeling that church-going somehow keeps them in order, and out of doings that would be less reassuring. When they exhibit any genuine religious fervor, its sexual character is usually so obvious that even the majority of men are cognizant of it. Women never go flocking ecstatically to a church in which the agent of God in the pulpit is an elderly asthmatic with a watchful wife. When one finds them driven to frenzies by the merits of the saints, and weeping over the sorrows of the heathen, and rushing out to haul the whole vicinage up to grace, and spending hours on their knees in hysterical abasement before the heavenly throne, it is quite safe to assume, even without an actual visit, that the ecclesiastic who has worked the miracle is a fair and toothsome fellow, and a good deal more aphrodisiacal than learned.

Women, in fact, are indifferent Christians in the primitive sense, just as they are in the antagonistic modern sense, and particularly on the side of ethics. If they actually accept the renunciations commanded by the Sermon on the Mount, it is only in an effort to flout their substance under cover of their appearance. No woman is really humble; she is merely politic. No woman, with a free choice before her, chooses self-immolation; the most she genuinely desires in that direction is a spectacular and preferably bogus martyrdom. No woman delights in poverty. No woman yields when she can prevail. No woman is honestly meek.

The moment she finds herself confronted by an antagonist genuinely dangerous, either to her own security or to the well-being of the helpless creatures under her protection — say a child or a husband — she displays a bellicosity which stops at nothing, however outrageous. In the courts of law one occasionally encounters a male extremist who tells the truth, the whole truth and nothing but the truth, even when it is against his cause, but no such woman has been on view since the days of Justinian. It is, indeed, an axiom of the bar that women invariably lie upon the stand, and the whole effort of a barrister who has one for a client is devoted to keeping her within bounds, that the obtuse suspicions of the jury may not be unduly aroused. Women litigants almost always win their cases, not, as is commonly assumed, because the male jurymen fall in love with them, but simply and solely because they are clear-headed, resourceful, implacable and without qualms.

What is here visible in the halls of justice, in the face of a vast technical equipment for combating mendacity, is ten times more obvious in freer fields. Any man who is so unfortunate as to have a serious controversy with a woman, say in the department of finance, theology or amour, must inevitably carry away from it a sense of having passed through a dangerous and hair-raising experience. Women not only bite in the clinches; they bite even in open fighting; they have a dental reach, so to speak, of amazing length. No attack is so desperate that they will not undertake it, once they are aroused; no device is so unfair and horrifying that it stays them. In my early days, desiring to improve my prose, I served for a year or so as reporter for a newspaper in a police court, and during that time I heard perhaps four hundred cases of so-called wife-beating. The husbands, in their defense, almost invariably pleaded justification, and some of them told such tales of studied atrocity at the domestic hearth, both psychic and physical, that the learned magistrate discharged them with tears in his eyes and the very catchpolls in the courtroom had to blow their noses.

Many more men than women go insane, and many more married men than single men. The fact puzzles no one who has had the same opportunity that I had to find out what goes on, year in and year out, behind the doors of apparently happy homes. A woman, if she hates her husband (and many of them do), can make life so sour and obnoxious to him that even death upon the gallows seems sweet by comparison. This hatred, of course, is often, and perhaps almost invariably, quite justified. To be the wife of an ordinary man, indeed, is an experience that must be very hard to bear. The hollowness and vanity of the fellow, his petty meanness and stupidity, his puling sentimentality and credulity, his bombastic air of a cock on a dunghill, his anesthesia to all whispers and summonings of the spirit, above all, his loathsome clumsiness in amour — all these things must revolt any woman above the lowest. To be the object of the oafish affections of such a creature, even when they are honest and profound, cannot be expected to give any genuine joy to a woman of sense and refinement. His performance as a gallant, as Honoré de Balzac long ago observed, unescapably suggests a gorilla's efforts to play the violin.

Women survive the tragi-comedy only by dint of their great capacity for play-acting. They are able to act so realistically that often they deceive even themselves; the average woman's contentment, indeed, is no more than a tribute to her histrionism. But there must be innumerable revolts in secret, even so, and one sometimes wonders that so few women, with the thing so facile and so safe, poison their husbands. Perhaps it is not quite as rare as vital statistics make it out; the death-rate among husbands is very much higher than among wives. More than once, indeed, I have gone to the funeral of an acquaintance who died suddenly, and observed a curious glitter in the eyes of the inconsolable widow.

The Lady of Joy

From the same, pp. 186–92

THE PROSTITUTE is disesteemed today, not because her trade involves anything intrinsically degrading or even disagreeable to the kind of woman who engages in it, but because she is currently assumed to have been driven into it by dire necessity, against her dignity and inclination. That this assumption is usually unsound is no objection to it; nearly all the thinking of the world, particularly in the field of morals, is based upon unsound assumption, e.g., that God observes the fall of a sparrow and is shocked by the fall of a Sunday-school superintendent. The truth is that prostitution is one of the most attractive of the occupations practically open to the women who practise it, and that the prostitute commonly likes her work, and would not exchange places with a shop-girl or a waitress for anything in the world.

The notion to the contrary is propagated by unsuccessful prostitutes who fall into the hands of professional reformers, and who assent to the imbecile theories of the latter in order to cultivate their good will, just as convicts in prison, questioned by teetotalers, always ascribe their rascality to alcohol. No prostitute of anything resembling normal female intelligence is under the slightest duress; she is perfectly free to abandon her trade and go into a shop or factory or into domestic service whenever the impulse strikes her; all the recurrent gabble about white slaves comes from pious rogues who make a living by feeding such nonsense to the credulous. So long as the average prostitute is able to make a good living, she is quite content with her lot, and disposed to contrast it egotistically with the slavery of her virtuous sisters. If she complains of it, then you may be sure that her success is below her expectations. A starving lawyer always sees injustice in the courts. A physician without patients is a bitter critic of the American Medical Association. And when a clergyman is forced out of his cure by a vestry-room revolution he almost invariably concludes that the sinfulness of man is incurable, and sometimes he even begins to doubt some of the typographical errors in Holy Writ.

Even the most lowly prostitute is better off, in all worldly ways, than the virtuous woman of her own station in life. She has less work to do, it is less monotonous and dispiriting, she meets a far greater variety of men, and they are of classes distinctly beyond her own. Nor is her occupation hazardous and her ultimate fate tragic. Some years ago I observed a somewhat amusing proof of this last. At that time certain sentimental busybodies of the American city in which I live undertook an elaborate inquiry into prostitution therein, and some of them came to me in advance, as a practical journalist, for advice as to how to proceed. I found that all of them shared the common superstition that the professional life of the average prostitute is only five years long, and that she invariably ends in the gutter. They were enormously amazed when they unearthed the truth. This truth was to the effect that the average prostitute of that town ended her career, not in the morgue but at the altar of God, and that those who remained unmarried often continued in practise for ten, fifteen and even twenty years, and then retired on competences. It was established, indeed, that fully eighty per cent. married, and that they almost always got husbands who would have been far beyond their reach had they remained virtuous. For one who married a cabman or petty pugilist there were a dozen who married respectable mechanics, policemen, small shopkeepers and minor officials, and at least two or three who married well-to-do tradesmen and professional men. Among the thousands whose careers were studied there was actually one who ended as the wife of the town's richest banker — that is, one who bagged the best catch in the whole community. This woman had begun as a domestic servant, and abandoned that harsh and dreary life to enter a high-toned brothel. Her experiences there polished and civilized her, and in her old age she was a *grande dame* of great dignity.

Much of the sympathy wasted upon women of the ancient profession is grounded upon an error as to their own attitude toward it. An educated woman, hearing that a frail sister in a public stew is expected to be amiable to all sorts of bounders, thinks of how *she* would shrink from such contacts, and so concludes that the actual prostitute suffers acutely. What she overlooks is that these men, however gross and repulsive they may appear to her, are measurably superior to men of the prostitute's own class — say her father and brothers — and that communion with them, far from being disgusting, is often rather romantic. I well remember observing, during my collaboration with the vice-crusaders aforesaid, the delight of a lady of joy who had attracted the notice of a police lieutenant; she was intensely pleased by the idea of having a client of such haughty manners, such brilliant dress, and what seemed to her to be so dignified a profession.

This weakness is not confined to the abandoned, but runs through the whole female sex. The woman who could not imagine an illicit affair with a wealthy soap manufacturer or even with a lawyer finds it quite easy to imagine herself succumbing to an ambassador or a duke. There are very few exceptions to this rule. In the most reserved of modern societies the women who represent their highest flower are notoriously complaisant to royalty. And royal women, to complete the circuit, not infrequently yield to actors and musicians, *i.e.*, to men radiating a glamor not encountered even in princes.

A Loss to Romance

From THE BLUSHFUL MYSTERY, PREJUDICES: FIRST SERIES,
1919, pp. 199–200.
First printed in the *Smart Set*, Feb., 1916, p. 155

THE AMERICAN puella is no longer naïve and charming; she goes to the altar of God with a learned and even cynical glitter in her eye. The veriest school-girl of today knows as much as the midwife of 1885, and spends a good deal more time discharging and disseminating her information. All this, of course, is highly embarrassing to the more romantic and ingenuous sort of men, of whom I have the honor to be one. We are constantly in the position of General Mitchener in Shaw's one-acter, "Press Cuttings," when he begs Mrs. Farrell, the talkative charwoman, to reserve her confidences for her medical adviser. One often wonders, indeed, what women now talk of to doctors.

I do not object to this New Freedom on moral grounds, but on purely esthetic grounds. In the relations between the sexes all beauty is founded upon romance, all romance is founded upon mystery, and all mystery is founded upon ignorance, or, failing that, upon the deliberate denial of the known truth. To be in love is merely to be in a state of perceptual anesthesia — to mistake an ordinary young man for a Greek discus-thrower or an ordinary young woman for a goddess. But how can this condition of mind survive the deadly matter-of-factness which sex hygiene and the new science of eugenics impose? How can a woman continue to believe in the honor, courage and loving tenderness of a man after she has learned, perhaps by affidavit, that his hemoglobin count is 117%, that he is free from sugar and albumen, that his blood pressure is 112/79 and that his Wassermann reaction is negative? Moreover, all this new-fangled frankness tends to dam up, at least for civilized adults, one of the principal well-springs of art, to wit, impropriety. If women, continuing their present tendency to its logical goal, end by going stark naked, there will be no more poets and painters, but only dermatologists.

The Balance Sheet

From REFLECTIONS ON HUMAN MONOGAMY, PREJUDICES:
FOURTH SERIES, 1924, p. 123

MARRIAGE, as everyone knows, is chiefly an economic matter. But too often it is assumed that its economy concerns only the wife's hats; it also concerns, and perhaps more importantly, the husband's cigars. No man is genuinely happy, married, who has to drink worse whiskey than he used to drink when he was single.

Compulsory Marriage

From IN DEFENSE OF WOMEN, 1918; revised, 1922, pp. 90–94.
First printed in the New York *Evening Mail*, Feb. 6, 1918

IN the days when I was a great deal more the revolutionary than I am now, I proposed the abolition of sentimental marriage by law and the substitution of pairing by the common hangman. This plan, if adopted, would have several plain advantages. For one thing, it would purge the serious business of marriage of the romantic fol-de-rol that now corrupts it, and so make for the peace and happiness of what is, technically speaking, the human race. For another thing, it would work against the process which now selects out those men who are most fit, and so throws the chief burden of paternity upon the inferior, to the damage of posterity.

The hangman, if he made his selections arbitrarily, would try to give his office permanence and dignity by choosing men whose marriage would meet with public approbation, *i.e.*, men obviously of the soundest stock and talents, *i.e.*, the sort of men who now habitually escape. And if he made his selection by the hazard of the die, or by drawing numbers out of a hat, or by any other such method of pure chance, that pure chance would fall indiscriminately upon all orders of men, and the upper orders would thus lose their present comparative immunity. True enough, a good many men would endeavor to influence him privately to their own advantage, and it is probable that, like any other public official, he would occasionally succumb, but it must be plain that the men most likely to prevail in that enterprise would not be philosophers, but politicians, and so there would be some benefit to the race even here. Posterity surely suffers no very heavy loss when a Congressman, a member of the House of Lords or even an ambassador or Prime Minister dies childless, but when a Kant goes to the grave without leaving sons behind him there is a detriment to all the generations of the future.

Many other theoretical advantages might be mentioned, but the execution of the scheme is made impossible, not only by inherent defects, but also by a general disinclination to abandon the present system, which at least offers certain attractions to concrete men and women, despite its unfavorable effects upon the unborn. Women would oppose the substitution of chance or arbitrary fiat for the existing struggle for husbands for the plain reason that every woman is convinced, and sometimes rightly, that her own judgment is superior to that of either the common hangman or the gods, and that her own enterprise is more favorable to her opportunities. And men would oppose it because it would restrict their liberty. This liberty, of course, is largely imaginary. In its common manifestation, it is no more, at bottom, than the privilege of being bamboozled and made a mock of by the first woman who stoops to essay the business. But none the less it is quite as precious to men as any other of the ghosts that their vanity conjures up for their enchantment. They cherish the notion that unconditioned volition enters into the matter, and that under volition there is not only a high degree of sagacity but also a touch of the daring and the devilish. A man is often almost as much pleased and flattered by his own marriage as he would be by seducing a duchess. In the one case, as in the other, his emotion is one of triumph. The substitution of pure chance would take away that soothing unction.

The present system, to be sure, also involves chance. Every man realizes it, and even the most bombastic bachelor has moments in which he humbly whispers: "There, but for the grace of God, go I." But that chance has a sugar-coating; it is swathed

in egoistic illusion; it shows less stark and intolerable chanci-
ness, so to speak, than the bald hazard of the die. Thus men
prefer it, and shrink from the other. In the same way, I have
no doubt, the majority of foxes would object to choosing lots
to determine the victim of a projected fox-hunt. They prefer
to take their chances with the dogs.

Cavia Cobaya

FROM REFLECTIONS ON HUMAN MONOGAMY, PREJUDICES:
FOURTH SERIES, 1924, pp. 117–18.
First printed in the *Smart Set*, Aug., 1920, p. 59

I FIND the following in Theodore Dreiser's "Hey-Rub-a-Dub-
Dub":

Does the average strong, successful man confine himself
to one woman? Has he ever?

The first question sets an insoluble problem. How are we, in
such intimate matters, to say what is the average and what is
not the average? But the second question is easily answered, and
the answer is, He has. Here Dreiser's curious sexual obsession
simply led him into absurdity. His view of the traffic of the sexes
remained the naïve one of an ex-Baptist nymph in Greenwich
Village. Did he argue that Otto von Bismarck was not a "strong,
successful man"? If not, then he should have known that Bismarck was a strict monogamist — a man full of sin, but always
faithful to his Johanna. Again, there was Thomas Henry Huxley. Again, there was William Ewart Gladstone. Yet again,
there were Robert Schumann, Felix Mendelssohn, Johann Sebastian Bach, Ulysses S. Grant, Andrew Jackson, Louis Pasteur,
Martin Luther, Helmuth von Moltke, Stonewall Jackson, Robert Browning, William T. Sherman, Sam Adams, . . . I could
extend the list to pages. . . . Perhaps I am unfair to Dreiser.
His notion of a "strong, successful man" may have been, not
such a genuinely superior fellow as Bismarck or Bach, but such
a mere brigand as Yerkes or Jim Fisk. If so, he was still wrong.
If so, he ran aground on John D. Rockefeller.

Art and Sex

From THE BLUSHFUL MYSTERY, PREJUDICES: FIRST SERIES,
1919, pp. 197–98.
First printed in the *Smart Set*, May, 1919, p. 54

ONE of the favorite notions of the Puritan mullahs who special-
ize in pornography is that the sex instinct, if suitably repressed,
may be "sublimated," as they say, into idealism, and especially
into esthetic idealism. That notion is to be found in all their
books; upon it they ground the theory that the enforcement of
chastity by a huge force of spies, stool pigeons and police would
convert the Republic into a nation of moral esthetes. All this,
of course, is simply pious fudge. If the notion were actually
sound, then all the great artists of the world would come from
the ranks of the hermetically repressed, *i.e.*, from the ranks of
old maids, male and female. But the truth is, as everyone
knows, that the great artists of the world are never Puritans,
and seldom even ordinarily respectable. No moral man — that
is, moral in the Y.M.C.A. sense — has ever painted a picture
worth looking at, or written a symphony worth hearing, or a
book worth reading, and it is highly improbable that the thing
has ever been done by a virtuous woman.

Offspring

From IN DEFENSE OF WOMEN, 1918; revised, 1922, pp. 67–68

THE WOMAN who has not had a child remains incomplete, ill at
ease, and more than a little ridiculous. She is in the position of
a man who has never stood in battle; she has missed the most
colossal experience of her sex. Moreover, a social odium goes
with her loss. Other women regard her as a sort of permanent
tyro, and treat her with ill-concealed disdain, and deride the
very virtue which lies at the bottom of her experiential penury.
There would seem to be, indeed, but small respect among
women for virginity *per se*. They are against the woman who

has got rid of hers outside marriage, not because they think she has lost anything intrinsically valuable, but because she has made a bad bargain, and one that materially diminishes the sentimental respect for virtue held by men, and hence one against the general advantage and well-being of the sex. In other words, it is a guild resentment that they feel, not a moral resentment. Women, in general, are not actively moral, nor, for that matter, noticeably modest. Every man, indeed, who is in wide practise among them is occasionally astounded and horrified to discover, on some rainy afternoon, an almost complete absence of modesty in some women of the highest respectability.

Sex Hygiene

From THE BLUSHFUL MYSTERY, PREJUDICES: FIRST SERIES,
1919, p. 197.
First printed in the *Smart Set*, April, 1919, p. 52

EVEN the most serious and honest of the sex hygiene tomes are probably futile, for they are all founded upon a pedagogical error. That is to say, they are all founded upon an attempt to explain a romantic mystery in terms of an exact science. Nothing could be more absurd: as well attempt to interpret Beethoven in terms of mathematical physics — as many a fatuous contrapuntist, indeed, has tried to do. The mystery of sex presents itself to the young, not as a scientific problem to be solved, but as a romantic itch to be accounted for. The only result of the current endeavor to explain its phenomena by seeking parallels in botany is to make botany obscene.

Eugenics

From EDUCATION, PREJUDICES: THIRD SERIES, 1922, p. 259

FIRST-RATE men are never begotten by Knights of Pythias; the notion that they sometimes are is due to an optical delusion.

When they appear in obscure and ignoble circles it is no more than a proof that only an extremely wise sire knows his son. Adultery, in brief, is one of nature's devices for keeping the lowest orders of men from sinking to the level of downright simians: sometimes for a few brief years in youth, their wives and daughters are comely — and now and then the baron drinks more than he ought.

The Double Standard

*From the same, p. 114. First printed in the *Smart Set*, Jan., 1923, p. 55*

THE DOUBLE standard of morality will survive in this world so long as a woman whose husband has been lured away is favored with the sympathetic tears of other women, and a man whose wife has made off is laughed at by other men.

The Supreme Comedy

FROM APPENDIX ON A TENDER THEME, PREJUDICES:
SECOND SERIES, 1920, pp. 244–45

MARRIAGE, at best, is full of a sour and inescapable comedy, but it never reaches the highest peaks of the ludicrous save when efforts are made to escape its terms — that is, when efforts are made to loosen its bounds, and so ameliorate and denaturize it. All projects to reform it by converting it into a free union of free individuals are inherently absurd. The thing is, at bottom, the most rigid of existing conventionalities, and the only way to conceal the fact and so make it bearable is to submit to it philosophically. The effect of every revolt is merely to make the bonds galling, and, what is worse, obvious. Who are happy in marriage? Those with so little imagination that they cannot picture a better state, and those so shrewd that they prefer quiet slavery to hopeless rebellion.

Woman as Realpolitiker

From REFLECTIONS ON HUMAN MONOGAMY, PREJUDICES:
FOURTH SERIES, 1924, p. 113

WOMEN in general are far too realistic to have any respect for so-called ideas. One seldom hears of them suffering and dying from any of the bogus Great Truths that men believe in. When a woman is on good terms with her husband she is quite willing to accept his idiotic theorizings on any subject that happens to engage him, whether theological, economic, epistemological or political. When one hears of a Republican man who has a Democratic wife, or *vice versa*, it is always safe to assume that she has her eye on a handsomer, richer or more docile fellow, and is thinking of calling up a lawyer.

After-Thoughts

Mainly from notes hitherto unpublished

IN every theologian there is a larval Torquemada, in every politician there are hopes of a Hitler, and in every wife there are vague glints and rumblings of Ruth Snyder. . . .

Every man, at some time or other in his life, plays the scoundrel to some woman. The decentest man imaginable has done it only once. . . .

Women's dislike of men, like the dislike of Englishmen for Americans, is sharpened by a mingling of envy and contempt. Men's dislike of women, like the dislike of Americans for Englishmen, is diluted by a sneaking suspicion that they are actually superior. . . .

The natural emotion of a normal young man after a conquest is not remorse, but elation. He is delighted by the triumphant demonstration of his manhood, and takes a natural mammalian joy in the fact that he has been accepted as a sexual object. In all probability, the normal girl feels much the same.

Remorse requires a period of incubation, precisely like that of the possible bacteriological effects of looseness. . . .

The other day, having my shoes shined, I was forced to listen to the old song, "Love Me, and the World is Mine!" on the professor's radio. Some day I should like to hear from a man who, having been loved in 1905 or thereabout, is still full of confidence that the world is his. . . .

One of the incentives to marriage is the desire for property, which is a subdivision of the craving for power. A husband, to the average woman, is very valuable property. So, to the average man, is a wife. No other domestic animal is so useful, or so greatly gratifies the vanity of the owner.

Romantic Interlude

From In Defense of Women, 1918; revised, 1922, pp. 207–09

IT is the close of a busy and vexatious day — say half past five or six o'clock of a Winter afternoon. I have had a cocktail or two, and am stretched out on a divan in front of a fire, smoking. At the edge of the divan, close enough for me to reach her with my hands, sits a woman not too young, but still good-looking and well-dressed — above all, a woman with a soft, low-pitched, agreeable voice. As I snooze she talks — of anything, everything, all the things that women talk of: books, music, dress, men, other women. No politics. No business. No theology. No metaphysics. Nothing challenging and vexatious — but remember, she is intelligent; what she says is clearly expressed, and often picturesquely. I observe the fine sheen of her hair, the pretty cut of her frock, the glint of her white teeth, the arch of her eyebrow, the graceful curve of her arm. I listen to the exquisite murmur of her voice. Gradually I fall asleep — but only for an instant. At once, observing it, she raises her voice ever so little, and I am awake. Then to sleep again — slowly and charmingly down that slippery hill of dreams. And then awake again, and then asleep again, and so on.

I ask you seriously: could anything be more unutterably beautiful? The sensation of falling asleep is to me the most delightful in the world. I relish it so much that I even look forward to death itself with a sneaking wonder and desire. Well, here is sleep poetized and made doubly sweet. Here is sleep set to the finest music in the world. I match this situation against any that you can think of. It is not only enchanting; it is also, in a very true sense, ennobling. In the end, when the lady grows prettily miffed and throws me out, I return to my sorrows somehow purged and glorified. I am a better man in my own sight. I have grazed upon the fields of asphodel. I have been genuinely, completely and unregrettably happy.

Apologia

From the same, pp. 209–10

A MAN is inseparable from his congenital vanities and stupidities, as a dog is inseparable from its fleas. They reveal themselves in everything he says and does, but they reveal themselves most of all when he discusses the majestic mystery of woman. Just as he smirks and rolls his eyes in her actual presence, so he puts on a pathetic and unescapable clownishness when he essays to dissect her in the privacy of the laboratory. There is no treatise on woman by a man that is not a stupendous compendium of posturings and imbecilities. There are but two that show even a superficial desire to be honest — "The Unexpurgated Case Against Woman Suffrage," by Sir Almroth Wright, and this one. Wright made a gallant attempt to tell the truth, but before he got half way through his task his ineradicable donkeyishness as a male overcame his scientific frenzy as a pathologist, and so he hastily washed his hands of the business, and affronted the judicious with a half-baked and preposterous work. Perhaps I have failed too, and even more ingloriously. If so, I am full of sincere and indescribable regret.

IV. RELIGION

The Cosmic Secretariat

From HIGH AND GHOSTLY MATTERS, PREJUDICES: FOURTH SERIES,
1924, pp. 61–65.
First printed in the *American Mercury*, Jan., 1924, pp. 75–76

THE ARGUMENT from design, once the bulwark of Christian apologetics, has been shot so full of holes that it is no wonder it has had to be abandoned. The more, indeed, the theologian seeks to prove the wisdom and omnipotence of God by His works, the more he is dashed by the evidences of divine incompetence and stupidity that the advance of science is constantly turning up. The world is not actually well run; it is very badly run, and no Huxley was needed to labor the obvious fact. The human body, very cunningly designed in some details, is cruelly and senselessly bungled in other details, and every reflective first-year medical student must notice a hundred ways to improve it. How are we to reconcile this mixture of finesse and blundering with the concept of a single omnipotent Designer, to whom all problems are equally easy? If He could contrive so efficient and durable a machine as the human hand, then how did He come to make such botches as the tonsils, the gall-bladder, the ovaries and the prostate gland? If He could perfect the elbow and the ear, then why did He boggle the teeth?

Having never encountered a satisfactory — or even a remotely plausible — answer to such questions, I have had to go to the trouble of devising one myself. It is, at all events, quite simple, and in strict accord with all the known facts. In brief, it is this: that the theory that the universe is run by a single God must be abandoned, and that in place of it we must set up the theory that it is actually run by a board of gods, all of equal puissance and authority. Once this concept is grasped the difficulties that have vexed theologians vanish, and human experience instantly lights up the whole dark scene. We observe in everyday life what happens when authority is divided, and great decisions are reached by consultation and compromise. We know that the effects at times, particularly when one of the consultants runs away with the others, are very good, but we also know that they are usually extremely bad. Such a mixture, precisely, is on display in the cosmos. It presents a series of brilliant successes in the midst of an infinity of failures.

I contend that my theory is the only one ever put forward that completely accounts for the clinical picture. Every other theory, facing such facts as sin, disease and disaster, is forced to admit the supposition that Omnipotence, after all, may not be omnipotent — a plain absurdity. I need toy with no such blasphemous nonsense. I may assume that every god belonging to the council which rules the universe is infinitely wise and infinitely powerful, and yet not evade the plain fact that most of the acts of that council are ignorant and foolish. In truth, my assumption that a council exists is tantamount to an *a priori* assumption that its acts are ignorant and foolish, for no act of any conceivable council can be otherwise. Is the human hand perfect, or, at all events, practical and praiseworthy? Then I account for it on the ground that it was designed by some single member of the council — that the business was turned over to him by inadvertence or as a result of an irreconcilable difference of opinion among the others. Had more than one member participated actively in its design it would have been measurably less meritorious than it is, for the sketch offered by the original designer would have been forced to run the gauntlet of criticisms and suggestions from all the other councillors, and human experience teaches us that most of these criticisms and suggestions would have been inferior to the original idea — that many of them, in fact, would have had nothing in them save a petty desire to maul and spoil the original idea.

But do I here accuse the high gods of harboring discreditable human weaknesses? If I do, then my excuse is that it is impossible to imagine them doing the work universally ascribed to them without admitting their possession of such weaknesses. One cannot imagine a god spending weeks and months, and maybe whole geological epochs, laboring over the design of the human kidney without assuming him to have been moved by a powerful impulse to express himself vividly, to marshal and publish his ideas, to win public credit among his fellows — in brief, without assuming him to be egoistic. And one cannot assume him to be egoistic without assuming him to prefer the adoption of his own ideas to the adoption of any other god's. I defy anyone to make the contrary assumption without plunging instantly into clouds of mysticism. Ruling it out, one comes inevitably to the conclusion that the inept management of the universe must be ascribed to clashes of egos, *i.e.*, to spites and revenges, among the gods, for any one of them alone, since we must assume him to be infinitely wise and powerful, could run it perfectly. We suffer from bad stomachs simply because the god who first proposed making a stomach aroused thereby the ill-nature of those who had not thought of it, and because they proceeded instantly to wreak that ill-nature upon him by improving, *i.e.*, botching, his work. We must reproduce our species in the familiar arduous, uneconomic, indecent and almost pathological manner because the god who devised the excellent process prevailing among the protozoa had to be put in his place when he proposed to extend it to the Primates.

The Nature of Faith

From the same, pp. 65–76

MANY years ago, when I was more reckless intellectually than I am today, I proposed the application of Haeckel's biogenetic law — to wit, that the history of the individual rehearses the history of the species — to the domain of ideas. So applied, it leads to some superficially startling but probably quite sound conclusions, for example, that an adult poet is simply an individual in a state of arrested development — in brief, a sort of moron. Just as all of us, *in utero*, pass through a stage in which we are tadpoles, and almost indistinguishable from the tadpoles which afterward become frogs, so all of us pass through a stage, in our nonage, when we are poets. A youth of seventeen who is not a poet is simply a donkey: his development has been arrested even anterior to that of the tadpole. But a man of fifty who still writes poetry is either an unfortunate who has never developed, intellectually, beyond his teens, or a conscious buffoon who pretends to be something that he isn't — something far younger and juicier than he actually is.

At adolescence large numbers of individuals, and maybe even most, have similar attacks of piety, but that is only saying that their powers of perception, at that age, outrun their knowledge. They observe the tangled and terrifying phenomena of life, but cannot account for them. Later on, unless their development is arrested, they gradually emerge from that romantic and spookish fog, just as they emerge from the hallucinations of poetry. I speak here, of course, of individuals genuinely capable of education — always a small minority. If, as the Army tests of conscripts showed, nearly 50 per cent. of American adult males never get beyond the mental development of a twelve-year-old child, then it must be obvious that a much smaller number get beyond the mental development of a youth at the end of his teens. I put that number, at a venture, at 10 per cent. The remaining 90 per cent. never quite free themselves from religious superstitions. They may no longer believe it is an act of God every time an individual catches a cold, or sprains his ankle, or cuts himself shaving, but they are pretty sure to see some trace of divine intervention in it if he is struck by lightning, or hanged, or afflicted with leprosy or syphilis.

All modern religions are based, at least on their logical side, on this notion that there are higher powers which observe the doings of man and constantly take a hand in them, and in the fold of Christianity, which is a good deal more sentimental than any other major religion, the concept of interest and intervention is associated with a concept of benevolence. In other words, it is believed that God is predominantly good. No true Christian can tolerate the idea that God ever deliberately and wantonly injures him, or could conceivably wish him ill. The slings and arrows that he suffers, he believes, are brought down upon him by his own ignorance and contumacy. Unhappily, this doctrine of the goodness of God does not fit into what we know of the nature and operations of the cosmos today; it is a survival from a day of universal ignorance. All science is simply a great mass-ing of proofs that God, if He exists, is really neither good nor bad, but simply indifferent — an infinite Force carrying on the operation of unintelligible processes without the slightest re-gard, either one way or the other, for the comfort, safety and happiness of man.

Why, then, does this belief survive? Largely, I am convinced, because it is supported by that other hoary relic from the adoles-cence of the race, to wit, the weakness for poetry. The Jews fastened their religion upon the Western world, not because it was more reasonable than the religions of their contemporaries — as a matter of fact, it was vastly less reasonable than many of them — but because it was far more poetical. The poetry in it was what fetched the decaying Romans, and after them the barbarians of the North; not the so-called Christian evidences. No better has ever been written. It is so powerful in its effects that even men who reject its content *in toto* are more or less susceptible. One hesitates to flout it on purely esthetic grounds; however dubious it may be in doctrine, it is nevertheless almost perfect in form, and so even the most violent atheist tends to respect it, just as he respects a beautiful but deadly toadstool. For no man, of course, ever quite gets over poetry. He may seem to have recovered from it, just as he may seem to have recovered from the measles of his school-days, but exact observation teaches us that no such recovery is ever quite perfect; there al-ways remains a scar, a weakness and a memory.

Now, there is reason for maintaining that the taste for poetry, in the process of human development, marks a stage measurably later than the stage of religion. Savages so little cultured that they know no more of poetry than a cow have elaborate and often very ingenious theologies. If this be true, then it follows that the individual, as he rehearses the life of the species, is apt to carry his taste for poetry further along than he carries his religion — that if his development is arrested at any stage be-fore complete intellectual maturity that arrest is far more likely to leave hallucinations. Thus, taking men in the mass, there are many more natural victims of the former than of the latter — and here is where the artfulness of the ancient Jews does its execution. It holds countless thousands to the faith who are actually against the faith, and the weakness with which it holds them is their weakness for poetry, *i.e.*, for the beautiful but untrue. Put into plain, harsh words most of the articles they are asked to believe would revolt them, but put into sonorous dithyrambs the same articles fascinate and overwhelm them.

This persistence of the weakness for poetry explains the curious growth of ritualism in an age of skepticism. Almost every day theology gets another blow from science. So badly has it been battered during the past century, indeed, that educated men now give it little more credence than they give to sorcery, its ancient ally. But squeezing out the logical nonsense does no damage to the poetry; on the contrary, it frees, and, in a sense, dignifies the poetry. Thus there is a constant movement of Christians, and particularly of newly-intellectual Christians, from the more literal varieties of Christian faith to the more poetical varieties. The normal idiot, in the United States, is born a Methodist or a Baptist, but when he begins to lay by money he and his wife tend to go over to the American outhouse of the Church of England, which is not only more fashionable but also less revolting to the higher cerebral centers. His daughter, when she emerges from the finishing-school, is very High Church; his grand-daughter, if the family keeps its securities, may go the whole hog by embracing Rome.

In view of all this, I am convinced that the Christian church, as a going concern, is quite safe from danger in the United States, despite the rapid growth of agnosticism. The theology it merchants is full of childish and disgusting absurdities; practically all the other religions of civilized and semi-civilized man are more plausible. But all of these religions, including Moslemism, contain the fatal defect that they appeal primarily to the reason. Christianity will survive not only Modernism but also Fundamentalism, a much more difficult business. It will survive because it makes its first and foremost appeal to that moony sense of the poetic which lingers in all men — to that elemental sentimentality which, in men of arrested mental development, which is to say, in the average men of Christendom, passes for the passion to seek and know beauty.[1]

---

[1] The reader fetched by this argument will find more to his taste in my *Treatise on the Gods*, second edition, 1946, pp. 286–89.

The Restoration of Beauty

From the same, pp. 77–78. First printed in the *Smart Set*,
March, 1920, p. 51

THE CHRISTIANS of the Apostolic Age were almost exactly like
the modern Holy Rollers — men quite without taste or imagination, whoopers and shouters, low vulgarians, cads. So far as
is known, their public worship was wholly devoid of the sense of
beauty; their sole concern was with the salvation of their so-
called souls. Thus they left us nothing worth preserving — not
a single church, or liturgy, or even hymn. The objects of art
exhumed from the Catacombs are inferior to the drawings and
statuettes of Crô-Magnon man. All the moving beauty that
adorns the corpse of Christianity today came into being long
after the Fathers had perished. The faith was many centuries
old before Christians began to build cathedrals. We think of
Christmas as the typical Christian festival, and no doubt it is;
none other is so generally kept by Christian sects, or so rich in
charm and beauty. Well, Christmas, as we now have it, was
almost unknown in Christendom until the Eleventh Century,
when the relics of St. Nicholas of Myra, originally the patron
of pawnbrokers, were brought from the East to Italy. All this
time the Universal Church was already torn by controversies
and menaced by schisms, and the shadow of the Reformation
was plainly discernible in the West. Religions, in fact, like
castles, sunsets and women, never reach their maximum of
beauty until they are touched by decay.

Holy Clerks

From the same, pp. 79–84. First printed in the *American Mercury*,
June, 1924, p. 183

AROUND no class of men do more false assumptions cluster than
around the rev. clergy, our lawful commissioners at the Throne

of Grace. I proceed at once to a crass example: the assumption that clergymen are necessarily religious. Obviously, it is widely cherished, even by clergymen themselves. The most ribald of us, in the presence of a holy clerk, is a bit self-conscious. I am myself given to criticizing Divine Providence somewhat freely, but in the company of the rector of my parish, even at the *Biertisch,* I tone down my animadversions to a level of feeble and polite remonstrance. I know the fellow too well, of course, to have any actual belief in his piety. He is, in fact, rather less pious than the average right-thinking Americano, and I doubt gravely that the sorceries he engages in professionally every day awaken in him any emotion more lofty than boredom. I have heard him pray for the President and Congress, the heathen and for rain, but I have never heard him pray for himself. Nevertheless, the public assumption that he is highly devout, though I dispute it, colors all my intercourse with him, and deprives him of hearing some of my most searching and intelligent observations.

All that is needed to expose the hollowness of this ancient delusion is to consider the chain of causes which brings a young man to taking holy orders. Is it, in point of fact, an irresistible religious impulse that sets him to studying exegetics, homiletics and the dog-Greek of the New Testament, and an irresistible religious impulse only, or is it something quite different? I believe that it is something quite different, and that that something may be described briefly as a desire to shine in the world without too much effort. The young theologue, in brief, is commonly an ambitious but somewhat lazy fellow, and he studies theology instead of osteopathy, salesmanship or the law because it offers a quicker and easier route to an assured job and public respect. The sacred sciences may be nonsensical, but they at least have the vast virtue of short-circuiting, so to speak, the climb up the ladder of security. The young medical man, for a number of years after he is graduated, either has to work for nothing or to content himself with the dregs of practise, and the young lawyer, unless he has unusual influence or complete atrophy of the conscience, often teeters on the edge of actual starvation. But the young divine is a safe and distinguished man the moment he is ordained; indeed, his popularity, especially among the faithful who are fair, is often greater at that moment than it ever is afterward. His livelihood is assured instantly. At one stroke, he becomes a person of dignity and importance, eminent in his community, deferred to even by those who question his magic, and vaguely and pleasantly feared by those who credit it.

These facts, you may be sure, are not concealed from aspiring young men of the sort I have mentioned. Such young men have eyes, and even a certain capacity for ratiocination. They observe the nine sons of the police sergeant: one a priest at twenty-five, with a fine house to live in, invitations to all the birthday parties for miles around, and plenty of time to go to the ball-game on Summer afternoons; the others struggling desperately to make their livings as furniture-movers, tin-roofers and bus-drivers. They observe the young Protestant dominie in his Ford sedan, flitting about among the women while their husbands labor down in the yards district, a clean collar around his neck, a solid meal of fried chicken in his gizzard, and his name in the local paper every day. Only crazy women ever fall in love with young insurance solicitors, but every young clergyman, if he is so inclined, may have a whole seraglio. Even if he is celibate, the gals bathe him in their smiles; in truth, the more celibate he is, the more attention he gets from them. No wonder his high privileges and immunities propagate the sin of envy. No wonder there are still candidates for the holy shroud, despite the vast growth of atheism among us.

The daily duties of a professional man of God have nothing to do with religion, but are basically social or commercial. In so far as he works at all, he works as the general manager of a corporation, and only too often it is in financial difficulties and rent by factions among the stockholders. His specifically theological hocus-pocus is of a routine and monotonous nature, and must needs depress him mightily, as a surgeon is depressed by the endless opening of boils. He gets rid of spiritual exaltation by reducing it to a hollow formality, as a politician gets rid of patriotism and a lady of joy of love. He becomes, in the end, quite anesthetic to religion, and even hostile to it. The fact is made distressingly visible by the right rev. the bench of bishops. For a bishop to fall on his knees spontaneously and begin to pray to God would make almost as great a scandal as if he mounted his throne in a bathing-suit. The piety of the ecclesiastic, on such high levels, becomes wholly theoretical. The servant of God has been lifted so near to the saints and become so familiar with the inner workings of the divine machinery that all awe and wonder have oozed out of him. He can no more undergo a genuine religious experience than a veteran scene-shifter can laugh at the wheezes of the First Gravedigger. It is, perhaps, well that this is so. If the higher clergy were actually religious some of their own sermons and pastoral epistles would scare them to death.

The Collapse of Protestantism

From PROTESTANTISM IN THE REPUBLIC, PREJUDICES: FIFTH SERIES, 1926, pp. 104–19.
First printed in the *American Mercury*, March, 1925, pp. 286–88

THAT Protestantism in this great Christian realm is down with a wasting disease must be obvious to every amateur of ghostly pathology. One half of it is moving, with slowly accelerating speed, in the direction of the Harlot of the Seven Hills: the other is sliding down into voodooism. The former carries the greater part of Protestant money with it; the latter carries the greater part of Protestant libido. What remains in the middle may be likened to a torso without either brains to think with or legs to dance — in other words, something that begins to be professionally attractive to the mortician, though it still makes shift to breathe. There is no lack of life on the higher levels, where the more solvent Methodists and the like are gradually transmogrified into Episcopalians, and the Episcopalians shin up the ancient bastions of Holy Church, and there is no lack of life on the lower levels, where the rural Baptists, by the route of Fundamentalism, rapidly descend to the dogmas and practises of the Congo jungle. But in the middle there is desiccation and decay. Here is where Protestantism was once strongest. Here is the region of the plain and godly Americano, fond of devotion but distrustful of every hint of orgy — the honest fellow who suffers dutifully on Sunday, pays his tithes, and hopes for a few kind words from the pastor when his time comes to die. Today, alas, he tends to absent himself from pious exercises, and the news goes about that there is something the matter with the churches, and the denominational papers bristle with schemes to set it right, and many up-and-coming pastors, tiring of preaching and parish work, get jobs as the executive secretaries of these schemes, and go about the country expounding them to the faithful.

The extent to which Protestantism, in its upper reaches, has succumbed to the lascivious advances of Rome seems to be but little apprehended by the majority of connoisseurs. I was myself unaware of the whole truth until a recent Christmas, when, in the pursuit of a quite unrelated inquiry, I employed agents to attend all the services held in the principal Protestant basilicas of an eminent American city, and to bring in the best reports they could formulate upon what went on in the lesser churches. The substance of these reports, in so far as they related to churches patronized by the well-to-do, was simple: they revealed a head-long movement to the right, an almost precipitate flight over the mountain. Six so-called Episcopal churches held midnight services on Christmas Eve in obvious imitation of Catholic midnight masses, and one of them actually called its service a solemn high mass. Two invited the nobility and gentry to processions, and a third concealed a procession under the name of a pageant. One offered Gounod's St. Cecilia mass on Christmas morning, and another the Messe Solennelle by the same composer; three others, somewhat more timorous, contented themselves with parts of masses. One, throwing off all pretense and euphemism, summoned the faithful to no less than three Christmas masses, naming them by name — two low and one high. All six churches were aglow with candles, and two employed incense.

But that was not the worst. Two Presbyterian churches and one Baptist church, not to mention five Lutheran churches of different synods, had carol services in the dawn of Christmas morning, and the one attended by the only one of my agents who got up early enough — it was in a Presbyterian church —

was made gay with candles, and had a palpably Roman smack. Yet worse: a rich and conspicuous Methodist church, patronized by the leading Wesleyan wholesalers and money-lenders of the town, boldly offered a "medieval" carol service. Medieval? What did that mean? The Middle Ages ended on July 16, 1453, at 12 o'clock meridian, and the Reformation was not launched by Martin Luther until October 31, 1517, at 10.15 a.m. If medieval, in the sense in which it was here used, did not mean Roman Catholic, then I surely went to school in vain. My agent, born a Methodist, reported that the whole ceremony shocked him excessively. It began with trumpet blasts from the church spire and it concluded with an Ave Maria by a vested choir. Candles rose up in glittering ranks behind the chancel rail, and above them glowed a shining electric star. God help us all, indeed! What next? Will the rev. pastor, on some near tomorrow, defy the lightnings of Yahweh by appearing in alb and dalmatic? Will he turn his back upon the faithful? Will he put in a telephone-booth for auricular confession?

Certainly no one argues that the use of candles in public worship would have had the sanction of the *Ur*-Wesleyans, or that they would have consented to *Blasmusik* and a vested choir. Down to sixty or seventy years ago, in fact, the Methodists prohibited Christmas services altogether, as Romish and heathen. But now we have ceremonies almost operatic. As I have said, the Episcopalians — who, in most American cities, are largely ex-Methodists or ex-Presbyterians, or, in New York, ex-Jews — go still further. In three of the churches attended by my agents Holy Communion was almost indistinguishable from a mass — and in every one there was a good house and what the colored pastors call a good plate. Even the Methodists who remain Methodists begin to wobble. Tiring of the dreadful din that goes with the orthodox Wesleyan demonology, they take to goings-on that grow more and more stately and voluptuous. The sermon ceases to be a cavalry charge, and becomes soft and *pizzicato*. The choir abandons "Throw Out the Life-Line" and "Are You Ready for the Judgment Day?" and toys with Handel. It is an evolution that has, viewed from a tree, a certain merit. The stock of nonsense in the world is sensibly diminished and the stock of beauty augmented. But what would the old-time circuit-riders say of it, imagining them miraculously brought back from Hell?

So much for the volatilization that is going on above the diaphragm. What is in progress below? All I can detect is a rapid descent to mere barbaric devil-chasing. In all those parts of the Republic where Beelzebub is still real — for example, in the rural sections of the Middle West and everywhere in the South save a few walled towns — the evangelical sects plunge into an abyss of malignant imbecility, and declare a holy war upon every decency that civilized men cherish. They have thrown the New Testament overboard, and gone back to the Old, and particularly to the bloodiest parts of it. What one mainly notices about the clerics who lead them is their vast lack of sound information and sound sense. They constitute, perhaps, the most ignorant class of teachers ever set up to guide a presumably civilized people; they are even more ignorant than the county superintendents of schools. Learning, indeed, is not esteemed in the evangelical denominations, and any literate plow-hand, if the Holy Spirit inflames him, is thought to be fit to preach. Is he commonly sent, as a preliminary, to a training camp, to college? But what a college! You will find one in every mountain valley of the land, with its single building in its bare pasture lot, and its faculty of half-idiot pedagogues and broken-down preachers. One man, in such a college, teaches oratory, ancient history, arithmetic and Old Testament exegesis. The aspirant comes in from the barnyard, and goes back in a year or two to the village. His body of knowledge is that of a bus-driver or a vaudeville actor. But he has learned the clichés of his craft, and he has got him a black Sunday coat, and so he has made his escape from the harsh labors of his ancestors, and is set up as a fountain of light and learning.

Immune

From the *American Mercury*, March, 1930, p. 289.
First printed, in part, in the Baltimore *Evening Sun*, Dec. 9, 1929

THE MOST curious social convention of the great age in which we live is the one to the effect that religious opinions should be respected. Its evil effects must be plain enough to everyone. All it accomplishes is (*a*) to throw a veil of sanctity about ideas that violate every intellectual decency, and (*b*) to make every theologian a sort of chartered libertine. No doubt it is mainly to blame for the appalling slowness with which really sound notions make their way in the world. The minute a new one is launched, in whatever fields, some imbecile of a theologian is certain to fall upon it, seeking to put it down. The most effective way to defend it, of course, would be to fall upon the theologian, for the only really workable defense, in polemics as in war, is a vigorous offensive. But convention frowns upon that device as indecent, and so theologians continue their assault upon sense without much resistance, and the enlightenment is unpleasantly delayed.

There is, in fact, nothing about religious opinions that entitles them to any more respect than other opinions get. On the contrary, they tend to be noticeably silly. If you doubt it, then ask any pious fellow of your acquaintance to put what he believes into the form of an affidavit, and see how it reads. . . . "I, John Doe, being duly sworn, do say that I believe that, at death, I shall turn into a vertebrate without substance, having neither weight, extent nor mass, but with all the intellectual powers and bodily sensations of an ordinary mammal; . . . and that, for the high crime and misdemeanor of having kissed my sister-in-law behind the door, with evil intent, I shall be boiled in molten sulphur for one billion calendar years." Or, "I, Mary Roe, having the fear of Hell before me, do solemnly affirm and declare that I believe it was right, just, lawful and decent for the Lord God Jehovah, seeing certain little children of Beth-el laugh at Elisha's bald head, to send a she-bear from the wood, and to instruct, incite, induce and command it to tear forty-two

of them to pieces." Or, "I, the Right Rev. ——— ———,
Bishop of ———, D.D., LL.D., do honestly, faithfully and on
my honor as a man and a priest, declare that I believe that
Jonah swallowed the whale," or *vice versa*, as the case may be.

No, there is nothing notably dignified about religious ideas.
They run, rather, to a peculiarly puerile and tedious kind of
nonsense. At their best, they are borrowed from metaphysicians, which is to say, from men who devote their lives to
proving that twice two is not always or necessarily four. At their
worst, they smell of spiritualism and fortune-telling. Nor is there
any visible virtue in the men who merchant them professionally.
Few theologians know anything that is worth knowing, even
about theology, and not many of them are honest. One may
forgive a Communist or a Single Taxer on the ground that there
is something the matter with his ductless glands, and that a
Winter in the south of France would relieve him. But the
average theologian is a hearty, red-faced, well-fed fellow with
no discernible excuse in pathology. He disseminates his blather,
not innocently, like a philosopher, but maliciously, like a politician. In a well-organized world he would be on the stone-pile.
But in the world as it exists we are asked to listen to him, not
only politely, but even reverently, and with our mouths open.

A New Use for Churches

From Damn! A Book of Calumny, 1918, pp. 88–89

Granting the existence of God, a house dedicated to Him naturally follows. He is all-important; it is fit that man should take
some notice of Him. But why praise and flatter Him for
His unspeakable cruelties? Why forget so supinely His failures
to remedy the easily remediable? Why, indeed, devote the
churches exclusively to worship? Why not give them over, now
and then, to justifiable indignation meetings?

If God can hear a petition, there is no ground for holding
that He would not hear a complaint. It might, indeed, please
Him to find His creatures grown so self-reliant and reflective.

More, it might even help Him to get through His infinitely complex and difficult work. Theology, in fact, has already moved toward such notions. It has abandoned the primitive doctrine of God's arbitrariness and indifference, and substituted the doctrine that He is willing, and even eager, to hear the desires of His creatures — i.e., their private notions, born of experience, as to what would be best for them. Why assume that those notions would be any the less worth hearing and heeding if they were cast in the form of criticism, and even of denunciation? Why hold that the God who can understand and forgive even treason could not understand and forgive remonstrance?

Free Will

From the same, pp. 91–94

FREE will, it appears, is still an essential dogma to most Christians. Without it the cruelties of God would strain faith to the breaking-point. But outside the fold it is gradually falling into decay. Men of science have dealt it staggering blows, and among laymen of inquiring mind it seems to be giving way to an apologetic sort of determinism — a determinism, one may say, tempered by defective observation. Mark Twain, in his secret heart, was such a determinist. In his "What Is Man?" you will find him at his farewells to libertarianism. The vast majority of our acts, he argues, are determined, but there remains a residuum of free choices. Here we stand free of compulsion and face a pair or more of alternatives, and are free to go this way or that.

A pillow for free will to fall upon — but one loaded with disconcerting brickbats. Where the occupants of this last trench of libertarianism err is in their assumption that the pulls of their antagonistic impulses are exactly equal — that the individual is absolutely free to choose which one he will yield to. Such freedom, in practise, is never encountered. When an individual confronts alternatives, it is not alone his volition that chooses between them, but also his environment, his inherited prejudices, his race, his color, his condition of servitude. I may

kiss a girl or I may not kiss her, but surely it would be absurd to
say that I am, in any true sense, a free agent in the matter. The
world has even put my helplessness into a proverb. It says that
my decision and act depend upon the time, the place — and
even to some extent, upon the girl.

Examples might be multiplied *ad infinitum*. I can scarcely
remember performing a wholly voluntary act. My whole life, as
I look back upon it, seems to be a long series of inexplicable
accidents, not only quite unavoidable, but even quite unintelligible. Its history is the history of the reactions of my personality
to my environment, of my behavior before external stimuli. I
have been no more responsible for that personality than I have
been for that environment. To say that I can change the former
by a voluntary effort is as ridiculous as to say that I can modify
the curvature of the lenses of my eyes. I know, because I have
often tried to change it, and always failed. Nevertheless, it has
changed. I am not the same man I was in the last century. But
the gratifying improvements so plainly visible are surely not to
be credited to me. All of them came from without — or from
unplumbable and uncontrollable depths within.

The more the matter is examined the more the residuum of
free will shrinks and shrinks, until in the end it is almost impossible to find it. A great many men, of course, looking at
themselves, see it as something very large; they slap their chests
and call themselves free agents, and demand that God reward
them for their virtue. But these fellows are simply egoists devoid
of a critical sense. They mistake the acts of God for their own
acts. They are brothers to the fox who boasted that he had
made the hounds run.

The throwing overboard of free will is commonly denounced
on the ground that it subverts morality, and makes of religion
a mocking. Such pious objections, of course, are foreign to
logic, but nevertheless it may be well to give a glance to this
one. It is based upon the fallacious hypothesis that the determinist escapes, or hopes to escape, the consequences of his
acts. Nothing could be more untrue. Consequences follow acts
just as relentlessly if the latter be involuntary as if they be
voluntary. If I rob a bank of my free choice or in response to
some unfathomable inner necessity, it is all one; I go to the

same jail. Conscripts in war are killed just as often as volunteers.

Even on the ghostly side, determinism does not do much damage to theology. It is no harder to believe that a man will be damned for his involuntary acts than it is to believe that he will be damned for his voluntary acts, for even the supposition that he is wholly free does not dispose of the massive fact that God made him as he is, and that God could have made him a saint if He had so desired. To deny this is to flout omnipotence — a crime at which I balk. But here I begin to fear that I wade too far into the hot waters of the sacred sciences, and that I had better retire before I lose my hide. This prudent retirement is purely deterministic. I do not ascribe it to my own sagacity; I ascribe it wholly to that singular kindness which fate always shows me. If I were free I'd probably keep on, and then regret it afterward.

Sabbath Meditation

In part from the *American Mercury*, May, 1924, pp. 60–61, and in part from the *Smart Set*, Oct., 1923, pp. 138–42

MY essential trouble, I sometimes suspect, is that I am quite devoid of what are called spiritual gifts. That is to say, I am incapable of religious experience, in any true sense. Religious ceremonials often interest me esthetically, and not infrequently they amuse me otherwise, but I get absolutely no stimulation out of them, no sense of exaltation, no mystical *katharsis*. In that department I am as anesthetic as a church organist, an archbishop or an altar boy. When I am low in spirits and full of misery, I never feel any impulse to seek help, or even mere consolation, from supernatural powers. Thus the generality of religious persons remain mysterious to me, and vaguely offensive, as I am unquestionably offensive to them. I can no more understand a man praying than I can understand him carrying a rabbit's foot to bring him luck. This lack of understanding is a cause of enmities, and I believe that they are sound ones. I dislike any man who is pious, and all such men that I know dislike me.

I am anything but a militant atheist and haven't the slightest objection to church-going, so long as it is honest. I have gone to church myself more than once, honestly seeking to experience the great inward kick that religious persons speak of. But not even at St. Peter's in Rome have I sensed the least trace of it. The most I ever feel at the most solemn moment of the most pretentious religious ceremonial is a sensuous delight in the beauty of it — a delight exactly like that which comes over me when I hear, say, "Tristan and Isolde" or Brahms' fourth symphony. The effect of such music, in fact, is much keener than the effect of the liturgy. Brahms moves me far more powerfully than the holy saints.

As I say, this deficiency is a handicap in a world peopled, in the overwhelming main, by men who are inherently religious. It sets me apart from my fellows and makes it difficult for me to understand many of their ideas and not a few of their acts. I see them responding constantly and robustly to impulses that to me are quite inexplicable. Worse, it causes these folks to misunderstand me, and often to do me serious injustice. They cannot rid themselves of the notion that, because I am anesthetic to the ideas which move them most profoundly, I am, in some vague but nevertheless certain way, a man of aberrant morals, and hence one to be kept at a distance. I have never met a religious man who did not reveal this suspicion. No matter how earnestly he tried to grasp my point of view, he always ended by making an alarmed sort of retreat. All religions, in fact, teach that dissent is a sin; most of them make it the blackest of all sins, and all of them punish it severely whenever they have the power. It is impossible for a religious man to rid himself of the notion that such punishments are just. He simply cannot imagine a civilized rule of conduct that is not based upon the fear of God.

Let me add that my failing is in the fundamental religious impulse, not in mere theological credulity. I am not kept out of the church by an inability to believe the current dogmas. In point of fact, a good many of them seem to me to be reasonable enough, and I probably dissent from most of them a good deal less violently than many men who are assiduous devotees. Among my curious experiences, years ago, was that of convincing an ardent Catholic who balked at the dogma of papal infallibility. He was a very faithful son of the church and his inability to accept it greatly distressed him. I proved to him, at least to his satisfaction, that there was nothing intrinsically absurd in it — that if the dogmas that he already accepted were true then this one was probably true also. Some time later, when this man was on his death-bed, I visited him and he thanked me simply and with apparent sincerity for resolving his old doubt. But even he was unable to comprehend my own lack of religion. His last words to me were a pious hope that I would give over my lamentable contumacy to God and lead a better life. He died firmly convinced that I was headed for Hell, and, what is more, that I deserved it.

The Immortality of the Soul

From the *American Mercury*, Sept., 1932, pp. 125–26

WHEN it comes to the immortality of the soul, whatever that may be precisely, I can only say that it seems to me to be wholly incredible and preposterous. There is not only no plausible evidence for it: there is a huge mass of irrefutable evidence against it, and that evidence increases in weight and cogency every time a theologian opens his mouth. All the common arguments for it may be reduced to four. The first is logical and is to the effect that it would be impossible to imagine God creating so noble a beast as man, and then letting him die after a few unpleasant years on earth. The answer is simple: I can imagine it, and so can many other men. Moreover, there is no reason to believe that God regards man as noble: on the contrary, all the available theological testimony runs the other way. The second argument is that a belief in immortality is universal in mankind, and that its very universality is ample proof of its truth. The answer is (*a*) that many men actually dissent, some of them in a very violent and ribald manner, and (*b*) that even if all men said aye it would prove nothing, for all men once said aye to the existence of witches. The third argument is that the dead, speaking through the mouths of gifted mediums, frequently communicate with the living, and must thus be alive themselves. Unfortunately, the evidence for this is so dubious that it takes a special kind of mind to credit it, and that kind of mind is far from persuasive. The fourth and final argument is based frankly on revelation: the soul is immortal because God hath said it is.

I confess that this last argument seems to me to be rather more respectable than any of the others: it at least makes no silly attempt to lug in the methods of science to prove a proposition in theology. But all the same there are plenty of obvious holes in it. Its proponents get into serious difficulties when they undertake to say when and how the soul gets into the body, and where it comes from. Must it be specially created in each instance, or is it the offspring of the two parent souls? In either case, when does it appear, at the moment of conception or somewhat later? If the former, then what happens to the soul of a zygote cast out, say, an hour after fertilization? If the death of that soul ensues, then the soul is not immortal in all cases, which means that its immortality can be certain in none: and if, on the contrary, it goes to Heaven or Hell or some vague realm between, then we are asked to believe that the bishops and archbishops who swarm beyond the grave are forced to associate, and on terms of equality, with shapes that can neither think nor speak, and resemble tadpoles far more than they resemble Christians. And if it be answered that all souls, after death, develop to the same point and shed all the characters of the flesh, then every imaginable scheme of *post-mortem* jurisprudence becomes ridiculous.

The assumption that the soul enters the body at some time after conception opens difficulties quite as serious, but I shall not annoy you with them in this hot weather. Suffice it to say that it forces one to believe either that there is a time when a human embryo, though it is alive, is not really a human being, or that a human being can exist without a soul. Both notions revolt me — the first as a student of biology, and the second as a dutiful subject of a great Christian state. The answers of the professional theologians are all inadequate. The Catholics try to get rid of the problem by consigning the souls of the unbaptized to a Limbus Infantum which is neither Heaven nor Hell, but that is only a begging of the question. As for the Protestants, they commonly refuse to discuss it at all. Their position seems to be that everyone ought to believe in the immortality of the soul as a matter of common decency, and that, when one has got that far, the details are irrelevant. But my appetite for details continues to plague me. I am naturally full of curiosity about a doctrine which, if it can be shown to be true, is of the utmost personal importance to me. Failing light, I go on believing dismally that when the bells ring and the cannon are fired, and people go rushing about frantic with grief, and my mortal clay is stuffed for the National Museum at Washington, it will be the veritable end of the noble and lovely creature once answering to the name of Henry.

Miracles

From the *American Mercury*, May, 1924, p. 61

HAS it ever occurred to anyone that miracles may be explained, not on the ground that the gods have transiently changed their rules, but on the ground that they have gone dozing and forgotten to enforce them? If they slept for two days running the moon might shock and singe us all by taking a header into the sun. For all we know, the moon may be quite as conscious as a poet or a realtor, and extremely weary of its monotonous round. It may long, above all things, for a chance to plunge into the sun and end the farce. What keeps it on its track is simply some external will — maybe not will embodied in any imaginable being, but nevertheless will. Law without will is quite as unthinkable as steam without heat.

Quod est Veritas?

From DAMN! A BOOK OF CALUMNY, 1918, p. 95

ALL great religions, in order to escape absurdity, have to admit
a dilution of agnosticism. It is only the savage, whether of the
African bush or the American gospel tent, who pretends to
know the will and intent of God exactly and completely. "For
who hath known the mind of the Lord?" asked Paul of the Romans. "How unsearchable are His judgments, and His ways past
finding out!" "It is the glory of God," said Solomon, "to conceal
a thing." "Clouds and darkness," said David, "are around Him."
"No man," said the Preacher, "can find out the work of God."
. . . The difference between religions is a difference in their
relative content of agnosticism. The most satisfying and ecstatic
faith is almost purely agnostic. It trusts absolutely without pro-
fessing to know at all.

The Doubter's Reward

From DAMN! A BOOK OF CALUMNY, 1918, p. 96

DESPITE the common delusion to the contrary the philosophy
of doubt is far more comforting than that of hope. The doubter
escapes the worst penalty of the man of faith and hope; he is
never disappointed, and hence never indignant. The inexplicable
and irremediable may interest him, but they do not enrage him,
or, I may add, fool him. This immunity is worth all the dubious
assurances ever foisted upon man. It is pragmatically impregnable. Moreover, it makes for tolerance and sympathy. The
doubter does not hate his opponents; he sympathizes with
them. In the end he may even come to sympathize with God.
The old idea of fatherhood here submerges in a new idea
of brotherhood. God, too, is beset by limitations, difficulties,
broken hopes. Is it disconcerting to think of Him thus? Well,
is it any the less disconcerting to think of Him as able to ease
and answer, and yet failing?

Holy Writ

From the *Smart Set*, Oct., 1923, pp. 141–42

WHOEVER it was who translated the Bible into excellent French prose is chiefly responsible for the collapse of Christianity in France. Contrariwise, the men who put the Bible into archaic, sonorous and often unintelligible English gave Christianity a new lease of life wherever English is spoken. They did their work at a time of great theological blather and turmoil, when men of all sorts, even the least intelligent, were beginning to take a vast and unhealthy interest in exegetics and apologetics. They were far too shrewd to feed this disconcerting thirst for ideas with a Bible in plain English; the language they used was deliberately artificial even when it was new. They thus dispersed the mob by appealing to its emotions, as a mother quiets a baby by crooning to it. The Bible that they produced was so beautiful that the great majority of men, in the face of it, could not fix their minds upon the ideas in it. To this day it has enchanted the English-speaking peoples so effectively that, in the main, they remain Christians, at least sentimentally. Paine has assaulted them, Darwin and Huxley have assaulted them and a multitude of other merchants of facts have assaulted them, but they still remember the twenty-third Psalm when the doctor begins to shake his head, they are still moved beyond compare (though not, alas, to acts!) by the Sermon on the Mount, and they still turn once a year from their sordid and degrading labors to immerse themselves unashamed in the story of the manger. It is not much, but it is something. I do not admire the general run of American Bible-searchers — Methodists, United Brethren, Baptists, and such vermin. But try to imagine what the average low-browed Methodist would be if he were not a Methodist but an atheist!

The Latin Church, which I constantly find myself admiring, despite its frequent astounding imbecilities, has always kept clearly before it the fact that religion is not a syllogism, but a poem. It is accused by Protestant dervishes of withholding the Bible from the people. To some extent this is true; to the same extent the church is wise; again to the same extent it is prosperous. Its toying with ideas, in the main, have been confined to its clergy, and they have commonly reduced the business to a harmless play of technicalities — the awful concepts of Heaven and Hell brought down to the level of a dispute of doctors in long gowns, eager only to dazzle other doctors. Its greatest theologians remain unknown to 99% of its adherents. Rome, indeed, has not only preserved the original poetry in Christianity; it has also made capital additions to that poetry — for example, the poetry of the saints, of Mary, and of the liturgy itself. A solemn high mass must be a thousand times as impressive, to a man with any genuine religious sense in him, as the most powerful sermon ever roared under the big-top by a Presbyterian auctioneer of God. In the face of such overwhelming beauty it is not necessary to belabor the faithful with logic; they are better convinced by letting them alone.

Preaching is not an essential part of the Latin ceremonial. It was very little employed in the early church, and I am convinced that good effects would flow from abandoning it today, or, at all events, reducing it to a few sentences, more or less formal. In the United States the Latin brethren have been seduced by the example of the Protestants, who commonly transform an act of worship into a puerile intellectual exercise; instead of approaching God in fear and wonder these Protestants settle back in their pews, cross their legs, and listen to an ignoramus try to prove that he is a better theologian than the Pope. This folly the Romans now slide into. Their clergy begin to grow argumentative, doctrinaire, ridiculous. It is a pity. A bishop in his robes, playing his part in the solemn ceremonial of the mass, is a dignified spectacle, even though he may sweat freely; the same bishop, bawling against Darwin half an hour later, is seen to be simply an elderly Irishman with a bald head, the son of a respectable saloon-keeper in South Bend, Ind. Let the reverend fathers go back to Bach. If they keep on spoiling poetry and spouting ideas, the day will come when some extra-bombastic deacon will astound humanity and insult God by proposing to translate the liturgy into American, that all the faithful may be convinced by it.

The Powers of the Air

From SOUVENIRS OF A BOOK REVIEWER, PREJUDICES: SIXTH SERIES, 1927, pp. 125-31.
First printed in the *American Mercury*, May, 1927, pp. 123-25. A review of The History of Witchcraft and Demonology, by Montague Summers; New York, 1927. Summers died in 1948

THE AUTHOR of this tome, an English clergyman — his full name is the Rev. Alphonsus Joseph-Mary Augustus Montague Summers, M.A. — wastes no time trying to reconcile Christianity and science, a folly that has brought so many American scientists, including the eminent but mushy Dr. Robert Andrews Millikan, to grief. He is in favor of Christianity, not of science, and with it, in the manner of a true believer, he goes the whole hog. Does Exodus XXII, 18, say flatly that witches exist, and that it is the duty of every righteous man to butcher them when found? Then Summers accepts the fact and the duty without evasion, and proceeds to elaborate on both. He can't imagine a Christian who refuses to believe in demoniacal possession, and no more can I. Marshaling an array of proofs that must shake even an atheistic archbishop, he demonstrates with fine eloquence and impeccable logic that the air is full of sinister spirits, and that it is their constant effort to enter into the bodies of men and women, and so convert good Christians, made in God's image, into witches, sorcerers, spiritualists, biologists, and other such revolting shapes. The Bible is the rock of his argument, but he also makes frequent and very effective use of the revelations vouchsafed to Holy Church.

There has never been a time in Christian history, he shows, when its chief experts and wiseacres did not believe in demons. The Roman rite, accepting their existence as indubitable, provides elaborate machinery for their scotching to this day. That machinery, to be sure, is not put into effect lightly. So long as the medical faculty is convinced that the patient is suffering from nothing worse than a leaping tapeworm or delirium tremens, and hope of his cure by chemical and mechanical means is thus held out, he is resigned to the secular arm. But once it becomes manifest that a fiend or goblin has got into him, the business becomes a matter for supernatural intervention, and the subsequent proceedings must be carried on by an ordained pastor, and according to a formula set forth in the Rituale Romanum, and in use since the pontificate of Peter I.

This formula is extremely complicated, and I suspect that using it must be somewhat fatiguing to the officiating clergyman. He must be himself a man of mature years, guiltless of anything even approaching loose living, and, according to Summers, "a systematic student, and well versed in the latest trends and development of psychological science." He is required to make himself quite sure, before he begins his exorcism, that the patient before him is actually possessed by a demon — that he is not confronting a mere case of insanity, or, worse still, imposture. Once convinced, he proceeds with the utmost heat and diligence, never relenting until the unclean spirit takes wing, and so returns to Hell. Summers gives the words of the exorcism, translated into English; they are so terrifying that I hesitate to reprint them in a volume designed for reading aloud at the domestic hearth. The demon is denounced in words that sting like scorpions: no Baptist pastor, damning Darwin, ever scorched the air with worse. And if, at the first attack, they fail to dislodge him, they are to be used again, and then again, and so on until the exorcism is completed. The patient, it appears, is apt to fall asleep while they are being intoned: making him to do so is one of the Devil's favorite tricks. If it happens, then the exorcist must awaken him, and by any device that seems workable, including smart blows *a posteriori*. Ordinarily, all this must be done in a church, but if the patient is too ill to leave his bed the exorcist may visit him in his boarding-house. Idle spectators are forbidden, but the canon requires that, as at a baptism or electrocution, a number of official witnesses, of known piety and sober mien, shall be present. No unnecessary conversation with the demon is permitted. If he speaks through the mouth of the patient, he is to be heard politely, but when he has had a sufficient say he is to be shut off. In particular, he is not to be permitted to indulge in ribaldries.

It is commonly believed that Protestantism questions the actuality of demoniacal possession, but this is not so. True enough, the Unitarians and Universalists have doubts about it, but so far as I am aware no other Protestant sect has ever formally repudiated it. There is a canon of the Church of England which forbids a priest to exorcise demons without the "license or direction (*mandatum*)" of his bishop, but there is nothing to prevent a bishop issuing such a *mandatum*. The Lutherans, who are very orthodox, all believe in demons, and hence, by a necessary inference, in witches; if they did not they would have to put Martin Luther down as a liar. As for the Methodists, the Baptists and other such mudsills of the Lord, it must be obvious that doubts among them are confined to a few advanced intellectuals, debauched by reading the epicurean poetry of Edgar A. Guest. The Baptists, at least in the South, even believe in ghosts, especially the colored brethren. The colored pastors have an elaborate ceremonial for exorcising all varieties of spirits, good or evil; an important part of it is the free-will offering just before the curative anathema is launched. In my own native republic, the Saorstát Maryland, I once made an attempt to ascertain the number of people, regardless of creed, who believed in ghosts and witches. After elaborate inquiries through prudent agents, I came to the conclusion that 92% of the population believed in ghosts, and that 74% also believed in witches. In the latter group was the then Governor of the State. He believed that rheumatism was caused by witchcraft, and wore a string around his middle to ward it off. The Marylanders are a gay and liberty-loving people, and drink and drab, perhaps, somewhat more than is good for them, but atheism has never made much progress among them. At least one of the eminent professors in the Johns Hopkins Medical School, at Baltimore, was once publicly accused of believing in witches, and never, so far as I know, denied it.

Summers is equally honest, and I think he deserves all praise for being so. Most ecclesiastics, when they write upon such subjects, try to evade the clear issue. They seem to be convinced — on what ground I don't know — that the old belief in demons is now dying out in the world, and to be afraid that they will be laughed at if they confess to it. All I can say is that that is a poor way to get into Heaven *post mortem*. Such duckers and skulkers, you may be sure, will have extremely unpleasant sessions with St. Peter when they reach the Gates, and Peter will be well justified in razzing them. Either the Christian religion involves a belief in disembodied powers, good and evil, or it doesn't. If it doesn't, then its Sacred Scriptures are a mass of nonsense, and even its Founder was grossly misinformed. If it does, then everyone adhering to it ought to confess the fact frankly, and without ignominious equivocation. This is what Summers does. In detail, his colleagues in theology may sometimes reasonably challenge him, as when, for example, he lays down the doctrine that the heaving of tables at spiritualist séances is performed by demons from Hell. But his fundamental postulates stand beyond refutation. If he is wrong, then the whole science of Christian theology is a degraded imposture — something which no right-thinking, law-abiding, home-loving American, I am sure, will want to allege. I rejoice to find a holy man so forthright and courageous, and so irresistibly convincing. He has rescued demonology from its long neglect, and restored it to its old high place among the sacred sciences.

Memorial Service

From PREJUDICES: THIRD SERIES, 1922, pp. 232–37.
First printed in the *Smart Set*, March, 1922, pp. 41–42

WHERE is the graveyard of dead gods? What lingering mourner waters their mounds? There was a time when Jupiter was the king of the gods, and any man who doubted his puissance was *ipso facto* a barbarian and an ignoramus. But where in all the world is there a man who worships Jupiter today? And what of Huitzilopochtli? In one year — and it is no more than five hundred years ago — 50,000 youths and maidens were slain in sacrifice to him. Today, if he is remembered at all, it is only by some vagrant savage in the depths of the Mexican forest. Huitzilopochtli, like many other gods, had no human father; his mother was a virtuous widow; he was born of an apparently innocent flirtation that she carried on with the sun. When he frowned, his father, the sun, stood still. When he roared with rage, earthquakes engulfed whole cities. When he thirsted he was watered with 10,000 gallons of human blood. But today Huitzilopochtli is as magnificently forgotten as Allen G. Thurman. Once the peer of Allah, Buddha and Wotan, he is now the peer of Richmond P. Hobson, Alton B. Parker, Adelina Patti, General Weyler and Tom Sharkey.

Speaking of Huitzilopochtli recalls his brother Tezcatilpoca. Tezcatilpoca was almost as powerful: he consumed 25,000 virgins a year. Lead me to his tomb: I would weep, and hang a *couronne des perles*. But who knows where it is? Or where the grave of Quitzalcoatl is? Or Xiehtecutli? Or Centeotl, that sweet one? Or Tlazolteotl, the goddess of love? Or Mictlan? Or Xipe? Or all the host of Tzitzimitles? Where are their bones? Where is the willow on which they hung their harps? In what forlorn and unheard-of Hell do they await the resurrection morn? Who enjoys their residuary estates? Or that of Dis, whom Cæsar found to be the chief god of the Celts? Or that of Tarves, the bull? Or that of Moccos, the pig? Or that of Epona, the mare? Or that of Mullo, the celestial jackass? There was a time when the Irish revered all these gods, but today even the drunkest Irishman laughs at them.

But they have company in oblivion: the Hell of dead gods is as crowded as the Presbyterian Hell for babies. Damona is there, and Esus, and Drunemeton, and Silvana, and Dervones, and Adsalluta, and Deva, and Belisama, and Uxellimus, and Borvo, and Grannos, and Mogons. All mighty gods in their day, worshipped by millions, full of demands and impositions, able to bind and loose — all gods of the first class. Men labored for generations to build vast temples to them — temples with stones as large as hay-wagons. The business of interpreting their whims occupied thousands of priests, bishops, archbishops. To doubt them was to die, usually at the stake. Armies took to the field to defend them against infidels: villages were burned, women and children were butchered, cattle were driven off. Yet in the end they all withered and died, and today there is none so poor to do them reverence.

What has become of Sutekh, once the high god of the whole Nile Valley? What has become of:

Resheph	Baal
Anath	Astarte
Ashtoreth	Hadad
Nebo	Dagon
Melek	Yau
Ahijah	Amon-Re
Isis	Osiris
Ptah	Molech?

All these were once gods of the highest eminence. Many of them are mentioned with fear and trembling in the Old Testament. They ranked, five or six thousand years ago, with Yahweh Himself; the worst of them stood far higher than Thor. Yet they have all gone down the chute, and with them the following:

Arianrod	Nuada Argetlam
Morrigu	Tagd
Govannon	Goibniu
Gunfled	Odin
Dagda	Ogma
Ogyrvan	Marzin
Dea Dia	Mars
Iuno Lucina	Diana of Ephesus
Saturn	Robigus
Furrina	Pluto
Cronos	Vesta
Engurra	Zer-panitu
Belus	Merodach
Ubilulu	Elum
U-dimmer-an-kia	Marduk
U-sab-sib	Nin
U-Mersi	Persephone
Tammuz	Istar
Venus	Lagas
Beltis	Nirig
Nusku	Nebo
Aa	En-Mersi
Sin	Assur
Apsu	Beltu
Elali	Kuski-banda

Mami	Nin-azu
Zaraqu	Qarradu
Zagaga	Ueras

Ask the rector to lend you any good book on comparative religion: you will find them all listed. They were gods of the highest dignity — gods of civilized peoples — worshipped and believed in by millions. All were omnipotent, omniscient and immortal. And all are dead.

V. MORALS

❧

The Origin of Morality

From TREATISE ON RIGHT AND WRONG, New York, 1934, pp. 1–8

CHILDREN come into the world without any visible understanding of the difference between good and bad, right and wrong, but some sense of it is forced upon them almost as soon as they learn the difference between light and dark, hot and cold, sweet and sour. It is a kind of knowledge that seems to be natural and essential to all creatures living in societies, and it shows itself in many of the lower animals quite as well as in human beings. To be sure, they do not appear to formulate a concept of evil *per se*, and certainly they know nothing about the highly metaphysical abstraction that mankind calls sin, but many species are well acquainted with concrete acts of wickedness, and punish them severely. Theft and adultery are familiar examples. A dog will pursue and, if it can, castigate another dog which steals its bone, and an ape will try to kill any bachelor intruder which makes too free with its wives. This sharp and often bloody discrimination between *meum* and *tuum* is to be observed not only in mammals, but also in animals of lower orders, including birds, insects and even fishes. Much of the uproar that goes on among sparrows and starlings is caused by conflicts over property rights, and everyone has seen two goldfishes in a globe fighting over a speck of food, with one claiming it and trying to gobble it and the other seeking to make off with it.

A German popular naturalist, Dr. Theodor Zell, has gone to the length of writing a treatise called "Moral in der Tierwelt" (Morality in the Animal World), in which he argues that many species, especially among the social insects, entertain not only the somewhat negative idea of vice but also the positive idea of virtue. The ants, he says, are better citizens than the members of any known human society, for they never go on strike.

99

If the workers of a given colony should quit work their queen would starve, and each of them would enjoy thereby the democratic privilege of aspiring to her power and circumstance, but they never cease to feed her so long as any food is obtainable. Thus they are true patriots, and show a luxuriant development of that loyalty to the established order which is put so high among the virtues of human beings.

Here it may be argued that such acts and attitudes in the lower animals are purely instinctive, and that it would be irrational to dignify them by calling them moral. But to that it may be answered that the motives and impulses lying behind many of the moral concepts of human beings seem to be instinctive in exactly the same sense, and almost to the same extent. No teaching is required to induce a baby to recognize a given rattle as its own; all the power of pedagogy must be devoted to inducing it to surrender its property on demand. Nor is there any reason to believe that the various manifestations of sexual rivalry among men are any nobler in origin than those observed among apes or dogs; the whole tendency of an advancing culture is to obliterate them, not to nourish them. In the days when anthropology was a pseudo-science chiefly cultivated by missionaries there was a belief that the lower races of men had no morals at all — that they yielded to their impulses in a naïve and irrational manner, and had no conception whatever of property rights, whether in goods or in women, or of duties, whether to their gods or to their fellow men. But it is now known that savages are really rather more moral, if anything, than civilized men. Their ethical systems, in some ways, differ from ours, just as their grammatical systems differ, and their theological and governmental systems, but even the most primitive of them submit unquestioningly to complicated and onerous duties and taboos, and not only suffer punishment willingly when the Old Adam lures them into false steps, but also appear to be tortured by what, on higher levels, is called conscience — to the extent, at times, of falling into such vapors of remorse that they languish and die.

Primitive man, in this respect as in others, seems to have been much like the savages of today. At the time when we get our first vague glimpse of him, lurking in the dark of his spooky caves, he was already a family man, and hence had certain duties, rights and responsibilities. We know, of course, very little about him, but we are at least reasonably sure that he did not habitually share his wife with all comers, or kill and eat his children, or fail in what he conceived to be his duty to the gods. To that extent, at least, he was a moral agent, and as completely so as any Christian. Later on in human history, when men discovered the art of writing and began to record their thoughts and doings for posterity, they devoted almost as much time and energy to setting down their notions of right and wrong as they gave to recording their prodigies and glories. In the very first chapter of the collection of hoary documents which we call the Bible there are confident moral mandates, and similar ones are to be found in the ancient books of every other people. The earliest conquerors and despots of whom we have any news seem to have regarded themselves, precisely like their colleagues of today, as the heralds of an ethical enlightenment, and every one of them was apparently just as eager as the celebrated Hammurabi to be known as "the king of righteousness."

In the world that we now live in the moral sense seems to be universally dispersed, at all events among normal persons beyond infancy. No traveler has ever discovered a tribe which failed to show it. There are peoples so primitive that their religion is hard to distinguish from a mere fear of the dark, but there is none so low that it lacks a moral system, elaborate and unyielding. Nor is that system often challenged, at least on the lower cultural levels, by those who lie under it. The rebellious individual may evade it on occasion, but he seldom denies its general validity. To find any such denial on a serious scale one must return to Christendom, where a bold and impatient reexamination of the traditional ethical dogma has followed the collapse of the old belief in revelation. But even in Christendom the most formidable critics of the orthodox system are still, as a rule, profoundly moral men, and the reform they propose is not at all an abandonment of moral imperatives, but simply a substitution of what they believe to be good ones for what they believe to be bad ones. This has been true of every important iconoclast from Hobbes to Lenin, and it was preeminently true of the arch-iconoclast Nietzsche. His furious attack upon the Christian ideal of humility and abnegation has caused Christian critics to denounce him as an advocate of the most brutal egoism, but in point of fact he proposed only the introduction of a new and more heroic form of renunciation, based upon abounding strength rather than upon hopeless weakness; and in his maxim "Be hard!" there was just as much sacrifice of immediate gratification to ultimate good as you will find in any of the *principia* of Jesus.

The difference between moral systems is thus very slight, and if it were not for the constant pressure from proponents of virtues that have no roots in ordinary human needs, and hence appeal only to narrow and abnormal classes of men, it would be slighter still. All of the really basic varieties of moral good have been esteemed as such since the memory of mankind runneth not to the contrary, and all of the basic wickednesses have been reprehended. The Second Commandment preached by Jesus (Mark XII, 31) was preached by the Gautama Buddha six centuries before Him, and it must have been hoary with age when the Gautama Buddha made it the center of his system. Similarly, the Ten Commandments of Exodus and Deuteronomy were probably thousands of years old when the Jewish scribes first reduced them to writing. Finally, and in the same way, the Greeks lifted their concept of wisdom as the supreme good out of the stream of time, and if we think of them today as its inventors, it is only because we are more familiar with their ethical speculations than we are with those of more ancient peoples.

The five fundamental prohibitions of the Decalogue — those leveled at murder, theft, trespass, adultery and false witness — are to be found in every moral system ever heard of, and seem to be almost universally supported by human opinion. This support, of course, does not mean that they are observed with anything properly describable as pedantic strictness; on the contrary, they are evaded on occasion, both by savages and by civilized men, and some of them are evaded very often. In the United States, for example, the situations in which killing a fellow human being is held to be innocent are considerably more numerous than those in which it is held to be criminal, and even in England, the most moral of great nations, there are probably almost as many. So with adultery. So, again, with theft, trespass and false witness. Theft and trespass shade by imperceptible gradations into transactions that could not be incommoded without imperiling the whole fabric of society, and bearing false witness is so easy to condone that bishops are sometimes among its most zealous practitioners. But despite this vagueness of moral outline and this tolerance of the erring the fact remains that all normal and well-disposed men, whether civilized or uncivilized, hold it to be axiomatic that murder, theft, trespass, adultery and false witness, in their cruder and plainer forms, are anti-social and immoral enterprises, and no one argues seriously, save maybe in time of war, when all the customary moral sanctions are abandoned, that they should be countenanced. When they are perpetrated in a naked manner, without any concession of the ancient and ineradicable feeling against them, they are viewed with abhorrence, and the guilty are severely punished.

The Good Citizen

From the same, pp. 19–27, with additions

So far, the fundamentals: they are the same everywhere. But morality, like theology, is capable of accretion and growth, and new moral ideas are coming in all the time. In our time we have seen desperate efforts to give moral sanction to notions that were unheard of even a few hundred years ago — for example, the notion that it is sinful to use alcohol. And simultaneously, we have seen the rise of virtues that were rejected by the founders of the current Christian morality — for example, those which enter principally into the character of what we now call a good citizen. These virtues certainly do not come out of the Bible, for the Jews of the great days, despite what is observed in their descendants today, had a low view of industry and an even lower view of thrift, and were almost devoid of the banal sentimentalities which now pass under the name of patriotism. Their loyalty was to Yahweh rather than to the state or the community, and they were ever ready to defy and overthrow their rulers, and to make war upon their brethren. In brief, their moral system was that of separatists and individualists, impatient of every secular restraint and disdainful of all hard and continued social effort. They originated as a tribe of desert nomads, and their point of view remained that of nomads to the end of their bloody chapter.

Work, in their eyes, was not the glorious privilege it has come to be in our highly socialized society, but an unmitigated curse, laid upon Adam for his sins, as the pains of parturition were laid upon Eve for hers. "Because thou hast . . . eaten of the tree, . . . in the sweat of thy face shalt thou eat bread." This concept of work as expiation eventually made it more or less tolerable, but it never became anything properly describable as pleasant. The Jews always laid great stress — rare in their time and place — upon the Sabbath's function as a day of rest: "in it thou shalt not do any work, thou, nor thy son, nor thy daughter, thy manservant, nor thy maidservant, nor thy cattle, nor thy stranger that is within thy gates." This rest was the righteous and highly appreciated reward of piety: by serving God assiduously they escaped at least a seventh part of the burden of work. Almost always, in the Old Testament, that burden is bracketed with sorrow, as in Psalms xc, 10. If "the sleep of a laboring man is sweet," then it is only because his work is done. There is no subjective stimulation in it, and no durable good. "As he came forth of his mother's womb, naked shall he return to go as he came, and shall take nothing of his labor."

The idea that wealth can be a good in itself, that there is a mystic virtue in accumulating it by hard work and self-denial — this was as foreign to the thinking of the Jews as it was to that of the Greeks. A rich man, to them, was almost always a villain; in fact, he was the favorite villain, next to the idolator, of their moral homilies. Are there occasional friendly words, in Proverbs, for the "man diligent in his business"? Then Dr. James Henry Breasted tells us that they are only borrowings from an ancient Egyptian book, the Wisdom of Amenemope (*c.* 100 B.C.) — and that with them, and from the same source, came dire warnings that diligence might be easily carried too far. Did Solomon, to whom Proverbs is traditionally (but falsely) ascribed, counsel his son to emulate the laborious ant? Then Solomon himself was a money-grubber, and hence, by Jewish theory, a suspicious character. When we get into the New Testament we find him held up in contemptuous contrast to the lilies of the field, which "toil not, neither do they spin." Jesus had two rich followers, Zaccheus of Jericho and Joseph of Arimathea, but the former was induced to give half of his goods to the poor and the latter did not appear until after the Crucifixion.

The general view of wealth that He entertained is too well known to need recalling. Preaching, as He did, the imminent end of the world, He could imagine no valid reason for piling up property, and in His system of ethics there was thus no room for the virtues of Babbitt. "Verily, I say unto you that a rich man shall hardly enter into the Kingdom of Heaven. And again I say unto you, It is easier for a camel to go through the eye of a needle than for a rich man to enter the Kingdom of God." Many other familiar echoes of the Tenth Commandment will come to mind: "Lay not up for yourselves treasures upon earth. . . . The deceitfulness of riches . . . choke[s] the Word, and it becometh unfruitful. . . . Ye cannot serve God and Mammon." And even more plainly and uncompromisingly there is this:

Take no thought for your life, what ye shall eat, or what ye shall drink; nor yet for your body, what ye shall put on. . . . Behold the fowls of the air: for they sow not, neither do they reap, nor gather into barns; yet your heavenly Father feedeth them. Are ye not much better than they?

As for Paul, he saw in opulence only a ticket to Hell. "They that will be rich," he wrote to Timothy, "fall into temptation and a snare, and into many foolish and hurtful lusts, which drown men in destruction and perdition. For the love of money is the root of all evil." Here the counsel of Jesus is supported, as is so often the case with Paul, by the dicta of the Greek philosophers and their Roman followers. Both Greeks and Romans — with the exception, perhaps, of a few Stoics — viewed work much as the Jews did: as no more, at its best, than an unpleasant sacrifice to the gods for their somewhat grudging mercies. In the Golden Age men knew nothing of it, as Hesiod tells us. The Italian *Kulturkritiker*, Adriano Tilgher, in his "Homo Faber," recalls the fact that the Greek word for work, *ponos*, came from the same root as the Latin word for sorrow, *poena*. He says that the failure of the Greeks to apply some of their scientific discoveries was largely due to their disdain of labor, worldly enterprise, and the accumulation of property. They even had a certain contempt for artists; cutting statues and raising buildings, they thought, were not vocations for free men, but for slaves. Aristotle, always seeking a golden mean, allowed that riches might be useful on occasion, if only as a stimulus to liberality and justice, but he saw no virtue in the bare act of accumulating them, and he thought that they were unnecessary to most of the higher enterprises of man. The seeker after wisdom (which to him, as to Confucius, was the highest good that could be imagined) "needs no external apparatus; on the contrary, worldly goods may almost be said to be a hindrance to contemplation."

The Romans, being a far less idealistic people than the Greeks, with no great love of wisdom, took a rather more friendly view of wealth, but they had rigid views about the means of getting it. Work, in itself, was disgusting to them, and they resigned it to slaves whenever possible. The two really respectable ways of accumulating money among them were by cultivating the land and by engaging in what we now call Big Business, but the latter was esteemed only because, in Tilgher's phrase, it led to "honorable retirement into rural peace as a country gentleman." For ordinary thrift and diligence the Romans had only contempt. Shopkeepers and common traders were clowns to them, and workingmen were scarcely human.

The early Christian Fathers, when the hope of the Second Coming faded at last, had to fit their moral system to the realities of a disturbed and exigent world, and so the counsels of Jesus were delicately revised. In particular, some thought had to be given to the ever-approaching and always menacing morrow, and in consequence the accumulation of goods began to take on a certain respectability. But the notion that work could be a good in itself was still far off. To Augustine (354–430), as to the Jews, it remained a kind of sacrifice — if not an actual expiation for sin, then at least a device for reducing temptation. He believed that all monks should be compelled to work, for it wore them out and took their minds off lubricity and other evil concerns. But when it came to laymen he was somewhat vague: they were in duty bound to share their gains with the poor, but they were apparently not in duty bound to labor and save.

It was not until the Middle Ages, when society in Europe began to reorganize itself very painfully on a commercial basis, that a general obligation to work began to be heard of. St. Thomas Aquinas (*c.* 1226–74) preached it as a corollary to his doctrine of fixed and immovable social classes. It was the duty of certain lowly orders of men to labor diligently, as it was the duty of the noble and learned to cultivate the humanities, spread the True Faith, and smite the infidel. But there was no revelation in this, and not much theology. Thomas, as always, spoke thunderously *ex cathedra*, but he spoke as a sociologist rather than a theologian. In other words, his theory was simply a logical deduction from the social necessities of his time. Work was inescapably needful in a world in which money was becoming more and more important, and it thus had to be endured. But thrift was yet somewhat dubious. The first duty of a man who happened to accumulate a great deal of wealth was to spend it — a large part of it on the poor, but a part of it also on that conspicuous waste which was one of the major social phenomena of the age. A prince who showed caution in this department was held in low esteem, and likewise a prelate. Most of the great cathedrals were built, not primarily to the glory of God, but in gorgeous proof of the liberality of archbishops.

As the Middle Ages flowed into the Renaissance and sustained work became ever more necessary to the well-being of a rapidly changing society, it naturally became more and more virtuous. But the Catholic theologians granted it their approval, one suspects, only under harsh economic compulsion: in their hearts they apparently still cherished the old Christian view of it as burdensome and painful, and when they praised it roundly it was chiefly as penance. It remained for the heretic, Martin Luther, to discover that the thing was laudable in itself. He was the true inventor of the modern doctrine that there is something inherently dignified and praiseworthy about labor — that the man who bears a burden in the heat of the day is somehow more pleasing to God than the man who takes his ease in the shade. Here, as in other directions, he gave an eager theological ratification to the economic revolution that was going on around him, and could not be stayed. He was the champion of the new masters of Europe, the *bourgeois* men of business, against its old masters, the soldiers and priests. These men of business needed willing laborers, and the easiest way to make them willing was to convince them that by working hard they were serving and gratifying God.

But even Luther was suspicious of the mere capitalist, as opposed to the *entrepreneur*, and in his early sermons he denounced the taking of interest in terms recalling the philippics of the early Christian Fathers. Later on, facing an ever-mounting tide that he could not stem, he prudently modified his position, and his final doctrine granted that taking rent for the use of land was pleasing to God, provided the charge did not run beyond 5% of the value. He held also that it was moral to recover from a borrower if the lender lost a chance of profit by making the loan, or if he had to borrow himself to replace what he had lent. But he never went the whole way: to the end he had grave doubts about certain kinds of investments. His great contribution to latter-day Christian ethics did not lie in this hazardous and dubious direction: it was his invention of the dignity of work. "With him," says Tilgher, "the German word *Beruf*, meaning profession, took on a religious color which it was never to lose, and which from German passed into all the analogous words of Protestant countries. Profession and vocation or calling became synonymous. Luther placed a crown on the sweaty forehead of labor.

Free Will Again

From the same, pp. 64–66

THE STUDY of the massive and instructive phenomenon of sin always causes moral theologians to harbor larger and larger doubts of the freedom of the will, and some of the most talented of them, notably Augustine, Luther and Calvin, have been close to throwing it overboard altogether. How, indeed, is it to be rec-

onciled with the omniscience and omnipotence of God, that
first postulate of all revealed religion? If He knew that I was
going to put in this evening at work upon the present ribald
book, to the scandal of the True Faith and the menace of souls,
then why didn't He divert me to some more seemly labor? It is
impossible to imagine, at least in the light of that True Faith,
that He didn't know what I was up to, and equally impossible
to imagine that He couldn't stop me. *Ergo*, He must shoulder
at least a part of the blame for my sin, and will cut a sorry figure
if He undertakes to punish me for it in Hell.

But this, of course, is going a great deal further than any really
discreet moral theologian ever lets himself go. Before he comes
to the point of putting the whole blame upon God he always
transforms the divine omniprescience into something considerably less sweeping, usually with a disarming metaphysical name,
and thereby makes room for free will. The Catholic Molinists,
for example, split it neatly into three parts, *simplex intelligen-
tia, scientia visionis* and *scientia media*, none of them capable
of precise definition: thus the question is disposed of by making
it unintelligible to the vulgar. And thus, despite His infinite
wisdom and awful powers, God is left free to be surprised, disappointed, grieved or indignant, and man is left free to sin, and
to be roasted for it throughout eternity. This concession, I
fancy, gives some pain to the theologians in their rôle of logi-
cians, but as practical pastors they make it with good grace, for
making it is absolutely essential to their business. Take away
the idea of free sinning, freely arrived at, and revealed religion
ceases to be a going concern.

The secular philosophers proceed in the other direction, but
they arrive at substantially the same position. Their problem is
not to find a precarious foothold for free will under the universal
shadow of God, but to keep it within plausible evidential
bounds. The ideal savage, immersed as he is in his animistic
naïveté, sees will in everything that moves and in many objects
that do not, and can scarcely imagine it curbed and circumscribed in man, the lord of creation. If A kills B, even though it
be by plain inadvertence, A must pay the ordained penalty:
either his own life or a heavy indemnity. The will, in other
words, is assumed from the act; there is no legal difference be-

tween the most deliberate premeditation and what we would call mere chance. But this ideal savage and his jurisprudence exist only as abstractions in the more romantic sort of anthropology books. In the real world even the most primitive tribes think of free will with certain reasonable reservations. Homicide under one set of circumstances is felt to differ materially from homicide under another, and the concepts of the unintentional, the excusable and the compulsory creep in.

An Ethical Dilemma

From the *Smart Set*, April, 1920, p. 42

IT is still socially dangerous for an American man to have the reputation of being virtuous. Theoretically, he who preserves his chemical purity in the face of all temptations is a noble and upright fellow and the delight of the heavenly hierarchy; actually he is laughed at by women and viewed with contempt by men. Such are the disparities that engage and torture the student of practical ethics in this great moral republic. It is the only country in the civilized world, so far as I know, in which male virtue is inculcated officially. And yet of all countries this is precisely the one in which private conversation among men is most largely made up of boudoir braggadocio and eloquent eye-winkings.

Most such bragging, I am convinced, is mendacious. The ratio of conquests hinted at to conquests actually achieved is probably not far from ten thousand to one. The American man, in point of fact, is anything but a Don Juan. He is far too sentimental for the rôle. Moreover, he lacks the sort of courage that it demands; he is brave enough in a combat with clubs, injunctions or fists, but he is a very timid performer in a combat of wits. When there is a conquest in amour, he is not the conqueror but the victim. But whether conqueror or victim, he goes on boasting just the same — and his boasts are even gaudier when there has been no conquest at all. In brief, the vast majority of his deviltries are purely theoretical. He pretends to gallantry in order to hush the sneers of men who pretend to gallantry in order to hush *his* sneers. He is ashamed to admit that, by the moral code of the land, he has no reason to be ashamed.

Honor

From the *Smart Set*, Oct., 1919, p. 84

It is a commonplace of moral science that absolute morality is impossible — in other words, that *all* men sin. What is often overlooked is that the same fallibility shows itself upon the higher level of what is called honor, which is simply the morality of superior men. A man who views himself as honorable usually labors under the delusion that his honor is unsullied, but this is never literally true. Every man, however honorable, occasionally sacrifices honor to mere morality behind the door, just as every man of morals occasionally sacrifices morality to self-interest.

VI. CRIME AND PUNISHMENT

The Criminal Law

From the *Smart Set*, May, 1922, pp. 30–34

THE SCIENCE of penology, in these days, is chiefly in the hands of sentimentalists, and in consequence it shows all the signs of glycosuria. The idea seems to be to turn the dungeons and bull-pens of the law into laboratories of the uplift, so that the man who goes in a burglar will come out a Y.M.C.A. secretary. To this end all harsh handling of the felon is frowned upon, and on the slightest showing of renascent piety in him he is delivered from his cage, almost with apologies.

At the bottom of this softness, of course, there is a sound instinct, and that is the instinct of revolt against cruel and excessive punishments. We inherited such a system of punishments from the English Common Law; in the Bill of Rights there is the first evidence of a rebellion against them. But our current error lies in the fact that softness has not stopped with disposing of the punishments that were barbarous and excessive; it has also sorely limited and conditioned the punishments that were reasonable and fitting; and so the problem of dealing effectively with crime remains a puzzle, and crime itself continues to flourish.

When I say crime, of course, I mean the thing in its conventional sense. In the abstract it scarcely has any existence. Practically all so-called crimes are justifiable on occasion, and nine-tenths of them, to certain kinds of men, are unavoidable on occasion. It is a platitude that you will find quite as many intelligent and honest men in the average prison as you will find in the average club, and when it comes to courage, enterprise and determination — in brief, to the special virtues which mark the superior man — you will probably find a great many more. But society, in order to protect the weak and botched against the bold and original, has had to proclaim certain human acts, under certain circumstances, as too dangerous to be permitted, and hence as what we call criminal. Most of us aspire to the majority of those acts in secret, and some of us commit them surreptitiously, but the man who performs them in such a manner that the fact becomes notorious is a menace to the security of the rest of us, and we go through the solemn hocus-pocus of seizing him and trying him, and pump up indignation over his rascality, and finally visit upon him the thing called punishment.

The trouble with this so-called punishment, in a great many cases, is that it is hypocritical and dishonest at bottom, and thus at constant war with abstract justice and common sense. What we find practically is a crowd of poltroons in the jury box venting their envious hatred of enterprise and daring upon a man who, at worst, is at least as decent as they are; and a scoundrel on the bench lording it over a scoundrel in the dock because the latter is less clever than he is. In the old days this ill nature took the form of floggings, mutilations and damnations. In our own days, with an evil conscience gnawing the gizzard of the world, it takes the shape of formalities which tend to grow more and more ineffective, sentimental and meaningless. In particular, it takes the shape of a grotesquely circumscribed répertoire of penalties, so that the business of fitting the punishment to the crime becomes more and more difficult, even to the stray judge with intelligence. In a few rare cases he may condemn a prisoner to death; in all other cases he has a Hobson's choice between a mulcting in damages which seldom punishes at all, and a deprivation of liberty which usually punishes inappropriately, and often too much. The medieval judge had an almost unlimited series of choices; if no habitual punishment suited his purposes, he could devise a new one to fit the case. But the modern judge must forever oscillate absurdly between fine and imprisonment — in other words, between allowing one prisoner to pay a bribe for his liberty, and taking away the liberty of another prisoner because he hasn't got the bribe.

It is a deep consciousness of this absurdity which lies at the bottom of all the fantastic experiments of modern penology, and of many of the extravagances which we witness on the bench. It seemed ridiculous, perhaps, for Judge Kenesaw Mountain

Landis, LL.B., to fine the Standard Oil Company $29,240,000, but in its essence it was an honest effort to bring an offender to something approaching scientifically exact justice. It seems (and may be) sugarishly sentimental for uplifters to transform prisons into moving-picture parlors, but underneath it there is the sound doctrine that locking up a man in a cell is, for most crimes, too harsh, and that its effect on the man is precisely the opposite of the one intended, for it makes him a more determined antagonist of so stupid and cruel a society than ever he was before. What we need is a thorough overhauling of our punishments — an overhauling looking to their rescue from formalism and imbecility. They must be made more fluent, more intelligible, more various. We must get rid of the mawkish and false humanity which shrinks from simple and forthright penalties, and restore the true humanity which makes the criminal stop doing what he is doing, and yet halts before it has made a hopeless wreck of him. If revenge is admitted (and I suppose it always will be), it must be admitted openly and unblushingly, and not swathed in that dishonest concealment which now seeks to make it appear as something else.

In medieval law, as I have hinted, there are suggestions that should engage the penological reformer of tomorrow. The medieval mind was unburdened by transcendental theories as to the nature and causes of crime. It was realistic in habit, and disdained to seek behind the palpable fact for hidden portents and significances. In particular, it disdained to conceal its workings beneath gossamers of fabulous purpose. It thus defined its crimes simply and clearly, and punished them frankly. For the runaway clod-hopper the obvious punishment was hamstringing, and, being obvious, it was executed without further ado. For the perjurer, the removal of his offending tongue. For the scoundrel who bit in clinches, extraction of the incisors. For the rowdy housewife and husband-baiter, prolonged immersion in a horse-pond — that is, enforced and painful silence. For the habitual thief, branding of the forehead with a large and warning T. For the short-weight grocer, three hours in the pillory, that his victims might pay him up with his own eggs and mark him well for future avoidance.

A judge, in those naïve and far-off days, had to be a fellow of resource and ingenuity, a man capable of quick and accurate reasoning. His public expected him, not merely to punish crime, but to punish it in some germane and felicitous fashion. If he could get a touch of humor into his sentence, so much the better, for the common people, then as now, remembered a jocosity much longer than they remembered a syllogism. In any event he had to maintain some intelligible connection between the offense and the penalty, that its lesson might be plain. If, finding the application of capsicum plasters to the pantaloons an efficient punishment for napping catchpolls, he next day prescribed it for a pirate, a witch, or a well-poisoner, then he was himself laughed at as a jackass, and perhaps even cashiered. In brief, he had to keep his wits about him if he would go on wallowing in the ermine. The law presumed him to be a man of sagacity, of ingenuity, of resource; and if, by any stupidity, he showed that he wasn't, its wrath consumed him.

The judge of today needs no such virtues. He is not the agent and exponent of justice, but its mere lackey. A great body of intricate law and precedent protects the felon against his effort to ferret out and determine the crime, and another great body of law protects the felon against his effort to fit the punishment to it. Consider, for example, the difficulties confronting him when he faces a very familiar task: the sentencing of a convicted pickpocket. Two or three considerations must inevitably flit through his darkened mind in this situation. One is that picking pockets requires a very high degree of manual skill — that it is an avocation as difficult technically as dentistry or playing the piano. Another, following upon the first, is that it is almost always pursued professionally — that, generally speaking, the pickpocket always devotes his whole time to it. A third is that, having thus entered the profession deliberately, and mastered its excessive difficulties, and taken over its known risks, he is firmly set in it, and cannot be shaken out by any process which leaves his actual expertness undamaged.

In other words, the pickpocket is a deliberate, habitual and incurable criminal, and neither chaining him by the leg nor forcing him to view moral moving-picture shows will ever cure him. To be bagged now and then, to make occasional sojourns in prison — all that, to him, is mere professional risk. When, by some mischance, he is taken and jailed, he lays the business to the fortunes of war, as a surgeon does when a patient dies on the table or a lawyer when a client is caught. As soon as he has paid his debt to the law he resumes the practise of his profession. If anything, a term in prison heartens and emboldens him, for he commonly debits it, not to the acts preceding it, but to the acts to follow it. In brief, he regards it as a sort of fee or license, paid to the community for the privilege of extracting wallets. No one ever heard of a reformed pickpocket; he exists only in the dreams of sentimental penologists. He may give up the business when his eyes give out, or his fingers get too stiff, but so long as he can snatch a pocketbook and get away he will keep on at it. And yet, so absurd is our law that we try to cure him by making him stop temporarily — by locking him up for two or three years, or maybe for only six months. As well try to cure a poet by forbidding him, for six months, to get drunk.

But what better offers? Something enormously better. The simple device, in brief, of condemning the detected pickpocket to lose the third phalange of the index finger of his right hand — a quick, safe, wholly painless operation, almost as easy as having a boil lanced. And yet quite as certain in its effects as life imprisonment. The pickpocket is not appreciably mutilated. The loss of that one phalange does not show itself. He is fit for almost any honest work that can be imagined. But he can no more pick a pocket, with the chief of his highly trained tools gone, than a fiddler, in like case, could play a cadenza. All of his special capacity for crime is gone, and with it his special temptation is gone, too. At every other variety of felony he is as much an amateur and blunderer as the judge on the bench.

I present only this one concrete example of what might be accomplished if we could rid our criminal laws of falsehood and sentimentality, and restore them to sense. The mind of every reflective judge must be full of simple, just and effective punishments that he would inflict if he could — punishments enormously more apt and efficient than the fine which penalizes too little and the imprisonment which penalizes arbitrarily, unintelligibly and usually too much. Why jail embezzlers? Why not put them to work as slaves of their victims, and make them work out what they have stolen? Why jail wife-beaters? Why not try to discourage them with a few strokes of the bastinado? Why jail grafters in office? Why not simply seize their stealings, strip them bare, and then forbid them the city, state and country?

Many old punishments deserve revival: ducking, whipping, transportation, branding, forfeiture of goods. They are simpler and cheaper than those we have; it is obvious that they would work better. In the South Seas we have scores of almost uninhabited islands. Why not ship our felons out there and let them learn discipline by preying on one another? Or send them to Arkansas to butcher the politicians and clergy? It is not only a way to get rid of them, and of the heavy expense of keeping them; it is a way to civilize Arkansas and the South Seas. Criminals are like the rest of us. Given the right kind of chance, they show their sound metal. Australia was settled by them, so were Maryland, and part of Virginia. Who notices it, or even remembers it, today?

In the forfeiture of goods there are the same great possibilities. This punishment would be the best of all weapons against stock-waterers, trade-restrainers, war-profiteers and other such powerful recalcitrants. Personally, I am in favor of these scoundrels, but if they are criminals by law, then let us deal with them in a way that will dispose of them. The fine of $29,240,000, even if collected, would not have hurt John D. Rockefeller. But a decree of forfeiture, taking over all his goods and making invalid any contract made with him or any security owned by him, would have converted him into a penniless Baptist colporteur overnight, and so brought down the price of gasoline.

Every day, by extra-legal means, our judges try to reach out for these new and more effective penalties. The punishment provided by law for one of the commonest of police court offenses — the stupid yielding to amorous suggestion called seduction — is a complex and unworkable combination of fine by instalments and threat of imprisonment. No sane judge ever inflicts it. What he does is to make the victim marry the party of the first part. The device is just and sensible, and it works. The victim is appropriately penalized for his numskullery, and the damage that society might have suffered from it is obliterated.

This is what we need in punishments — first, a reasonable fitness and justice, and secondly, a removal of the damage or menace to social order and security. Our present system fails in both departments. It is arbitrary, unintelligent and alternately too cruel and too soft; and it wholly fails to make crime difficult and unattractive.

The Penalty of Death

From FOUR MORAL CAUSES, PREJUDICES: FIFTH SERIES, 1926, pp. 21–27. With additions from the Baltimore *Evening Sun*, Feb. 23, 1925, and April 5, 1926

OF the arguments against capital punishment that issue from uplifters, two are commonly heard most often, to wit:

1. That hanging a man (or frying him or gassing him) is a dreadful business, degrading to those who have to do it and revolting to those who have to witness it.

2. That it is useless, for it does not deter others from the same crime.

The first of these arguments, it seems to me, is plainly too weak to need serious refutation. All it says, in brief, is that the work of the hangman is unpleasant. Granted. But suppose it is? It may be quite necessary to society for all that. There are, indeed, many other jobs that are unpleasant, and yet no one thinks of abolishing them — that of the plumber, that of the soldier, that of the garbage-man, that of the priest hearing confessions, that of the sand-hog, and so on. Moreover, what evidence is there that any actual hangman complains of his work? I have heard none. On the contrary, I have known many who delighted in their ancient art, and practised it proudly.

In the second argument of the abolitionists there is rather more force, but even here, I believe, the ground under them is shaky. Their fundamental error consists in assuming that the whole aim of punishing criminals is to deter other (potential) criminals — that we hang or electrocute A simply in order to so alarm B that he will not kill C. This, I believe, is an assumption which confuses a part with the whole. Deterrence, obviously, is *one* of the aims of punishment, but it is surely not the only one. On the contrary, there are at least half a dozen, and some are probably quite as important. At least one of them, practically considered, is *more* important. Commonly, it is described as revenge, but revenge is really not the word for it. I borrow a better term from the late Aristotle: *katharsis. Katharsis,* so used, means a salubrious discharge of emotions, a healthy letting off of steam. A school-boy, disliking his teacher, deposits a tack upon the pedagogical chair; the teacher jumps and the boy laughs. This is *katharsis.* What I contend is that one of the prime objects of all judicial punishments is to afford the same grateful relief (*a*) to the immediate victims of the criminal punished, and (*b*) to the general body of moral and timorous men.

These persons, and particularly the first group, are concerned only indirectly with deterring other criminals. The thing they crave primarily is the satisfaction of seeing the criminal actually before them suffer as he made them suffer. What they want is the peace of mind that goes with the feeling that accounts are squared. Until they get that satisfaction they are in a state of emotional tension, and hence unhappy. The instant they get it they are comfortable. I do not argue that this yearning is noble; I simply argue that it is almost universal among human beings. In the face of injuries that are unimportant and can be borne without damage it may yield to higher impulses; that is to say, it may yield to what is called Christian charity. But when the injury is serious Christianity is adjourned, and even saints reach for their sidearms. It is plainly asking too much of human nature to expect it to conquer so natural an impulse. A keeps a store and has a bookkeeper, B. B steals $700, employs it in playing at dice or bingo, and is cleaned out. What is A to do? Let B go? If he does so he will be unable to sleep at night. The sense of injury, of injustice, of frustration will haunt him like pruritus. So he turns B over to the police, and they hustle B to prison. Thereafter A can sleep. More, he has pleasant dreams. He pictures B chained to the wall of a dungeon a hundred feet underground, devoured by rats and scorpions. It is so agreeable that it makes him forget his $700. He has got his *katharsis.*

The same thing precisely takes place on a larger scale when

there is a crime which destroys a whole community's sense of security. Every law-abiding citizen feels menaced and frustrated until the criminals have been struck down — until the communal capacity to get even with them, and more than even, has been dramatically demonstrated. Here, manifestly, the business of deterring others is no more than an afterthought. The main thing is to destroy the concrete scoundrels whose act has alarmed everyone, and thus made everyone unhappy. Until they are brought to book that unhappiness continues; when the law has been executed upon them there is a sigh of relief. In other words, there is *katharsis*.

I know of no public demand for the death penalty for ordinary crimes, even for ordinary homicides. Its infliction would shock all men of normal decency of feeling. But for crimes involving the deliberate and inexcusable taking of human life, by men openly defiant of all civilized order — for such crimes it seems, to nine men out of ten, a just and proper punishment. Any lesser penalty leaves them feeling that the criminal has got the better of society — that he is free to add insult to injury by laughing. That feeling can be dissipated only by a recourse to *katharsis*, the invention of the aforesaid Aristotle. It is more effectively and economically achieved, as human nature now is, by wafting the criminal to realms of bliss.

The real objection to capital punishment doesn't lie against the actual extermination of the condemned, but against our brutal American habit of putting it off so long. After all, every one of us must die soon or late, and a murderer, it must be assumed, is one who makes that sad fact the cornerstone of his metaphysic. But it is one thing to die, and quite another thing to lie for long months and even years under the shadow of death. No sane man would choose such a finish. All of us, despite the Prayer Book, long for a swift and unexpected end. Unhappily, a murderer, under the irrational American system, is tortured for what, to him, must seem a whole series of eternities. For months on end he sits in prison while his lawyers carry on their idiotic buffoonery with writs, injunctions, mandamuses, and appeals. In order to get his money (or that of his friends) they have to feed him with hope. Now and then, by the imbecility of a judge or some trick of juridic science, they actually justify it. But let us say that, his money all gone, they finally throw up their hands. Their client is now ready for the rope or the chair. But he must still wait for months before it fetches him.

That wait, I believe, is horribly cruel. I have seen more than one man sitting in the death-house, and I don't want to see any more. Worse, it is wholly useless. Why should he wait at all? Why not hang him the day after the last court dissipates his last hope? Why torture him as not even cannibals would torture their victims? The common answer is that he must have time to make his peace with God. But how long does that take? It may be accomplished, I believe, in two hours quite as comfortably as in two years. There are, indeed, no temporal limitations upon God. He could forgive a whole herd of murderers in a millionth of a second. More, it has been done.

On Hanging a Man

From my Foreword to By the Neck, by my brother, August Mencken; Hastings House, publishers, New York, 1940. With additions from the Baltimore *Evening Sun*, Aug. 16, 1926

In my capacity of newspaper reporter I have been a spectator at nine hangings. It is my firm impression that this operation, if competently carried out, is a humane method of putting criminals to death, though perhaps it is not quite as quick as electrocution. The drop now used in the United States could be improved, as I shall indicate, but it is seldom that it causes any unnecessary physical pain or mental anguish. The blow delivered to the criminal's upper works when he reaches suddenly the end of the rope is at least as formidable as a crack on the head with an ax, and I believe that in most cases it causes immediate unconsciousness, or, at all events, such a scattering of the faculties that the condemned is hardly able to suffer. The rope, if properly knotted, thereupon presses heavily upon the blood vessels supplying the brain, and if any trace of consciousness survives it must be suspended by anoxemia in not more than eight or ten seconds. It is highly probable that this pressure, producing an irreversible cerebral anemia, is the actual cause of death in most cases. Fracture or dislocation of the cervical vertebræ is the exception rather than the rule, and asphyxia is scarcely more than a by-product. A criminal executed by a competent hangman shows no sign of suffering. He drops straight through the trap, and when he comes to rest remains hanging motionless. There is no struggle. After a little while the legs draw up a bit, but not violently. The heart keeps up a gradual diminishing beating for ten or twelve minutes, but all consciousness has departed, and the criminal dies without apparent pain.

In England a ring is inserted at the end of the rope, with the other end passing through it, and as a result the pressure that I have mentioned is more violent, and the criminal probably loses his senses almost instantly. The hangman's knot that is generally favored in the United States is rather less efficient, if only because rope slides across rope less facilely than across metal. But when the knot is made by competent hands it works very well, and is not cruel. An advantage of hanging is that it does not mutilate the body of the victim. The rope naturally leaves marks on the soft tissues of the neck, but it does not break the skin, and the marks themselves have almost disappeared before the body leaves the place of execution. Electrocution, as everyone knows, sometimes produces burns, and moreover, it involves shaving at least a part of the head. Putting a man to death with poisonous gases is even worse, for it causes a general discoloration, and there is no reason to believe that it is either quick or painless.

It is unpleasant, I grant you, to see a man put to death, but the brutality of it is immensely overestimated by those who have never enjoyed that honor. They forget this technical skill that can make even killing painless and humane. And they forget that the victim himself is almost always a brute with little more sensitiveness than an ox. This was certainly true of the late Whittemore, whose exitus I witnessed recently.[1] He went

[1] Russell Whittemore was hanged at the Maryland Penitentiary, Baltimore, on Aug. 13, 1926. He was a Baltimorean, but practised mainly in New York. The courts there failed to convict him, but when he tried his

to his death with a swagger, and obviously full of an imbecile delight in the attention he was attracting. His occupations in his last days were those of a happy half-wit, and his final message, delivered through the tabloid newspaper, the Baltimore *Post*, was precisely the sort of defiant rubbish that such a moron would be expected to formulate and delight in. The whole thing, to him, was a gaudy show, and it was quite impossible for any rational man, observing him at the end, to have any very active sympathy for him.

A new State law has got rid of the obscene crowds that used to flock to hangings, and of the bungling that once made them revolting. The gallows at the Penitentiary is admirably designed. Whittemore dropped at least ten feet, and he was unconscious instantly. Save for one brief drawing up of the legs as he died he didn't move an inch. The old-time jail yard gallows was a wooden structure with a high step, and the condemned had to climb up that step. It was a dreadful ordeal. He could see the noose a long way off. But Whittemore, stepping out of a second-story door on to a high platform, was on the trap before he saw the rope at all. If he had not delayed the proceedings to bawl a nonsensical farewell [2] he would have been dead in less than a minute after he emerged. As it was, he dropped in less than two minutes. Was the thing horrible as a spectacle? No more than the most trivial surgery. One does not see a man hanged. One sees a black bag.

I have spoken of Whittemore as a moron. The term is probably flattering. His farewell message in the *Post* and his philosophical autobiography in the same instructive paper, published a few months ago, showed the mentality of a somewhat backward boy of ten. Such professional killers, I believe, are

---

art in Maryland he was sent to the Penitentiary. While there he killed a guard in an attempt to escape, and was promptly sentenced to death.

[2] His last words, as I recall them, were "All I've got to say is good-by. That's the best I could say to anyone." Thereupon he was shoved on the trap and dropped. On my way out of the Penitentiary I heard one spectator say to another: "Did you hear what he said? It was 'Let's go.'" He said nothing of the sort, but this tale spread in the Baltimore saloons next day, and was widely believed. Most of the other spectators, indeed, were ready to testify that they had heard "Let's go" themselves. The hatching of such legends is a familiar phenomenon to every old newspaper reporter.

nearly all on the same level: a Gerald Chapman is very rare among them, as a man of honor is rare in Congress. The sentimentalists, observing the fact, employ it as an argument against capital punishment. It is immoral, they contend, for the State to take the life of a creature so palpably stupid, and hence so little capable of sound judgment and decent behavior. But all this, it seems to me, is full of bad logic. The State of Maryland did not kill Whittemore because he was a moron: it killed him because he had demonstrated conclusively that his continued existence was incompatible with the reasonable safety of the rest of us. What difference did it make whether his criminality was due to lack of intelligence, or, as in the case of Chapman, to intelligence gone rancid? The only important thing was that he was engaged habitually, and apparently incorrigibly, in gross and intolerable attacks upon the public security. What was to be done about it? He had been sent to prison without effect. He had actually committed a murder in prison. There remained only the device of taking his life, and so getting rid of a dangerous and demoralizing nuisance.

To argue that society, confronted by such a rogue, has no right to take his life is to argue that it has no rights at all — that it cannot even levy a tax or command a service without committing a crime. There are, to be sure, men who so argue, and some of their arguments are very ingenious. But they have not converted any considerable body of reflective men and women. The overwhelming majority of people believe that, when a man adopts murder as his trade, society is justified in putting him to death. They have believed it in all ages and under all forms of government, and I am convinced that they still believe it today. The execution of Whittemore was almost unanimously approved in Maryland. If he had escaped the gallows there would have been an uproar, and it would have been justified.

The opponents of capital punishment have firmer ground under them when they object to the infliction of the death penalty upon criminals other than professional murderers. The public opinion of Christendom long ago revolted against its employment to put down minor crimes: for example, theft. There has been, of late, a revolt against its use even in certain varieties of murder, and that revolt, I believe, is largely responsible for the increasing difficulty of getting convictions in capital cases, and the increasing tendency of the courts to upset convictions by legal quackery. The truth is that our criminal codes need a thorough overhauling. The old categories of crime are only too often archaic and irrational. It is absurd to hang an aggrieved husband for killing his wife and her lover, and let a professional murderer live because, in a given case, the State is unable to prove premeditation. The test should be, not the instant intention, but the antecedent circumstances. Every one of us, under easily imaginable conditions, may commit a premeditated murder. But that possibility does not make us professional criminals, and it does not necessarily justify the death penalty in case we succumb. Juries obviously have felt that way, for many a murderer has escaped under the so-called unwritten law.

Judge Frederick Bausman, of the State of Washington, a very intelligent jurist, once suggested a way out. All crimes, he said, should be divided into two new categories; those which a reasonable and otherwise reputable man, under the circumstances confronting the accused, might be imagined as committing, and those showing only deliberate and gratuitous criminality. Under the first heading would fall many crimes of passion and many ordinary thefts. Under the second would fall the doings of the Chapmans and Whittemores. The man who commits the former is now often used too harshly; the man who commits the latter is almost always used too softly. What sense is there in the old rule of evidence that the record of an accused, save he go on the stand himself, may not be brought against him on his trial? It is hypocritical and vain, for juries consider it notwithstanding. It is unjust, for the record often contributes to a sound judgment, as it did in the Whittemore case. The important thing is not to play a game according to a set of tight and stupid rules but to punish and put down crime. The way to do that is to proceed swiftly and harshly against professional criminals. I believe that every gunman should be hanged after his first shot, whether it kills or not. To stop short of that is to put the rights that he has deliberately forfeited above the public security. In other words, it is to convert the judicial process into a scheme for protecting and fostering crime.

Cops and Their Ways

From the *American Mercury*,.Jan., 1931, pp. 121–22.
A review of THE THIRD DEGREE, by Emanuel Lavine; New York, 1930

MR. LAVINE is a police reporter of long practise in New York. In a way his book proves it, for it is written in slipshod and often irritating journalese, but in another way it conceals the fact, for he deals with the police in a frank and objective manner that is very rare among men of his craft. Most of them, after a year or two at headquarters, become so coppish themselves that they are quite unable to discuss the constabulary art and mystery with any show of sense. They fade into what Mr. Lavine himself calls police buffs; that is, police enthusiasts, police fans. A headquarters detective, though he may present to the judicious eye only the spectacle of an ill-natured and somewhat thievish jackass, becomes a hero to them, and they regard an inspector with his gold badge in the wistful, abject fashion proper to the contemplation of the Holy Saints. Every American newspaper of any size has such a police reporter on its staff; there must be at least a thousand in the whole country. But they never write anything about cops that is either true or interesting, and so the literature of the subject is a blank.

Mr. Lavine's book is scarcely to be called literature; nevertheless, it makes a beginning. His discussion of the contents of the average policeman's mind is searching, accurate, and withal humane. He does not ask men of a useful but still humble profession to be philosophers, but on the other hand he does not exaggerate such modest mental gifts as they really have. He sees them as fellows who, in the main, are as honest as the next man, but labor under a stupidity which makes them close to helpless before rogues in general and wholly helpless before rogues of their own corps. The tone of the craft, unfortunately, is set by the last-named. They perform the outrages that have come, in the United States, to be associated with the name of policeman, and they are safe behind the fact that the average cop would rather conceal and protect them than run any risk of besmirching the force in general. Thus it is hard for reformers to get evidence against police grafters, and it is almost unheard of for other cops to expose them.

As his title indicates, Mr. Lavine devotes a large part of his book to describing the so-called third degree. His accounts of it have the gaudy picturesqueness of good war correspondence. Blood not only flows in streams; it spouts and gurgles. He tells of criminals so badly beaten by police-station Torquemadas that they went *mashuggah*, and Sing Sing had to yield them to Matteawan. But he manages to get through his account without any show of moral indignation. It is very uncommon, he says, for an innocent man to be thus ill used. The cops seldom get out their rubber-hose shillelahs and lengths of automobile tire save when they have a clearly guilty man before them, and are trying to force something out of him — say the names of his accomplices — that will aid them in their art. Few professional criminals are able to withstand a really brisk third degree. They may hold out long enough to be somewhat severely mauled, but by the time the ceiling begins to show bloodstains and their bones begin to crack they are eager to betray their friends and get to hospital. Many a time such a session *in camera* has yielded enough evidence to fill the death-house. Thus, while the third degree is clearly illegal, it is justified by the national pragmatism, for it undoubtedly works.

The curse of the cops, speaking professionally, is the sensitiveness of the district attorney's office to political and other pressure. Every day they see perfectly good cases fall to pieces in the courtroom. As a result their most arduous labors, sometimes at the risk of their lives, go for naught, and they are naturally upset and full of woe. Not infrequently they beat up a prisoner because they fear that he will be able to escape any other punishment. They know that he is guilty, but they also know that he has a sharp lawyer, so they fan him while they have him. This fanning — or massaging, as they call it — is greatly dreaded by criminals. Says Mr. Lavine:

> Strong-arm men, gorillas and tough gangsters who cheerfully commit dastardly and murderous assaults are usually not afraid of a mere arrest. . . . But massaging by the police is a different affair. The same gangster who would kick

a stranger in the abdomen or use a blackjack on a passing citizen for refusing him the price of a drink will either whimper or scream with fear when the workout begins.

There is here a hint for lawmakers. Let them restore the bastinado, as has been done in England, and they will not have to resort to Baumes laws and other such extravagant and desperate devices, most of which do not work. The English, when they take a tough boy in an assault with firearms, give him what, in America, would be regarded as a very short term of imprisonment, but they keep him jumping while he is behind the bars by cowhiding him at regular intervals. In consequence there are very few gunmen in England. In the United States any such programme would bring loud protests from so-called humanitarians. But there is really no reason why whipping should be inhumane. In England its aim is not to butcher the culprit but simply to hurt him — above all, to invade and make a mock of his professional dignity. It is hard for him, when he gets out, to posture as a hero, for all of his associates know that he has been flogged like a schoolboy, and they can imagine his piteous and unmanly yells.

VII. DEACH

🙠

On Suicide

From The Human Mind, Prejudices: Sixth Series, 1927, pp. 85–91.
First printed in the Baltimore *Evening Sun*, Aug. 9, 1926

THE SUICIDE rate, so I am told by an intelligent mortician, in going up. It is good news to his profession, which has been badly used of late by the progress of medical science, and scarcely less so by the rise of cut-throat, go-getting competition within its own ranks. It is also good news to those romantic optimists who like to believe that the human race is capable of rational acts. What could be more logical than suicide? What could be more preposterous than keeping alive? Yet nearly all of us cling to life with desperate devotion, even when the length of it remaining is palpably slight, and filled with agony. Half the time of all medical men is wasted keeping life in human wrecks who have no more intelligible reason for hanging on than a cow has for giving milk.

In part, no doubt, this absurd frenzy has its springs in the human imagination, or, as it is more poetically called, the human reason. Man, having acquired the high faculty of visualizing death, visualizes it as something painful and dreadful. It is, of course, seldom anything of the sort. The proceedings anterior to it are sometimes (though surely not always) painful, but death itself appears to be devoid of sensation, either psychic or physical. The candidate, facing it at last, simply loses his faculties. It is no more to him than it is to a coccus. The dreadful, like the painful, is not in it. It is far more likely to show elements of the grotesque. I speak here, of course, of natural death. Suicide is plainly more unpleasant, if only because there is some uncertainty about it. The candidate hesitates to shoot himself because he fears, with some show of reason, that he may fail to kill himself, and only hurt himself. Moreover, this shooting, along with most of the other more common aids to an artificial exitus, involves a kind of affront to his dignity: it is apt to make a mess. But that objection, it seems to me, is one that is bound to disappear with the progress of science. Safe, sure, easy and sanitary methods of departing this life will be invented. Some, in truth, are already known, and perhaps the fact explains the increase in suicides, so satisfactory to my mortician friend.

I pass over the theological objections to self-destruction as too sophistical to be worth a serious answer. From the earliest days Christianity has depicted life on this earth as so sad and vain that its value is indistinguishable from that of a damn. Then why cling to it? Simply because its vanity and unpleasantness are parts of the will of a Creator whose love for His creatures takes the form of torturing them. If they revolt in this world they will be tortured a million times worse in the next. I present the argument as a typical specimen of theological reasoning, and proceed to more engaging themes. Specifically, to my original thesis: that it is difficult, if not impossible, to discover any evidential or logical reason, not instantly observed to be full of fallacy, for keeping alive. The universal wisdom of the world long ago concluded that life is mainly a curse. Turn to the proverbial philosophy of any race, and you will find it full of a sense of the futility of the mundane struggle. Anticipation is better than realization. Disappointment is the lot of man. We are born in pain and die in sorrow. The lucky man died a' Wednesday. He giveth His beloved sleep. I could run the list to pages. If you disdain folk-wisdom, secular or sacred, then turn to the works of William Shakespeare. They drip with such pessimism from end to end. If there is any general idea in them, it is the idea that human existence is a painful futility. Out, out, brief candle!

Yet we cling to it in a muddled physiological sort of way — or, perhaps more accurately, in a pathological way — and even try to fill it with a gaudy hocus-pocus. All men who, in any true sense, are sentient strive mightily for distinction and power, *i.e.*, for the respect and envy of their fellowmen, *i.e.*, for the ill-natured admiration of an endless series of miserable and ridiculous bags of rapidly disintegrating amino acids. Why? If I knew, I'd certainly not be writing books in this infernal American climate; I'd be sitting in state in a hall of crystal and gold, and people would be paying $10 a head to gape at me through peep-holes. But though the central mystery remains, it is possible, perhaps, to investigate the superficial symptoms to some profit. I offer myself as a laboratory animal. Why have I worked so hard for years and years, desperately striving to accomplish something that remains impenetrable to me to this day? Is it because I desire money? Bosh! I can't recall ever desiring it for an instant: I have always found it easy to get all I wanted. Is it, then, notoriety that I am after? Again the answer must be no. The attention of strangers is unpleasant to me, and I avoid it as much as possible. Then is it a yearning to Do Good that moves me? Bosh and blah! If I am convinced of anything, it is that Doing Good is in bad taste.

Once I ventured the guess that men worked in response to a vague inner urge for self-expression. But that was probably a shaky theory, for some men who work the hardest have nothing to express. A hypothesis with rather more plausibility in it now suggests itself. It is that men work simply in order to escape the depressing agony of contemplating life — that their work, like their play, is a mumbo-jumbo that serves them by permitting them to escape from reality. Both work and play, ordinarily, are illusions. Neither serves any solid and permanent purpose. But life, stripped of such illusions, instantly becomes unbearable. Man cannot sit still, contemplating his destiny in this world, without going frantic. So he invents ways to take his mind off the horror. He works. He plays. He accumulates the preposterous nothing called property. He strives for the coy eye-wink called fame. He founds a family, and spreads his curse over others. All the while the thing that moves him is simply the yearning to lose himself, to forget himself, to escape the tragi-comedy that is himself. Life, fundamentally, is not worth living. So he confects artificialities to make it so. So he erects a gaudy structure to conceal the fact that it is *not* so.

Perhaps my talk of agonies and tragi-comedies may be a bit misleading. The basic fact about human existence is not that it is a tragedy, but that it is a bore. It is not so much a war as an endless standing in line. The objection to it is not that it is predominantly painful, but that it is lacking in sense. What is ahead for the race? Even theologians can see nothing but a gray emptiness, with a burst of irrational fireworks at the end. But there is such a thing as human progress. True. It is the progress that a felon makes from the watch-house to the jail, and from the jail to the death-house. Every generation faces the same intolerable boredom.

I speak as one who has had what must be regarded, speaking statistically, as a happy life. I work a great deal, but working is more agreeable to me than anything else I can imagine. I am conscious of no vast, overwhelming and unattainable desires. I want nothing that I can't get. But it remains my conclusion, at the gate of senility, that the whole thing is a grandiose futility, and not even amusing. The end is always a vanity, and usually a sordid one, without any noble touch of the pathetic. The means remain. In them lies the secret of what is called contentment, *i.e.*, the capacity to postpone suicide for at least another day. They are themselves without meaning, but at all events they offer a way of escape from the paralyzing reality. The central aim of life is to simulate extinction. We have been yelling up the wrong rain-spout.

Under the Elms

From the Trenton, N. J., *Sunday Times*, April 3, 1927. Early in 1927 several suicides were reported from college campuses, and the newspapers played them up in a melodramatic manner and tried to show that there was an epidemic. In this they were supported by various alarmed pedagogues, one of whom, Dr. John Martin Thomas, president of Rutgers, told the *Times* that the cause was "too much Mencken." The *Times* asked me to comment on this, and I sent in the following. Thomas, a Presbyterian pastor turned pedagogue, was president of Rutgers from 1925 to 1930. He resigned to enter the insurance business

I SEE nothing mysterious about these suicides. The impulse to self-destruction is a natural accompaniment of the educational process. Every intelligent student, at some time or other during his college career, decides gloomily that it would be more sensible to die than to go on living. I was myself spared the intellectual humiliations of a college education, but during my late teens, with the enlightening gradually dawning within me, I more than once concluded that death was preferable to life. At that age the sense of humor is in a low state. Later on, by the mysterious working of God's providence, it usually recovers.

What keeps a reflective and skeptical man alive? In large part, I suspect, it is this sense of humor. But in addition there is curiosity. Human existence is always irrational and often painful, but in the last analysis it remains interesting. One wants to know what is going to happen tomorrow. Will the lady in the mauve frock be more amiable than she is today? Such questions keep human beings alive. If the future were known, every intelligent man would kill himself at once, and the Republic would be peopled wholly by morons. Perhaps we are really moving toward that consummation now.

I hope no one will be upset and alarmed by the fact that various bishops, college presidents, Rotary lecturers and other such professional damned fools are breaking into print with highfalutin discussions of the alleged wave of student suicides. Such men, it must be manifest, seldom deal with realities. Their whole lives are devoted to inventing bugaboos, and then laying them. Like the news editors, they will tire of this bogus wave after a while, and go yelling after some other phantasm. Meanwhile, the world will go staggering on. Their notions are never to be taken seriously. Their one visible function on earth is to stand as living proofs that education is by no means synonymous with intelligence.

What I'd like to see, if it could be arranged, would be a wave of suicides among college presidents. I'd be delighted to supply the pistols, knives, ropes, poisons and other necessary tools. Going further, I'd be delighted to load the pistols, hone the knives, and tie the hangman's knots. A college student, leaping uninvited into the arms of God, pleases only himself. But a college president, doing the same thing, would give keen and permanent joy to great multitudes of persons. I drop the idea, and pass on.

Exeunt Omnes

From PREJUDICES: SECOND SERIES, 1920, pp. 180–91.
First published in the *Smart Set*, Dec., 1919, pp. 138–43

Go to any public library and look under "Death: Human" in
the card index, and you will be surprised to find how few books
there are on the subject. Worse, nearly all the few are by psychical researchers who regard death as a mere removal from one
world to another or by mystics who appear to believe that it is
little more than a sort of illusion. Once, seeking to find out
what death was physiologically — that is, to find out just what
happened when a man died — I put in a solid week without result. There seemed to be nothing whatever on the subject,
even in the medical libraries. Finally, after much weariness, I
found what I was looking for in Dr. George W. Crile's "Man:
An Adaptive Mechanism." [1] Crile said that death was acidosis
— that it was caused by the failure of the organism to maintain
the alkalinity necessary to its normal functioning — and in the
absence of any proofs or even argument to the contrary I accepted his notion forthwith and have cherished it ever since. I
thus think of death as a sort of deleterious fermentation, like
that which goes on in a bottle of Château Margaux when it becomes corked. Life is a struggle, not against sin, not against the
Money Power, not against malicious animal magnetism, but
against hydrogen ions. The healthy man is one in whom those
ions, as they are dissociated by cellular activity, are immediately fixed by alkaline bases. The sick man is one in whom the
process has begun to lag, with the hydrogen ions getting ahead.
The dying man is one in whom it is all over save the charges of
fraud.

But here I get into chemical physics, and not only run afoul
of revelation but also reveal, perhaps, a degree of ignorance
verging upon the indecent. The thing I started out to do was
simply to call attention to the only full-length and first-rate
treatise on death that I have ever encountered or heard of, to
wit, "Aspects of Death and Correlated Aspects of Life," by

[1] New York, 1916. Dr. Crile died in 1943.

Dr. F. Parkes Weber,[2] a fat, hefty and extremely interesting tome, the fruit of truly stupendous erudition. What Dr. Weber has attempted is to bring together in one volume all that has been said or thought about death since the time of the first human records, not only by poets, priests and philosophers, but also by painters, engravers, soldiers, monarchs and the populace generally. One traces, in chapter after chapter, the ebb and flow of human ideas upon the subject, of the human attitude to the last and greatest mystery of them all — the notion of it as a mere transition to a higher plane of life, the notion of it as a benign panacea for all human suffering, the notion of it as an incentive to this or that way of living, the notion of it as an impenetrable enigma, inevitable and inexplicable. Few of us quite realize how much the contemplation of death has colored human thought throughout the ages, despite the paucity of formal books on the subject. There have been times when it almost shut out all other concerns; there has never been a time when it has not bulked enormously in the racial consciousness. Well, what Dr. Weber does is to detach and set forth the salient ideas that have emerged from all that consideration and discussion — to isolate the chief theories of death, ancient and modern, pagan and Christian, scientific and mystical, sound and absurd.

The material thus accumulated and digested comes from sources of great variety. The learned author, in addition to written records, has canvassed prints, medals, paintings, engraved gems and monumental inscriptions. His authorities range from St. John on what is to happen at the Day of Judgment to Sir William Osler on what happens upon the normal human deathbed, and from Socrates on the relation of death to philosophy to Havelock Ellis on the effects of Christian ideas of death upon the medieval temperament. The one field that Dr. Weber overlooked is that of music, a somewhat serious omission. It is hard to think of a great composer who never wrote a funeral march, or a requiem, or at least a sad song to some departed love. Even old Papa Haydn had moments when he ceased to be merry, and let his thought turn stealthily upon the doom ahead. To me, at all events, the slow movement of the Military Symphony is the saddest of music — an elegy, I take it, on some young fellow

[2] New York, 1919.

who went out in the incomprehensible wars of those times and got himself horribly killed in a far place. The trumpet blasts toward the end fling themselves over his hasty grave in a remote cabbage field; one hears, before and after them, the honest weeping of his comrades into their wine-pots. Beethoven, a generation later, growled at death surlily, but Haydn faced it like a gentleman. The romantic movement brought a sentimentalization of the tragedy; it became a sort of orgy. Whenever Wagner dealt with death he treated it as if it were some sort of gaudy tournament or potlatch — a thing less dreadful than ecstatic. Consider, for example, the *Char-Freitag* music in "Parsifal" — death music for the most memorable death in the history of the world. Surely no one hearing it for the first time, without previous warning, would guess that it had to do with anything so gruesome as a crucifixion. On the contrary, I have a notion that the average auditor would guess that it was a musical setting for some lamentable fornication between a baritone seven feet in height and a soprano weighing three hundred pounds.

But if Dr. Weber thus neglects music, he at least gives full measure in all other departments. His book, in fact, is encyclopedic; he almost exhausts the subject. One idea, however, I do not find in it: the conception of death as the last and worst of all the practical jokes played upon poor mortals by the gods. That idea apparently never occurred to the Greeks, who thought of almost everything else, but nevertheless it has an ingratiating plausibility. The hardest thing about death is not that men die tragically, but that most of them die ridiculously. If it were possible for all of us to make our exits at great moments, swiftly, cleanly, decorously, and in fine attitudes, then the experience would be something to face heroically and with high and beautiful words. But we commonly go off in no such gorgeous, poetical way. Instead, we died in raucous prose — of arteriosclerosis, of diabetes, of toxemia, of a noisome perforation in the ileocaecal region, of carcinoma of the liver. The abominable acidosis of Dr. Crile sneaks upon us, gradually paralyzing the adrenals, flabbergasting the thyroid, crippling the poor old liver, and throwing its fog upon the brain. Thus the ontogenetic process is recapitulated in reverse order, and we pass into the mental obscurity of infancy, and then into the blank unconsciousness of the prenatal state, and finally into the condition of undifferentiated protoplasm. A man does not die quickly and brilliantly, like a lightning stroke; he passes out by inches, hesitatingly and, one may almost add, gingerly.

It is hard to say just when he is fully dead. Long after his heart has ceased to beat and his lungs have ceased to swell him up with the vanity of his species, there are remote and obscure parts of him that still live on, quite unconcerned about the central catastrophe. Dr. Alexis Carrel used to cut them out and keep them alive for months. No doubt there are many parts of the body, and perhaps even whole organs, which wonder what it is all about when they find that they are on the way to the crematory. Burn a man's mortal remains, and you inevitably burn a good portion of him alive, and no doubt that portion sends alarmed messages to the unconscious brain, like dissected tissue under anesthesia, and the resultant shock brings the deceased before the hierarchy of Heaven in a state of collapse, with his face white, sweat bespangling his forehead and a great thirst upon him. It would not be pulling the nose of reason to argue that many a cremated pastor, thus confronting the ultimate in the aspect of a man taken with the goods, has been put down as suffering from an uneasy conscience when what actually ailed him was simply surgical shock. The cosmic process is not only incurably idiotic; it is also indecently unjust.

Thus the human tendency to make death dramatic and heroic has little excuse in the facts. No doubt you remember the scene in the last act of "Hedda Gabler," in which Dr. Brack comes in with the news of Lövborg's suicide. Hedda immediately thinks of him putting the pistol to his temple and dying instantly and magnificently. The picture fills her with romantic delight. When Brack tells her that the shot was actually through the breast she is disappointed, but soon begins to romanticize even *that*. "The breast," she says, "is also a good place. . . . There is something beautiful in this!" A bit later she recurs to the charming theme, "In the breast — ah!" Then Brack tells her the plain truth — in the original, thus: *"Nej, — det traf ham i underlivet!"* . . . Edmund Gosse, in his first English translation of the play, made the sentence: "No — it struck him in the abdomen." In the last edition William Archer makes it "No — in the bowels!"

Abdomen is nearer to *underlivet* than bowels, but belly would probably render the meaning better than either. What Brack wants to convey to Hedda is the news that Lövborg's death was not romantic in the least — that he went to a brothel, shot himself, not through the cerebrum or the heart, but the duodenum or perhaps the jejunum, and is at the moment of report awaiting autopsy at the Christiania Allgemeinekrankenhaus. The shock floors her, but it is a shock that all of us must learn to bear. Men upon whom we lavish our veneration reduce it to an absurdity at the end by dying of cystitis, or by choking on marshmallows or dill pickles. Women whom we place upon pedestals worthy of the holy saints come down at last with mastoid abscesses or die obscenely of female weakness. And we ourselves? Let us not have too much hope. The chances are that, if we go to war, eager to leap superbly at the cannon's mouth, we'll be finished on the way by being run over by an army truck driven by a former bus-boy and loaded with imitation Swiss cheeses made in Oneida, N. Y. And that if we die in our beds, it will be of cholelithiasis.

The aforesaid Crile, in one of his other books, "A Mechanistic View of War and Peace," [3] has a good deal to say about death in war, and in particular, about the disparity between the glorious and inspiring passing imagined by the young soldier and the messy finish that is normally in store for him. He shows two pictures, the one ideal and the other real. The former is the familiar print, "The Spirit of '76," with the three patriots springing grandly to the attack, one of them with a neat and romantic bandage around his head — apparently, to judge by his liveliness, to cover a wound no worse than a bee-sting. The latter picture is a close-up of a French soldier who was struck just below the mouth by a German one-pounder shell — a soldier suddenly converted into the hideous simulacrum of a cruller. What one notices especially is the curious expression upon what remains of his face — an expression of the utmost surprise and indignation. No doubt he marched off to the front firmly convinced that, if he died at all, it would be at the climax of some heroic charge, up to his knees in blood and with his bayonet run clear through a Bavarian at least four feet in diameter.

[3] New York, 1915.

He imagined the clean bullet through the heart, the stately last gesture, the final words: "Thérèse! Sophie! Olympe! Marie! Suzette! Odette! Dénise! Julie! . . . France!" Go to the book and see what he got.

Alas, the finish of a civilian in a luxurious hospital, with trained nurses fluttering over him and his pastor whooping and heaving for him at the foot of his bed, is often quite as unesthetic as any form of exitus witnessed in war. "No. 8," says the apprentice nurse in faded pink, tripping down the corridor with a hooch of rye for the diabetic in No. 2, "has just passed out." "Which is No. 8?" asks the new nurse. "The one whose wife wore that awful hat this afternoon?" . . . But all the authorities, it is pleasant to know, report that the final scene, though it may be full of horror, is commonly devoid of terror. The dying man doesn't struggle much and he isn't much afraid. As his alkalies give out he succumbs to a blest stupidity. His mind fogs. His will power vanishes. He submits decently. He scarcely gives a damn.

Clarion Call to Poets

From PREJUDICES: SIXTH SERIES, 1927, pp. 103–112

ONE of the crying needs of the time in this incomparable Republic is for a suitable Burial Service for the admittedly damned. I speak as one who has of late attended the funeral orgies of several such gentlemen, each time to my esthetic distress. The first of them, having a great abhorrence of rhetoric in all its branches, left strict orders that not a word was to be said at his obsequies. The result was two extremely chilly and uncomfortable moments: when six of us walked into his house in utter silence and carried out his clay, and when we stood by as it was shoved, in the same crawling silence, into the fire-box of the crematory. The whole business was somehow unnatural and even a shade indecent: it violated one of the most ancient sentiments of *Homo sapiens* to dispatch so charming a fellow in so cavalier a fashion. One felt almost irresistibly impelled to say good-by to him in some manner or other, if only, soldier fashion, by blowing a bugle and rolling a drum. Even the mortician, an eminent star of one of the most self-possessed of professions, looked a bit uneasy and ashamed.

The second funeral was even worse. The deceased had been a Socialist of the militantly anti-clerical variety, and threatened, on his death-bed, to leap from his coffin with roars if a clergyman were hired to snuffle over him. His widow accordingly asked two of his Socialist colleagues to address the mourners. They prepared for the business by resorting to the jug, and in consequence both of them were garrulous and injudicious. One of them traced the career of Karl Marx in immense detail, and deduced from it a long series of lessons for ambitious American boys. The other, after first denouncing the New York *Times*, read twenty or thirty cantos of execrable poetry from the *Free-thinker*. If the widow had not performed a series of very realistic sobs — leaning for support, I may add, upon a comrade who soon afterward succeeded to the rights of the deceased in her person and real estate — the ceremony would have been indistinguishable from a session of the House of Representatives.

The third funeral was conducted by Freemasons, who came in plug hats and with white aprons over their cow-catchers. They entered the house of mourning in a long file, with their hats held over their left breasts in the manner of a President reviewing an inaugural parade, and filed past the open coffin at a brisk parade march. As each passed he gave a swift, mechanical glance at the fallen brother: there was in it the somewhat metallic efficiency of an old hand. These Freemasons brought their own limousines and took a place in the funeral procession ahead of the hearse. At the cemetery they deployed around the grave, and as soon as the clergyman hired by the pious widow had finished his mumbo-jumbo, began a ceremonial of their own. Their leader, standing at the head of the grave with his plug hat on, first read a long series of quasi-theological generalities — to the general effect, so far as I could make out, that Freemasons are immune to Hell, as they are notoriously immune to hanging — , and then a brother at the foot of the grave replied. After that there was a slight pause, and in rather ragged chorus the rest of

the brethren said "So mote [1] it be!" This went on almost endlessly; I was heartily glad when it was over. The whole ceremony,
in fact, was tedious and trashy. As for me, I'd rather have been
planted by a Swedenborgian, whiskers and all. Or even by a
grand goblin of the Ethical Culture Society.

What is needed, and what I bawl for politely, is a service that
is free from the pious but unsupported asseverations that revolt
so many of our best minds, and yet remains happily graceful
and consoling. It will be very hard, I grant you, to concoct
anything as lasciviously beautiful as the dithyrambs in the Book
of Common Prayer. Who wrote them originally I don't know,
but whoever did it was a poet. They put the highly improbable
into amazingly luscious words, and the palpably not-true into
words even more caressing and disarming. It is impossible to
listen to them, when they are intoned by a High Church rector
of sepulchral gifts, without harboring a sneaking wish that, by
some transcendental magic, they could throw off their lowly
poetical character and take on the dignity and reliability of
prose — in other words, that the departed could be actually imagined as leaping out of the grave on the Last Morn, his split
colloids all restored to their pristine complexity, his clothes
neatly scoured and pressed, and every molecule of him thrilling
with a wild surmise. I have felt this wish at the funerals of many
virtuous and earnest brethren, whose sole sin was their refusal
to swallow such anecdotes as the one in II Kings II, 23–24. It
seems a pity that men of that sort should be doomed to Hell,
and it seems an even greater pity that they should be laid away
to the banal chin-music of humorless Freemasons and stewed
Socialists.

But, so far as I know, no suitable last rites for them have ever
been drawn up. Between the service in the Book of Common
Prayer (and its various analogues, nearly all of them greatly inferior) and the maudlin mortuary dialogues of the Freemasons,
Knights of Pythias and other such assassins of beauty there is

---

[1] This verb is ancient in English, but has been archaic for centuries. No
doubt the Freemasons retain it to support their claim to a venerable antiquity. It occurs in Beowulf, Cædmon, Chaucer and Spenser, and was
used by Byron and Scott as a conscious archaism. In meaning it is roughly
equivalent to *may*.

absolutely nothing. Even the professional agnostics, who are violently literary, have never produced anything worthy to be considered; their best is indistinguishable from the text of a flag-drill or high-school pageant. Thus the average American skeptic, when his time comes to return to earth, is commonly turned off with what, considering his prejudices, may be best described as a razzing. His widow, disinclined to risk scandal by burying him without any ceremonies at all, calls in the nearest clergyman, and the result is a lamentable comedy, creditable neither to honest faith nor to honest doubt. More than once, in attendance upon such an affair, I have observed a sardonic glitter in the eye of the pastor, especially when he came to the unequivocal statement that the deceased would infallibly rise again. Did he secretly doubt it? Or was he poking fun at a dead opponent, now persuaded of the truth of revelation at last? In either case there was something unpleasant in the spectacle. A suitable funeral for doubters, full of lovely poetry, but devoid of any specific pronouncement on the subject of a future life, would make such unpleasantness unnecessary.

We have the poets for the job, and I incline to suspect that their private theological ideas fit them for it. Skepticism, in fact, runs with their cynical trade. Most Americans, as everyone knows, give their ecclesiastical affiliations in "Who's Who in America" — especially Congressmen, pedagogues, bank presidents and uplifters. But not the poets. The sole exception in recent years, so far as I can make out, has been Vachel Lindsay, who reported that he was a member of the "Christian (Disciples) Church," a powerful sect in the No-More-Scrub-Bulls Belt, with a private Hell of its own, deep and hot. Even Edgar Albert Guest is silent on the subject, though he mentions the fact that he is a 33° Mason. Frost, Sandburg and the rest keep suspiciously mum. I suggest that they meet in some quiet saloon and draw up the ritual I advocate. Let Edna St. Vincent Millay be added to give the thing a refined voluptuousness. Here Holy Church shows the way. Its funeral service is a great deal less forensic than operatic.

There is some need, too, for a Marriage Service for the damned, and at different times attempts have been made to supply it. But all such works seem to emanate from radicals showing a characteristic lack of humor — and humor is as necessary to a Marriage Service as poetry is to a Funeral Service: a fact that the astute authors of the Book of Common Prayer did not overlook. However, the need here is not pressing, for in most American States civil marriage is sufficient, and heretics may be safely united without going before a sorcerer at all. Court clerks and police magistrates perform the job, mumbling unintelligibly out of a mysterious book, perhaps only a stolen Gideon Bible, excavated to hold cigarettes. The main thing is to pay the fee. Marriages after midnight cost double, and if the bridegroom has the fumes of wine in his head, he is apt to lose his watch as well as his liberty.

As I say, the Marriage Services drawn up by antinomians for the use of unbelievers lack humor. Worse, they are full of indignation — against the common theory that a wife is bound to give some care to her husband's goods, against the convention that she shall adopt his surname, and so on. It is hard to give serious attention to such grim notions at a time immemorially viewed as festive and jocose. One hears frequently of wedding guests getting drunk and fighting, but when they are drawn into sociological controversy it is too much. Such revolutionary Marriage Services, in point of fact, have never gained much popularity. Now and then a pair of Marxians resorts to one, but even Marxians appear to prefer the harsh, mechanical offices of a court clerk.

But these are side issues. The main thing is that the poets, though most of them seem to have departed from the precincts and protection of Holy Church and her schismatic colonies — since when has a first-rate American poet written a hymn? — have failed, so far, to rise to the occasion when, even among heretics, poets are most pressingly needed. I don't insist, of course, that their service for the doubting dead be wholly original. The authors of the Book of Common Prayer, though they were poets of great talent, certainly did not trust only to their private inspiration. They borrowed copiously from the old missals, and they borrowed, too, directly from Holy Writ. What they concocted finally was a composite, but it was very discreetly and delicately put together, and remains impregnable to this day, despite many furious efforts to undo it.

All I propose is that the committee of poets imitate them, but with an avoidance of strophes objectionable to heathen doctrine. Isn't there material enough in the books? There is enough, and to spare. I point to the works of Walt Whitman — to those parts, at least, of a non-erotic and non-political nature. I point to certain memorable stanzas of William Cullen Bryant. I point to Blake, Tennyson, Milton, Shelley, Keats, even Swinburne; what gaudy stuff for the purpose is in "Ave Atque Vale," "Tristram of Lyonesse" and "Atalanta in Calydon!" There is here a sweet soothing, a healing reassurance, a divine booziness — in brief, all the stuff of A No. 1 poetry. It would bring comfort, I believe, to many a poor widow who now groans as the Freemasons intone their balderdash, or flounces her veil, fidgets and blushes as a radical orator denounces Omnipotence for permitting stock dividends — it would bring her a great deal more comfort, certainly, than the positive statement, made defiantly by the unwilling rector of the parish, that her departed John, having been earthy and as the beasts, has now become gaseous and immortal. Such a libretto for the inescapable last act would be humane and valuable. I renew my suggestion that the poets spit upon their hands and confect it at once.

VIII. GOVERNMENT

❦

Its Inner Nature

From MATTERS OF STATE, PREJUDICES: THIRD SERIES, 1922, pp. 289–92.
First printed in the *Smart Set*, Dec., 1919, pp. 71–72

ALL government, in its essence, is a conspiracy against the superior man: its one permanent object is to oppress him and cripple him. If it be aristocratic in organization, then it seeks to protect the man who is superior only in law against the man who is superior in fact; if it be democratic, then it seeks to protect the man who is inferior in every way against both. One of its primary functions is to regiment men by force, to make them as much alike as possible and as dependent upon one another as possible, to search out and combat originality among them. All it can see in an original idea is potential change, and hence an invasion of its prerogatives. The most dangerous man, to any government, is the man who is able to think things out for himself, without regard to the prevailing superstitions and taboos. Almost inevitably he comes to the conclusion that the government he lives under is dishonest, insane and intolerable, and so, if he is romantic, he tries to change it. And even if he is not romantic personally he is very apt to spread discontent among those who are.

There is seldom, if ever, any evidence that the new government proposed would be any better than the old one. On the contrary, all the historical testimony runs the other way. Political revolutions do not often accomplish anything of genuine value; their one undoubted effect is simply to throw out one gang of thieves and put in another. After a revolution, of course, the successful revolutionists always try to convince doubters that they have achieved great things, and usually they hang any man who denies it. But that surely doesn't prove their case. In Russia, for many years, the plain people were taught that getting rid of the Czar would make them all rich and happy, but now that they have got rid of him they are poorer and unhappier than ever before. Even the American colonies gained little by their revolt in 1776. For twenty-five years after the Revolution they were in far worse condition as free states than they would have been as colonies. Their government was more expensive, more inefficient, more dishonest, and more tyrannical. It was only the gradual material progress of the country that saved them from starvation and collapse, and that material progress was due, not to the virtues of their new government, but to the lavishness of nature. Under the British hoof they would have got on just as well, and probably a great deal better.

The ideal government of all reflective men, from Aristotle onward, is one which lets the individual alone — one which barely escapes being no government at all. This ideal, I believe, will be realized in the world twenty or thirty centuries after I have passed from these scenes and taken up my public duties in Hell.

More of the Same

From MEMOIRS OF A SUBJECT OF THE UNITED STATES, PREJUDICES:
SIXTH SERIES, 1927, pp. 53–61.
First printed in the *American Mercury*, Feb., 1925, pp. 158–60

THE AVERAGE man, whatever his errors otherwise, at least sees clearly that government is something lying outside him and outside the generality of his fellow men — that it is a separate, independent and often hostile power, only partly under his control, and capable of doing him great harm. In his romantic moments, he may think of it as a benevolent father or even as a sort of *jinn* or god, but he never thinks of it as part of himself. In time of trouble he looks to it to perform miracles for his benefit; at other times he sees it as an enemy with which he must do constant battle. Is it a fact of no significance that robbing the government is everywhere regarded as a crime of less magnitude than robbing an individual, or even a corporation?

In the United States today it carries a smaller penalty and infinitely less odium than acts that are intrinsically trivial — for example, marrying two wives, both willing.

What lies behind all this, I believe, is a deep sense of the fundamental antagonism between the government and the people it governs. It is apprehended, not as a committee of citizens chosen to carry on the communal business of the whole population, but as a separate and autonomous corporation, mainly devoted to exploiting the population for the benefit of its own members. Robbing it is thus an act almost devoid of infamy — an exploit rather resembling those of Robin Hood and the eminent pirates of tradition. When a private citizen is robbed a worthy man is deprived of the fruits of his industry and thrift; when the government is robbed the worst that happens is that certain rogues and loafers have less money to play with than they had before. The notion that they have earned that money is never entertained; to most sensible men it would seem ludicrous. They are simply rascals who, by accidents of law, have a somewhat dubious right to a share in the earnings of their fellow men. When that share is diminished by private enterprise the business is, on the whole, far more laudable than not.

The intelligent man, when he pays taxes, certainly does not believe that he is making a prudent and productive investment of his money; on the contrary, he feels that he is being mulcted in an excessive amount for services that, in the main, are useless to him, and that, in substantial part, are downright inimical to him. He may be convinced that a police force, say, is necessary for the protection of his life and property, and that an army and navy safeguard him from being reduced to slavery by some vague foreign kaiser, but even so he views these things as extravagantly expensive — he sees in even the most essential of them an agency for making it easier for the exploiters constituting the government to rob him. In those exploiters themselves he has no confidence whatever. He sees them as purely predatory and useless; he believes that he gets no more net benefit from their vast and costly operations than he gets from the money he lends to his wife's brother. They constitute a power that stands over him constantly, ever alert for new chances to squeeze him. If they could do so safely they would strip him to his hide. If they leave him anything at all, it is simply prudentially, as a farmer leaves a hen some of her eggs.

This gang is well-nigh immune to punishment. Its worst extortions, even when they are baldly for private profit, carry no certain penalties under our laws. Since the first days of the Republic less than a dozen of its members have been impeached, and only a few obscure understrappers have ever been put into prison. The number of men sitting at Atlanta and Leavenworth for revolting against the extortions of the government is always ten times as great as the number of government officials condemned for oppressing the taxpayers to their own gain. Government, today, has grown too strong to be safe. There are no longer any citizens in the world; there are only subjects. They work day in and day out for their masters; they are bound to die for their masters at call. Out of this working and dying they tend to get less and less. On some bright tomorrow, a geological epoch or two hence, they will come to the end of their endurance, and then such newspapers as survive will have a first-page story well worth its black headlines.

The Politician

From a lecture before the Institute of Arts and Sciences,
Columbia University, Jan. 4, 1940

AFTER damning politicians up hill and down dale for many years, as rogues and vagabonds, frauds and scoundrels, I sometimes suspect that, like everyone else, I often expect too much of them. Though faith and confidence are surely more or less foreign to my nature, I not infrequently find myself looking to them to be able, diligent, candid, and even honest. Plainly enough, that is too large an order, as anyone must realize who reflects upon the manner in which they reach public office. They seldom if ever get there by merit alone, at least in democratic states. Sometimes, to be sure, it happens, but only by a kind of miracle. They are chosen normally for quite different reasons, the chief of which is simply their power to impress and enchant the intellectually underprivileged. It is a talent like any other, and when it is exercised by a radio crooner, a movie actor or a bishop, it even takes on a certain austere and sorry respectability. But it is obviously not identical with a capacity for the intricate problems of statecraft.

Those problems demand for their solution — when they are soluble at all, which is not often — a high degree of technical proficiency, and with it there should go an adamantine kind of integrity, for the temptations of a public official are almost as cruel as those of a glamor girl or a dipsomaniac. But we train a man for facing them, not by locking him up in a monastery and stuffing him with wisdom and virtue, but by turning him loose on the stump. If he is a smart and enterprising fellow, which he usually is, he quickly discovers there that hooey pleases the boobs a great deal more than sense. Indeed, he finds that sense really disquiets and alarms them — that it makes them, at best, intolerably uncomfortable, just as a tight collar makes them uncomfortable, or a speck of dust in the eye, or the thought of Hell. The truth, to the overwhelming majority of mankind, is indistinguishable from a headache. After trying a few shots of it on his customers, the larval statesman concludes sadly that it must hurt them, and after that he taps a more humane keg, and in a little while the whole audience is singing "Glory, glory, hallelujah," and when the returns come in the candidate is on his way to the White House.

I hope no one will mistake this brief account of the political process under democracy for exaggeration. It is almost literally true. I do not mean to argue, remember, that all politicians are villains in the sense that a burglar, a child-stealer, or a Darwinian are villains. Far from it. Many of them, in their private characters, are very charming persons, and I have known plenty that I'd trust with my diamonds, my daughter or my liberty, if I had any such things. I happen to be acquainted to some extent with nearly all the gentlemen, both Democrats and Republicans, who are currently itching for the Presidency, including the present incumbent, and I testify freely that they are all pleasant fellows, with qualities above rather than below the common. The worst of them is a great deal better company than most generals in the army, or writers of murder mysteries,

or astrophysicists, and the best is a really superior and wholly
delightful man — full of sound knowledge, competent and prudent, frank and enterprising, and quite as honest as any American can be without being clapped into a madhouse. Don't ask
me what his name is, for I am not in politics. I can only tell
you that he has been in public life a long while, and has not
been caught yet.

But will this prodigy, or any of his rivals, ever unload any
appreciable amount of sagacity on the stump? Will any of
them venture to tell the plain truth, the whole truth and nothing but the truth about the situation of the country, foreign
or domestic? Will any of them refrain from promises that he
knows he can't fulfill — that no human being *could* fulfill? Will
any of them utter a word, however obvious, that will alarm and
alienate any of the huge packs of morons who now cluster at
the public trough, wallowing in the pap that grows thinner
and thinner, hoping against hope? Answer: maybe for a few
weeks at the start. Maybe before the campaign really begins.
Maybe behind the door. But not after the issue is fairly joined,
and the struggle is on in earnest. From that moment they will
all resort to demagogy, and by the middle of June of election
year the only choice among them will be a choice between amateurs of that science and professionals.

They will all promise every man, woman and child in the
country whatever he, she or it wants. They'll all be roving
the land looking for chances to make the rich poor, to remedy
the irremediable, to succor the unsuccorable, to unscramble the
unscrambleable, to dephlogisticate the undephlogisticable. They
will all be curing warts by saying words over them, and paying
off the national debt with money that no one will have to earn.
When one of them demonstrates that twice two is five, another
will prove that it is six, six and a half, ten, twenty, n. In brief,
they will divest themselves of their character as sensible, candid
and truthful men, and become simply candidates for office,
bent only on collaring votes. They will all know by then, even
supposing that some of them don't know it now, that votes
are collared under democracy, not by talking sense but by talking nonsense, and they will apply themselves to the job with a
hearty yo-heave-ho. Most of them, before the uproar is over,

will actually convince themselves. The winner will be whoever promises the most with the least probability of delivering anything.

Some years ago I accompanied a candidate for the Presidency on his campaign-tour. He was, like all such rascals, an amusing fellow, and I came to like him very much. His speeches, at the start, were full of fire. He was going to save the country from all the stupendous frauds and false pretenses of his rival. Every time that rival offered to rescue another million of poor fish from the neglects and oversights of God he howled his derision from the back platform of his train. I noticed at once that these blasts of common sense got very little applause, and after a while the candidate began to notice it too. Worse, he began to get word from his spies on the train of his rival that the rival was wowing them, panicking them, laying them in the aisles. They threw flowers, hot dogs and five-cent cigars at him. In places where the times were especially hard they tried to unhook the locomotive from his train, so that he'd have to stay with them awhile longer, and promise them some more. There were no Gallup polls in those innocent days, but the local politicians had ways of their own for finding out how the cat was jumping, and they began to join my candidate's train in the middle of the night, and wake him up to tell him that all was lost, including honor. This had some effect upon him — in truth, an effect almost as powerful as that of sitting in the electric chair. He lost his intelligent manner, and became something you could hardly distinguish from an idealist. Instead of mocking he began to promise, and in a little while he was promising everything that his rival was promising, and a good deal more.

One night out in the Bible country, after the hullabaloo of the day was over, I went into his private car along with another newspaper reporter, and we sat down to gabble with him. This other reporter, a faithful member of the candidate's own party, began to upbraid him, at first very gently, for letting off so much hokum. What did he mean by making promises that no human being on this earth, and not many of the angels in Heaven, could ever hope to carry out? In particular, what was his idea in trying to work off all those preposterous bile-beans and snake-oils on the poor farmers, a class of men who had been fooled and rooked by every fresh wave of politicians since Apostolic times? Did he really believe that the Utopia he had begun so fervently to preach would ever come to pass? Did he honestly think that farmers, as a body, would ever see all their rosy dreams come true, or that the share-croppers in their lower ranks would ever be more than a hop, skip and jump from starvation? The candidate thought awhile, took a long swallow of the coffin-varnish he carried with him, and then replied that the answer in every case was no. He was well aware, he said, that the plight of the farmers was intrinsically hopeless, and would probably continue so, despite doles from the treasury, for centuries to come. He had no notion that anything could be done about it by merely human means, and certainly not by political means: it would take a new Moses, and a whole series of miracles. "But you forget, Mr. Blank," he concluded sadly, "that our agreement in the premises must remain purely personal. You are not a candidate for President of the United States. *I am.*" As we left him his interlocutor, a gentleman grown gray in Washington and long ago lost to every decency, pointed the moral of the episode. "In politics," he said, "man must learn to rise above principle." Then he drove it in with another: "When the water reaches the upper deck," he said, "follow the rats."

Governmental Theories

From the *Smart Set*, Feb., 1922, p. 26

IN every age the advocates of the dominant political theory seek to give it dignity by identifying it with whatever contemporaneous desire of man happens to be most powerful. In the days of monarchy, monarchy was depicted as the defender of the faith. In our present era of democracy, democracy is depicted as the only safe guardian of liberty. And the communism or super-communism of tomorrow, I suppose, will be sold to the booboisie as the only true palladium of peace, justice and plenty. All of these attempts to hook up cause and effect are nonsensical.

Monarchy was fundamentally not a defender of the faith at all, but a rival and enemy to the faith. Democracy does not promote liberty; it diminishes and destroys liberty. And communism, as the example of Russia already shows, is not a fountain that gushes peace, justice and plenty, but a sewer in which they are drowned.

Note on a Cuff

From the Baltimore *Evening Sun*, Dec. 9, 1929

THE SADDEST life is that of a political aspirant under democracy. His failure is ignominious and his success is disgraceful.

IX. DEMOCRACY

Its Origins

From NOTES ON DEMOCRACY, 1926, pp. 3–9

WHAT we now call democracy came into the Western World
to the tune of sweet, soft music. There was, at the start, no harsh
bawling from below; there was only a dulcet twittering from
above. Democratic man thus began as an ideal being, full of
ineffable virtues and romantic wrongs — in brief, as Rousseau's
noble savage in smock and jerkin, brought out of the tropical
wilds to shame the lords and masters of the civilized lands. The
fact continues to have important consequences to this day. It
remains impossible, as it was in the Eighteenth Century, to
separate the democratic idea from the theory that there is a
mystical merit, an esoteric and ineradicable rectitude, in the
man at the bottom of the scale — that inferiority, by some
strange magic, becomes a sort of superiority — nay, the superiority of superiorities. Everywhere on earth, save where the enlightenment of the modern age is confessedly in transient
eclipse, the movement is toward the completer and more en-
amored enfranchisement of the lower orders. Down there, one
hears, lies a deep, illimitable reservoir of righteousness and wisdom, unpolluted by the corruption of privilege. What baffles
statesmen is to be solved by the people, instantly and by a sort
of seraphic intuition. Their yearnings are pure; they alone are
capable of a perfect patriotism; in them is the only hope of
peace and happiness on this lugubrious ball. The cure for the
evils of democracy is more democracy.

This notion, as I hint, originated in the poetic fancy of gentlemen on the upper levels — sentimentalists who, observing to
their distress that the ass was overladen, proposed to reform
transport by putting him into the cart. A stale Christian bilge
ran through their veins. They were the direct ancestors of the

more saccharine Liberals of today, who yet mouth their tattered phrases and dream their preposterous dreams. I can find no record that these phrases, in the beginning, made much impression upon the actual objects of their rhetoric. Early democratic man seems to have given little thought to the democratic ideal, and less veneration. What he wanted was something concrete and highly materialistic — more to eat, less work, higher wages, lower taxes. He had no apparent belief in the acroamatic virtue of his own class, and certainly none in its capacity to rule. His aim was not to exterminate the baron, but simply to bring the baron back to a proper discharge of baronial business. When, by the wild shooting that naturally accompanies all mob movements, the former end was accidentally accomplished, as in France, and men out of the mob began to take on baronial airs, the mob itself quickly showed its opinion of them by butchering them deliberately and in earnest. Once the pikes were out, indeed, it was a great deal more dangerous to be a tribune of the people than to be an ornament of the old order. The more copiously the blood gushed, the nearer that old order came to resurrection. The Paris proletariat, having been misled into killing its King in 1793, devoted the next two years to killing those who had misled it, and by the middle of 1796 it had another King in fact, and in three years more he was King *de jure*, with an attendant herd of barons, counts, marquises and dukes, some of them new but most of them old, to guard, symbolize and execute his sovereignty. And he and they were immensely popular — so popular that half France leaped to suicide that their glory might blind the world.

Meanwhile, of course, there has been a certain seeping down of democratic theory from the metaphysicians to the mob — obscured by the uproar, but still going on. Rhetoric, like a stealthy plague, was doing its immemorial work. Where men were confronted by the harsh, exigent realities of battle and pillage, as they were everywhere on the Continent, it got into their veins only slowly, but where they had time to listen to oratory, as in England and, above all, in America, it fetched them more quickly. Eventually, as the world grew exhausted and the wars passed, it began to make its effects felt everywhere. Democratic man, contemplating himself, was suddenly warmed by the spectacle. His condition had plainly improved. Once a slave, he was now only a serf. Once condemned to silence, he was now free to criticize his masters, and even to flout them, and the ordinances of God with them. As he gained skill and fluency at that sombre and fascinating art, he began to heave in wonder at his own merit. He was not only, it appeared, free to praise and damn, challenge and remonstrate; he was also gifted with a peculiar rectitude of thought and will, and a high talent for ideas, particularly on the political plane. So his wishes, in his mind, began to take on the dignity of legal rights, and by the same token the wishes of his masters sank to the level of mere ignominious lusts. By 1828 in America and by 1848 in Europe the doctrine had arisen that all moral excellence, and with it all pure and unfettered sagacity, resided in the inferior four-fifths of mankind. In 1867 a philosopher out of the ghetto pushed that doctrine to its logical conclusion. He taught that the superior minority had no virtues at all, and hence no rights at all — that the world belonged exclusively and absolutely to those who hewed its wood and drew its water. In half a century he had more followers in the world, open and covert, than any other sophist since Apostolic times.

Since then, to be sure, there has been a considerable recession from that extreme position. The dictatorship of the proletariat, tried here and there, has turned out to be — if I may venture a prejudiced judgment — somewhat impracticable. Even the most advanced Liberals, observing the thing in being, have been moved to cough sadly behind their hands. But it would certainly be going beyond the facts to say that the underlying democratic dogma has been abandoned, or even appreciably overhauled. To the contrary, it is now more prosperous than ever before. The war of 1914–18 was fought in its name, and it was embraced with loud hosannas by all the defeated nations. Everywhere in Christendom it is now official, save in a few benighted lands where God is temporarily asleep. Everywhere its fundamental axioms are accepted: (*a*) that the great masses of men have an inalienable right, born of the very nature of things, to govern themselves, and (*b*) that they are competent to do it. Are they occasionally detected in gross and lamentable imbecilities? Then it is only because they are misinformed by those who would exploit them. The remedy is more education. Are they, at times, seen to be a trifle naughty, even swinish? Then it is only a natural reaction against the oppressions they suffer: the remedy is to deliver them. The central aim of all the Christian governments of today, in theory if not in fact, is to further their liberation, to augment their power, to drive ever larger and larger pipes into the great reservoir of their natural wisdom. That government is called good which responds most quickly and accurately to their desire and ideas. That is called bad which conditions their omnipotence and puts a question mark after their omniscience.

A Glance Ahead

From the same, pp. 202–06

For all I know, democracy may be a self-limiting disease, as civilization itself seems to be. There are thumping parodoxes in its philosophy, and some of them have a suicidal smack. It offers John Doe a means to rise above his place beside Richard Roe, and then, by making Roe his equal, it takes away the chief usufructs of the rising. I here attempt no pretty logical gymnastics: the history of democratic states is a history of disingenuous efforts to get rid of the second half of that dilemma. There is not only the natural yearning of Doe to use and enjoy the superiority that he has won; there is also the natural tendency of Roe, as an inferior man, to acknowledge it. Democracy, in fact, is always inventing class distinctions, despite its theoretical abhorrence of them. The baron has departed, but in his place stand the grand goblin, the supreme worthy archon, the sovereign grand commander. Democratic man is quite unable to think of himself as a free individual; he must belong to a group, or shake with fear and loneliness — and the group, of course, must have its leaders. It would be hard to find a country in which such brummagem serene highnesses are revered with more passionate devotion than they get in the United States. The distinction that goes with mere office runs far ahead of the distinction that goes with actual achievement. A Harding is regarded as superior to a Halsted, no doubt because his doings are better understood.

But there is a form of human striving that is understood by democratic man even better than Harding's, and that is the striving for money. Thus the plutocracy, in a democratic state, tends inevitably, despite its theoretical infamy, to take the place of the missing aristocracy, and even to be mistaken for it. It is, of course, something quite different. It lacks all the essential characters of a true aristocracy: a clean tradition, culture, public spirit, honesty, honor, courage — above all, courage. It stands under no bond of obligation to the state; it has no public duty; it is transient and lacks a goal. Its most puissant dignitaries of today came out of the mob only yesterday — and from the mob they bring all its peculiar ignobilities. As practically encountered, the plutocracy stands quite as far from the *honnête homme* as it stands from the holy saints. Its main character is its incurable timorousness; it is for ever grasping at the straws held out by demagogues. Half a dozen gabby Jewish youths, meeting in a back room to plan a revolution — in other words, half a dozen kittens preparing to upset the Matterhorn — are enough to scare it half to death. Its dreams are of banshees, hobgoblins, bugaboos. The honest, untroubled snores of a Percy or a Hohenstaufen are quite beyond it.

The plutocracy is comprehensible to the mob because its aspirations are essentially those of inferior men: it is not by accident that Christianity, a mob religion, paves heaven with gold and precious stones, *i.e.*, with money. There are, of course, reactions against this ignoble ideal among men of more civilized tastes, even in democratic states, and sometimes they arouse the mob to a transient distrust of certain of the plutocratic pretensions. But that distrust seldom arises above mere envy, and the polemic which engenders it is seldom sound in logic or impeccable in motive. What it lacks is aristocratic disinterestedness, born of aristocratic security. There is no body of opinion behind it that is, in the strictest sense, a free opinion. Its chief exponents, by some divine irony, are pedagogues of one sort or another — which is to say, men chiefly marked by their haunting fear of losing their jobs. Living under such terrors, with the plutocracy policing them harshly on one side and the mob congenitally suspicious of them on the other, it is no wonder that their revolt usually peters out in metaphysics, and that they tend to abandon it as their families grow up, and the costs of heresy become prohibitive. The pedagogue, in the long run, shows the virtues of the Congressman, the newspaper editorial writer or the butler, not those of the aristocrat. When, by any chance, he persists in contumacy beyond thirty, it is only too commonly a sign, not that he is heroic, but simply that he is pathological. So with most of his brethren of the Utopian Fife and Drum Corps, whether they issue out of his own seminary or out of the wilderness. They are fanatics; not statesmen. Thus politics, under democracy, resolves itself into impossible alternatives. Whatever the label on the parties, or the war cries issuing from the demagogues who lead them, the practical choice is between the plutocracy on the one side and a rabble of preposterous impossibilists on the other. It is a pity that this is so. For what democracy needs most of all is a party that will separate the good that is in it theoretically from the evils that beset it practically, and then try to erect that good into a workable system. What it needs beyond everything is a party of liberty. It produces, true enough, occasional libertarians, just as despotism produces occasional regicides, but it treats them in the same drum-head way. It will never have a party of them until it invents and installs a genuine aristocracy, to breed them and secure them.

The Democratic Citizen

From Memoirs of a Subject of the United States, Prejudices: Sixth Series, 1927, pp. 61–70

That the life of man is a struggle and an agony was remarked by the sages of the remotest antiquity. The idea runs like a *Leitmotiv* through the literature of the Greeks and the Jews alike. "Vanity of vanities," saith the Preacher, "vanity of vanities; all is vanity!" "O ye deathward-going tribes of men," chants

Sophocles, "what do your lives mean except that they go to nothingness?" But not placidly, not unresistingly, not without horrible groans and gurgles. Man is never honestly the fatalist, nor even the stoic. He fights his fate, often desperately. He is forever entering bold exceptions to the rulings of the bench of gods. This fighting, no doubt, makes for human progress, for it favors the strong and the brave. It also makes for beauty, for lesser men try to escape from a hopeless and intolerable world by creating a more lovely one of their own. Poetry, as everyone knows, is a means to that end — facile, and hence popular. The aim of poetry is to give a high and voluptuous plausibility to what is palpably not true. I offer the Twenty-third Psalm as an example: "The Lord is my shepherd: I shall not want." It is immensely esteemed by the inmates of almshouses, and by gentlemen waiting to be hanged. I have to limit my own reading of it, avoiding soft and yielding moods, for I too, in my way, am a gentleman waiting to be hanged, as you are.

The struggle is always the same, but in its details it differs in different ages. There was a time when it was mainly a combat between the natural instincts of the individual and his yearning to get into Heaven. That was an unhealthy time, for throttling the instincts is almost as deleterious as breathing bad air: it makes for an unpleasant clamminess. The Age of Faith, seen in retrospect, looks somehow pale and puffy: one admires its saints and anchorites without being conscious of any very active desire to shake hands with them and smell them. Today the yearning to get into Heaven is in abeyance, at least among the vast majority of humankind, and so the ancient struggle takes a new form. In the main, it is a struggle of man with society — a conflict between his desire to be respected and his impulse to follow his own bent. Society usually wins. There are, to be sure, free spirits in the world, but their freedom, in the last analysis, is not much greater than that of a canary in a cage. They may leap from perch to perch; they may bathe and guzzle at their will; they may flap their wings and sing. But they are still in the cage, and soon or late it conquers them. What was once a great itch for long flights and the open spaces is gradually converted into a fading memory and nostalgia, sometimes stim-

ulating but more often merely blushful. The free man, made in
God's image, is converted into a Freudian case.

Democracy produces swarms of such men, and their secret
shames and sorrows, I believe, are largely responsible for the
generally depressing tone of democratic society. Old Freud,
living in a more urbane and civilized world, paid too little heed
to that sort of repression. He assumed fatuously that what was
repressed was always, or nearly always, something intrinsically
wicked, or, at all events, anti-social — for example, the natural
impulse to drag a pretty woman behind the barn, regardless of
her husband's protests. But under democracy that is only half
the story. The democrat with a yearning to shine before his
fellows must not only repress all the common varieties of natural sin; he must also repress many of the varieties of natural
decency. His impulse to tell the truth as he sees it, to speak his
mind freely, to be his own man, comes into early and painful
collision with the democratic dogma that such things are not
nice — that the most worthy and laudable citizen is that one
who is most like all the rest. In youth, as every one knows, this
dogma is frequently challenged, and sometimes with great as-
perity, but the rebellion, taking one case with another, is not
of long duration. The campus Nietzsche, at thirty, begins to
feel the suction of Rotary.

But his early yearning for freedom and its natural concomi-
tants is still not dead; it is merely imprisoned, to adopt the
Freudian jargon, in the depths of his subconscious. Down there
it drags out its weary and intolerable years, protesting silently
but relentlessly against its durance. We know, by Freud's evidence, what the suppression of concupiscence can do to the
individual — how it can shake his reason on its throne, and
even give him such things as gastritis, migraine and angina pec-
toris. Every Sunday-school in the land is full of such wrecks;
they recruit the endless brigades of wowsers. A vice-crusader is
simply an unfortunate who goes about with a brothel in his own
cellar; a teetotaler is one who has buried rum, but would have
been safer drinking it. All this is now a commonplace of knowledge to every American school-girl. But so far no psychoanalyst
has done a tome on the complexes that issue out of the moral

struggles against common decency, though they are commoner under democracy than the other kind, and infinitely more ferocious. A man who has throttled a bad impulse has at least some consolation in his agonies, but a man who has throttled a good one is in a bad way indeed. Yet this great Republic swarms with such men, and their sufferings are under every eye. We have more of them, perhaps, than all the rest of Christendom, with heathendom thrown in to make it unanimous.

A Blind Spot

From the *Smart Set*, April, 1920, pp. 43–44

No doubt my distaste for democracy as a political theory is, like every other human prejudice, due to an inner lack — to a defect that is a good deal less in the theory than in myself. In this case it is very probably my incapacity for envy. That emotion, or weakness, or whatever you choose to call it, is quite absent from my make-up; where it ought to be there is a vacuum. In the face of another man's good fortune I am as inert as a curb broker before Johann Sebastian Bach. It gives me neither pleasure nor distress. The fact, for example, that John D. Rockefeller had more money than I have is as uninteresting to me as the fact that he believed in total immersion and wore detachable cuffs. And the fact that some half-anonymous ass or other has been elected President of the United States, or appointed a professor at Harvard, or married to a rich wife, or even to a beautiful and amiable one: this fact is as meaningless to me as the latest piece of bogus news from eastern Europe.

The reason for all this does not lie in any native nobility or acquired virtue. Far from it, indeed. It lies in the accidental circumstance that the business I pursue in the world seldom brings me into very active competition with other men. I have, of course, rivals, but they do not rival me directly and exactly, as one delicatessen dealer or clergyman or lawyer or politician rivals another. It is only rarely that their success costs me anything, and even then the fact is usually concealed. I have always had enough money to meet my modest needs, and have always found it easy to get more than I actually want. A skeptic as to all ideas, including especially my own, I have never suffered a pang when the ideas of some other imbecile prevailed.

Thus I am never envious, and so it is impossible for me to feel any sympathy for men who are. *Per corollary*, it is impossible for me to get any glow out of such hallucinations as democracy and Puritanism, for if you pump envy out of them you empty them of their very life blood: they are all immovably grounded upon the inferior man's hatred of the man who is having a better time. One often hears them accounted for, of course, in other ways. Puritanism is represented as a lofty sort of obedience to God's law. Democracy is depicted as brotherhood, even as altruism. All such notions are in error. There is only one honest impulse at the bottom of Puritanism, and that is the impulse to punish the man with a superior capacity for happiness — to bring him down to the miserable level of "good" men, *i.e.*, of stupid, cowardly and chronically unhappy men. And there is only one sound argument for democracy, and that is the argument that it is a crime for any man to hold himself out as better than other men, and, above all, a most heinous offense for him to prove it.

What I admire most in any man is a serene spirit, a steady freedom from moral indignation, an all-embracing tolerance — in brief, what is commonly called good sportsmanship. Such a man is not to be mistaken for one who shirks the hard knocks of life. On the contrary, he is frequently an eager gladiator, vastly enjoying opposition. But when he fights he fights in the manner of a gentleman fighting a duel, not in that of a longshoreman cleaning out a waterfront saloon. That is to say, he carefully guards his *amour propre* by assuming that his opponent is as decent a man as he is, and just as honest — and perhaps, after all, right. Such an attitude is palpably impossible to a democrat. His distinguishing mark is the fact that he always attacks his opponents, not only with all arms, but also with snorts and objurgations — that he is always filled with moral indignation — that he is incapable of imagining honor in an antagonist, and hence incapable of honor himself. Such fellows I do not like. I do not share their emotion. I can't understand their indignation, their choler. In particular, I can't fathom their envy. And so I am against them.

Rivals to Democracy

From Notes on Democracy, 1926, pp. 118–21

The mob has its flatterers and bosh-mongers; the king has his courtiers. But there is a difference, and I think it is important. The courtier, at his worst, at least performs his genuflections before one who is theoretically his superior, and is surely not less than his equal. He does not have to abase himself before swine with whom, ordinarily, he would disdain to have any traffic. He is not compelled to pretend that he is a worse man than he really is. He needn't hold his nose in order to approach his benefactor. Thus he may go into office without having dealt his honor a fatal wound, and once he is in, he is under no pressure to sacrifice it further, and may nurse it back to health and vigor. His sovereign, at worst, has a certain respect for it, and hesitates to strain it unduly; the mob has no sensitiveness on that point, and, indeed, no knowledge that it exists. The courtier's sovereign, in other words, is apt to be a man of honor himself. When, in 1848 or thereabout, Wilhelm I of Prussia was offered the imperial crown by a so-called parliament of his subjects, he refused it on the ground that he could take it only from his equals, *i.e.*, from the sovereign princes of the *Reich*. To the democrats of the world this attitude was puzzling, and on reflection it began to seem contemptible and offensive. But that was not to be marveled at. To a democrat any attitude based upon a concept of honor, dignity and integrity seems contemptible and offensive.

The democratic politician, facing such plain facts, tries to save his *amour propre* in a characteristically human way; that is to say, he denies them. We all do that. We convert our degradations into renunciations, our self-seeking into public spirit, our swinishness into heroism. No man, I suppose, ever admits to himself candidly that he gets his living in a dishonorable way, not even a biter off of puppies' tails. The democratic politician, confronted by the dishonesty and stupidity of his master, the mob, tries to convince himself and all the rest of us that it is really full of rectitude and wisdom. This is the origin of the doctrine that, whatever its transient errors, democracy always comes to right decisions in the long run. Perhaps — but on what evidence, by what reasoning, and for what motives! Go examine the long history of the anti-slavery agitation in America: it is a truly magnificent record of buncombe, false pretenses, and imbecility. This notion that the mob is wise, I fear, is not to be taken seriously: it was invented by mob-masters to save their faces. Whenever democracy, by an accident, produces a genuine statesman, he is found to be proceeding on the assumption that it is not true. And on the assumption that it is difficult, if not impossible to go to the mob for support, and still retain the ordinary decencies.

The best democratic statesmanship, like the best non-democratic statesmanship, tends to safeguard the honor of the higher officers of state by relieving them of that degrading necessity. As every schoolboy knows, such was the intent of the Fathers, as expressed in Article II, Sections 1 and 2, of the Constitution. To this day it is a common device, when this or that office becomes steeped in intolerable corruption, to take it out of the gift of the mob, and make it appointive. The aspirant, of course, still has to seek it, for under democracy it is very rare that office seeks the man, but seeking it of the President, or even of the Governor of a State, is felt to be appreciably less humiliating and debasing than seeking it of the mob. The President may be a Coolidge, and the Governor may be a Blease or a Ma Ferguson, but he (or she) is at least able to understand plain English, and need not be put into good humor by the arts of the circus clown or Baptist evangelist.

To sum up: the essential objection to feudalism (the perfect antithesis to democracy) was that it imposed degrading acts and attitudes upon the vassal; the essential objection to democracy is that, with few exceptions, it imposes degrading acts and attitudes upon the men responsible for the welfare and dignity of the state. The former was compelled to do homage to his suzerain, who was very apt to be a brute and an ignoramus.

The latter are compelled to do homage to their constituents, who in overwhelming majority are certain to be both.

Last Words

From the same, pp. 206–212

ONE of the merits of democracy is quite obvious: it is perhaps the most charming form of government ever devised by man. The reason is not far to seek. It is based upon propositions that are palpably not true — and what is not true, as everyone knows, is always immensely more fascinating and satisfying to the vast majority of men than what is true. Truth has a harshness that alarms them, and an air of finality that collides with their incurable romanticism. They turn, in all the great emergencies of life, to the ancient promises, transparently false but immensely comforting, and of all those ancient promises there is none more comforting than the one to the effect that the lowly shall inherit the earth. It is at the bottom of the dominant religious system of the modern world, and it is at the bottom of the dominant political system. Democracy gives it a certain appearance of objective and demonstrable truth. The mob man, functioning as citizen, gets a feeling that he is really important to the world — that he is genuinely running things. Out of his maudlin herding after rogues and mountebanks there comes to him a sense of vast and mysterious power — which is what makes archbishops, police sergeants and other such magnificoes happy. And out of it there comes, too, a conviction that he is somehow wise, that his views are taken seriously by his betters — which is what makes United States Senators, fortune-tellers and Young Intellectuals happy. Finally, there comes out of it a glowing consciousness of a high duty triumphantly done — which is what makes hangmen and husbands happy.

All these forms of happiness, of course, are illusory. They don't last. The democrat, leaping into the air to flap his wings and praise God, is forever coming down with a thump. The seeds of his disaster lie in his own stupidity: he can never get

rid of the naïve delusion — so beautifully Christian! — that happiness is something to be got by taking it away from the other
fellow. But there are seeds, too, in the very nature of things:
a promise, after all, is only a promise, even when it is supported
by divine revelation, and the chances against its fulfilment may
be put into a depressing mathematical formula. Here the irony
that lies under all human aspiration shows itself: the quest for
happiness, as usual, brings only *un*happiness in the end. But
saying that is merely saying that the true charm of democracy
is not for the democrat but for the spectator. That spectator, it
seems to me, is favored with a show of the first cut and calibre.
Try to imagine anything more heroically absurd! What grotesque false pretenses! What a parade of obvious imbecilities!
What a welter of fraud! But is fraud unamusing? Then I retire
forthwith as a psychologist. The fraud of democracy, I contend,
is more amusing than any other — more amusing even, and by
miles, than the fraud of religion. Go into your praying-chamber
and give sober thought to any of the more characteristic democratic inventions. Or to any of the typical democratic prophets.
If you don't come out paled and palsied by mirth then you
will not laugh on the Last Day itself, when Presbyterians step
out of the grave like chicks from the egg, and wings blossom
from their scapulæ, and they leap into interstellar space with
roars of joy.

I have spoken hitherto of the possibility that democracy may
be a self-limiting disease, like measles. It is, perhaps, something
more: it is self-devouring. One cannot observe it objectively
without being impressed by its curious distrust of itself — its
apparently ineradicable tendency to abandon its whole philosophy at the first sign of strain. I need not point to what happens
invariably in democratic states when the national safety is menaced. All the great tribunes of democracy, on such occasions,
convert themselves, by a process as simple as taking a deep
breath, into despots of an almost fabulous ferocity. Nor is this
process confined to times of alarm and terror: it is going on day
in and day out. Democracy always seems bent upon killing
the thing it theoretically loves. All its axioms resolve themselves
into thundering paradoxes, many amounting to downright contradictions in terms. The mob is competent to rule the rest of

us — but it must be rigorously policed itself. There is a government, not of men, but of laws — but men are set upon benches to decide finally what the law is and may be. The highest function of the citizen is to serve the state — but the first assumption that meets him, when he essays to discharge it, is an assumption of his disingenuousness and dishonor. Is that assumption commonly sound? Then the farce only grows the more glorious.

I confess, for my part, that it greatly delights me. I enjoy democracy immensely. It is incomparably idiotic, and hence incomparably amusing. Does it exalt dunderheads, cowards, trimmers, frauds, cads? Then the pain of seeing them go up is balanced and obliterated by the joy of seeing them come down. Is it inordinately wasteful, extravagant, dishonest? Then so is every other form of government: all alike are enemies to decent men. Is rascality at the very heart of it? Well, we have borne that rascality since 1776, and continue to survive. In the long run, it may turn out that rascality is an ineradicable necessity to human government, and even to civilization itself — that civilization, at bottom, is nothing but a colossal swindle. I do not know. I report only that when the suckers are running well the spectacle is infinitely exhilarating. But I am, it may be, a somewhat malicious man: my sympathies, when it comes to suckers, tend to be coy. What I can't make out is how any man can believe in democracy who feels for and with them, and is pained when they are debauched and made a show of. How can any man be a democrat who is sincerely a democrat?

X. AMERICANS

❧❦❧

The Anglo-Saxon

From THE AMERICAN TRADITION, PREJUDICES: FOURTH SERIES,
1924, pp. 23–42.
First printed in the Baltimore *Evening Sun*, July 16, 1923

WHEN I speak of Anglo-Saxons, of course, I speak inexactly and
in the common phrase. Even within the bounds of that phrase
the American of the dominant stock is Anglo-Saxon only partially, for there is probably just as much Celtic blood in his
veins as Germanic, and his norm is to be found, not south of
the Tyne and west of the Severn, but on the two sides of the
northern border. Among the first English colonists there were
many men of almost pure Teutonic stock from the east and
south of England, and their influence is yet visible in many
characteristic American folkways, in certain traditional American ideas — some of them now surviving only in national hypoc-
risies — and, above all, in the fundamental peculiarities of the
American dialect of English. But their Teutonic blood was early
diluted by Celtic strains from Scotland, from the north of Ireland, from Wales, and from the west of England, and today
those Americans who are regarded as being most thoroughly
Anglo-Saxons — for example, the mountaineers of the Appa-
lachian slopes from Pennsylvania to Georgia — are obviously
far more Celtic than Teutonic, not only physically but also
mentally. They are leaner and taller than the true English, and
far more given to moral obsessions and religious fanaticism. A
Methodist revival is not an English phenomenon; it is Welsh.
So is the American tendency, marked by every foreign student
of our history, to turn all political combats into moral crusades.
The English themselves, of course, have been greatly polluted
by Scotch, Irish and Welsh blood during the past three centuries, and for years past their government has been largely in

the hands of Celts, but though this fact, by making them more like Americans, has tended to conceal the difference that I am discussing, it has certainly not sufficed to obliterate it altogether. The English notion of humor remains different from the American notion, and so does the English view of personal liberty, and on the same level of primary ideas there are many other obvious differences.

But though I am thus convinced that the American Anglo-Saxon wears a false label, and grossly libels both of the great races from which he claims descent, I can imagine no good in trying to change it. Let him call himself whatever he pleases. Whatever he calls himself, it must be plain that the term he uses designates a genuinely distinct and differentiated race — that he is separated definitely, in character and habits of thought, from the men of all other recognizable strains — that he represents, among the peoples of the earth, almost a special species, and that he runs true to type. The traits that he developed when the first mixture of races took place in colonial days are the traits that he still shows; despite the vast changes in his material environment, he is almost precisely the same, in the way he thinks and acts, as his forefathers were. Some of the other great races of men, during the past two centuries, have changed very noticeably, but the American Anglo-Saxon has stuck to his hereditary guns. Moreover, he tends to show much less variation than other races between man and man. No other race, save it be the Chinese, is so thoroughly regimented.

The good qualities of this so-called Anglo-Saxon are many, and I am certainly not disposed to question them, but I here pass them over without apology, for he devotes practically the whole of his literature and fully a half of his oral discourse to celebrating them himself, and so there is no danger that they will ever be disregarded. No other known man, indeed, is so violently the blowhard, save it be his English kinsman. In this fact lies the first cause of the ridiculous figure he commonly cuts in the eyes of other people: he brags and blusters so incessantly that, if he actually had the combined virtues of Socrates, the Cid and the Twelve Apostles, he would still go beyond the facts, and so appear a mere Bombastes Furioso. This habit, I believe, is fundamentally English, but it has been exaggerated in the

Americano by his larger admixture of Celtic blood. In late years in America it has taken on an almost pathological character, and is to be explained, perhaps, only in terms of the Freudian necromancy. Braggadocio, in the 100% American — "we won the war," "it is our duty to lead the world," and so on — is probably no more than a protective mechanism erected to conceal an inescapable sense of inferiority.

That this inferiority is real must be obvious to any impartial observer. Whenever the Anglo-Saxon, whether of the English or of the American variety, comes into sharp conflict with men of other stocks, he tends to be worsted, or, at best, to be forced back upon extraneous and irrelevant aids to assist him in the struggle. Here in the United States his defeat is so palpable that it has filled him with vast alarms, and reduced him to seeking succor in grotesque and extravagant devices. In the fine arts, in the sciences and even in the more complex sorts of business the children of the later immigrants are running away from the descendants of the early settlers. To call the roll of Americans eminent in almost any field of human endeavor above the most elemental is to call a list of strange and often outlandish names; even the panel of Congress presents a startling example. Of the Americans who have come into notice during the past fifty years as poets, as novelists, as critics, as painters, as sculptors and in the minor arts, less than half bear Anglo-Saxon names, and in this minority there are few of pure Anglo-Saxon blood. So in the sciences. So in the higher reaches of engineering and technology. So in philosophy and its branches. So even in industry and agriculture. In those areas where the competition between the new and the old bloodstreams is most sharp and clear-cut, say in New York, in seaboard New England and in the farming States of the upper Middle West, the defeat of the so-called Anglo-Saxon is overwhelming and unmistakable. Once his predominance everywhere was actual and undisputed; today, even where he remains superior numerically, it is largely sentimental and illusory.

The descendants of the later immigrants tend generally to move upward; the descendants of the first settlers, I believe, tend plainly to move downward, mentally, spiritually and even physically. Civilization is at its lowest mark in the United States precisely in those areas where the Anglo-Saxon still presumes to rule. He runs the whole South — and in the whole South there are not as many first-rate men as in many a single city of the mongrel North. Wherever he is still firmly in the saddle, there we look for such pathological phenomena as Fundamentalism, Prohibition and Ku Kluxery, and there they flourish. It is not in the northern cities, with their mixed population, that the death-rate is highest, and politics most corrupt, and religion nearest to voodooism, and every decent human aspiration suspect; it is in the areas that the recent immigrations have not penetrated, where "the purest Anglo-Saxon blood in the world" still flows. I could pile up evidences, but they are not necessary. The fact is too plain to be challenged. One testimony will be sufficient: it comes from two inquirers who made an exhaustive survey of a region in southeastern Ohio, where "the people are more purely Americans than in the rest of the State":

> Here gross superstition exercises strong control over the thought and action of a large proportion of the people. Syphilitic and other venereal diseases are common and in-creasing over whole counties, while in some communities nearly every family is afflicted with inherited or infectious disease. Many cases of incest are known; inbreeding is rife. Imbeciles, feeble-minded, and delinquents are numerous, politics is corrupt, and selling of votes is common, petty crimes abound, the schools have been badly managed and poorly attended. Cases of rape, assault, and robbery are of almost weekly occurrence within five minutes' walk of the corporation limits of one of the county seats, while in an-other county political control is held by a self-confessed criminal. Alcoholic intemperance is excessive. Gross im-morality and its evil results are by no means confined to the hill districts, but are extreme also in the towns.[1]

As I say, the American of the old stock is not unaware of this steady, and, of late, somewhat rapid deterioration — this grad-ual loss of his old mastery in the land his ancestors helped to

[1] Since the above was written there has been unqualified confirmation of it by a distinguished English authority, to wit, Arnold J. Toynbee. See his Study of History, Vol. I, pp. 466–67, and Vol. II, pp. 311–12.

wring from the Indian and the wildcat. He senses it, indeed, very painfully, and, as if in despair of arresting it in fact, makes desperate efforts to dispose of it by denial and concealment. These efforts often take grotesque and extravagant forms. Laws are passed to hobble and cage the citizen of newer stocks in a hundred fantastic ways. It is made difficult and socially dangerous for him to teach his children the speech of his fathers, or to maintain the cultural attitudes that he has inherited from them. Every divergence from the norm of the low-cast Anglo-Saxon is treated as an *attentat* against the commonwealth, and punished with eager ferocity.

It so happens that I am myself an Anglo-Saxon — one of far purer blood, indeed, than most of the half-bleached Celts who pass under the name in the United States and England. I am in part Angle and in part Saxon, and what else I am is safely white, Nordic, Protestant and blond. Thus I feel free, without risk of venturing into bad taste, to regard frankly the *soi-disant* Anglo-Saxon of this incomparable Republic and his rather less dubious cousin of the Motherland. How do the two appear to me, after years spent largely in accumulating their disfavor? What are the characters that I discern most clearly in the so-called Anglo-Saxon type of man? I may answer at once that two stick out above all others. One is his curious and apparently incurable incompetence — his congenital inability to do any difficult thing easily and well, whether it be isolating a bacillus or writing a sonata. The other is his astounding susceptibility to fears and alarms — in short, his hereditary cowardice.

To accuse so enterprising and successful a race of cowardice, of course, is to risk immediate derision; nevertheless, I believe that a fair-minded examination of its history will bear me out. Nine-tenths of the great feats of derring-do that its sucklings are taught to venerate in school — that is, its feats as a race, not the isolated exploits of its extraordinary individuals, most of them at least partly of other stocks — have been wholly lacking in even the most elementary gallantry. Consider, for example, the events attending the extension of the two great empires, English and American. Did either movement evoke any genuine courage and resolution? The answer is plainly no. Both empires were built up primarily by swindling and butchering unarmed savages, and after that by robbing weak and friendless nations. Neither produced a hero above the average run of those in the movies; neither exposed the folks at home to any serious danger of reprisal. Almost always, indeed, mercenaries have done the Anglo-Saxon's fighting for him — a high testimony to his common sense, but scarcely flattering, I fear, to the truculence he boasts of. The British empire was won mainly by Irishmen, Scotchmen and native allies, and the American empire, at least in large part, by Frenchmen and Spaniards. Moreover, neither great enterprise cost any appreciable amount of blood; neither presented grave and dreadful risks; neither exposed the conqueror to the slightest danger of being made the conquered. The British won most of their vast dominions without having to stand up in a single battle against a civilized and formidable foe, and the Americanos won their continent at the expense of a few dozen puerile skirmishes with savages. The total cost of conquering the whole area from Plymouth Rock to the Golden Gate and from Lake George to the Everglades, including even the cost of driving out the French, Dutch, English and Spaniards, was less than the cost of defending Verdun.

So far as I can make out there is no record in history of any Anglo-Saxon nation entering upon any great war without allies. The French have done it, the Dutch have done it, the Germans have done it, the Japs have done it, and even such inferior nations as the Danes, the Spaniards, the Boers and the Greeks have done it, but never the English or Americans. Can you imagine the United States resolutely facing a war in which the odds against it were as huge as they were against Spain in 1898? The facts of history are wholly against any such fancy. The Anglo-Saxon always tries to take a gang with him when he goes into battle, and even when he has it behind him he is very uneasy, and prone to fall into panic at the first threat of genuine danger. Here I put an unimpeachably Anglo-Saxon witness on the stand, to wit, the late Charles W. Eliot. I find him saying, in an article quoted with approbation by the *Congressional Record*, that during the Revolutionary War the colonists now hymned so eloquently in the school-books "fell into a condition of despondency from which nothing but the steadfastness of Washington and the Continental army *and the aid from France* saved them," and that "when the War of 1812 brought grave losses a considerable portion of the population experienced a moral collapse, from which they were rescued only by the exertions of a few thoroughly patriotic statesmen and the exploits of three or four American frigates on the seas" — to say nothing of an enterprising Corsican gentleman, Bonaparte by name.

In both these wars the Americans had enormous and obvious advantages, in terrain, in allies and in men; nevertheless, they fought, in the main, very badly, and from the first shot to the last a majority of them stood in favor of making peace on almost any terms. The Mexican and Spanish Wars I pass over as perhaps too obscenely ungallant to be discussed at all; of the former, U. S. Grant, who fought in it, said that it was "the most unjust war ever waged by a stronger against a weaker nation." Who remembers that, during the Spanish War, the whole Atlantic Coast trembled in fear of the Spaniards' feeble fleet — that all New England had hysterics every time a strange coal-barge was sighted on the sky-line, that the safe-deposit boxes of Boston were emptied and their contents transferred to Worcester, and that the Navy had to organize a patrol to save the coast towns from depopulation? Perhaps those Reds, atheists and pro-Germans remember it who also remember that during World War I the entire country went wild with fear of an enemy who, without the aid of divine intervention, obviously could not strike it a blow at all — and that the great moral victory was gained at last with the assistance of twenty-one allies and at odds of eight to one.[2]

But the American Civil War remains? Does it, indeed? The almost unanimous opinion of the North, in 1861, was that it would be over after a few small battles; the first soldiers were actually enlisted for but three months. When, later on, it turned unexpectedly into a severe struggle, recruits had to be driven to the front by force, and the only Northerners remaining in favor

---

[2] The case of World War II was even more striking. The two enemies that the United States tackled had been softened by years of a hard struggle with desperate foes, and those foes continued to fight on. Neither enemy could muster even a tenth of the materials that the American forces had the use of. And at the end both were outnumbered in men by odds truly enormous.

of going on were Abraham Lincoln, a few ambitious generals and the profiteers. I turn to Dr. Eliot again. "In the closing year of the war," he says, "large portions of the Democratic party in the North *and of the Republican party*, advocated surrender to the Confederacy, *so downhearted were they*." Downhearted at odds of three to one! The South was plainly more gallant, but even the gallantry of the South was largely illusory. The Confederate leaders, when the war began, adopted at once the traditional Anglo-Saxon device of seeking allies. They tried and expected to get the aid of England, and they actually came very near succeeding. When hopes in that direction began to fade (*i.e.*, when England concluded that tackling the North would be dangerous), the common people of the Confederacy threw up the sponge, and so the catastrophe, when it came at last, was mainly internal. The South failed to bring the quaking North to a standstill because, to borrow a phrase that Dr. Eliot uses in another connection, it "experienced a moral collapse of unprecedented depth and duration." The folks at home failed to support the troops in the field, and the troops in the field began to desert. Even so early as Shiloh, indeed, many Confederate regiments were already refusing to fight.

This reluctance for desperate chances and hard odds, so obvious in the military record of the English-speaking nations, is also conspicuous in times of peace. What a man of another and superior stock almost always notices, living among so-called Anglo-Saxons, is (*a*) their incapacity for prevailing in fair rivalry, either in trade, in the fine arts or in what is called learning — in brief, their general incompetence, and (*b*) their invariable effort to make up for this incapacity by putting some inequitable burden upon their rivals, usually by force. The Frenchman, I believe, is the worst of chauvinists, but once he admits a foreigner to his country he at least treats that foreigner fairly, and does not try to penalize him absurdly for his mere foreignness. The Anglo-Saxon American is always trying to do it; his history is a history of recurrent outbreaks of blind rage against peoples who have begun to worst him. Such movements would be inconceivable in an efficient and genuinely self-confident people, wholly assured of their superiority, and they would be equally inconceivable in a truly gallant and courageous people, disdaining unfair advantages and overwhelming odds. Theoretically launched against some imaginary inferiority in the non-Anglo-Saxon man, either as patriot, as democrat or as Christian, they are actually launched at his general superiority, his greater fitness to survive in the national environment. The effort is always to penalize him for winning in fair fight, to handicap him in such a manner that he will sink to the general level of the Anglo-Saxon population, and, if possible, even below it. Such devices, of course, never have the countenance of the Anglo-Saxon minority that is authentically superior, and hence self-confident and tolerant. But that minority is pathetically small, and it tends steadily to grow smaller and feebler. The communal laws and the communal *mores* are made by the folk, and they offer all the proof that is necessary, not only of its general inferiority, but also of its alarmed awareness of that inferiority. The normal American of the "pure-blooded" majority goes to rest every night with an uneasy feeling that there is a burglar under the bed, and he gets up every morning with a sickening fear that his underwear has been stolen.

This Anglo-Saxon of the great herd is, in many important respects, the least civilized of white men and the least capable of true civilization. His political ideas are crude and shallow. He is almost wholly devoid of esthetic feeling. The most elementary facts about the visible universe alarm him, and incite him to put them down. Educate him, make a professor of him, teach him how to express his soul, and he still remains palpably third-rate. He fears ideas almost more cravenly than he fears men. His blood, I believe, is running thin; perhaps it was not much to boast of at the start; in order that he may exercise any functions above those of a trader, a pedagogue or a mob orator, it needs the stimulus of other and less exhausted strains. The fact that they increase is the best hope of civilization in America. They shake the old race out of its spiritual lethargy, and introduce it to disquiet and experiment. They make for a free play of ideas. In opposing the process, whether in politics, in letters or in the ages-long struggle toward the truth, the prophets of Anglo-Saxon purity and tradition only make themselves ridiculous.

American Culture

From THE NATIONAL LETTERS, PREJUDICES: SECOND SERIES,
1920, pp. 65–78.
First printed in the *Yale Review*, June, 1920, pp. 804–17

THE CAPITAL defect in the culture of These States is the lack of
a civilized aristocracy, secure in its position, animated by an
intelligent curiosity, skeptical of all facile generalizations, superior to the sentimentality of the mob, and delighting in the
battle of ideas for its own sake. The word I use, despite the
qualifying adjective, has got itself meanings, of course, that I
by no means intend to convey. Any mention of an aristocracy,
to a public fed upon democratic fustian, is bound to bring up
images of stockbrokers' wives lolling obscenely in opera boxes,
or of haughty Englishmen slaughtering whole generations of
grouse in an inordinate and incomprehensible manner, or of
bogus counts coming over to work their magic upon the daughters of breakfast-food and bathtub kings. This misconception belongs to the general American tradition. Its depth and extent
are constantly revealed by the naïve assumption that the so-
called fashionable folk of the large cities — chiefly wealthy
industrials in the interior-decorator and country-club stage of
culture — constitute an aristocracy, and by the scarcely less remarkable assumption that the peerage of England is identical
with the gentry — that is, that such men as Lord Northcliffe,
Lord Riddel and even Lord Reading were English gentlemen.

Here, as always, the worshiper is the father of the gods, and
no less when they are evil than when they are benign. The inferior man must find himself superiors, that he may marvel at
his political equality with them, and in the absence of recognizable superiors *de facto* he creates superiors *de jure*. The sublime principle of one man, one vote must be translated into
terms of dollars, diamonds, fashionable intelligence; the equality of all men before the law must have clear and dramatic
proofs. Sometimes, perhaps, the thing goes further and is more
subtle. The inferior man needs an aristocracy to demonstrate,
not only his mere equality, but also his actual superiority. The

society columns in the newspapers may have some such origin. They may visualize once more the accomplished journalist's understanding of the mob mind that he plays upon so skillfully, as upon some immense and cacophonous organ, always going *fortissimo*. What the inferior man and his wife see in the sinister revels of those brummagem first families, I suspect, is often a massive witness to their own higher rectitude — in brief, to their firmer grasp upon the immutable axioms of Christian virtue, the one sound boast of the nether nine-tenths of humanity in every land under the cross.

But this bugaboo aristocracy is actually bogus, and the evidence of its bogusness lies in the fact that it is insecure. One gets into it only onerously, but out of it very easily. Entrance is effected by dint of a long and bitter struggle, and the chief incidents of that struggle are almost intolerable humiliations. The aspirant must school and steel himself to sniffs and sneers; he must see the door slammed upon him a hundred times before ever it is thrown open to him. To get in at all he must show a talent for abasement — and abasement makes him timorous. Worse, that timorousness is not cured when he succeeds at last. On the contrary, it is made even more tremulous, for what he faces within the gates is a scheme of things made up almost wholly of harsh and often unintelligible taboos, and the penalty for violating even the least of them is swift and disastrous. He must exhibit exactly the right social habits, appetites and prejudices, public and private. He must harbor exactly the right enthusiasms and indignations. He must have a hearty taste for exactly the right sports and games. His attitude toward the fine arts must be properly tolerant and yet not a shade too eager. He must read and like exactly the right books, pamphlets and public journals. He must put up at the right hotels when he travels. His wife must patronize the right milliners. He himself must stick to the right haberdashery. He must live in the right neighborhood. He must even embrace the right doctrines of religion. It would ruin him, for all society column purposes, to move to Union Hill, N. J., or to drink coffee from his saucer, or to marry a chambermaid with a gold tooth, or to join the Seventh Day Adventists. Within the boundaries of his curious order he is worse fettered than a monk in a cell. Its obscure conception of propriety, its nebulous notion that this or that is honorable, hampers him in every direction, and very narrowly. What he resigns when he enters, even when he makes his first deprecating knock at the door, is every right to attack the ideas that happen to prevail within. Such as they are, he must accept them without question. And as they shift and change he must shift and change with them, silently and quickly.

Obviously, that order cannot constitute a genuine aristocracy, in any rational sense. A genuine aristocracy is grounded upon very much different principles. Its first and most salient character is its interior security, and the chief visible evidence of that security is the freedom that goes with it — not only freedom in act, the divine right of the aristocrat to do what he damn well pleases, so long as he does not violate the primary guarantees and obligations of his class, but also and more importantly freedom in thought, the liberty to try and 'err, the right to be his own man. It is the instinct of a true aristocracy, not to punish eccentricity by expulsion, but to throw a mantle of protection about it — to safeguard it from the suspicions and resentments of the lower orders. Those lower orders are inert, timid, inhospitable to ideas, hostile to changes, faithful to a few maudlin superstitions. All progress goes on on the higher levels. It is there that salient personalities, made secure by artificial immunities, may oscillate most widely from the normal track. It is within that entrenched fold, out of reach of the immemorial certainties of the mob, that extraordinary men of the lower orders may find their city of refuge, and breathe a clear air. This, indeed, is at once the hall-mark and the justification of a genuine aristocracy — that it is beyond responsibility to the general masses of men, and hence superior to both their degraded longings and their no less degraded aversions. It is nothing if it is not autonomous, curious, venturesome, courageous, and everything if it is. It is the custodian of the qualities that make for change and experiment; it is the class that organizes danger to the service of the race; it pays for its high prerogatives by standing in the forefront of the fray.

No such aristocracy, it must be plain, is now on view in the United States. The makings of one were visible in the Virginia of the Eighteenth Century, but with Jefferson and Washington the promise died. In New England, it seems to me, there was never anything of the sort, either in being or in nascency: there was only a theocracy that degenerated very quickly into a plutocracy on the one hand and a caste of sterile pedants on the other — the passion for God splitting into a lust for dollars and a weakness for mere words. Despite the common notion to the contrary — a notion generated by confusing literacy with intelligence — the New England of the great days never showed any genuine enthusiasm for ideas. It began its history as a slaughterhouse of ideas, and it is today not easily distinguishable from a cold-storage plant. Its celebrated adventures in mysticism, once apparently so bold and significant, are now seen to have been little more than an elaborate hocus-pocus — respectable Unitarians shocking the peasantry and scaring the horned cattle in the fields by masquerading in the robes of Rosicrucians. The notions that it embraced in those austere and far-off days were stale, and when it had finished with them they were dead. So in politics. Since the Civil War it has produced fewer political ideas, as political ideas run in the Republic, than any average county in Kansas or Nebraska. Appomattox seemed to be a victory for New England idealism. It was actually a victory for the New England plutocracy, and that plutocracy has dominated thought above the Housatonic ever since. The sect of professional idealists has so far dwindled that it has ceased to be of any importance, even as an opposition. When the plutocracy is challenged now, it is challenged by the proletariat.

Well, what is on view in New England is on view in all other parts of the nation, sometimes with ameliorations, but usually with the colors merely exaggerated. What one beholds, sweeping the eye over the land, is a culture that, like the national literature, is in three layers — the plutocracy on top, a vast mass of undifferentiated human blanks bossed by demagogues at the bottom, and a forlorn *intelligentsia* gasping out a precarious life between. I need not set out at any length, I hope, the intellectual deficiencies of the plutocracy — its utter failure to show anything even remotely resembling the makings of an aristocracy. It is badly educated, it is stupid, it is full of low-caste superstitions and indignations, it is without decent traditions or informing vision; above all, it is extraordinarily lacking in the most elemental independence and courage. Out of this class comes the grotesque fashionable society of our big towns, already described. It shows all the stigmata of inferiority — moral certainty, cruelty, suspicion of ideas, fear. Never does it function more revealingly than in the recurrent *pogroms* against radicalism, *i.e.*, against humorless persons who, like Andrew Jackson, take the platitudes of democracy seriously. And what is the theory at the bottom of all these proceedings? So far as it can be reduced to comprehensible terms it is much less a theory than a fear — a shivering, idiotic, discreditable fear of a mere banshee — an overpowering, paralyzing dread that some extra-eloquent Red, permitted to emit his balderdash unwhipped, may eventually convert a couple of courageous men, and that the courageous men, filled with indignation against the plutocracy, may take to the highroad, burn down a nail-factory or two, and slit the throat of some virtuous profiteer.

Obviously, it is out of reason to look for any hospitality to ideas in a class so extravagantly fearful of even the most palpably absurd of them. Its philosophy is firmly grounded upon the thesis that the existing order must stand forever free from attack, and not only from attack, but also from mere academic criticism, and its ethics are as firmly grounded upon the thesis that every attempt at any such criticism is a proof of moral turpitude. Within its own ranks, protected by what may be regarded as the privilege of the order, there is nothing to take the place of this criticism. In other countries the plutocracy has often produced men of reflective and analytical habit, eager to rationalize its instincts and to bring it into some sort of relationship to the main streams of human thought. The case of David Ricardo at once comes to mind, and there have been many others: John Bright, Richard Cobden, George Grote. But in the United States no such phenomenon has been visible. Nor has the plutocracy ever fostered an inquiring spirit among its intellectual valets and footmen, which is to say, among the gentlemen who compose headlines and leading articles for its newspapers. What chiefly distinguishes the daily press of the United States from the press of all other countries pretending to culture is not its lack of truthfulness or even its lack of dignity and honor, for these deficiencies are common to newspapers every-

where, but its incurable fear of ideas, its constant effort to evade
the discussion of fundamentals by translating all issues into a
few elemental fears, its incessant reduction of all reflection to
mere emotion. It is, in the true sense, never well-informed. It is
seldom intelligent, save in the arts of the mob-master. It is never
courageously honest. Held harshly to a rigid correctness of
opinion, it sinks rapidly into formalism and feebleness. Its yellow section is perhaps its best section, for there the only vestige
of the old free journalist survives. In the more respectable papers one finds only a timid and petulant animosity to all ques-
tioning of the existing order, however urbane and sincere — a
pervasive and ill-concealed dread that the mob now heated up
against the orthodox hobgoblins may suddenly begin to unearth
hobgoblins of its own, and so run amok.

For it is upon the emotions of the mob, of course, that the
whole comedy is played. Theoretically, the mob is the repository of all political wisdom and virtue; actually, it is the ultimate
source of all political power. Even the plutocracy cannot make
war upon it openly, or forget the least of its weaknesses. The
business of keeping it in order must be done discreetly, warily,
with delicate technique. In the main that business consists in
keeping alive its deep-seated fears — of strange faces, of unfamiliar ideas, of unhackneyed gestures, of untested liberties and
responsibilities. The one permanent emotion of the inferior
man, as of all the simpler mammals, is fear — fear of the unknown, the complex, the inexplicable. What he wants beyond
everything else is security. His instincts incline him toward a society so organized that it will protect him at all hazards, and not
only against perils to his hide but also against assaults upon his
mind — against the need to grapple with unaccustomed problems, to weigh ideas, to think things out for himself, to scrutinize the platitudes upon which his everyday thinking is based.

XI. THE SOUTH

The Sahara of the Bozart

From PREJUDICES: SECOND SERIES, 1920, pp. 136–54. This was first printed, in shorter form, in the New York *Evening Mail*, Nov. 13, 1917. It produced a ferocious reaction in the South, and I was belabored for months, and even years afterward in a very extravagant manner. The essay in its final form, as it is here reproduced, dates sadly, but I have let it stand as a sort of historical document. On the heels of the violent denunciations of the elder Southerners there soon came a favorable response from the more civilized youngsters, and there is reason to believe that my attack had something to do with that revival of Southern letters which followed in the middle 1920s

Alas, for the South! Her books have grown fewer —
She never was much given to literature.

IN the lamented J. Gordon Coogler, author of these elegiac lines, there was the insight of a true poet. He was the last bard of Dixie, at least in the legitimate line. Down there a poet is now almost as rare as an oboe-player, a dry-point etcher or a metaphysician. It is, indeed, amazing to contemplate so vast a vacuity. One thinks of the interstellar spaces, of the colossal reaches of the now mythical ether. Nearly the whole of Europe could be lost in that stupendous region of worn-out farms, shoddy cities and paralyzed cerebrums: one could throw in France, Germany and Italy, and still have room for the British Isles. And yet, for all its size and all its wealth and all the "progress" it babbles of, it is almost as sterile, artistically, intellectually, culturally, as the Sahara Desert. There are single acres in Europe that house more first-rate men than all the states south of the Potomac; there are probably single square miles in America. If the whole of the late Confederacy were to be engulfed by a tidal wave tomorrow, the effect upon the civilized minority of men in the world would be but little greater than that of a flood on the Yang-tse-kiang. It would be impossible in all history to match so complete a drying-up of a civilization.

I say a civilization because that is what, in the old days, the South had, despite the Baptist and Methodist barbarism that reigns down there now. More, it was a civilization of manifold excellences — perhaps the best that the Western Hemisphere had ever seen — undoubtedly the best that These States have ever seen. Down to the middle of the last century, and even beyond, the main hatchery of ideas on this side of the water was across the Potomac bridges. The New England shopkeepers and theologians never really developed a civilization; all they ever developed was a government. They were, at their best, tawdry and tacky fellows, oafish in manner and devoid of imagination; one searches the books in vain for mention of a salient Yankee gentleman; as well look for a Welsh gentleman. But in the South there were men of delicate fancy, urbane instinct and aristocratic manner — in brief, superior men — in brief, gentry. To politics, their chief diversion, they brought active and original minds. It was there that nearly all the political theories we still cherish and suffer under came to birth. It was there that the crude dogmatism of New England was refined and humanized. It was there, above all, that some attention was given to the art of living — that life got beyond and above the state of a mere infliction and became an exhilarating experience. A certain notable spaciousness was in the ancient Southern scheme of things. The Ur-Confederate had leisure. He liked to toy with ideas. He was hospitable and tolerant. He had the vague thing that we call culture.

But consider the condition of his late empire today. The picture gives one the creeps. It is as if the Civil War stamped out every last bearer of the torch, and left only a mob of peasants on the field. One thinks of Asia Minor, resigned to Armenians, Greeks and wild swine, of Poland abandoned to the Poles. In all that gargantuan paradise of the fourth-rate there is not a single picture gallery worth going into, or a single orchestra capable of playing the nine symphonies of Beethoven, or a single opera-house, or a single theater devoted to decent plays, or a single public monument that is worth looking at, or a single

workshop devoted to the making of beautiful things. Once you
have counted James Branch Cabell (a lingering survivor of the
ancien régime: a scarlet dragon-fly imbedded in opaque amber)
you will not find a single Southern prose writer who can actually
write. And once you have — but when you come to critics, musical composers, painters, sculptors, architects and the like, you
will have to give it up, for there is not even a bad one between
the Potomac mud-flats and the Gulf. Nor a historian. Nor a
philosopher. Nor a theologian. Nor a scientist. In all these fields
the South is an awe-inspiring blank — a brother to Portugal,
Serbia and Albania.

Consider, for example, the present estate and dignity of Virginia — in the great days indubitably the premier American
state, the mother of Presidents and statesmen, the home of the
first American university worthy of the name, the *arbiter ele-
gantiarum* of the Western World. Well, observe Virginia today. It is years since a first-rate man, save only Cabell, has come
out of it; it is years since an idea has come out of it. The old
aristocracy went down the red gullet of war; the poor white trash
are now in the saddle. Politics in Virginia are cheap, ignorant,
parochial, idiotic; there is scarcely a man in office above the rank
of a professional job-seeker; the political doctrine that prevails
is made up of hand-me-downs from the bumpkinry of the Middle West — Bryanism, Prohibition, all that sort of filthy claptrap; the administration of the law is turned over to professors
of Puritanism and espionage; a Washington or a Jefferson,
dumped there by some act of God, would be denounced as a
scoundrel and jailed overnight.

Elegance, *esprit,* culture? Virginia has no art, no literature, no
philosophy, no mind or aspiration of her own. Her education
has sunk to the Baptist seminary level; not a single contribution
to human knowledge has come out of her colleges in twenty-
five years; she spends less than half upon her common schools,
per capita, than any Northern state spends. In brief, an intellectual Gobi or Lapland. Urbanity, *politesse,* chivalry? Go to! It
was in Virginia that they invented the device of searching for
contraband whiskey in women's underwear. . . . There remains,
at the top, a ghost of the old aristocracy, a bit wistful and infinitely charming. But it has lost all its old leadership to fabu-

lous monsters from the lower depths; it is submerged in an industrial plutocracy that is ignorant and ignominious. The mind of the state, as it is revealed to the nation, is pathetically naïve and inconsequential. It no longer reacts with energy and elasticity to great problems. It has fallen to the bombastic trivialities of the camp-meeting and the stump. One could no more imagine a Lee or a Washington in the Virginia of today than one could imagine a Huxley in Nicaragua.

I choose the Old Dominion, not because I disdain it, but precisely because I esteem it. It is, by long odds, the most civilized of the Southern states, now as always. It has sent a host of creditable sons northward; the stream kept running into our own time. Virginians, even the worst of them, show the effects of a great tradition. They hold themselves above other Southerners, and with sound pretension. If one turns to such a commonwealth as Georgia the picture becomes far darker. There the liberated lower orders of whites have borrowed the worst commercial bounderism of the Yankee and superimposed it upon a culture that, at bottom, is but little removed from savagery. Georgia is at once the home of the cotton-mill sweater, of the Methodist parson turned Savonarola and of the lynching bee. A self-respecting European, going there to live, would not only find intellectual stimulation utterly lacking; he would actually feel a certain insecurity, as if the scene were the Balkans or the China Coast. There is a state with more than half the area of Italy and more population than either Denmark or Norway, and yet in thirty years it has not produced a single idea. Once upon a time a Georgian printed a couple of books that attracted notice, but immediately it turned out that he was little more than an amanuensis for the local blacks — that his works were really the products, not of white Georgia, but of black Georgia. Writing afterward *as* a white man, he swiftly subsided into the fifth rank. And he is not only the glory of the literature of Georgia; he is, almost literally, the whole of the literature of Georgia — nay, of the entire art of Georgia.[1]

Virginia is the best of the South today, and Georgia is perhaps the worst. The one is simply senile; the other is crass, gross, vulgar and obnoxious. Between lies a vast plain of mediocrity,

---

[1] The reference here, of course, was to Joel Chandler Harris.

stupidity, lethargy, almost of dead silence. In the North, of course, there is also grossness, crassness, vulgarity. The North, in its way, is also stupid and obnoxious. But nowhere in the North is there such complete sterility, so depressing a lack of all civilized gesture and aspiration. One would find it difficult to unearth a second-rate city between the Ohio and the Pacific that isn't struggling to establish an orchestra, or setting up a little theater, or going in for an art gallery, or making some other effort to get into touch with civilization. These efforts often fail, and sometimes they succeed rather absurdly, but under them there is at least an impulse that deserves respect, and that is the impulse to seek beauty and to experiment with ideas, and so to give the life of every day a certain dignity and purpose. You will find no such impulse in the South. There are no committees down there cadging subscriptions for orchestras; if a string quartet is ever heard there, the news of it has never come out; an opera troupe, when it roves the land, is a nine days' wonder. The little theater movement has swept the whole country, enormously augmenting the public interest in sound plays, giving new dramatists their chance, forcing reforms upon the commercial theater. Everywhere else the wave rolls high — but along the line of the Potomac it breaks upon a rock-bound shore. There is no little theater beyond. There is no gallery of pictures. No artist ever gives exhibitions. No one talks of such things. No one seems to be interested in such things.

As for the cause of this unanimous torpor and doltishness, this curious and almost pathological estrangement from everything that makes for a civilized culture, I have hinted at it already, and now state it again. The South has simply been drained of all its best blood. The vast hemorrhage of the Civil War half exterminated and wholly paralyzed the old aristocracy, and so left the land to the harsh mercies of the poor white trash, now its masters. The war, of course, was not a complete massacre. It spared a decent number of first-rate Southerners — perhaps even some of the very best. Moreover, other countries, notably France and Germany, have survived far more staggering butcheries, and even showed marked progress thereafter. But the war not only cost a great many valuable lives; it also brought bankruptcy, demoralization and despair in its train — and so the majority of the first-rate Southerners that were left, broken in spirit and unable to live under the new dispensation, cleared out. A few went to South America, to Egypt, to the Far East. Most came north. They were fecund; their progeny is widely dispersed, to the great benefit of the North. A Southerner of good blood almost always does well in the North. He finds, even in the big cities, surroundings fit for a man of condition. His peculiar qualities have a high social value, and are esteemed. He is welcomed by the codfish aristocracy as one palpably superior. But in the South he throws up his hands. It is impossible for him to stoop to the common level. He cannot brawl in politics with the grandsons of his grandfather's tenants. He is unable to share their fierce jealousy of the emerging black — the cornerstone of all their public thinking. He is anesthetic to their theological and political enthusiasms. He finds himself an alien at their feasts of soul. And so he withdraws into his tower, and is heard of no more. Cabell is almost a perfect example. His eyes, for years, were turned toward the past; he became a professor of the grotesque genealogizing that decaying aristocracies affect; it was only by a sort of accident that he discovered himself to be an artist. The South is unaware of the fact to this day; it regards Woodrow Wilson and John Temple Graves as much finer stylists, and Frank L. Stanton as an infinitely greater poet. If it has heard, which I doubt, that Cabell has been hoofed by the Comstocks, it unquestionably views that assault as a deserved rebuke to a fellow who indulges a lewd passion for fancy writing, and is a covert enemy to the Only True Christianity.

What is needed down there, before the vexatious public problems of the region may be intelligently approached, is a survey of the population by competent ethnologists and anthropologists. The immigrants of the North have been studied at great length, and anyone who is interested may now apply to the Bureau of Ethnology for elaborate data as to their racial strains, their stature and cranial indices, their relative capacity for education, and the changes that they undergo under American *Kultur*. But the older stocks of the South, and particularly the emancipated and dominant poor white trash, have never been investigated scientifically, and most of the current generalizations about them are probably wrong. For example, the generalization that they are purely Anglo-Saxon in blood. This I doubt very seriously. The chief strain down there, I believe, is Celtic rather than Saxon, particularly in the hill country. French blood, too, shows itself here and there, and so does Spanish, and so does German. The last-named entered from the northward, by way of the limestone belt just east of the Alleghenies. Again, it is very likely that in some parts of the South a good many of the plebeian whites have more than a trace of Negro blood. Interbreeding under concubinage produced some very light halfbreeds at an early day, and no doubt appreciable numbers of them went over into the white race by the simple process of changing their abode. Not long ago I read a curious article by an intelligent Negro, in which he stated that it is easy for a very light Negro to pass as white in the South on account of the fact that large numbers of Southerners accepted as white have distinctly negroid features. Thus it becomes a delicate and dangerous matter for a train conductor or a hotel-keeper to challenge a suspect. But the Celtic strain is far more obvious than any of these others. It not only makes itself visible in physical stigmata — *e.g.*, leanness and dark coloring — but also in mental traits. For example, the religious thought of the South is almost precisely identical with the religious thought of Wales. There is the same naïve belief in an anthropomorphic Creator but little removed, in manner and desire, from an evangelical bishop; there is the same submission to an ignorant and impudent sacerdotal tyranny, and there is the same sharp contrast between doctrinal orthodoxy and private ethics. Read Caradoc Evans's ironical picture of the Welsh Wesleyans in his preface to "My Neighbors," and you will be instantly reminded of the Georgia and Carolina Methodists. The most booming sort of piety, in the South, is not incompatible with the theory that lynching is a benign institution. Two generations ago it was not incompatible with an ardent belief in slavery.

It is highly probable that some of the worst blood of western Europe flows in the veins of the Southern poor whites, now poor no longer. The original strains, according to every honest historian, were extremely corrupt. Philip Alexander Bruce (a Virginian of the old gentry) says in his "Industrial History of Virginia in the Seventeenth Century" that the first native-born generation was largely illegitimate. "One of the most common offenses against morality committed in the lower ranks of life in Virginia during the Seventeenth Century," he says, "was bastardy." The mothers of these bastards, he continues, were chiefly indentured servants, and "had belonged to the lowest class in their native country." Fanny Kemble Butler, writing of the Georgia poor whites of a century later, described them as "the most degraded race of human beings claiming an Anglo-Saxon origin that can be found on the face of the earth — filthy, lazy, ignorant, brutal, proud, penniless savages." The Sunday-school and the chautauqua, of course, have appreciably mellowed the descendants of these "savages," and their economic progress and rise to political power have done perhaps even more, but the marks of their origin are still unpleasantly plentiful. Every now and then they produce a political leader who puts their secret notions of the true, the good and the beautiful into plain words, to the amazement and scandal of the rest of the country. That amazement is turned into downright incredulity when news comes that his platform has got him high office, and that he is trying to execute it.

In the great days of the South the line between the gentry and the poor whites was very sharply drawn. There was absolutely no intermarriage. So far as I know there is not a single instance in history of a Southerner of the upper class marrying one of the bondwomen described by Mr. Bruce. In other societies characterized by class distinctions of that sort it is common for the lower class to be improved by extra-legal crosses. That is to say, the men of the upper class take women of the lower class as mistresses, and out of such unions spring the extraordinary plebeians who rise sharply from the common level, and so propagate the delusion that all other plebeians would do the same thing if they had the chance — in brief, the delusion that class distinctions are merely economic and conventional, and not congenital and genuine. But in the South the men of the upper classes sought their mistresses among the blacks, and after a few generations there was so much white blood in the black women that they were considerably more attractive than the unhealthy and bedraggled women of the poor whites. This preference continued into our own time. A Southerner of good family once told me in all seriousness that he had reached his majority before it ever occurred to him that a white woman might make quite as agreeable a mistress as the octaroons of his jejune fancy. If the thing has changed of late, it is not the fault of the Southern white man, but of the Southern mulatto women. The more sightly yellow girls of the region, with improving economic opportunities, have gained self-respect, and so they are no longer as willing to enter into concubinage as their grand-dams were.

As a result of this preference of the Southern gentry for mulatto mistresses there was created a series of mixed strains containing the best white blood of the South, and perhaps of the whole country. As another result the poor whites went unfertilized from above, and so missed the improvement that so constantly shows itself in the peasant stocks of other countries. It is a commonplace that nearly all Negroes who rise above the general are of mixed blood, usually with the white predominating. I know a great many Negroes, and it would be hard for me to think of an exception. What is too often forgotten is that this white blood is not the blood of the poor whites but that of the old gentry. The mulatto girls of the early days despised the poor whites as creatures distinctly inferior to Negroes, and it was thus almost unheard of for such a girl to enter into relations with a man of that submerged class. This aversion was based upon a sound instinct. The Southern mulatto of today is a proof of it. Like all other half-breeds he is an unhappy man, with disquieting tendencies toward anti-social habits of thought, but he is intrinsically a better animal than the pure-blooded descendant of the old poor whites, and he not infrequently demonstrates it. It is not by accident that the Negroes of the South are making faster progress, culturally, than the masses of the whites. It is not by accident that the only visible esthetic activity in the South is in their hands. No Southern composer has ever written music so good as that of half a dozen white-black composers who might be named. Even in politics, the Negro reveals a curious superiority. Despite the fact that the race question has been the main political concern of the Southern whites for two generations, to the practical exclusion of everything else, they have contributed nothing to its discussion that has impressed the rest of the world so deeply and so favorably as three or four books by Southern Negroes.

Entering upon such themes, of course, one must resign one's self to a vast misunderstanding and abuse. The South has not only lost its old capacity for producing ideas; it has also taken on the worst intolerance of ignorance and stupidity. Its prevailing mental attitude for several decades past has been that of its own hedge ecclesiastics. All who dissent from its orthodox doctrines are scoundrels. All who presume to discuss its ways realistically are damned. I have had, in my day, several experiences in point. Once, after I had published an article on some phase of the eternal race question,[2] a leading Southern newspaper replied by printing a column of denunciation of my father, then dead nearly twenty years — a philippic placarding him as an ignorant foreigner of dubious origin, inhabiting "the Baltimore ghetto" and speaking a dialect recalling that of Weber & Fields — two thousand words of incandescent nonsense, utterly false and beside the point, but exactly meeting the latter-day Southern notion of effective controversy. Another time, I published a short discourse on lynching, arguing that the sport was popular in the South because the backward culture of the region denied the populace more seemly recreations. Among such recreations I mentioned those afforded by brass bands, symphony orchestras, boxing matches, amateur athletic contests, horse races, and so on. In reply another great Southern journal denounced me as a man "of wineshop temperament, brass-jewelry tastes and pornographic predilections." In other words, brass bands, in the South, are classed with brass jewelry, and both are snares of the devil! To advocate setting up symphony orchestras is pornography! . . . Alas, when the touchy Southerner attempts a greater urbanity, the result is often even worse. Some time ago a colleague of mine printed an article deploring the arrested cultural development of Georgia. In reply he received a number of protests from patriotic Georgians, and all of them solemnly listed the glories of the state. I indulge in a few specimens:

[2] Si Mutare Potest Aethiops Pellum Suam, *Smart Set*, Sept., 1917, pp. 138–42.

Who has not heard of Asa G. Candler, whose name is synonymous with Coca-Cola, a Georgia product?

The first Sunday-school in the world was opened in Savannah.

Who does not recall with pleasure the writings of . . . Frank L. Stanton, Georgia's brilliant poet?

Georgia was the first state to organize a Boys' Corn Club in the South — Newton county, 1904.

The first to suggest a common United Daughters of the Confederacy badge was Mrs. Raynes, of Georgia.

The first to suggest a state historian of the United Daughters of the Confederacy was Mrs. C. Helen Plane (Macon convention, 1896).

The first to suggest putting to music Heber's "From Greenland's Icy Mountains" was Mrs. F. R. Goulding, of Savannah.

And so on, and so on. These proud boasts came, remember, not from obscure private persons, but from "leading Georgians" — in one case, the state historian. Curious sidelights upon the ex-Confederate mind! Another comes from a stray copy of a Negro paper. It describes an ordinance passed by the city council of Douglas, Ga., forbidding any trousers presser, on penalty of forfeiting a $500 bond, to engage in "pressing for both white and colored." This in a town, says the Negro paper, where practically all of the white inhabitants have "their food prepared by colored hands," "their babies cared for by colored hands," and "the clothes which they wear right next to their skins washed in houses where Negroes live" — houses in which the said clothes "remain for as long as a week at a time." But if you marvel at the absurdity, keep it dark! A casual word, and the united press of the South will be upon your trail, denouncing you bitterly as a scoundrelly damnyankee, a Bolshevik Jew.

Obviously, it is impossible for intelligence to flourish in such an atmosphere. Free inquiry is blocked by the idiotic certainties of ignorant men. The arts, save in the lower reaches of the gospel hymn, the phonograph and the political harangue, are all held in suspicion. The tone of public opinion is set by an upstart class but lately emerged from industrial slavery into commercial enterprise — the class of "bustling" business men, of "live wires," of commercial club luminaries, of "drive" managers, of forward-lookers and right-thinkers — in brief, of third-rate Southerners inoculated with all the worst traits of the Yankee sharper. One observes the curious effects of an old tradition of truculence upon a population now merely pushful and impudent, of an old tradition of chivalry upon a population now quite without imagination. The old repose is gone. The old romanticism is gone. The philistinism of the new type of town-boomer Southerner is not only indifferent to the ideals of the Old South; it is positively antagonistic to them. That philistinism regards human life, not as an agreeable adventure, but as a mere trial of rectitude and efficiency. It is overwhelmingly utilitarian and moral. It is inconceivably hollow and obnoxious. What remains of the ancient tradition is simply a certain charming civility in private intercourse — often broken down, alas, by the hot rages of Puritanism, but still generally visible. The Southerner, at his worst, is never quite the surly cad that the Yankee is. His sensitiveness may betray him into occasional bad manners, but in the main he is a pleasant fellow — hospitable, polite, good-humored, even jovial. . . . But a bit absurd. . . . A bit pathetic.

The Confederate Mind

From the *Smart Set*, Oct., 1921, pp. 42–43

MANY of the curious phenomena which engage and delight the psychologist in the late Confederate States are probably explicable as effects of a tradition of truculence operating upon a population that is congenitally timorous and even poltroonish. That tradition comes down from the Southern aristocracy of the old days, which bred it as a part of the general tradition of feudalism. The old-time Southerner of the ruling caste was primarily a cavalier, *i.e.*, a cavalry officer, and cultivated all the qualities that go with the trade. He carried arms and knew how to use them; he cultivated a chivalrous attitude toward women;

he was quick to resent injuries, and enjoyed combat; he tried to model himself, not upon Cromwell, but upon the Cid. This tradition, as I say, survives, but the actual cavalier is almost extinct. In his place, making his gestures and trying absurdly to think his thoughts, there is the Southerner of today, a man usually of very humble origin and often of true proletarian instincts. His great-grandfather was not a gentleman, but a farm laborer, and very probably one bound by terms which made him almost a slave. When, now, this scion of an inferior stock, moved by what he regards as his duty as a Southerner, rolls his eye in the best Chevalier Bayard manner, reaches for his weapon and tries to scare the vulgar to death — when this spectacle is unfolded the effect is not unlike that of a sheep trying to bark.

No actual gallantry is left in the South, save as the private possession of a small minority of surviving first-rate Southerners. The thing that the new lords of the soil have on tap is simply a puerile imitation of it. In place of dueling they mob. Instead of the old high tone of controversy there is nothing but doggery brawling. These new Southerners, at bottom, are no better and no worse than any other men of their class. If they follow their natural instincts they would be no more obnoxious than the newly emancipated and enriched proletarians of any other region. But the fatal tradition of truculence lies upon them, and, yielding to it, they become nuisances. It is as if so many Russian *muzhiks* should put on horn-rimmed spectacles and set up shop as philosophers.

The Calamity of Appomattox

From the *American Mercury*, Sept., 1930, pp. 29–31

No American historian, so far as I know, has ever tried to work out the probable consequences if Grant instead of Lee had been on the hot spot at Appomattox. How long would the victorious Confederacy have endured? Could it have surmounted the difficulties inherent in the doctrine of States' Rights, so often inconvenient and even paralyzing to it during the war? Could it have remedied its plain economic deficiencies, and become a self-sustaining nation? How would it have protected itself against such war heroes as Beauregard and Longstreet, Joe Wheeler and Nathan B. Forrest? And what would have been its relations to the United States, socially, economically, spiritually and politically?

I am inclined, on all these counts, to be optimistic. The chief evils in the Federal victory lay in the fact, from which we still suffer abominably, that it was a victory of what we now call Babbitts over what used to be called gentlemen. I am not arguing here, of course, that the whole Confederate army was composed of gentlemen; on the contrary, it was chiefly made up, like the Federal army, of innocent and unwashed peasants, and not a few of them got into its corps of officers. But the impulse behind it, as everyone knows, was essentially aristocratic, and that aristocratic impulse would have fashioned the Confederacy if the fortunes of war had run the other way. Whatever the defects of the new commonwealth below the Potomac, it would have at least been a commonwealth founded upon a concept of human inequality, and with a superior minority at the helm. It might not have produced any more Washingtons, Madisons, Jeffersons, Calhouns and Randolphs of Roanoke, but it would certainly not have yielded itself to the Heflins, Caraways, Bilbos and Tillmans.

The rise of such bounders was a natural and inevitable consequence of the military disaster. That disaster left the Southern gentry deflated and almost helpless. Thousands of the best young men among them had been killed, and thousands of those who survived came North. They commonly did well in the North, and were good citizens. My own native town of Baltimore was greatly enriched by their immigration, both culturally and materially; if it is less corrupt today than most other large American cities, then the credit belongs largely to Virginians, many of whom arrived with no baggage save good manners and empty bellies. Back home they were sorely missed. First the carpetbaggers ravaged the land, and then it fell into the hands of the native white trash, already so poor that war and Reconstruction could not make them any poorer. When things began to improve they seized whatever was seizable, and their heirs and

assigns, now poor no longer, hold it to this day. A raw plutocracy owns and operates the New South, with no challenge save
from a proletariat, white and black, that is still three-fourths
peasant, and hence too stupid to be dangerous. The aristocracy
is almost extinct, at least as a force in government. It may survive in backwaters and on puerile levels, but of the men who
run the South today, and represent it at Washington, not 5%,
by any Southern standard, are gentlemen.

If the war had gone with the Confederates no such vermin
would be in the saddle, nor would there be any sign below the
Potomac of their chief contributions to American *Kultur* — Ku
Kluxry, political ecclesiasticism, nigger-baiting, and the more
homicidal variety of wowserism. Such things might have arisen
in America, but they would not have arisen in the South. The
old aristocracy, however degenerate it might have become,
would have at least retained sufficient decency to see to that.
New Orleans, today, would still be a highly charming and civilized (if perhaps somewhat zymotic) city, with a touch of Paris
and another of Port Said. Charleston, which even now sprouts
lady authors, would also sprout political philosophers. The University of Virginia would be what Jefferson intended it to be,
and no shouting Methodist would haunt its campus. Richmond
would be, not the dull suburb of nothing that it is now, but a
beautiful and consoling second-rate capital, comparable to Buda-
pest, Brussels, Stockholm or The Hague. And all of us, with the
Middle West pumping its revolting silo juices into the East and
West alike, would be making frequent leaps over the Potomac,
to drink the sound red wine there and breathe the free air.

My guess is that the two Republics would be getting on pretty
amicably. Perhaps they'd have come to terms as early as 1898,
and fought the Spanish-American War together. In 1917 the
confiding North might have gone out to save the world for democracy, but the South, vaccinated against both Wall Street
and the Liberal whim-wham, would have kept aloof — and
maybe rolled up a couple of billions of profit from the holy crusade. It would probably be far richer today, independent, than
it is with the clutch of the Yankee mortgage-shark still on its
collar. It would be getting and using his money just the same,
but his toll would be less. As things stand, he not only exploits

the South economically; he also pollutes and debases it spiritually. It suffers damnably from low wages, but it suffers even more from the Chamber of Commerce metaphysic.

No doubt the Confederates, victorious, would have abolished slavery by the middle 80s. They were headed that way before the war, and the more sagacious of them were all in favor of it. But they were in favor of it on sound economic grounds, and not on the brummagem moral grounds which persuaded the North. The difference here is immense. In human history a moral victory is always a disaster, for it debauches and degrades both the victor and the vanquished. The triumph of sin in 1865 would have stimulated and helped to civilize both sides.

Today the way out looks painful and hazardous. Civilization in the United States survives only in the big cities, and many of them — notably Boston and Philadelphia — seem to be sliding down to the cow country level. No doubt this standardization will go on until a few of the more resolute towns, headed by New York, take to open revolt, and try to break out of the Union. Already, indeed, it is talked of. But it will be hard to accomplish, for the tradition that the Union is indissoluble is now firmly established. If it had been broken in 1865 life would be far pleasanter today for every American of any noticeable decency. There are, to be sure, advantages in Union for everyone, but it must be manifest that they are greatest for the worst kinds of people. All the benefit that a New Yorker gets out of Kansas is no more than what he might get out of Saskatchewan, the Argentine pampas, or Siberia. But New York to a Kansan is not only a place where he may get drunk, look at dirty shows and buy bogus antiques; it is also a place where he may enforce his dunghill ideas upon his betters.

A Class A Blunder

From MISCELLANEOUS NOTES, PREJUDICES: FIFTH SERIES,
1926, pp. 291–92.
First printed in the *American Mercury*, April, 1925, p. 449

THE SOUTHERN gentry made a capital mistake when they yielded
to pressure from the poor white trash and connived at the dis-
franchisement of the colored brother. Had they permitted him
to vote they would have retained political control of all the
Southern States, for the black, like the peasant everywhere else,
would have followed his natural masters. As it was, control
quickly passed to the white trash, who still maintain it, though
some of them have ceased to be poor. The gentry now struggle
in vain to get back in the saddle; they lack the votes to achieve
the business unaided, and the blacks, who were ready to follow
them in 1870, have become incurably suspicious of them. The
result is that politics in the South remains fathomlessly swinish.
Every civilized Southerner knows it and is ashamed of it, but
the time has apparently passed to do anything about it. To get
rid of its demagogues the South would have to wait until the
white trash were themselves civilized. This would be a matter
demanding almost as much patience as the long vigil of the
Seventh Day Adventists.

XII. HISTORY

Historians

From DAMN! A BOOK OF CALUMNY, 1918, pp. 32–33

IT is the misfortune of humanity that its history is chiefly written by third-rate men. The first-rate man seldom has any impulse to record and philosophize; his impulse is to act; life, to him, is an adventure, not a syllogism or an autopsy. Thus the writing of history is left mainly to professors, moralists, theorists, dunderheads. Few historians, great or small, have shown any capacity for the affairs they presume to describe and interpret. Gibbon was an inglorious failure as a member of Parliament. Thucydides made such a mess of his naval command that he was exiled from Athens for twenty years and finally assassinated. Flavius Josephus, serving as governor of Galilee, lost the whole province to the Romans, and had to flee for his life. Momssen, elected to the Prussian Landtag, became an easy mark for the Socialists.

How much better we would understand the habits and nature of man if there were more historians like Julius Cæsar, or even like Niccolo Machiavelli. Remembering the sharp and devastating character of their rough notes, think what marvelous histories Bismarck and Frederick the Great might have written. Such men are privy to the facts; the usual historians have to depend on deductions, rumors, guesses. Again, such men know how to tell the truth, however unpleasant; they are wholly free of that puerile moral obsession which marks the professor. . . . But how seldom it is that they tell it.

Forgotten Men

From the *American Mercury*, March, 1928, pp. 280–82

HAPPY nations, said Cesare Bonesano Beccaria, have no history. Nor, it appears, have intelligent men; at all events, they are seldom remembered generally, and almost never with respect. All the great heroes of the human race have preached things palpably not true, and practised things palpably full of folly. Their imbecilities, surviving, constitute the massed wisdom of *Homo sapiens*, lord of the lion and the whale, the elephant and the wolf, though not, as yet, of the gnat and the fly, the cockroach and the rat. So surviving, these august imbecilities conceal the high probability that, when they were new, they must have been challenged sharply by doubting and dare-devil men — that sober reason must have revolted against them contemporaneously, as it does today. But of that revolt, in most cases, nothing is known. The penalty of intelligence is oblivion.

Consider, for example, the case of those ancient Jews whose banal speculations about the origin of things still afflict the whole of Christendom, to say nothing of Islam. Is it possible to believe that, in the glorious Eighth and Ninth Centuries B.C., *all* Jews swallowed that preposterous rubbish — that the race was completely devoid of intelligent men, and knew nothing of an enlightened public opinion? I find it hard to go so far. The Jews, at that time, had already proved that they were the best of the desert tribes, and by long odds, and they were fast moving to the front as city folks, *i.e.*, as civilized men. Yet the only Jewish document that comes down to us from that great day is part of the Book of Genesis, a farrago of nonsense so wholly absurd that even Sunday-school scholars have to be threatened with Hell to make them accept it. The kind of mind it reveals is the kind one encounters today among New York wash-room attendants, Mississippi newspaper editors, and Tenneseee judges. It is barely above the level of observation and ratiocination of a bright young jackass.

Are we to assume that this appalling mind was the best Jewish mind of the time — that Genesis represents the finest flowering of the Jewish national genius? To ask the question is to answer it. The Jews, you may rest assured, were not unanimously of such low mental visibility. There were enlightened men among them as well as sorcerers and theologians. They had shrewd and sophisticated fellows who were to Moses and the other patriarchs as Thomas Henry Huxley was to Gladstone. They had lost and happy souls who laughed at Genesis quite as loudly the day it was released as it is laughed at today by the current damned. But of these illuminati not a word survives in the records of the Jews. Of their animadversions upon Moses's highfalutin tosh — and no doubt those animadversions were searching and devastating — we lack even so much as the report of a report. Thus all we know today of the probably brilliant and enterprising intellectual life of the ante-Exile Jews is contained in a compilation of balderdash by certain of their politicians and ecclesiastics. It is as if their descendants of our own time were to be measured by the sonorous rumble-bumble of Rabbi Stephen S. Wise and Otto H. Kahn. It is as if the American civilization we sweat and prosper under were to go down into history in terms of Calvin Coolidge, Henry Ford and Arthur Brisbane.

Well, why not? Those, perhaps, are the precise terms in which it *is* to go down. On second thought, I change perhaps into no doubt. What has happened invariably in the past will keep on happening to the end of the chapter. Certainly we can't expect to escape the fate of Greece and Rome — and both Greece and Rome are chiefly remembered today (and venerated by the learned and unintelligent) by the records of their second- and third-rate men. Is it seriously argued that Plato was the most enlightened Greek of his age? Then it may be argued with equal plausibility that Upton Sinclair has been the most enlightened American of this one. Item by item the two match: as political scientists, as professors of esthetics, as experts on the natural processes. In some ways, true enough, Plato was clearly superior to Sinclair: for one thing, he was better versed in the jargon of metaphysics, heavenly maid — which is to say, in the jargon of organized nonsense. But I think that no one will undertake to deny that Sinclair beats him on the pharmacology of alcohol, on the evils of voluptuousness, and on the electronic vibrations of the late Dr. Albert Abrams.

Plato survives today as one of the major glories of Greece. Put upon oath in a court of law, more specialists in dead ideas would probably rate him as the greatest Greek of them all. But you may be sure that there were Athenians in his own day who, dropping in to hear his Message, carried away a different notion. Some of them were very bright fellows, and privy to the philosophical arcana. They had heard all the champions, and had their private views. I suggest somewhat diffidently that there were ideas in the Republic and the Laws that made them retire to the nearby wine-shops to snigger. But no one remembers those immune Athenians today, nor the hard-boiled fellows who guffawed at the court of Philip of Macedon. The world recalls only Plato.

Here, I sincerely hope, I shall not be mistaken for one who seeks to cry that great man down. On the contrary, I venerate him. There is implicit in his writings, though not often explicit, the operation of an intellect of a superior order. Whatever may be said against him, he at least refrained from ratifying the political, theological and epistemological notions that were current in his time. He was no Athenian Rotarian, but his very intelligence made him remember, when he got up before his customers, that it was necessary to adapt his speculations to their capacities and prejudices. Like Woodrow Wilson in a later age, he had a weakness for oratory, and got himself enmeshed in its snares. Some of his principal works are no more than reports of his harangues, and the heat in them singes the sense. He suffered, as all reflective men must suffer, from the fact that what is put into words for the general ear can never come within even the remotest reach of what is pondered in the privacy of the study or praying-room.

The case of Abraham Lincoln immediately recalls itself. He was, I believe, one of the most intelligent men ever heard of in his realm — but he was also a politician, and, in his last years, President of the Federal Union. The fact worked an immemorial cruelty upon him when he visited the battlefield of Gettysburg, on November 19, 1863. One may easily imagine the reflections that the scene and the occasion must have inspired in so sagacious and unconventional a man — at all events, one may imagine the more obvious of them. They were, it is highly probable, of an extremely acrid and unpleasant nature. Before him stretched row upon row of new-made graves; around him ranged the gaunt cinders of a witless and abominable war. The thought must have occurred to him at once that —

But before him there also stretched an acre or two of faces — the faces of dull Pennsylvania peasants from the adjacent farms, with here and there the jowls of a Philadelphia politician gleaming in the pale Winter sunlight. It was too cold that day to his badly-cushioned bones for a long speech, and the audience would have been mortally offended by a good one. So old Abe put away his reflections, and launched into the tried and sure-fire stuff. Once started, the *furor loquendi* dragged him on. Abandoning the simple and crystal-clear English of his considered utterance, he stood a sentence on its head, and made a pretty parlor ornament of it. Proceeding, he described the causes and nature of the war in terms of the current army press bureau. Finally, he launched a sonorous, meaningless epigram, and sat down. There was immense applause. The Pennsylvania oafs were delighted. And the speech remains in all the school-books to this day.

Lincoln had too much humor in him to leave a diary, and so we do not know what he thought of it the day following, or a month later, or a year. But it is safe to assume, I believe, that he vacillated often between laughing at it sourly and hanging himself. For he was far too intelligent to believe in any such Kiwanian bombast. He could no more have taken it seriously than he took the strutting of Mr. Secretary Seward seriously, or the cerebral steam-pressure of General Grant. He knew it, you may be sure, for what it was. He was simply doomed, like many another good man before and after him, to keep his soundest and loftiest thoughts to himself. Just as Plato had to adapt his most penetrating and revolutionary thoughts to the tastes and comprehension of the sophomores assembled to hear him, so Lincoln had to content himself, on a great occasion, with ideas comprehensible to Pennsylvania Dunkards, which is to say, to persons to whom genuine ideas were not comprehensible at all. Knowing their theological principles, he knew that, in the political field, they grazed only on pansies.

Nor is this all. The highest flights of human intellect are not only inordinately offensive to the overwhelming majority of men; they are also, at least in large part, incapable of reduction to words. Thus the best thought of the human race does not appear in its written records. What is set down in orderly and seemly sentences, even today, always has some flavor in it of the stilted rubbish that the Sumerian kings used to engrave upon their tombs. The current *clichés* get into it inevitably; it is never quite honest. Complete honesty, intellectually, seldom expresses itself in formal words: its agents of notification are rather winks and sniggers, hip flasks and dead cats. The language was not made for it. Reading Shakespeare, a man of penetrating intelligence, one frequently observes him trying to put a really novel and apposite thought into words — and falling helplessly into mere sound and fury, signifying nothing. The groundlings pulled him and the deficiencies of human speech pushed him. The result is many a magnificent salvo of nonsense, vastly esteemed by the persons who esteem that sort of thing.

I propose no remedy. In fact, I am convinced that no remedy is possible, or even imaginable. The human race seems doomed to run, intellectually, on its lowest gear. Sound ideas, when by chance they become articulate, annoy it and terrify it; it prefers the sempiternal slobber.

Revolution

From the Baltimore *Evening Sun*, Dec. 22, 1930

IT is the law of political revolution that the actual upset of a government is always preceded by concessions to the malcontent party. So long as Porfirio Diaz ruled Mexico like a house of correction he was perfectly safe, but the moment he released Francisco Madero from jail and began to talk of reforming the judiciary, dividing the big estates and widening the suffrage his doom was sealed, and within a year he was a fugitive and Madero was President. So with the Czar of Russia. He signed his own death warrant when he signed the decree calling the first Duma: even if a World War had never come he would have lost his throne inevitably, and his head with it. So in many another case, ancient and modern. There has never been a successful revolution out of the clear sky. Always the doomed despot has prepared for it by making concessions to his enemies.

The psychology behind this phenomenon is so simple that even a psychoanalyst should be able to penetrate it. What protects the despot, so long as he lays about him boldly, is the fact that very few men, even among rebels, have any appreciable courage. Whether physically or morally, they seldom attack a power that can really hurt them, and is plainly willing and eager to do so. But the moment that power shows any sign of fading into weakness, they become very daring and are hot for defying it. Next to outright abdication, the chief sign of such weakening, at least to most men, is a readiness to compromise. They have no belief whatever in the excuses commonly given for it: generosity, a sense of justice, conversion to new ideas, and so on. They always see it, and perhaps quite rightly, as simply a cloak for fear.

Thus the despot who hedges, no matter how exalted his motives may be in his own view, appears to his enemies as one who has lost his grip, and at the first chance they fly at his throat, usually to the tune of loud protestations of altruism. The leaders among them appear suddenly to be full of courage, for courage is always a relative matter, and the man who runs from a lion in the full possession of its faculties will pull the tail of a lion down with the palsy. Simultaneously, the camp-followers and me-toos, hitherto discreetly silent, begin to beat heroically on washtubs and to demand a chance to get at him.

New England

From The Last New Englander, Prejudices: Fifth Series, 1926, pp. 244–54

Orthodox American history assumes that the witch-burners and infant-damners had it all their own way in New England, even down to Revolutionary times. They actually met with sturdy opposition from the start. All their seaports gradually filled up with sailors who were anything but pious Christian men, and even the back-country had its heretics, as the incessant wars upon them demonstrate. The fact that only Puritans could vote in the towns has deceived the historians; they mistake what was the law for what was really said and done. We have had proofs in our own time that that error is easy. Made by students of early New England, it leads to multiple absurdities.

The fact is that the civilization that grew up in the region, such as it was, owed very little to the actual Puritans; it was mainly the product of anti-Puritans, either home-bred or imported. Even the school system, so celebrated in legend, owed whatever value was in it to what were currently regarded as criminals. The Puritans did not found their schools for the purpose of propagating what is now known as learning; they founded them simply as nurseries of orthodoxy. Beyond the barest rudiments nothing of any worldly value was taught in them. The principal subject of study, first and last, was theology, and it was theology of the most grotesque and insane sort ever cherished by man. Genuine education began in New England only when the rising minority of anti-Puritans, eventually to become a majority, rose against this theology, and tried to put it down. The revolt was first felt at Harvard; it gradually converted a seminary for the training of Puritan pastors into something resembling an actual university. Harvard delivered New England, and made civilization possible there. All the men who adorned that civilization in the days of its glory — Emerson, Hawthorne and all the rest of them — were essentially anti-Puritans.

Today, save in its remoter villages, New England is no more Puritan than, say, Maryland or Missouri. There is scarcely a Protestant clergyman in the entire region who, if the Mathers could come back to life, would not be condemned by them instantly as a heretic, and even as an atheist. The dominant theology is mild, skeptical and wholly lacking in passion. The evangelical spirit has completely disappeared. Save in a small minority of atavistic fanatics, there is a tolerance that is almost indistinguishable from indifference. Roman Catholicism and Christian Science are alike viewed amiably. The old heat is gone. Where it lingers in America is in far places — on the Methodist prairies of the Middle West, in the Baptist back-waters of the South. There, I believe, it still retains not a little of its old vitality. There Puritanism survives, not merely as a system of theology, but also as a way of life. It colors every human activity; it is powerful in politics; learning wears its tinge. To charge a Harvard professor of today with agnosticism would sound as banal as to charge him with playing the violoncello. But his colleague of Kansas, facing the same accusation, would go damp upon the forehead, and his colleague of Texas would leave town between days.

New Deal No. 1

From the Baltimore *Evening Sun*, Dec. 31, 1934

THE STATE of affairs in France in 1845 was a great deal like the state of affairs in the United States in 1928. The country, after some heavy grunting and contriving, had at last recovered from the Napoleonic wars, there was an immensely stupid but immensely respectable King on the throne, the Cabinet, headed by F. P. G. Guizot, was committed to the principle of "Peace and no reform," business was good and getting better, the prices of all stocks and bonds were striking new highs, wages were soaring with them, and the whole landscape seemed to be covered with molasses. The English, glowering across the channel, and the Germans, stealing dark glances over the Rhine, were frankly envious, and it was at this time, I believe, that the latter invented one of the most eloquent of their phrases, *wie Gott in Frankreich.*

But in 1847 something slipped, and before the year was out France was tortured by billions of ants in its pantaloons. No one seemed to know just what had happened. One day everything was lovely, and the next day there was a panic on the Stock Exchange, the shops of Paris were suddenly empty, factories were closing down everywhere, and hundreds of thousands of Frenchmen were out of work. The politicians, of course, all had glib explanations, some saying one thing and

some another, and the professors at the Sorbonne issued a great
many contradictory graphs and tables of statistics, but the plain
people distrusted the former as rogues and the latter as idiots,
and in consequence there was much murmuring in the land.

It went on *pianissimo* for six months or so, and then rose unpleasantly to *forte*, with frequent bursts of *sforzando*. Simultaneously a great many new wizards began to rove the country,
many of them preaching a novel gospel called Socialism, lately
invented by a man named Karl Marx. The whole trouble, said
these wizards, was due to the Rotten Rich. France, it appears,
was still bursting with wealth, but the Rotten Rich were hog-
ging all of it. Look at their elegant carriages in the Bois, with
red wheels, plate-glass doors and coachmen arrayed like ambassadors. Regard the obscene way in which they drape silks,
satins, pearls, rubies and diamonds upon their wives, daughters
and concubines. Take a peep, *mon cher*, into their baroque
mansions, and observe the immoral displays of gilt chairs,
leopard-skin rugs, and hand-painted oil paintings. Above all, my
little rabbit, think of their tight hold upon their docile serf,
that false and wicked King, Louis Philippe.

So on February 24, 1848, Louis Philippe was heaved out, and
a provisional government was set up in his place. This government, it turned out later, was operated from behind the scenes
by professional politicians, but all the plain people could see of
it at the start was an impressive Brain Trust, then something
new in the world. There have been many Brain Trusts since,
and some of them have glittered with genius, but certainly there
has never been another that took the shine off this first one. For
it not only included all the political and economic advanced
thinkers of the time, from Louis Blanc to Louis Blanqui, and
from Jacques Cavaignac to Alexandre Ledru-Rollin; it also could
show a gifted proletarian metaphysician, Alexandre Albert, and
a celebrated poet, Alphonse de Lamartine.

These talented men proceeded at once to give France a
Planned Economy. The capitalistic system was abolished overnight, and in place of it there was established a system of Shared
Wealth, not unlike the late Huey Long's. It was ordained that
the old inequality between man and woman should cease, and

that every freeborn French citizen should have in future, not
what he could get, but what he yearned for. But where was the
money to come from? From the Rotten Rich, of course. Hadn't
they been grinding the faces of the poor since the days of
Charlemagne? Weren't they known to be so full of their ill-
gotten spoils that their very hides were nigh to bursting?

Unfortunately, making them disgorge was not as easy as it
looked. Large numbers of them had departed for Palo Alto with
Louis Philippe, and many had managed to take their gold and
chattels with them. The rest protested that they were broke like
everyone else. Their baroque mansions were boarded up and
their anthropophagous factories were shut down. All through the
Winter jobs became scarcer and scarcer. People began to tramp
through the streets of Paris demanding bread. The Brain Trust
labored day and night on its revolutionary plans to make society
over, but even its boldest and most forward-looking devices
could not keep pace with the backward slosh of events.

Finally, it came out with a new scheme, and announced that
the problem was solved at last. The trouble hitherto, it explained, had been that the plain people had depended too
much on the Rotten Rich for jobs. Now all that would be
done away with. Henceforth, the dishing out of all jobs would
be in the hands of the Government, which is to say, of the
Brain Trust. Public factories would be erected at once, and
every workman who wanted to work would be accommodated.
There would be no more unemployment in France, and the
workers, instead of yielding up 99% of the fruits of their labor
to capital, would henceforth take all.

The erection of these factories was intrusted to a young advanced thinker with the charming name of Marie, and he fell
to work furiously. In addition, he prepared to undertake open-
air public works on an enormous scale — the construction of two
huge railway stations in Paris, the dredging of the River Oise,
the building of new canals and railways in all directions, and
so on. But for some reason undetermined — maybe the secret
machinations of the outlawed capitalists, maybe the sinister
workings of the law of supply and demand — all the jobs thus
made failed to accommodate the hordes of jobless. In fact, their

numbers kept on increasing, and soon there were riots in Paris, and M. Marie was out of a job himself, and a bright young professor named Thomas was put in his place.

But Professor Thomas came a cropper, too, and by the end of 1848 France was in a far worse state than it had been at the beginning of its New Deal. Many members of the original Brain Trust had been sent packing by now, but others always turned up, and these recruits kept on functioning with increasing assiduity as the dismal year wore on. Every day they announced some new and grander scheme to bring in the millennium, and every day they abandoned some busted one. Meanwhile, the plain people went on looking for jobs and not finding them, and the politicians behind the scenes waited for their chance. It came in December. Within the space of a few days they turned the Brain Trust out and made the accommodating Louis Napoleon President of France. At once the Rotten Rich began to creep back, the closed factories began to reopen, and there began to be jobs again. Three years later Louis Napoleon became Emperor.

Some of the details of this story are worth noting. One is that the Brain Trust, despite all its highfalutin pretensions, was never anything save a sort of falseface for politicians. They let it rave on so long as the plain people believed in its magic, but when that magic was seen to be bogus by everyone they emerged from behind the arras, and took over their old business at the old stand. Another is that the Brain Trust, though it was made up of the self-confessed first intellects of the time, scored a complete goose egg. Not a single one of its fine schemes to bring in the More Abundant Life really worked. At the end of its operations all that it had to show was a gigantic public debt, the highest tax rate ever heard of in France, and an almost endless line of unemployed.

What this adventure cost the country, first and last, I don't know, but certainly it must have been many millions of francs. Its goat was the French taxpayer. He had to pay, in the end, for all the crazy building of gaudy railway stations, and all that frantic dredging of rivers and digging of canals. Starting out with the thesis that the Rotten Rich were scoundrels and ought to be squeezed, the Brain Trust proceeded easily to the thesis that any man who had any property whatsoever was a scoundrel, too, and ought to be squeezed equally. The rich, in the main, managed to escape, but the little fellow could not get away, and squeezed he surely was.

And what became of the Brain Trust when the show was over? It disappeared as mysteriously as it had come together, leaving scarcely a trace. The only genius on its roll who was a man of any actual distinction in the world was the poet, Lamartine. After it blew up, he decided to go in for politics professionally, and in 1849 he ran for President of France against Louis Napoleon. Beaten by millions of votes, he returned to the poetical business, but even at that he could no longer make a living, and in his last days the French Government had to put him on the dole. Of such sort were the smart and saucy fellows who undertook, in the France of a century ago, to overthrow the capitalistic system, redistribute wealth, abolish poverty, find a job for everyone, and bring in the New Jerusalem.

The Greeks

From the *American Mercury*, Oct., 1927, pp. 254–55. A review of
The Cambridge Ancient History, Vol. V; Cambridge (England), 1927

THE GREEKS of the palmy days remain the most overestimated people in all history. Ever since the Renaissance it has been a high indecorum to question their genius, and never a month passes that another book does not come out, praising them in loud, astounding terms. More men of the first rank were assembled in the Athens of Pericles, we are told, than any other city, or even any other nation, has ever housed. Going further, we are told that they remain unsurpassed to this day, in quality as in quantity. Greek science is depicted as the father of all modern science, Greek art as the *Ur*-art, Greek philosophy as the last word in reason, and the Greek government of Pericles's time as democracy made perfect. In all this, alas, there is mainly only buncombe. The plain facts are that Greek science, even at its best, would be hard to distinguish from the science prevailing among Hottentots, Haitians and Mississippi Baptists today, that Greek art was chiefly only derivative and extremely narrow in range, that Greek philosophy was quite as idiotic as any other philosophy, and that the government of the Greeks, even at its best, was worse than the worst of Tammany. One discovers plenty of proofs of all this in the present massive volume. It was written by scholars sharing the usual academic prejudice in favor of everything Greek, but nevertheless they manage to tell the truth in it, at least between the lines. They show that the salient Greek philosophers of Pericles's time were almost identical with the chautauqua orators of bucolic America, and that the more enlightened Greeks regarded them as public nuisances. They show that beauty, to the Greeks, was not something for everyday, but a rare luxury and means of display. They show that the Greek government was knavish and incompetent — that it was constantly engaging in crooked enterprises abroad, and frequently became so corrupt and oppressive at home that the decent people of Athens had to rise up and reform it. And they show that most of the genuinely intelligent Greeks were foreigners, and that such natives as showed sense, *e.g.*, Aristophanes, were commonly thrown out of the country.

The Greek language was the first lost tongue recovered in modern times, and the men who recovered it naturally made as much as they could of the ideas that came with it. Ever since the Renaissance it has been a mark of intellectual distinction to know Greek, though there is no record that knowing it has ever helped any man to think profitable thoughts. That distinction, to be sure, now begins to fade and wear thin, but there was a time, just before the beginning of the current rapid increase of knowledge, when it rose above all other forms of intellectual eminence, and it was during that period that the world was saddled with the exalted view of Greece and the Greeks that still survives. In so far as it is not a mere sentimentality, it is grounded, I believe, upon the scantiness of our records of other peoples, contemporaneous with the Greeks or preceding them. If the history of Greek philosophy were known accurately, it would probably turn out to be no more than an imitation of some earlier philosophy, now forgotten — and maybe abandoned by its inventors as nonsense. In architecture and the other arts, it is certainly absurd to say that the Greeks invented anything. They got the column from the Egyptians, who had perfected it a thousand years before the Parthenon, and they slavishly followed the Egyptians in their neglect of the arch. Their excellent materials were accidental, and in working them they showed no originality. Was the Greek drama really indigenous? I shall believe it when it is proved that the Sanskrit drama was also indigenous, and not an imitation of some Persian, or maybe even Assyrian prototype. Were the Greeks scientists? Then so are the modern chiropractors. What they had of exact knowledge, in fact, was mainly borrowed, and most of it was spoiled in the borrowing. And the Greek religion? The best that one may say of it is that none of the intelligent foreigners who frequented Athens believed in it, and that many of them were jailed, exiled and even put to death for making fun of it. As for the Greek genius for politics, it revealed its true measure in the fact that no Greek government ever lasted for more than a century, and that most of them ended in scandal and disaster.

Here I make no fatuous attempt to read the Greeks out of court altogether. They were, for their time, an enterprising and progressive people, and they left us an immensely rich heritage, partly of sound ideas and partly of pleasant delusions and superstitions. But we probably owe a great deal more to the Egyptians, and quite as much to the lesser peoples who infested the eastern shores of the Mediterranean, notably the Phoenicians, the earlier Minoans, the Jews, and the forerunners of the later Arabs. The one genuinely solid contribution of the Greeks to human progress lay in their attempt to synthesize and organize whatever knowledge was afloat in the world of their day. This business they achieved with great skill. But out of their own heads they produced little that is valid and important to modern man, save perhaps in the dreams of pedagogues seeking to astonish schoolboys. The Greeks themselves, restored to earth, would laugh at the pretension to the contrary, as they laughed at the Grecomaniac Romans. If they had any virtue above all others, it was the virtue of skepticism. They were, in that department at least, the first of modern men. The barbaric surges and thunders of the Odyssey, in these twilight days of Christendom, are moving only to professors of Greek — which is to say, to men whose opinion on any other subject would be rejected even by their fellow professors — and the enjoyment of Greek tragedy, that unparalleled bore, is confined almost wholly to actresses who have grown too fat for Ibsen; but the ideas of Lucian and Aristophanes still live, and so do those of the Four Hundred.

War

From the *American Mercury*, Sept., 1929, pp. 23–24

WAR naturally sucks in those who can be most profitably spared, and lets go most of those whose talents are really useful. One hears, now and then, of promising young men cut down too soon, but the science of statistics scarcely justifies the accompanying mourning. Let us turn, for example, to the Civil War. In the Union Army, during the four years of the war, there were 2,666,999 men who reached the field, and of this number 110,070 were killed in battle or died of wounds, 199,720 died of disease, and 40,154 perished otherwise — murdered, killed by accident, or done to death in prisons. Of those who were murdered or died of accident or disease, probably 100,000 would have died anyhow. Deducting that number, the total net loss comes to about 250,000. How many men were wounded is not certain, but probably the number ran to at least 1,000,000.

We don't know, of course, what the dead men would have done if they had lived, but we may reach some approximation to it by examining the wounded who survived. How many of them, after the war, contributed anything that was genuinely interesting to civilization? Searching the record for weary days and nights I can find but three names: those of Major Ambrose Bierce, Captain Oliver Wendell Holmes, Jr., and Private George Westinghouse. The typical eminentissimo who survived the Civil War was not of this company; he was the shallow political plug, McKinley. All the really important men of the post-Civil War era, all the men who developed and fecundated such culture as we now have, from John D. Rockefeller to Walt Whitman, from Grover Cleveland to William James, from Mark

Twain to Cyrus Field, from Andy Carnegie to Mark Hanna, from William Dean Howells to Bronson Howard, from John Fiske to James Russell Lowell, and from Willard Gibbs to Brigham Young — all these men were slackers, and leaped not to the cannon's roar. The three exceptions that research reveals I have listed. Apply the ratio to those who perished, and it appears that the Civil War cost American *Kultur* exactly three-fourths of a really valuable man. Call Fitz-James O'Brien, who died of his wounds, the other fourth — and the net loss comes to one man.

The melancholy conclusion that the science of statistics thus points to is amply confirmed by a study of military history. Of all the arts practised by man, the art of the soldier seems to call for the least intelligence and to develop the least professional competency. Every battle recorded in history appears as a series of almost incredible blunders and imbecilities — always, at least, on one side, and usually, on both. One marvels, reading the chronicles, that any major engagement was ever won. Even the greatest generals — for example, Bonaparte — walk idiotically into palpable traps, and waste thousands of lives getting themselves out. The lesser fry proceed heroically from disaster to disaster, as Burnside did during the Civil War and Joffre during the World War. The simplest problem of their ancient and elemental business flabbergasts them. They seem to be congenitally incapable of reasoning clearly, even when all the facts are before them. And at the enterprise of unearthing those facts they show only the gross and pathetic ineptitude of a second-rate lawyer or a third-rate pedagogue.

Whenever, at the practise of their art in the field, they confront a problem of any complexity, they have to get help from civilians, *i.e.*, from men not paralyzed by training in their professional numskullery. It was so, as everyone knows, in the war of 1914–18. The great captains on the two sides lay locked in a bloody and horrible embrace until engineers, chemists and press-agents came to their rescue and pried them loose. All the while, behind the lines, they were laboriously drilling their recruits in the archaic marchings and counter-marchings of the Old Dessauer. . . . Yet the human race, after watching such bunglers perform their gory buffooneries, cheers them when they come home, dazed and empty-headed, and thrusts its highest honors upon them. What a certificate to its judgment, its common sense, its sense of humor, its right to survive on earth!

A Bad Guess

From the Baltimore *Evening Sun*, Nov. 11, 1931. Nations, like men, seldom learn by experience. England made the same mistake again on September 3, 1939, and the United States followed docilely two years later. The consequences are now spread before a candid world

MOST of England's appalling troubles today are due to a bad guess: she went into the war on the wrong side in 1914. The theory of her statesmen, in those days, was that, by joining France and Russia, she would give a death-blow to a dangerous rival, Germany, and so be free to run the world. But the scheme failed to work; moreover, it had unexpected and almost fatal results. Not only did Germany come out of the mess a dangerous rival still; France also became a rival, and a very formidable one. Worse, the United States was pumped up to immense proportions, and began to challenge England's control of the world's markets. The results are now visible: England has three competitors instead of one, and is steadily going downhill. If she had gone into the war on the German side she'd be in a much better situation today. The Germans would be grateful for the help, and willing to pay for it (while the French are not); the French would be down and out, and hence unable to menace the peace of Europe; Germany would have Russia in Europe and there would be no Bolshevik nuisance; England would have all of Siberia and Central Asia, and there would be no Japanese threat and no Indian revolt; and the United States would still be a docile British colony, as it was in 1914. English foreign policy, once so simple and direct, is now confused and irresolute. It confronts three huge problems, all of them probably insoluble — to hamstring and dephlogisticate both France and Germany, to bamboozle the United States (*e.g.*, in the matter of naval "disarmament"), and to keep the colonies and dominions from flying off into space. Yet the English put up monuments to the "statesmen" who got them into this mess. And even taller monuments to King Edward VII, who prepared the way for it by preferring the patchouli of Paris to the malt liquor of Berlin.

The United States made a similar mistake in 1917. Our real interests at the time were on the side of the Germans, whose general attitude of mind is far more American than that of any other people. If we had gone in on their side, England would be moribund today, and the dreadful job of pulling her down, which will now take us forty or fifty years, would be over. We'd have a free hand in the Pacific, and Germany would be running the whole Continent like a house of correction. In return for our connivance there she'd be glad to give us whatever we wanted elsewhere. There would be no Bolshevism in Russia and no Fascism in Italy. Our debtors would all be able to pay us. The Japs would be docile, and we'd be reorganizing Canada and probably also Australia. But we succumbed to a college professor who read Matthew Arnold, just as the English succumbed to a gay old dog who couldn't bear to think of Prussian M.P.'s shutting down the Paris night-clubs.

As for the mistake that the Russians made, I leave it to history.

Undying Glories

From the *Smart Set*, Nov., 1921, p. 36

THE HAPSBURGS seem to be quite down and out. The archdukes of the house, once so steadily in the newspapers, are now heard of no longer, and the Emperor Karl appears to be a jackass almost comparable to an American Congressman. But what a family in the past! To one member Haydn dedicated the Kaiser quartette, to another Beethoven dedicated the Erzherzog trio, and to a third old Johann Strauss dedicated the Kaiser waltz. Match that record in all human history.

XIII. STATESMEN

Pater Patriæ

From DAMN! A BOOK OF CALUMNY, 1918, pp. 7–8

IF George Washington were alive today, what a shining mark he would be for the whole camorra of uplifters, forward-lookers and professional patriots! He was the Rockefeller of his time, the richest man in the United States, a promoter of stock companies, a land-grabber, an exploiter of mines and timber. He was a bitter opponent of foreign entanglements, and denounced their evils in harsh, specific terms. He had a liking for forthright and pugnacious men, and a contempt for lawyers, schoolmasters and all other such obscurantists. He was not pious. He drank whiskey whenever he felt chilly, and kept a jug of it handy. He knew far more profanity than Scripture, and used and enjoyed it more. He had no belief in the infallible wisdom of the common people, but regarded them as inflammatory dolts, and tried to save the Republic from them. He advocated no sure cure for all the sorrows of the world, and doubted that such a panacea existed. He took no interest in the private morals of his neighbors.

Inhabiting These States today, George would be ineligible for any office of honor or profit. The Senate would never dare confirm him; the President would not think of nominating him. He would be on trial in the newspapers for belonging to the Money Power. The Sherman Act would have him in its toils; he would be under indictment by every grand jury south of the Potomac; the Methodists of his native State would be denouncing him (he had a still at Mount Vernon) as a debaucher of youth, a recruiting officer for insane asylums, a poisoner of the home. And what a chance there would be for that ambitious young district attorney who thought to shadow him on his peregrinations — and grab him under the Mann Act!

Abraham Lincoln

FROM FIVE MEN AT RANDOM, PREJUDICES: THIRD SERIES,
1922, pp. 171–76.
First printed, in part, in the *Smart Set*, May, 1920, p. 141

SOME time ago a publisher told me that there are four kinds of books that seldom, if ever, lose money in the United States — first, murder stories; secondly, novels in which the heroine is forcibly overcome by the hero; thirdly, volumes on spiritualism, occultism and other such claptrap, and fourthly, books on Lincoln. But despite all the vast mass of Lincolniana and the constant discussion of old Abe in other ways, even so elemental a problem as that of his religious ideas — surely an important matter in any competent biography — is yet but half solved. Was he a Christian? Did he believe in the Divinity of Jesus? I am left in doubt. He was very polite about it, and very cautious, as befitted a politician in need of Christian votes, but how much genuine conviction was in that politeness? And if his occasional references to Jesus were thus open to question, what of his rather vague avowals of belief in a personal God and in the immortality of the soul? Herndon and some of his other early friends always maintained that he was an atheist, but the Rev. William E. Barton, one of the best of the later Lincolnologists, argues that this atheism was simply disbelief in the idiotic Methodist and Baptist dogmas of his time — that nine Christian churches out of ten, if he were alive today, would admit him to their high privileges and prerogatives without anything worse than a few warning coughs. As for me, I still wonder.

Lincoln becomes the American solar myth, the chief butt of American credulity and sentimentality. Washington, of late years, has been perceptibly humanized; every schoolboy now knows that he used to swear a good deal, and was a sharp trader, and had a quick eye for a pretty ankle. But meanwhile the varnishers and veneerers have been busily converting Abe into a plaster saint, thus making him fit for adoration in the Y.M.C.A.'s. All the popular pictures of him show him in his robes of state, and wearing an expression fit for a man about to be hanged. There is, so far as I know, not a single portrait of him showing him smiling — and yet he must have cackled a good deal, first and last: who ever heard of a storyteller who didn't? Worse, there is an obvious effort to pump all his human weaknesses out of him, and so leave him a mere moral apparition, a sort of amalgam of John Wesley and the Holy Ghost. What could be more absurd? Lincoln, in point of fact, was a practical politician of long experience and high talents, and by no means cursed with idealistic superstitions. Until he emerged from Illinois they always put the women, children and clergy to bed when he got a few gourds of corn aboard, and it is a matter of unescapable record that his career in the State Legislature was indistinguishable from that of a Tammany Nietzsche. Even his handling of the slavery question was that of a politician, not that of a messiah. Nothing alarmed him more than the suspicion that he was an Abolitionist, and Barton tells of an occasion when he actually fled town to avoid meeting the issue squarely. An Abolitionist would have published the Emancipation Proclamation the day after the first battle of Bull Run. But Lincoln waited until the time was more favorable — until Lee had been hurled out of Pennsylvania, and more important still, until the political currents were safely running his way. Even so, he freed the slaves in only a part of the country: all the rest continued to clank their chains until he himself was an angel in Heaven.

Like William Jennings Bryan, he was a dark horse made suddenly formidable by fortunate rhetoric. The Douglas debate launched him, and the Cooper Union speech got him the Presidency. His talent for emotional utterance was an accomplishment of late growth. His early speeches were mere empty fireworks — the hollow rhodomontades of the era. But in middle life he purged his style of ornament and it became almost baldly simple — and it is for that simplicity that he is remembered today. The Gettysburg speech is at once the shortest and the most famous oration in American history. Put beside it, all the whoopings of the Websters, Sumners and Everetts seem gaudy and silly. It is eloquence brought to a pellucid and almost gem-like perfection — the highest emotion reduced to a few poetical phrases. Nothing else precisely like it is to be found in the whole range of oratory. Lincoln himself never even remotely approached it. It is genuinely stupendous.

But let us not forget that it is poetry, not logic; beauty, not sense. Think of the argument in it. Put it into the cold words of everyday. The doctrine is simply this: that the Union soldiers who died at Gettysburg sacrificed their lives to the cause of self-determination — "that government of the people, by the people, for the people," should not perish from the earth. It is difficult to imagine anything more untrue. The Union soldiers in that battle actually fought *against* self-determination; it was the Confederates who fought for the right of their people to govern themselves. What was the practical effect of the battle of Gettysburg? What else than the destruction of the old sovereignty of the States, *i.e.*, of the people of the States? The Confederates went into battle free; they came out with their freedom subject to the supervision and veto of the rest of the country — and for nearly twenty years that veto was so effective that they enjoyed scarcely more liberty, in the political sense, than so many convicts in the penitentiary.

Portrait of an Immortal

From the *American Mercury*, Feb., 1929, pp. 251–53. A review of Meet General Grant, by W. E. Woodward; New York, 1928

THE DREADFUL title of Mr. Woodward's book is not the least of its felicities. If they had been saying such things in his day it seems unquestionable that Grant would have said, "Meet the wife." He was precisely that sort of man. His imagination was the imagination of a respectable hay and feed dealer, and his virtues, such as they were, were indistinguishable from those of a county court clerk. Mr. Woodward, trying to be just to him, not infrequently gives him far more than he deserves. He was not, in point of fact, a man of any great competence, even as a soldier. All the major strategy of the war, including the final advance on Richmond, was planned by other men, notably Sherman. He was a ham as a tactician, and habitually wasted his men. He was even a poor judge of other generals, as witness his admiration for Sheridan and his almost unbelievable underrating of Thomas and Meade. If he won battles, it was because he had the larger battalions, and favored the primitive device of heaving them into action, callously, relentlessly, cruelly, appallingly.

Thinking was always painful to Grant, and so he never did any of it if he could help it. He had a vague distaste for war, and dreamed somewhat boozily of a day when it would be no more. But that distaste never stayed his slaughters; it only made him keep away from the wounded. He had no coherent ideas on any subject, and changed his so-called opinions overnight, and for no reason at all. He entered the war simply because he needed a job, and fought his way through it without any apparent belief in its purposes. His wife was a slaveholder to the end. At Appomattox he showed a magnanimity that yet thrills schoolboys, but before he became President he went over to the Radical Republicans, and was largely to blame for the worst horrors of Reconstruction. His belief in rogues was congenital, touching and unlimited. He filled Washington with them, and defended them against honest men, even in the face of plain proofs of their villainy. Retired to private life at last, he sought out the worst scoundrel of them all, gave the fellow control of his whole modest fortune, and went down to inglorious bankruptcy with him. The jail gates, that time, were uncomfortably close; if Grant had not been Grant he would have at least gone on trial. But he was completely innocent. He was too stupid to be anything else.

Yet, for all his colossal imbecilities, he helped in a wholesale way to pave Hell with good intentions. Like Joseph Conrad's Almayer, he always wanted to do the right thing. The trouble with him was that he could seldom find out what it was. Once he had got beyond a few elemental ideas, his brain refused to function. Thereafter he operated by hunches, some of them good ones, but others almost idiotic. Commanding his vast armies in the field, he wandered around like a stranger, shabby, uncommunicative and only defectively respected. In the White House he was a primeval Harding, without either the diamond scarf-pin or the cutie hiding in the umbrella closet. He tried, in his dour, bashful manner, to be a good fellow. There was no flummery about him. He had no false dignity. But he was the easiest mark ever heard of. It was possible to put anything over on him, however fantastic. Now and then, by a flash of what must be called, I suppose, insight, he penetrated the impostures which surrounded him, and struck out in his Berserker way for common decency. But that was not often. His eight years in the White House were scarlet with scandal. He had a Teapot Dome on his hands once a month.

Mr. Woodward's portrait, despite its mercies, is an extraordinarily brilliant one. The military automaton of the "Memoirs" and the noble phrase-maker of the school-books disappears, and there emerges a living and breathing man, simple-minded, more than a little bewildered, and infinitely pathetic. Grant went to the high pinnacles of glory, but he also plunged down the black steeps of woe. I don't think that his life was a happy one, even as happiness is counted among such primitive organisms. He was miserable as a boy, he was miserable at West Point, and he was miserable in the old army. The Mexican War revolted him, and he took to drink and lost his commission. For years he faced actual want. The Civil War brought him little satisfaction, save for a moment at the end. He was neglected in his early days in a manner that was wormwood to him, and after luck brought him opportunity he was surrounded by hostile intrigue. He made costly and egregious blunders, notably at Shiloh and Cold Harbor; he knew the sting of professional sneers; he quailed before Lee's sardonic eye. His eight years in the White House were years of tribulation and humiliation. His wife was ill-favored; his only daughter made a bad marriage; his relatives, both biological and in-law, harassed and exploited him. He died almost penniless, protesting that he could no longer trust a soul. He passed out in gusts of intolerable pain. It is hard to imagine harder lines.

If, in this chronicle, he sometimes recedes into the background, and seems no more than a bystander at the show, then it is because he was often that in life. Other men had a way of running him — John A. Rawlins during the war, Hamilton Fish at Washington, Ferdinand Ward afterward. His relations to the first-named are discussed in one of Mr. Woodward's most interesting chapters. Rawlins was the Grant family lawyer at Galena, and had no military experience when the war began. Grant made him his brigade adjutant, and thereafter submitted docilely to his domination. Rawlins was a natural pedagogue, a sort of school-ma'am with a beard. He supervised and limited Grant's guz-zling; he edited Grant's orders; he made and unmade all other subordinates. "I have heard him curse at Grant," said Charles A. Dana, "when, according to his judgment, the general was doing something that he thought he had better not do. . . . With-out him Grant would have not been the same man." Gossip in the army went even further; it credited Rawlins with actually sharing command. "The two together," said James H. Wilson, "constituted a military character of great simplicity, force and singleness of purpose, which has passed into history under the name of Grant."

A Good Man in a Bad Trade

From the *American Mercury*, Jan., 1933, pp. 125–27. A review of Grover
Cleveland: a Study in Courage, by Allan Nevins; New York, 1932

WE have had more brilliant Presidents than Cleveland, and one or two who were considerably more profound, but we have never had one, at least since Washington, whose fundamental charac-ter was solider and more admirable. There was never any string tied to old Grover. He got on in politics, not by knuckling to politicians, but by scorning and defying them, and when he found himself opposed in what he conceived to be sound and honest courses, not only by politicians but by the sovereign peo-ple, he treated them to a massive dose of the same medicine. No more self-sufficient man is recorded in modern history. There were times, of course, when he had his doubts like the rest of us, but once he had made up his mind he stood immovable. No conceivable seduction could weaken him. There was some-thing almost inhuman about his fortitude, and to millions of his contemporaries it seemed more satanic than godlike. No President since Lincoln, not even the melancholy Hoover, has been more bitterly hated, or by more people. But Cleveland, though he certainly did not enjoy it — he was, indeed, singularly lacking in the shallower and more comforting sort of egoism — yet did not let it daunt him. He came into office his own man, and he went out without yielding anything of that character for an instant.

In his time it was common to ascribe a good part of this vast steadfastness to his mere bulk. He had a huge girth, shoulders like the Parthenon, a round, compact head, and the slow movements of any large animal. He was not very tall, but he looked, somehow, like an enormous natural object — say, the Jungfrau or Cape Horn. This aspect of the stupendous, almost of the terrific, was tempting to the primeval psychologists of that innocent day, and they succumbed to it easily. But in the years that have come and gone since then we have learned a great deal about fat men. It was proved, for example, by W. H. Taft that they could be knocked about and made to dance with great facility, and it was proved by Hoover that their texture may be, not that of Alps, but that of chocolate éclairs. Cleveland, though he was also fat, was the complete antithesis of these gentlemen. There was far more to him than beam and tonnage. When enemies had at him they quickly found that his weight was the least of their difficulties; what really sent them sprawling was the fact that his whole huge carcass seemed to be made of iron. There was no give in him, no bounce, no softness. He sailed through American history like a steel ship loaded with monoliths of granite.

He came of an excellent family, but his youth had been a hard one, and his cultural advantages were not of the best. He learned a great deal about human nature by sitting with pleasant fellows in the Buffalo saloons, but he seems to have made but little contact with the finer and more elusive parts of the spiritual heritage of man, and in consequence his imagination was not awakened, and he remained all his days a somewhat stodgy and pedantic fellow. There is no sign in his writings of the wide and fruitful reading of Roosevelt I, and they show none of the sleek, shiny graces of Wilson. His English, apparently based upon Eighteenth Century models, was a horrible example to the young. It did not even roar; it simply heaved, panted and grunted. He made, in his day, some phrases, and a few of them are still remembered, but they are all études in ponderosity — *innocuous desuetude, communism of pelf,* and so on. The men he admired were all solid men like himself. He lived through the Gilded Age, the Mauve Decade and the Purple Nineties without being aware of them. His heroes were largely lawyers of the bow-wow type, and it is significant that he seems to have had little acquaintance with Mark Twain, though Mark edited a paper in Buffalo during his terms as mayor there. His favorite American author was Richard Watson Gilder.

The one man who seems to have had any genuine influence upon him was Richard Olney, first his Attorney-General and then his Secretary of State. He had such great respect for Olney's professional skill as a lawyer that he was not infrequently blind to the man's defects as a statesman. It was Olney who induced him to send troops to Chicago to put down the Pullman strike, and Olney who chiefly inspired the celebrated Venezuela message. Cleveland, at the start, seems to have been reluctant to intervene in Chicago, but Olney convinced him that it was both legal and necessary. In the Venezuelan matter something of the same sort appears to have occurred. It was characteristic of Cleveland that, once he had made up his mind, he stuck to his course without the slightest regard for consequences. Doubts never beset him. He banged along like a locomotive. If man or devil got upon the track, then so much the worse for man or devil. "God," he once wrote to Gilder, "has never failed to make known to me the path of duty."

Any man thus obsessed by a concept of duty is bound to seek support for it somewhere outside himself. He must rest it on something which seems to him to be higher than mere private inclination or advantage. Cleveland, never having heard of Kant's categorical imperatives and being almost as innocent of political theory, naturally turned to the Calvinism of his childhood. His father had been a Presbyterian clergyman, and he remained a communicant of the family faith to the end. But the Calvinism that he subscribed to was a variety purged of all the original horrors. He translated predestination, with its sharp cocksureness and its hordes of damned, into a sort of benign fatalism, not unmixed with a stealthy self-reliance. God, he believed, ordained the order of the world, and His decrees must ever remain inscrutable, but there was nevertheless a good deal to be said for hard work, a reasonable optimism, and a sturdy fidelity to what seemed to be the right. Duty, in its essence, might be transcendental, but its mandates were issued in plain English, and no honest man could escape them. There is no record that Cleveland ever tried to escape them. He was not averse to popularity, but he put it far below the approval of conscience. In him all the imaginary virtues of the Puritans became real.

It is not likely that we shall see his like again, at least in the present age. The Presidency is now closed to the kind of character that he had so abundantly. It is going, in these days, to more politic and pliant men. They get it by yielding prudently, by changing their minds at the right instant, by keeping silent when speech is dangerous. Frankness and courage are luxuries confined to the more comic varieties of runners-up at national conventions. Thus it is pleasant to remember Cleveland, and to speak of him from time to time. He was the last of the Romans. If pedagogy were anything save the puerile racket that it is he would loom large in the schoolbooks. As it is, he is subordinated to Lincoln, Roosevelt I and Wilson. This is one of the things that are the matter with the United States.

Roosevelt I

From ROOSEVELT: AN AUTOPSY, PREJUDICES: SECOND SERIES, 1920, pp. 107–28.
First printed, in part, in the *Smart Set*, March, 1920, pp. 138–44

ROOSEVELT's reaction to World War I must occupy a large part of any adequate account of him, for that reaction was probably more comprehensively typical of the man than any other business of his life. It displayed not only his whole stock of political principles, but also his whole stock of political tricks. It plumbed, on the one hand, the depths of his sagacity, and on the other hand the depths of his insincerity. Fundamentally, I am convinced, he was quite out of sympathy with, and even quite unable to comprehend the body of doctrine upon which the Allies, and later the United States, based their case. To him it must have seemed insane when it was not hypocritical, and hypocritical when it was not insane. His instincts were profoundly against a new loosing of democratic fustian upon the world; he believed in strongly centralized states, founded upon power and devoted to enterprises far transcending mere internal government; he was an imperialist of the type of Cecil Rhodes, Treitschke and Delcassé.

But the fortunes of domestic politics jockeyed him into the position of standing as the spokesman of an almost exactly contrary philosophy. The visible enemy before him was Wilson. What he wanted as a politician was something that he could get only by wresting it from Wilson, and Wilson was too cunning to yield it without making a tremendous fight, chiefly by chicane — whooping for peace while preparing for war, playing mob fear against mob fear, concealing all his genuine motives and desires beneath clouds of chautauqua rhetoric, leading a mad dance whose tune changed at every swing. Here was an opponent that more than once puzzled Roosevelt, and in the end flatly dismayed him. Here was a mob-master with a technique infinitely more subtle and effective than his own. So lured into an unequal combat, the Rough Rider got bogged in absurdities so immense that only the democratic anesthesia to absurdity saved him. To make any progress at all he was forced into fighting against his own side. He passed from the scene bawling piteously for a cause that, at bottom, it is impossible to imagine him believing in, and in terms of a philosophy that was as foreign to his true faith as it was to the faith of Wilson. In the whole affair there was a colossal irony. Both contestants were intrinsically frauds.

When, soon after his death, I ventured in a magazine article to call attention to Roosevelt's philosophical kinship to the Kaiser [1] I received letters of denunciation from all parts of the United States, and not a few forthright demands that I recant on penalty of lynch law. Prudence demanded that I heed these demands. We live in a curious and often unsafe country. Haled

---

[1] Roosevelt and Others, *Smart Set*, March, 1920, pp. 138–44.

before a Roosevelt judge for speeding my automobile, or spitting on the sidewalk, or carrying a jug, I might have been railroaded for ten years under some constructive corollary of the Espionage Act. But there were two things that supported me in my contumacy to the departed. One was a profound reverence for and fidelity to the truth, sometimes almost amounting to fanaticism. The other was the support of the eminent Iowa right-thinker and patriot, Prof. Dr. S. P. Sherman. Writing in the *Nation*, Prof. Dr. Sherman put the thing in plain terms. "With the essentials in the religion of the militarists of Germany," he said, "Roosevelt was utterly in sympathy." [2]

Utterly? Perhaps the adverb was a bit too strong. There was in the man a certain instinctive antipathy to the concrete aristocrat and in particular to the aristocrat's private code — the produce, no doubt, of his essentially *bourgeois* origin and training. But if he could not go with the Junkers all the way, he could at least go the whole length of their distrust of the third order — the undifferentiated masses of men below. Here, I daresay, he owed a lot to Nietzsche. He was always reading German books, and among them, no doubt, were "Also sprach Zarathustra" and "Jenseits von Gut und Böse." In fact, the echoes were constantly sounding in his own harangues. Years ago, as an intellectual exercise while confined to hospital, I devised and printed a giveaway of the Rooseveltian philosophy in parallel columns — in one column, extracts from "The Strenuous Life"; in the other, extracts from Nietzsche. The borrowings were numerous and unescapable. Theodore had swallowed Friedrich as a farm-wife swallows Peruna — bottle, cork, label and testimonials. Worse, the draft whetted his appetite, and soon he was swallowing the Kaiser of the *Garde-Kavallerie*-mess and battleship-launching speeches — another somewhat defective Junker. In his palmy days it was often impossible to distinguish his politico-theological bulls from those of Wilhelm; during the war, indeed, I suspect that some of them were boldly lifted by the British press bureau, and palmed off as felonious imprudences out of Potsdam. Wilhelm was his model in *Weltpolitik*, and in sociology, exegetics, administration, law, sport and connubial polity no less. Both roared for doughty armies, eternally prepared — for

[2] Roosevelt and the National Psychology, *Nation*, Nov. 8, 1919.

the theory that the way to prevent war is to make all conceivable enemies think twice, thrice, ten times. Both dreamed of gigantic navies, with battleships as long as Brooklyn Bridge. Both preached incessantly the duty of the citizen to the state, with the soft pedal upon the duty of the state to the citizen. Both praised the habitually gravid wife. Both delighted in the armed pursuit of the lower fauna. Both heavily patronized the fine arts. Both were intimates of God, and announced His desires with authority. Both believed that all men who stood opposed to them were prompted by the devil and would suffer for it in Hell.

If, in fact, there was any difference between them, it was all in favor of Wilhelm. For one thing, he made very much fewer speeches; it took some colossal event, such as the launching of a dreadnaught or the birthday of a colonel-general, to get him upon his legs; the Reichstag was not constantly deluged with his advice and upbraiding. For another thing, he was a milder and more modest man — one more accustomed, let us say, to circumstance and authority, and hence less intoxicated by the greatness of his high estate. Finally, he had been trained to think, not only of his own immediate fortunes, but also of the remote interests of a family that, in his heyday, promised to hold the throne for many years, and so he cultivated a certain prudence, and even a certain ingratiating suavity. He could, on occasion, be extremely polite to an opponent. But Roosevelt was never polite to an opponent; perhaps a gentleman, by what pass as American standards, he was surely never a gentle man. In a political career of nearly forty years he was never even fair to an opponent. All his gabble about the square deal was merely so much protective coloration. No man, facing him in the heat of controversy, ever actually got a square deal. He took extravagant advantages; he played to the worst idiocies of the mob; he hit below the belt almost habitually. One never thinks of him as a duelist, say of the school of Disraeli, Palmerston and, to drop a bit, Blaine. One always thinks of him as a glorified bouncer engaged eternally in cleaning out bar-rooms — and not too proud to gouge when the inspiration came to him, or to bite in the clinches, or to oppose the relatively fragile brass knuckles of the code with chair-legs, bung-starters, cuspidors, demijohns, and ice-picks.

Lawrence Abbott and William Roscoe Thayer, in their official lives,[3] made elaborate efforts to depict their hero as one born with a deep loathing of the whole Prussian scheme of things. Abbott even went so far as to hint that the attentions of the Kaiser, during Roosevelt's historic tour of Europe on his return from Africa, were subtly revolting to him. Nothing could be more absurd. Sherman, in the article I have mentioned, blows up that nonsense by quoting from a speech made by the tourist in Berlin — a speech arguing for the most extreme sort of militarism in a manner that must have made even some of the Junkers blow their noses dubiously. The disproof need not be piled up; the America that Roosevelt dreamed of was always a sort of swollen Prussia, truculent without and regimented within. There was always a clank of the saber in his discourse; he could not discuss the tamest matter without swaggering in the best dragoon fashion. Abbott gets into yet deeper waters when he sets up the doctrine that the invasion of Belgium threw his darling into an instantaneous and tremendous fit of moral indignation, and that the curious delay in the public exhibition thereof, so much discussed afterward, was due to his (Abbott's) fatuous interference — a *faux pas* later regretted with much bitterness. Unluckily, the evidence he offers leaves me full of doubts. What the doctrine demands that one believe is simply this: that the man who, for mere commercial advantage and (in Frederick's famous phrase) "to make himself talked of in the world," tore up the treaty of 1848 between the United States and Colombia (*geb.* New Granada), whereby the United States forever guaranteed the "sovereignty and ownership" of the Colombians in the isthmus of Panama — that this same man, thirteen years later, was horrified into a fever when Germany, facing powerful foes on two fronts, tore up the treaty of 1832, guaranteeing, not the sovereignty, but the bald neutrality of Belgium — a neutrality already destroyed, according to the evidence before the Germans, by Belgium's own acts.

[3] Impressions of Theodore Roosevelt, by Abbott, New York, 1920; Theodore Roosevelt, by Thayer; New York, 1920.

It is hard, without an inordinate strain upon the credulity, to believe any such thing, particularly in view of the fact that this instantaneous indignation of the most impulsive and vocal of men was diligently concealed for at least six weeks, with reporters camped upon his doorstep day and night, begging him to say the very thing that he left so darkly unsaid. Can one imagine Roosevelt, with red-fire raging within him and sky-rockets bursting in his veins, holding his peace for a month and a half? I have no doubt whatever that Abbott, as he says, desired to avoid embarrassing Wilson — but think of Roosevelt showing any such delicacy! For one, I am not equal to the feat. All that unprecedented reticence, in fact, is far more readily explicable on other and less lofty grounds. What really happened I presume to guess. My guess is that Roosevelt, like the great majority of other Americans, was *not* instantly and automatically outraged by the invasion of Belgium. On the contrary, he probably viewed it as a regrettable, but not unexpected or unparalleled device of war — if anything, as something rather thrillingly gaudy and effective — a fine piece of virtuosity, pleasing to a military connoisseur.

But then came the deluge of Belgian atrocity stories, and the organized campaign to enlist American sympathies. It succeeded very quickly. By the middle of August the British press bureau was in full swing; by the beginning of September the country was flooded with inflammatory stuff; six weeks after the war opened it was already hazardous for a German in America to state his country's case. Meanwhile, the Wilson administration had declared for neutrality, and was still making a more or less sincere effort to practise it, at least on the surface. Here was Roosevelt's opportunity, and he leaped to it with sure instinct. On the one side was the administration that he detested, and that all his self-interest (*e.g.*, his yearning to get back his old leadership and to become President again in 1917) prompted him to deal a mortal blow, and on the other side was a ready-made issue, full of emotional possibilities, stupendously pumped up by extremely clever propaganda, and so far unembraced by any other rabble-rouser of the first magnitude. Is it any wonder that he gave a whoop, jumped upon his cayuse, and began screaming for war? In war lay the confusion of Wilson, and the melodramatic renaissance of the Rough Rider, the professional hero, the national Barbarossa.

In all this, of course, I strip the process of its plumes and spangles, and expose a chain of causes and effects that Roosevelt himself, if he were alive, would denounce as grossly contumelious to his native purity of spirit — and perhaps in all honesty. It is not necessary to raise any doubts as to that honesty. No one who has given any study to the development and propagation of political doctrine in the United States can have failed to notice how the belief in issues among politicians tends to run in exact ratio to the popularity of those issues. Let the populace begin suddenly to swallow a new panacea or to take fright at a new bugaboo, and almost instantly nine-tenths of the masterminds of politics begin to believe that the panacea is a sure-cure for all the malaises of the Republic, and the bugaboo an immediate and unbearable menace to all law, order and domestic tranquillity.

At the bottom of this singular intellectual resilience, of course, there is a good deal of hard calculation; a man must keep up with the procession of crazes, or his day is swiftly done. But in it there are also considerations a good deal more subtle, and maybe less discreditable. For one thing, a man devoted professionally to patriotism and the wisdom of the fathers is very apt to come to a resigned sort of acquiescence in all the doctrinaire rubbish that lies beneath the national scheme of things — to believe, let us say, if not that the plain people are gifted with an infallible sagacity, then at least that they have an inalienable right to see their follies executed. Poll-parroting nonsense as a matter of daily routine, the politician ends by assuming that it is sense, even though he doesn't believe it. For another thing, there is the contagion of mob enthusiasm — a much underestimated murrain. No man is so remote and arctic that he is wholly safe from that contamination; it explains many extravagant phenomena of a democratic society; in particular, it explains why the mob leader is so often a victim to his mob.

Roosevelt, a perfectly typical politician, devoted to the trade, not primarily because he was gnawed by ideals, but because he frankly enjoyed its rough-and-tumble encounters and its gaudy rewards, was probably moved in both ways — and also by the hard calculation that I have mentioned. If, by any ineptness of the British press-agents and tear-squeezers, indignation over the invasion of Belgium had failed to materialize — if, worse still, some gross infringement of American rights by the English had caused it to be forgotten completely — if, finally, Wilson had been whooping for war with the populace firmly against him — in such event it goes without saying that the moral horror of Roosevelt would have stopped short at a very low amperage, and that he would have refrained from making it the center of his polity. But with things as they were, lying neatly to his hand, he permitted it to take on an extraordinary virulence, and before long all his old delight in German militarism had been converted into a lofty detestation of German militarism, and its chief spokesman on this side of the Atlantic became its chief opponent. Getting rid of that old delight, of course, was not easily achieved. The concrete enthusiasm could be throttled, but the habit of mind remained. Thus one beheld the curious spectacle of militarism belabored in terms of militarism — of the Kaiser arraigned in unmistakably *kaiserliche* tones.

Such violent swallowings and regurgitations were no novelties to the man. His whole political career was marked, in fact, by performances of the same sort. The issues that won him most votes were issues that, at bottom, he didn't believe in; there was always a mental reservation in his rhetoric. He got into politics, not as a tribune of the plain people, but as an amateur reformer of the snobbish type common in the eighties, by the *Nation* out of the Social Register. He was a young Harvard man scandalized by the discovery that his town was run by men with such names as Michael O'Shaunnessy and Terence Googan — that his social inferiors were his political superiors. His sympathies were essentially anti-democratic. He believed in strong centralization — the concentration of power in a few hands, the strict regimentation of the nether herd, the abandonment of platitudes. His heroes were such Federalists as Morris and Hamilton; he made his first splash in the world by writing about them and praising them. Worse, his daily associations were with the old Union League crowd of high-tariff Republicans — men almost apoplectically opposed to every movement from below — safe and sane men, highly conservative and suspicious men — the profiteers of peace, as they afterward became the profiteers of war. His early adventures in politics were not very fortunate, nor did they reveal any capacity for leadership. The bosses of the day took him in rather sportively, played him for what they could get out of him, and then turned him loose. In a few years he became disgusted and went West. Returning after a bit, he encountered catastrophe: as a candidate for Mayor of New York he was drubbed unmercifully. He went back to the West. He was, up to this time, a comic figure — an anti-politician victimized by politicians, a pseudo-aristocrat made ridiculous by the mob-masters he detested.

But meanwhile something was happening that changed the whole color of the political scene, and was destined, eventually, to give Roosevelt his chance. That something was a shifting in what might be called the foundations of reform. Up to now it had been an essentially aristocratic movement — superior, sniffish and anti-democratic. But hereafter it took on a strongly democratic color and began to adopt democratic methods. More, the change gave it new life. What Harvard, the Union League Club and Godkin's *Nation* had failed to accomplish, the plain people now undertook to accomplish. This invasion of the old citadel of virtue was first observed in the West, and its manifestations out there must have given Roosevelt a good deal more disquiet than satisfaction. It is impossible to imagine him finding anything to his taste in the outlandish doings of the Populists, the wild schemes of the pre-Bryan dervishes. His instincts were against all that sort of thing. But as the movement spread toward the East it took on a certain urbanity, and by the time it reached the seaboard it had begun to be almost civilized.

With this new brand of reform Roosevelt now made terms. It was full of principles that outraged all his pruderies, but it at least promised to work. His entire political history thereafter, down to the day of his death, was a history of compromises with the new forces — of a gradual yielding, for strategic purposes, to ideas that were intrinsically at odds with his congenital prejudices. When, after a generation of that sort of compromising, the so-called Progressive party was organized and he seized the leadership of it from the Westerners who had founded it, he performed a feat of wholesale englutination that must forever hold a high place upon the roll of political prodigies. That is to say, he swallowed at one gigantic gulp, and out of the same herculean jug, the most amazing mixture of social, political and economic sure-cures ever got down by one hero, however valiant, however athirst — a cocktail made up of all the elixirs hawked among the boobery in his time, from woman suffrage to the direct primary, and from the initiative and referendum to the short ballot, and from Prohibition to public ownership, and from trust-busting to the recall of judges.

This homeric achievement made him the head of the most tatterdemalion party ever seen in American politics — a party composed of such incompatible ingredients and hung together so loosely that it began to disintegrate the moment it was born. In part it was made up of mere disordered enthusiasts — believers in anything and everything, pathetic victims of the credulity complex, habitual followers of jitney messiahs, incurable hopers and snufflers. But in part it was also made up of rich converts like Roosevelt himself — men eager for office, disappointed by the old parties, and now quite willing to accept any aid that half-idiot doctrinaires could give them. I have no doubt that Roosevelt himself, carried away by the emotional hurricanes of the moment and especially by the quasi-religious monkey-shines that marked the first Progressive convention, gradually convinced himself that at least some of the doctrinaires, in the midst of all their imbecility, yet preached a few ideas that were workable, and perhaps even sound. But at bottom he was against them, and not only in the matter of their specific remedies, but also in the larger matter of their childish faith in the wisdom and virtue of the plain people.

Roosevelt, for all his fluent mastery of democratic counterwords, democratic gestures and all the rest of the armamentarium of the mob-master, had no such faith in his heart of hearts. He didn't believe in democracy; he believed simply in government. His remedy for all the great pangs and longings of existence was not a dispersion of authority, but a hard concentration of authority. He was not in favor of unlimited experiment; he was in favor of a rigid control from above, a despotism of inspired prophets and policemen. He was not for democracy as his followers understood democracy, and as it actually is and must be; he was for a paternalism of the true Bismarckian pattern, almost of the Napoleonic pattern — a paternalism concerning itself with all things, from the regulation of coal-mining and meat-packing to the regulation of spelling and marital rights. His instincts were always those of the property-owning Tory, not those of the romantic Liberal. Even when, for campaign purposes, he came to terms with the Liberals his thoughts always ranged far afield. When he tackled the trusts the thing that he had in his mind's eye was not the restoration of competition but the subordination of all private trusts to one great national trust, with himself at its head. And when he attacked the courts it was not because they put their own prejudices before the law but because they refused to put *his* prejudices before the law.

In all his career no one ever heard him make an argument for the rights of the citizen; his eloquence was always expended in expounding the duties of the citizen. I have before me a speech in which he pleaded for "a spirit of kindly justice toward every man and woman," but that seems to be as far as he ever got in that direction — and it was the gratuitous justice of the absolute monarch that he apparently had in mind, not the autonomous and inalienable justice of a free society. The duties of the citizen, as he understood them, related not only to acts, but also to thoughts. There was, to his mind, a simple body of primary doctrine, and dissent from it was the foulest of crimes. No man could have been more bitter against opponents, or more unfair to them, or more ungenerous. In this department, indeed, even so gifted a specialist in dishonorable controversy as Wilson seldom surpassed him. He never stood up to a frank and chivalrous debate. He dragged herrings across the trail. He made seductive faces at the gallery. He capitalized his enormous talents as an entertainer, his rank as a national hero, his public influence and consequence. The two great law-suits in which he was engaged were screaming burlesques upon justice. He tried them in the newspapers before ever they were called; he befogged them with irrelevant issues; his appearances in court were not the appearances of a witness standing on a level with other witnesses, but those of a comedian sure of his crowd. He was, in his dealings with concrete men as in his dealings with men in the mass, a charlatan of the very highest skill — and there was in him, it goes without saying, the persuasive charm of the charlatan as well as the daring deviousness, the humanness of naïveté as well as the humanness of chicane. He knew how to woo — and not only boobs.

The appearance of such men, of course, is inevitable under democracy. Consummate showmen, they arrest the wonder of the mob, and so put its suspicions to sleep. What they actually believe is of secondary consequence; the main thing is what they say; even more, the way they say it. Obviously, their activity does a great deal of damage to the democratic theory, for they are standing refutations of the primary doctrine that the common folk choose their leaders wisely. They damage it again in another and more subtle way. That is to say, their ineradicable contempt for the minds they must heat up and bamboozle leads them into a fatalism that shows itself in a cynical and opportunistic politics, a deliberate avoidance of fundamentals. The policy of a democracy thus becomes an eternal improvisation, changing with the private ambitions of its leaders and the transient and often unintelligible emotions of its rank and file. Roosevelt, incurably undemocratic in his habits of mind, often found it difficult to gauge those emotional oscillations. The fact explains his frequent loss of mob support, his periodical journeys into Coventry. There were times when his magnificent talents as a public comedian brought the proletariat to an almost unanimous groveling at his feet, but there were also times when he puzzled and dismayed it, and so awakened its hostility.

I have a notion that he died too soon. His best days were probably not behind him, but ahead of him. Had he lived ten years longer, he might have enjoyed a great rehabilitation, and exchanged his old false leadership of the inflammatory and fickle mob for a sound and true leadership of the civilized minority. For the more one studies his mountebankeries as mob-master, the more one is convinced that there was a shrewd man beneath the motley, and that his actual beliefs were anything but nonsensical. The truth of them, indeed, emerges more clearly day by day. The old theory of a federation of free and autonomous states has broken down by its own weight, and we are moved toward centralization by forces that have long been powerful and are now quite irresistible. So with the old theory of national isolation: it, too, has fallen to pieces. The United States can no longer hope to lead a separate life in the world, undisturbed by the pressure of foreign aspirations. Roosevelt, by whatever route of reflection or intuition, arrived at a sense of these facts at a time when it was still somewhat scandalous to state them, and it was the capital effort of his life to reconcile them, in some dark way or other, to the prevailing platitudes, and so get them heeded. Today no one seriously maintains, as all Americans once maintained, that the States can go on existing together as independent commonwealths, each with its own laws, its own legal theory and its own view of the common constitutional bond. And today no one seriously maintains, as all Americans once maintained, that the nation may safely potter on without adequate means of defense. However unpleasant it may be to contemplate, the fact is plain that the American people, during the next century, will have to fight to maintain their place in the sun.

Roosevelt lived just long enough to see his notions in these directions take on life, but not long enough to see them openly adopted. To the extent of his prevision he was a genuine leader of the nation, and perhaps in the years to come, when his actual ideas are disentangled from the demagogic fustian in which he had to wrap them, his more honest pronunciamentoes will be given canonical honors, and he will be ranked among the prophets. He saw clearly more than one other thing that was by no means obvious to his age — for example, the inevitability of frequent wars under the new world-system of extreme nationalism; again, the urgent necessity, for primary police ends, of organizing the backward nations into groups of vassals, each under the hoof of some first-rate power; yet again, the probability of the breakdown of the old system of free competition; once more, the high social utility of the Spartan virtues and the grave dangers of sloth and ease; finally, the incompatibility of free speech and democracy. I do not say that he was always quite honest, even when he was most indubitably right. But in so far as it was possible for him to be honest and exist at all politically, he inclined toward the straightforward thought and the candid word. That is to say, his instinct prompted him to tell the truth, just as the instinct of Wilson prompted him to shift and dissimulate. What ailed him was the fact that his lust for glory, when it came to a struggle, was always vastly more powerful than his lust for the eternal verities. Tempted sufficiently, he would sacrifice anything and everything to get applause. Thus the statesman was debauched by the politician, and the philosopher was elbowed out of sight by the popinjay.

What he stood most clearly in opposition to was the superior pessimism of the three Adams brothers — the notion that the public problems of a democracy are unworthy the thought and effort of a civilized and self-respecting man — the same error that lies in wait for all of us who hold ourselves above the general. Against this suicidal aloofness Roosevelt always hurled himself with brave effect. Enormously sensitive and resilient, almost pathological in his appetite for activity, he made it plain to everyone that the most stimulating sort of sport imaginable was to be obtained in fighting, not for mere money, but for ideas. There was no aristocratic reserve about him. He was not, in fact, an aristocrat at all, but a quite typical member of the upper *bourgeoisie*. The marks of the thoroughbred were simply not there. The man was blatant, crude, overly confidential, devious, tyrannical, vainglorious, sometimes quite childish. One often observed in him a certain pathetic wistfulness, a reaching out for a grand manner that was utterly beyond him. But the sweet went with the bitter. He had all the virtues of the fat and complacent burgher. His disdain of affectation and prudery was magnificent. He hated all pretension save his own pretension. He had a sound respect for hard effort, for loyalty, for thrift, for honest achievement.

His worst defects were the defects of his race and time. Aspiring to be the leader of a nation of third-rate men, he had to stoop to the common level. When he struck out for realms above that level he always came to grief: this was the "unsafe" Roosevelt, the Roosevelt who was laughed at, the Roosevelt retired suddenly to cold storage. This was the Roosevelt who, in happier times and a better place, might have been. Well, one does what one can.

In Memoriam: W. J. B.

From PREJUDICES: FIFTH SERIES, 1926, pp. 64–74. In its first form this was printed in the Baltimore *Evening Sun*, July 27, 1925, the day after Bryan's death at Dayton, Tenn. I reworked it for the *American Mercury*, Oct., 1925, pp. 158–60. My adventures as a newspaper correspondent at the Scopes trial are told in my Newspaper Days; New York, 1943, pp. 214–38

HAS it been duly marked by historians that William Jennings Bryan's last secular act on this globe of sin was to catch flies? A curious detail, and not without its sardonic overtones. He was the most sedulous fly-catcher in American history, and in many ways the most successful. His quarry, of course, was not *Musca domestica* but *Homo neandertalensis*. For forty years he tracked it with coo and bellow, up and down the rustic backways of the Republic. Wherever the flambeaux of Chautauqua smoked and guttered, and the bilge of idealism ran in the veins, and Baptist pastors dammed the brooks with the sanctified, and men gathered who were weary and heavy laden, and their wives who were full of Peruna and as fecund as the shad (*Alosa sapidissima*), there the indefatigable Jennings set up his traps and spread his bait. He knew every country town in the South and West, and he could crowd the most remote of them to suffocation by simply winding his horn. The city proletariat, transiently flustered by him in 1896, quickly penetrated his buncombe and would have no more of him; the cockney gallery jeered him at every Democratic national convention for twenty-five years. But out where the grass grows high, and the horned cattle dream away the lazy afternoons, and men still fear the powers and principalities of the air — out there between the corn-rows he held his old puissance to the end. There was no need of beaters to drive in his game. The news that he was coming was enough. For miles the flivver dust would choke the roads. And when he rose at the end of the day to discharge his Message there would be such breathless attention, such a rapt and enchanted ecstasy, such a sweet rustle of amens as the world had not known since Johann fell to Herod's ax.

There was something peculiarly fitting in the fact that his last days were spent in a one-horse Tennessee village, beating off the flies and gnats, and that death found him there. The man felt at home in such simple and Christian scenes. He liked people who sweated freely, and were not debauched by the refinements of the toilet. Making his progress up and down the Main street of little Dayton, surrounded by gaping primates from the upland valleys of the Cumberland Range, his coat laid aside, his bare arms and hairy chest shining damply, his bald head sprinkled with dust — so accoutred and on display, he was obviously happy. He liked getting up early in the morning, to the tune of cocks crowing on the dunghill. He liked the heavy, greasy victuals of the farmhouse kitchen. He liked country lawyers, country pastors, all country people. He liked country sounds and country smells.

I believe that this liking was sincere — perhaps the only sincere thing in the man. His nose showed no uneasiness when a hillman in faded overalls and hickory shirt accosted him on the street, and besought him for light upon some mystery of Holy Writ. The simian gabble of the cross-roads was not gabble to him, but wisdom of an occult and superior sort. In the presence of city folks he was palpably uneasy. Their clothes, I suspect, annoyed him, and he was suspicious of their too delicate manners. He knew all the while that they were laughing at him — if not at his baroque theology, then at least at his alpaca pantaloons. But the yokels never laughed at him. To them he was not the huntsman but the prophet, and toward the end, as he gradually forsook mundane politics for more ghostly concerns, they began to elevate him in their hierarchy. When he died he was the peer of Abraham. His old enemy, Wilson, aspiring to the same white and shining robe, came down with a thump. But Bryan made the grade. His place in Tennessee hagiography is secure. If the village barber saved any of his hair, then it is curing gall-stones down there today.

But what label will he bear in more urbane regions? One, I fear, of a far less flattering kind. Bryan lived too long, and descended too deeply into the mud, to be taken seriously hereafter by fully literate men, even of the kind who write schoolbooks. There was a scattering of sweet words in his funeral notices, but it was no more than a response to conventional sentimentality. The best verdict the most romantic editorial writer could dredge up, save in the humorless South, was to the general effect that his imbecilities were excused by his earnestness — that under his clowning, as under that of the juggler of Notre Dame, there was the zeal of a steadfast soul. But this was apology, not praise; precisely the same thing might be said of Mary Baker G. Eddy. The truth is that even Bryan's sincerity will probably yield to what is called, in other fields, definitive criticism. Was he sincere when he opposed imperialism in the Philippines, or when he fed it with deserving Democrats in Santo Domingo? Was he sincere when he tried to shove the Prohibitionists under the table, or when he seized their banner and began to lead them with loud whoops? Was he sincere when he bellowed against war, or when he dreamed of himself as a tin-soldier in uniform, with a grave reserved at Arlington among the generals? Was he sincere when he fawned over Champ Clark, or when he betrayed Clark? Was he sincere when he pleaded for tolerance in New York, or when he bawled for the faggot and the stake in Tennessee?

This talk of sincerity, I confess, fatigues me. If the fellow was sincere, then so was P. T. Barnum. The word is disgraced and degraded by such uses. He was, in fact, a charlatan, a mountebank, a zany without sense or dignity. His career brought him into contact with the first men of his time; he preferred the company of rustic ignoramuses. It was hard to believe, watching him at Dayton, that he had traveled, that he had been received in civilized societies, that he had been a high officer of state. He seemed only a poor clod like those around him, deluded by a childish theology, full of an almost pathological hatred of all learning, all human dignity, all beauty, all fine and noble things. He was a peasant come home to the barnyard. Imagine a gentleman, and you have imagined everything that he was not. What animated him from end to end of his grotesque career was simply ambition — the ambition of a common man to get his hand upon the collar of his superiors, or, failing that, to get his thumb into their eyes. He was born with a roaring voice, and it had the trick of inflaming half-wits. His whole career was devoted to raising those half-wits against their betters, that he himself might shine.

His last battle will be grossly misunderstood if it is thought of as a mere exercise in fanaticism — that is, if Bryan the Fundamentalist Pope is mistaken for one of the bucolic Fundamentalists. There was much more in it than that, as everyone knows who saw him on the field. What moved him, at bottom, was simply hatred of the city men who had laughed at him so long, and brought him at last to so tatterdemalion an estate. He lusted for revenge upon them. He yearned to lead the anthropoid rabble against them, to punish them for their execution upon him by attacking the very vitals of their civilization. He went far beyond the bounds of any merely religious frenzy, however inordinate. When he began denouncing the notion that man is a mammal even some of the hinds at Dayton were agape. And when, brought upon Clarence Darrow's cruel hook, he writhed and tossed in a very fury of malignancy, bawling against the veriest elements of sense and decency like a man frantic — when he came to that tragic climax of his striving there were snickers among the hinds as well as hosannas.

Upon that hook, in truth, Bryan committed suicide, as a legend as well as in the body. He staggered from the rustic court ready to die, and he staggered from it ready to be forgotten, save as a character in a third-rate farce, witless and in poor taste. It was plain to everyone who knew him, when he came to Dayton, that his great days were behind him — that, for all the fury of his hatred, he was now definitely an old man, and headed at last for silence. There was a vague, unpleasant manginess about his appearance; he somehow seemed dirty, though a close glance showed him as carefully shaven as an actor, and clad in immaculate linen. All the hair was gone from the dome of his head, and it had begun to fall out, too, behind his ears, in the obscene manner of Samuel Gompers. The resonance had departed from his voice; what was once a bugle blast had become reedy and quavering. Who knows that, like Demosthenes, he had a lisp? In the old days, under the magic of his eloquence, no one noticed it. But when he spoke at Dayton it was always audible.

When I first encountered him, on the sidewalk in front of the office of the rustic lawyers who were his associates in the Scopes case, the trial was yet to begin, and so he was still expansive and amiable. I had printed in the *Nation*, a week or so before, an article arguing that the Tennessee anti-evolution law, whatever its wisdom, was at least constitutional — that the ya-hoos of the State had a clear right to have their progeny taught whatever they chose, and kept secure from whatever knowledge violated their superstitions. The old boy professed to be de-lighted with the argument, and gave the gaping bystanders to understand that I was a publicist of parts. Not to be outdone, I admired the preposterous country shirt that he wore — sleeve-less and with the neck cut very low. We parted in the manner of two ambassadors.

But that was the last touch of amiability that I was destined to see in Bryan. The next day the battle joined and his face be-came hard. By the end of the week he was simply a walking fever. Hour by hour he grew more bitter. What the Christian Scientists call malicious animal magnetism seemed to radiate from him like heat from a stove. From my place in the court-room, standing upon a table, I looked directly down upon him, sweating horribly and pumping his palm-leaf fan. His eyes fasci-nated me; I watched them all day long. They were blazing points of hatred. They glittered like occult and sinister gems. Now and then they wandered to me, and I got my share, for my reports of the trial had come back to Dayton, and he had read them. It was like coming under fire.

Thus he fought his last fight, thirsting savagely for blood. All sense departed from him. He bit right and left, like a dog with rabies. He descended to demagogy so dreadful that his very associates at the trial table blushed. His one yearning was to keep his yokels heated up — to lead his forlorn mob of imbeciles against the foe. That foe, alas, refused to be alarmed. It in-sisted upon seeing the whole battle as a comedy. Even Darrow, who knew better, occasionally yielded to the prevailing spirit. One day he lured poor Bryan into the folly I have mentioned: his astounding argument against the notion that man is a mam-mal. I am glad I heard it, for otherwise I'd never believe it. There stood the man who had been thrice a candidate for the Presidency of the Republic — there he stood in the glare of the world, uttering stuff that a boy of eight would laugh at. The artful Darrow led him on: he repeated it, ranted for it, bellowed it in his cracked voice. So he was prepared for the final slaughter. He came into life a hero, a Galahad, in bright and shining armor. He was passing out a poor mountebank.

The Archangel Woodrow

FROM MEMOIRS OF A SUBJECT OF THE UNITED STATES, PREJUDICES: SIXTH SERIES, 1927, pp. 43–44, and from the *Smart Set*, Jan., 1921, pp. 142–43

WILSON was a typical Puritan — of the better sort, perhaps, for he at least toyed with the ambition to appear as a gentleman, but nevertheless a true Puritan. Magnanimity was simply beyond him. Confronted, on his death-bed, with the case of poor Debs, all his instincts compelled him to keep Debs in jail. I daresay that, as a purely logical matter, he saw clearly that the old fellow ought to be turned loose; certainly he must have known that Washington would not have hesitated, or Lincoln. But Calvinism triumphed as his intellectual faculties decayed. In the full bloom of health, with a plug hat on his head, he aped the gentry of his wistful adoration very cleverly, but lying in bed, stripped like Thackeray's Louis XIV, he reverted to his congenital Puritanism, which is to say, bounderism.

There is a truly devastating picture of him in "The Story of a Style," by Dr. William Bayard Hale. Hale was peculiarly equipped for the business, for he was at one time high in the literary and philosophical confidence of the late Messiah, and learned to imitate his gaudy rhetoric with great skill — so perfectly, indeed, that he was delegated to write one of the Woodrovian books, to wit, "The New Freedom," once a favorite text of *New Republic* Liberals, deserving Democrats, and the tender-minded in general. But in the end he revolted against both the new Euphuism and its eminent pa, and when he wrote his book he tackled both with considerable ferocity, and, it must be added, vast effect. His analysis of the whole Wilsonian buncombe, in fact, is appallingly cruel. He shows its ideational hollowness, its ludicrous strutting and bombast, its heavy dependence upon greasy and meaningless words, its frequent descents to mere

sound and fury, signifying nothing. In particular, he devotes
himself to a merciless study of what, after all, must remain the
deceased Moses's chief contribution to both history and beautiful letters, *viz.*, his biography of Washington. This incredible
work is an almost inexhaustible mine of bad writing, faulty gen-
eralizing, childish pussyfooting, ludicrous posturing, and naïve
stupidity. To find a match for it one must try to imagine a
biography of the Duke of Wellington by his barber. Well, Hale
spreads it out on his operating table, sharpens his snickersnee
upon his bootleg, and proceeds to so harsh an anatomizing that
it nearly makes me sympathize with the author. Not many of
us — writers, and hence vain and artificial fellows — could undergo so relentless an examination without damage. But not
many of us, I believe, would suffer quite so horribly as Woodrow. The book is a mass of puerile affectations, and as Hale un-
veils one after the other he performs a sound service for American scholarship and American letters.

I say that his book is cruel, but I must add that his laparotomies are carried on with every decorum — that he by no means
rants and rages against his victim. On the contrary, he keeps his
temper even when there is strong temptation to lose it, and his
inquiry maintains itself upon the literary level as much as possible, without needless descents to political and personal matters.
More than once, in fact, he says very kind things about Woodrow — a man probably quite as mellow and likable within as
the next man, despite his strange incapacity for keeping his
friends. The Woodrovian style, at the height of the Wilson
hallucination, was much praised by cornfed connoisseurs. I read
editorials, in those days, comparing it to the style of the Biblical
prophets, and arguing that it vastly exceeded the manner of any
living literatus. Looking backward, it is not difficult to see how
that doctrine arose. Its chief sponsors, first and last, were not
men who actually knew anything about writing English, but
simply editorial writers on party newspapers, *i.e.*, men who related themselves to literary artists in much the same way that
an Episcopal bishop relates himself to Paul of Tarsus. What
intrigued such gentlemen was the plain fact that Wilson was
their superior in their own special field — that he accomplished
with a great deal more skill than they did themselves the great

task of reducing all the difficulties of the hour to a few sonorous and unintelligible phrases, often with theological overtones — that he knew better than they did how to arrest and enchant the boobery with words that were simply words, and nothing else. The vulgar like and respect that sort of balderdash. A discourse packed with valid ideas, accurately expressed, is quite incomprehensible to them. What they want is the sough of vague and comforting words — words cast into phrases made familiar to them by the whooping of their customary political and ecclesiastical rabble-rousers, and by the highfalutin style of the newspapers that they read. Woodrow knew how to conjure up such words. He knew how to make them glow, and weep. He wasted no time upon the heads of his dupes, but aimed directly at their ears, diaphragms and hearts.

But reading his speeches in cold blood offers a curious experience. It is difficult to believe that even idiots ever succumbed to such transparent contradictions, to such gaudy processions of mere counter-words, to so vast and obvious a nonsensicality. Hale produces sentence after sentence that has no apparent meaning at all — stuff quite as bad as the worst bosh of Warren Gamaliel Harding. When Wilson got upon his legs in those days he seems to have gone into a sort of trance, with all the peculiar illusions and delusions that belong to a pedagogue gone *mashugga*. He heard words giving three cheers; he saw them race across a blackboard like Marxians pursued by the *Polizei*; he felt them rush up and kiss him. The result was the grand series of moral, political, sociological and theological maxims which now lodges imperishably in the cultural heritage of the American people, along with Lincoln's "government of the people, by the people," etc., Perry's "We have met the enemy, and they are ours," and Vanderbilt's "The public be damned." The important thing is not that a popular orator should have uttered such vaporous and preposterous phrases, but that they should have been gravely received, for weary years, by a whole race of men, some of them intelligent. Here is a matter that deserves the sober inquiry of competent psychologists. The boobs took fire first, but after a while even college presidents — who certainly ought to be cynical men, if ladies of joy are cynical women — were sending up sparks, and for a long while anyone who laughed was in danger of the calaboose.

Coolidge

From the *American Mercury*, April, 1933, pp. 388–90.
First printed, in part, in the Baltimore *Evening Sun*, Jan. 30, 1933.
Coolidge died Jan. 5, 1933

THE EDITORIAL writers who had the job of concocting mortuary tributes to the late Calvin Coolidge, LL.D., made heavy weather of it, and no wonder. Ordinarily, an American public man dies by inches, and there is thus plenty of time to think up beautiful nonsense about him. More often than not, indeed, he threatens to die three or four times before he actually does so, and each threat gives the elegists a chance to mellow and adorn their effusions. But Dr. Coolidge slipped out of life almost as quietly and as unexpectedly as he had originally slipped into public notice, and in consequence the brethren were caught napping and had to do their poetical embalming under desperate pressure. The common legend is that such pressure inflames and inspires a true journalist, and maketh him to sweat masterpieces, but it is not so in fact. Like any other literary man, he functions best when he is at leisure, and can turn from his tablets now and then to run down a quotation, to eat a plate of ham and eggs, or to look out of the window.

The general burden of the Coolidge memoirs was that the right hon. gentleman was a typical American, and some hinted that he was the most typical since Lincoln. As the English say, I find myself quite unable to associate myself with that thesis. He was, in truth, almost as unlike the average of his countrymen as if he had been born green. The Americano is an expansive fellow, a back-slapper, full of amiability; Coolidge was reserved and even muriatic. The Americano has a stupendous capacity for believing, and especially for believing in what is palpably not true; Coolidge was, in his fundamental metaphysics, an agnostic.

The Americano dreams vast dreams, and is hag-ridden by a demon; Coolidge was not mount but rider, and his steed was a mechanical horse. The Americano, in his normal incarnation, challenges fate at every step and his whole life is a struggle; Coolidge took things as they came.

Some of the more romantic of the funeral bards tried to convert the farmhouse at Plymouth into a log-cabin, but the attempt was as vain as their effort to make a Lincoln of good Cal. His early days, in fact, were anything but pinched. His father was a man of substance, and he was well fed and well schooled. He went to a good college, had the clothes to cut a figure there, and made useful friends. There is no record that he was brilliant, but he took his degree with a respectable mark, proceeded to the law, and entered a prosperous law firm on the day of his admission to the bar. Almost at once he got into politics, and by the time he was twenty-seven he was already on the public payroll. There he remained without a break for exactly thirty years, always moving up. Not once in all those years did he lose an election. When he retired in the end, it was at his own motion, and with three or four hundred thousand dollars of tax money in his tight jeans.

In brief, a darling of the gods. No other American has ever been so fortunate, or even half so fortunate. His career first amazed observers, and then dazzled them. Well do I remember the hot Saturday in Chicago when he was nominated for the Vice-Presidency on the ticket with Harding. Half a dozen other statesmen had to commit political suicide in order to make way for him, but all of them stepped up docilely and bumped themselves off. The business completed, I left the press-stand and went to the crypt below to hunt a drink. There I found a group of colleagues listening to a Boston brother who knew Coolidge well, and had followed him from the start of his career.

To my astonishment I found that this gentleman was offering to lay a bet that Harding, if elected, would be assassinated before he had served half his term. There were murmurs, and someone protested uneasily that such talk was injudicious, for A. Mitchell Palmer was still Attorney-General and his spies were all about. But the speaker stuck to his wager.

"I am simply telling you," he roared, "what I *know*. I know

Cal Coolidge inside and out. He is the luckiest goddam ————
———— in the whole world."

It seemed plausible then, and it is certain now. No other
President ever slipped into the White House so easily, and none
other ever had a softer time of it while there. When, at Rapid
City, S. D., on August 2, 1927, he loosed the occult words, "I
do not choose to run in 1928," was it prescience or only luck?
For one, I am inclined to put it down to luck. Surely there was
no prescience in his utterances and maneuvers otherwise. He
showed not the slightest sign that he smelt black clouds ahead;
on the contrary, he talked and lived only sunshine. There was a
volcano boiling under him, but he did not know it, and was
not singed. When it burst forth at last, it was Hoover who got
its blast, and was fried, boiled, roasted and fricasseed. How Dr.
Coolidge must have chuckled in his retirement, for he was not
without humor of a sad, necrotic kind. He knew Hoover well,
and could fathom the full depths of the joke.

In what manner he would have performed himself if the holy
angels had shoved the Depression forward a couple of years —
this we can only guess, and one man's hazard is as good as another's. My own is that he would have responded to bad times
precisely as he responded to good ones — that is, by pulling
down the blinds, stretching his legs upon his desk, and snoozing
away the lazy afternoons. Here, indeed, was his one peculiar
Fach, his one really notable talent. He slept more than any other
President, whether by day or by night. Nero fiddled, but Coolidge only snored. When the crash came at last and Hoover began to smoke and bubble, good Cal was safe in Northampton,
and still in the hay.

There is sound reason for believing that this great gift of his
for self-induced narcolepsy was at the bottom of such modest
popularity as he enjoyed. I mean, of course, popularity among
the relatively enlightened. On lower levels he was revered simply because he was so plainly just folks — because what little he
said was precisely what was heard in every garage and barber-
shop. He gave the plain people the kind of esthetic pleasure
known as recognition, and in horse-doctor's doses. But what got
him customers higher up the scale of humanity was something
else, and something quite different. It was the fact that he not

only said little, and that little of harmless platitudes all compact, but did even less. The kind of government that he offered the country was government stripped to the buff. It was government that governed hardly at all. Thus the ideal of Jefferson was realized at last, and the Jeffersonians were delighted.

Well, there is surely something to say for that abstinence, and maybe a lot. I can find no relation of cause and effect between the Coolidge somnolence and the Coolidge prosperity, but it is nevertheless reasonable to argue that if the former had been less marked the latter might have blown up sooner. We suffer most, not when the White House is a peaceful dormitory, but when it is a jitney Mars Hill, with a tin-pot Paul bawling from the roof. Counting out Harding as a cipher only, Dr. Coolidge was preceded by one World Saver and followed by two more. What enlightened American, having to choose between any of them and another Coolidge, would hesitate for an instant? There were no thrills while he reigned, but neither were there any headaches. He had no ideas, and he was not a nuisance.

Imperial Purple

From the Baltimore *Evening Sun*, Aug. 17, 1931

MOST of the rewards of the Presidency, in these days, have come to be very trashy. The President continues, of course, to be an eminent man, but only in the sense that Jack Dempsey, Lindbergh, Babe Ruth and Henry Ford have been eminent men. He sees little of the really intelligent and amusing people of the country: most of them, in fact, make it a sort of point of honor to avoid him. His time is put in mainly with shabby politicians and other such designing fellows — in brief, with rogues and ignoramuses. When he takes a little holiday his customary companions are vermin that no fastidious man would consort with. Dr. Harding, forced to entertain them, resorted to poteen as an analgesic; Dr. Coolidge loaded them aboard the *Mayflower*, and then fled to his cabin, took off his vest and shirt, and went to sleep; Dr. Hoover hauled them to the Rapidan at 60 miles an hour, and back at 80 or 90.

The honors that are heaped upon a President are seldom of a kind to impress and content a civilized man. People send him turkeys, opossums, pieces of wood from the *Constitution*, goldfish, carved peach kernels, models of the State capitols of Wyoming and Arkansas, and pressed flowers from the Holy Land. Once a year some hunter in Montana or Idaho sends him 20 pounds of bearsteak, usually collect. It arrives in a high state, and has to be fed to the White House dog. He receives 20 or 30 chain-prayer letters every day, and fair copies of 40 or 50 sets of verse. Colored clergymen send him illustrated Bibles, madstones and boxes of lucky powders, usually accompanied by applications for appointment as collector of customs at New Orleans, Mobile or Wilmington, N. C., or as Register of the Treasury. His public rewards come in the form of LL.D.'s from colleges eager for the publicity — and on the same day others precisely like it are given to a champion lawn-tennis player, a banker known to be without heirs of his body, and a general in the Army. No one ever thinks to give him any other academic honor; he is never made a Litt.D., a D.D., an S.T.D., a D.D.S., or a J.U.D., but always an LL.D. Dr. Hoover, to date, has 30 or 40 such degrees. He apparently knows as little about law as a court catchpoll, but he is more solidly *legum doctor* than Blackstone or Pufendorf.

The health of a President is watched very carefully, not only by the Vice-President but also by medical men detailed for the purpose by the Army or Navy. These medical men have high-sounding titles, and perform the duties of their office in full uniform, with swords on one side and stethoscopes on the other. The diet of their imperial patient is rigidly scrutinized. If he eats a few peanuts they make a pother; if he goes in for some steamed hard crabs at night, washed down by what passes in Washington for malt liquor, they complain to the newspapers. Every morning they look at his tongue, take his pulse and temperature, determine his blood pressure, and examine his eyegrounds and his knee-jerks. The instant he shows the slightest sign of being upset they clap him into bed, post Marines to guard him, put him on a regimen fit for a Trappist, and issue bulletins to the newspapers.

When a President goes traveling he never goes alone, but always with a huge staff of secretaries, Secret Service agents, doctors, nurses, and newspaper reporters. Even so stingy a fellow as Dr. Coolidge had to hire two whole Pullman cars to carry his entourage. The cost, to be sure, is borne by the taxpayers, but the President has to put up with the company. As he rolls along thousands of boys rush out to put pennies on the track, and now and then one of them loses a finger or a toe, and the train has to be backed up to comfort his mother, who, it usually turns out, cannot speak English. When the train arrives anywhere all the town bores and scoundrels gather to greet the Chief Magistrate, and that night he has to eat a bad dinner, and to listen to three hours of bad speeches.

The President has less privacy than any other American. Thousands of persons have the right of access to him, beginning with the British Ambassador and running down to the secretary of the Republican county committee of Ziebach county, South Dakota. Among them are the 96 members of the United States Senate, perhaps the windiest and most tedious group of men in Christendom. If a Senator were denied admission to the White House the whole Senate would rise in indignation. And if the minister from Albania were kicked out even the French and British Ambassadors would join in protesting. Many of these gentlemen drop in, not because they have anything to say, but simply to prove to their employers or customers that they can do it. How long they stay is only partly determined by the President himself. Dr. Coolidge used to get rid of them by falling asleep in their faces, but that device is impossible to Presidents with a more active interest in the visible world. It would not do to have them heaved out by the Secret Service men or by the White House police, or to insult and affront them otherwise, for many of them have wicked tongues. On two occasions within historic times Presidents who were irritable with such bores were reported in Washington to be patronizing the jug, and it took a lot of fine work to put down the scandal.

All day long the right hon. lord of us all sits listening solemnly to bores and quacks. Anon a secretary rushes in with the news that some eminent movie actor or football coach has died, and the President must seize a pen and write a telegram of condolence to the widow. Once a year he is repaid by receiving a cable on his birthday from King George. Such things are cherished by Presidents, and they leave them, *post mortem,* to the Library of Congress. Anon there comes a day of public ceremonial, and a chance to make a speech. Alas, it must be made at the annual banquet of some organization that is discovered, at the last minute, to be made up mainly of gentlemen under indictment, or at the tomb of some statesman who escaped impeachment by a hair. Twenty million voters with IQ's below 60 have their ears glued to the radio; it takes four days' hard work to concoct a speech without a sensible word in it. Next day a dam must be opened somewhere. Four Senators get drunk and try to neck a lady politician built like an overloaded tramp steamer. The Presidential automobile runs over a dog. It rains.

XIV. AMERICAN IMMORTALS

Mr. Justice Holmes

From the *American Mercury*, May, 1930, pp. 122–24. A review of The Dissenting Opinions of Mr. Justice Holmes, arranged by Alfred Lief, with a foreword by George W. Kirchwey; New York, 1930. With additions from the *American Mercury*, May, 1932, pp. 123–26

MR. JUSTICE HOLMES's dissenting opinions have got so much fawning praise from Liberals that it is somewhat surprising to discover that Mr. Lief is able to muster but fifty-five of them, and even more surprising to hear from Dr. Kirchwey that in only one case did the learned justice stand quite alone, and that the cases "in which he has given expression to the judgment of the court, or in which he has concurred in its judgment, far outnumber, in the ratio of eight or ten to one, those in which he felt it necessary to record his dissent."

There is even more surprising stuff in the opinions themselves. In three Espionage Act cases, including the Debs case, one finds a clear statement of the doctrine that, in war time, the rights guaranteed by the First Amendment cease to have any substance, and may be set aside summarily by any jury that has been sufficiently inflamed by a district attorney itching for higher office. In *Fox vs. the State of Washington* we learn that any conduct "which shall tend to encourage or advocate disrespect for the law" may be made a crime, and that the protest of a man who believes that he has been jailed unjustly, and threatens to boycott his persecutors, may be treated as such a crime. In *Moyer vs. Peabody* it appears that the Governor of a State, "without sufficient reason but in good faith," may call out the militia, declare martial law, and jail anyone he happens to suspect or dislike, without laying himself open "to an action after he is out of office on the ground that he had no reasonable ground for his belief." And in *Weaver vs. Palmer Bros. Co.* there is the plain inference that in order to punish a theoretical man, A, who is suspected of wrong-doing, a State Legislature may lay heavy and intolerable burdens upon a real man, B, who has admittedly done no wrong at all.

I find it hard to reconcile such notions with any plausible concept of Liberalism. They may be good law, but it is impossible to see how they can conceivably promote liberty. My suspicion is that the hopeful Liberals of the 20s, frantically eager to find at least one judge who was not violently and implacably against them, seized upon certain of Mr. Justice Holmes's opinions without examining the rest, and read into them an attitude that was actually as foreign to his ways of thinking as it was to those of Mr. Chief Justice Hughes. Finding him, now and then, defending eloquently a new and uplifting law which his colleagues proposed to strike off the books, they concluded that he was a sworn advocate of the rights of man. But all the while, if I do not misread his plain words, he was actually no more than an advocate of the rights of law-makers. There, indeed, is the clue to his whole jurisprudence. He believed that the law-making bodies should be free to experiment almost *ad libitum*, that the courts should not call a halt upon them until they clearly passed the uttermost bounds of reason, that everything should be sacrificed to their autonomy, including, apparently, even the Bill of Rights. If this is Liberalism, then all I can say is that Liberalism is not what it was when I was young.

In those remote days, sucking wisdom from the primeval springs, I was taught that the very aim of the Constitution was to keep law-makers from running amok, and that it was the highest duty of the Supreme Court, following *Marbury vs. Madison*, to safeguard it against their forays. It was not sufficient, so my instructors maintained, for Congress or a State Legislature to give assurance that its intentions were noble; noble or not, it had to keep squarely within the limits of the Bill of Rights, and the moment it went beyond them its most virtuous acts were null and void. But Mr. Justice Holmes apparently thought otherwise. He held, it would seem, that violating the Bill of Rights is a rare and difficult business, possible only by summoning up deliberate malice, and that it is the chief business of the Supreme Court to keep the Constitution loose and elastic, so that blasting holes through it may not be too onerous. Bear this doctrine in mind, and you will have an adequate explanation, on the one hand, of those forward-looking opinions which console the Liberals — for example, in *Lochner vs. New York* (the bakery case), in the child labor case, and in the Virginia case involving the compulsory sterilization of imbeciles — and on the other hand, of the reactionary opinions which they so politely overlook — for example, in the Debs case, in *Bartels vs. Iowa* (a war-time case, involving the prohibition of foreign-language teaching), in the Mann Act case (in which Dr. Holmes concurred with the majority of the court, and thereby helped pave the way for the wholesale blackmail which Mr. Justice McKenna, who dissented, warned against), and finally in the long line of Volstead Act cases.

Like any other man, of course, a judge sometimes permits himself the luxury of inconsistency. Mr. Justice Holmes, it seems to me, did so in the wiretapping case and again in the Abrams case, in which his dissenting opinion was clearly at variance with the prevailing opinion in the Debs case, written by him. But I think it is quite fair to say that his fundamental attitude was precisely as I have stated it. Over and over again, in these opinions, he advocated giving the legislature full head-room, and over and over again he protested against using the Fourteenth Amendment to upset novel and oppressive laws, aimed frankly at helpless minorities. If what he said in some of those opinions were accepted literally there would be scarcely any brake at all upon lawmaking, and the Bill of Rights would have no more significance than the Code of Manu.

The weak spot in his reasoning, if I may presume to suggest such a thing, was his tacit assumption that the voice of the legislature was the voice of the people. There is, in fact, no reason for confusing the people and the legislature: the two, in these later years, are quite distinct. The legislature, like the executive, has ceased, save indirectly, to be even the creature of the people: it is the creature, in the main, of pressure groups, and most of them, it must be manifest, are of dubious wisdom and even more dubious honesty. Laws are no longer made by a rational process of public discussion; they are made by a process of blackmail and intimidation, and they are executed in the same manner. The typical lawmaker of today is a man wholly devoid of principle — a mere counter in a grotesque and knavish game. If the right pressure could be applied to him he would be cheerfully in favor of polygamy, astrology or cannibalism.

It is the aim of the Bill of Rights, if it has any remaining aim at all, to curb such prehensile gentry. Its function is to set a limitation upon their power to harry and oppress us to their own private profit. The Fathers, in framing it, did not have powerful minorities in mind; what they sought to hobble was simply the majority. But that is a detail. The important thing is that the Bill of Rights sets forth, in the plainest of plain language, the limits beyond which even legislatures may not go. The Supreme Court, in *Marbury vs. Madison*, decided that it was bound to execute that intent, and for a hundred years that doctrine remained the corner-stone of American constitutional law. But in late years the court has taken the opposite line, and public opinion seems to support it. Certainly Dr. Holmes did not go as far in that direction as some of his brother judges, but equally certainly he went far enough. To call him a Liberal is to make the word meaningless.

Let us, for a moment, stop thinking of him as one, and let us also stop thinking of him as a *littérateur*, a reformer, a sociologist, a prophet, an evangelist, a metaphysician; instead, let us think of him as something that he undoubtedy was in his Pleistocene youth and probably remained ever after, to wit, a soldier. Let us think of him, further, as a soldier extraordinarily ruminative and articulate — in fact, so ruminative and articulate as to be, in the military caste, almost miraculous. And let us think of him still further as a soldier whose natural distaste and contempt for civilians, and corollary yearning to heave them all into Hell, was cooled and eased by a stream of blood that once flowed through the Autocrat of the Breakfast Table — in brief, as a soldier beset by occasional doubts, hesitations, flashes of humor, bursts of affability, moments of sneaking pity. Observe that I insert the wary word, "occasional"; it surely belongs there. On at least three days out of four, during his long years on the bench, the learned justice remained the soldier — precise, pedantic, unimaginative, even harsh. But on the fourth day a strange amiability overcame him, and a strange impulse to play with heresy, and it was on that fourth day that he acquired his singular repute as a sage.

There is no evidence in Dr. Holmes's decisions that he ever gave any really profound thought to the great battle of ideas which raged in his time. He was interested in those ideas more or less, and now and then his high office forced him to take a hand in the battle, but he never did so with anything properly describable as passionate conviction. The whole uproar, one gathers, seemed fundamentally foolish to him. Did he have any genuine belief in democracy? Apparently the answer must be no. It amused him as a spectacle, and there were times when he was in the mood to let that spectacle run on, and even to help it on, but there were other times when he was moved to haul it up with a sharp command. That, no doubt, is why his decisions show so wide a spread and so beautiful an inconsistency, baffling to those who would get him into a bottle. He could, on occasion, state the case for the widest freedom, whether of the individual citizen or of the representative lawmaker, with a magnificent clarity, but he could also on occasion give his vote to the most brutal sort of repression. It seems to me that the latter occasions were rather more numerous than the former. And it seems to me again, after a very attentive reading of his decisions, that what moved him when he was disposed to be complacent was far less a positive love of liberty than an amiable and half contemptuous feeling that those who longed for it ought to get a horse-doctor's dose of it, and thereby suffer a really first-rate belly-ache.

This easy-going cynicism of his is what gave his decisions their peculiar salacity, and made them interesting as literature. It separated them sharply from the writings of his fellow judges, most of whom were frankly dull dogs. He had a considerable talent for epigram, and like any other man who possesses it was not shy about exercising it. I do not go so far as to allege that it colored and conditioned his judgment, that the apt phrase actually seduced him, but certainly it must be plain that once his mood had brought him to this or that judgment the announcement of it was sometimes more than a little affected by purely literary impulses. Now and then, alas, the result was far more literature than law. I point, for example, to one of his most celebrated epigrams: "Three generations of morons are enough." It is a memorable saying, and its essential soundness need not be questioned, but is it really judicial, or even legal, in form and content; does it offer that plain guidance which the higher courts are supposed to provide? What of the *two* generations: are they too little? I should not want to be a *nisi prius* judge if all the pronunciamentoes of the Supreme Court were so charmingly succinct and memorable — and so vague.

The average American judge, as everyone knows, is a mere rabbinical automaton, with no more give and take in his mind than you will find in the mind of a terrier watching a rathole. He converts the law into a series of rubber-stamps, and brings them down upon the scalped skulls of the just and unjust alike. The alternative to him, as commonly conceived, is quite as bad — an uplifter in a black robe, eagerly gulping every new brand of Peruna that comes out, and converting his pulpit into a sort of soap-box. Mr. Justice Holmes was neither, and he was better than either. He was under no illusions about the law. He knew very well that its aim was not to bring in the millennium, but simply to keep the peace. But he believed that keeping the peace was an art that could be practised in various ways, and that if one of them was by using a club then another was by employing a feather. Thus the Liberals, who long for tickling with a great and tragic longing, were occasionally lifted to the heights of ecstasy by the learned judge's operations, and in fact soared so high that they were out of earshot of next day's thwack of the club. I suspect that Dr. Holmes himself, when he heard of their enthusiasm, was quite as much amused as flattered. Such misunderstandings are naturally grateful to a skeptic, and they are doubly grateful to a skeptic of the military order, with his professional doubt of all persons who think that they think. I can imagine this skepticism — or, if you chose, cynicism — giving great aid and comfort to him on January 1, 1932, when he entered the chamber of the Supreme Court for the last time, and read his last opinion.

The case was that of one James Dunne, an humble bootician of Eureka, Calif., and the retiring justice delivered the majority opinion. Dunne had been tried in California on an indictment embracing three counts. The first charged him with keeping liquor for sale, the second with possessing it unlawfully, and the third with selling it. The jury acquitted him on the second and third counts, but found him guilty on the first. His counsel thereupon appealed. The evidence as to all three offenses, it was shown, was precisely the same. If the prisoner was innocent of two of them, then how could he be guilty of the third? Mr. Justice Holmes, speaking for himself and all his fellow justices save one, swept away this question in the following words:

> Consistency in the verdict is not necessary. Each count in an indictment is regarded as if it was a separate offense. If separate indictments had been presented against the defendant for possession and for maintenance of a nuisance, and had been separately tried, the same evidence being offered in support of each, an acquittal on one could not be pleaded as *res judicata* of the other. Where the offenses are separately charged in the counts of a single indictment the same rule must hold.

I am not learned in the law, but the special gifts of a lawyer are surely not necessary to see that this judgment disposed completely of the prohibition of double jeopardy in Article I of the Bill of Rights. What it said, in plain English, is that a man may be tried over and over again for what is essentially the same offense, and that if one, two, three or *n* juries acquit him he may yet be kept in the dock, and so on *ad infinitum* until a jury is found that will convict him. And what such a series of juries may do may be done by one single jury — by the simple device of splitting his one offense into two, three, four or *n* offenses, and then trying him for all of them. In order to go free he must win verdicts of not guilty on every count. But in order to jail him all the prosecuting attorney needs is a verdict of guilty on one.

I commend this decision to Liberals who still cherish the delusion that Dr. Holmes belonged to their lodge. Let them paste it in their Sunday go-to-meeting hats. And I commend to them also the astounding but charming fact that the one judge who dissented was Mr. Justice Pierce Butler, for many years the chief demon in their menagerie. This is what he said:

Excluding the possession negatived by the finding under the second count, there is nothing of substance left in the first count, for its specifications were limited to the keeping for sale of the identical drinks alleged in the second count to have been unlawfully possessed. . . . The evidence having been found insufficient to establish such possession, it cannot be held adequate to warrant conviction under the first count. The finding of not guilty is a final determination that possession, the gravamen of both counts, was not proved.

Professor Veblen

From PREJUDICES: FIRST SERIES, 1919, pp. 59–83. An expansion of Prof. Veblen and the Cow, which appeared in the *Smart Set* for May, 1919, pp. 138–44, and made a considerable pother. The events dealt with in this essay seem far away today, and perhaps a bit incredible, but they deserve to be recalled, for another and even more preposterous Veblen may be on us tomorrow. On the advent of the New Deal in 1933 some of the wizards at Washington tried to revive him, but this time he did not take and was soon forgotten again. I never met him, but years after 1919 I heard from some of his friends that my onslaught had greatly upset him, and, in fact, made him despair of the Republic. He died in 1929

BACK in the year 1909, being engaged in a bombastic discussion with what was then known as an intellectual Socialist (like the rest of the *intelligentsia*, he succumbed to the first fife-corps of World War I, pulled down the red flag, damned Marx as a German spy, and began whooping for Woodrow Wilson and Otto Kahn), I was greatly belabored and incommoded by his long quotations from a certain Prof. Thorstein Veblen, then quite unknown to me. My antagonist manifestly attached a great deal of importance to these borrowed sagacities, for he often heaved them at me in lengths of a column or two, and urged me to read every word of them. I tried hard enough, but found it impossible going. The more I read them, in fact, the less I could make of them, and so in the end, growing impatient and impolite, I denounced this Prof. Veblen as a geyser of pish-posh, refused to waste any more time upon his incomprehensible syllogisms, and applied myself to the other Socialist witnesses in the case, seeking to set fire to their shirts.

That old debate, which took place by mail (for the Socialist lived in levantine luxury on his country estate and I was a wageslave attached to a city newspaper), was afterward embalmed in a dull book, and got the mild notice of a day. The book, by name, "Men vs. the Man," [1] is now as completely forgotten as Baxter's "Saint's Rest" or the Constitution of the United States. I myself am perhaps the only man who remembers it at all, and the only thing I can recall of my opponent's argument (beyond the fact that it not only failed to convert me to Marxism, but left me a bitter and incurable scoffer at democracy in all its forms) is his curious respect for the aforesaid Veblen, and his delight in the learned gentleman's long, tortuous and (to me, at least) intolerably flapdoodlish phrases.

There was, indeed, a time when I forgot even this — when my mind was empty of the professor's very name. That was, say, from 1909 or thereabout to the middle of 1917. During those years, having lost all my former interest in Socialism, even as a species of insanity, I ceased to read its literature, and thus lost track of its Great Thinkers. The periodicals that I then gave an eye to, setting aside newspapers, were chiefly the familiar American imitations of the English weeklies of opinion, and in these the dominant Great Thinker was, first, the late Dr. William James, and, after his decease in 1910, Dr. John Dewey. The reign of James, as the illuminated will recall, was long and glorious. For three or four years running he was mentioned in every one of those American *Spectators* and *Saturday Reviews* at least once a week, and often a dozen times. Among the less somber gazettes of the republic, to be sure, there were other heroes: Maeterlinck, Rabindranath Tagore, Judge Ben B. Lindsey, and so on, and still further down the literary and intellectual scale there were yet others: Hall Caine, Brieux and Jack Johnson among them, with paper-bag cookery and the twilight sleep to dispute their popularity. But on the majestic level of the pre-Villard *Nation*, among the white and lavender peaks of professorial ratiocination, there was scarcely a serious rival to James. Now and then, perhaps, Jane Addams had a month of vogue,

[1] New York, 1910. The Socialist was Robert Rives La Monte.

and during one Winter there was a rage for Bergson, but taking one day with another James held his own against the field.

His ideas, immediately they were stated, became the ideas of every pedagogue from Harvard to Leland Stanford, and the pedagogues rammed them into the skulls of the lesser *cerebelli*. When he died his ghost went marching on: it took three or four years to interpret and pigeon-hole his philosophical remains and to take down and redact his messages (via Sir Oliver Lodge, Little Brighteyes, Wah-Wah the Indian Chief, and other gifted psychics) from the spirit world. But then, gradually, he achieved the ultimate, stupendous and irrevocable act of death, and there was a vacancy. To it Prof. Dr. Dewey was elected by the acclamation of all right-thinking and forward-looking men. He was an expert in pedagogics, metaphysics, psychology, ethics, logic, politics, pedagogical metaphysics, metaphysical psychology, psychological ethics, ethical logic, logical politics and political pedagogics. He was *artium magister, philosophiæ doctor* and twice *legum doctor*. He had written a book called "How to Think." He sat in a professor's chair and caned sophomores for blowing spit-balls. *Ergo*, he was the ideal candidate, and so he was nominated, elected and inaugurated, and for three years, more or less, he enjoyed a glorious reign in the groves of sapience, and the inferior *umbilicarii* venerated him as they had once venerated James.

I myself greatly enjoyed and profited by the discourses of this Prof. Dewey and was in hopes that he would last. Born of indestructible Vermont stock and a man of the highest bearable sobriety, he seemed likely to peg along almost *ad infinitum*, a gentle and charming volcano of correct thought. But it was not, alas, to be. Under cover of pragmatism, the serpent's metaphysic that James had left behind him, there was unrest beneath the surface. Young professors in remote and obscure universities, apparently as harmless as so many convicts in the death-house, were secretly flirting with new and red-hot ideas. Whole squads of them yielded in stealthy privacy to rebellious and often incomprehensible yearnings. Now and then, as if to reveal what was brewing, a hellmouth blazed and a Dr. Scott Nearing went sky-hooting through its smoke. One heard whispers of strange heresies — economic, sociological, even political. Gossip had it that pedagogy was hatching vipers, nay, was already brought to bed. But not much of this got into the home-made *Saturday Reviews* and *Athenæums* — a hint or two maybe, but no more. In the main they kept to their old resolute demands for a pure civil-service, the budget system in Congress, the abolition of hazing at the Naval Academy, an honest primary, and justice to the Filipinos, with extermination of the Prussian monster added after August, 1914. And Dr. Dewey, on his remote Socratic Alp, pursued the calm reënforcement of the philosophical principles underlying these and all other lofty and indignant causes.

Then, of a sudden, Siss! Boom! Ah! Then, overnight, the up-springing of intellectual soviets, the headlong assault upon all the old axioms of pedagogical speculation, the nihilistic de-thronement of Prof. Dewey — and rah, rah, rah for Prof. Dr. Thorstein Veblen! Veblen? Could it be — ? Aye, it was! My old acquaintance! The *doctor obscurus* of my half-forgotten bout with the so-called intellectual Socialist! The Great Thinker redivivus! Here, indeed, he was again, and in a few months — almost it seemed a few days — he was all over the *Nation*, the *Dial*, the *New Republic* and the rest of them, his books and pamphlets began to pour from the presses, the newspapers re-ported his every wink and whisper, and everybody who was any-body began gabbling about him. The spectacle, I do not hesi-tate to say, somewhat disconcerted me and even distressed me. On the one hand, I was sorry to see so learned and interesting a man as Dr. Dewey sent back to the insufferable dungeons of Columbia, there to lecture in imperfect Yiddish to classes of Grand Street Platos. And on the other hand, I shrunk supinely from the appalling job, newly rearing itself before me, of re-reading the whole canon of the singularly laborious and muggy, the incomparably tangled and unintelligible works of Prof. Veblen.

But if a sense of duty tortures a man, it also enables him to achieve prodigies, and so I managed to get through the whole infernal job. I read "The Theory of the Leisure Class" (1899), I read "The Theory of Business Enterprise" (1904), and then I read "The Instinct of Workmanship" (1914). A hiatus fol-lowed; I was racked by a severe neuralgia, with delusions of per-secution. On recovering I tackled "Imperial Germany and the

Industrial Revolution" (1915). Marasmus for a month, and then "The Nature of Peace and the Terms of Its Perpetuation" (1917). What ensued was never diagnosed; probably it was some low infection of the mesentery or spleen. When it passed off, leaving only an asthmatic cough, I read "The Higher Learning in America" (1918), and then went to Mt. Clemens to drink the Glauber's salts. Eureka! the business was done! It had strained me, but now it was over. Alas, a good part of the agony had been needless. What I found myself aware of, coming to the end, was that practically the whole system of Prof. Veblen was in his first book and his last — that is, in "The Theory of the Leisure Class," and "The Higher Learning in America." [2] I pass on the news to literary archeologists. Read these two, and you won't have to read the others. And if even two daunt you, then read the first. Once through it, though you will have missed many a pearl and many a pain, you will have an excellent grasp of the gifted metaphysician's ideas.

For those ideas, in the main, were quite simple, and often anything but revolutionary in essence. What was genuinely remarkable about them was not their novelty, or their complexity, nor even the fact that a professor should harbor them; it was the astoundingly grandiose and rococo manner of their statement, the almost unbelievable tediousness and flatulence of the gifted headmaster's prose, his unprecedented talent for saying nothing in an august and heroic manner. There are tales of an actress of the last generation, probably Sarah Bernhardt, who could put pathos and even terror into a recitation of the multiplication table. Something of the same talent, raised to a high power, was in this Prof. Veblen. If one tunneled under his great moraines and stalagmites of words, dug down into his vast kitchen-midden of discordant and raucous polysyllables, blew up the hard, thick shell of his almost theological manner, what one found in his discourse was chiefly a mass of platitudes — the self-evident made horrifying, the obvious in terms of the staggering.

Marx, I daresay, had said a good deal of it long before him, and what Marx overlooked had been said over and over again by his heirs and assigns. But Marx, at this business, labored

[2] He wrote four books between The Higher Learning and his death in 1929, but they were only reboilings of old bones, and attracted no notice.

under a technical handicap; he wrote in German, a language he actually understood. Prof. Veblen submitted himself to no such disadvantage. Though born, I believe, in These States, and resident here all his life, he achieved the effect, perhaps without employing the means, of thinking in some unearthly foreign language — say Swahili, Sumerian or Old Bulgarian — and then painfully clawing his thoughts into a copious but uncertain and book-learned English. The result was a style that affected the higher cerebral centers like a constant roll of subway expresses. The second result was a sort of bewildered numbness of the senses, as before some fabulous and unearthly marvel. And the third result, if I make no mistake, was the celebrity of the professor as a Great Thinker. In brief, he stated his hollow nothings in such high, astounding terms that inevitably arrested and blistered the right-thinking mind. He made them mysterious. He made them shocking. He made them portentous. And so, flinging them at naïve and believing souls, he made them stick and burn.

Consider this specimen — the first paragraph of Chapter XIII of "The Theory of the Leisure Class":

In an increasing proportion as time goes on, the anthropomorphic cult, with its code of devout observances, suffers a progressive disintegration through the stress of economic exigencies and the decay of the system of status. As this disintegration proceeds, there come to be associated and blended with the devout attitude certain other motives and impulses that are not always of an anthropomorphic origin, nor traceable to the habit of personal subservience. Not all of these subsidiary impulses that blend with the bait of devoutness in the later devotional life are altogether congruous with the devout attitude or with the anthropomorphic apprehension of sequence of phenomena. Their origin being not the same, their action upon the scheme of devout life is also not in the same direction. In many ways they traverse the underlying norm of subservience or vicarious life to which the code of devout observances and the ecclesiastical and sacerdotal institutions are to be traced as their substantial basis. Through the presence of these alien motives the social and industrial regime of status gradually disintegrates, and the canon of personal subservience loses the support derived from an unbroken tradition. Extraneous habits and proclivities encroach upon the field of action occupied by this canon, and it presently comes about that the ecclesiastical and sacerdotal structures are partially converted to other uses, in some measure alien to the purpose of the scheme of devout life as it stood in the days of the most vigorous and characteristic development of the priesthood.

Well, what have we here? What does this appalling salvo of rhetorical artillery signify? What was the sweating professor trying to say? Simply that in the course of time the worship of God is commonly corrupted by other enterprises, and that the church, ceasing to be a mere temple of adoration, becomes the headquarters of these other enterprises. More simply still, that men sometimes vary serving God by serving other men, which means, of course, serving themselves. This bald platitude, which must be obvious to any child who has ever been to a church bazaar, was here tortured, worried and run through rollers until it spread out to 241 words, of which fully 200 were unnecessary. The next paragraph was even worse. In it the master undertook to explain in his peculiar dialect the meaning of "that non-reverent sense of æsthetic congruity with the environment which is left as a residue of the latter-day act of worship after elimination of its anthropomorphic content." Just what did he mean by this "non-reverent sense of æsthetic congruity"? I studied the whole paragraph for three days, halting only for prayer and sleep, and I came to certain conclusions. What I concluded was this: he was trying to say that many people go to church, not because they are afraid of the devil but because they enjoy the music, and like to look at the stained glass, the potted lilies and the rev. pastor. To get this profound and highly original observation upon paper, he wasted, not merely 241, but more than 300 words. To say what might have been said on a postage stamp he took more than a page in his book.

And so it went, alas, alas, in all his other volumes — a cent's worth of information wrapped in a bale of polysyllables. In

"The Higher Learning in America" the thing perhaps reached its damndest and worst. It was as if the practise of that incredibly obscure and malodorous style were a relentless disease, a sort of progressive intellectual diabetes, a leprosy of the horse sense. Words were flung upon words until all recollection that there must be a meaning in them, a ground and excuse for them, were lost. One wandered in a labyrinth of nouns, adjectives, verbs, pronouns, adverbs, prepositions, conjunctions and participles, most of them swollen and nearly all of them unable to walk. It was, and is, impossible to imagine worse English, within the limits of intelligible grammar. It was clumsy, affected, opaque, bombastic, windy, empty. It was without grace or distinction and it was often without the most elementary order. The professor got himself enmeshed in his gnarled sentences like a bull trapped by barbed wire, and his efforts to extricate himself were quite as furious and quite as spectacular. He heaved, he leaped, he writhed; at times he seemed to be at the point of yelling for the police. It was a picture to bemuse the vulgar and to give the judicious grief.

Worse, there was nothing at the bottom of all this strident wind-music — the ideas it was designed to set forth were, in the overwhelming main, poor ideas, and often they were ideas that were almost idiotic. The concepts underlying, say, "The Theory of the Leisure Class" were simply Socialism and well water; the concepts underlying "The Higher Learning in America" were so childishly obvious that even the poor drudges who wrote editorials for newspapers often voiced them, and when, now and then, the professor tired of this emission of stale bosh and attempted flights of a more original character, he straightway came tumbling down into absurdity. What the reader then had to struggle with was not only intolerably bad writing, but also loose, flabby, cocksure and preposterous thinking. . . . Again I take refuge in an example. It is from Chapter IV of "The Theory of the Leisure Class." The problem before the author here had to do with the social convention which, in pre-Prohibition 1899, frowned upon the consumption of alcohol by women — at least to the extent to which men might consume it decorously. Well, then, what was his explanation of this convention? Here, in brief, was his process of reasoning:

1. The leisure class, which is the predatory class of feudal times, reserves all luxuries for itself, and disapproves their use by members of the lower classes, for this use takes away their charm by taking away their exclusive possession.

2. Women are chattels in the possession of the leisure class, and hence subject to the rules made for inferiors. "The patriarchal tradition . . . says that the woman, being a chattel, should consume only what is necessary to her sustenance, except so far as her further consumption contributes to the comfort or the good repute of her master."

3. The consumption of alcohol contributes nothing to the comfort or good repute of the woman's master, but "detracts sensibly from the comfort or pleasure" of her master. *Ergo*, she is forbidden to drink.

This, I believe, was a fair specimen of the Veblenian ratio cination. Observe it well, for it was typical. That is to say, it started off with a gratuitous and highly dubious assumption, proceeded to an equally dubious deduction, and then ended with a platitude which begged the whole question. What sound reason was there for believing that exclusive possession was the hall-mark of luxury? There was none that I could see. It might be true of a few luxuries, but it was certainly not true of the most familiar ones. Did I enjoy a decent bath because I knew that John Smith could not afford one — or because I delighted in being clean? Did I admire Beethoven's Fifth Symphony because it was incomprehensible to Congressmen and Methodists — or because I genuinely loved music? Did I prefer kissing a pretty girl to kissing a charwoman because even a janitor may kiss a charwoman — or because the pretty girl looked better, smelled better and kissed better?

Confronted by such considerations, it seemed to me that there was little truth left in Prof. Veblen's theory of conspicuous consumption and conspicuous waste — that what remained of it, after it was practically applied a few times, was no more than a wraith of balderdash. What could have been plainer than his failure in the case of the human female? Starting off with a platitude, he ended in absurdity. No one could deny, I was willing to grant, that in a clearly limited sense, women occupied a place in the world — or, more accurately, aspired to a place in the world — that had some resemblance to that of a chattel. Marriage, the goal of their only honest and permanent hopes, invaded their individuality; a married woman (I was thinking, remember, of 1899) became the function of another individuality. Thus the appearance she presented to the world was often the mirror of her husband's egoism. A rich man hung his wife with expensive clothes and jewels for the same reason, among others, that he drove an expensive car: to notify everybody that he could afford it — in brief, to excite the envy of Marxians. But he also did it, let us hope, for another and far more powerful reason, to wit, that he delighted in her, that he loved her — and so wanted to make her gaudy and happy. This reason, to be sure, was rejected by the Marxians of the time, as it is rejected by those of ours, but nevertheless, it continued to appeal very forcibly, and so continues in our own day, to the majority of normal husbands in the nations of the West. The American husband, in particular, dresses his wife like a circus horse, not primarily because he wants to display his wealth upon her person, but because he is a soft and moony fellow and ever ready to yield to her desires, however preposterous. If any conception of her as a chattel were actively in him, even unconsciously, he would be a good deal less her slave. As it is, her vicarious practise of conspicuous waste commonly reaches such a development that her master himself is forced into renunciations — which brought Prof. Dr. Veblen's theory to self-destruction.

His final conclusion was as unsound as his premises. All it came to was a plain begging of the question. Why does a man forbid his wife to drink all the alcohol she can hold? Because, he said, it "detracts sensibly from his comfort or pleasure." In other words, it detracts from his comfort and pleasure because it detracts from his comfort and pleasure. Meanwhile, the real answer is so plain that even a professor should know it. A man forbids his wife to drink too much because, deep in his secret archives, he has records of the behavior of other women who drank too much, and is eager to safeguard his wife's connubial rectitude and his own dignity against what he knows to be certain invasion. In brief, it is a commonplace of observation, familiar to all males beyond the age of twenty-one, that once a woman is drunk the rest is a mere matter of time and place: the girl is already there. A husband, viewing this prospect, perhaps shrinks from having his chattel damaged. But let us be soft enough to think that he may also shrink from seeing humiliation and bitter regret inflicted upon one who is under his protection, and one whose dignity and happiness are precious to him, and one whom he regards with deep and (I surely hope) lasting affection. A man's grandfather is surely not his chattel, even by the terms of the Veblen theory, yet I am sure that no sane man would let the old gentleman go beyond a discreet cocktail or two if a bout of genuine bibbing were certain to be followed by the complete destruction of his dignity, his chastity and (if a Presbyterian) his immortal soul.

One more example of the Veblenian logic and I must pass on. On page 135 of "The Theory of the Leisure Class" he turned his garish and buzzing searchlight upon another problem of the domestic hearth, this time a double one. First, why do we have lawns around our country houses? Secondly, why don't we use cows to keep them clipped, instead of employing Italians, Croatians and blackamoors? The first question was answered by an appeal to ethnology: we delight in lawns because we are the descendants of "a pastoral people inhabiting a region with a humid climate" — because our dolicho-blond ancestors had flocks, and thus took a keen professional interest in grass. (The Marx *motif*! The economic interpretation of history in E flat.) But why don't *we* keep flocks? Why do we renounce cows and hire Jugo-Slavs? Because "to the average popular apprehension a herd of cattle so pointedly suggests thrift and usefulness that their presence . . . would be intolerably cheap." Plowing through a bad book from end to end, I could find nothing sillier than this. Here, indeed, the whole "theory of conspicuous waste" was exposed for precisely what it was: one per cent. platitude and ninety-nine per cent. nonsense. Had the genial professor, pondering his great problems, ever taken a walk in the country? And had he, in the course of that walk, ever crossed a pasture inhabited by a cow (*Bos taurus*)? And had he, making that crossing, ever passed astern of the cow herself? And had he, thus passing astern, ever stepped carelessly, and —

John D.

From the *American Mercury*, Dec., 1932, pp. 508–10. A review of God's Gold: the Story of Rockefeller and His Times, by John T. Flynn; New York, 1932

WHEN the tale of old John D. Rockefeller's long days and heroic deeds is summed up at last, it will probably turn out that his career in business was really the least interesting part of him. His era saw many more picturesque ornaments of that great mystery, and not a few of them were his partners — Archbold, H. H. Rogers, Henry M. Flagler, and so on. Any one of these would make a better book than Mr. Flynn's — in fact, they are largely responsible for the goodness of his book as it stands. Some of them were pirates and some were poets. There was a vast saltiness in all of them; they gave a pungent flavor to their times. But Rockefeller, as Mr. Flynn well says, was only a sort of sublimated bookkeeper. While the others were out in the highways and byways, bellowing and brawling, he remained at home casting accounts. It was his natural gift for that science which brought him his billion. He knew how to arrange things neatly, and how to do them cheaply. He made the oil business a going concern by introducing economy into it, and neatness, and honest arithmetic, and all the other kinds of virtue that certified public accountants esteem. He converted its enormous wastes into enormous profits, and most of those profits stayed where they belonged, which is to say, in his own pocket. The rest got lots of money too, but he always got the most. After thirty years' hard study of moral theology I can only say that I believe he deserved it.

Far more interesting than his story of his acquisitions is the story of his spendings. There is no evidence that he had a sense of humor, but in days of his first grandeurs he developed a very good substitute for it, and that substitute sufficed to save him from the follies which usually consume American millionaires. When he moved to New York in the early 80s he was already quite rich enough to bust into what then passed for fashionable society there. He had at least as much money as the Astors and probably considerably more than the Vanderbilts. There was no reason why he should not have bought a yacht for himself, and begun to train his children for polo and polygamy. But he did nothing of the sort. Instead, he kept himself and his house steadfast to the austere Baptist theology of his youth, and had no truck whatever with Ward McAllister's fleshpots. On Sunday mornings he got into a long-tailed coat, put on a plug hat, and went to church. If Mrs. Rockefeller happened to be detained at home by household business he made notes of the sermon, and on his return, re-preached it to her, with pauses for applause. The children were brought up on the strictest Baptist principles, and knew little of luxury. There was one tricycle for the four of them: "if they have just one they will learn to give up to one another."

Nor was old John an easy mark for the chiselers who always beset rich Americans, flattering them and seeking to rook them. Upon all of their customary rackets he cast a fishy eye, for he had notions of his own about the disposition of his money. The chief of them was to the effect that it was wasteful and foolish to pay out hard dollars for mere ameliorations. Thus he did not relieve the concrete poor; he tried to devise schemes that would work against poverty in general. He put up no hospitals for the indigent sick: instead, he staked medical research with millions, and so tried to make sickness less likely. Even in the religious field he was a hard nut for touring missionaries and other such racketeers to crack. Sometimes, to be sure, he gave them money, but always he added a plan for the reorganization and delousing of their business. In brief, he did not cease to be a bookkeeper when he shut his actual books, and retired to fight (and conquer) the ulcers that adorned his gastric mucosa, and filled him with sadness. On the contrary, he simply took on more and wider bookkeeping, and in the course of a few years he had pretty well revolutionized American philanthropy.

Whether or not his scheme was a good one is not yet demonstrated with any certainty. His chief enterprise, the Rockefeller Foundation, has unquestionably made some useful contributions to medical science, but the cost, in all probability, has gone beyond the net return. Perhaps it would have been more sensible, instead of trying to set up a sort of Standard Research

Company, to have spread the money among the multitude of smaller units, searching always for the genuine genius and giving him the equipment he so often lacks. But that plan would have presented enormous difficulties, and perhaps Rockefeller did the best thing possible, considering the circumstances of the time and his own lack of special knowledge. His chief almoner was always the Rev. Frederick Taylor Gates, a go-getting Baptist clergyman. No doubt an adviser less dependent upon the Holy Spirit for light would have done better, but it must be said for Pastor Gates that, taking one day with another, he did pretty well.

There is no evidence that Rockefeller was ever beset by any doubts about the simple theology of his youth. His innocent faith, for many years, made him a heavy contributor to the Anti-Saloon League, and hence one of the chief promoters of the pestilence of snooping, spying, slugging and blackmail that so long demoralized the Republic. When, in the end, he began to have doubts about the matter he quietly withdrew his support and went into prayer, and in due course there emanated from him, through his son John, a blast so devastating that what was left of Prohibition collapsed overnight. The Baptist clergy were flabbergasted, and their indignation was immense. But not many of them gave voice to it, for it was beyond their daring to flout a Rockefeller. The two Johns, indeed, remained the most eminent and authoritative Baptists extant, though the younger one also upset the *Geistliche* by patronizing a tabernacle which subscribes to open communion and is thus full of suspicious characters, Baptistically speaking.

Perhaps the most interesting thing about the Rockefellers, in the last analysis, was their fidelity to this rustic and preposterous shamanism. Most Americans, when they accumulate money, climb the golden rainspout of the nearest Episcopal Church, wherein the crude Yahweh of the backwoods is polished and perfumed, and speaks the vulgate with an English *a*. But the Rockefellers clung to the primeval rain-god of the American hinterland, and never showed any sign of being ashamed of Him. The old Hell of the Bible was Hell enough for them.

XV. ODD FISH

A Good Man Gone Wrong

A review of Doomed Ship, by Judd Gray; New York, 1928, in the American Mercury, Feb., 1929, pp. 254–55. Part of this was first printed in the Baltimore Evening Sun, Jan. 2, 1928. After the review appeared I received a letter from one of Mr. Gray's closest relatives, approving and supporting my theory as to the origins of his crime

MR. GRAY went to the electric chair in Sing Sing on January 11, 1928, for his share in the butchery of Mrs. Ruth Snyder's husband. The present book was composed in his last days, and appears with the imprimatur of his devoted sister. From end to end of it he protests pathetically that he was, at heart, a good man. I believe him. The fact, indeed, is spread all over his singularly naïve and touching record. He emerges from it as the almost perfect model of the Y.M.C.A. alumnus, the conscientious husband and father, the Christian business man, the virtuous and God-fearing Americano. It was his very virtue, festering within him, that brought him to his appalling doom. Another and more wicked man, caught in the net of La Snyder, would have wriggled out and gone on his way, scarcely pausing to thank God for the fun and the escape. But once poor Judd had yielded to her brummagem seductions, he was done for and he knew it. Touched by sin, he shriveled like a worm on a hot stove. From the first exchange of wayward glances to the final agony in the chair the way was straight and inevitable.

All this sounds like paradox, but I offer it seriously, and as a psychologist of high gifts. What finished the man was not his banal adultery with his suburban sweetie, but his swift and overwhelming conviction that it was mortal sin. The adultery itself was simply in bad taste: it was, perhaps, something to be ashamed of, as stealing a poor taxi-driver's false teeth would be something to be ashamed of, but it was no more. Elks and

Shriners do worse every day, and suffer only transient qualms. But to Gray, with his Presbyterian upbringing and his idealistic view of the corset business, the slip was a catastrophe, a calamity. He left his tawdry partner in a daze, marveling that there could be so much wickedness in the world, and no belch of fire from Hell to stop it. Thereafter his demoralization proceeded from step to step as inexorably and as beautifully as a case of Bright's disease. The woman horrified him, but his very horror became a kind of fascination. He resorted to her as a Christian dipsomaniac resorts to the jug, protestingly, tremblingly and helplessly. In his blinking eyes she became an amalgam of all the Loreleis, with the Rum Demon peeping over her shoulder. Whatever she ordered him to do he did at once, like a man stupefied by some diabolical drug. When, in the end, she ordered him to butcher her oaf of a husband, he proceeded to the business almost automatically, wondering to the last instant why he obeyed and yet no more able to resist than he was able, on the day of retribution, to resist his 2,000 volts.

In his narrative he makes much of this helplessness, and speculates somewhat heavily upon its cause. That cause, as I hint, is clear enough: he was a sincere Presbyterian, a good man. What is the chief mark of such a good man? That he cannot differentiate rationally between sin and sin — that a gnat gags him as badly as a camel. So with poor Gray. His initial peccadillo shocked him so vastly that he could think of himself thereafter only as a sinner unspeakable and incorrigible. In his eyes the step from adultery to murder was as natural and inevitable as the step from the cocktail-shaker to the gutter in the eyes of a Methodist bishop. He was rather astonished, indeed, that he didn't beat his wife and embezzle his employers' funds. Once the conviction of sin had seized him he was ready to go the whole hog. He went, as a matter of record, somewhat beyond it. His crime was of the peculiarly brutal and atrocious kind that only good men commit. An Elk or a Shriner, persuaded to murder Snyder, would have done it with a certain decency. Moreover, he would have demanded a plausible provocation. But Gray, being a good man, performed the job with sickening ferocity, and without asking for any provocation at all. It was sufficient for him that he was full of sin, that God had it in for him, that he was hopelessly damned. His crime, in fact, was a sort of public ratification of his damnation. It was his way of confessing. If he had any logical motive it was his yearning to get into Hell as soon as possible. In his book, to be sure, he speaks of Hell under the name of Heaven. But that is mere blarney, set down for the comfort of his family. He was too good a Presbyterian to have any illusions on the point: he was, in fact, an amateur theologian of very respectable attainments. He went to the chair fully expecting to be in Hell in twenty seconds.

It seems to me that his story is a human document of immense interest and value, and that it deserves a great deal more serious study than it will probably get. Its moral is plain. Sin is a dangerous toy in the hands of the virtuous. It should be left to the congenitally sinful, who know when to play with it and when to let it alone. Run a boy through a Presbyterian Sunday-school and you must police him carefully all the rest of his life, for once he slips he is ready for anything.

Valentino

From Prejudices: Sixth Series, 1927, pp. 305–11. Valentino died Aug. 23, 1926. This piece first appeared in the Baltimore *Evening Sun*, Aug. 30, 1926

By one of the chances that relieve the dullness of life and make it instructive, I had the honor of dining with this celebrated gentleman in New York, a week or so before his fatal illness. I had never met him before, nor seen him on the screen; the meeting was at his instance, and, when it was proposed, vaguely puzzled me. But soon its purpose became clear enough. Valentino was in trouble and wanted advice. More, he wanted advice from an elder and disinterested man, wholly removed from the movies and all their works. Something that I had written, falling under his eye, had given him the notion that I was a judicious fellow. So he requested one of his colleagues, a lady of the films, to ask me to dinner at her hotel.

The night being infernally warm, we stripped off our coats,

and came to terms at once. I recall that he wore suspenders of extraordinary width and thickness. On so slim a young man they seemed somehow absurd, especially on a hot Summer night. We perspired horribly for an hour, mopping our faces with our handkerchiefs, the table napkins, the corners of the tablecloth, and a couple of towels brought in by the humane waiter. Then there came a thunderstorm, and we began to breathe. The hostess, a woman as tactful as she is charming, disappeared mysteriously and left us to commune.

The trouble that was agitating Valentino turned out to be very simple. The ribald New York papers were full of it, and that was what was agitating him. Some time before, out in Chicago, a wandering reporter had discovered, in the men's wash-room of a gaudy hotel, a slot-machine selling talcum-powder. That, of course, was not unusual, but the color of the talcum-powder was. It was pink. The news made the town giggle for a day, and inspired an editorial writer on the Chicago *Tribune* to compose a hot weather editorial. In it he protested humorously against the effeminization of the American man, and laid it lightheartedly to the influence of Valentino and his sheik movies. Well, it so happened that Valentino, passing through Chicago that day on his way east from the Coast, ran full tilt into the editorial, and into a gang of reporters who wanted to know what he had to say about it. What he had to say was full of fire. Throwing off his 100% Americanism and reverting to the *mores* of his fatherland, he challenged the editorial writer to a duel, and, when no answer came, to a fist fight. His masculine honor, it appeared, had been outraged. To the hint that he was less than he, even to the extent of one half of one per cent., there could be no answer save a bath of blood.

Unluckily, all this took place in the United States, where the word honor, save when it is applied to the structural integrity of women, has only a comic significance. When one hears of the honor of politicians, of bankers, of lawyers, of the United States itself, everyone naturally laughs. So New York laughed at Valentino. More, it ascribed his high dudgeon to mere publicity-seeking: he seemed a vulgar movie ham seeking space. The poor fellow, thus doubly beset, rose to dudgeons higher still. His Italian mind was simply unequal to the situation.

.So he sought counsel from the neutral, aloof and seasoned. Unluckily, I could only name the disease, and confess frankly that there was no remedy — none, that is, known to any therapeutics within my ken. He should have passed over the gibe of the Chicago journalist, I suggested, with a lofty snort — perhaps, better still, with a counter gibe. He should have kept away from the reporters in New York. But now, alas, the mischief was done. He was both insulted and ridiculous, but there was nothing to do about it. I advised him to let the dreadful farce roll along to exhaustion. He protested that it was infamous. Infamous? Nothing, I argued, is infamous that is not true. A man still has his inner integrity. Can he still look into the shaving-glass of a morning? Then he is still on his two legs in this world, and ready even for the Devil. We sweated a great deal, discussing these lofty matters. We seemed to get nowhere.

Suddenly it dawned upon me — I was too dull or it was too hot for me to see it sooner — that what we were talking about was really not what we were talking about at all. I began to observe Valentino more closely. A curiously naïve and boyish young fellow, certainly not much beyond thirty, and with a disarming air of inexperience. To my eye, at least, not handsome, but nevertheless rather attractive. There was some obvious fineness in him; even his clothes were not precisely those of his horrible trade. He began talking of his home, his people, his early youth. His words were simple and yet somehow very eloquent. I could still see the mime before me, but now and then, briefly and darkly, there was a flash of something else. That something else, I concluded, was what is commonly called, for want of a better name, a gentleman. In brief, Valentino's agony was the agony of a man of relatively civilized feelings thrown into a situation of intolerable vulgarity, destructive alike to his peace and to his dignity — nay, into a whole series of such situations.

It was not that trifling Chicago episode that was riding him; it was the whole grotesque futility of his life. Had he achieved, out of nothing, a vast and dizzy success? Then that success was hollow as well as vast — a colossal and preposterous nothing. Was he acclaimed by yelling multitudes? Then every time the multitudes yelled he felt himself blushing inside. The old story of Diego Valdez once more, but with a new poignancy in it.

Valdez, at all events, was High Admiral of Spain. But Valentino, with his touch of fineness in him — he had his commonness, too, but there was that touch of fineness — Valentino was only the hero of the rabble. Imbeciles surrounded him in a dense herd. He was pursued by women — but what women! (Consider the sordid comedy of his two marriages — the brummagem, star-spangled passion that invaded his very death-bed!) The thing, at the start, must have only bewildered him. But in those last days, unless I am a worse psychologist than even the professors of psychology, it was revolting him. Worse, it was making him afraid.

I incline to think that the inscrutable gods, in taking him off so soon and at a moment of fiery revolt, were very kind to him. Living, he would have tried inevitably to change his fame — if such it is to be called — into something closer to his heart's desire. That is to say, he would have gone the way of many another actor — the way of increasing pretension, of solemn artiness, of hollow hocus-pocus, deceptive only to himself. I believe he would have failed, for there was little sign of the genuine artist in him. He was essentially a highly respectable young man, which is the sort that never metamorphoses into an artist. But suppose he had succeeded? Then his tragedy, I believe, would have only become the more acrid and intolerable. For he would have discovered, after vast heavings and yearnings, that what he had come to was indistinguishable from what he had left. Was the fame of Beethoven any more caressing and splendid than the fame of Valentino? To you and me, of course, the question seems to answer itself. But what of Beethoven? He was heard upon the subject, *viva voce*, while he lived, and his answer survives, in all the freshness of its profane eloquence, in his music. Beethoven, too, knew what it meant to be applauded. Walking with Goethe, he heard something that was not unlike the murmur that reached Valentino through his hospital window. Beethoven walked away briskly. Valentino turned his face to the wall.

Here was a young man who was living daily the dream of millions of other young men. Here was one who was catnip to women. Here was one who had wealth and fame. And here was one who was very unhappy.

An American Bonaparte

From the *American Mercury*, Dec., 1924, pp. 444–46.
Bonaparte died June 28, 1921

So far, to my considerable amazement, no vandalic psychographer has violated the tomb of one of the strangest Americans ever seen on land or sea, to wit, the Hon. Charles Joseph Bonaparte, LL.D., Secretary of the Navy and later Attorney-General in the Cabinet of the illustrious Roosevelt I. This neglect is hard to understand, for he was unquestionably *sui generis* — a truly fabulous compound of Sicilian brigand and Scotch bluenose, a pawky and cruel wit and yet the most humorless of men, a royalist in his every instinct and yet a professional democrat and Puritan wowser all his days long. When he died, alas, he was already forgotten, but he surely deserves to be blown up with literary gases and made to dance before connoisseurs of the preposterous and incredible.

Bonaparte was a grandson of that younger brother of Napoleon I who married the fair Betsy Patterson, of Baltimore, daughter to an eminent Babbitt of the time, Scotch in origin. This young brother, Jerome, deserted Betsy at Napoleon's order, but not before she became the mother of a son. The son, who called himself Jerome Bonaparte-Patterson, was the father, in his turn, of two sons, one of whom was Charles Joseph. Betsy herself, after Jerome deserted her, returned to America, and lived to a great age. She did not die, in fact, until 1879, and during her last years she accumulated a very large property. Old Baltimore remembered her as she plodded about the town in rain and shine, collecting her rents. She took charge of the education of her grandsons, sent Charles Joseph to Harvard, set him up as a lawyer, and when she died left him a million in gilt-edged real estate.

The other grandson, Jerome Napoleon, was never heard of, but Charles Joseph began to make a noise in his native Baltimore in the 70s, when he was just out of Harvard. The public school in America was then just getting on its legs, and Bonaparte, who had been brought up as a Catholic, was violently against it. His opposition, characteristically, was carried on in a very doctrinaire manner; he argued, in the end, that it was as outrageous for the State to supply free schools as it would be for it to provide free soup-houses. Some wit thereupon gave him the nickname of Soup-House Charlie, and it stuck to him for thirty years. But the public schools did not long detain him. In the early 80s, when Civil Service Reform began to be heard of, he joined its legions with a whoop, and thereafter, until his death, he spent half of his free energies bawling for the merit system in public office and the other half trying to wreck it as a Republican politician.

It was through the National Civil Service Reform League that Roosevelt first came into contact with him. They had many things in common. Both were reformers who were yet adept at every trick of practical politics. Both sobbed for democracy, and distrusted the concrete democrat. Both consecrated themselves to Service, and were yet highly alert to the main chance. Bonaparte, I suspect, had secret doubts about Roosevelt, as he had about all men, but on Roosevelt's side it was a genuine love affair. He not only admired Bonaparte's caustic wit and immense (if disorderly) learning; he was also greatly flattered by the attentions of a man whom he looked upon as of royal blood. When he became President he put Bonaparte into the Cabinet at the first opportunity, and made frequent references thereafter to the fact that a member of an imperial house sat at his table. Bonaparte was the worst Secretary of the Navy ever heard of. It was not so much that he was incompetent as that he was indolent. For weeks running his attendance at his office was confined to an hour a day. He left Baltimore by the 11 o'clock train, got to Washington at noon, dashed to the Navy Department, and then caught the 1 o'clock train back to Baltimore. Only on Cabinet days did he linger longer in the capital.

Nevertheless, Roosevelt was delighted with him, and presently made him Attorney-General. In this high office his indolence was of the utmost value to all predatory gentlemen of wealth. He sat for three years, and during the whole time the trusts were well and happy. Nevertheless, there is a record that, on one occasion, at least, he bestirred himself. This was when Roosevelt made one of his periodical onslaughts upon the anarchists — the predecessors, in political buncombe, of the modern Reds. Certain Italians at Paterson, N. J., printed a small anarchist newspaper, in Italian, and sent it through the mails. It had only the most meagre circulation, and its contents were so mild that prosecuting the editors was out of the question, but Roosevelt wanted to make a sensation by barring it from the mails. The problem was put up to Bonaparte as Attorney-General. After weeks of cogitation he produced an opinion which, years later, was to be the foundation-stone of all the patriotic endeavors of Burleson, Palmer, Daugherty and Burns. In brief, he decided that, while there was no warrant in law for barring the paper from the mails, it should be done anyhow, for the Italians who ran it would have no practicable means of redress after the business was accomplished. In other words, he laid down the rule that it is all right to invade a citizen's right so long as he can't help himself. This principle, which Roosevelt adopted instantly and gladly, is now embodied in many of the decisions of our highest courts, and is thus firmly established in American jurisprudence. Roosevelt and Bonaparte put it there.

Bonaparte, as I have said, was a Catholic. In fact, he was a very earnest one, and was never absent from his pew in the Baltimore Cathedral at high mass on Sunday morning. But he had more Scotch blood in him than Latin, and so he became, in his old age, that strangest of hybrids, a Catholic Puritan. Had he lived long enough and kept his vigor he would have been the most violent of Prohibitionists. As it was he, he specialized in the pursuit of the scarlet woman. For years he was one of the chief backers of the Baltimore Anti-Vice Society, and his enthusiasm kept up even after the grand archon of the organization, a Methodist clergyman, had been taken in homosexual practises at the Y.M.C.A. and had to leave town between days. It was common gossip in Baltimore that the Bonaparte estate included a number of old rookeries that were rented by ladies of joy. Nevertheless, Bonaparte demanded the blood of these fair creatures in season and out of season, and in the end he stirred up the town to such an extent that vice was formally prohibited and abolished, absolutely and forever. From that day to this, so I hear, not a single act of illicit carnality has ever been perpetrated in Baltimore.

Bonaparte lived to be nearly seventy, and died childless and relatively poor. His property had gradually slipped through his fingers, though he was the most assiduous of business men, and seldom missed a day at his office. It was only in public office that he was indolent. He belonged to all known reform organizations, made endless speeches against public and private sin, and wrote incessantly. His style was extremely florid and complex. It was common for him to write sentences of five hundred words. In my newspaper days I often handled his pronunciamentoes. Not infrequently I would make two or three paragraphs out of a single sentence. But for all this copiousness he wrote clearly: his longest sentence, given wind enough, could be parsed. His books, once widely read by believers in the reforms he advocated, are now forgotten. His speeches and essays moulder in newspaper files. Few persons seem to recall him at all.

Yet he was an enormously racy and amusing fellow and his story, done with any sort of skill, would make an extremely interesting book. I mention one thing more about him, and then resign him to the literary anatomists. He got into the Roosevelt Cabinet mainly, if not solely, because he was a Bonaparte: the fact caressed Roosevelt's vanity. The same fact got him an audience the moment he was out of Harvard, and so opened the way for his career as a reformer. All his life he was chiefly conspicuous, not on his own account, but as the grand-nephew of Napoleon I. Nevertheless, the relationship seemed to interest him personally not at all. He never made any public reference to it; he never visited France, nor had any visible communication with the rest of the Bonaparte family. Once, denounced as a Frenchman and hence sinful, he defended himself by maintaining that he hadn't a drop of French blood — that he was Italian and Scotch. Beyond that, so far as I know, he never mentioned the Bonapartes.

Sister Aimée

From the Baltimore *Evening Sun*, Dec. 13, 1926. This was written at the height of La McPherson's stormy career. Earlier in 1926 she had mysteriously disappeared, and there was a dreadful hullabaloo among her customers. When she returned just as mysteriously she told an incredible tale of having been kidnapped. It was soon established that she had been on a love-trip with one of her employés, a baldheaded and one-legged electrician, and she was thereupon charged with perjury and put on trial. She escaped easily enough, but the scandal badly damaged her business, and she was soon supplanted as the ranking ecclesiastic of the United States by Bishop James Cannon, Jr. She died, almost forgotten, in 1944

THE REV. sister in God, I confess, greatly disappointed me. Arriving in Los Angeles out of the dreadful deserts of Arizona and New Mexico, I naturally made tracks to hear and see the town's most distinguished citizen. Her basilica turned out to be at a great distance from my hotel, far up a high hill and in the midst of a third-rate neighborhood. It was a cool and sunshiny Sunday afternoon, the place was packed, and the whisper had gone around that Aimée was heated up by the effort to jail her, and would give a gaudy show. But all I found myself gaping at, after an hour, was an orthodox Methodist revival, with a few trimmings borrowed from the Baptists and the Holy Rollers — in brief, precisely the sort of thing that goes on in the shabby suburbs and dark back streets of Baltimore, three hundred nights of every year.

Aimée, of course, is richer than most evangelists, and so she has got herself a plant that far surpasses anything ever seen in shabby suburbs. Her temple to the One God is immensely wide — as wide, almost, as the Hippodrome in New York — and probably seats 2,500 customers. There is a full brass band down in front, with a grand piano to one side of it and an organ to the other. From the vast gallery, built like that of a theater, runways run along the side walls to what may be called the proscenium arch, and from their far ends stairways lead down to the platform. As in many other evangelical bull-rings, there are theater seats instead of pews. Some pious texts are emblazoned on the wall behind the platform: I forget what they say. There are no stained-glass windows. The architecture, in and out, is of the Early Norddeutscher-Lloyd Rauchzimmer school, with modifications suggested by the filling-stations of the Standard Oil Company of New Jersey. The whole building is very cheaply made. It is large and hideous, but I don't think it cost much. Nothing in Los Angeles appears to have cost much. The town is inconceivably shoddy.

As I say, Aimée has nothing on tap to make my eyes pop, old revival fan that I am. The proceedings began with a solemn march by the brass band, played about as well as the average Salvation Army could have done it, but no better. Then a brother from some remote outpost filed down the aisle at the head of a party of fifty or sixty of the faithful. They sang a hymn, the brother made a short speech, and then he handed Aimée a check for $500 for her Defense Fund. A quartet followed, male, a bit scared, and with Army haircuts. Two little girls then did a duet, to the music of a ukulele played by one of them. Then Aimée prayed. And then she delivered a brief harangue. I could find nothing in it worthy of remark. It was the time-honored evangelical hokum, made a bit more raucous than usual by the loud-speakers strewn all over the hall. A brother who seemed to be a sort of stage manager held the microphone directly under Aimée's nose. When, warmed by her homiletic passion, she turned this way or that, he followed her. It somehow suggested an attentive deck steward, plying his useful art on a rough day. Aimée wore a long white robe, with a very low-cut collar, and over it there was a cape of dark purple. Her thick hair, piled high, turned out to be of mahogany brown. I had heard that it was a flaming red.

The rest of the orgy went on in the usual way. Groups of four, six, eight or twenty got up and sang. A large, pudgy, soapy-looking brother prayed. Aimée herself led the choir in a hymn with a lively tune and very saucy words, chiefly aimed at her enemies. Two or three times more she launched into brief addresses. But mostly she simply ran the show. While the quartets bawled and the band played she was busy at a telephone behind the altar or hurling orders in a loud stage-whisper at sergeants and corporals on the floor. Obviously, a very managing woman, strongly recalling the madame of a fancy-house on

a busy Saturday night. A fixed smile stuck to her from first
to last.

What brought this commonplace and transparent mountebank to her present high estate, with thousands crowding her tabernacle daily and money flowing in upon her from whole regiments of eager dupes? The answer, it seems to me, is as plain as mud. For years she had been wandering about the West, first as a side-show wriggler, then as a faith healer, and finally as a cow-town evangelist. One day, inspired by God, she decided to try her fortune in Los Angeles. Instantly she was a roaring success. And why? For the plain reason that there were more morons collected in Los Angeles than in any other place on earth — because it was a pasture foreordained for evangelists, and she was the first comer to give it anything low enough for its taste and comprehension.

The osteopaths, chiropractors and other such quacks had long marked and occupied it. It swarmed with swamis, spiritualists, Christian Scientists, crystal-gazers and the allied necromancers. It offered brilliant pickings for real estate speculators, oil-stock brokers, wire-tappers and so on. But the town pastors were not up to its opportunities. They ranged from melancholy High Church Episcopalians, laboriously trying to interest retired Iowa alfalfa kings in ritualism, down to struggling Methodists and Baptists, as earnestly seeking to inflame the wives of the same monarchs with the crimes of the Pope. All this was over the heads of the trade. The Iowans longed for something that they could get their teeth into. They wanted magic and noise. They wanted an excuse to whoop.

Then came Aimée, with the oldest, safest tricks out of the pack of Dr. Billy Sunday, Dr. Gipsy Smith and the rest of the old-time hell-robbers, and to them she added capers from her circus days. In a month she had Los Angeles sitting up. In six months she had it in an uproar. In a year she was building her rococo temple and her flamboyant Bible College and the half-wits were flocking in from twenty States. Today, if her temple were closed by the police, she could live on her radio business alone. Every word she utters is carried on the air to every forlorn hamlet in those abominable deserts, and every day the mail brings her a flood of money.

The effort to jail her has disingenuousness in it, and the more civilized Angeleños all sympathize with her, and wish her well. Her great success raised up two sets of enemies, both powerful. One was made up of the regular town clergy, who resented her raids upon their customers. The other was composed of the town Babbitts who began to fear that her growing celebrity was making Los Angeles ridiculous. So it was decided to bump her off, and her ill-timed morganatic honeymoon with the bald-headed and wooden-legged Mr. Ormiston offered a good chance. But it must be manifest to any fair observer that there is very little merit in the case against her. What she is charged with, in essence, is perjury, and the chief specification is that, when asked if she had been guilty of unchastity, she said no. I submit that no self-respecting judge in the Maryland Free State, drunk or sober, would entertain such a charge against a woman, and that no Maryland grand jury would indict her. It is unheard of, indeed, in any civilized community for a woman to be tried for perjury uttered in defense of her honor. But in California, as everyone knows, the process of justice is full of unpleasant novelties, and so poor Aimée, after a long and obscene hearing, has been held for trial.

The betting odds in the Los Angeles saloons are 50 to 1 that she will either hang the jury or get a clean acquittal. I myself, tarrying in the town, invested some money on the long end, not in avarice, but as a gesture of sympathy for a lady in distress. The local district attorney has the newspapers on his side, and during the progress of Aimée's hearing he filled one of them, in the chivalrous Southern California manner, with denunciations of her. But Aimée herself has the radio, and I believe that the radio will count most in the long run. Twice a day, week in and week out, she caresses the anthropoids of all that dusty, forbidding region with her lubricious coos. And twice a day she meets her lieges of Los Angeles face to face, and has at them with her shiny eyes, her mahogany hair, her eloquent hips, and her lascivious voice. It will be a hard job, indeed, to find twelve men and true to send her to the hoosegow. Unless I err grievously, our Heavenly Father is with her.

XVI. ECONOMICS

To Him That Hath

From the *Smart Set*, May, 1920, pp. 33–34

PERHAPS the most valuable of all human possessions, next to an aloof and sniffish air, is the reputation of being well-to-do. Nothing else so neatly eases one's way through life. There is in 90% of all men — and in 99% of all Marxists, who value money far beyond its worth, and are always thinking of it and itching for it — an irresistible impulse to crook the knee to wealth, to defer to the power that it carries with it, to see all sorts of superiorities in the man who has it, or is said to have it. True enough, envy goes with the craven neck, but it is envy somehow purged of menace: the inferior man, at bottom, is afraid to do evil to the man with money; he is even afraid to *think* evil of him — that is, in any patent and offensive way. What stays his natural hatred of his superior, I daresay, is the sneaking hope that he may get some of the money by being polite — that it will pay him better to caress than to strike.

Whatever the psychological process, he always arrives at a great affability. Give out the news that one has just made a killing in the stock market, or robbed some confiding widow of her dower, or swindled the government in some patriotic enterprise, and at once one will discover that one's shabbiness is a charming eccentricity, and one's judgment of wines worth hearing, and one's political hallucinations worthy of attention. The man who is thought to be poor never gets a fair chance. No one wants to listen to him. No one gives a damn what he thinks or knows or feels. No one has any desire for his good opinion. I discovered this principle early in life, and have put it to use ever since. I have got a great deal more out of men (and women) by having the name of being a well-heeled fellow than I have ever got by being decent to them, or by dazzling them with my sagacity, or by hard industry, or by a personal beauty that is singular and ineffable.

Capitalism

From the Baltimore *Evening Sun*, Jan. 14, 1935

ALL the quacks and cony-catchers now crowding the public trough at Washington seem to be agreed upon one thing, and one thing only. It is the doctrine that the capitalistic system is on its last legs, and will presently give place to something nobler and more "scientific." There is, of course, no truth in this doctrine whatsoever. It collides at every point with the known facts. There is not the slightest reason for believing that capitalism is in collapse, or that anything proposed by the current wizards would be any better. The most that may be said is that the capitalistic system is undergoing changes, some of them painful. But those changes will probably strengthen it quite as often as they weaken it.

We owe to it almost everything that passes under the general name of civilization today. The extraordinary progress of the world since the Middle Ages has not been due to the mere expenditure of human energy, nor even to the flights of human genius, for men had worked hard since the remotest times, and some of them had been of surpassing intellect. No, it has been due to the accumulation of capital. That accumulation permitted labor to be organized economically and on a large scale, and thus greatly enhanced its productiveness. It provided the machinery that gradually diminished human drudgery, and liberated the spirit of the worker, who had formerly been almost indistinguishable from a mule. Most of all, it made possible a longer and better preparation for work, so that every art and handicraft greatly widened its scope and range, and multitudes of new and highly complicated crafts came in.

We owe to capital the fact that the medical profession, for example, is now really useful to mankind, whereas formerly it was useful only to the charlatans who practised it. It took accumulated money to provide the long training that medicine began to demand as it slowly lifted itself from the level of a sorry trade to that of a dignified art and science — money to keep the student while he studied and his teachers while they instructed him, and more money to pay for the expensive housing and materials that they needed. In the main, all that money came from private capitalists. But whether it came from private capitalists or from the common treasury, it was always capital, which is to say, it was always part of an accumulated surplus. It never could have been provided out of the hand-to-mouth income of a non-capitalistic society.

When the Bolsheviki, a gang of frauds almost comparable to our own Brain Trust, took over the control of affairs in Russia, they had to throw overboard at once one of the cardinal articles of their ostensible creed. That article was to the effect that all the sorrows of the world were due to the fact that the workingman, under capitalism, had lost ownership in his tools. All the classical authorities on Socialism, from Marx and Engels downward, had stressed this loss heavily, and the Utopia they visioned was always one in which the workingman should get his tools back, and become an independent producer, working for himself alone, and giving none of the value he created to a wicked capitalist. But the moment the Bolsheviki came into power they had to shelve all this, and since then nothing has been heard about it save from their American gulls. A shrewd set of shysters, eager only to run Russia as their private preserve, they saw instantly that their main job was to accumulate capital, for without it half of their victims would starve. The old capital of the country had been destroyed by war. An easy way to get more would have been to borrow it, but no one would lend, so the Bolsheviki had to accumulate fresh capital of their own.

This they managed to do by sweating the Russian workers in a manner never before seen on earth, at all events in modern times. The workers, at the start, resisted, especially the farmers, and in consequence Russia had a couple of famines, and the hat had to be passed in the capitalistic countries to feed the starving. But by slaughtering the rebellious farmers and organizing the jobless into a huge army, the Bolsheviki presently managed to bring the workers of Russia to heel, and since then those poor fish have been worked like prisoners in a chain gang, and have got pretty much the same wages. All the produce of their labor, over and above subsistence far more suitable to rats than to men, has gone into the coffers of the Bolsheviki. Thereby the Bolsheviki have accumulated a store of new capital, and now they use it not only to build ever larger and larger factories, each manned by hordes of workers who own nothing but their hands, but also to provide luxurious quarters for themselves, including an embassy at Washington so gaudy that it is the envy of every banker in the town.

Thus one of the fundamental principles of Marxism has been reduced to absurdity in the house of its professed disciples. They may be scoundrels, and no doubt they are, but they also have a considerable cunning, and are thus well aware that nothing properly describable as modern civilization can be carried on without capital. And by capital I mean precisely what they mean when they denounce it for foreign consumption — that is, I mean a surplus accumulated, not in the pockets of workers, but in the pockets of persons who provide them with the means to work, and not under control of those who produce it, but under the control of those who have managed to collar it. The shabby politicians, puerile pedagogues and briefless lawyers who have raged and roared at Washington since 1933 would go the same way if they had the chance. Some of them, perhaps, are actually stupid enough to believe that the world could get along without capitalism, but others surely must be shrewd enough to note what has happened in Russia. But whether they are only plain idiots or clever rogues, they all talk grandly about capitalism's decay, and even those who allege that they are trying to save it keep on mouthing the nonsense that it is on its deathbed. You will find the same hollow blah in all the organs of the More Abundant Life, and every day it issues from some dotty pedagogue yearning for a Government job.

There is no sense in it whatever. The modern world could no more get along without accumulated capital than it could get along without police or paved streets. The greatest change imaginable is simply the change that has occurred in Russia —

a transfer of capital from private owners to professional politicians. If you think this would do the individual any good, then all you need do to be undeceived is to ask any American letter-carrier. He works for a master capitalist named Uncle Sam — and he will be glad to tell you how hard he has to sweat for every nickel he gets.

On Getting a Living

From the Baltimore *Evening Sun*, May 12, 1924

SINCE the great reform in medical education in America, launched by the American Medical Association some years ago, it has become, to all intents and purposes, a sheer impossibility for a medical student to work his way to a degree. He could do it very readily in the old days. Everywhere there were medical colleges that would accept a youth direct from the plow and turn him out a full-fledged M.D. in three years of easy work. But no more. Today he must have an A.B. or at least the half of it before he may even begin to study, and then he must put in four years of extremely hard work before he gets his M.D., and pledge himself to service a year or two more as an interne before he begins to practise.

It seems harsh, but why should the rest of us get into a sweat about it? For one, I see no sound reason. I haven't the slightest objection to being dosed and consoled, when I am ill, by a medical man whose father (or someone else) paid for his education, and who thus got it in comfort and with an easy mind. I can discern absolutely no ground for believing that the doctor who had to spend half or two-thirds of his time in college getting a living should be any more competent. Nor, for that matter, any more humane in his charges. It is not well-to-do men who love money most, but men who are needy. I do not say, of course, that *every* student who works his way must necessarily succumb to the fumes of the dollar; I merely say that he is enormously more apt to succumb than his brother of easier means. His attention is concentrated too constantly and painfully upon the question of getting a living, and that sort of attitude is obviously a bad one to bring into any of the arts or sciences. The artist and the scientist — and the physician, in a sense, is both — is a man who is presumed to be interested primarily in his work, not in its emoluments. He can do genuinely good work, indeed, only to the extent that he *is* so interested. The moment he begins habitually to engage in enterprises that offer him only profit he ceases to be either an artist or a scientist, and becomes a mere journeyman artisan.

True enough, a medical man who is intensely interested in his work, without regard to its material rewards — such a medical man often makes a great deal of money. If he has genuine ability, indeed, he almost invariably does so. But it is extremely difficult to put the cart before the horse. That is to say, it is extremely difficult to practise medicine primarily as a business, and at the same time keep up its dignity as an art and a science. The man who does so is on the wrong track. He is heading toward the chiropractors, not toward the Oslers.

The change that has come over medical education is relatively recent. With it has come a tremendous improvement in the equipment of the young medical man. In the old days he often entered college defectively prepared, and after struggling through found that he was barely started. Some men, of unusual resolution, kept up the struggle — getting a living, so to speak, with one hand and continuing their professional training with the other. But the majority succumbed to a few easy formulæ and got no further; the country was crowded with half-educated and incompetent doctors. Today there is a palpable improvement. The Class A medical schools, to be sure, cannot engage to turn out only first-rate men, but they can at least get rid of the hopeless incompetents — they can at least guarantee that no man will be launched upon the public unless he is decently equipped and of reasonable fitness for his work.

This will work a hardship upon the young man who cannot meet the new standards, and it will work a hardship scarcely less upon the young man who can meet them only by dint of herculean effort and sacrifice. But what these men lose the general public will gain, and surely that gain is not to be

sniffed at. Now and then, perhaps, a young man of great promise, well fitted naturally for medical work, will be kept out,
but for every such man a hundred utter incompetents will be
kept out. The bitter must go with the sweet. Eventually, no
doubt, there will be funds for the assistance of likely students
who can't pay their own way, as there are already funds for the
assistance of young men who aspire to the sacerdotal art and
mystery. Meanwhile, the study of medicine will tend to be restricted to the sons of well-to-do fathers. Well, why not? I see
no reason for believing that the sons of well-to-do fathers, taking one with another, are apt to be less fitted for it than the
sons of poor fathers: on the contrary, I am convinced that they
are apt to be far more fitted for it. In any case, we patients
have no reason to complain — and there are many more of us
than there are of medical students.

All the professions in America would be materially improved
in dignity and usefulness if they became more snobbish — that
is, if they were less accessible to novices from the sub-profes-
sional classes. There is no impediment in this grand and
puissant Republic to the rise of any family from the lowest
economic depths to the heights of learning, power and honor,
and no reflective man would have it otherwise; but nothing, I
submit, is accomplished by speeding the process unduly, or by
attempting to short-circuit it. A family ought to seek economic
security before it aspires higher; its first business should be to
get the means to pay its way. This is surely not a difficult enterprise, for it is accomplished every day by thousands of persons
of very modest capacities. We all hear so much about the millionaires that we overlook the much more numerous fellows,
obscure Babbitts, most of them, who succeed less gaudily but
every bit as surely — the hundreds of thousands of Americans
who accumulate enough to keep the wolf from the door and
to give their children good starts in life. The children of the
millionaires are often crushed beneath their money, and the
children of the poor are crippled and ruined by the lack of it.
But the children of the Babbitts have the world before them.
They can do whatever they want to do — and that freedom is
of immense value to them in whatever they undertake.

I believe that it would be a very good thing for the country if they monopolized the professions, as they do in almost all other countries. Frederick the Great, asked why he gave commissions in the Prussian army only to *Junker*, replied simply, "Because they will not lie and cannot be bought." A profound saying. The essence of a genuine professional man is that he cannot be bought. He is least apt to be bought, I believe, when his need of money is least exigent and desperate.

Personal Note

From the Baltimore *Evening Sun*, June 12, 1922

THE EASIEST job I have ever tackled in this world is that of making money. It is, in fact, almost as easy as losing it. Almost, but not quite.

XVII. PEDAGOGY

ᕫᘞᕫ

The Educational Process

From EDUCATION, PREJUDICES: THIRD SERIES, 1922, pp. 238–65.
First printed in the New York *Evening Mail*, Jan. 23, 1918

NEXT to the clerk in holy orders, the fellow with the foulest job in the world is the schoolmaster. Both are underpaid, both fall steadily in authority and dignity, and both wear out their hearts trying to perform the impossible. How much the world asks of them, and how little they can actually deliver! The clergyman's business is to save the human race from Hell. If he saves one-eighth of one per cent., even within the limits of his narrow flock, he does magnificently. The schoolmaster's is to spread the enlightenment, to make the great masses of the plain people think — and thinking is precisely the thing that the great masses of the plain people are congenitally and eternally incapable of.

Is it any wonder that the poor birchman, facing this labor that would have staggered Sisyphus, seeks refuge from its essential impossibility in a Chinese maze of empty technic? The ghost of Pestalozzi, once bearing a torch and beckoning toward the heights, now leads down dark stairways into the black and forbidding dungeons of Teachers College, Columbia. The art of pedagogics becomes a sort of puerile magic, a thing of preposterous secrets, a grotesque compound of false premises and illogical conclusions. Every year sees a craze for some new solution of the teaching enigma, an endless series of flamboyant arcana. The worst extravagances of *privat dozent* experimental psychology are gravely seized upon; the uplift pours in its ineffable principles and discoveries; mathematical formulæ are marked out for every emergency; there is no sure-cure so idiotic that some superintendent of schools will not swallow it. The aim seems to be to reduce the whole teaching process to a sort of automatic reaction, to discover some master formula that will not only take the place of competence and resourcefulness in the teacher but that will also create an artificial receptivity in the child. Teaching becomes a thing in itself, separable from and superior to the thing taught. Its mastery is a special business, a sort of transcendental high jumping. A teacher well grounded in it can teach anything to any child, just as a sound dentist can pull any tooth out of any jaw.

All this, I need not point out, is in sharp contrast to the old theory of teaching. By that theory mere technic was simplified and subordinated. All that it demanded of the teacher told off to teach, say, geography, was that he master the facts in the geography book and provide himself with a stout rattan. Thus equipped, he was ready for a test of his natural pedagogical genius. First he exposed the facts in the book, then he gilded them with whatever appearance of interest and importance he could conjure up, and then he tested the extent of their transference to the minds of his pupils. Those pupils who had ingested them got apples; those who had failed got fanned. Followed the second round, and the same test again, with a second noting of results. And then the third, and fourth, and the fifth, and so on until the last and least pupil had been stuffed to his subnormal and perhaps moronic brim.

I was myself grounded in the underlying delusions of what is called knowledge by this austere process, and despite the eloquence of those who support newer ideas, I lean heavily in favor of it, and regret to hear that it is no more. It was crude, it was rough, and it was often not a little cruel, but it at least had two capital advantages over all the systems that have succeeded it. In the first place, its machinery was simple; even the stupidest child could understand it; it hooked up cause and effect with the utmost clarity. And in the second place, it tested the teacher as and how he ought to be tested — that is, for his actual capacity to teach, not for his mere technical virtuosity. There was, in fact, no technic for him to master, and hence none for him to hide behind. He could not conceal a hopeless inability to impart knowledge beneath a correct professional method.

That ability to impart knowledge, it seems to me, has very

little to do with technical method. It may operate at full function without any technical method at all, and contrariwise, the most elaborate of technical methods cannot make it operate when it is not actually present. And what does it consist of? It consists, first, of a natural talent for dealing with children, for getting into their minds, for putting things in a way that they can comprehend. And it consists, secondly, of a deep belief in the interest and importance of the thing taught, a concern about it amounting to a kind of passion. A man who knows a subject thoroughly, a man so soaked in it that he eats it, sleeps it and dreams it — this man can almost always teach it with success, no matter how little he knows of technical pedagogy. That is because there is enthusiasm in him, and because enthusiasm is as contagious as fear or the barber's itch. An enthusiast is willing to go to any trouble to impart the glad news bubbling within. He thinks that it is important and valuable for to know; given the slightest glow of interest in a pupil to start with, he will fan that glow to a flame. No hollow hocus-pocus cripples him and slows him down. He drags his best pupils along as fast as they can go, and he is so full of the thing that he never tires of expounding its elements to the dullest.

This passion, so unordered and yet so potent, explains the capacity for teaching that one frequently observes in scientific men of high attainments in their specialties — for example, Huxley, Ostwald, Karl Ludwig, Jowett, William G. Sumner, Halsted and Osler — men who knew nothing whatever about the so-called science of pedagogy, and would have derided its alleged principles if they had heard them stated. It explains, too, the failure of the general run of high-school and college teachers — men who are competent, by the professional standards of pedagogy, but who nevertheless contrive only to make intolerable bores of the things they presume to teach. No intelligent student ever learns much from the average drover of undergraduates; what he actually carries away has come out of his textbooks, or is the fruit of his own reading and inquiry. But when he passes to the graduate school, and comes among men (if he is lucky) who really understand the subjects they teach, and, what is more, who really love them, his store of knowledge increases rapidly, and in a very short while, if he has any intelligence at all, he learns to think in terms of the thing he is studying.

So far, so good. But an objection still remains, the which may be couched in the following terms: that in the average college or high school, and especially in the elementary school, most of the subjects taught are so bald and uninspiring that it is difficult to imagine them arousing the passion I have been describing — in brief, that only a donkey could be enthusiastic about them. In witness, think of the four elementals: reading, penmanship, arithmetic and spelling. This objection, at first blush, seems dismaying, but only a brief inspection is needed to show that it is really of very small validity. It is made up of a false assumption and a false inference. The false assumption is that there are no donkeys in our schools and colleges today. The false inference is that there is any sound reason for prohibiting teaching by donkeys, if only the donkeys know how to do it, and to do it well. The facts stand in almost complete antithesis to these notions. The truth is that the average schoolmaster, on all the lower levels, is and always must be essentially and next door to an idiot, for how can one imagine an intelligent man engaging in so puerile an avocation? And the truth is that it is precisely his inherent idiocy, and not his technical equipment as a pedagogue, that is responsible for whatever modest success he now shows.

I here attempt no heavy jocosity, but mean exactly what I say. Consider, for example, penmanship. A legible handwriting, it must be obvious, is useful to all men, and particularly to the lower orders of men. It is one of the few things capable of acquirement in school that actually helps them to make a living. Well, how is it taught today? It is taught, in the main, by schoolmarms so enmeshed in a complex and unintelligible technic that, even supposing them able to write clearly themselves, they find it quite impossible to teach their pupils. Every few years sees a radical overhauling of the whole business. First the vertical hand is to make it easy; then certain curves are the favorite magic; then there is a return to slants and shadings. No department of pedagogy sees a more hideous cavorting of quacks. In none is the natural talent and enthusiasm of the teacher more depressingly crippled. And the result? The result is that our American school children write abominably — that a clerk or stenographer with a simple, legible hand becomes almost as scarce as one with Greek.

Go back, now, to the old days. Penmanship was then taught, not mechanically and ineffectively, by unsound and shifting formulæ, but by passionate penmen with curly patent-leather hair and far-away eyes — in brief, by the unforgettable professors of our youth, with their flourishes, their heavy downstrokes and their lovely birds-with-letters-in-their-bills. You remember them, of course. Asses all! Preposterous popinjays and numskulls! Pathetic imbeciles! But they loved penmanship, they believed in the glory and beauty of penmanship, they were fanatics, devotees, almost martyrs of penmanship — and so they got some touch of that passion into their pupils. Not enough, perhaps, to make more flourishers and bird-blazoners, but enough to make sound penmen. Look at your old writing book; observe the excellent legibility, the clear strokes of your "Time is money." Then look at your child's.

Such idiots, despite the rise of "scientific" pedagogy, have not died out in the world. I believe that our schools are full of them, both in pantaloons and in skirts. There are fanatics who love and venerate spelling as a tom-cat loves and venerates catnip. There are grammatomaniacs; schoolmarms who would rather parse than eat; specialists in an objective case that doesn't exist in English; strange beings, otherwise sane and even intelligent and comely, who suffer under a split infinitive as you or I would suffer under gastro-enteritis. There are geography cranks, able to bound Mesopotamia and Beluchistan. There are zealots for long division, experts in the multiplication table, lunatic worshipers of the binomial theorem. But the system has them in its grip. It combats their natural enthusiasm diligently and mercilessly. It tries to convert them into mere technicians, clumsy machines. It orders them to teach, not by the process of emotional osmosis which worked in the days gone by, but by formulæ that are as baffling to the pupil as they are paralyzing to the teacher. Imagine what would happen to one of them who stepped to the blackboard, seized a piece of chalk, and engrossed a bird that held the class spell-bound — a bird with a thousand flowing feathers, wings bursting with parabolas and epicycloids, and long ribbons streaming from its bill. Imagine the fate of one who began "Honesty is the best policy" with an H as florid and — to a child — as beautiful as the initial of a medieval manuscript. Such a teacher would be cashiered and handed over to the secular arm; the very enchantment of the assembled infantry would be held as damning proof against him. And yet it is just such teachers that we should try to discover and develop. Pedagogy needs their enthusiasm, their naïve belief in their own grotesque talents, their capacity for communicating their childish passion to the childish.

But this would mean exposing the children of the Republic to contact with monomaniacs, half-wits? Well, what of it? The vast majority of them are already exposed to contact with half-wits in their own homes; they are taught the word of God by half-wits on Sundays; they will grow up into Knights of Pythias, Odd Fellows, Red Men and other such half-wits in the days to come. Moreover, as I have hinted, they are already fact to face with half-wits in the actual schools, at least in three cases out of four. The problem before us is not to dispose of this fact, but to utilize it. We cannot hope to fill the schools with persons of high intelligence, for persons of high intelligence simply refuse to spend their lives teaching such banal things as spelling and arithmetic. Among the teachers male we may safely assume that 95% are of low mentality, else they would depart for more appetizing pastures. And even among the teachers female the best are inevitably weeded out by marriage, and only the worst (with a few romantic exceptions) survive.

The task before us, as I say, is not to make a vain denial of this cerebral inferiority of the pedagogue, nor to try to combat and disguise it by concocting a mass of technical balderdash, but to search out and put to use the value lying concealed in it. For even stupidity, it must be plain, has its uses in the world, and some of them are uses that intelligence cannot meet. One would not tell off a Galileo to drive an ash-cart or an Ignatius Loyola to be a stock-broker, or a Mozart to lead the orchestra in a night-club. By the same token, one would not ask a Duns Scotus to instruct sucklings. Such men would not only be wasted at the job; they would also be incompetent. The business of dealing with children, in fact, demands a certain jejunity of mind. The best teacher, until one comes to adult pupils, is not the one who knows most, but the one who is most capable of reducing knowledge to that simple compound of the obvious and the wonderful which slips into the infantile comprehension. A man of high intelligence, perhaps, may accomplish the thing by a conscious intellectual feat. But it is vastly easier to the man (or woman) whose habits of mind are naturally on the plane of a child's. The best teacher of children, in brief, is one who is essentially childlike.

If I had my way I should expose all candidates for berths in the grade-schools to the Binet-Simon test, and reject all those who revealed a mentality of more than fifteen years. Plenty would still pass. Moreover, they would be secure against contamination by the new technic of pedagogy. Its vast wave of pseudo-psychology would curl and break against the hard barrier of their innocent and passionate intellects — as it probably does, in fact, even now. They would know nothing of learning situations, integration, challenges, emphases, orthogenics, mind-sets, differentia, and all the other fabulous fowl of the Teachers College aviary. But they would see in reading, writing and arithmetic the gaudy charms of profound knowledge, and they would teach these ancient branches, now so abominably in decay, with passionate gusto, and irresistible effectiveness, and a gigantic success.

Travail

From the Baltimore *Evening Sun*, Oct. 8, 1928

IT always makes me melancholy to see the boys going to school. During the half hour before 9 o'clock they stagger through the square in front of my house in Baltimore with the despondent air of New Yorkers coming up from the ferries to work. It happens to be uphill, but I believe they'd lag as much if they were going down. Shakespeare, in fact, hints as much in the Seven Ages. In the afternoon, coming home, they leap and spring like gazelles. They are tired, but they are happy, and happiness in the young always takes the form of sharp and repeated contractions of the striped muscles, especially in the legs, arms and larynx.

The notion that schoolboys are generally content with their lot seems to me to be a sad delusion. They are, in the main, able to bear it, but they like it no more than a soldier enjoys life in a foxhole. The need to endure it makes actors of them; they learn how to lie — perhaps the most valuable thing, to a citizen of Christendom, that they learn in school. No boy genuinely loves and admires his teacher; the farthest he can go, assuming him to have all of his wits, is to tolerate her as he tolerates castor oil. She may be the loveliest flower in the whole pedagogical garden, but the most he can ever see in her is a jailer who might conceivably be worse.

School-days, I believe, are the unhappiest in the whole span of human existence. They are full of dull, unintelligible tasks, new and unpleasant ordinances, brutal violations of common sense and common decency. It doesn't take a reasonably bright boy long to discover that most of what is rammed into him is nonsense, and that no one really cares very much whether he learns it or not. His parents, unless they are infantile in mind, tend to be bored by his lessons and labors, and are unable to conceal the fact from his sharp eyes. His first teachers he views simply as disagreeable policemen. His later ones he usually sets down quite accurately as asses.

It is, indeed, one of the capital tragedies of youth — and youth is the time of real tragedy — that the young are thrown mainly with adults they do not quite respect. The average boy of my time, if he had had his free choice, would have put in his days with Amos Rusie or Jim Corbett; a bit later he would have chosen Roosevelt. But a boy sees such heroes only from afar. His actual companions, forced upon him by the inexorable decrees of a soulless and irrational state, are schoolma'ams, male and female, which is to say, persons of trivial and un-romantic achievement, and no more capable of inspiring emulation in a healthy boy than so many midwives or dog-catchers.

It is no wonder that schoolboys so often turn for stimulus from their teachers to their fellows. The fact, I believe, is largely to blame for the juvenile lawlessness that prevails in America, for it is the relatively daring and lawless boys who stand out from the mass, and so attract their weaker brethren. But whatever the consequences, the thing itself is quite natural, for a boy with superabundant energy flogging him yearns for experiment and adventure. What he gets out of his teachers is mainly the opposite. On the female side they have the instincts of duennas, and on the male side they seldom rise above the level of scout-masters and Y.M.C.A. secretaries. It would be hard enough for a grown man, with alcohol and cynicism aiding him, to endure such society. To a growing boy it is torture.

I believe that things were better in the days before maudlin harridans, searching the world for atrocities to put down, alarmed the school boards into abolishing corporal punishment. The notion that it was degrading to boys is silly. In the main, their public opinion indorsed it as both just and humane. I went to a school where rattanning was resorted to when needed. Its effects, I am convinced, were excellent. It preserved the self-respect of the teachers, and so tended to make the boys respect them. Given command, they actually exercised it. I never heard of a boy complaining, after the smarting in his gluteus maximus had passed off, that he had been used cruelly or unjustly. He sometimes bawled during the operation, but he was content afterward. The teachers in that school were not only respected by the boys, but more or less liked. The males among them seemed to be men, not milksops.

But even so, attendance upon their séances was a dull business far more often than it was exhilarating, and every boy in their classes began thinking of the closing bell the instant the opening bell clanged. Keeping up with the pace they set was cruel to the stupid boys, and holding back to it was even more cruel to the intelligent ones. The things that they regarded as important were not, as a rule, interesting to the boys, and the things that the boys liked they only too often appeared to regard as low. I incline to believe, looking backward, that the boys were right far oftener than they were wrong.

Today the old pedagogy has gone out, and a new and complicated science has taken its place. Unluckily, it is largely the confection of imbeciles, and so the unhappiness of the young continues. In the whole realm of human learning there is no faculty more fantastically incompetent than that of pedagogy. If you doubt it, go read the pedagogical journals. Better still, send for an armful of the theses that *Kandidaten* write and publish when they go up for their Ph.D.'s. Nothing worse is to be found in the literature of astrology, scientific salesmanship, or Christian Science. But the poor schoolma'ams, in order to get on in their trade, must make shift to study it, and even to master it. No wonder their dreams are of lawful domestic love, even with the curse of cooking thrown in.

The school-children of today are exposed to this cataract of puerility from the time they escape from the kindergarten until the time they escape into college or wage-slavery. Are their lives happy? Ask yourself if you would be happy if you had to listen six or seven hours a day to speeches by spiritualists and Seventh Day Adventists. It must be dreadful for a bright child to submit to such vivisection, and its discomforts are surely not ameliorated by the fact that the poor ma'am is suffering too. It is no longer sufficient that she love her art and practise it diligently. She must also sweat through Summer-school every year, damning her luck and boldly laying on more and more rouge. In the end her mind is a black abyss of graphs and formulæ, by bogus statistics out of snide psychology, and she is no more fit to teach than an adding machine.

There should be more sympathy for school-children. The idea that they are happy is of a piece with the idea that the lobster in the pot is happy. They are, in more ways than one, the worst and most pathetic victims of the complex of inanities and cruelties called civilization. The human race is so stupid that it has never managed to teach them its necessary tricks and delusions in a painless and pleasant manner. The cats and dogs do better by their young, and so, in fact, do savages. All that is taught to the end of grammar school could be imparted to an intelligent child, by genuinely scientific methods, in two years and without any cruelty worse than that involved in pulling a tooth. But now it takes nine years, and in a long series of laparotomies without anesthetics.

Is anything really valuable ever learned at school? I sometimes doubt it. Moreover, many wiser men doubt it, though they commonly make an exception of reading and writing. The ma'am, they say, can teach her customers to read and write: afterward, whatever they learn they pick up themselves. I go further. I believe that even in the matter of reading and writing children commonly teach themselves, or one another. The ma'am may show them how to learn, and make them want to do so, but she seldom actually teaches them. She is too busy making out reports, passing examinations, and trying to find out what the innumerable super-gogues who beset her desire her to do and say. She is as unhappy as her charges, and hates learning quite as bitterly.

I suggest hanging all the professors of pedagogy, arming the ma'am with a rattan, and turning her loose. Back to Bach! The new pedagogy has got so complicated that it often forgets the pupil altogether, just as the new medicine often forgets the patient. It is driving the poor ma'ams crazy, and converting the children into laboratory animals. I believe that the old sing-song system, with an occasional fanning of the posterior, was better. At all events, it was simpler. One could grasp it without graphs.

Classical Learning

From the New York *American*, January 20, 1936

A PALL of medievalism still hangs over the universities of the world, including even some of the universities of this great free Republic. The highest degree that the latter offer in course is still called the doctorate in philosophy, though philosophy itself is only a gaudy kind of logic-chopping, and hardly more valid as a science than astrology. And in most universities

Latin retains something of the academic respectability that it had in the year 1350. To be sure, all of the boys are not forced to master it, but those who do so are still thought to be more refined and scholarly than those who do not.

During the Middle Ages, when every educated man spoke it, Latin was esteemed for its everyday utility, and for no other reason. It was the *lingua franca* of Christendom, and no man could get around in the world who lacked it. But not a single soul, so far as I have been able to make out, ever ventured to argue that acquiring its complicated and irrational grammar was an elevating intellectual exercise, or that the literature written in it was better than any other literature. These imbecilities were invented after Latin had ceased to be useful, not while it was in use by all educated men. The medieval student had no illusions about it. He studied it because it enabled him to learn other things, not because he had any respect for it in itself. He regarded his struggles with it as a filthy chore, to be accomplished as quickly as possible, and he read its classical literature so little that most of the chief works thereof went out of print, so to speak, and were almost forgotten.

Their revival by pedagogues of later ages has proved only that the medieval student was right. In them, in fact, one finds precious little that is worth reading. The literatures of England, France and Germany have immensely more to offer in every department of thought, and even the literature of Spain, Italy and Russia offer quite as much. No rational man can go through the endless volumes of the Loeb Library without concluding that the Romans were an essentially dull and practical people, without much more fancy in them than a Congressman or a cow doctor. They had their high virtues, of course, but a lush and charming imagination was certainly not one. They were not poets, but policemen and lawyers.

The Boon of Culture

From the *American Mercury*, Sept., 1931, pp. 36–48

EVERY American college president, it appears, is in duty bound to write and utter at least one book upon the nature, aims and usufructs of the Higher Education. That responsibility lies upon him as heavily as the obligation to edit at least one edition of "The Deserted Village" lies upon every professor of English. As a rule, he puts it off to his later Autumn days, when the hemlock of senility has begun to dull the edge of his troubles, but he seldom dodges it altogether. I have on my shelves a long row of such books, and I have read all of them in a respectful and hopeful spirit, for I think I may call myself, without vanity, a fan of learned men. But I must add in all honesty that I have yet to find, in any such tome, anything properly describable as wisdom.

What afflicts all of them — or, at all events, all of them that I have collected and read — is the assumption that the chief if not the only end of education is education. This, in the United States, is very far from true. Only a small minority of boys and girls go to college for the purpose of stuffing their heads with knowledge, whether real or false; the majority go there simply because it has come to be the prudent thing to do. What they get out of it is mainly what they will get, later on, out of joining country clubs, Rotary, the Nobles of the Mystic Shrine, and other such fraternities — a feeling that they have somehow plunged into the main current of correct American thought, that they have emerged from the undifferentiated mass and gained admittance into an organized and privileged class, that they have ceased to be nobodies and come to be somebodies.

The impulse to make this grade is not to be confused with mere social pushing, which may go on (and usually does) on much lower levels. Nor is it to be confused, on the other hand, with genuine intellectual aspiration. The basic motive is probably a desire for security rather than a yearning for superiority. The virtue of a college degree is that it shuts off the asking of certain kinds of questions, some of them embarrassing. It is a certificate of safety, both to the holder and to the nation in general. A graduate is one who has been trained to act according to a pattern that is publicly considered to be normal and trustworthy. When he gets his diploma he makes a change, not in mere station, but in status. It lifts him over a definite fence, and maketh him to lie down in greener pastures.

Perhaps all of this should have been put into the past tense instead of the present. The general confidence in "education" has greatly multiplied the candidates for it, and this mutiplication has encouraged the proliferation of colleges. They spring up, in fact, in every third country town, and operating them becomes a kind of racket, carried on by all sorts of dubious persons, lay and clerical. They are even spattered over such barbaric States as Mississippi and North Dakota, where it would be dangerous to be educated in any real sense. The result is somewhat unhappy. The public belief that four years in college make a boy measurably more reliable, socially speaking, than he was before is still entertained, but it begins to be suspected that one college is not precisely like another. Thus there is a noticeable movement among the lesser ones to imitate, as closely as possible, the greater ones — first, by throwing off their theological obsessions (the real moving springs, in many cases, of their being), and secondly, by going in for gaudy Gothic buildings, and other such prodigalities.

But these gestures fool only the most naïve. Everyone who knows anything at all knows that a boy who has been through Harvard or Yale is apt to run far nearer to the American ideal than a boy who has been through, say, the Hardshell Baptist "University" of Smithville, Okla. He has been broken to an older, and hence to a better esteemed tradition, he has encountered more ornaments of it, and he has seen more impressive evidences of its value. No one knows this better than the graduate of the Hardshell seminary. It doesn't take him long to discover that what he sweated to attain was not quite attained, after all — that if he has escaped from the scullery he is not yet admitted to the first table in the hall. He is somewhat in the position of a conscript who went through all the pains of training, and then missed service at the front. Such a conscript is, of course, a war hero, but he is plainly a war hero of a lesser sort.

I suspect that a growing realization of all this is gradually filling the United States with inferiority complexes of a peculiarly malignant type. We are turning out thousands of college graduates who will have to go through life explaining and apologizing, which is precisely what college training among us is mainly designed to prevent. They have got the appearance without the essence. In fact, such one-legged collegians are already innumerable, for there have been bad colleges in the country since the earliest days. One cannot fail to observe their discomfort in the presence of graduates of the more tasty and reliable seminaries. They have, in many cases, far more actual education than the latter, but they lack the inner assurance; they are not so confident that sound American opinion respects and trusts them. Nor does it. It is a sad state of mind to be in.

If I had a son I should send him to Harvard, for more is to be had for the money there than anywhere else — more that is real, and will last. I don't think he'd learn more at Cambridge than he could learn at Siwash (given any desire to learn at all), but I believe a Harvard diploma would help him a great deal more in his later life, American ideas being what they are, whether God cast him for the rôle of metaphysician or for that of investment securities broker.

Bearers of the Torch

From the Baltimore *Evening Sun*, March 12, 1923

THE GREAT problems of human society are plainly too vexatious and difficult to be set before college undergraduates or pupils yet lower down the scale. The best that the teacher can hope to do, considering the short time at his disposal and the small attention that he can engage, is to fill his students with certain broad generalizations and conclusions. But precisely *what* generalizations and conclusions? Obviously, the safest are those that happen to be official at the moment, not only because they are most apt to slip into the minds of the pupils with least resistance, but also and more importantly because they are most apt to coincide with the prejudices, superstitions and ways of thought of the pedagogue himself, an ignorant and ninth-rate man.

In brief, the teaching process, as commonly observed, has nothing to do with the investigation and establishment of facts, assuming that actual facts may ever be determined. Its sole purpose is to cram the pupils, as rapidly and as painlessly as possible, with the largest conceivable outfit of current axioms, in all departments of human thought — to make the pupil a good citizen, which is to say, a citizen differing as little as possible, in positive knowledge and habits of mind, from all other citizens. In other words, it is the mission of the pedagogue, not to make his pupils think, but to make them think *right*, and the more nearly his own mind pulsates with the great ebbs and flows of popular delusion and emotion, the more admirably he performs his function. He may be an ass, but that is surely no demerit in a man paid to make asses of his customers.

This central aim of the teacher is often obscured by pedagogical pretension and bombast. The pedagogue, discussing himself, tries to make it appear that he is a sort of scientist. He is actually a sort of barber, and just as responsive to changing fashions. That this is his actual character is now, indeed, a part of the official doctrine that he must inculcate. On all hands, he is told plainly by his masters that his fundamental function in America is to manufacture an endless corps of sound Americans. A sound American is simply one who has put out of his mind all doubts and questionings, and who accepts instantly, and as incontrovertible gospel, the whole body of official doctrine of his day, whatever it may be and no matter how often it may change. The instant he challenges it, no matter how timorously and academically, he ceases by that much to be a loyal and creditable citizen of the Republic.

XVIII. PSYCHOLOGY

❦

Psychologists in a Fog

From the *American Mercury*, July, 1927, pp. 382–83. A review of Psychology: a simplification, by Loyd Ring Coleman and Saxe Commins: New York, 1927

THE SO-CALLED science of psychology is now in chaos, with no sign that order is soon to be restored. It is hard to find two of its professors who agree, and when the phenomenon is encountered it usually turns out that one of them is not a psychologist at all, but simply a teacher of psychology. Even the Freudians, whose barbaric raid first demoralized and scattered the placid experts of the old school, now quarrel among themselves. Worse, the same psychologist frequently turns upon and devours himself. The case of Dr. William McDougall, late of Harvard, comes to mind at once.[1] Every time he prints a new book, which is very frequently, he changes his list of instincts. Some of the others go much further: Dr. McDougall, indeed, is a conservative. These gay boys, at short intervals, throw overboard their whole baggage. There are psychologists in America who started out with the classical introspective psychology, abandoned two-thirds of it in order to embrace Freudism, then took headers into Behaviorism, and now incline toward the *Gestalt* revelation of Köhler and Koffka. Some say one thing and some another. It is hard for the layman to keep his head in this whirl. Not even anthropology offers a larger assortment of conflicting theories, or a more gaudy band of steaming and blood-sweating professors.

Nevertheless, certain general tendencies show themselves, and in the long run they may lay the foundation of a genuinely rational and scientific psychology. The chief of them is the tendency to examine the phenomena of the mind objectively, and

[1] McDougall left Harvard for Duke in 1927. He died in 1938.

with some approach to a scientific method. The old-time psychologist did not bother with such inquiries, some of which are very laborious. He simply locked himself in his study, pondered on the processes of his own pondering, and then wrote his book. If, as an aid to his speculations, he went to the length of mastering the elements of physiology, he regarded himself as very advanced, and was so regarded by his customers. Basically, he was a metaphysician, not a scientist. His concepts of the true were constantly mellowed and ameliorated by concepts of the what ought to be true. These old-time psychologists, like the metaphysicians, had a great gift for inventing terminology, and their masterpieces still harass the students in the more backward seminaries of learning. Most of them, again like the metaphysicians, believed that they had sufficiently described a thing when they had given it a name.

But the psychology of today is mainly experimental. Its professors do not attempt to account for the thought process by introspection, but by observation. Their learning is not on philosophy, but on physiology. So far, it must be confessed, they have failed to solve any of the fundamental problems of psychology — for example, the problem of consciousness — but they have swept away a great mass of futile speculation, and unearthed a large number of interesting, if often embarrassing facts. Here the Behaviorists, who are relatively recent comers in the field, have done some good work. Being psychologists, they are of course inclined to nonsense, and so one finds them plunging into doctrines that war upon common observation — for example, the doctrine that the qualities of the mind are never inherited, but spring wholly out of environmental causes —, but they have at least cleared off the old view of the mental machine as a mechanism working in a sort of vacuum, with no relation to the other organs of the body. These Behaviorists have proved, what should have been obvious long ago: that a man thinks with his liver as well as with his brain — in brief, that the organism is an actual organism, and not a mere congeries of discordant units. In their studies of children, in particular, they have got at some simple and useful facts, and so disposed of a formidable accumulation of idle speculations. But their formula is too simple to be wholly true, and they seem very likely to ruin it by trying to get more work out of it than it is capable of.

So with the Freudians. So with the *Gestalt* enthusiasts. So with the endocrine psychologists. So with all the rest. Why don't they get together as the pathologists, physiologists and other scientists get together, pool their facts, scrap their theories, and so lay the foundations of a rational psychology? Messrs. Coleman and Commins hint at the reason. No professional *kudos* is to be got by pooling facts. The one way to make a splash in psychology is to come out with a new and revolutionary theory. In other words, public opinion among psychologists is not yet genuinely enlightened. They paddle around in what ought to be a science, but they are not quite scientists. Some day, perhaps, they will make the grade, and so become brothers to the pathologists. But at this moment they are nearer the osteopaths.

The Mind of the Slave

From CONTRIBUTIONS TO THE STUDY OF VULGAR PSYCHOLOGY,
PREJUDICES: FOURTH SERIES, 1924, pp. 261–68

ONE of the forgotten divisions between men and men is that separating those who enjoy the work they have to do in the world and those who suffer it only as a necessary evil. The distinction, despite its neglect by psychologists, is probably very important — certainly far more important than the current divisions between producers and exploiters, dolichocephalic Nordic blonds and brachycephalic Mediterraneans, Darwinians and Christians, Republicans and Democrats, Protestants and Catholics. A man's politics, theology and other vices engage his attention, after all, only in his moments of leisure, and the shape of his cranium has very little demonstrable influence upon what habitually goes on within it, but the nature of the work he does in the world conditions every thought and impulse of his life, and his general attitude toward it is almost indistinguishable from his general attitude toward the cosmos.

At the one extreme lies the unmitigated slave — the man

who has to spend his whole life performing tasks that are incurably uninteresting, and that offer no soothing whatever to his vanity. At the other extreme is what Beethoven called the free artist — the man who makes a living, with no boss directly over him, doing things that he enjoys enormously, and that he would keep on doing gladly, even if all economic pressure upon him disappeared. To the second category belong all the happiest men in the world, and hence, perhaps, all the most useful men. For what is done with joy is always better done, whether it be fashioning a material object, thinking out a problem or kissing a girl; and the man who can make the rest of humanity pay him for being happy is obviously a better man than the general, or, at all odds, a luckier one. Here luck and superiority are one and the same. The fact that Joseph Conrad could write better than I was, in a sense, a matter of pure chance. He was born with his talent; he did not earn it. Nevertheless, it was just as real as if he had got it by Christian endeavor, and his superiority to me was thus perfectly genuine.

The slave is always conscious of his slavery, and makes constant and often desperate efforts to mitigate it or to get rid of it altogether. Sometimes he seeks that mitigation in outside activities that promise to give him the sense of dignity and importance that his daily labor denies him; sometimes he tries to give a false appearance of dignity to his work itself. The last phenomenon must be familiar to every American; it is responsible for various absurd devices to pump up lowly trades by giving them new and high-sounding names. I point, for example, to those of the real-estate agent and the undertaker. Neither trade, it must be obvious, offers any stimulation to men of genuine superiority. One could not imagine a Beethoven, a Lincoln or even a Coolidge getting any joy out of squeezing apartment-house tenants or pickling Odd Fellows. Both jobs, indeed, fail to satisfy the more imaginative sort of men among those compelled to practise them. Hence these men try to dignify them with hocus-pocus. The real-estate agent, seeking to conceal his real purpose in life, lets it be known grandly that he is an important semi-public functionary, that he has consecrated himself to Service and is a man of Vision — and to prove it he immerses himself in a private office with a secretary to insult his customers, joins Rotary, and begins to call himself a *realtor*, a word as idiotic as *flu, pep* or *gent*. The ambitious washer of the dead, until very lately a sort of pariah in all civilized societies, like the hangman and the dog-catcher, proceeds magnificently along the same route. At regular intervals I receive impressive literature from a trade-union of undertakers calling themselves the Selected Morticians. By this literature it appears that the members thereof are professional men of a rank and dignity comparable to judges or archbishops, and they are hot for the subtlest and most onerous kind of Service, and even eager to offer their advice to the national government. In brief, the realtor complex all over again. I do not laugh at these soaring embalmers; I merely point out that their nonsense proves how little the mere planting of martyred lodge brothers satisfies their interior urge to be important and distinguished — an urge that is in all of us.

But most of the trades pursued by slaves, of course, offer no such opportunities for self-deceptive flummery. The clerk working in the lime and cement warehouse of some remote town of the Foreign Missions Belt cannot conceivably convince himself that his profession is noble; worse, he cannot convince anyone else. And so with millions of other men in this great Republic, both urban and rural — millions of poor fellows doomed their life long to dull, stupid and tedious crafts — the lower sort of clerks, truck-drivers, farmers, petty officials, grabbers of odd jobs. They must be downright idiots to get any satisfaction out of their work. Happiness, the feeling that they too are somebody, the sense of being genuinely alive, must be sought in some other direction. In the big cities, that need is easily met. Here there is a vast and complex machinery for taking the slave's mind off his desolateness of spirit — movie cathedrals to transport him into a land of opulence and romance, where men (whom he always identifies with himself) are brave, rich and handsome, and women (whom he identifies with his wife — or perchance with her younger sister) are clean, well-dressed and beautiful; newspapers to delight and instruct him with their sports pages, their comic strips and their eloquent appeals to his liberality, public spirit and patriotism; radio to play the latest jazz for him; baseball, races, gambling, harlotry and games in arenas; a thousand devices to make him forget his woes. It is this colossal opportunity to escape from life that brings yokels swarming to the cities, not any mere lust for money. The yokel is actually far more comfortable on his native soil; the city crowds and exploits him, and nine times out of ten he remains desperately poor. But the city at least teaches him how to forget his poverty; it amuses him and thrills him while it is devouring him.

But millions of the slaves, of course, must remain in the small towns or on the land; the cities can't absorb all of them, nor even half of them. They thus confront the problem of making life bearable out of their own meagre resources. The devices that they adopt — political, religious and social — are familiar to all of us, and account fully, it seems to me, for some of the phenomena of American life that are most puzzling to foreign observers. The hoop-la revival with its psychopathological basis; the violent bitterness of rural politics; the prosperity of the clownish fraternal orders; the persistent popularity of barbarities of a dozen varieties — all these things are no more than manifestations of the poor hind's pathetic effort to raise himself out of his wallow, to justify and dignify his existence, to escape from the sordid realities that daily confront him. To snort and froth at a revival makes him conspicuous, prominent, a man of mark; it is therefore easy to induce him to do it. To hold a petty country office is eminence; hence he struggles for it frantically. To belong to the Red Men gives him a mysterious and sinister dignity, and fills him with a sense of power and consequence; he falls for it as quickly as a city intellectual falls for the *Légion d'honneur* or an LL.D. All these things make him forget, at least transiently, that he remains a miserable worm, and of little more actual importance on earth than his own hogs.

Long ago, I suggested that a good way to diminish lynching in the South would be to establish brass bands in all the country towns. The bad music, I argued, would engage and enchant both the blackamoors and the poor white trash, and so discourage the former from crime and the latter from seeking a savage satisfaction in its punishment. I now improve and embellish that suggestion. That is to say, I propose that the band scheme be shelved, and that bull-fighting be established as a substitute. Why not, indeed? Cattle have to be killed, and the Southern poor white is admittedly a savage. Why not combine the necessary slaughter of horned quadrupeds with a show that will give that savage a thrill and take his mind from his lowly lot, and turn him from seeking escape in politics, murder and voodoo? Bull-fights in the South would not only abolish lynchings; they would also undermine Fundamentalism. Life would be safer and happier in Georgia if the pure Anglo-Saxons down there could work off their steam by going weekly to a *plaza de toros,* and there see official *picadores, banderilleros,* and *matadors,* all of them good Democrats and baptized men, lynch and burn (or even merely geld) a reluctant and protesting male of *Bos taurus.*

The Crowd

From DAMN! A BOOK OF CALUMNY, 1918, pp. 45–47

GUSTAVE LE BON and his school, in their discussions of the psychology of crowds, put forward the doctrine that the individual man, cheek by jowl with the multitude, drops down an intellectual peg or two, and so tends to show the mental and emotional reactions of his inferiors. It is thus that they explain the well-known violence and imbecility of crowds. The crowd, as a crowd, performs acts that many of its members, as individuals, would never be guilty of. Its average intelligence is very low; it is inflammatory, vicious, idiotic, almost simian. Crowds, properly worked up by skillful demagogues, are ready to believe anything, and to do anything.

Le Bon, I daresay, is partly right, but also partly wrong. His theory is probably too flattering to the average numskull. He accounts for the extravagance of crowds on the assumption that the numskull, along with the superior man, is knocked out of his wits by suggestion — that he, too, does things in association that he would never think of doing singly. The fact may be accepted, but the reasoning raises a doubt. The numskull runs amok in a crowd, not because he has been inoculated with new rascality by the mysterious crowd influence, but because his habitual rascality now has its only chance to function safely. In other words, the numskull is vicious, but a poltroon. He refrains from all attempts at lynching *a cappella*, not because it takes suggestion to make him desire to lynch, but because it takes the protection of a crowd to make him brave enough to try it.

What happens when a crowd cuts loose is not quite what Le Bon and his followers describe. The few superior men in it are not straightway reduced to the level of the underlying stoneheads. On the contrary, they usually keep their heads, and often make efforts to combat the crowd action. But the stoneheads are too many for them; the fence is torn down or the blackamoor is burned. And why? Not because the stoneheads, normally virtuous, are suddenly criminally insane. Nay, but because they are suddenly conscious of the power lying in their numbers — because they suddenly realize that their natural viciousness and insanity may be safely permitted to function. In other words, the particular swinishness of a crowd is permanently resident in the majority of its members — in all those members, that is, who are naturally ignorant and vicious — say 90%. All studies of mob psychology are defective in that they underestimate this viciousness. The lower orders of men are actually incurable rascals, either individually or collectively. Decency, self-restraint, the sense of justice, courage — these virtues belong to a small minority of men. This minority seldom runs amok. Its most distinguishing character, in truth, is its resistance to all running amok. The third-rate man, though he may wear the false whiskers of a first-rate man, may always be detected by his inability to keep his head in the face of an appeal to his emotions. A whoop strips off his disguise.

The Art Eternal

From CONTRIBUTIONS TO THE STUDY OF VULGAR PSYCHOLOGY,
PREJUDICES: FOURTH SERIES, 1924, pp. 269–77.
First printed in the New York *Evening Mail*, July 5, 1918

ONE of the laudable by-products of the Freudian quackery is the discovery that lying, in most cases, is involuntary and inevitable — that the liar can no more avoid it than he can avoid blinking his eyes when a light flashes or jumping when a bomb goes off behind him. At its worst, indeed, this necessity takes on a downright pathological character, and is thus as innocent as sciatica. It is part of the morbid baggage of hysterics and neurasthenics: their lying is simply a symptom of their convulsive effort to adjust themselves to an environment which bears upon them too harshly for endurance. The rest of us are not quite so hard pushed, but pushed we all are. In us the thing works through the inferiority complex, which no man can escape. He who lacks it entirely is actually reckoned insane by the fact: his satisfaction with his situation in the world is indistinguishable from a delusion of grandeur. The great majority of us — all, in brief, who are normal — pass through life in constant revolt against our limitations, objective and subjective. Our conscious thought is largely devoted to plans and specifications for cutting a better figure in human society, and in our unconscious the business goes on much more steadily and powerfully. No healthy man, in his secret heart, is content with his destiny. He is tortured by dreams and images as a child is tortured by the thought of a state of existence in which it would live in a candy-store and have two stomachs.

Lying is the product of the unconscious yearning to realize such visions, and if the policeman, conscience, prevents the lie being put into plain words, then it is at least put into more or less plausible acts. We all play parts when we face our fellowmen, as even poets have noticed. No man could bring himself to reveal his true character, and, above all, his true limitations as a citizen and a Christian, his true meannesses, his true imbecilities, to his friends, or even to his wife. Honest autobiography is therefore a contradiction in terms: the moment a man considers himself, even *in petto*, he tries to gild and fresco himself. Thus a man's wife, however realistic her view of him, always flatters him in the end, for the worst she sees in him is appreciably better, by the time she sees it, than what is actually there. What she sees, even at times of the most appalling domestic revelation and confidence, is not the authentic man at all, but a compound made up in part of the authentic man and in part of his projection of a gaudy ideal. The man who is most respected by his wife is the one who makes this projection most vivid — that is, the one who is the most daring and ingratiating liar. He can never, of course, deceive her utterly, but if he is skillful he may at least deceive her enough to make her happy.

Omnis homo mendax: thus the Psalmist. So far the Freudians merely parrot him. What is new in their gospel is the doctrine that lying is instinctive, normal, and unavoidable — that a man is forced into it by his very will-to-live. This doctrine purges the business of certain ancient embarrassments, and restores innocence to the heart. Think of a lie as a compulsion neurose, and you think of it more kindly. I need not add, I hope, that this transfer of it from the department of free will to that of determinism by no means disposes of the penalty that traditionally pursues it, supposing it to be detected and resented. The proponents of free will always make the mistake of assuming that the determinists are simply evil fellows looking for a way to escape the just consequences of their transgressing. No sense is in that assumption. If I lie on the witness-stand and am detected by the judge, I am jailed for perjury forthwith, regardless of my helplessness under compulsion. Here justice refuses absolutely to distinguish between a misfortune and a tort: the overt act is all it is concerned with. But as jurisprudence grows more intelligent and more civilized it may change its tune, to the benefit of liars, which is to say, to the benefit of humanity. Science is unflinchingly deterministic, and it has begun to force its determinism into morals. On some shining tomorrow a psychoanalyst may be put into the box to prove that perjury is simply a compulsion neurose, like beating time with the foot at a concert or counting the lampposts along the highway.

However, I have but small faith in millenniums, and do not formally predict this one. Nor do I pronounce any moral judgment, pro or con: moral judgments, as old Friedrich used to say, are foreign to my nature. But let us not forget that lying, *per se*, is not forbidden by the moral code of Christendom. Holy Writ dismisses it cynically, and the statutes of all civilized states are silent about it. Only the Chinese, indeed, make it a penal offense. Perjury, of course, is prohibited everywhere, and also any mendacity which amounts to fraud and deprives a fellow-man of his property. But that far more common form of truth-stretching which has only the lesser aim of augmenting the liar's personal dignity and consequence is looked upon with a very charitable eye. So is that form which has the aim of helping another person in the same way. In the latter direction lying may even take on the stature of a positive virtue. The late King Edward VII, when Prince of Wales, attained to great popularity throughout Christendom by venturing into downright perjury. Summoned into a court of law to give expert testimony regarding some act of adultery, he lied like a gentleman, as the phrase goes, to protect a woman. The lie, to be sure, was intrinsically useless; no one believed that the lady was innocent. Nevertheless, every decent Christian applauded the perjurer for his good intentions, including even the judge on the bench, sworn to combat false witness by every resource of forensics. All of us, worms that we are, occasionally face the alternatives that confronted Edward. On the one hand, we may tell the truth, regardless of consequences, and on the other hand we may mellow it and sophisticate it to make it humane and tolerable.

For the habitual truth-teller and truth-seeker, indeed, the world has very little liking. He is always unpopular, and not infrequently his unpopularity is so excessive that it endangers his life. Run your eye back over the list of martyrs, lay and clerical: nine-tenths of them, you will find, stood accused of nothing worse than honest efforts to find out and announce the truth. Even today, with the scientific passion become familiar in the world, the general view of such fellows is highly unfavorable. The typical scientist, the typical critic of institutions, the typical truth-seeker in every field is held under suspicion by the great majority of men, and variously beset by posses of relentless foes. If he tries to find out the truth about arteriosclerosis, or surgical shock, or cancer, he is denounced as a scoundrel by the Christian Scientists, the osteopaths and the anti-vivisectionists. If he tries to tell the truth about the government, its agents seek to silence him and punish him. If he turns to fiction and endeavors to depict his fellow-men accurately, he has the Comstocks on his hands. In no field can he count upon a friendly audience, and freedom from assault. Especially in the United States is his whole enterprise viewed with bilious eye. The men the American people admire most extravagantly are the most daring liars; the men they detest most violently are those who try to tell them the truth. A Galileo could no more be elected President of the United States than he could be elected Pope of Rome. Both high posts are reserved for men favored by God with an extraordinary genius for swathing the bitter facts of life in bandages of soft illusion.

XIX. SCIENCE

❧❦❧

Hypothesis

From the Baltimore *Evening Sun*, April 6, 1931

IN the sciences hypothesis always precedes law, which is to say, there is always a lot of tall guessing before a new fact is established. The guessers are often quite as important as the fact-finders; in truth, it would not be difficult to argue that they are more important. New facts are seldom plucked from the clear sky; they have to be approached and smelled out by a process of trial and error, in which bold and shrewd guessing is an integral part. The Greeks were adepts at such guessing, and the scientists of the world have been following the leads they opened for more than two thousand years. Unluckily, the supply of Greek guesses is now running out, and so science begins to show a lack of imagination. What is needed is a new supply of guessers. Mathematical physics has produced a pretty good one in the person of Dr. Einstein, but some of the other sciences seem to have none, and suffer badly from that lack — for example, physiology. It has been piling up facts for more than a century past, but the meaning of most of them remains occult. If it could develop a Class A guesser he would soon be one of its magnificoes, and of a rank comparable to that of Du Bois-Reymond, Johannes Müller, Lavoisier, Malpighi or Harvey.

Darwin

From the same, April 6, 1931

THE TROUBLE with human progress is that it tends to go too fast — that is, too fast for the great majority of comfortable

329

and incurious men. Its agents are always in a hurry, and so become unpopular. If Darwin had printed "The Origin of Species" as a serial running twenty or thirty years he might have found himself, at the end of it, a member of the House of Lords or even Archbishop of Canterbury. But he disgorged it in one stupendous and appalling dose, and in consequence he alarmed millions, including many of his fellow scientists, and got an evil name. To this day, though all of the soundest (and thus most revolutionary) of his ideas have become platitudes, he continues to be thought of much as Simon Legree, Thomas Paine and John Wilkes Booth are thought of. To name a new public-school after him would cause almost as grave a scandal as to name it after Lillian Russell. In at least two-thirds of the American States one of the easiest ways to get into public office is to denounce him as a scoundrel. But by the year 2030, I daresay, what remains of his doctrine, if anything, will be accepted as complacently as the Copernican cosmography is now accepted. His offense was simply that he was too precipitate.

Caveat Against Science

From the *American Mercury*, Sept., 1927, pp. 126–27.
A review of SCIENCE: THE FALSE MESSIAH, by C. E. Ayres;
Indianapolis, 1927

MR. AYRES, formerly a member of the staff of the *New Republic*, has served his time as a professor of philosophy, and, like any other metaphysician in a machine age, is full of vague fevers and shooting pains. In the present volume he endeavors gallantly to reduce them to a series of theses, with supporting syllogisms, but though he enjoys the gift of utterance and is, in fact, extraordinarily articulate for a philosopher, his argument remains, nevertheless, somewhat inchoate. What I gather from it chiefly is the sad thought that science, after all, cannot teach us how to live. It accumulates immense pyramids of facts, but the facts turn out, on examination, to be meaningless. What if the astronomers discover that the temperature at the core of a certain star is 750,000 degrees Centigrade? What if the electron reveals itself as a speck of vacuum performing a witless and eternal dance? What if epinephrin is synthesized, and even Gordon gin? What if a distinguished movie actor is found to be a perfect specimen of *Eoanthropus dawsoni?* What if someone proves that a straight line is no longer the shortest distance between two points? All the really important human problems remain unsolved. Nothing in any of the triumphs of science will help a man to determine whether, having $50 to invest, he will do better to put it in the missionary box or buy some worthy girl a set of necking tools. Mr. Ayres, it appears, long ago gave up any hope of light from the purely physical sciences: chemistry, physics, pathology, physiology, zoölogy, chiropractic, golf, etc. But psychology still lured him, and he began to investigate it — just in time to see the behaviorists turn Man into a teetotum, not unlike the electron. There remained anthropology, but now even anthropology runs to graphs and tables of statistics, laws and more laws, all impersonal, all devoid of metaphysical content, all extremely mortifying to a philosopher.

Mr. Ayres seems to have a fear that the end is not yet — that science, having turned its back upon the moral order of the world, will one day return to put it down, maybe by force — that is, that we are facing scientific tyranny almost as bad as the old theological tyranny or the current political tyranny. "When science has become supreme," he says, in the last sentence of his book, "any attempt to rectify its formulæ will be persecuted as heresy." But here, I believe, he is simply judging science in terms of the crimes of philosophy. There is not the slightest sign that science, in itself, has any such malign ambition. Its aim is simply to establish the facts. It has no more interest in the moral significance of those facts than it has in the moral significance of a streptococcus. It must be amoral by its very nature: the minute it begins separating facts into the two categories of good ones and bad ones it ceases to be science and becomes a mere nuisance, like theology. Nevertheless, there is a certain uncomfortable reason in Mr. Ayres's fears. Science itself will never send him to the stake, but the quacks who hang about its flanks may one day try to do so.

Such quacks are already numerous, and they tend to disguise themselves as scientists, and to be accepted by the world in that character. I point, for example, to the so-called hygienists, and especially to those who are also public jobholders. Theoretically and by their own representation, these singularly cocksure men are scientists; actually they are simply moralists, and of the same lineage as Prohibition agents. The body of exact facts lying under their pretensions is of very modest dimensions, and so far as I am aware not one of those facts was unearthed by their own efforts. They are to pathology as astrologers are to astronomy. It is certainly by no mere coincidence that they are the only claimants to scientific authority in the whole modern world who make any demand that the police enforce their decrees.

But there is no reason why Mr. Ayres should permit these hygienists to alarm him. Their present high puissance is not due to the fact that science is running amok, but to the fact that science is still impotent. If it had the authority that he sees in his unpleasant visions, and the moral fervor that he seems to think must go therewith, it would be hanging hygienists today. But I don't believe that it would actually hang them, even if it had the power. To science, a hygienist is simply a natural phenomenon, like a philosopher or a Congressman; all three stand upon an equal footing in its sight. Their moral passion is no more to be put down by force than is a bishop's passion to cultivate the rich; it is simply something to be studied calmly, as the habits of the crayfish are studied. Is that study sterile? Of course it is — to the sort of man to whom it is sterile. That sort of man is not content with facts; he also craves advice. It is the business of philosophers to give him that advice. Functioning as theologians, as publicists, as metaphysicians and what not, they have been doing so for five or six thousand years. No doubt it has done him a lot of good.

But there are also men who do not crave such advice. Those are the men to whom science is a reality. They believe that there is something intrinsically agreeable about learning something not hitherto known. They get the same stimulation out of widening their knowledge that the customer of the theologians and metaphysicians gets out of being instructed in his duties toward God, the Armenians, his brother-in-law, and the memory of Woodrow Wilson. It is a form of effort that is relatively new in the world, and hence it is not mentioned in the sacred books. No known church teaches that a man could get into Heaven by discovering the hypothetical element lying between molybdenum and ruthenium, or by determining the exact value of π. More, no man could hope to be elected President for doing it, or even to membership in the Elks, or the American Academy of Arts and Letters, or the Actors' Equity. Nevertheless, as I say, there are men who are interested in such achievements, and esteem their fruits. They constitute a very small minority of the human race. They alone are concerned with science, or have any understanding of its peculiar values. It is as impossible to imagine them engaging in the tyranny that Mr. Ayres fears as it is to imagine the rest of mankind comprehending their attitude — or escaping tyranny at other hands.

The Eternal Conundrum

From the *American Mercury*, Feb., 1931, pp. 252–54.
A review of The Mysterious Universe, by Sir James Jeans;
New York, 1930

WHEN I was a boy it was commonly taught that all astronomers, soon or late, went crazy. In this theory there was probably no truth, but it was based nevertheless on a sound observation, to wit, that the astronomers of that day, more than any other men of science, ran to daring speculations about the nature and goal of the universe, and the purpose behind it. Their successors still do so, and it is no wonder, for their business brings them far closer than any other scientists ever come to the fundamental mysteries of creation.

Contrast that business, for example, with the daily work of a biologist. The phenomena that a biologist has to do with nearly all lie within narrow limits of space and time, and the questions that he asks himself about them are almost always answerable in ways consonant with everyday experience. When he has explained this one in terms of surface tension, that one in terms of osmosis, and a third one in terms of Mendel's law, he has pretty well satisfied his professional curiosity, and that of his customers. All the materials of his trade are to be found in his own small corner of the visible universe, and the actions and reactions that he observes going on among them all seem perfectly logical, and follow natural laws that are not hard to comprehend.

Even life itself, considered biologically, is not very mysterious. No biologist, so far, has ever set it going in inert matter, but there is nothing in its apparent nature, as revealed by investigation and experiment, which forbids the hope of setting it going at some time hereafter. Thus biologists seldom give any time to speculating about the ultimate constitution of matter, or about the origin of the universe, or about the motives, if any, behind the natural laws that they observe and record. Most of them care little for such exercises, and it is rare to find one who shows any leaning toward mystical ways of thought. They are, as a class, a hard-headed and matter-of-fact lot. When one chances to be born with a mystical taint, he usually forsakes biology at the first opportunity, and, like Alfred Russel Wallace, William James and Hans Driesch, gives himself over to frank metaphysics.

With astronomers, and with physicists in general, the case is different. They are constantly colliding with questions which take them beyond the superficial flow of phenomena and into the realm of ultimates. They do a great deal of their work, not on the safe ground where knowledge is abundant and may be arranged in orderly systems, but on the borderline between the known and the unknowable, where every equation is bound to have a couple of x's in it. Proceeding, say, from the molecule, of which a lot may be learned, to the atom, of which less may be learned, and then to the electron, of which still less may be learned, they presently find themselves confronting shapes and forces of which nothing, it would seem, can be learned. If they were all ideal scientific men they would sit down at this place, and wait patiently for further light. But having gone so far into the unknown, they pant to go further, and it is thus common

for them, in the absence of objective facts, to resort to subjective speculations.

If they are thorough materialists, as sometimes happens, they
entertain us with pictures of an infinite, irrational and intrinsically incomprehensible universe, running without motive power
but otherwise not unlike an immense internal-combustion engine. But if there is any trace of the common Christian heritage
in them — and, alas, there often is — they begin to speculate
about the nature of the motive power, and soon they are con-
juring up a will behind it, and inflicting one more God upon
a sweating and distracted world. That God, as usual, follows
the pattern of themselves. Dr. Robert A. Millikan's is an elderly
Unitarian born in Morrison, Ill., who took his Ph.D. at Columbia in 1895, got the Nobel Prize in 1923, and is a member of
the Valley Hunt Club of Pasadena, Calif. Dr. A. S. Eddington's is a Quaker imperfectly denaturized at Cambridge and
now a don there. By the same token, Sir James Jeans's is a
mathematician.

This Jeans God shows rather more plausibility than the
others, and is much more refined. He lacks both the hearty,
beefy bucolicity of Millikan's Middle Western Corn-God and
the sickly chlorosis of Eddington's gaseous Quaker. He neither
belches nor swoons. His tastes and habits of mind, as described by His creator, correspond very aptly with the way the
universe seems to be run. If a human mathematician ran it, it
would be, in fact, pretty much what it is now. In particular,
positing a mathematical God disposes neatly of certain difficulties that have long badgered physicists. This is no place to
describe them in detail: suffice it to say that they involve a
number of apparent irregularities in the flow of phenomena —
a number of unaccountable variations in what has been regarded as natural law. Sometimes, it appears, electrons do not
jump according to a regular system, but irregularly, like grasshoppers in a meadow. Again, light does not move in a straight
line, but along some sort of curve. Yet again, time has a vari-
able value, according to the place and the observer. Such aberrations are hard to fit into a strictly mechanical universe, but
they slip very smoothly into one operated on a mathematical
plan, for mathematics, as everyone knows, does not confine it-

self to immutable phenomena, but also takes an interest in the wavering and fickle kind. A whole, and very important branch of the science is devoted to mere probabilities, and there are others, much used by statisticians, which try to get a certain rough order into downright chaos. It is Sir James's idea that many of the apparently unruly and intractable phenomena which now puzzle physicists (and especially astronomers) may be brought to something approaching coherence by thinking of them in mathematical terms. So he suggests that the whole universe may be no more than a prodigious exercise in some sort of calculus, and that God may be, not the engineer that many scientists have hitherto imagined, but a mathematician.

It is a charming conceit, and Sir James develops it with great skill and address. He is one of the most competent writers on physics now extant, with a really extraordinary gift for making the most difficult of scientific concepts understandable. Even the Einstein speculations about space and time, in his hands, take on a kind of clarity. Nevertheless, I can only report that, in the present case, he leaves at least one very friendly reader quite unconvinced. The "loose-jointedness" that he discovers in the universe by no means "destroys the case for absolutely strict causation." All it really brings us to is an uneasy realization that our present stock of knowledge is far from complete. Not only are there plain gaps in it; there are also parts of it that are obviously dubious. I believe that fully four-fifths of what cocksure physicists now tell us about the nature and behavior of electrons will be laughed at on some near tomorrow, and that most of the phenomena which now seem to be lawless and hence inexplicable will be reduced to law and order at the same time. All we really know is that we do not yet know what this law is. Physicists, as a class, are far too eager to make mysteries. Facing the dark, they are always seeing things. If chemists were similarly given to fanciful and mystical guessing, they would have hatched a quantum theory forty years ago to account for the variations that they observed in atomic weights. But they kept on plugging away in their laboratories without calling in either mathematicians or theologians to aid them, and eventually they discovered the isotopes, and what had been chaos was reduced to the most exact sort of order.

The same thing, no doubt, will happen in the domain of physics, once the physicists forget that they were once baptized, and begin to apply themselves honestly to the problems of their business. They have, in late years, made a great deal of progress, though it has been accompanied by a considerable quackery. Some of the notions which they now try to foist upon the world, especially in the astronomical realm and about the atom, are obviously nonsensical, and will soon go the way of all unsupported speculations. But there is nothing intrinsically insoluble about the problems they mainly struggle with, and soon or late really competent physicists will arise to solve them. These really competent physicists, I predict, will be too busy in their laboratories to give any time to either metaphysics or theology. Both are eternal enemies of every variety of sound thinking, and no man can monkey with them without losing something of his good judgment.

The Universe

From the *Smart Set*, Oct., 1922, pp. 142–44

ASTRONOMERS, it seems to me, dispose in too cavalier a manner of the notion (so often revived in the Hearst Sunday newspapers) that there may be life on planets other than the earth, and even on certain stars. Uranus and Neptune, they say, are too hot; Mercury is too hot on one side and too cold on the other (what of the regions where the two climates meet?); Venus suffers from the same defect; Mars lacks air and water; Jupiter is covered with a cloud of steam; so is Saturn; as for the moon, it has no air. But all these objections simply beg the question, for the most they prove (and in the case of Mars and Venus there is doubt even here) is that the planets of the solar system cannot support the sort of life that the earth supports — to wit, life based upon unstable compounds of carbon, hydrogen, oxygen and nitrogen. Is there any reason for believing that no other sort of life is possible? If so, then I have never heard of it. To me, at least, with my facile fancy, it is quite easy to imagine living forms composed, not of carbon, hydrogen, oxygen and nitrogen, but of platinum, tantalum, rhodium and tungsten, none of which melts at less than 3,000 degrees Fahrenheit. I go even further: I can imagine living beings whose bodies are not solid, but liquid — as, in fact, ours are, all save a small part. Or even gaseous. If the Lord God Almighty, by combining carbon and the three gases, can make an Ambassador at the Court of St. James's, I see absolutely no reason why he cannot make a monad of helium and fluorine. Here I, too, make a gratuitous supposition: I speak of a monad, *i.e.*, of a definite cell. But why should life be the exclusive function of cells? Isn't it possible to imagine living beings without definite form? The whole interstellar space, in fact, may be full of them, and their cavortings may be the cause of some of the phenomena observed by Dr. Einstein. There may be sun-worms that flourish as contentedly in the terrific temperature of the sun as a *Bierfisch* flourishes in a keg of Löwenbräu. There may be supermen on Neptune and Uranus with skulls of fire-brick and bowels of asbestos. It is neither probable nor improbable: we simply do not know. But it is certainly not impossible.

Even without abandoning the carbon concept of living matter we may easily conceive of life on Mercury, Venus, Mars, Jupiter and Saturn, to say nothing of the moon. If Jupiter and Saturn are surrounded by clouds of visible steam, then they cannot be quite as hot as certain astronomers assume, for visible steam is steam that is hovering about a temperature of 212 degrees Fahrenheit: above that it becomes as transparent as air. There are plenty of low organisms, even on the earth, that are able to survive a bath of live steam for a considerable time; on Jupiter and Saturn they may be able to survive it long enough to grow up, love, marry, beget and decay. As for the absence of air and water on Mars and the moon, it is a deficiency of very small importance. If the Martians need hydrogen and oxygen, as we do, they may get both out of the solid crust of their planet — as we'd probably try to do if all the rivers ran dry and the air began to grow too thin for us. Many low organisms exist without free oxygen, and there are probably some that get along with little, if any, hydrogen. The extreme cold of some of the planets — running down, perhaps, to absolute zero, or minus 273 degrees Centigrade — offers an obstacle of even less importance. It is very probable that there exist on earth today a number of primitive forms of life that could survive this temperature: a Scotsman could do it if whiskey did not freeze at minus 130. Thus I incline to suspect that some of the planets may swarm with life, just as the earth does, and that it is just as useless and obscene as it is here. The theory that the earth is improved by its fauna — to such a degree, indeed, that it is the special care and concern of Divinity — is one that I find myself unable to subscribe to. The most charming spots on earth, in fact, are precisely those in which living creatures, whether insects or men, are rarest.

The Boons of Civilization

From the *American Mercury*, Jan., 1931, pp. 33–35

"What we call progress," said Havelock Ellis, "is the exchange of one nuisance for another nuisance." The thought is so obvious that it must occur now and then even to the secretary of the Greater Zenith Booster League. There may be persons who actually enjoy the sound of the telephone bell, but if they exist I can only say that I have never met them. It is highly probable that the telephone, as it stands today, represents more sheer brain power than any other familiar invention. A truly immense ingenuity has gone into perfecting it, and it is as far beyond its progenitor of 1880 as a battleship is beyond Fulton's *Clermont*. But all the while no one has ever thought of improving the tone of its bell. The sound remains intolerably harsh and shrill, even when efforts are made to damp it. With very little trouble it might be made deep, sonorous and even soothing. But the telephone engineers let it remain as it was at the start, and millions of people suffer under its assault at every hour of the day.

The telephone, I believe, is the greatest boon to bores ever invented. It has set their ancient art upon a new level of efficiency and enabled them to penetrate the last strongholds of privacy. All the devices that have been put into service against them have failed. I point, for example, to that of having a private telephone number, not listed in the book. Obviously, there is nothing here to daunt bores of authentic gifts. Obtaining private telephone numbers is of the elemental essence of their craft. Thus the poor victim of their professional passion is beset quite as much as if he had his telephone number limned upon the sky in smoke. But meanwhile his friends forget it at critical moments and he misses much pleasant gossip and many an opportunity for vinous relaxation.

It is not only hard to imagine a world without telephones; it becomes downright impossible. They have become as necessary to the human race, at least in the United States, as window glass, newspapers or aspirin. Every now and then one hears of a man who has moved to some remote village to get rid of them, and there proposes to meditate and invite his soul in the manner of the Greek philosophers, but almost always it turns out that his meditations run in the direction of Rosicrucianism, the Single Tax, farm relief, or some other such insanity. I have myself ordered my telephone taken out at least a dozen times, but every time I found urgent use for it before the man arrived, and so had to meet him with excuses and a drink. A telephone bigwig tells me that such orders come in at the rate of scores a day, but that none has ever been executed. I now have two telephones in my house, and am about to put in a third. In the years to come, no doubt, there will be one in every room, as in hotels.

Despite all this, I remain opposed to the telephone theoretically, and continue to damn it. It is a great invention and of vast value to the human race, but I believe it has done me, personally, almost as much harm as good. How often a single call has blown up my whole evening's work, and so exacerbated my spirit and diminished my income! I am old enough to remember when telephones were very rare, and romantic enough to believe that I was happier then. But at worst I get more out of them than I get out of any of the other current wonders: for example, the radio, the phonograph, the movie, and the automobile. I am perhaps the first American ever to give up automobiling, formally and honestly. I sold my car so long ago as

1919, and have never regretted it. When I must move about in a city too large for comfortable walking I employ a taxicab, which is cheaper, safer and far less trouble than a private car. When I travel further I resort to the Pullman, by long odds the best conveyance yet invented by man. The radio, I admit, has potentialities, but they will remain in abeyance so long as the air is laden and debauched by jazz, idiotic harangues by frauds who do not know what they are talking about, and the horrible garglings of ninth-rate singers. The phonograph is just as bad, and the movie is ten times worse.

Of all the great inventions of modern times the one that has given me most comfort and joy is one that is seldom heard of, to wit, the thermostat. I was amazed, some time ago, to hear that it was invented at least a generation ago. I first heard of it during the War of 1914–18, when some kind friend suggested that I throw out the coal furnace that was making steam in my house and put in a gas furnace. Naturally enough, I hesitated, for the human mind is so constituted. But the day I finally succumbed must remain ever memorable in my annals, for it saw me move at one leap from an inferno into a sort of paradise. Everyone will recall how bad the coal was in those heroic days. The patriotic anthracite men loaded their culm-piles on cars, and sold them to householders all over the East. Not a furnace-man was in practise in my neighborhood: all of them were working in the shipyards at $15 a day. So I had to shovel coal myself, and not only shovel coal, but sift ashes. It was a truly dreadful experience. Worse, my house was always either too hot or too cold. When a few pieces of actual coal appeared in the mass of slate the temperature leaped up to 85 degrees, but most of the time it was between 45 and 50.

The thermostat changed all that, and in an instant. I simply set it at 68 degrees, and then went about my business. Whenever the temperature in the house went up to 70 it automatically turned off the gas under the furnace in the cellar, and there was an immediate return to 68. And if the mercury, keeping on, dropped to 66, then the gas went on again, and the temperature was soon 68 once more. I began to feel like a man liberated from the death-house. I was never too hot or too cold. I had no coal to heave, no ashes to sift. My house became so clean that I could wear a shirt five days. I began to feel like work, and rapidly turned out a series of imperishable contributions to the national letters. My temper improved so vastly that my family began to suspect senile changes. Moreover, my cellar became as clean as the rest of the house, and as roomy as a barn. I enlarged my wine-room by 1000 cubic metres. I put in a cedar closet big enough to hold my whole wardrobe. I added a vault for papers, a carpenter shop, and a praying chamber.

For all these boons and usufructs I was indebted to the inventor of the thermostat, a simple device but incomparable. I'd print his name here, but unfortunately I forget it. He was one of the great benefactors of humanity. I wouldn't swap him for a dozen Marconis, a regiment of Bells, or a whole army corps of Edisons. Edison's life-work, like his garrulous and nonsensical talk, has been mainly a curse to humanity: he has greatly augmented its stock of damned nuisances. But the man who devised the thermostat, at all events in my private opinion, was a hero comparable to Shakespeare, Michelangelo or Beethoven.

XX. QUACKERY

Christian Science

From the Baltimore *Evening Sun*, Feb. 28, 1927

IN more than one American State, I gather, a Christian Science practitioner is forbidden to accept fees from the faithful. That is, he may not accept fees as fees. If a grateful patient, cured of cancer or hydrophobia by his sorcery, tips him $5 or $10, it is apparently all right, but if he sends in a bill he may be jailed for it. What could be more idiotic? Either the citizen of this great Republic is a free man or he is not a free man. If he is, then he has a plain right, when he is ill, to consult any medicine man he fancies, and quite as plain a right to pay that medicine man for his services — openly, without impediment, and according to a scale satisfactory to him. If that right be taken away, then one of his essential liberties is taken away — and the moment a Christian Scientist begins to lose an essential liberty, then all the rest of us begin to lose ours.

The fact that a certain section of medical opinion supports the existing laws is surely no argument for their justice and reasonableness. A certain section of medical opinion, in late years, has succumbed to the messianic delusion. Its spokesmen are not content to deal with the patients who come to them for advice; they conceive it to be their duty to force their advice upon everyone, including especially those who don't want it. That duty is purely imaginary. It is born of vanity, not of public spirit. The impulse behind it is not altruism, but a mere yearning to run things. A physician, however learned, has no more right to intrude his advice upon persons who prefer the advice of a Christian Scientist, a chiropractor or a pow-wow doctor than he has to intrude it upon persons who prefer the advice of some other physician.

Here, I hope, I shall not be suspected of inclining toward the

343

Eddyan buncombe. It seems to me to be pure balderdash. I believe that the services a Christian Science practitioner offers to his customers are no more valuable than the service a foot-wash evangelist offers to a herd of country jakes. But the right to freedom obviously involves the right to be foolish. If what I say must be passed on for its sagacity by censors, however wise and prudent, then I have no free speech. And if what I may believe — about gall-stones, the Constitution, castor-oil, or God — is conditioned by law, then I am not a free man.

It is constantly argued by the proponents of legislation against quacks that it is necessary for the public safety — that if it is not put upon the books, the land will be ravaged by plagues, and that the death-rate will greatly increase, to the immense damage of the nation. But in all this there are a great many more assumptions than facts, and even more false inferences than assumptions. What reason is there for believing that a high death-rate, in itself, is undesirable? To my knowledge none whatever. The plain fact is that, if it be suitably selective, it is extremely salubrious. Suppose it could be so arranged that it ran to 100% a year among politicians, executive secretaries, drive chairmen, and the homicidally insane? What rational man would object?

I believe that the quack healing cults set up a selection that is almost as benign and laudable. They attract, in the main, two classes: first, persons who are incurably ill, and hence beyond the reach of scientific medicine, and second, persons of congenitally defective reasoning powers. They slaughter these unfortunates by the thousand — even more swiftly and surely than scientific medicine (say, as practised by the average neighborhood doctor) could slaughter them. Does anyone seriously contend that this butchery is anti-social? It seems to me to be quite the reverse. The race is improved as its misfits and half-wits are knocked off. And life is thereby made safer and cheaper for the rest of us.

The section of medical opinion that I have mentioned stands against these obvious facts. It contends that the botched and incompetent should be kept alive against their will, and in the face of their violent protests. To what end? To the end, first, that the rest of us may go on carrying them on our backs. To the end, second, that they may multiply gloriously, and so burden our children and grandchildren. But to the end, mainly, that hordes of medical busybodies, unequal to the strain of practise, may be kept in comfort.

Every now and then one of these busybodies, discovering that some imbecile woman is having her child treated for a fractured skull or appendicitis by a Christian Scientist, fills the newspapers with clamor and tries to rush the poor woman to jail. A great sobbing ensues: it appears at once that it is the duty of the government (*i.e.*, of certain jobholders) to rescue children from the follies of their parents. Is that duty real? If so, then let us extend it a bit. If it arises when a foolish mother tries to cure her child of diabetes by calling in a healer to read nonsense out of "Science and Health," then doesn't it arise equally when another foolish mother feeds her darling indigestible victuals? And if bad food is sufficient reason to summon the *Polizei*, then what of bad ideas?

The truth is that the inhumanity of Christian Science mothers is grossly exaggerated. They are, in the main, exactly like other mothers. So long as little Otto is able to yell they try home remedies — whether castor oil or Christian Science is all one. But when it becomes plain that he is seriously ill, they send for the doctor — and the ensuing hocus-pocus is surely not to be laid at their doors. What is the actual death-rate among the offspring of Christian Scientists? If it can be proved to be more than 5% above the death-rate among the infant patrons of free clinics I shall be glad to enter a monastery and renounce the world.

As a lifelong patriot and fan for human progress I should rejoice if it were five times what it is. Is it desirable to preserve the lives of children whose parents read and take seriously such dreadful bilge as is in "Science and Health"? If so, then it is also desirable to cherish the children of parents who believe that a horse-hair put into a bottle of water will turn into a snake. Such strains are manifestly dysgenic. Their persistence unchecked would quickly bring the whole human race down to an average IQ of 10 or 15. Being intelligent would become a criminal offense everywhere, as it already is in Mississippi and Tennessee. Thus a genuinely enlightened State would endow

Christian Science and chiropractic on eugenic principles, as our great universities already endow football. Failing that, it is the plain duty of statesmanship to let nature take its course.

Chiropractic

From DIVES INTO QUACKERY, PREJUDICES: SIXTH SERIES, 1927, pp. 217–27.
First printed in part in the Baltimore *Evening Sun*, Dec. 8, 1924, and in part in the Chicago *Tribune*, Feb. 13, 1927

THIS preposterous quackery flourishes lushly in the back reaches of the Republic, and begins to conquer the less civilized folk of the big cities. As the old-time family doctor dies out in the country towns, with no competent successor willing to take over his dismal business, he is followed by some hearty blacksmith or ice-wagon driver, turned into a chiropractor in six months, often by correspondence. In Los Angeles the Damned there are probably more chiropractors than actual physicians, and they are far more generally esteemed. Proceeding from the Ambassador Hotel to the heart of the town, along Wilshire boulevard, one passes scores of their gaudy signs; there are even many chiropractic "hospitals." The morons who pour in from the prairies and deserts, most of them ailing, patronize these "hospitals" copiously, and give to the chiropractic pathology the same high respect that they accord to the theology of the town sorcerers. That pathology is grounded upon the doctrine that all human ills are caused by the pressure of misplaced vertebræ upon the nerves which come out of the spinal cord — in other words, that every disease is the result of a pinch. This, plainly enough, is buncombe. The chiropractic therapeutics rest upon the doctrine that the way to get rid of such pinches is to climb upon a table and submit to a heroic pummeling by a retired piano-mover. This, obviously, is buncombe doubly damned.

Both doctrines were launched upon the world by an old quack named Andrew T. Still, the father of osteopathy. For years the osteopaths merchanted them, and made money at the trade. But as they grew opulent they grew ambitious, *i.e.*, they began to study anatomy and physiology. The result was a gradual abandonment of Papa Still's ideas. The high-toned osteopath of today is a sort of eclectic. He tries anything that promises to work, from tonsillectomy to the x-rays. With four years' training behind him, he probably knows more anatomy than the average graduate of the Johns Hopkins Medical School, or at all events, more osteology. Thus enlightened, he seldom has much to say about pinched nerves in the back. But as he abandoned the Still revelation it was seized by the chiropractors, led by another quack, one Palmer. This Palmer grabbed the pinched nerve nonsense and began teaching it to ambitious farm-hands and out-at-elbow Baptist preachers in a few easy lessons. Today the backwoods swarm with chiropractors, and in most States they have been able to exert enough pressure on the rural politicians to get themselves licensed.[1] Any lout with strong hands and arms is perfectly equipped to become a chiropractor. No education beyond the elements is necessary. The takings are often high, and so the profession has attracted thousands of recruits — retired baseball players, work-weary plumbers, truck-drivers, longshoremen, bogus dentists, dubious preachers, cashiered school superintendents. Now and then a quack of some other school — say homeopathy — plunges into it. Hundreds of promising students come from the intellectual ranks of hospital orderlies.

Such quackeries suck in the botched, and help them on to bliss eternal. When these botched fall into the hands of competent medical men they are very likely to be patched up and turned loose upon the world, to beget their kind. But massaged along the backbone to cure their lues, they quickly pass into the last stages, and so their pathogenic heritage perishes with them. What is too often forgotten is that nature obviously intends the botched to die, and that every interference with that benign process is full of dangers. That the labors of quacks tend to propagate epidemics and so menace the lives of all of us, as is alleged by their medical opponents — this I doubt. The fact

---

[1] It is not altogether a matter of pressure. Large numbers of rustic legislators are themselves believers in chiropractic. So are many members of Congress.

is that most infectious diseases of any seriousness throw out such alarming symptoms and so quickly that no sane chiropractor is likely to monkey with them. Seeing his patient breaking out in pustules, or choking, or falling into a stupor, he takes to the woods at once, and leaves the business to the nearest medical man. His trade is mainly with ambulant patients; they must come to his studio for treatment. Most of them have lingering diseases; they tour all the neighborhood doctors before they reach him. His treatment, being nonsensical, is in accord with the divine plan. It is seldom, perhaps, that he actually kills a patient, but at all events he keeps many a worthy soul from getting well.

The osteopaths, I fear, are finding this new competition serious and unpleasant. As I have said, it was their Hippocrates, the late Dr. Still, who invented all of the thrusts, lunges, yanks, hooks and bounces that the lowly chiropractors now employ with such vast effect, and for years the osteopaths had a monopoly of them. But when they began to grow scientific and ambitious their course of training was lengthened until it took in all sorts of tricks and dodges borrowed from the regular doctors, or resurrection men, including the plucking of tonsils, adenoids and appendices, the use of the stomach-pump, and even some of the legerdemain of psychiatry. They now harry their students furiously, and turn them out ready for anything from growing hair on a bald head to frying a patient with the x-rays. All this new striving, of course, quickly brought its inevitable penalties. The osteopathic graduate, having sweated so long, was no longer willing to take a case of delirium tremens for $2, and in consequence he lost patients. Worse, very few aspirants could make the long grade. The essence of osteopathy itself could be grasped by any lively farm-hand or night watchman in a few weeks, but the borrowed magic baffled him. Confronted by the phenomenon of gastrulation, or by the curious behavior of heart muscle, or by any of the current theories of immunity, he commonly took refuge, like his brother of the orthodox faculty, in a gulp of laboratory alcohol, or fled the premises altogether. Thus he was lost to osteopathic science, and the chiropractors took him in; nay, they welcomed him. He was their meat. Borrowing that primitive part of osteopathy which was comprehensible to the meanest understanding, they threw the rest overboard, at the same time denouncing it as a sorcery invented by the Medical Trust. Thus they gathered in the garage mechanics, ash-men and decayed welter-weights, and the land began to fill with their graduates. Now there is a chiropractor at every cross-roads.

I repeat that it eases and soothes me to see them so prosperous, for they counteract the evil work of the so-called science of public hygiene, which now seeks to make imbeciles immortal. If a man, being ill of a pus appendix, resorts to a shaved and fumigated longshoreman to have it disposed of, and submits willingly to a treatment involving balancing him on McBurney's spot and playing on his vertebræ as on a concertina, then I am willing, for one, to believe that he is badly wanted in Heaven. And if that same man, having achieved lawfully a lovely babe, hires a blacksmith to cure its diphtheria by pulling its neck, then I do not resist the divine will that there shall be one less radio fan later on. In such matters, I am convinced, the laws of nature are far better guides than the fiats and machinations of medical busybodies. If the latter gentlemen had their way, death, save at the hands of hangmen, policemen and other such legalized assassins, would be abolished altogether, and the present differential in favor of the enlightened would disappear. I can't convince myself that that would work any good to the world. On the contrary, it seems to me that the current coddling of the half-witted should be stopped before it goes too far — if, indeed, it has not gone too far already. To that end nothing operates more cheaply and effectively than the prosperity of quacks. Every time a bottle of cancer oil goes through the mails *Homo americanus* is improved to that extent. And every time a chiropractor spits on his hands and proceeds to treat a gastric ulcer by stretching the backbone the same high end is achieved.

But chiropractic, of course, is not perfect. It has superb potentialities, but only too often they are not converted into concrete cadavers. The hygienists rescue many of its foreordained customers, and, turning them over to agents of the Medical Trust, maintained at the public expense, get them cured. Moreover, chiropractic itself is not certainly fatal: even an Iowan with diabetes may survive its embraces. Yet worse, I have a suspicion that it sometimes actually cures. For all I know (or any orthodox pathologist seems to know) it *may* be true that certain malaises are caused by the pressure of vagrom vertebræ upon the spinal nerves. And it *may* be true that a hearty ex-boilermaker, by a vigorous yanking and kneading, may be able to relieve that pressure. What is needed is a scientific inquiry into the matter, under rigid test conditions, by a committee of men learned in the architecture and plumbing of the body, and of a high and incorruptible sagacity. Let a thousand patients be selected, let a gang of selected chiropractors examine their backbones and determine what is the matter with them, and then let these diagnoses be checked up by the exact methods of scientific medicine. Then let the same chiropractors essay to cure the patients whose maladies have been determined. My guess is that the chiropractors' errors in diagnosis will run to at least 95% and that their failures in treatment will push 99%. But I am willing to be convinced.

Where is such a committee to be found? I undertake to nominate it at ten minutes' notice. The land swarms with men competent in anatomy and pathology, and yet not engaged as doctors. There are thousands of hospitals, with endless clinical material. I offer to supply the committee with cigars and music during the test. I offer, further, to supply both the committee and the chiropractors with sound wet goods. I offer, finally, to give a bawdy banquet to the whole Medical Trust at the conclusion of the proceedings.[2]

[2] This offer was made in 1927. There were no takers. After World War II the jobholders at Washington, many of them patrons of chiropractic themselves, decided that any veteran who longed to study the science was eligible to receive assistance under the G.I. Bill of Rights. Thus a multitude of fly-by-night chiropractic schools sprang up, and their students were ranked, officially, precisely on all fours with those who studied at Harvard.

The Fruits of Comstockery

From FOUR MORAL CAUSES, PREJUDICES: FIFTH SERIES, 1926, pp. 15–16.
Comstock was born in 1844 and died in 1915

IN 1873, when the late Anthony Comstock began his great Christian work, the American flapper, or, as she was then called, the young lady, read *Godey's Ladies' Book*. Today she reads — but if you want to find out what she reads simply take a look at the fiction magazines which rise mountain-high from every news-stand. It is an amusing and at the same time highly instructive commentary upon the effectiveness of moral legislation. The net result of long years of Comstockery is complete and ignominious failure. All its gaudy raids and alarms have simply gone for naught.

In Comstock's heyday "Three Weeks" was still regarded as a very salacious book. The wives of Babbitts read it in the kitchen, with the blinds down; it was hidden under every pillow in every finishing school in the land. Today "Three Weeks" would be dismissed as intolerably banal by school girls of thirteen. I began reviewing current American fiction in 1908. The change that I note since then is immense. When I started out a new novel dealing frankly with the physiology and pathology of sex was still something of a novelty. It was, indeed, so rare that I always called attention to it. Today it is a commonplace. The surprise now comes when a new novel turns out to be chemically pure. Try to imagine an American publisher, in these days, getting alarmed about Dreiser's "Sister Carrie" and suppressing it before publication. The oldest and most dignified houses would print it without question; they print far worse every day. Yet in 1900 it seemed so lewd and lascivious that the publisher who put it into type got into a panic of fright, and hid the whole edition in the cellar. Today that same publisher is advertising an edition of Walt Whitman's "Leaves of Grass," with "A Woman Waits for Me" printed in full.

Comstock was a Puritan of the old school, and had no belief whatever in virtue *per se*. A good woman, to him, was simply one who was efficiently policed. Unfortunately for him, there rose up, within the bounds of his own sect, a school of uplifters, to wit, the sex hygienists, who began to merchant quite contrary ideas. They believed that sin was often caused by ignorance — that many a virtuous girl was undone simply because she didn't know what her young man was doing. These uplifters held that unchastity was not the product of a congenital tendency to it in the female, but of the sinister enterprise of the male, flowing out of his superior knowledge and sophistication. So they set out to spread the enlightenment. If all girls of sixteen, they argued not unplausibly, knew as much about the dreadful consequences of sin as the average police lieutenant or midwife, there would be no more seductions, and in accordance with that theory, they began printing books describing the discomforts of parturition and the terminal symptoms of lues. These books they broadcast in numerous and immense editions. Comstock, of course, was bitterly against the scheme. He had no faith in the solemn warnings; he saw only the new and startling frankness, and he believed firmly that its one effect would be to "arouse a libidinous passion . . . in the mind of a modest woman." But he lost the battle, and, with it, the war. After the young had read the sex hygiene books they began to observe that what was set out in novels was very evasive, and that much of it was downright untrue. So they began to murmur, to snicker, to boo. One by one the old-time novelists went on the shelf. I could make up a long and melancholy roll of them. Their sales dropped off; they began to be laughed at. In place of them rose a new school, and its aim was to Tell All. With this new school Comstock and his heirs have been wrestling ever since, and with steadily increasing bad fortune. Every year they make raids, perform in the newspapers and predict the end of the world, but every year the average is worse than the worst of the year before.

As a book-worm I have got so used to lewd and lascivious books that I no longer notice them. They pour in from all directions. The most virtuous lady novelists write things that would have made a bartender blush to death two decades ago. If I open a new novel and find nothing about copulation in it, I suspect at once that it is simply a reprint of some forgotten novel of 1885, with a new name. When I began reviewing I used to send my review copies, after I had sweated through them, to the Y.M.C.A. By 1920 I was sending all discarded novels to a medical college.

The Foundations of Quackery

From the Baltimore *Evening Sun*, June 4, 1923

No democratic delusion is more fatuous than that which holds that all men are capable of reason, and hence susceptible to conversion by evidence. If religions depended upon evidence for their prolongation, then all of them would collapse. It is not only that the actual evidence they offer is extremely dubious; it is mainly that the great majority of the men they seek to reach are quite incapable of comprehending any evidence, good or bad. They must get at such men through their feelings or resign getting at them altogether.

So in all other regions of the so-called mind. I have often pointed out how politics, under democracy, invariably translates itself from the domain of logical ideas to the domain of mere feelings, usually simple fear — how every great campaign in American history, however decorously it started with a statement of principles, has always ended with a violent pursuit of hobgoblins. The great majority of the half-wits who followed William Jennings Bryan in his three Presidential battles were certainly not attracted to him by his complex and nonsensical economic doctrines; those doctrines, in fact, dealt with such unfamiliar and difficult concepts that not one in ten thousand of the loudest Bryanites could understand them at all. What attracted them was not Bryan's economics but his adroit demonology; an evangelist by divine inspiration, he invented demons that palsied them and took their breath, and so they stormed after him.

The number of men eligible to membership in such mobs is always underestimated. That is to say, the number of men capable of anything properly describable as logical reasoning is always put too high. Worse, the great progress of all the exact sciences in our own time tends to diminish it constantly. There was a time, and it was much less than a century ago, when any man of sound sense and fair education could understand all of the concepts commonly employed in the physical sciences, and even most of those used in the speculative sciences. In medicine, for example, there was nothing beyond the comprehension of the average intelligent layman. But of late that has ceased to be true, to the great damage of the popular respect for knowledge. Only too often, when a physician of today tries to explain to his patient what is the matter with him, he finds it impossible to get the explanation into terms within the patient's understanding. The latter, if he is intelligent enough, will face the fact of his lack of training without rancor, and content himself with whatever parts of the exposition he can grasp. But that sort of intelligence, unluckily, is rather rare in the world; it is confined, indeed, to men of the sort who are said to have the scientific mind, *i.e.*, a very small minority of men. The average man, finding himself getting beyond his depth, instantly concludes that what lies beyond is simply nonsense.

It is this fact which accounts for the great current prosperity of such quackeries as osteopathy, chiropractic and Christian Science. The agents of such quackeries gain their converts by the simple process of reducing the inordinately complex to the absurdly simple. Unless a man is already equipped with a considerable knowledge of chemistry, bacteriology and physiology, no one can ever hope to make him understand what is meant by the term anaphylaxis, but any man, if only he be idiot enough, can grasp the whole theory of chiropractic in twenty minutes. The fact that such imbeciles prosper increasingly in the world, and gain adherents in constantly superior circles — that is, among persons of more and more apparent education and culture — is no more than proof that the physical sciences are becoming increasingly recondite and difficult, and that the relative numbers of persons congenitally incapable of comprehending them is growing year by year.

Hooey from the Orient

From the *American Mercury*, Nov., 1931, pp. 379–80.
A review of The Mysterious Madame, by C. E. Bechofer Roberts;
New York, 1931

THE LIKENESS of Helena Petrovna Blavatsky (1831–91), *geb.* Kahn, founder and for sixteen years grand panjandrum of the Theosophical Society, to Mrs. Mary Baker G. Eddy must strike every connoisseur of the higher mountebankery. Both emerged from obscure and stupid family circles, both invented romantic biographies for themselves, both played heavily with love before giving it up as a bad job, both began their professional careers as conventional magicians and only gradually developed their own arcana, both were copious and shameless plagiarists, both suffered from life-long malaises, both were constantly beset by demons, both loved money and knew how to get it, both suspected their immediate followers of evil designs, and both have been purged *post mortem* of their plentiful blunders and rascalities, and elevated to what amounts substantially to sainthood.

La Eddy, on the whole, must be set down as the more respectable character. Her three marriages are hard to explain, and her stealings from Quimby and other such forerunners defy explanation altogether, but her New England upbringing saved her from the more gross and overt kinds of indecorum. La Blavatsky, a Russian of mixed Slavic, Jewish, and German ancestry, was a far rougher person. She smoked incessantly in a day when it was simply not done by ladies, she swore like a second mate, and there is sound reason for believing that she once committed bigamy. But these peccadilloes add to her charm almost as much as they take away from her respectability. She was, indeed, a most salty and amusing old harridan.

Also, she was a fraud pure and unadulterated — a fraud deliberate, unconscionable and unmitigated. She started out in life as a professional spiritualist, and the banal tricks of that amusing trade were always her chief reliances. She materialized the forms of Koot Hoomi and her other preposterous mahatmas

precisely as the hard-working mediums in back streets materialize the forms of Wah-Wah the Indian chief. That is to say, she
had them confected of stuffed pillows and other such lowly
stuff, and then danced them before her dupes in dark rooms.
She had a cabinet with a sliding door in the back, and from it
she produced letters from Tibet (all written in her own hand,
with curious Russified letters) and other such marvels. Her
books were all clumsy plagiarisms. In "Isis Unveiled" a diligent
critic discovered 2000 passages borrowed from other treatises
on occultism, not to mention 700 blunders "in names, words
and numbers" and 600 "mis-statements of fact." She was caught
over and over again. Her very assistants exposed her more than
once, with exact specifications. But she relied confidently upon
the illimitable credulity of her followers, and was not disappointed. Like the patrons of Mrs. Eddy, they were insatiable
gluttons for punishment. The more she was exposed, the more
firmly they believed in her.

Thousands of them continue to do so to this day. Theosophy
has never made the worldly success of Christian Science, but it
still has a ponderable following, both in Europe and in America, and every now and then the faithful are worked by some
new operator. Its tenets are unanimously nonsensical. They are
not merely dubious; they are downright insane. In part they are
borrowed from the mooney speculations of such European
mystics as Jakob Böhme, in part they come from the common
claptrap of professional occultists (which is to say, of persons
on a level, morally and intellectually, with mind-readers at
county fairs), and in part they are a stale and ignorant rehash
of so-called oriental philosophy. This oriental philosophy is the
product of Hindus who believe that cows have souls, that adepts
can fly through the air without the use of wings or gasoline,
and that a man who permits his daughter to go unmarried so
much as twenty-four hours beyond the onset of puberty is
doomed to Hell. In brief, it is the product of degraded ignoramuses who make India a sewer of superstition.

How does it come that such imbecilities win converts in the
West, and are even spoken of respectfully, now and then, by
presumably learned men? There are two reasons. The first is
that they are embodied in scriptures which also include a great

deal of metaphysics — and metaphysics, to certain types of mind, always seems profound, even when it is palpably balderdash. The other is that not a few of the more ancient Indian ideas, working their way westward by way of Persia, Egypt and Greece, were embedded in Christianity by the Early Fathers, and have thus come to have a familiar and pious flavor. But they are just as silly in the Book of Revelation and in the lucubrations of Athanasius, Tertullian and Augustine as they are in the Indian Vedas. To discuss them seriously is to turn one's back upon every intellectual decency. They are precisely equivalent to the philosophizing of phrenologists, chiropractors and Communists.

One Blavatsky tells far more about the human race than a whole herd of psychologists. Her works offer massive proof that, even in the midst of what seems to be civilization, Neanderthal Man is still with us.

The Executive Secretary

From Prejudices: Sixth Series, 1927, pp. 266–72

Some time ago, encountering a bishop of my acquaintance on a train, I found him suffering from a bad cold and what used to be called a fit of the vapors. The cause of his dual disorder soon became manifest. He was smarting under the slings and arrows of executive secretaries. By virtue of his transcendental office, he was naturally a man of wide influence in the land, and so they tried to enlist his interest in their multitudinous and often nefarious schemes. Every morning at 8 o'clock, just as he was rolling over for a last brief dream of Heaven, he was dragged to the telephone to hear their night-letters, and there, on unlucky days, he stood for as much as half an hour, with his episcopal feet bare, and rage gradually mounting in his episcopal heart. Thus, on a cold morning, he had caught his cold, and thus he had acquired his bad humor.

This holy man, normally a most amiable fellow, told me that he believed the number of executive secretaries in the United

States was increasing at the rate of at least a thousand a week. He said that he knew of 30,000 in the field of Christian and moral endeavor alone. He estimated that the average number of dues-paying members behind each one did not run much beyond half a dozen. Nine-tenths of them, he said, were supported by two or three well-heeled fanatics. These fanatics, mainly retired Babbitts and their wives, longed to make a noise in the world, and so escape oblivion. It was the essence of the executive secretary's art and mystery to show them how to do it. Chiefly it was done by discovering bugaboos and giving chase to them. But secondarily it was done by hauling poor ecclesiastics out of bed on frosty mornings, and making them listen to endless night-letters about the woes of the Jews, the need of intensive missionary effort in Siam, the plot of Moscow to set up soviets in Lowell, Mass., and the absolute necessity of deeper waterways from the Lakes to the Atlantic.

The executive secretary is relatively new in the world. Like his colleague in well-paid good works, the Y.M.C.A. secretary, he has come into being since the Civil War. Compared to him, his predecessor of ante-bellum days was an amateur and an idiot. That predecessor had no comfortable office in a gaudy skyscraper, he got no lavish salary, and he had no juicy expense-account. On the contrary, he paid his own way, and, especially when he worked for Abolition, which was usually, he sometimes had to take a beating into the bargain. The executive secretary of today is something else again. He belongs to the order of live wires. He speaks the language of up-and-coming men, and is not sparing with it at the sessions of Rotary and Kiwanis. Not uncommonly a shady and unsuccessful newspaper reporter or a press-agent out of a job, he quickly becomes, by virtue of his craft, a Man of Vision. The cause that he represents for cash in hand is not merely virtuous; it is, nine times out of ten, divinely inspired. If it fails, then civilization will also fail.

It is a good job that he has — far better than legging it on the street for some gorilla of a city editor — far, far better than traversing the sticks ahead of a No. 4 company. There is no need to get up at 7 a.m. and there is no need to fume and strain after getting up. Once three or four — or maybe even only one or two — easy marks with sound bank accounts have been snared, the new "national" — or perhaps it is "international" — association is on its legs, and all that remains is to have brilliant stationery printed, put in a sightly stenographer, and begin deluging bishops, editors and the gullible generally with literature. The executive secretary, if he has any literary passion in him, may prepare this literature himself, but more often he employs experts to do it. Once a year he launches a drive. But it is only for publicity. The original suckers pay the freight. When they wear out, the executive secretary starts a new association.

Such sharks now swarm in every American city. The office-buildings are full of them. Their prosperity depends very largely upon the singular complaisance of the newspapers. Some time ago Mr. Stanley Walker, a New York journalist of sense and experience, examined a typical copy of one of the great New York dailies. He found that there were sixty-four items of local news in it — and that forty-two of them could be plainly traced to executive secretaries, and other such space-grabbers. The executive secretary, of course, does not have at his editors crudely. He seldom accompanies his item of "news" with any intimation that he is paid a good salary for planting it, and he discourages all inquiries into the actual size, aims and personnel of his organization. Instead he commonly postures as the mere agent of men and women known to be earnest and altruistic philanthropists. These philanthropists are the suckers upon whom he feeds. They pay his salary, maintain his office, and keep up his respectability in newspaper offices. What do they get out of it themselves? In part, no doubt, an honest feeling that they are doing good: the executive secretary, in fact, has to convince them of it before he is in a position to tackle the newspapers at all. But in part, also, they enjoy the publicity — and maybe other usufructs too. In the United States, indeed, doing good has come to be, like patriotism, a favorite device of persons with something to sell.

Some time ago, sweating under this assault of executive secretaries, the editors of a great American newspaper hit upon a scheme of relief. It took the form of a questionnaire — something not seldom used, and to vast effect, by executive secretaries themselves. This questionnaire had a blank in which the executive secretary was asked to write his full name and address, and the amount of his annual salary. In other blanks there was room for putting down the total income and outgo of his association, with details of every item amounting to more than 1% of the whole, and for a full list of its contributors and employés, with the amount given by every one of the former contributing more than 1% and the salary received by every one of the latter getting more than 1%. This simple questionnaire cut down the mail received from executive secretaries by at least one half. Many of them did not answer at all. Many others, answering, revealed the not surprising fact that their high-sounding national and international organizations were actually small clubs of a few men and women, and that they themselves consumed most of the revenues. It is a device that might be employed effectively by other American newspapers. When the executive secretaries return their answers by mail, which is usually the case, they are under pressure to answer truthfully, for answering otherwise is using the mails to obtain money by fraud, and many worthy men are jugged at Atlanta and Leavenworth for that offense.

The Husbandman

From PREJUDICES: FOURTH SERIES, 1924, pp. 43–60.
First printed in the *American Mercury*, March, 1924, pp. 293–96

LET the farmer, so far as I am concerned, be damned forevermore. To Hell with him, and bad luck to him. He is a tedious fraud and ignoramus, a cheap rogue and hypocrite, the eternal Jack of the human pack. He deserves all that he ever suffers under our economic system, and more. Any city man, not insane, who sheds tears for him is shedding tears of the crocodile.

No more grasping, selfish and dishonest mammal, indeed, is known to students of the *Anthropoidea*. When the going is good for him he robs the rest of us up to the extreme limit of our endurance; when the going is bad he comes bawling for help out of the public till. Has anyone ever heard of a farmer making any sacrifice of his own interests, however slight, to the common good? Has anyone ever heard of a farmer practising or advocating any political idea that was not absolutely self-seeking — that was not, in fact, deliberately designed to loot the rest of us to his gain? Greenbackism, free silver, the government guarantee of prices, bonuses, all the complex fiscal imbecilities of the cow State John Baptists — these are the contributions of the virtuous husbandmen to American political theory. There has never been a time, in good seasons or bad, when his hands were not itching for more; there has never been a time when he was not ready to support any charlatan, however grotesque, who promised to get it for him. Only one issue ever fetches him, and that is the issue of his own profit. He must be promised something definite and valuable, to be paid to him alone, or he is off after some other mountebank. He simply cannot imagine himself as a citizen of a commonwealth, in duty bound to give as well as take; he can imagine himself only as getting all and giving nothing.

Yet we are asked to venerate this prehensile moron as the *Ur*-burgher, the citizen *par excellence*, the foundation-stone of the state! And why? Because he produces something that all of us must have — that we must get somehow on penalty of death. And how do we get it from him? By submitting helplessly to his unconscionable blackmailing — by paying him, not under any rule of reason, but in proportion to his roguery and incompetence, and hence to the direness of our need. I doubt that the human race, as a whole, would submit to that sort of high-jacking, year in and year out, from any other necessary class of men. But the farmers carry it on incessantly, without challenge or reprisal, and the only thing that keeps them from reducing us, at intervals, to actual famine is their own imbecile knavery. They are all willing and eager to pillage us by starving us, but they can't do it because they can't resist attempts to swindle each other. Recall, for example, the case of the cotton-growers in the South. Back in the 1920s they agreed among themselves to cut down the cotton acreage in order to inflate the price — and instantly every party to the agreement began planting *more* cotton in order to profit by the abstinence of his neighbors. That abstinence being wholly imaginary, the price of cotton fell instead of going up — and then the entire pack of scoundrels began demanding assistance from the national treasury — in brief, began demanding that the rest of us indemnify them for the failure of their plot to blackmail us.

The same demand is made sempiternally by the wheat farmers of the Middle West. It is the theory of the zanies who perform at Washington that a grower of wheat devotes himself to that banal art in a philanthropic and patriotic spirit — that he plants and harvests his crop in order that the folks of the cities may not go without bread. It is the plain fact that he raises wheat because it takes less labor than any other crop — because it enables him, after working no more than sixty days a year, to loaf the rest of the twelve months. If wheat-raising could be taken out of the hands of such lazy *fellahin* and organized as the production of iron or cement is organized, the price might be reduced by two-thirds, and still leave a large profit for *entrepreneurs*. But what would become of the farmers? Well, what rational man gives a hoot? If wheat went to $10 a bushel tomorrow, and all the workmen of the cities became slaves in name as well as in fact, no farmer in this grand land of freedom would consent voluntarily to a reduction of as much as ⅛ of a cent a bushel. "The greatest wolves," said E. W. Howe, a graduate of the farm, "are the farmers who bring produce to town to sell." Wolves? Let us not insult *Canis lupus*. I move the substitution of *Hyæna hyæna*.

Meanwhile, how much truth is in the common theory that the husbandman is harassed and looted by our economic system, that the men of the cities prey upon him — specifically, that he is the chronic victim of such devices as the tariff, railroad regulation, and the banking system? So far as I can make out, there is none whatever. The net effect of our present banking system is that the money accumulated by the cities is used to finance the farmers, and that they employ it to blackmail the cities. As for the tariff, is it a fact that it damages the farmer, or benefits him? Let us turn for light to the worst tariff act ever heard of in human history: that of 1922. It put a duty of 30 cents a bushel on wheat, and so barred out Canadian wheat, and gave the American farmer a vast and unfair advantage. For months running the difference in the price of wheat on the two sides of the American-Canadian border — wheat raised on farms not a mile apart — ran from 25 to 30 cents a bushel. Danish butter was barred out by a duty of 8 cents a pound — and the American farmer pocketed the 8 cents. Potatoes carried a duty of 50 cents a hundredweight — and the potato-growers of Maine, eager to mop up, raised such an enormous crop that the market was glutted, and they went bankrupt, and began bawling for government aid. High duties were put, too, upon meats, upon cheese, upon wool — in brief, upon practically everything that the farmer produced. But his profits were taken from him by even higher duties upon manufactured goods, and by high freight rates? Were they, indeed? There was, in fact, no duty at all upon many of the things he consumed. There was no duty, for example, upon shoes. The duty upon woolen goods gave a smaller advantage to the manufacturer than the duty on wool gave to the farmer. So with the duty on cotton goods. Automobiles were cheaper in the United States than anywhere else on earth. So were all agricultural implements. So were groceries. So were fertilizers.

But here I come to the brink of an abyss of statistics, and had better haul up. The enlightened reader is invited to investigate them for himself; they will bring him, I believe, some surprises. They by no means exhaust the case against the consecrated husbandman. I have said that the only political idea he can grasp is one which promises him a direct profit. It is, alas, not quite true: he can also grasp one which has the sole effect of annoying and damaging his enemy, the city man. The same mountebanks who get to Washington by promising to augment his gains and make good his losses devote whatever time is left over from that enterprise to saddling the rest of us with oppressive and idiotic laws, all hatched on the farm. There, where the cows low through the still night, and the jug of Peruna stands behind the stove, and bathing begins, as at Biarritz, with the vernal equinox — there is the reservoir of all the nonsensical legislation which makes the United States a buffoon among the great nations. It was among country Methodists, practitioners of a theology degraded almost to the level of voodooism, that Prohibition was invented, and it was by country Methodists, nine-tenths of them actual followers of the plow, that it was fastened upon the rest of us, to the damage of our bank accounts, our dignity and our viscera. What lay under it, and under all the other crazy enactments of its category, was no more and no less than the yokel's congenital and incurable hatred of the city man — his simian rage against everyone who, as he sees it, is having a better time than he is.

The same animus is visible in innumerable other moral statutes, all ardently supported by the peasantry. For example, the Mann Act. The aim of this amazing law, of course, is not to put down adultery; it is simply to put down that variety of adultery which is most agreeable. What got it upon the books was the constant gabble in the rural newspapers about the byzantine debaucheries of urban antinomians — rich stockbrokers who frequented Atlantic City from Friday to Monday, movie actors who traveled about the country with beautiful wenches, and so on. Such aphrodisiacal tales, read beside the kitchen-stove by hinds condemned to monogamous misery with stupid, unclean and ill-natured wives, naturally aroused in them a vast detestation of errant cockneys, and this detestation eventually rolled up enough force to attract the attention of the quacks who make laws at Washington. The result was the Mann Act. Since then a number of the cow States have passed Mann Acts of their own, usually forbidding the use of automobiles "for immoral purposes." But there is nowhere a law forbidding the use of cow-stables, hay-ricks and other such familiar rustic ateliers of sin. That is to say, there is nowhere a law forbidding yokels to drag virgins into infamy by the crude technic practised since Tertiary times on the farms; there are only laws forbidding city youths to do it according to the refined technic of the great Babylons.

Such are the sweet-smelling and altruistic agronomists whose sorrows are the *Leitmotiv* of our politics, whose welfare is alleged to be the chief end of democratic statecraft, whose patriotism is the so-called bulwark of this so-called Republic.

Zoos

From Damn! A Book of Calumny, 1918, pp. 80–85.
First printed in the New York *Evening Mail*, Feb. 2, 1918

I often wonder how much sound and nourishing food is fed to the animals in the zoölogical gardens of America every week, and try to figure out what the public gets in return for the cost thereof. The annual bill must surely run into millions; one is constantly hearing how much beef a lion downs at a meal, and how many tons of hay an elephant dispatches in a month. And to what end? To the end, principally, that a horde of superintendents and keepers may be kept in easy jobs. To the end, secondarily, that the least intelligent minority of the population may have an idiotic show to gape at on Sunday afternoons, and that the young of the species may be instructed in the methods of amour prevailing among chimpanzees and become privy to the technic employed by jaguars, hyenas and polar bears in ridding themselves of lice.

So far as I can make out, after laborious visits to some of the chief zoos of the nation, no other imaginable purpose is served by their existence. One hears constantly, true enough (mainly from the gentlemen they support) that they are educational. But how? Just what sort of instruction do they radiate, and what is its value? I have never been able to find out. The sober truth is that they are no more educational than so many firemen's parades or displays of skyrockets, and that all they actually offer to the public in return for the taxes spent upon them is a form of idle and witless amusement, compared to which a visit to a penitentiary, or even to a State Legislature in session, is informing, stimulating and ennobling.

. Education your grandmother! Show me a schoolboy who has ever learned anything valuable or important by watching a mangy old lion snoring away in its cage or a family of monkeys fighting for peanuts. To get any useful instruction out of such a spectacle is palpably impossible. The most it can imaginably impart is that the stripes of a certain sort of tiger run one way and the stripes of another sort some other way, that hyenas

and polecats smell worse than Greek 'bus boys, that the Latin
name of the raccoon (who was unheard of by the Romans) is
Procyon lotor. For the dissemination of such banal knowledge,
absurdly emitted and defectively taken in, the taxpayers of the
United States are mulcted. As well make them pay for teaching policemen the theory of least squares, or for instructing
roosters in the laying of eggs.

But zoos, it is argued, are of scientific value. They enable
learned men to study this or that. Again the facts blast the
theory. No scientific discovery of any value whatsoever, even
to the animals themselves, has ever come out of a zoo. The zoo
scientist is the old woman of zoölogy, and his alleged wisdom
is usually exhibited, not in the groves of actual learning, but
in the Sunday newspapers. He is to biology what the late Ca-
mille Flammarion was to astronomy, which is to say, its court
jester and *reductio ad absurdum*. When he leaps into public
notice with some new pearl of knowledge, it commonly turns
out to be no more than the news that Marie Bashkirtseff, the
Russian lady walrus, has had her teeth plugged with zinc and
is expecting twins. Or that Pishposh, the man-eating alligator,
is down with locomotor ataxia. Or that Damon, the grizzly,
has just finished his brother Pythias in the tenth round, chew-
ing off his tail, nose and remaining ear.

Science, of course, has its uses for the lower animals. A diligent study of their livers and lights helps to an understanding
of the anatomy and physiology, and particularly of the pathology, of man. They are necessary aids in devising and manufacturing many remedial agents, and in testing the virtues of those
already devised; out of the mute agonies of a rabbit or a dog
may come relief for a baby with diphtheria, or means for an
archdeacon to escape the consequences of his youthful follies.
Moreover, something valuable is to be got out of a mere study
of their habits, instincts and ways of mind — knowledge that,
by analogy, may illuminate the parallel doings of the *genus
homo*, and so enable us to comprehend the primitive mental
processes of the rev. clergy.

But it must be obvious that none of these studies can be
made in a zoo. The zoo animals, to begin with, provide no
material for the biologist; he can find out no more about their

insides than what he discerns from a safe distance and through the bars. He is not allowed to try his germs and specifics upon them; he is not allowed to vivisect them. If he would find out what goes on in the animal body under this condition or that, he must turn from the inhabitants of the zoo to the customary guinea pigs and dogs, and buy or steal them for himself. Nor does he get any chance for profitable inquiry when zoo animals die (usually of lack of exercise or ignorant doctoring), for their carcasses are not handed to him for autopsy, but at once stuffed with gypsum and excelsior and placed in some museum.

Least of all do zoos produce any new knowledge about animal behavior. Such knowledge must be got, not from animals penned up and tortured, but from animals in a state of nature. A professor studying the habits of the giraffe, for example, and confining his observations to specimens in zoos, would inevitably come to the conclusion that the giraffe is a sedentary and melancholy beast, standing immovable for hours at a time and employing an Italian to feed him hay and cabbages. As well proceed to a study of the psychology of a jurisconsult by first immersing him in Sing Sing, or of a juggler by first cutting off his hands. Knowledge so gained is inaccurate and imbecile knowledge. Not even a professor, if sober, would give it any faith and credit.

There remains, then, the only true utility of a zoo: it is a childish and pointless show for the unintelligent, in brief, for children, nurse-maids, visiting yokels and the generality of the defective. Should the taxpayers be forced to sweat millions for such a purpose? I think not. The sort of man who likes to spend his time watching a cage of monkeys chase one another, or a lion gnaw its tail, or a lizard catch flies, is precisely the sort of man whose mental weakness should be combatted at the public expense, and not fostered. He is a public liability and public menace, and society should seek to improve him. Instead of that, we spend a lot of money to feed his degrading appetite and further paralyze his mind. It is precisely as if the community provided free champagne for dipsomaniacs, or hired lecturers to convert the Army to the doctrines of the Quakers.

XXI. THE HUMAN BODY

Pathological Note

From the *Smart Set*, Dec., 1919, pp. 66–67

THE EXACT nature of disease is a matter that still gives pause to MM. the pathologists. All that may be said about it with any certainty is that a given condition is an apparent departure from the normal balance, and it tends to destroy the organism and produce death. When one comes to non-lethal abnormality, it would be absurd to assume that it is to be regarded, *ipso facto*, as regrettable. The perfectly normal human being, the absolutely average man, is surely anything but an ideal creature. A great many admittedly abnormal men, even in the direction of what is called disease, are his obvious superiors, and this class includes many so-called men of genius. As for the fact that disease tends to produce death, this is a matter of small significance. Life itself tends to produce death; living is a sort of gradual dying. All that distinguishes what is known as a healthy man from what is known as a diseased man is that the latter promises to die sooner — and even this probability is not always borne out by the event. Men afflicted with diseases regarded as fatal often live so long that their physicians begin to regard them as personal enemies and have to get them out of the way, by giving them doses out of the black bottle.

The fact is that certain diseased states are very favorable to the higher functioning of the organism — more favorable, indeed, than states of health. One of the diseases that American gobs were saved from in 1917 by the virtuous watchfulness of the Hon. Josephus Daniels is of such curious effect upon the mental powers that, under certain conditions, it would be much more sensible to call it a benefit than a handicap. True enough, ninety-nine out of a hundred victims who show signs of its mental effect move toward insanity, but the hundredth moves toward genius. Beethoven, Nietzsche and Schopenhauer were such victims, if the word may be used of giants. The mild toxemia accompanying the disease kept them keyed up to stupendous effort. All three died of it in the end, but while they lived it acted upon them like some extraordinarily powerful stimulant, and there is little doubt that their great achievements were at least partly due to it.

In this case, of course, ideas of loathsomeness reinforce mere fear, and so most sane men would rather do without the stimulation than face the disease. But there are other maladies, not popularly regarded as loathsome, which also seem to prick up the intellect. One of them is tuberculosis. It is perfectly possible that the superior mental development of the white races may be due to the fact that they have suffered from tuberculosis for many centuries. History shows a vast number of extraordinary consumptives, and it is common observation that even the stupidest man, once he is attacked by the tubercle bacilli, begins to exhibit a certain alertness. Perhaps the time will come when promising young men, instead of being protected from such diseases at all hazards, will be deliberately infected with them, just as soils are now inoculated with nitrogen-liberating bacteria.

This plan, of course, will tend to diminish the length of their days, but that will be no objection to it, for its aim will not be to improve the candidates quantitatively, but to improve them qualitatively. The science of hygiene, which is largely in the hands of quacks, lays too much stress upon mere longevity, and when it gets beyond longevity it seeks only the good of common men. To produce better stockbrokers, Knights of Pythias, Sons of the Revolution, corner grocerymen, labor leaders and other such *cocci*, it is necessary, of course, to keep them physically well, for if they are valuable at all, it is chiefly as physical machines. They serve to reverse and complete the great nitrogen-fixing process of vegetable life. But if it were possible to produce a Chopin with a few doses of tubercle bacilli, even at the cost of killing him at thirty-nine, it would surely be worth while. And if a technique is ever worked out for producing a Beethoven, or even making measurably more likely the production of a Beethoven, with any other pathogenic organisms, then certainly only idiots will complain if they kill him at fifty-seven.

The Striated Muscle Fetish

From the *American Mercury*, June, 1931, pp. 156–58

IN the American colleges, anon and anon, there goes on a crusade against the gross over-accentuation of athletic sports and pastimes, but it is not likely that it will ever yield any substantial reform. On the one hand, college authorities, and especially college presidents, are far too politic a class of men to take any really effective steps against an enterprise that brings in such large sums of money, and on the other hand they are far too conventional to challenge the common delusion that athletics, in themselves, are uplifting and hence laudable. The most one hears, even from the radicals among them, is that it is somehow immoral for college stadiums to cost five times as much as college libraries; no one ever argues that the stadiums ought to be abolished altogether. Yet it is plain that that position might be very plausibly maintained.

The popular belief in athletics is grounded upon the theory that violent exercise makes for bodily health, and that bodily health is necessary to mental vigor. Both halves of this theory are highly dubious. There is, in fact, no reason whatever for believing that such a game as, say, football improves the health of those who play it. On the contrary, there is every reason for believing that it is deleterious. The football player is not only exposed constantly to a risk of grave injury, often of an irremediable kind; he is also damaged in his normal physiological processes by the excessive strains of the game, and the exposure that goes with playing it. If it were actually good for half-grown boys to wallow for several hours a day in a muddy field, with their heads bare and the bleak autumnal skies overhead, then it would also be good for them to be sprayed with a firehose before going to bed. And if it were good for their non-playing schoolmates to sit watching them on cold and windy bleachers then it would also be good for those schoolmates to hear their professors in the same place.

The truth is that athletes, as a class, are not above the normal in health, but below it. Despite all the attention that they get from dietitians, rubbers and the medical faculty, they are forever beset by malaises, and it is almost unheard of for one of them to pass through an ordinary season without a spell of illness. When a college goes in for any given sport in the grand manner it always has to prepare five or six times as many players as the rules demand, for most of its stars are bound to be disabled at some time or other. Not a few, after a game or two, drop out altogether, and are heard of no more. Some are crippled on the field, but more succumb to the mere wear and tear. In other words, the exercise they get does not really improve their vigor; it only develops and reveals their lack of vigor. The survivors are not better animals than they were; they were simply better animals than the general in the first place.

The cult of health, indeed, has been carried to plainly preposterous lengths. It is whooped up, in large part, by medical men turned uplifters, *i.e.*, by men trained in medicine but with no talent for it, and an aversion to it. The public hygiene movement is chiefly in the hands of such quacks, and they seem to have a powerful and baleful influence upon colleagues who should know better. This influence shows itself, *inter alia*, in the current craze to employ heliotherapy in a wholesale and irrational manner, without any consideration whatever for the comfort of the patient or the nature of his disease. My prediction is that exposing sick people to glaring sunlight, or to any kind of artificial light that simulates it, will some day go as far out of fashion as bleeding them has gone today. The fact is that, to the higher varieties of civilized man, sunlight is often injurious, and their natural inclination to keep out of it is sound in instinct. If it were beneficial, then farmers would be healthier than city men, which they are surely not. Man has apparently sought the shade since his earliest days on earth, and all of his anthropoid ancestors seem to have been forest dwellers.

Fresh air is another medicament that will be trusted less hereafter than it is today. Everyone can recall the time when poor consumptives were exposed to the wintry blasts on mountaintops. Most of them, of course, died painful deaths, but the recovery of those who didn't was ascribed to the rarefied air. But now it begins to be understood that the only valuable part of this treatment was the rest, which the roaring of the winds ob-

viously impeded rather than helped. At about the same time
the pedagogues of the United States also succumbed to the
fresh air craze, and the taxpayers were rooked into laying out
millions for elaborate and costly ventilating systems for the
public schools. But now it has been found that the air which
comes in around the edges of an ordinary window is all the
pupils really need, and the pedagogues, abandoning their insane ventilating systems, begin to bellow for expensive quartz
window-panes, to let in the ultra-violet rays. This lunacy will
last a while, and then go out. Even pedagogues, it appears, have
a certain capacity for learning.

But not much. In the matter of athletics they are hampered
by bad training. Most of them, at least in the colleges, are themselves college graduates, and thus accept the campus scale of
values. Inasmuch as the average boy of eighteen would far
rather be heavy-weight champion of the world than Einstein,
that scale is heavily loaded in favor of mere physical prowess.
The poor 'gogues, subscribing to it, can never quite rid themselves of a sneaking admiration for football stars. Practically
every one of them, when he dreams at night, dreams that he is a
reincarnation of Sandow. Thus they cannot be trusted to make
any really vigorous onslaught upon the college athletic racket.
If a reform ever comes, it will not come from college faculties,
but from college trustees, most of whom are fortunately without college training. But these trustees, alas, have their dreams
too: they dream that they are J. P. Morgans. Thus the only way
to get rid of the combats of gorillas which now bring millions
to the colleges will be to invent some imbecility which brings in
even more. To that enterprise, I regret to have to report, I find
myself unequal.

Moral Tale

From the Baltimore *Sun*, April 11, 1935.
Welch was born in 1850 and died in 1934

THE LATE Dr. William H. Welch, one of the stars of the Johns
Hopkins Medical School, was a sort of walking *reductio ad ab-*

surdum of some of the most confident theories of his fellow resurrection-men. For diet he cared precisely nothing, yet he lived to be 84. In exercise he took so little interest that he never had a golf-stick or even a billiard-cue in his hands, yet he was hale and hearty until his last brief illness. And to top it all, he came into the world with the very sort of physique which, if the insurance statisticians are to be believed, means certain death before 50.

Dr. Welch was hardly more than five feet six inches in height, but he must have weighed close to 200 pounds. With his broad brow, fine eyes and closely-clipped beard, he was a very distinguished-looking man, yet it would have been difficult to prove legally that he had a neck. His massive head, in fact, sat directly on his sturdy chest, and a foot below it there were the beginnings of a majestic paunch. This is the build, according to the professors of such matters, that offers ideal soil for a long list of incurable malaises. It spells high blood-pressure, kidney deterioration and heart disease. When it is combined with a distaste for exercise, a habit of sitting up until all hours of the night and an enlightened appreciation of each and every variety of sound food and drink, it is tantamount, so we are told, to being sentenced to die in the electric-chair at 45. Yet Dr. Welch lived 14 years and 22 days beyond the canonical three-score and ten and had a grand time to the end. And when he died at last it was not of any of the diseases his colleagues had been warning him against for 60 years.

A year or so before his death I happened to sit beside him one day at lunch. The main dish was country ham and greens, and of it he ate a large portion, washing it down with several mugs of beer. There followed lemon meringue pie. He ate an arc of at least 75 degrees of it, and eased it into his system with a cup of coffee. Then he lighted a six-inch panatela and smoked it to the butt. And then he ambled off to attend a medical meeting and to prepare for dinner. The night before, so I gathered from his talk, he had been to a banquet, and sat until 11.30 listening to bad speeches and breathing tobacco smoke. The wines had been good enough for him to remember them and mention them. Returning to his bachelor quarters, he had read until 1 o'clock and then turned in. The morning before our meeting he had devoted to meditation in an easy-chair, cigar in hand. At the lunch itself, I forgot to say, he made a speech, beginning in English and finishing in German.

What are we to gather, brethren, from Dr. Welch's chart? Simply that pathology is still far from an exact science, especially in the department of forecasting. In the presence of what are assumed to be causes the expected effects do not always or necessarily follow. Here was a man who stood in the very front rank of the medical profession, and yet his whole life was a refutation of some of its most confident generalizations. He lived to be pallbearer to scores of colleagues who made 36 holes of golf a week a religious rite, and to scores more who went on strict diets at 30 and stuck to them heroically until they died at 50 or 60.

Comfort for the Ailing

From the *American Mercury*, March, 1930, pp. 288–89

To the gods who run the cosmos, disease and health probably look pretty much alike. I am not, of course, privy to the secret lucubrations of Yahweh, but it is certainly imaginable that a hearty, incandescent boil gives Him quite as much satisfaction as a damask cheek, and maybe a great deal more. The boil, I suspect, is harder to fashion, if only because it is more complex, and hence it must be more stimulating to the artist. As for a carcinoma, a strangulated hernia or a case of paralysis agitans, it must needs fill its eminent Designer with a very soothing professional warmth. Second-rate gods, it is manifest, could never have invented such things. They show a high degree of ingenuity, and something hard to distinguish from esthetic passion.

What is the thing called health? Simply a state in which the individual happens transiently to be perfectly adapted to his environment. Obviously, such states cannot be common, for the environment is in constant flux. Am I perfectly well today, with the temperature 55 and a light wind blowing? Then I can't be perfectly well tomorrow, with the mercury at 30, and a wild gale roaring out of the North. Moreover, I am abstemious to-

day, for it is my saint's day, and in consequence my poor duodenum is quiescent; tomorrow will be my Uncle Wolfgang's
birthday, and I must gorge and guzzle. A week hence, according to the insurance actuaries, the chances are one in so many
that my heart will begin to cut capers, for I am getting into the
age for it. Twenty years hence it is at least a ten to one bet that
I'll be stuffed and in the National Museum at Washington.
And so, as they say, it goes.

Uninterrupted health is probably possible only to creatures of
very simple structure, beginning, say, with the *Rhizopoda* and
running up to schoolboys. They have little conflict with their
environment, for they make few demands upon it. So long as
it does not bombard them in a gross and overwhelming manner, like a falling house, they are scarcely conscious of it. But on
higher levels there is a vastly greater sensitiveness, and so there
is much more illness. History tells us of few really distinguished
men who were completely healthy: the biography of the high-
toned is always largely concerned with aches and malaises. In
the great days of the Greeks only the athletes were good insurance risks — and of the athletes, then as now, we hear nothing
save that they were athletes. There must have been thousands
of them, first and last, but not one of them, as he grew older,
ever amounted to anything. No doubt the average hero of the
games spent his last days keeping a wine-shop or serving as
night-watchman at the Academy. Meanwhile, the philosophers
pored over the works of Hippocrates, and were steady customers
of all the quacks who swarmed in from the East.

Happiness, like health, is probably also only a passing accident. For a moment or two the organism is irritated so little
that it is not conscious of it; for the duration of that moment
it is happy. Thus a hog is always happier than a man, and a
bacillus is happier than a hog. The laws of the cosmos seem
to be as little concerned about human felicity as the laws of the
United States are concerned about human decency. Whoever
set them in motion apparently had something quite different in
mind — something that we cannot even guess at. The very life
of man seems to be no more than one of their inconsidered
by-products. One may liken it plausibly to the sparks that fly
upward when a blacksmith fashions a horse-shoe. The sparks

are undoubtedly more brilliant than the horse-shoe, but all the
while they remain secondary to it. If the iron could speak, it
would probably complain of them as a disease. In the same way,
I daresay, man is a disease of the cosmos. . . . But here I begin to argue in a circle, for I started out by suggesting that disease itself may be only a higher form of normalcy. Perhaps I
had better shut down.

Eugenic Note

From the same, June, 1924, pp. 188–89

HAS anyone ever given credit to the Black Death for the Renaissance — in other words, for modern civilization? I can find
no mention of any such theory in the books; most of them try
to make it appear, vaguely and unpersuasively, that the Renaissance was somehow set off by the fall of Constantinople in
1453. But how could the fall of one of the most civilized of
cities have stimulated the progress of civilization? Somehow, I
detect a *non sequitur* here. Other authorities allege that the
Renaissance began when scholars from the East appeared at
Rome, some of them from Constantinople and some from other
places: this, we are told, was about the year 1400. But there is
really very little evidence for the fact. Scholars from the East
had been familiar to the Romans for at least a thousand years,
and yet they had left few marks upon Italian thought. Moreover, the Renaissance, when it got under way at last, was carried forward, not by scholars from the East, but by Italians. All
the great names of the time, in every field from architecture to
politics, are Western, not Eastern. There is, indeed, no more
evidence in the records that scholars from the East had anything to do with the business than there is that Sioux Indians
had a hand in it. The Renaissance was thoroughly occidental;
its greatest achievements would have been utterly unintelligible
to an Eastern pundit. It did not revive and carry on a work
dropped at Constantinople when the Turks approached; it began a work that Constantinople knew absolutely nothing about.

But if Italians launched the Renaissance, with Germans and Frenchmen following after, then why did they wait until the Fourteenth Century to do it? If they were barbarians in the year 1300, how did they manage to convert themselves into highly civilized men — perhaps the most civilized ever seen on earth; certainly vastly more civilized than the grossly overrated Greeks — by 1450? Are we to assume that they were suddenly inspired by God? Or that large numbers of them began to mutate in a De Vriesian manner, highly astonishing to the biologist? I do not believe that it is necessary to dally with any such theories. The Renaissance, it seems to me, is easily and sufficiently explained by the fact that the Black Death, raging from 1334 to 1351, exterminated such huge masses of the European proletariat that the average intelligence and enterprise of the race were greatly lifted, and that this purged and improved society suddenly functioned splendidly because it was no longer hobbled from below. For a thousand years the population of Europe had been steadily increasing, and its best men had been forced, in consequence, to devote themselves to the wasteful business of politics — the grabbing of new territories, the opening of markets, the policing of the proletariat. Their ability thus had no opportunity to function in a dignified and splendid manner; they were condemned to such dull, degrading tasks as harass United States Senators, generals in the Army, Tammany bosses, college presidents and captains of industry. Then, like a bolt from the blue, came the Black Death. In less than twenty years it reduced the population of Europe by at least 50% — and yet it left substantially all of the wealth of Europe untouched. More, it killed its millions selectively; the death-rate among the upper classes, as every Sunday-school scholar reading the Decameron of Boccaccio knows, was immensely less than the death-rate among the submerged. The net result was that Europe emerged from the pandemic with the old pressure of population relieved, all the worst problems of politics in abeyance, plenty of money, and a newly-found leisure. The best brains of the time, thus suddenly emancipated, began to function freely and magnificently. There ensued what we call the Renaissance.

XXII. UTOPIAN FLIGHTS

⧓

A Purge for Legislatures

From PREJUDICES: SIXTH SERIES, 1927, pp. 44–53. First printed in the *American Mercury*, Aug., 1926, pp. 414–16. I repeated my proposal in The Law-Making Racket, Baltimore *Evening Sun*, April 13, 1931

A MOOD of constructive criticism being upon me, I propose forthwith that the method of choosing legislators now prevailing in the United States be abandoned and that the method used in choosing juries be substituted. That is to say, I propose that the men who make our laws be chosen by chance and against their will, instead of by fraud and against the will of all the rest of us, as now. But isn't the jury system itself imperfect? Isn't it occasionally disgraced by gross abuse and scandal? Then so is the system of justice devised and ordained by the Lord God Himself. Didn't He assume that the Noachian Deluge would be a lasting lesson to sinful humanity — that it would put an end to all manner of crime and wickedness, and convert mankind into a race of Presbyterians? And wasn't Noah himself, its chief beneficiary, lying drunk, naked and uproarious within a year after the ark landed on Ararat? All I argue for the jury system, invented by man, is that it is measurably better than the scheme invented by God. It has its failures and its absurdities, its abuses and its corruptions, but taking one day with another it manifestly works. It is not the fault of juries that so many murderers go unwhipped of justice, and it is not the fault of juries that so many honest men are harassed by preposterous laws. The juries find the gunmen guilty: it is functionaries higher up, all politicians, who deliver them from the noose, and turn them out to resume their butcheries.

So I propose that our Legislatures be chosen as our juries are now chosen — that the names of all the men eligible in each assembly district be put into a hat (or, if no hat can be found that is large enough, into a bathtub), and that a blind moron, preferably of tender years, be delegated to draw out one. Let the constituted catchpolls then proceed swiftly to this man's house, and take him before he can get away. Let him be brought into court forthwith, and put under bond to serve as elected, and if he cannot furnish the bond, let him be kept until the appointed day in the nearest jail.

The advantages that this system would offer are so vast and so obvious that I hesitate to venture into the banality of rehearsing them. It would in the first place, save the commonwealth the present excessive cost of elections, and make political campaigns unnecessary. It would in the second place, get rid of all the heart-burnings that now flow out of every contest at the polls, and block the reprisals and charges of fraud that now issue from the heart-burnings. It would, in the third place, fill all the State Legislatures with men of a peculiar and unprecedented cast of mind — men actually convinced that public service is a public burden, and not merely a private snap. And it would, in the fourth and most important place, completely dispose of the present degrading knee-bending and trading in votes, for nine-tenths of the legislators, having got into office unwillingly, would be eager only to finish their duties and go home, and even those who acquired a taste for the life would be unable to do anything to increase the probability, even by one chance in a million, of their reëlection.

The disadvantages of the plan are very few, and most of them, I believe, yield readily to analysis. Do I hear argument that a miscellaneous gang of tin-roofers, delicatessen dealers and retired bookkeepers, chosen by hazard, would lack the vast knowledge of public affairs needed by makers of laws? Then I can only answer (*a*) that no such knowledge is actually necessary, and (*b*) that few, if any, of the existing legislators possess it. The great majority of public problems, indeed, are quite simple, and any man may be trusted to grasp their elements in ten days who may be — and is — trusted to unravel the obfuscations of two gangs of lawyers in the same time. In this department the so-called expertness of so-called experts is largely imaginary. My scheme would have the capital merit of barring them from the game. They would lose their present enormous advantages as a class, and so their class would tend to disappear.

Would that be a disservice to the state? Certainly not. On the contrary, it would be a service of the first magnitude, for the worst curse of democracy, as we suffer under it today, is that it makes public office a monopoly of a palpably inferior and ignoble group of men. They have to abase themselves in order to get it, and they have to keep on abasing themselves in order to hold it. The fact reflects itself in their general character, which is obviously low. They are men congenitally capable of cringing and dishonorable acts, else they would not have got into public life at all. There are, of course, exceptions to that rule among them, but how many? What I contend is simply that the number of such exceptions is bound to be smaller in the class of professional job-seekers than it is in any other class, or in the population in general. What I contend, second, is that choosing legislators from that population, by chance, would reduce immensely the proportion of such slimy men in the halls of legislation, and that the effects would be instantly visible in a great improvement in the justice and reasonableness of the laws.

Are juries ignorant? Then they are still intelligent enough to be entrusted with your life and mine. Are they venal? Then they are still honest enough to take our fortunes into their hands. Such is the fundamental law of the Germanic peoples, and it has worked for nearly a thousand years. I have launched my proposal that it be extended upward and onward, and the mood of constructive criticism passes from me. My plan belongs to any reformer who cares to lift it.

A Chance for Millionaires

From the New York *Evening Mail*, 1918

On the general stupidity and hunkerousness of millionaires a formidable tome might be written — a job I resign herewith to anyone diligent enough to assemble the facts. Not only do they gather in their assets by processes which never show any originality, but are always based upon a few banal principles of swindling; they also display the same lack of resource and ingenuity in getting rid of them. It is years since any American millionaire got his money in any new and stimulating way, and it is years since any American millionaire got rid of his money by any device worthy the admiration of connoisseurs.

Setting aside the pathetic dullards who merely hang on to their accumulations, like dogs hoarding bones, the rich men of the Republic may be divided into two grand divisions, according to their varying notions of what is a good time. Those in the first division waste their funds upon idiotic dissipation or personal display. They are the Wine Jacks, social pushers and horsy fellows — the Thaws, Goulds and so on. Those in the second division devote themselves to buying public esteem by gaudy charities and a heavy patronage of the arts and sciences. They are the Rockefellers, Carnegies, Morgans, *et al.*

The second crowd, it seems to me, are even more dull and unimaginative than the first, and show less originality. One never hears of them doing anything new; they are forever imitating one another in something old. They build hospitals, or establish libraries, or collect works of art, or endow colleges, or finance some scientific institution or other — and after that their fancy is exhausted. John D. Rockefeller, probably the most intelligent of them, actually did nothing new with his billions. He staked a few charities, he trustified certain religious enterprises, he capitalized medical research — and that is all. Every one of these things had been done before. John did not invent them, and neither did he greatly improve them. The late John Pierpont Morgan I was even less original. The only use he could find for his money was to lavish it on art collections. With the passion of a miser piling up gold, he scoured the world for pictures, pots, furniture and fabrics, taking the good with the bad, and often, if rumor is to be believed, the bogus with the real. His accumulations finally surpassed those of all other men, living or dead. He was the champion of champions, the John L. Sullivan of art patrons. And then he died, and left all that chaos of beauty and ugliness to his son, who dispersed a large part of it, just as a less opulent son sells off his dead father's wornout clothes.

Such frenzied inordinateness is obviously empty, and perhaps almost maniacal. Morgan's actual taste was probably that of any other rich banker; there are hints of its true dignity in the fact that he bought the original manuscript of Dickens's "Christmas Carol," and regarded it as a lofty work, and had it read aloud to him every Christmas. Had he been poorer he would have collected, I daresay, gaudy sets of Bulwer Lytton, Guy de Maupassant and Balzac, or Denby Sadler etchings, or Rogers groups. He was simply a Philistine with an unlimited bank account. His services to art were scarcely greater than those of a moderately intelligent dealer.

I need not call a further roll. You will think of other examples yourself, and you will see at once how little ingenuity they have brought to the spending of their money. The trouble with nearly all of them is simple. Their primary motive in pouring out millions is to gain the good will and adulation of the general public, which is to say, of the general mass of dolts and noodles, and so they are restricted to enterprises which fall within the comprehension of such noodles, and excite their admiration. This bars out at once all schemes that are likely to appeal to a civilized man, for it is a peculiarity of such a man that he is usually in favor of whatever the mob is against, and against whatever it is in favor of. The millionaire who would make a genuine splash with his money must reject this common motive and adopt a contrary motive. That is to say, he must set himself to do, not what is popular, but precisely what is most *un*popular. So far not one of the fraternity has shown imagination enough for that business.

Meanwhile, the opportunities are so numerous and so inviting that they bring tears to the eyes. Even old ideas may be improved, embellished, made mellow. Think, for example, of the scheme of the late D. O. Mills. He erected the two so-called Mills hotels in New York — and was canonized as a great philanthropist. But suppose he had built them, not in New York, but at Newport, Palm Beach or the Virginia Hot Springs. Suppose he had set them down in the very midst of American snobdom, and then invited all his decayed mechanics, unsuccessful peddlers and gentlemen out of work to come in and make themselves at home. As things stand, Mills is remembered by one American in 2,000,000; even many of his guests have scarcely heard of him. Had he been a man of originality his name would be as immortal as that of Lorenzo Borgia.

On the theological side many stimulating enterprises invite. I often think of the noble divertissement that John D. Rockefeller could have got by giving $100,000,000 to the Mormons, first to finance a nation-wide campaign in favor of polygamy, then to buy legislation authorizing it from the State Legislatures, and then to pay for a fight to a finish before the Supreme Court of the United States, with all the leading barristers of the nation for the defense. The combat would have been gaudy, thrilling, incomparable. Millions of Americans would have been converted; the newspapers would have fallen one by one; in the end it might have been possible to put through a constitutional amendment not only authorizing polygamy, but even making it obligatory. John got no such fun out of the Rockefeller Institute, nor out of his gifts to Baptist missions in Cochin-China. Carnegie got no such fun out of his libraries. Morgan got no such fun out of his squirrel-like hoarding up of dingy paintings and moth-eaten old sofas.

A still more gorgeous opportunity offers itself in the South. Among the native fauna down there are 10,000,000 colored folk of defective culture and inflammable habits. Theoretically, these Moors are all Christians, but as a matter of fact their faith is still adulterated by many ideas inherited from their African ancestors. The average religious ceremony among them is wild and vociferous. Not infrequently, indeed, the gendarmes have to shut off their deafening supplications, that the adjacent gentry may be able to get some sleep. These facts have often suggested to the judicious that Christianity, in its authentic form, is a cult not quite suited to the genius of the darker races. In Africa, where it has had to meet the competition of Moslemism, it has, in fact, usually succumbed. Hundreds of thousands of native Africans, converted by the gallant efforts of our own missionaries, have later gone over to the Crescent with a whoop, and sometimes butchered their late pastors in celebration of their apostasy. From end to end of the Dark Continent, indeed, Mohammedanism has swept like a whirlwind. No other known faith appeals so eloquently to the untutored Ethiop.

What I here hint at is the millionaire who imported a ship-load of Moslem evangelists from Arabia, schooled them in English by intensive cultivation, and then turned them loose in Georgia — that such a millionaire, at all events, would suffer little from boredom during the ensuing carnage, and that his name would have an assured place in the history of the Confederate States. I am a poor man, but if the hat is passed I shall be glad to contribute to the project $1,000,000 in Mississippi bonds of the issue of 1838.

The Malevolent Jobholder

From the *American Mercury*, June, 1924, pp. 156–59. This was written long before the New Deal afflicted the country with a great mass of new administrative law and a huge horde of new and extra-tyrannical jobholders. I am more than ever convinced that it embodied a good idea

IN the immoral monarchies of the continent of Europe, now happily abolished by God's will, there was, in the old days of sin, an intelligent and effective way of dealing with delinquent officials. Not only were they subject, when taken in downright corruption, to the ordinary processes of the criminal laws; in addition they were liable to prosecution in special courts for such offenses as were peculiar to their offices. In this business the abominable Prussian state, though founded by Satan, took the lead. It maintained a tribunal in Berlin that devoted itself wholly to the trial of officials accused of malfeasance, corruption, tyranny and incompetence, and any citizen was free to lodge a complaint with the learned judges. The trial was public and in accord with rules fixed by law. An official found guilty could be punished summarily and in a dozen different ways. He could be reprimanded, reduced in rank, suspended from office for a definite period, transferred to a less desirable job, removed from the rolls altogether, fined, or sent to jail. If he was removed from office he could be deprived of his right to a pension in addition, or fined or jailed in addition. He could be made to pay damages to any citizen he had injured, or to apologize publicly.

All this, remember, was in addition to his liability under the ordinary law, and the statutes specifically provided that he could be punished twice for the same offense, once in the ordinary courts and once in the administrative court. Thus, a Prussian official who assaulted a citizen, invaded his house without a warrant, or seized his property without process of law, could be deprived of his office and fined heavily by the administrative court, sent to jail by an ordinary court, and forced to pay damages to his victim by either or both. Had a Prussian judge in those far-off days of despotism, overcome by a brain-storm of *kaiserliche* passion, done any of the high-handed and irrational things that our own judges, Federal and State, do almost every day, an aggrieved citizen might have haled him before the administrative court and recovered heavy damages from him, besides enjoying the felicity of seeing him transferred to some dismal swamp in East Prussia, to listen all day to the unintelligible perjury of anthropoid Poles. The law specifically provided that responsible officials should be punished, not more leniently than subordinate or ordinary offenders, but more severely. If a corrupt policeman got six months a corrupt chief of police got two years. More, these statutes were enforced with Prussian barbarity, and the jails were constantly full of errant officials.

I do not propose, of course, that such medieval laws be set up in the United States. We have, indeed, gone far enough in imitating the Prussians already; if we go much further the moral and enlightened nations of the world will have to unite in a crusade to put us down. As a matter of fact, the Prussian scheme would probably prove ineffective in the Republic, if only because it involved setting up one gang of jobholders to judge and punish another gang. It worked very well in Prussia before the country was civilized by force of arms because, as everyone knows, a Prussian official was trained in ferocity from infancy, and regarded every man arraigned before him, whether a fellow official or not, as guilty *ipso facto*; in fact, any thought of a prisoner's possible innocence was abhorrent to him as a reflection upon the *Polizei*, and by inference, upon the Throne, the whole monarchical idea, and God. But in America, even if they had no other sentiment in common, which would be rarely, judge and prisoner would often be fellow Democrats or fellow Republicans, and hence jointly interested in protecting their party against scandal and its members against the loss of their jobs. Moreover, the Prussian system had another plain defect: the punishments it provided were, in the main, platitudinous and banal. They lacked dramatic quality, and they lacked ingenuity and appropriateness. To punish a judge taken in judicial *crim. con.* by fining him or sending him to jail is a bit too facile and obvious. What is needed is a system (*a*) that does not depend for its execution upon the good-will of fellow jobholders, and (*b*) that provides swift, certain and unpedantic punishments, each fitted neatly to its crime.

I announce without further ado that such a system, after due prayer, I have devised. It is simple, it is unhackneyed, and I believe that it would work. It is divided into two halves. The first half takes the detection and punishment of the crimes of jobholders away from courts of impeachment, congressional smelling committees, and all the other existing agencies — *i.e.*, away from other jobholders — and vests it in the whole body of free citizens, male and female. The second half provides that any member of that body, having looked into the acts of a jobholder and found him delinquent, may punish him instantly and on the spot, and in any manner that seems appropriate and convenient — and that, in case this punishment involves physical damage to the jobholder, the ensuing inquiry by the grand jury or coroner shall confine itself strictly to the question whether the jobholder deserved what he got. In other words, I propose that it shall be no longer *malum in se* for a citizen to pummel, cowhide, kick, gouge, cut, wound, bruise, maim, burn, club, bastinado, flay or even lynch a jobholder, and that it shall be *malum prohibitum* only to the extent that the punishment exceeds the jobholder's deserts. The amount of this excess, if any, may be determined very conveniently by a petit jury, as other questions of guilt are now determined. The flogged judge, or Congressman, or other jobholder, on being discharged from hospital — or his chief heir, in case he has perished — goes before a grand jury and makes complaint, and, if a true bill is found, a petit jury is empaneled and all the evidence is put before it. If it decides that the jobholder deserves the punishment inflicted upon him, the citizen who inflicted

it is acquitted with honor. If, on the contrary, it decides that
this punishment was excessive, then the citizen is adjudged
guilty of assault, mayhem, murder, or whatever it is, in a degree
apportioned to the difference between what the jobholder deserved and what he got, and punishment for that excess follows
in the usual course.

The advantages of this plan, I believe, are too patent to need
argument. At one stroke it removes all the legal impediments
which now make the punishment of a recreant jobholder so
hopeless a process, and enormously widens the range of possible
penalties. They are now stiff and, in large measure, illogical;
under the system I propose they could be made to fit the crime
precisely. Say a citizen today becomes convinced that a certain
judge is a jackass — that his legal learning is defective, his sense
of justice atrophied and his conduct of cases before him tyrannical and against decency. As things stand, it is impossible to
do anything about it. A judge cannot be impeached on the
mere ground that he is a jackass; the process is far too costly
and cumbersome, and there are too many judges liable to the
charge. Nor is anything to be gained by denouncing him publicly and urging all good citizens to vote against him when he
comes up for reëlection, for his term may run for ten or fifteen
years, and even if it expires tomorrow and he is defeated the
chances are good that his successor will be quite as bad, and
maybe even worse. Moreover, if he is a Federal judge he never
comes up for reëlection at all, for once he has been appointed
by the President of the United States, on the advice of his more
influential clients and with the consent of their agents in the
Senate, he is safe until he is so far gone in senility that he has
to be propped on the bench with pillows.

But now imagine any citizen free to approach him in open
court and pull his nose. Or even, in aggravated cases, to cut off
his ears, throw him out of the window, or knock him in the
head with an ax. How vastly more attentive he would be to his
duties! How diligently he would apply himself to the study of
the law! How careful he would be about the rights of litigants
before him! How polite and even suave he would become! For
judges, like all the rest of us, are vain fellows: they do not enjoy
having their noses pulled. The ignominy resident in the opera-

tion would not be abated by the subsequent trial of the puller, even if he should be convicted and jailed. The fact would still be brilliantly remembered that at least one citizen had deemed the judge sufficiently a malefactor to punish him publicly, and to risk going to jail for it. A dozen such episodes, and the career of any judge would be ruined and his heart broken, even though the jails bulged with his critics. He could not maintain his air of aloof dignity on the bench; even his catchpolls would snicker at him behind their hands, especially if he showed a cauliflower ear, a black eye or a scar over his bald head. Moreover, soon or late some citizen who had at him would be acquitted by a petit jury, and then, obviously, he would have to retire. It might be provided by law, indeed, that he should be compelled to retire in that case — that an acquittal would automatically vacate the office of the offending jobholder.

Portrait of an Ideal World

From PREJUDICES: FOURTH SERIES, 1924, pp. 173–79.
First printed in the *American Mercury*, Feb., 1924, pp. 201–03

THAT alcohol in dilute aqueous solution, when taken into the human organism, acts as a depressant, not as a stimulant, is now so much a commonplace of knowledge that even the more advanced varieties of physiologists are beginning to be aware of it. The intelligent layman no longer resorts to the jug when he has important business before him, whether intellectual or manual; he resorts to it after his business is done, and he desires to release his taut nerves and reduce the steam-pressure in his spleen. Alcohol, so to speak, unwinds us. It raises the threshold of sensation and makes us less sensitive to external stimuli, and particularly to those that are unpleasant. Putting a brake upon all the qualities which enable us to get on in the world and shine before our fellows — for example, combativeness, shrewdness, diligence, ambition —, it releases the qualities which mellow us and make our fellows love us — for example, amiability, generosity, toleration, humor, sympathy. A man who has taken aboard two or three cocktails is less competent than he was before to steer a battleship down the Ambrose Channel, or to cut off a leg, or to draw up a deed of trust, or to conduct Bach's B minor mass, but he is immensely more competent to entertain a dinner party, or to admire a pretty girl, or to *hear* Bach's B minor mass. The harsh, useful things of the world, from pulling teeth to digging potatoes, are best done by men who are as starkly sober as so many convicts in the death-house, but the lovely and useless things, the charming and exhilarating things, are best done by men with, as the phrase is, a few sheets in the wind. *Pithecanthropus erectus* was a teetotaler, but the angels, you may be sure, know what is proper at 5 p.m.

All this is so obvious that I marvel that no utopian has ever proposed to abolish all the sorrows of the world by the simple device of getting and keeping the whole human race gently stewed. I do not say drunk, remember; I say simply gently stewed — and apologize, as in duty bound, for not knowing how to describe the state in a more seemly phrase. The man who is in it is a man who has put all of his best qualities into his show-case. He is not only immensely more amiable than the cold sober man; he is immeasurably more decent. He reacts to all situations in an expansive, generous and humane manner. He has become more liberal, more tolerant, more kind. He is a better citizen, husband, father, friend. The enterprises that make human life on this earth uncomfortable and unsafe are never launched by such men. They are not makers of wars; they do not rob and oppress anyone. All the great villainies of history have been perpetrated by sober men, and chiefly by teetotalers. But all the charming and beautiful things, from the Song of Songs to terrapin à la Maryland, and from the nine Beethoven symphonies to the Martini cocktail, have been given to humanity by men who, when the hour came, turned from well water to something with color to it, and more in it than mere oxygen and hydrogen.

I am well aware, of course, that getting the whole human race stewed and keeping it stewed, year in and year out, would present formidable technical difficulties. It would be hard to make the daily dose of each individual conform exactly to his private needs, and hard to get it to him at precisely the right time. On the one hand there would be the constant danger that large minorities might occasionally become cold sober, and so start wars, theological disputes, moral reforms, and other such unpleasantnesses. On the other hand, there would be danger that other minorities might proceed to actual intoxication, and so annoy us all with their fatuous bawling or maudlin tears. But such technical obstacles, of course, are by no means insurmountable. Perhaps they might be got around by abandoning the administration of alcohol *per ora* and distributing it instead by impregnating the air with it. I throw out the suggestion, and pass on. Such questions are for men skilled in therapeutics, government and business efficiency. They exist today and their enterprises often show a high ingenuity, but, being chiefly sober, they devote too much of their time to harassing the rest of us. Half-stewed, they would be ten times as genial, and perhaps at least half as efficient. Thousands of them, relieved of their present anti-social duties, would be idle, and eager for occupation. I trust to them in this small matter. If they didn't succeed completely, they would at least succeed partially.

The objection remains that even small doses of alcohol, if each followed upon the heels of its predecessor before the effects of the latter had worn off, would have a deleterious effect upon the physical health of the race — that the death-rate would increase, and whole categories of human beings would be exterminated. The answer here is that what I propose is not lengthening the span of life, but augmenting its joys. Suppose we assume that its duration is reduced 20%. My reply is that its delights will be increased at least 100%. Misled by statisticians, we fall only too often into the error of worshiping mere figures. To say that A will live to be eighty and B will die at forty is certainly not to argue plausibly that A is more to be envied than B. A, in point of fact, may have to spend all of his eighty years in Kansas or Arkansas, with nothing to eat save corn and hog-meat and nothing to drink save polluted river water, whereas B may put in his twenty years of discretion upon the Côte d'Azur, *wie Gott im Frankreich*. It is my contention that the world I picture, assuming the average duration of human life to be cut down even 50%, would be an infinitely happier and more charming world than that we live in today — that no intelligent human being, having once tasted its peace and joy, would go back voluntarily to the harsh brutalities and stupidities that we now suffer, and idiotically strive to prolong. If intelligent Americans, in these depressing days, still cling to life and try to stretch it out longer and longer, it is surely not logically, but only instinctively. It is the primeval brute in them that hangs on, not the man. The man knows only too well that ten years in a genuine civilized and happy country would be infinitely better than a geological epoch under the curses he must now face and endure every day.

Moreover, there is no need to admit that the moderate alcoholization of the whole race would materially reduce the duration of life. A great many of us are moderately alcoholized already, and yet manage to survive quite as long as the blue-noses. As for the blue-noses themselves, who would repine if breathing alcohol-laden air brought them down with delirium tremens and so sterilized and exterminated them? The advantage to the race in general would be obvious and incalculable. All the worst strains — which now not only persist, but even prosper — would be stamped out in a few generations, and so the average human being would move appreciably away from, say, the norm of a Baptist clergyman in Georgia and toward the norm of Shakespeare, Mozart and Goethe. It would take æons, of course, to go all the way, but there would be progress with every generation, slow but sure. Today, it must be manifest, we make no progress at all; instead we slip steadily backward. That the average civilized man of today is inferior to the average civilized man of two or three generations ago is too plain to need arguing. He has less enterprise and courage; he is less resourceful and various; he is more like a rabbit and less like a lion. Harsh oppressions have made him what he is. He is the victim of tyrants. Well, no man with two or three cocktails in him is a tyrant. He may be foolish, but he is not cruel. He may be noisy, but he is also tolerant, generous and kind. My proposal would restore Christianity to the world. It would rescue mankind from moralists, pedants and brutes.

XXIII. SOUVENIRS OF A JOURNALIST

❧

The Hills of Zion

From PREJUDICES: FIFTH SERIES, 1926, pp. 75–86. In its first form this was a dispatch to the Baltimore *Evening Sun*. I wrote it on a roaring hot Sunday afternoon in a Chattanooga hotel room, naked above the waist and with only a pair of BVDs below·

IT was hot weather when they tried the infidel Scopes at Dayton, Tenn., but I went down there very willingly, for I was eager to see something of evangelical Christianity as a going concern. In the big cities of the Republic, despite the endless efforts of consecrated men, it is laid up with a wasting disease. The very Sunday-school superintendents, taking jazz from the stealthy radio, shake their fire-proof legs; their pupils, moving into adolescence, no longer respond to the proliferating hormones by enlisting for missionary service in Africa, but resort to necking instead. Even in Dayton, I found, though the mob was up to do execution upon Scopes, there was a strong smell of antinomianism. The nine churches of the village were all half empty on Sunday, and weeds choked their yards. Only two or three of the resident pastors managed to sustain themselves by their ghostly science; the rest had to take orders for mail-order pantaloons or work in the adjacent strawberry fields; one, I heard, was a barber. On the courthouse green a score of sweating theologians debated the darker passages of Holy Writ day and night, but I soon found that they were all volunteers, and that the local faithful, while interested in their exegesis as an intellectual exercise, did not permit it to impede the indigenous debaucheries. Exactly twelve minutes after I reached the village I was taken in tow by a Christian man and introduced to the favorite tipple of the Cumberland Range: half corn liquor and half Coca-Cola. It seemed a dreadful dose to me, but I found that the Dayton illuminati got it down with gusto, rubbing their tummies and rolling their eyes. I include among them the chief local proponents of the Mosaic cosmogony. They were all hot for Genesis, but their faces were far too florid to belong to teetotalers, and when a pretty girl came tripping down the main street, which was very often, they reached for the places where their neckties should have been with all the amorous enterprise of movie actors. It seemed somehow strange.

An amiable newspaper woman of Chattanooga, familiar with those uplands, presently enlightened me. Dayton, she explained, was simply a great capital like any other. That is to say, it was to Rhea county what Atlanta was to Georgia or Paris to France. That is to say, it was predominantly epicurean and sinful. A country girl from some remote valley of the county, coming into town for her semi-annual bottle of Lydia Pinkham's Vegetable Compound, shivered on approaching Robinson's drug-store quite as a country girl from up-State New York might shiver on approaching the Metropolitan Opera House. In every village lout she saw a potential white-slaver. The hard sidewalks hurt her feet. Temptations of the flesh bristled to all sides of her, luring her to Hell. This newspaper woman told me of a session with just such a visitor, holden a few days before. The latter waited outside one of the town hot-dog and Coca-Cola shops while her husband negotiated with a hardware merchant across the street. The newspaper woman, idling along and observing that the stranger was badly used by the heat, invited her to step into the shop for a glass of Coca-Cola. The invitation brought forth only a gurgle of terror. Coca-Cola, it quickly appeared, was prohibited by the country lady's pastor, as a levantine and Hell-sent narcotic. He also prohibited coffee and tea — and pies! He had his doubts about white bread and boughten meat. The newspaper woman, interested, inquired about ice-cream. It was, she found, not specifically prohibited, but going into a Coca-Cola shop to get it would be clearly sinful. So she offered to get a saucer of it, and bring it out to the sidewalk. The visitor vacillated — and came near being lost. But God saved her in the nick of time. When the newspaper woman emerged from the place she was in full flight up the street. Later on her husband, mounted on a mule, overtook her four miles out the mountain pike.

This newspaper woman, whose kindness covered city infidels

as well as Alpine Christians, offered to take me back in the hills
to a place where the old-time religion was genuinely on tap.
The Scopes jury, she explained, was composed mainly of its
customers, with a few Dayton sophisticates added to leaven the
mass. It would thus be instructive to climb the heights and observe the former at their ceremonies. The trip, fortunately,
might be made by automobile. There was a road running out
of Dayton to Morgantown, in the mountains to the westward,
and thence beyond. But foreigners, it appeared, would have to
approach the sacred grove cautiously, for the upland worshipers
were very shy, and at the first sight of a strange face they would
adjourn their orgy and slink into the forest. They were not to be
feared, for God had long since forbidden them to practise assas-
sination, or even assault, but if they were alarmed a rough trip
would go for naught. So, after dreadful bumpings up a long
and narrow road, we parked our car in a little woodpath a mile
or two beyond the tiny village of Morgantown, and made the
rest of the approach on foot, deployed like skirmishers. Far off
in a dark, romantic glade a flickering light was visible, and out
of the silence came the rumble of exhortation. We could distinguish the figure of the preacher only as a moving mote in the
light: it was like looking down the tube of a dark-field micro-
scope. Slowly and cautiously we crossed what seemed to be a
pasture, and then we stealthily edged further and further. The
light now grew larger and we could begin to make out what was
going on. We went ahead on all fours, like snakes in the grass.

From the great limb of a mighty oak hung a couple of crude
torches of the sort that car inspectors thrust under Pullman cars
when a train pulls in at night. In the guttering glare was the
preacher, and for a while we could see no one else. He was an
immensely tall and thin mountaineer in blue jeans, his collar-
less shirt open at the neck and his hair a tousled mop. As he
preached he paced up and down under the smoking flambeaux,
and at each turn he thrust his arms into the air and yelled
"Glory to God!" We crept nearer in the shadow of the corn-
field, and began to hear more of his discourse. He was preaching
on the Day of Judgment. The high kings of the earth, he roared,
would all fall down and die; only the sanctified would stand up
to receive the Lord God of Hosts. One of these kings he men-

tioned by name, the king of what he called Greece-y.[1] The king of Greece-y, he said, was doomed to Hell. We crawled forward a few more yards and began to see the audience. It was seated on benches ranged round the preacher in a circle. Behind him sat a row of elders, men and women. In front were the younger folk. We crept on cautiously, and individuals rose out of the ghostly gloom. A young mother sat suckling her baby, rocking as the preacher paced up and down. Two scared little girls hugged each other, their pigtails down their backs. An immensely huge mountain woman, in a gingham dress, cut in one piece, rolled on her heels at every "Glory to God!" To one side, and but half visible, was what appeared to be a bed. We found afterward that half a dozen babies were asleep upon it.

The preacher stopped at last, and there arose out of the darkness a woman with her hair pulled back into a little tight knot. She began so quietly that we couldn't hear what she said, but soon her voice rose resonantly and we could follow her. She was denouncing the reading of books. Some wandering book agent, it appeared, had come to her cabin and tried to sell her a specimen of his wares. She refused to touch it. Why, indeed, read a book? If what was in it was true, then everything in it was already in the Bible. If it was false, then reading it would imperil the soul. This syllogism from the Caliph Omar complete, she sat down. There followed a hymn, led by a somewhat fat brother wearing silver-rimmed country spectacles. It droned on for half a dozen stanzas, and then the first speaker resumed the floor. He argued that the gift of tongues was real and that education was a snare. Once his children could read the Bible, he said, they had enough. Beyond lay only infidelity and damnation. Sin stalked the cities. Dayton itself was a Sodom. Even Morgantown had begun to forget God. He sat down, and a female aurochs in gingham got up. She began quietly, but was soon leaping and roaring, and it was hard to follow her. Under cover of the turmoil we sneaked a bit closer.

A couple of other discourses followed, and there were two or three hymns. Suddenly a change of mood began to make itself felt. The last hymn ran longer than the others, and dropped gradually into a monotonous, unintelligible chant. The leader

[1] Grecia? Cf. Daniel VIII, 21.

beat time with his book. The faithful broke out with exultations. When the singing ended there was a brief palaver that
we could not hear, and two of the men moved a bench into the
circle of light directly under the flambeaux. Then a half-grown
girl emerged from the darkness and threw herself upon it. We
noticed with astonishment that she had bobbed hair. "This
sister," said the leader, "has asked for prayers." We moved a
bit closer. We could now see faces plainly, and hear every
word. At a signal all the faithful crowded up to the bench and
began to pray — not in unison, but each for himself. At another
they all fell on their knees, their arms over the penitent. The
leader kneeled facing us, his head alternately thrown back dramatically or buried in his hands. Words spouted from his lips
like bullets from a machine-gun — appeals to God to pull the
penitent back out of Hell, defiances of the demons of the air,
a vast impassioned jargon of apocalyptic texts. Suddenly he rose
to his feet, threw back his head and began to speak in the
tongues [2] — blub-blub-blub, gurgle-gurgle-gurgle. His voice rose
to a higher register. The climax was a shrill, inarticulate squawk,
like that of a man throttled. He fell headlong across the pyramid of supplicants.

From the squirming and jabbering mass a young woman
gradually detached herself — a woman not uncomely, with a
pathetic homemade cap on her head. Her head jerked back, the
veins of her neck swelled, and her fists went to her throat as
if she were fighting for breath. She bent backward until she
was like half a hoop. Then she suddenly snapped forward. We
caught a flash of the whites of her eyes. Presently her whole
body began to be convulsed — great throes that began at the
shoulders and ended at the hips. She would leap to her feet,
thrust her arms in air, and then hurl herself upon the heap.
Her praying flattened out into a mere delirious caterwauling. I
describe the thing discreetly, and as a strict behaviorist. The
lady's subjective sensations I leave to infidel pathologists, privy
to the works of Ellis, Freud and Moll. Whatever they were,
they were obviously not painful, for they were accompanied by
vast heavings and gurglings of a joyful and even ecstatic nature.
And they seemed to be contagious, too, for soon a second peni-

[2] Mark XVI, 17.

tent, also female, joined the first, and then came a third, and a
fourth, and a fifth. The last one had an extraordinary violent
attack. She began with mild enough jerks of the head, but in a
moment she was bounding all over the place, like a chicken
with its head cut off. Every time her head came up a stream
of hosannas would issue out of it. Once she collided with a
dark, undersized brother, hitherto silent and stolid. Contact
with her set him off as if he had been kicked by a mule. He
leaped into the air, threw back his head, and began to gargle
as if with a mouthful of BB shot. Then he loosed one tremendous, stentorian sentence in the tongues, and collapsed.

By this time the performers were quite oblivious to the profane universe and so it was safe to go still closer. We left our
hiding and came up to the little circle of light. We slipped into
the vacant seats on one of the rickety benches. The heap of
mourners was directly before us. They bounced into us as they
cavorted. The smell that they radiated, sweating there in that
obscene heap, half suffocated us. Not all of them, of course, did
the thing in the grand manner. Some merely moaned and rolled
their eyes. The female ox in gingham flung her great bulk on
the ground and jabbered an unintelligible prayer. One of the
men, in the intervals between fits, put on his spectacles and
read his Bible. Beside me on the bench sat the young mother
and her baby. She suckled it through the whole orgy, obviously
fascinated by what was going on, but never venturing to take
any hand in it. On the bed just outside the light the half a dozen
other babies slept peacefully. In the shadows, suddenly appearing and as suddenly going away, were vague figures, whether of
believers or of scoffers I do not know. They seemed to come and
go in couples. Now and then a couple at the ringside would
step out and vanish into the black night. After a while some
came back, the males looking somewhat sheepish. There was
whispering outside the circle of vision. A couple of Model T
Fords lurched up the road, cutting holes in the darkness with
their lights. Once someone out of sight loosed a bray of
laughter.

All this went on for an hour or so. The original penitent, by
this time, was buried three deep beneath the heap. One caught
a glimpse, now and then, of her yellow bobbed hair, but then

she would vanish again. How she breathed down there I don't know; it was hard enough six feet away, with a strong five-cent cigar to help. When the praying brothers would rise up for a bout with the tongues their faces were streaming with perspiration. The fat harridan in gingham sweated like a longshoreman. Her hair got loose and fell down over her face. She fanned herself with her skirt. A powerful old gal she was, plainly equal in her day to a bout with obstetrics and a week's washing on the same morning, but this was worse than a week's washing. Finally, she fell into a heap, breathing in great, convulsive gasps.

Finally, we got tired of the show and returned to Dayton. It was nearly eleven o'clock — an immensely late hour for those latitudes — but the whole town was still gathered in the courthouse yard, listening to the disputes of theologians. The Scopes trial had brought them in from all directions. There was a friar wearing a sandwich sign announcing that he was the Bible champion of the world. There was a Seventh Day Adventist arguing that Clarence Darrow was the beast with seven heads and ten horns described in Revelation XIII, and that the end of the world was at hand. There was an evangelist made up like Andy Gump, with the news that atheists in Cincinnati were preparing to descend upon Dayton, hang the eminent Judge Raulston, and burn the town. There was an ancient who maintained that no Catholic could be a Christian. There was the eloquent Dr. T. T. Martin, of Blue Mountain, Miss., come to town with a truck-load of torches and hymn-books to put Darwin in his place. There was a singing brother bellowing apocalyptic hymns. There was William Jennings Bryan, followed everywhere by a gaping crowd. Dayton was having a roaring time. It was better than the circus. But the note of devotion was simply not there; the Daytonians, after listening a while, would slip away to Robinson's drug-store to regale themselves with Coca-Cola, or to the lobby of the Aqua Hotel, where the learned Raulston sat in state, judicially picking his teeth. The real religion was not present. It began at the bridge over the town creek, where the road makes off for the hills.

Dempsey vs. Carpentier

From the New York *World*, July 3, 1921. During the 20s and 30s I often undertook newspaper commissions, and always enjoyed them vastly. I covered the Dempsey-Carpentier fight in Boyle's Thirty Acres, Jersey City, N. J., July 2, 1921, for the *World* and the Baltimore *Sun* jointly. Carpentier was the favorite, not only of the populace but also of the sporting reporters, mainly because Dempsey was disliked for evading service in World War I. These sporting reporters were nearly all inclined to see what they wanted to see, to wit, the severe punishment of Dempsey by Carpentier. Accordingly, they reported that Dempsey had been almost knocked out in the second or third round. This rapidly developed into a sort of superstition, which was not laid until both Carpentier and Dempsey denounced it as untrue

In the great combat staged there in that colossal sterilizer beneath the harsh Jersey sun there was little to entertain the fancier of gladiatorial delicacies. It was simply a brief and hopeless struggle between a man full of romantic courage and one overwhelmingly superior in every way. This superiority was certainly not only in weight nor even in weight and reach.

As a matter of fact, the difference in weight was a good deal less than many another championship battle has witnessed, and Carpentier's blows seldom failed by falling short. What ailed them was that they were not hard enough to knock out Dempsey or even to do him any serious damage. Whenever they landed Dempsey simply shook them off. And in the intervals between them he landed dozens and scores of harder ones. It was a clean fight, if not a beautiful one. It was swift, clear-cut, brilliant and honest.

Before half of the first round was over it must have been plain to even the policemen and Follies girls at the ringside that poor Carpentier was done for. Dempsey heaved him into the ropes, indeed, at the end of the first minute and thereafter gave him such a beating that he was plainly gone by the time he got to his corner. Blow after blow landed upon his face, neck, ribs, belly and arms. Two-thirds of them were upper cuts at very short range — blows which shook him, winded him, confused him, hurt him, staggered him. A gigantic impact was behind them. His face began to look blobby; red marks appeared all over his front.

Where was his celebrated right? Obviously he was working hard for a chance to unlimber it. He walked in boldly, taking terrific punishment with great gallantry. Suddenly the opportunity came and he let it fly. It caught Dempsey somewhere along the frontiers of his singularly impassive face. The effect upon him was apparently no greater than that of a somewhat angry slap upon an ordinary ox. His great bulk hardly trembled. He blinked, snuffled amiably and went on. Five seconds later Carpentier was seeking cover behind the barricade of his own gloves, and Dempsey was delivering colossal wallops under it, over it and headlong through it.

He fought with both hands, and he fought all the time. Carpentier, after that, was in the fight only intermittently. His right swings reached Dempsey often enough, but as one followed another they hurt him less and less. Toward the end he scarcely dodged them. More and more they clearly missed him, shooting under the arms or sliding behind his ears.

In the second round, of course, there was a moment when Carpentier appeared to be returning to the fight. The crowd, eager to reward his heroic struggle, got to its legs and gave him a cheer. He waded into Jack, pushed him about a bit, and now and then gave him a taste of that graceful right. But there was no left to keep it company, and behind it there was not enough amperage to make it burn. Dempsey took it, shook it off, and went on.

Clout, clout, clout! In the space of half a minute Carpentier stopped twenty-five sickening blows — most of them short, and all of them cruelly hard. His nose began to melt. His jaw sagged. He heaved pathetically. Because he stood up to it gamely, and even forced the fighting, the crowd was for him, and called it his round. But this view was largely that of amateurs familiar only with rough fights between actors at the Lambs club. Observed more scientifically, the round was Jack's. When it closed he was as good as new — and Carpentier was beginning to go pale.

It was not in the second, but in the third round that Carpentier did his actual best. Soon after the gong he reached Jack with a couple of uppers that seemed to have genuine steam in them, and Jack began to show a new wariness. But it was only for a moment. Presently Carpentier was punching holes through the air with wild rights that missed the champion by a foot, and the champion was battering him to pieces with shorts that covered almost every square inch of his upper works. They came in pairs, right and left, and then in quartets, and then in octets, and then almost continuously.

Carpentier decayed beneath them like an Autumn leaf in Vallombrosa. Gently and pathetically he fluttered down. His celebrated right by this time gave Jack no more concern. It would have taken ten of them to have knocked out even Fatty Arbuckle. They had the effect upon the iron champion of petting with a hot water bag. Carpentier went to his corner bloody and bowed. It was all over with the high hopes of that gallant France. He had fought a brave fight; he had kept the faith — but the stars were set for Ireland and the Mormons.

The last round was simply mopping up. Carpentier was on the floor in half a minute. I doubt that Dempsey hit him hard in this round. A few jabs, and all the starch was out of his neck. He got up at nine, and tried a rush. Jack shoved him over, and gave him two or three light ones for good measure as he went down again. He managed to move one of his legs, but above the waist he was dead. When the referee counted ten Dempsey lifted him to his feet and helped him to his stool.

With his arms outstretched along the ropes, he managed to sit up, but all the same he was a very badly beaten pug. His whole face was puffy and blood ran out of his nose and mouth. His façade was one great mass of hoof-prints. Between them his skin had the whiteness of a mackerel's belly. Gone were all his hopes. And with them, the hard francs and centimes, at ruinous rates of exchange, of all the beauty and chivalry of France. Many Frenchmen were in the stand. They took it as Carpentier fought — bravely and stoically. It was a hard and a square battle, and there was no dishonor in it for the loser.

But as a spectacle, of course, it suffered by its shortness and its one-sidedness. There was never the slightest doubt in any cultured heart, from the moment the boys put up their dukes, that Dempsey would have a walk-over.

As I say, it was not only or even mainly a matter of weight. Between the two of them, as they shook hands, there was no very noticeable disparity in size and bulk. Dempsey was the larger, but he certainly did not tower over Carpentier. He was also a bit the thicker and solider, but Carpentier was thick and solid too. What separated them so widely was simply a difference in fighting technique. Carpentier was the lyrical fighter, prodigal with agile footwork and blows describing graceful curves. He fought nervously, eagerly and beautifully. I have seen far better boxers, but I have never seen a more brilliant fighter — that is, with one hand.

Dempsey showed none of that style and passion. He seldom moved his feet, and never hopped, skipped or jumped. His strategy consisted in the bare business: (a) of standing up to it as quietly and solidly as possible; and (b) of jolting, bumping, thumping, bouncing and shocking his antagonist to death with the utmost convenient despatch.

This method is obviously not one for gladiators born subject to ordinary human weaknesses and feelings; it presents advantages to an antagonist who is both quick and strong; it grounds itself, when all is said, rather more on mere toughness than on actual skill at fighting. But that toughness is certainly a handy thing to have when one hoofs the fatal rosin. It gets one around bad situations. It saves the day when the vultures begin to circle overhead.

To reinforce his left Dempsey has a wallop in his right hand like the bump of a ferryboat into its slip. The two work constantly and with lovely synchronization. The fighter who hopes to stand up to them must be even tougher than Jack is, which is like aspiring to be even taller than the late Cy Sulloway. Carpentier simply fell short. He could not hurt Dempsey, and he could not live through the Dempsey bombardment. So he perished there in that Homeric stewpan, a brave man but an unwise one.

The show was managed with great deftness, and all the antecedent rumors of a frame-up were laid in a manner that will bring in much kudos and mazuma to Mons. Tex Rickard, the manager, hereafter. I have never been in a great crowd that was more orderly, or that had less to complain of in the way of avoidable discomforts.

Getting out of the arena, true enough, involved some hot work with the elbows; the management, in fact, put in small fry after the main battle in order to hold some of the crowd back, and so diminish the shoving in the exits, which were too few and too narrow. If there had been a panic in the house, thousands would have been heeled to death. But getting in was easy enough, the seats though narrow were fairly comfortable, and there was a clear view of the ring from every place in the monster bowl. Those who bought bleacher tickets, in fact, saw just as clearly as those who paid $50 apiece for seats at the ringside.

The crowd in the more expensive sections was well-dressed, good-humored and almost distinguished. The common allegation of professional moralists that prize fights are attended by thugs was given a colossal and devastating answer. No such cleanly and decent looking gang was ever gathered at a Billy Sunday meeting, or at any other great moral outpouring that I have ever attended. All the leaders of fashionable and theatrical society were on hand, most of them in checkerboard suits and smoking excellent cigars, or, if female, in new hats and pretty frocks.

Within the range of my private vision, long trained to esthetic alertness, there was not a single homely gal. Four rows ahead of me there were no less than half a dozen who would have adorned the "Follies." Behind me, clad in pink, was a creature so lovely that she caused me to miss most of the preliminaries. She rooted for Carpentier in the French language, and took the count with heroic fortitude.

How Legends are Made

From the Baltimore *Evening Sun*, July 5, 1921

THE LATE herculean combat between Prof. Dempsey and Mons. Carpentier, in addition to all its other usufructs, also had some lessons in it for the psychologist — that is, if any psychologist can be found who is not an idiot. One was a lesson in the ways and means whereby legends are made, that man may be kept misinformed and happy on this earth, and hence not too willing to go to Hell. I allude specifically to a legend already in full credit throughout the length and breadth of Christendom, to wit, the legend that Carpentier gave Dempsey some fearful wallops in the second round of their joust, and came within a micromillimeter of knocking him out. Loving the truth for its own sake, I now tell it simply and hopelessly. No such wallops were actually delivered. Dempsey was never in any more danger of being knocked out than I was, sitting there in the stand with a very pretty gal just behind me and five or six just in front.

In brief, the whole story is apocryphal, bogus, hollow and null, imbecile, devoid of substance. The gallant Frog himself, an honest as well as a reckless man, has testified clearly that, by the time he came to the second round, he was already substantially done for, and hence quite incapable of doing any execution upon so solid an aurochs as Dempsey. His true finish came, in fact, in the first round, when Dempsey, after one of Carpentier's flashy rights, feinted to his head, caused him to duck, and then delivered a devastating depth-bomb upon the back of his neck. This blow, says Carpentier, produced a general agglutination of his blood corpuscles, telescoped his vertebræ, and left him palsied and on the verge of Cheyne-Stokes breathing. To say that any pug unaided by supernatural assistance, after such a colossal shock, could hit von Dempsey hard enough to hurt him is to say that a Sunday-school superintendent could throw a hippopotamus. Nevertheless, there stands the legend, and Christendom will probably believe it as firmly as it believes that Jonah swallowed the whale. It has been printed multitudinously. It has been cabled to all the four quarters of the earth. It enters into the intellectual heritage of the human race. How is it to be accounted for? What was the process of its genesis?

Having no belief in simple answers to the great problems of being and becoming, I attempt a somewhat complex one. It may be conveniently boiled down to the following propositions:

(*a*) The sympathies of a majority of the intelligentsia present were with M. Carpentier, because (1) he was matched with a man plainly his superior, (2) he had come a long way to fight, (3) he was the challenger, (4) he was an ex-soldier, whereas his opponent had ducked the draft.

(*b*) He was (1) a Frenchman, and hence a beneficiary of the romantic air which hangs about all things French, particularly to Americans who question the constitutionality of Prohibition and the Mann Act; he was (2) of a certain modest social pretension, and hence palpably above Professor Dempsey, a low-brow.

(*c*) He was polite to newspaper reporters, the surest means to favorable public notice in America, whereas the oaf, Dempsey, was too much afraid of them to court them.

(*d*) He was a handsome fellow, and made love to all the sob-sisters.

(*e*) His style of fighting was open and graceful, and grounded itself upon active footwork and swinging blows that made a smack when they landed, and so struck the inexperienced as deft and effective.

All these advantages resided within M. de Carpentier himself. Now for a few lying outside him:

(*a*) The sporting reporters, despite their experience, often succumb to (*e*) above. That is, they constantly overestimate the force and effect of spectacular blows, and as constantly underestimate the force and effect of short, close and apparently unplanned blows.

(*b*) They are all in favor of prize-fighting as a sport, and seek to make it appear fair, highly technical and romantic; hence their subconscious prejudice is against a capital fight that is one-sided and without dramatic moments.

(*c*) They are fond, like all the rest of us, of airing their technical knowledge, and so try to gild their reports with accounts of mysterious transactions that the boobery looked at but did not see.

(*d*) After they have predicted confidently that a given pug will give a good account of himself, they have to save their faces by describing him as doing it.

(*e*) They are, like all other human beings, sheep-like, and docilely accept any nonsense that is launched by a man who knows how to impress them.

I could fish up other elements out of the hocus-pocus, but here are enough. Boiled down, the thing simply amounts to this: that Carpentier practised a style of fighting that was more spectacular and attractive than Dempsey's, both to the laiety present and to the experts; that he was much more popular than Dempsey, at least among the literati and the nobility and gentry; and that, in the face of his depressing defeat, all his partisans grasped eagerly at the apparent recovery he made in the second round — when, by his own confession, he was already quite out of it — and converted that apparent recovery into an onslaught which came within an ace of turning the tide for him.

But why did *all* the reporters and spectators agree upon the same fiction? The answer is easily given: *all* of them did *not* agree upon it. Fully a half of them knew nothing about it when they left the stand; it was not until the next day that they began to help it along. As for those who fell upon it at once, they did so for the simple reason that the second round presented the only practicable opportunity for arguing that Carpentier was in the fight at all, save perhaps as an unfortunate spectator. If they didn't say that he had come near knocking out Dempsey in that round, they couldn't say it at all. So they said it — and now every human being on this favorite planet of Heaven believes it, from remote missionaries on the Upper Amazon to lonely Socialists in the catacombs of Leavenworth, and from the Hon. Warren Gamaliel Harding on his alabaster throne to the meanest Slovak in the bowels of the earth. I sweat and groan on this hot night to tell you the truth, but you will not believe me. The preponderance of evidence is against me. In six more days, no doubt, I'll be with you, rid of my indigestible facts and stuffed with the bosh that soothes and nourishes man. . . . Aye, why wait six days? Tomorrow I'll kiss the book, and purge my conscience.

Meanwhile, I take advantage of my hours of grace to state the ribald and immoral truth in plain terms, that an occasional misanthrope may be rejoiced. Carpentier never for a single instant showed the slightest chance of knocking out Dempsey. His fighting was prettier than Dempsey's; his blows swung from the shoulder; he moved about gracefully; when he struck the spot he aimed at (which was very seldom), it was with a jaunty and charming air. But he was half paralyzed by that clout on the posterior neck in the very first round, and thereafter his wallops were no more dangerous to Dempsey than so many cracks with a bag stuffed with liberty cabbage. When, in the second round, he rushed in and delivered the two or three blows to the jaw that are alleged to have shaken up the ex-non-conscript, he got in exchange for them so rapid and so powerful a series of knocks that he came out of the round a solid mass of bruises from the latitude of McBurney's point to the bulge of the frontal escarpment.

Nor did Dempsey, as they say, knock him out finally with a right to the jaw, or with a left to the jaw, or with any single blow to any other place. Dempsey knocked him out by beating him steadily and fearfully, chiefly with short-arm jabs — to the jaw, to the nose, to the eyes, to the neck front and back, to the ears, to the arms, to the ribs, to the *kishkas*. His collapse was gradual. He died by inches. In the end he simply dropped in his tracks, and was unable to get up again — perhaps the most scientifically and thoroughly beaten a man that ever fought in a championship mill. It was, to my taste, almost the ideal fight. There was absolutely no chance to talk of an accidental blow, or of a foul. Carpentier fought bravely, and, for the first minute or two, brilliantly. But after that he went steadily down hill, and there was never a moment when the result was in doubt. The spectators applauded the swinging blows and the agile footwork, but it was the relentless pummeling that won the fight.

Such are the facts. I apologize for the Babylonian indecency of printing them.

Lodge

From the Baltimore *Evening Sun*, June 15, 1920. Written on my return from the Republican National Convention in Chicago, which nominated Warren G. Harding for the Presidency. Henry Cabot Lodge, then a Senator from Massachusetts and one of the leaders of the Republican party, was permanent chairman of the convention. I came back from Chicago on the same train that carried him, and in fact had the compartment next to his. The weather was very hot and there was no air-conditioning. In the morning coming into Washington he astounded humanity by appearing in the corridor in his shirt-sleeves. Harding died on Aug. 2, 1923, and Lodge on Nov. 9, 1924

WHAT Lodge thinks of it, viewing all that ghastly combat of mountebanks in ironical retrospect, would make an interesting story — perhaps the most interesting about the convention that could be told, or even imagined. He presided over the sessions from a sort of aloof intellectual balcony, far above the swarming and bawling of the common herd. He was there in the flesh, but his soul was in some remote and esoteric Cathay. Perhaps even the presence of the flesh was no more than an optical delusion, a mirage due to the heat. At moments when the whole infernal hall seemed bathed in a steam produced by frying delegates and alternates alive, he was as cool as an undertaker at a hanging. He did not sweat like the general. He did not puff. He did not fume. If he put on a fresh collar every morning it was mere habit and foppishness — a sentimental concession to the Harvard tradition. He might have worn the same one all week.

It was delightful to observe the sardonic glitter in his eye, his occasional ill-concealed snort, his general air of detachment from the business before him. For a while he would watch the show idly, letting it get more and more passionate, vociferous and preposterous. Then, as if suddenly awakened, he would stalk into it with his club and knock it into decorum in half a minute. I call the thing a club; it was certainly nothing properly describable as a gavel. The head of it was simply a large globe of hard wood, as big as an ordinary cantaloupe. The handle was perhaps two feet long. The weight of it I can't estimate. It must have been light, else so frail a man would have found it too much for him. But it made a noise like the breaking in a door, and before that crash whole delegations went down.

Supporting it was the Lodge voice, and behind the voice the Lodge sneer. That voice seemed quite extraordinary in so slim and ancient a man. It had volume, resonance, even a touch of music: it was pleasant to hear, and it penetrated that fog of vaporized humanity to great depth. No man who spoke from the platform spoke more clearly, more simply or more effectively. Lodge's keynote speech, of course, was bosh, but it was bosh delivered with an air — bosh somehow dignified by the manner of its emission. The same stuff, shoveled into the atmosphere by any other statesman on the platform, would have simply driven the crowd out of the hall, and perhaps blown up the convention then and there. But Lodge got away with it because he was Lodge — because there was behind it his unescapable confidence in himself, his disarming disdain of discontent below, his unapologetic superiority.

This superiority was and is quite real. Lodge is above the common level of his party, his country and his race, and he knows it very well, and is not disposed toward the puerile hypocrisy of denying it. He has learning. He has traditions behind him. He is absolutely sure of himself in all conceivable American societies. There was a profound irony in the rôle that he had to play at Chicago, and it certainly did not escape him. One often detected him snickering into his beard as the obscene farce unrolled itself before him. He was a nurse observing sucklings at their clumsy play, a philosopher shooing chickens out of the corn. His delight in the business visibly increased as the climax was approached. It culminated in a colossal chuckle as the mob got out of hand, and the witches of crowd folly began to ride, and the burlesque deliberations of five intolerable days came to flower in the half-frightened, half-defiant nomination of Harding — a tin-horn politician with the manner of a rural corn doctor and the mien of a ham actor.

I often wonder what such a man as Lodge thinks secretly of the democracy he professes to cherish. It must interest him enormously, at all events as spectacle, else he would not waste his time upon it. He might have given over his days to the writing of bad history — an avocation both amusing and re-

spectable, with a safe eminence as its final reward. He might
have gone in for diplomacy and drunk out of the same jug with
kings. He might have set up general practise as a Boston intellectual, groaning and sniffing an easy way through life in the
lofty style of the Adams brothers. Instead he dedicated himself
to politics, and spent years mastering its complex and yet fundamentally childish technique.

Well, what reward has it brought him? At 73 he is a boss in
the Senate, holding domination over a herd of miscellaneous
mediocrities by a loose and precarious tenure. He has power,
but men who are far beneath him have more power. At the
great quadrennial pow-wow of his party he plays the part of
bellwether and chief of police. Led by him, the rabble complains bitterly of lack of leadership. And when the glittering
prize is fought for, he is shouldered aside to make way for a
gladiator so bogus and so preposterous that the very thought of
him must reduce a scion of the Cabots to sour and sickly mirth.

A superior fellow? Even so. But superior enough to disdain
even the Presidency, so fought for by fugitives from the sewers?
I rather doubt it. My guess is that the gaudy glamor of the
White House has intrigued even Henry Cabot — that he would
leap for the bauble with the best of them if it were not clearly
beyond his reach. The blinding rays, reflected from the brazen
front of Roosevelt, bathed him for a while; he had his day on
the steps of the throne, and I suspect that he was not insensitive to the thrill of it. On what other theory can one account
for his sober acceptance of the whole Roosevelt hocus-pocus
save on this theory of bedazzlement? Imagine the prince of
cynics actually bamboozled by the emperor of mountebanks!
Think of Swift reading Nick Carter, Edward Bok and Harold
Bell Wright!

He came back from Chicago on the same train that carried
Harding. Harding traveled in one car and Lodge in another.
So far as I could observe their communications were confined
to a few politenesses. Lodge sat in a compartment all alone,
gazing out of the window with his inscrutable ghost of a smile.
He breakfasted alone. He lunched alone. He dined alone. His
job was done, and he was once more serenely out of it.

The Perihelion of Prohibition

From the Sydney (Australia) *Bulletin*, July 20, 1922. This piece, of course, is now of only antiquarian interest, but I am printing it to recall to America what went on during the glaring noonday of Prohibition, when its agents controlled all branches of the government at Washington and in most of the States, and its end seemed far away. There is yet no adequate history of those years. Americans always tend to forget things so disagreeable. They have put the memory of Prohibition out of their minds just as they have put the memory of the great influenza epidemic of 1918–19

PROHIBITION by constitutional amendment has been in force in the United States for three years, everywhere with the full power of the Federal Government behind it, and in most of the 48 States with stringent State laws to help. The results of that colossal effort to enforce it may be briefly summarized as follows:

1. The State and Federal Governments, taken together, have lost the $500,000,000 annual revenue that was formerly derived from excises and licenses, and general taxation has had to be increased to make it up.

2. There has been created, at a cost of $50,000,000 a year, a great army of Prohibition detectives, spies and *agents provocateurs*, four-fifths of whom are already corrupt.

3. There has been created another army of so-called bootleggers, dealing partly in wines and liquors smuggled from Canada and the West Indies, and partly in beers, wines and liquors manufactured illicitly at home, and its members take a joint profit that is certainly not less than $750,000,000 a year, and probably runs to $1,500,000,000.

4. Brewing and distilling and wine-making have been re-established as home industries, and the business of supplying the necessary materials — malt syrup, bottles, corks, etc. — has taken on gigantic proportions.

5. In every American city, and in nine-tenths of the American towns, every known alcoholic beverage is still obtainable — at prices ranging from 100% to 500% above those of pre-Prohibition days — and even in the most re-

mote country districts there is absolutely no place in which any man who desires to drink alcohol cannot get it.

In brief, Prohibition is a failure, and it grows a worse failure every day. There was a time, shortly after the Eighteenth Amendment went into effect, when it showed some promise of being a success, especially in the farming regions, and on the strength of that promise very optimistic reports were sent broadcast by the extremely diligent press-agents of the Anti-Saloon League, and a number of confiding foreigners — for example, Sir Arthur Newholme, the Englishman — were made to believe that the New Jerusalem was actually at hand. But that was simply because the great majority of Americans had not been taking the thing seriously — because they had been caught unawares by the extraordinarily drastic provisions of the Volstead Enforcement Act. The instant they realized what was upon them they applied the national ingenuity and the national talent for corruption to the problem, and in six months it was solved. On the one hand they devised a great multitude of schemes for circumventing the law; on the other hand they proceeded gallantly to the business of debauching the officers sworn to enforce it. Since then there has been a continuous struggle between guns and armament, with guns gradually drawing into the lead. No man, not even the most romantic Prohibitionist, argues that there is anything remotely resembling a general enforcement of Prohibition today. And no unbiased and reflective man, so far as I know, sees the slightest sign that it will ever be enforced hereafter.

The business of evading it and making a mock of it, in fact, has ceased to wear any of the customary aspects of crime, and has become a sort of national sport. The criminal, in the public eye, is not the bootlegger and certainly not his customer, but the enforcement officer. This new-fangled agent of justice has begun to take on an almost legendary character. He is looked upon by the plain people as corruption incarnate — a villainous snooper and blackmailer whose sole public function is to increase the price of drinks. When he comes into court for attacking an illicit distiller with firearms, as happens often, juries handle him roughly. Not infrequently he is mobbed while he is at his work. The effects of this public sentiment are obviously very damaging to the *morale* of the service. In the Federal branch there is a constant changing of personnel, and the average agent now lasts no more than six months. In that time, if he is honest, he has become disgusted by the work he is called upon to do, and alarmed by the general view of it. And if, as is probably more usual, he has gone into it simply to get as much as he can while the getting is good, he has made enough to retire. I have heard of one Federal agent in New York who, on a salary of $2000 a year, paid $4000 rent for his apartment, and kept two automobiles.

Most of the strong liquors sold in the large cities of the East come either from Canada or from the Bahamas. Those from Canada are brought across the international border in large motor-lorries, and the business is so extensive and so well organized that the bribes paid to the officers employed to oppose it, both on the Canadian side and on the American side, are standardized, and so, barring accident, a bootlegger can estimate the cost of his goods to within a few dollars a case, and prepare for financing his operations accordingly. The supplies that come from the Bahamas are transported in small schooners. Some put in by night at lonely places along the immense American coast, where motor transportation awaits their cargoes. Others boldly enter the ports, and the Customs officers are either deceived with false manifests or boldly bribed.

Most of the stuff thus brought in is Scotch whiskey. In pre-Prohibition days it sold in New York at from $30 to $40 a case. Now it brings from $80 to $110, according to the supply. In the main, it is honest goods. But some of the lesser bootleggers — those who sell it, not by the case, but by the bottle — sophisticate it with home-made imitations, chiefly compounded of cologne spirits, prune-juice, pepper and creosote. Very little gin is imported, for it is too easily made at home. As for wines, the bootleggers chiefly confine their attentions to champagne, which brings $120 a case in New York. Under the Volstead Act it is perfectly lawful to import wines for "medicinal and sacramental" purposes. The bootleggers import champagne as "medicine," and then trust to the venality of the Prohibition enforcement officers to get it released for the general trade. The business of bringing in still wines is now almost entirely in the hands of Jewish rabbis in the ghettos of the coast towns. The law allows a Jew in good standing to buy 15 gallons of wine a year for ritualistic use. These gentlemen of God, in return for a profit of from $10 to $15 a case, inscribe all solvent comers on their books as orthodox Ashkenazim — and if the customer has money enough, he may go upon the books of a dozen different rabbis, and under a dozen different safely Jewish names.

As I have said, very little gin is imported, though the widespread popularity of the cocktail makes a steady and immense demand for it. It is manufactured at illicit distilleries, or by the simple process of diluting grain alcohol to 50% strength and adding a few drops of juniper oil and glycerine to the quart. It sells at from $40 to $65 a case, according to quality. All the known liqueurs are made by the same bootleggers, even absinthe. The necessary oils and herbs are imported from France, Italy and Germany, and added to a mixture of alcohol, water and syrup. Some of the liqueurs thus concocted are of surprisingly good quality. In fact, the absinthe now on tap in New York is quite as good as the Swiss absinthe formerly sold in the bars. It costs $15 a quart. Everywhere south of New York so-called corn whiskey, made of maize, is manufactured in stupendous quantities; in one southern State there are said to be no less than 10,000 stills in operation. It is an extremely bad drink, but the native palate, particularly in the country, favors it — and in the cities it is often transformed by devious arts into a very fair rye whiskey. It sells for from $10 to $30 a gallon.

I have left beers and light native wines to the last. The extent to which brewing has been revived in the home in the United States is almost incredible. In some States every second housewife has become a brewer, and some of the beers and ales thus produced are extremely agreeable. A batch of wort may be cooked in an hour, the fermentation is over in four or five days, and two weeks after bottling the brew is fit to drink. In one American city of 750,000 inhabitants there are now 100 shops devoted exclusively to the sale of beer-making supplies, and lately the proprietor of one of them, by no means the largest, told me that he sold 2000 pounds of malt-syrup a day. Two thousand pounds of malt-syrup will make 4000 gallons of prime ale. It costs 2 cents a pint-bottle to make. When the breweries were still running the cheapest beer cost about 4 cents.

Before Prohibition the American people drank very little wine. They were, in fact, just beginning to appreciate their excellent California wines when the Eighteenth Amendment was passed. Some of the California grape-growers, in despair, plowed up their vineyards and planted oranges and olives. Now they wish that they had been less hasty. Last Autumn wine was made in hundreds of thousands of American households, and the price of grapes rose to $125 a ton. I know of no American home, indeed, in which some sort of brewing, wine-making or distilling is not going on. Even in the country, where belief in Prohibition still persists, practically every housewife at least makes a jug or two of blackberry cordial. Every known fruit is expectantly fermented; in the cities raisins and currants are in enormous demand. Even the common dandelion, by some process unknown to me, is converted into a beverage that gently caresses.

Well, if the American people are thus so diligently alcoholic — in the city folk patronize the bootleggers and make beer, and the far-flung yokels experiment with wines and set up stills — why does Prohibition remain the law of the land? In the large cities the majority against it is now at least 4 to 1; in the country it loses public confidence steadily. Then, why isn't it abandoned, and the vast losses that go with it saved, and the inconceivable corruption abated? The answer is too complex to be made in the space that I have remaining. Part of it lies in the fact that the process of amending the Constitution in the United States is very deliberate and vexatious; it took fully 75 years of persistent agitation to get Prohibition adopted, and it will take years of attack to get it formally rejected. But another part of the answer lies in the curious power that fanatical minorities have in American politics — a power that enables them, by playing upon the weaknesses of the two great parties, to overcome their lack of votes.

The End of Prohibition

From The Wet Wets Triumph, Making of a President, 1932, pp. 133–
46. A Chicago dispatch to the Baltimore *Evening Sun*, June 30, 1932. In
those days I always covered the national conventions of the two great parties for the *Sunpapers*. The Republicans, led by the unfortunate Hoover,
adopted a compromise plank on Prohibition at the 1932 convention. It
was already apparent to everyone that the dry millennium was drawing to a
close, but Hoover believed that it would nevertheless last through what he
hoped would be his second term, and thus insisted on placating the drys.
Roosevelt II, the chief Democratic candidate, went even further. He sent
A. Mitchell Palmer to Chicago with a plank that was actually more favorable to the drys than Hoover's. But this only aroused the eager and panting
wets, and they staged a revolt in the resolutions committee. To the surprise
of everyone they got enough support from the South and Middle West to
put over their minority, or wet wet plank, and it was thus the majority
plank when it reached the floor of the convention. One of the few major
politicos to hold out against it was Cordell Hull. The rest joined the procession, and by the end of the year the Eighteenth Amendment and the
Volstead Act were only evil memories

SINCE one o'clock this morning Prohibition has been a fugitive
in the remote quagmires of the Bible Belt. The chase began
thirteen hours earlier, when the resolutions committee of the
convention retired to the voluptuous splendors of the Rose
Room at the Congress Hotel. For four hours nothing came out
of its stronghold save the moaning of converts in mighty travail. Then the Hon. Michael L. Igoe, a round-faced Chicago
politician,[1] burst forth with the news that the wet wets of the
committee had beaten the damp wets by a vote of 35 to 17.
There ensued a hiatus, while the quarry panted and the blood-
hounds bayed. At 7 in the evening the chase was resumed in
the convention hall, and four hours later Prohibition went out
of the window to the stately tune of 934¾ votes to 213¼, or
more than four to one. So the flight to the fastnesses of Zion
began.

But even down there where Genesis has the police behind it,
and an unbaptized man is as rare as a metaphysician, the fugitive is yet harried and oppressed. Only two States, Georgia and

[1] Born in St. Paul, Minn., in 1885; appointed a Federal district judge,
1939. An Elk and a Catholic.

Mississippi, showed a solid dry front on the poll, and in Georgia there were plenty of wets lurking behind the unit rule. All the other great commonwealths of the late Confederacy cast votes for the immediate repeal of the Eighteenth Amendment and the Volstead Act, led by Texas with its solid 46, and South Carolina with its solid 18. Even Tennessee, the Baptist Holy Land, went 18 dripping wet to 6 not so wet. Taking all the Confederate States together, with Kentucky thrown in, they cast 165 votes for the forthright and uncompromising plank of the majority, and only 123 for the pussyfooting plank of the minority. In the Middle West the carnage was even more appalling. Kansas voted 12 to 8 for the minority straddle, but Iowa went the whole hog with loud hosannas, and so did North Dakota, and so did Indiana and Illinois. Even Ohio, the citadel of the Anti-Saloon League, went over to the enemy by 49 to 2, and Nebraska, the old home of William Jennings Bryan, voted nearly two to one for rum and rebellion.

It was a gorgeous affair while it lasted, and the consolations for the poor drys were precious few and not very stimulating. They held Mississippi, the Worst American State,[2] and they held Oklahoma, and the better part of Arkansas, Alabama and North Carolina, but these States are all wobbling, and not even the most optimistic friend of the late holy cause expects them to hold out much longer.

The fight in the resolutions committee was full of dramatic surprises, but by the time it was transferred to the floor of the convention the end was plainly in sight, and so it narrowly escaped becoming a bore. When the really wet wets, led by Senator David I. Walsh, of Massachusetts,[3] and Major E. Brooke Lee, of Maryland, went into the committee room they had but twenty-three States pledged to their side, and they needed twenty-eight. Major Lee professed to be sure that he could snare them, but his confidence was anything but visible in his

2 In September, October and November, 1931, I had printed in the *American Mercury* three articles inquiring into the relative degree of civilization of the forty-eight States, supported by 106 tables of statistics. I found that Mississippi, on almost all accounts, was entitled to "the lamentable preëminence of the Worst American State."

3 Born in 1872; Senator, 1919–47; died 1947.

face. A long, long wait followed, with a gang of reporters buzzing around the keyhole. Nothing came out of it, and the statesmen who emerged at intervals turned out to be deaf and dumb. The hotel was as hot as a boiler-room, and every time the door opened the eminent men within could be seen mopping their bald heads.

Suddenly, at 3 o'clock, the Hon. Mr. Igoe popped out.

"The vote," he bawled, "is 35 to 18."

"For what?" demanded the reporters.

"Against the majority plank."

"Do you mean that the wet wets have substituted the Walsh plank?"

"Not yet," replied Igoe. "One thing at a time. First we had to reject the majority plank. Now we'll take up — "

But at that precise moment another statesman burst out with the news that it was done — that the Walsh plank had been substituted by a vote of 35 to 17. What became of the odd vote was never made plain. Perhaps it was Igoe's, and he forgot to cast it.

The session of the convention, meanwhile, had been postponed from noon to 1 o'clock, and then to 3, and then to 7. Everyone looked for the resolutions committee to wrestle with the Prohibition plank all afternoon, and maybe far into the night. But when the plank was reached, after a long and innocuous debate over the tariff, war debts and free silver, the fight was over in ten minutes. For the wet wets, reinforced by twelve converts, demanded a showdown instantly, and it proved that they had an overwhelming majority. Moreover, it proved that the majority on the floor would be very much larger, for in committee each State had only one vote, whereas on the floor it would cast a vote for every one of its delegates, and the big States were all on the wet wet side.

Thus the combat on the floor last night was really only a sham battle, though it lasted more than three hours. When former Senator Gilbert M. Hitchcock, of Nebraska,[4] got on his legs to read the report of the committee — which is to say, to read the platform — there was such turmoil in the hall that Chairman Walsh had to bang for order over and over again. But

[4] Born in 1859; Senator, 1911–23; died 1934.

when Mr. Hitchcock approached the Prohibition plank there was a sudden hush, and the instant the first sentence of it was out of his mouth the roof was shaken by a stupendous cheer. At once the delegations began parading, led by South Carolina from the traitorous Bible Belt and Iowa from the recreant open spaces of the Middle West. Mississippi held out, and so did Virginia, Washington, Oklahoma, Delaware, North Carolina and Alabama, but there was almost as much politeness in this as fidelity, for three hours later the seven of them were to yield 38½ wet wet votes.

The first rhetorician put up to speak for the minority report, which had been the majority report until the catastrophe in the Rose Room, was the Hon. Cordell Hull, of Tennessee. Hull is a Prohibitionist of long service and heroic deeds, and only three days ago Col. Patrick H. Callahan, the lone Catholic dry,[5] was telling me that he would be the last stalwart to surrender to the rum demon. And yet here he was pleading for resubmission of the Eighteenth Amendment! Not a word did he utter in favor of Prohibition. All he had to say was that it would be better to put it on trial in a decorous and judicial manner, and not butcher it out of hand. The crowd yelled him down.

"You are proposing to repeal Prohibition," he yelled, "after only a few hours' consideration."

"Twelve years," yelled someone in the gallery, and once more Chairman Thomas J. Walsh[6] had to get out his bung-starter and clout for order. It came after a while and the long debate proceeded. All sorts of orators were put up. Some of them hollered for as little as two minutes. Most of them were local dignitaries, eager only to reach the radio audience back home. They offered little in the way of argument and nothing in the way of eloquence. Four-fifths of them seemed to be hotly in favor of the wet wet plank, but sometimes it was difficult to make out which side a given speaker was on.

One such was a gentleman from Texas, whose name seemed to be Hughes. He was introduced as a defender of what was

---

[5] In his youth a professional baseball player; later a varnish manufacturer. Born 1886; died 1940.

[6] Born 1859; Senator from Montana, 1913–33; died 1933.

now the minority plank and the crowd started to boo him, but at once he announced that Texas had decided unanimously to join the wet wets and so the boos began to be drowned in cheers. As he proceeded it appeared that he was actually arguing for the majority plank, which is to say, for light wines and beers immediately and the harder stuff on some near and blest tomorrow. Whether Chairman Walsh made a mistake in introducing him or he became converted to the wet wet doctrine while he was on his legs never appeared clearly. But the crowd decided that he was all right and when the gavel cut him short he was given a rousing hullabaloo for his pains.

The so-called debate went on in the brutal, clumsy, ribald manner that is almost as characteristic of a national convention as the Summer heat. Delegate after delegate, some male and some female, climbed up on the platform to heave another projectile at the vanishing shadow of Prohibition. They came not only from the traditionally wet and antinomian States but also from such former paradises of Christian Endeavor as Florida, Iowa and South Carolina. Their names were often unintelligible, and what they had to say was only half heard. But now and then a notable was recognized and got his round of huzzahs. Thus it was that Jouett Shouse, of Kansas, leaping eagerly from his political tomb, was given his chance to hymn his fellow-corpse, the Hon. John J. Raskob, and to say all over again that Prohibition is, was and of a right ought to be a great curse to humanity.[7]

Some of these snorters against it looked to me to be very recent converts. In fact, not a few of them appeared to be still packing Bibles on their hips, and more than one did his stuff in the ecstatic singsong of a retrieved hell-cat at a revival. The debate was supposed to proceed in the orthodox manner, with each side using half the time, but it was soon apparent that the opponents of the wet wet plank had very few word-heavers on their string, and that none of them was actually dry. The best was probably a gentleman from Idaho, who looked like a pros-

---

[7] Shouse had been chairman of the executive committee of the Democratic National Committee from 1929 until July 1, 1932. Raskob had been chairman of the whole committee during the Al Smith campaign of 1928 and until succeeded by James A. Farley in 1932.

perous cattleman, and made a plea for a simple resubmission
of the Eighteenth Amendment without any party commitment
either one way or the other. He was heard more or less politely
until he squared off and demanded "Is it fair to say that in
order to qualify as a Democrat a man must be wet?" Shouts
of "Yes! Yes!" went up from both the floor and the galleries
and the services had to be halted to give the ultra-wets a chance
to howl off some of their libido.

The setpiece of the debate was the speech of Al Smith. When
he suddenly appeared on the platform, his face a brilliant scarlet and his collar wet and flapping about his neck, he got a
tremendous reception and the overgrown pipe organ let loose
with "East Side, West Side" in an almost terrifying manner,
with every stop wide open and a ton or so of extra weight on
the safety valve. Al did a very good job. He had at Hoover with
some excellent wisecracks, he made some amusing faces, and he
got a huge and friendly laugh by pronouncing the word *radio*
in his private manner, with two *d*'s. He had sense enough to
shut down before he wore out his welcome, so he got another
ear-splitting hand as he finished, with the organ booming again
and the band helping.

Governor Albert C. Ritchie of Maryland [8] had been told off
to second Al's efforts, but a lot of obscure wet wets were panting
to be heard by the folk back home, and he had to wait nearly
two hours. He put in the time on the platform, mopping his
neck, for the heat increased as the evening wore on, and by
midnight it was that of Washington on a muggy August afternoon. In the end the Governor came near being robbed of his
chance by a stout old fellow named W. C. Fitts, with a glittering bald head and bushy white eyebrows.

Fitts turned out to be from Birmingham, Ala., and he arose
to plead with the delegates to abate their wet fervor a trifle,
so as to avoid putting the party on a series of red-hot spots in
the surviving dry strongholds of the Bible country. He had a
plausible case, and he urged it in a reasonable manner. Not a
word directly in favor of Prohibition came out of him. He simply asked that the Southern delegates be spared the need of
going home smelling too powerfully of the devil's brews. But

[8] Born 1876; died 1936.

the crowd was hot for the wettest imaginable wetness, and pretty soon it began to boo him and to demand a vote. The old boy, however, stuck to the microphone, and whenever his syllogisms and exhortations were drowned out by the uproar Chairman Walsh went furiously to his rescue. He kept going, first and last, for at least twenty minutes and in the end he had his say. But he had got the galleries into such a lather that it began to look like suicide for Governor Ritchie to follow him.

Nevertheless, the Governor stepped into it, and at sight of him the crowd shed its impatience magically, and he got a rousing reception,[9] with the organ booming "Maryland, My Maryland" and "Dixie." He had prepared a speech running to a column in the *Evening Sun*, and it had been sent out to the four corners of the Republic by the press associations, but he wisely abandoned it and gave them something shorter and snappier. It made an excellent success, and when he sat down there was another roar, and the organ took another herculean hack at "Maryland, My Maryland."

When the voting on the platform began at midnight it was apparent at once that the extreme wets had it all their own, and that the resubmission plank of the minority, though it went further than the Republican straddle, was too mild to poll any considerable vote. When Alabama split and Arizona cast its six votes for the majority plank the whole audience, delegates and visitors alike, began to cheer, and thereafter the voting was carried on in the traditional Democratic manner, to the tune of howls, bellowings and charges of fraud. Three delegations demanded polls and caused long delays, and there were numerous hot exchanges between the chair and the floor. But the wet vote rolled up steadily, and by the time Kansas was reached it was running two to one. When Massachusetts threw in thirty-six wet votes it rose to three to one, and at the end, as I have said, it was better than four to one.

Despite the slow tempo, the polling was full of dramatic episodes. Just as Iowa, for long a happy hunting ground for the

[9] Ritchie was very popular at the convention, and was the second choice for the presidential nomination of more than half the delegates. But Al Smith bungled the Stop Roosevelt movement so badly that by the time it came to a vote there was no second choice.

Anti-Saloon League, went dripping wet with all its delegates on their legs, yelling and waving their hats, a courier entered the press stand with the news that Senator George W. Norris, of Nebraska, one of the last of the honest drys in Washington, had come out for resubmission and confessed that Prohibition was a cooked goose. Ten minutes later the Nebraska Democrats cast nine votes for the wet wet plank and only five for the damp one, with one delegate absent and another too alarmed and upset to vote. The sweep was really colossal. No comfort whatever was left for the drys. Two weeks ago the Republican convention threw them some bones, but the Democrats refused to do so. The plank adopted is the wettest ever proposed by even the most fanatical wet — in fact, it goes beyond anything that was so much as imagined a month ago or even two weeks ago. After the Republican convention the professional drys were full of hope that they would be able to intimidate the Democrats into compromise and futility. But the Democrats simply refused to be intimidated. Instead, they fell upon Prohibition with raucous hosannas, gave it a dreadful beating and then chased it back to the Bible swamps whence it came.

The professional drys gave up the fight yesterday morning. They are astute fellows and they saw, even before the wet leaders, which way the thing was going. I tried to find Bishop Cannon to hear his last words, but though he seemed to be in Chicago no one could locate him.[10] He and his friends will now call a conference and prepare to arouse the Southern Bible students for Hoover again. But it will be much harder this time and they know it. In 1928 they had a candidate who could help them, for the legend of the Great Engineer was still in full blast. But now they are strapped to a corpse and the

[10] This was written in the early morning, after the historic session adjourned. Next day Roosevelt was nominated — and promptly swallowed the wet wet plank, though he had pulled against it. I found Bishop Cannon during the day. He was sitting lugubriously in an upstairs corridor of the Congress Hotel, and told me that the sudden collapse of Prohibition had been a great surprise to him. While we palavered a photographer came along and made a picture of us, head to head. When it was printed it made a painful impression upon the bosses of the Anti-Saloon League, for to them I was one of Beelzebub's agents. But the bishop was too despondent to care.

once so amiable Yahweh of the club and the search-warrant has deserted them.

The New Deal

From Wizards, Baltimore *Evening Sun*, May 27, 1935. I offer this as a specimen of my polemic against the New Deal, which started in the Spring of 1933 and went on until the approach of the American entrance into World War II adjourned free speech on public questions. I choose the following because it recalls facts about the New Deal .personnel and *modus operandi* that tend to be forgotten

I TAKE the following from the celebrated *New Republic:*

In the Autumn of 1933, after General Johnson and his Blue Eagle had done their part, business began rapidly to decline. On a train coming back from a social workers' meeting, Harry Hopkins and his assistant, Aubrey Williams, discussed with apprehension the coming Winter. . . . Hopkins said: "Let's take a real crack at this. Let's give everyone a job." The title, the Civil Works Administration, was contributed by Jacob Baker.

And the following from the eminent *Nation:*

It is characteristic of Hopkins that he wasted no time meditating upon the stupendous problems and conflicts such a revolutionary scheme might engender. He talked it over with his aides — Baker, Williams and Corrington Gill — and from their discussion there emerged an equally brief memorandum outlining the scheme. With this memorandum in hand he trotted off to the White House one Wednesday afternoon in November. He went merely to enlist Roosevelt's interest. He expected to be told to develop the idea and come back with a fuller outline. He still expected that when he left the White House that evening. But it so happened that he had caught the New Deal Messiah in one of his periods of infatuation with the spending art, and Hopkins literally woke up the next morning to discover that Roosevelt without further ado had proclaimed the CWA in effect.

The money began to pour out on November 16, 1933, to the tune of a deafening hullabaloo. By December 1 more than 1,000,000 men were on the CWA pay roll; by January 18, 1934, the number reached 4,100,000. Press agents in eight-hour shifts worked day and night to tell a panting country what it was all about. The Depression, it was explained, was being given a series of adroit and fatal blows, above, below and athwart the belt. In six months there would be no more unemployment, the wheels of industry would be spinning, and the More Abundant Life would be on us. Brains had at last conquered the fear of fear.

What actually happened belongs to history. By the opening of Spring Hopkins had got rid of his billion, and the whole scheme had blown up with a bang. More people were out of work than ever before. The wheels of industry resolutely refused to spin. The More Abundant Life continued to linger over the sky line. There ensued a pause for taking breath, and then another stupendous assault was launched upon the taxpayer. This time the amount demanded was $4,880,000,000. It is now in hand, and plans are under way to lay it out where it will do the most good in next year's campaign.

Go back to the two clippings and read them again. Consider well what they say. Four preposterous nonentities, all of them professional uplifters, returning from a junket at the taxpayer's expense, sit in a smoking car munching peanuts and talking shop. Their sole business in life is spending other people's money. In the past they have always had to put in four-fifths of their time cadging it, but now the New Deal has admitted them to the vast vaults of the public treasury, and just beyond the public treasury, shackled in a gigantic lemon-squeezer worked by steam, groans the taxpayer. They feel their oats, and are busting with ideas. For them, at least, the More Abundant Life has surely come in.

Suddenly one of them, biting down hard on a peanut, has an inspiration. He leaps to his feet exultant, palpitating like a crusader shinning up the walls of Antioch. How, now, comrade, have you bitten into a worm? Nay, gents, I have thought of a good one, a swell one, the damndest you ever heard tell of. Why not put *everyone* to work? Why not shovel it out in a really Large Way? Why higgle and temporize? We won't be here forever, and when we are gone we'll be gone a long while.

But the *Führer*? Wasn't he babbling again, only the other day, of balancing the budget? Isn't it a fact that he shows some sign of wobbling of late — that the flop of the NRA has given him to think? Well, we can only try. We have fetched him before, and maybe we can fetch him again. So the train reaches Washington, the porter gets his tip from the taxpayer's pocket, and the next day the four brethren meet to figure out the details. But they never get further than a few scratches, for the *Führer* is in one of his intuitive moods, and his Christian Science smile is in high gear. Say no more, Harry, it is done! The next morning the money begins to gush and billow out of the Treasury. Six months later a billion is gone, and plans are under way to collar five times as much more.

Such is government by the Brain Trust. Such is the fate of the taxpayer under a Planned Economy. Such is the Utopia of damned fools. I have been careful to take the evidence from unimpeachable sources. If it had come from the *Congressional Record* I'd have been suspicious of it, for both Houses, as we heard lately from the *Führer* himself, are full of liars. But the *Nation* and the *New Republic* always tell the precise truth, and in the precise sense that it is defined by all idealistic men. Both were howling for a Planned Economy long before the *Führer* himself ever heard of it, and both hailed the setting up of the Brain Trust as a step forward in government comparable to the Northern Securities decision or the emancipation of the slaves.

Well, then, who is this Hopkins who had that facile inspiration on the train, and made off with that billion so swiftly and so light-heartedly, and is now preparing to get rid of $4,800,000,000 more? I turn to the *Nation* and the *New Republic* again: the former printed a monograph on him on May 22, and the latter on April 10. He is, it appears, the son of an honest harness-maker in Sioux City, Iowa. In 1910 or thereabout he was graduated from a fresh-water college in his native wilds, and made tracks for New York. In a little while he had a nice job with the Association for Improving the Condition of the Poor, and then, in 1918, he got a nicer one with the Board of Child Welfare. By 1922 he was beginning to be known as a promising uplifter, and in that year the Red Cross made him its divisional manager and wikinski at New Orleans. In 1924 he was back in New York to take a better job with the Association for the Improvement of the Condition of the Poor, and a few years later he fell into a still better one as director of the New York Tuberculosis and Health Association. Here he shined so effulgently that when, in 1932, the *Führer*, then Governor of New York, set up a Temporary Emergency Relief Administration, good Harry was made its director at $12,500 a year. His translation to Washington followed naturally. When he arrived there, according to the *New Republic's* biographer, he was "received uproariously by the Administration's left wing, and within three months was a national figure."

Of such sort are the wizards who now run the country. Here is the perfect pattern of a professional world-saver. His whole life has been devoted to the art and science of spending other people's money. He has saved millions of the down-trodden from starvation, pestilence, cannibalism, and worse — always at someone else's expense, and usually at the taxpayer's. He has been going it over and over again at Washington. And now, with $4,800,000,000 of your money and mine in his hands, he is preparing to save fresh multitudes, that they may be fat and optimistic on the Tuesday following the first Monday in November, 1936, and so mark their ballots in the right box.

About his associates in this benign work for humanity I can tell you less, for the *Nation* and the *New Republic* have failed, so far, to print treatises on them, and "Who's Who in America" is silent about them. "Who's Who" is so hospitable that no less than 31,081 head of Americans, male and female, qualify for its present edition. They include all sorts of one-book authors, third-rate clergymen, superannuated Chautauqua lecturers, and neighborhood busybodies, but a diligent search fails to reveal the Hon. Messrs. Jacob Baker, Aubrey Williams and Corrington Gill. There is an Ezra Baker who is chairman of the Bunker Hill Monument Association and was formerly chairman of the Boston Licensing Board, and a Rev. George

Randolph Baker who is associate secretary of the Board of Education of the Northern Baptist Convention, but the ineffable Jacob is *non est*. Among the Williamses there is an Anita who is a professional uplifter down in sunny Tennessee and refuses coyly to give the date of her birth, and a Charles B. who is professor of Greek and ethics at Union "University" in the same great State, and an Edward L. F. who is a lecturer in Summer schools, a Rotarian and the editor of the *Kadelphian Review* of Tiffin, Ohio, but I can't find the genius, Aubrey. Finally, there are eight Gills, including one who wrote "Forest Facts for Schools" and another who is an Elk, a Knight of Pythias and a Woodman of the World, but nowhere in the book is there any mention of that inspired young man, Corrington.

Of such sort are the young wizards who now sweat to save the plain people from the degradations of capitalism, which is to say, from the degradations of working hard, saving their money, and paying their way. This is what the New Deal and its Planned Economy come to in practise — a series of furious and irrational raids upon the taxpayer, planned casually by professional do-gooders lolling in smoking cars, and executed by professional politicians bent only upon building up an irresistible machine. This is the *Führer's* inspired substitute for constitutional government and common sense.

XXIV. CRITICISM

The Critical Process

From FOOTNOTE ON CRITICISM, PREJUDICES: THIRD SERIES,
1922, pp. 85–104.
First printed, in part, in the *Smart Set*, Dec., 1921, p. 25

NEARLY all the discussions of criticism that I am acquainted with start off with a false assumption, to wit, that the primary motive of the critic, the impulse which makes a critic of him instead of, say, a politician or a stockbroker, is pedagogical — that he writes because he is possessed by a passion to advance the enlightenment, to put down error and wrong, to disseminate some specific doctrine: psychological, epistemological, historical, or esthetic. But this is true, it seems to me, only of bad critics, and its degree of truth increases in direct ratio to their badness. The motive of the critic who is really worth reading — the only critic of whom, indeed, it may be said truthfully that it is at all possible to read him, save as an act of mental penitence — is something quite different. That motive is not the motive of the pedagogue, but the motive of the artist. It is no more and no less than the simple desire to function freely and beautifully, to give outward and objective form to ideas that bubble inwardly and have a fascinating lure in them, to get rid of them dramatically and make an articulate noise in the world.

When, years ago, I devoted myself diligently to critical pieces upon the writings of Theodore Dreiser, I found that practically everyone who took any notice of my proceedings at all fell into either one of two assumptions about my underlying purpose: (*a*) that I had a fanatical devotion to Mr. Dreiser's ideas and desired to propagate them, or (*b*) that I was an ardent patriot, and yearned to lift up American literature. Both assumptions were false. I had, in fact, very little interest in many of Mr. Dreiser's main ideas; when we met we usually quarreled about them. And I was and am wholly devoid of public spirit, and haven't the least lust to improve American literature; if it ever came to what I regard as perfection my job would be gone. What, then, was my motive in writing about Mr. Dreiser so copiously? My motive, well known to Mr. Dreiser himself and to everyone else who knew me as intimately as he did, was simply and solely to sort out and give coherence to the ideas of Mr. Mencken, and to put them into suave and ingratiating terms, and to discharge them with a flourish, and maybe with a phrase of pretty song into the dense fog that blanketed the Republic.

The critic's choice of criticism rather than of what is called creative writing is chiefly a matter of temperament, with accidents of education and environment to help. The feelings that happen to be dominant in him at the moment the scribbling frenzy seizes him are feelings inspired, not directly by life itself, but by books, pictures, music, sculpture, architecture, religion, philosophy — in brief, by some other man's feelings about life. They are thus, in a sense, second-hand, and it is no wonder that creative artists so easily fall into the theory that they are also second-rate. Perhaps they usually are. If, indeed, the critic continues on this plane — if he lacks the intellectual agility and enterprise needed to make the leap from the work of art to the vast and mysterious complex of phenomena behind it — then they *always* are, and he remains no more than a fugleman or policeman to his betters. But if anything resembling a genuine artist is concealed within him — if his feelings are in any sense profound and original, and his capacity for self-expression above the average of educated men — then he moves inevitably from the work of art to life itself, and begins to take on a dignity that he formerly lacked.

It is impossible to think of a man of any actual force and originality, universally recognized as having those qualities, who spent his whole life appraising and describing the work of other men. Did Goethe, or Carlyle, or Matthew Arnold, or Sainte-Beuve, or Macaulay, or even, to come down a few pegs, Lewes, or Lowell, or Hazlitt? Certainly not. The thing that becomes most obvious about the writings of all such men, once they are examined carefully, is that the critic is always being swallowed

up by the creative artist — that what starts out as the review of
a book, or a play, or other work of art, usually develops very
quickly into an independent essay upon the theme of that work
of art, or upon some theme that it suggests — in a word, that
it becomes a fresh work of art, and only indirectly related to the
one that suggested it. This fact, indeed, is so plain that it
scarcely needs statement. What the pedagogues always object
to in, for example, the *Quarterly* reviewers is that they forgot
the books they were supposed to review, and wrote long papers
— often, in fact, small books — expounding ideas suggested (or
not suggested) by the books under review. But every critic who
is worth reading falls inevitably into the same habit. He cannot
stick to his ostensible task: what is before him is always infinitely less interesting to him than what is within him. If he is
genuinely first-rate — if what is within him stands the test of
type, and wins an audience, and produces the reactions that
every artist craves — then he usually ends by abandoning the
criticism of specific works of art altogether, and setting up shop
as a merchant in general ideas, *i.e.*, as an artist working in the
materials of life itself.

Mere reviewing, however conscientiously and competently it
is done, is plainly a much inferior business. Like writing poetry,
it is chiefly a function of intellectual immaturity. The young
literatus just out of the university, having as yet no capacity
for grappling with the fundamental mysteries of existence, is
put to writing reviews of books, or plays, or music, or painting.
Very often he does it pretty well; it is, in fact, not hard to do
well, for even decayed pedagogues often do it. But if he continues to do it, whether well or ill, it is a sign to all the world
that his growth ceased when they made him *artium bacca-
laureus*. Gradually he becomes, whether in or out of the academic grove, a professor, which is to say, a man devoted to
diluting and retailing the ideas of his superiors — not an artist,
not even a bad artist, but almost the antithesis of an artist. He
is learned, he is sober, he is painstaking and accurate — but he
is as hollow as a jug. Nothing is in him save the ghostly echoes
of other men's thoughts and feelings. If he were a genuine artist
he would have thoughts and feelings of his own, and the impulse to give them objective form would be irresistible. An art-

ist can no more withstand that impulse than a politician can withstand the temptations of a job. There are no mute, inglorious Miltons, save in the hallucinations of poets. The one sound test of a Milton is that he functions as a Milton. His difference from other men lies precisely in the superior vigor of his impulse to self-expression, not in the superior beauty and loftiness of his ideas. Other men, in point of fact, often have the same ideas, or perhaps even loftier ones, but they are able to suppress them, usually on grounds of decorum, and so they escape being artists, and are respected by right-thinking persons, and die with money in the bank, and are forgotten in two weeks.

Obviously, the critic whose performance we are commonly called upon to investigate is a man standing somewhere along the path leading from the beginning that I have described to the goal. He has got beyond being a mere cataloguer and valuer of other men's ideas, but he has not yet become an autonomous artist — he is not yet ready to challenge attention with his own ideas alone. But it is plain that his motion, in so far as he is moving at all, must be in the direction of that autonomy, that is, unless one imagines him sliding backward into senile infantilism — a spectacle not unknown to literary pathology, but too pathetic to be discussed here. Bear this motion in mind, and the true nature of his aims and purposes becomes clear; more, the incurable falsity of the aims and purposes usually credited to him becomes equally clear. He is not actually trying to perform an impossible act of arctic justice upon the artist whose work gives him a text. He is not trying with mathematical passion to find out exactly what was in that artist's mind at the moment of creation, and to display it precisely and in an ecstasy of appreciation. He is not trying to bring the work discussed into accord with some transient theory of esthetics, or ethics, or truth, or to determine its degree of departure from that theory. He is not trying to lift up the fine arts, or to defend democracy against sense, or to promote happiness at the domestic hearth, or to convert sophomores into right-thinkers, or to serve God. He is not trying to fit a group of novel phenomena into the orderly process of history. He is not even trying to discharge the catalytic office that I myself, in a romantic moment, once sought to force upon him.[1] He is, first and last, simply trying to express himself. He is trying to arrest and challenge a sufficient body of readers, to make them pay attention to him, to impress them with the charm and novelty of his ideas, to provoke them into an agreeable (or shocked) awareness of him, and he is trying to achieve thereby for his own inner ego the grateful feeling of a function performed, a tension relieved, a *katharsis* attained which Wagner achieved when he wrote "Die Wal-küre," and a hen achieves every time she lays an egg.

Joseph Conrad was moved by that necessity to write romances; Mozart was moved to write music; poets are moved to write poetry; critics are moved to write criticism. The form is nothing; the only important thing is the motive power, and it is the same in all cases. It is the pressing yearning of nearly every man who has actual ideas in him to empty them upon the world, to hammer them into plausible and ingratiating shapes, to compel the attention and respect of his equals, to lord it over his inferiors. So seen, the critic becomes a far more transparent and agreeable fellow than ever he was in the discourses of the psychologists who sought to make him a mere appraiser in an intellectual customs house, a gauger in a distillery of the spirit, a just and infallible judge upon the cosmic bench. Such offices, in point of fact, never fit him. He always bulges over their confines. When he is thus labeled and estimated, it inevitably turns out that the critic under examination is a very bad one, or no critic at all.

But when he is thought of, not as pedagogue, but as artist, then he begins to take on reality, and, what is more, dignity. Carlyle was surely no just and infallible judge; on the contrary, he was full of prejudices, biles, naïvetés, humors. Yet he is read, consulted, attended to. Macaulay was unfair, inaccurate, fanciful, lyrical — yet his essays live. Arnold had his faults too, and so did Sainte-Beuve, and so did Goethe, and so did many another of that line — and yet they are remembered today, and all the learned and conscientious critics of their time, laboriously concerned with the precise intent of the artists under re-

[1] In Criticism of Criticism of Criticism, Prejudices: First Series, 1919, pp. 9–31. This essay, in shorter form, was first printed in the New York *Evening Mail*, July 1, 1919.

view, and passionately determined to set it forth with god-like care and to relate it exactly to this or that great stream of ideas — all these pedants are forgotten. What saved Carlyle, Macaulay and company is as plain as day. They were first-rate artists. They could make the thing charming, and that is always a million times more important than making it true.

Truth, indeed, is something that is believed in completely only by persons who have never tried personally to pursue it to its fastnesses and grab it by the tail. It is the adoration of second-rate men — men who always receive it as second-hand. Pedagogues believe in immutable truths and spend their lives trying to determine them and propagate them; the intellectual progress of man consists largely of a concerted effort to block and destroy their enterprise. Nine times out of ten, in the arts as in life, there is actually no truth to be discovered; there is only error to be exposed. In whole departments of human inquiry it seems to me quite unlikely that the truth ever *will* be discovered. Nevertheless, the rubber-stamp thinking of the world always makes the assumption that the exposure of an error is identical with the discovery of the truth — that error and truth are simply opposites. They are nothing of the sort. What the world turns to, when it has been cured of one error, is usually simply another error, and maybe one worse than the first one. This is the whole history of the intellect in brief. The average man of today does not believe in precisely the same imbecilities that the Greek of the Fourth Century before Christ believed in, but the things that he *does* believe in are often quite as idiotic.

Perhaps this statement is a bit too sweeping. There is, year by year, a gradual accumulation of what may be called, provisionally, truths — there is a slow accretion of ideas that somehow manage to meet all practicable human tests, and so survive. But even so, it is risky to call them absolute truths. All that one may safely say of them is that no one, as yet, has demonstrated that they are errors. Soon or late, if experience teaches us anything, they are likely to succumb too. The profoundest truths of the Middle Ages are now laughed at by schoolboys. The profoundest truths of democracy will be laughed at, a few centuries hence, even by school-teachers.

In the department of esthetics, wherein critics mainly disport themselves, it is almost impossible to think of a so-called truth that shows any sign of being permanently true. The most profound of principles begins to fade and quiver almost as soon as it is stated. But the work of art, as opposed to the theory behind it, has a longer life, particularly if that theory be obscure and questionable, and so cannot be determined accurately. "Hamlet," the Mona Lisa, "Dixie," "Parsifal," "Mother Goose," "Annabel Lee," "Huckleberry Finn" — these things, so baffling to pedagogy, so contumacious to the categories, so mysterious in purpose and utility — these things live. And why? Because there is in them the flavor of salient, novel and attractive personality, because the quality that shines from them is not that of correct demeanor but that of creative passion, because they pulse and breathe and speak, because they are genuine works of art.

So with criticism. Let us forget all the heavy effort to make a science of it; it is a fine art, or nothing. If the critic, retiring to his cell to concoct his treatise upon a book or play or whatnot, produces a piece of writing that shows sound structure, and brilliant color, and the flash of new and persuasive ideas, and civilized manners, and the charm of an uncommon personality in free function, then he has given something to the world that is worth having, and sufficiently justified his existence. Is Carlyle's "Frederick" true? Who cares? As well ask if the Parthenon is true, or the C Minor Symphony, or "Wiener Blut." Let the critic who is an artist leave such necropsies to professors of esthetics, who can no more determine the truth than he can, and will infallibly make it unpleasant and a bore.

It is, of course, not easy to practise this abstention. Two forces, one within and one without, tend to bring even a Hazlitt under the campus pump. One is the almost universal human susceptibility to messianic delusions — the irresistible tendency to practically every man, once he finds a crowd in front of him, to strut and roll his eyes. The other is the public demand, born of such long familiarity with conventional criticism that no other kind is readily conceivable, that the critic teach something as well as say something — in the Rotarian phrase, that he be constructive. Both operate powerfully against his free functioning, and especially the former. He finds it hard to resist the flattery of his customers, however little he may actually esteem it. If he knows anything at all, he knows that his following, like that of every other artist in ideas, is chiefly made up of the congenitally subaltern type of man and woman — natural converts, lodge joiners, me-toos, stragglers after parades. It is precious seldom that he ever gets a positive idea out of them; what he usually gets is mere unintelligent ratification. But this troop, despite its obvious failings, corrupts him in various ways. For one thing, it enormously reënforces his belief in his own ideas, and so tends to make him stiff and dogmatic — in brief, precisely everything that he ought not to be. And for another thing, it tends to make him (by a curious contradiction) a bit pliant and politic: he begins to estimate new ideas, not in proportion as they are amusing or beautiful, but in proportion as they are likely to please. So beset, front and rear, he sometimes sinks supinely to the level of a professor, and his subsequent proceedings are interesting no more.

The true aim of a critic is certainly not to make converts. He must know that very few of the persons who are susceptible to conversion are worth converting. Their minds are intrinsically flabby and parasitical, and it is certainly not sound sport to agitate minds of that sort. Moreover, the critic must always harbor a grave doubt about most of the ideas that they lap up so greedily — it must occur to him not infrequently, in the silent watches of the night, that much that he writes is sheer buncombe. As I have said, I can't imagine any idea — that is, in the domain of esthetics — that is palpably and incontrovertibly sound. All that I am familiar with, and in particular all that I announce most vociferously, seem to me to contain a core of quite obvious nonsense. I thus try to avoid cherishing them too lovingly, and it always gives me a shiver to see anyone else gobble them at one gulp. Criticism, at bottom, is indistinguishable from skepticism. Both launch themselves, the one by esthetic presentations and the other by logical presentations, at the common human tendency to accept whatever is approved, to take in ideas ready-made, to be responsive to mere rhetoric and gesticulation. A critic who believes in anything absolutely is bound to that something quite as helplessly as a Christian is bound to the Freudian garbage in the Book of Revelation. To that extent, at all events, he is unfree and unintelligent, and hence a bad critic.

The demand for "constructive" criticism is based upon the ancient assumption that immutable truths exist in the arts, and that the artist will be improved by being made aware of them. This notion, whatever the form it takes, is always absurd — as much so, indeed, as its brother delusion that the critic, to be competent, must be a practitioner of the specific art he ventures to deal with, *i.e.*, that a doctor, to cure a belly-ache, must have a belly-ache. As practically encountered, it is disingenuous as well as absurd, for it comes chiefly from bad artists who tire of serving as performing monkeys, and crave the greater ease and safety of sophomores in class. They demand to be taught in order to avoid being knocked about. In their demand is the theory that instruction, if they could get it, would profit them — that they are capable of doing better work than they do. As a practical matter, I doubt that this is ever true. Bad poets never actually grow any better; they invariably grow worse and worse. In all history there has never been, to my knowledge, a single practitioner of any art who, as a result of "constructive" criticism, improved his work. The curse of all the arts, indeed, is the fact that they are constantly invaded by persons who are not artists at all — persons whose yearning to express their ideas and feelings is unaccompanied by the slightest capacity for charming expression — in brief, persons with absolutely nothing to say.

This is particularly true of the art of letters, which interposes very few technical obstacles to the vanity and garrulity of such invaders. Any effort to teach them to write better is an effort wasted, as every editor discovers for himself; they are as incapable of it as they are of jumping over the moon. The only sort of criticism that can deal with them to any profit is the sort that employs them frankly as laboratory animals. It cannot cure them, but it can at least make an amusing and perhaps edifying show of them. It is idle to argue that the good in them is thus destroyed with the bad. The simple answer is that there *is* no good in them. Suppose Poe had wasted his time trying to dredge good work out of Rufus Dawes, author of "Geraldine."

He would have failed miserably — and spoiled a capital essay, still diverting after a century. Suppose Beethoven, dealing with Gottfried Weber, had tried laboriously to make an intelligent music critic of him. How much more apt, useful and durable the simple note: "Arch-ass! Double-barreled ass!" Here was absolutely sound criticism. Here was a judgment wholly beyond challenge. Moreover, here was a small but perfect work of art.

Upon the low practical value of "constructive" criticism I can offer testimony out of my own experience. My books have been commonly reviewed at length, and many critics have devoted themselves to pointing out what they conceive to be my errors, both of fact and of taste. Well, I cannot recall a case in which any suggestion offered by a "constructive" critic has helped me in the slightest, or even actively interested me. Every such wet-nurse of letters has sought fatuously to make me write in a way differing from that in which the Lord God Almighty, in His infinite wisdom, impels me to write — that is, to make me write stuff which, coming from me, would be as false as an appearance of decency in a Congressman. All the benefits I have ever got from the critics of my work have come from the destructive variety. A hearty slating always does me good, particularly if it be well written. It begins by enlisting my professional respect; it ends by making me examine my ideas coldly in the privacy of my chamber. Not, of course, that I usually revise them, but I at least examine them. If I decide to hold fast to them, they are all the dearer to me thereafter, and I expound them with a new passion and plausibility. If, on the contrary, I discern holes in them, I shelve them in a *pianissimo* manner, and set about hatching new ones to take their place. But "constructive" criticism irritates me. I do not object to being denounced, but I can't abide being schoolmastered, especially by men I regard as imbeciles.

I find, as a practising critic, that very few men who write books are even as tolerant as I am — that most of them, soon or late, show signs of extreme discomfort under criticism, however polite its terms. Perhaps this is why enduring friendships between authors and critics are so rare. All artists, of course, dislike one another more or less, but that dislike seldom rises to implacable enmity, save between opera singer and opera singer, and creative author and critic. Even when the latter two keep up an outward show of good-will, there is always bitter antagonism under the surface. Part of it, I daresay, arises out of the impossible demands of the critic, particularly if he be tinged with the constructive madness. Having favored an author with his good opinion, he expects the poor fellow to live up to that good opinion without the slightest compromise or faltering, and this is commonly beyond human power. He feels that any let-down compromises *him* — that his hero is stabbing him in the back, and making him ridiculous — and this feeling rasps his vanity. The most bitter of all literary quarrels are those between critics and creative artists, and most of them arise in just this way. As for the creative artist, he on his part naturally resents the critic's air of pedagogical superiority and he resents it especially when he has an uneasy feeling that he has fallen short of his best work, and that the discontent of the critic is thus justified. Injustice is relatively easy to bear; what stings is justice.

Under it all, of course, lurks the fact that I began with: the fact that the critic is himself an artist, and that his creative impulse, soon or late, is bound to make him neglect the punctilio. When he sits down to compose his criticism, his artist ceases to be a friend and becomes mere raw material for his work of art. It is my experience that artists invariably resent this cavalier use of them. They are pleased so long as the critic confines himself to the modest business of interpreting them — preferably in terms of their own estimate of themselves — but the moment he proceeds to adorn their theme with variations of his own, the moment he brings new ideas to the enterprise and begins contrasting them with their ideas, that moment they grow restive. It is precisely at this point, of course, that criticism becomes genuine criticism; before that it was mere reviewing. When a critic passes it he loses his friends. By becoming an artist, he becomes the foe of all other artists.

But the transformation, I believe, has good effects upon him: it makes him a better critic. Too much *Gemütlichkeit* is as fatal to criticism as it would be to surgery or politics. When it rages unimpeded it leads inevitably either to a dull professorial sticking on of meaningless labels or to log-rolling, and often it leads to both. One of the most hopeful signs in the Republic is the revival of acrimony in criticism — the renaissance of the doctrine that esthetic matters are important, and that it is worth the while of a healthy male to take them seriously, as he takes business, sport and amour. In the days when American literature was showing its first vigorous growth, the native criticism was extraordinarily violent and even vicious; in the days when American literature swooned upon the tomb of the Puritan *Kultur* it became flaccid and childish. The typical critic of the first era was Poe, as the typical critic of the second was Howells. Poe carried on his critical jehads with such ferocity that he sometimes got into law-suits, and now and again ran no little risk of having his head cracked. He regarded literary questions as exigent and momentous. The lofty aloofness of the don was simply not in him. When he encountered a book that seemed to him to be bad, he attacked it almost as sharply as an archbishop would attack Jesus. His opponents replied in the same Berserker manner. Much of Poe's surviving ill-fame, as a drunkard and dead-beat, is due to their inordinate denunciations of him. They were not content to refute him; they constantly tried to dispose of him altogether. The very ferocity of that ancient row shows that the native literature, in those days, was in a healthy state. Books of genuine value were produced.

Literature always thrives best, in fact, in an atmosphere of hearty strife. Poe, surrounded by admiring professors, never challenged, never aroused to the emotions of revolt, would probably have written poetry indistinguishable from the hollow stuff of, say, George E. Woodberry. It took the persistent (and often grossly unfair and dishonorable) opposition of Griswold *et al.* to stimulate him to his highest endeavors. He needed friends, true enough, but he also needed enemies.

Examination for Critics

From THE NATIONAL LETTERS, PREJUDICES: SECOND SERIES, 1920, pp. 24–25

HERE are the tests that the late Clayton Hamilton proposed for the dramatic critics of 1917, *i.e.*, for gentlemen chiefly employed in reviewing such compositions as the Ziegfeld Follies, "Up in Mabel's Room," "Ben-Hur" and "The Witching Hour":

1. Have you ever stood bareheaded in the nave of Amiens?
2. Have you ever climbed to the Acropolis by moonlight?
3. Have you ever walked with whispers into the hushed presence of the Frari Madonna of Bellini?

XXV. LITERATURE

The Divine Afflatus

From Prejudices: Second Series, 1920, pp. 155–71.
First printed in part in the New York *Evening Mail*, Nov. 16, 1917

Every man who writes, or paints, or composes knows by hard experience that there are days when his ideas flow freely and clearly and days when they are dammed up damnably. On his good days, for some reason quite incomprehensible to him, all the processes and operations of his mind take on an amazing ease and slickness. Almost without conscious effort he solves technical problems that have badgered him for weeks. He is full of novel expedients, extraordinary efficiencies, strange cunnings. He has a feeling that he has suddenly and unaccountably broken through a wall, dispersed a fog, got himself out of the dark. So he does a double or triple stint of the best work that he is capable of — maybe of far better work than he has ever been capable of before — and goes to bed impatient for the morrow. And on the morrow he discovers to his consternation that he has become almost idiotic, and quite incapable of any work at all.

This unpleasant experience overtakes poets and contrapuntists, critics and dramatists, painters and sculptors, and also, no doubt, philosophers and journalists; it may even be shared, so far as I know, by advertisement writers and the rev. clergy. The characters that all anatomists of melancholy mark in it are the irregular ebb and flow of the tides, and the impossibility of getting them under any sort of rational control. The brain, as it were, stands to one side and watches itself pitching and tossing, full of agony but essentially helpless. Here the man of creative imagination pays a ghastly price for all his superiorities and immunities; nature takes revenge upon him for dreaming of improvements in the scheme of things. Sitting there in his lonely room, gnawing the handle of his pen, racked by his infernal quest, horribly bedeviled by incessant flashes of itching, tooth-ache, eye-strain and festering conscience — thus tortured, he makes atonement for his crime of having ideas. The normal man, the healthy and honest man, the good citizen and house-holder — this man, I daresay, knows nothing of all that travail. It is the particular penalty of those who pursue strange butter-flies into dark forests, and go fishing in enchanted and for-bidden streams.

How are we to account for it? My question, of course, is purely rhetorical. Explanations exist; they have existed for all times, for there is always an easy solution to every human prob-lem — neat, plausible, and wrong. The ancients laid the blame upon the gods: sometimes they were remote and surly, and sometimes they were kind. In the Middle Ages lesser powers took a hand, and one reads of works of art inspired by Our Lady, by the Blessed Saints, by the souls of the departed, and even by the devil. In our own day there are explanations less supernatural but no less fanciful — to wit, the explanation that the whole thing is a matter of pure chance, and not to be re-solved into any orderly process — to wit, the explanation that the controlling factor is external circumstance, that the artist happily married to a dutiful wife is thereby inspired — finally, to make an end, the explanation that it is all a question of Freudian complexes, themselves lurking in impenetrable shad-ows. But all these explanations fail to satisfy the mind that is not to be put off with mere words. Some of them are palpably absurd; others beg the question. The problem of the how re-mains, even when the problem of the why is disposed of. What is the precise machinery whereby the cerebrum is bestirred to such abnormal activity on one day that it sparkles and splutters like an arc-light, and reduced to such feebleness on another day that it smokes and gutters like a tallow dip?

In this emergency, having regard for the ages-long and un-relieved sufferings of artists great and small, I offer a new, simple, and at all events not ghostly solution. It is supported by the observed facts, by logical analogies and by the soundest known principles of biology, and so I present it without apolo-gies. It may be couched, for convenience, in the following brief terms: that inspiration, so-called, is a function of metabolism, and that it is chiefly conditioned by the state of the intestinal flora — in larger words, that a man's flow of ideas is controlled and determined, both quantitatively and qualitatively, not by the whims of the gods, nor by the terms of his armistice with his wife, nor by the combinations of some transcendental set of dice, but by the chemical content of the blood that lifts itself from his liver to his brain, and that this chemical content is mainly determined in his digestive tract, particularly south of the pylorus. A man may write great poetry when he is in liquor, when he is cold and miserable, when he is bankrupt, when he has a black eye, when his wife glowers at him across the table, when his children lie dying of smallpox; he may even write it during an earthquake, or while crossing the English channel, or in New York. But I am so far gone in materialism that I am disposed to deny flatly and finally, and herewith do deny flatly and finally, that there has lived a poet in the whole history of the world, ancient or modern, near or far, who ever managed to write great poetry, or even passably fair and decent poetry, at a time when he was suffering from stenosis at any point along the thirty-four foot *via dolorosa* running from the pylorus to the sigmoid flexure. In other words, when he was —

But perhaps I had better leave your medical adviser to explain. After all, it is not necessary to go any further in this direction; the whole thing may be argued in terms of the blood stream — and the blood stream is respectable, as the sigmoid is an outcast. It is the blood and the blood only, in fact, that the cerebrum is aware of; of what goes on elsewhere it can learn only by hearsay. If all is well below, then the blood that enters the brain through the internal carotid is full of the elements necessary to bestir the brain-cells to their highest activity; if, on the contrary, anabolism and katabolism are going on ineptly, if the blood is not getting the supplies that it needs and not getting rid of the wastes that burden it, then the brain-cells will be both starved and poisoned, and not all the king's horses and all the king's men can make them do their work with any show of ease and efficiency. In the first case the man whose psyche dwells in the cells will have a moment of inspiration — that is, he will find it a strangely simple and facile matter to write his poem, or iron out his syllogism, or make his bold modulation from F sharp minor to C major, or get his flesh-tone, or maybe only perfect his swindle. But in the second case he will be stumped and helpless. The more he tries, the more vividly he will be conscious of his impotence. Sweat will stand out in beads upon his brow, he will fish patiently for the elusive thought, he will try coaxing and subterfuge, he will retire to his ivory tower, he will tempt the invisible powers with black coffee, tea, alcohol and the alkaloids, he may even curse God and invite death — but he will not write his poem, or iron out his syllogism, or find his way into C major, or get his flesh-tone, or perfect his swindle.

Fix your eye upon this hypothesis of metabolic inspiration, and at once you will find the key to many a correlative mystery. For one thing, it quickly explains the observed hopelessness of trying to pump up inspiration by mere hard industry — the essential imbecility of the 1,000 words a day formula. Let there be stenosis below, and not all the industry of a Hercules will suffice to awaken the lethargic brain. Here, indeed, the harder the striving, the worse the stagnation — as every artist knows only too well. And why not? Striving in the face of such an interior obstacle is the most cruel of enterprises — a business more nerve-wracking and exhausting than reading a newspaper or watching a bad play. The pain thus produced, the emotions thus engendered, react upon the liver and the result is a steady increase in the intestinal demoralization, and a like increase in the pollution of the blood. In the end the poor victim, beset on the one hand by impotence and on the other hand by an impatience grown pathological, gets into a state indistinguishable from the frantic. It is at such times that creative artists suffer most atrociously. It is then that they pay a grisly supertax upon their superiority to the great herd of law-abiding and undistinguished men. The men of this herd never undergo any comparable torture; the agony of the artist is quite beyond their experience and even beyond their imagination. No catastrophe that could conceivably overtake a lime and cement dealer, a curb broker, a plumber or a Presbyterian is to be mentioned in the same breath with the torments that, to the most minor of poets, are familiar incidents of his professional life, and, to such a man as Poe or Beethoven are the commonplaces of every day. Beethoven suffered more during the composition of the Fifth symphony than all the judges on the benches of the world have suffered jointly since the time of Pontius Pilate.

Again, my hypothesis explains the fact that inspiration, save under extraordinary circumstances, is never continuous for more than a relatively short period. A banker, a barber or used car dealer does his work day after day without any noticeable rise or fall of efficiency; save when he is drunk, jailed or ill in bed the curve of his achievement is flattened out until it becomes almost a straight line. But the curve of an artist, even of the greatest of artists, is frightfully zig-zagged. There are moments when it sinks below the bottom of the chart, and immediately following there may be moments when it threatens to run off the top. Some of the noblest passages written by Shakespeare are in his worst plays, cheek by jowl with padding and banality; some of the worst music of Wagner is in his finest music dramas. There is, indeed, no such thing as a flawless masterpiece. Long labored, it may be gradually enriched with purple passages — the high inspirations of widely separated times crowded together —, but even so it will remain spotty, for those purple passages will be clumsily joined, and their joints will remain as apparent as so many false teeth. Only the most elementary knowledge of physiology is needed to show the cause of this zig-zagging. It lies in the elemental fact that the chemical constitution of the blood changes every hour, almost every minute. What it is at the beginning of digestion is not what it is at the end of digestion, and in both cases it is enormously affected by the nature of the substances digested. No man, within twenty-four hours after eating a meal in a Pennsylvania Railroad dining-car, could conceivably write anything worth reading. A tough beefsteak, I daresay, has ditched many a promising sonnet, and bad beer, as everyone knows, has spoiled hundreds of sonatas. Thus inspiration rises and falls, and even when it rises twice to the same height it usually shows some qualitative difference — there is the inspiration, say, of Spring vegetables and there is the inspiration of Autumn fruits. In a long work the products of greatly differing inspirations, of greatly differing streams of blood, are hideously intermingled, and the result is the inevitable spottiness that I have mentioned. No one but a maniac argues that "Die Meistersinger" is *all* good. One detects in it days when Wagner felt, as the saying goes, like a fighting cock, but one also detects days when he arose in the morning full of acidosis and despair — days when he turned heavily from the Pierian spring to castor oil.

Moreover, it must be obvious that the very conditions under which works of art are produced tend to cause great aberrations in metabolism. The artist is forced by his calling to be a sedentary man. Even a poet, perhaps the freest of artists for he is wholly emancipated from fact, must spend a good deal of time bending over a desk. He may conceive his poems in the open air, as Beethoven conceived his music, but the work of reducing them to actual words requires diligent effort *in camera*. Here it is a sheer impossibility for him to enjoy the ideal hygienic conditions which surround the farmhand, the policeman and the sailor. His viscera are congested; his eyes are astrain; his muscles are without necessary exercise. Furthermore, he probably breathes bad air and goes without needed sleep. The result is inevitably some disturbance of metabolism, with a vitiated blood supply and a starved cerebrum. One is always surprised to encounter a poet who is ruddy and stout; the standard model is a pale and flabby stenotic, kept alive by patent medicines. So with the painter, the musical composer, the sculptor, the artist in prose. There is no more confining work known to man than instrumentation. The composer who has spent a day at it is invariably nervous and ill. For hours his body is bent over his music-paper, the while his pen engrosses little dots upon thin lines. I have known composers, after a week or so of such labor, to come down with autointoxication in its most virulent forms. Perhaps the notorious ill health of Beethoven, and the mental break-downs of Schumann, Tschaikowsky and Hugo Wolf had their origin in this direction. It is difficult, going through the history of music, to find a single composer in the grand manner who was physically and mentally up to par.

I do not advance it as a formal corollary, but no doubt this stenosis hypothesis also throws some light upon two other immemorial mysteries, the first being the relative esthetic sterility

of women, and the other being the low esthetic development
of certain whole classes, and even races of men, *e.g.*, the Puritans, the Welsh and the Confederate Americans. That women
suffer from stenosis far more than men is a commonplace of
internal medicine; the weakness is chiefly to blame, rather than
the functional peculiarities that they accuse, for their liability
to headache. A good many of them, in fact, are habitually in
the state of health which, in the artist, is accompanied by an
utter inability to work. This state of health, as I said, does
not inhibit *all* mental activity. It leaves the power of observation but little impaired; it does not corrupt common sense; it
is not incompatible with an intelligent discharge of the ordinary duties of life. Thus a hardware dealer, in the midst of it,
may function almost as well as when his metabolic processes
are perfectly normal, and by the same token a woman chronically a victim to it may yet show all the sharp mental competence which characterizes her sex. But here the thing stops. To
go beyond — to enter the realm of creative thinking, to abandon the mere application of old ideas and essay to invent new
ideas, to precipitate novel concepts out of the chaos of memory
and perception — this is quite impossible to the stenotic. *Ergo*,
it is unheard of among classes and races of men who feed
grossly and neglect personal hygiene; the pill-swallower is the
only artist in such groups. One may thus argue that the elder
Beecham saved poetry in England, as the younger Beecham
saved music. . . . But, as I say, I do not stand behind the
hypothesis in this department, save, perhaps, in the matter of
women. I could amass enormous evidence in favor of it, but
against them there would always loom the disconcerting contrary evidence of the Bulgarians. Among them, I suppose, stenosis must be unknown — but so are all the fine arts.

The artist is normally anything but a healthy animal. Perfect
health, indeed, is a boon that very few men above the rank of
clodhoppers ever enjoy. What health means is a degree of
adaptation to the organism's environment so nearly complete
that there is no irritation. Such a state, it must be obvious, is
not often to be observed in organisms of the highest complexity. It is common, perhaps, in the earthworm. This elemental beast makes few demands upon its environment, and is

thus subject to few diseases. It seldom gets out of order until the sands of its life are run, and then it suffers one grand illness and dies forthwith. But man is forever getting out of order, for he is enormously complicated — and the higher he rises in complexity, the more numerous and the more serious are his derangements. There are whole categories of disease that afflict chiefly the more civilized and delicate ranks of men, leaving the inferior orders unscathed. Good health in man, indeed, is almost invariably a function of inferiority. A professionally healthy man, *e.g.*, an acrobat, a cavalry lieutenant or an ice-wagon driver, is always stupid. In the Greece of the great days the athletes we hear so much about were mainly slaves. Not one of the eminent philosophers, poets or statesmen of Greece was a good high-jumper. Nearly all of them, in fact, suffered from the same malaises which afflict their successors of today, as you will quickly discern by examining their compositions. The esthetic impulse, like the thirst for truth, might well be called a disease. It seldom if ever appears in a perfectly healthy man.

The Poet and His Art

From PREJUDICES: THIRD SERIES, 1922, pp. 150–70.
First printed in part in the *Smart Set*, June, 1920, pp. 138–43

POETRY is two quite distinct things, and may be either or both. One is a series of words that are intrinsically musical, in clang-tint and rhythm, as the single words *cellar-door* and *sarcoma* are musical. The other is a series of ideas, false in themselves, that offer a means of emotional and imaginative escape from the harsh realities of everyday. In brief, poetry is a comforting piece of fiction set to more or less lascivious music — a slap on the back in waltz time — a grand release of longings and repressions to the tune of flutes, harps, sackbuts, psalteries and the usual strings.

As I say, poetry may be either the one thing or the other — caressing music or caressing assurance. It need not necessarily be both. Consider a familiar example from "Othello":

> Not poppy, nor mandragora,
> Nor all the drowsy syrups of the world
> Shall ever medicine thee to that sweet sleep
> Which thou owed'st yesterday.

Here the sense, at best, is surely very vague. Probably not one auditor in a hundred, hearing an actor recite those glorious lines, attaches any intelligible meaning to the archaic word *owed'st*, the cornerstone of the whole sentence. Nevertheless, the effect is stupendous. The passage assaults and benumbs the faculties like the slow movement of Schumann's Rhenish symphony; hearing it is a sensuous debauch; the man anesthetic to it could stand unmoved in Sainte-Chapelle. One easily recalls many other such bursts of pure music, almost meaningless but infinitely delightful — in Poe, in Swinburne, in Marlowe. Two-thirds of the charm of reading Chaucer (setting aside the Rabelaisian comedy) comes out of the mere burble of the words; the meaning, to a modern, is often extremely obscure, and sometimes downright undecipherable. The whole fame of Poe, as a poet, is based upon five short poems. Of them, three are almost pure music. Their intellectual content is of the vaguest. No one would venture to reduce them to plain English. Even Poe himself always thought of them, not as statements of poetic ideas, but as simple utterances of poetic (*i.e.,* musical) sounds.

It was Sidney Lanier, himself a poet, who first showed the dependence of poetry upon music. He had little to say, unfortunately, about the clang-tint of words; what concerned him almost exclusively was rhythm. In "The Science of English Verse," he showed that the charm of this rhythm could be explained in the technical terms of music — that all the old gabble about dactyls and spondees was no more than a dog Latin invented by men who were fundamentally ignorant of the thing they discussed. Lanier's book was the first (and last) intelligent work ever published upon the nature and structure of the sensuous content of English poetry. He struck out into such new and far paths that the professors of prosody still lag behind him, quite unable to understand a poet who was also a shrewd critic and a first-rate musician. But if, so deeply concerned with rhythm, he marred his treatise by forgetting clang-tint, he marred it still more by forgetting content. Poetry that is all music is obviously relatively rare, for only a poet who is also a natural musician can write it, and natural musicians are much rarer in the world than poets. Ordinary poetry, average poetry, thus depends in part upon its ideational material, and perhaps even chiefly. It is the *idea* expressed in a poem, and not the mellifluousness of the words used to express it, that arrests and enchants the average connoisseur. Often, indeed, he disdains this mellifluousness, and argues that the idea ought to be set forth without the customary pretty jingling, or, at most, with only the scant jingling that lies in rhythm — in brief, he wants his ideas in the altogether, and so advocates *vers libre*.

It was another American, this time F. C. Prescott, who first gave scientific attention to the intellectual content of poetry. His book is called "Poetry and Dreams." Its virtue lies in the fact that it rejects all the customary mystical and romantic definitions of poetry, and seeks to account for the thing in straightforward psychological terms. Poetry, says Prescott, is simply the verbal materialization of a day-dream, an attempt to satisfy a longing by saying that it is satisfied. In brief, poetry represents imagination's bold effort to escape from the cold and clammy facts that hedge us in — to soothe the wrinkled and fevered brow with beautiful balderdash. On the precise nature of this beautiful balderdash you can get all the information you need by opening at random the nearest book of verse. The ideas you will find in it may be divided into two main divisions. The first consists of denials of objective fact; the second of denials of subjective fact. Specimen of the first sort:

> God's in His heaven,
> All's right with the world.

Specimen of the second:

> I am the master of my fate;
> I am the captain of my soul.

All poetry (forgetting, for the moment, its possible merit as mere sound) may be resolved into either the one or the other of these imbecilities — its essential character lies in its bold flouting of what every reflective adult knows to be the truth. The poet, imagining him to be sincere, is simply one who disposes of all the horrors of life on this earth, and of all the difficulties presented by his own inner weaknesses no less, by the elementary device of denying them. Is it a well-known fact that love is an emotion that is almost as perishable as eggs — that it is biologically impossible for a given male to yearn for a given female more than a few brief years? Then the poet disposes of it by assuring his girl that he will nevertheless love her forever — more, by pledging his word of honor that he believes that *she* will love *him* forever. Is it equally notorious that there is no such thing as justice in the world — that the good are tortured insanely and the evil go free and prosper? Then the poet composes a piece crediting God with a mysterious and unintelligible system of jurisprudence, whereby the torture of the good is a sort of favor conferred upon them for their goodness. Is it of almost equally widespread report that no healthy man likes to contemplate his own inevitable death — that even in time of war, with a vast pumping up of emotion to conceal the fact, every soldier hopes and believes that he, personally, will escape? Then the poet, first carefully introducing himself into a bombproof, achieves strophes declaring that he is free from all such weakness — that he will deliberately seek a rendezvous with death, and laugh ha-ha when the bullet finds him.

The precise nature of the imbecility thus solemnly set forth depends, very largely, of course, upon the private prejudices and yearnings of the poet, and the reception that is given it depends, by the same token, upon the private prejudices and yearnings of the reader. That is why it is often so difficult to get any agreement upon the merits of a definite poem, *i.e.*, to get any agreement upon its capacity to soothe. There is the man who craves only the animal delights of a sort of Moslem-Methodist paradise: to him "The Frost is on the Pumpkin" is a noble poem. There is the man who yearns to get out of the visible universe altogether and tread the fields of asphodel: for him there is delight only in the mystical stuff of Crashaw, Donne, Thompson and company. There is the man who revolts against the sordid Christian notion of immortality — an eternity to be spent flapping wings with pious greengrocers and

Anglican bishops; he finds *his* escape in the gorgeous blasphe-
mies of Swinburne. There is, to make an end, the man who,
with an inferiority complex eating out of his heart, is moved
by a great desire to stalk the world in heroic guise: he may go
to the sonorous swanking of Kipling, or he may go to something more subtle, to some poem in which the boasting is more
artfully concealed, say Christina Rossetti's "When I am Dead."
Many men, many complexes, many secret yearnings! They collect, of course, in groups; if the group happens to be large
enough the poet it is devoted to becomes famous. Kipling's
fame is thus easily explained. He appealed to the commonest
of all types of men, next to the sentimental type — which is to
say, he appealed to the bully and braggart type, the chest-
slapping type, the patriot type. Less harshly described, to the
boy type. All of us have been Kiplingomaniacs at some time or
other. I was myself a very ardent one at 17, and wrote many
grandiloquent sets of verse in the manner of "Tommy Atkins"
and "Fuzzy-Wuzzy." But if the gifts of observation and reflection have been given to us, we get over it. There comes a time
when we no longer yearn to be heroes, but seek only ease —
maybe even hope for quick extinction. Then we turn to Swinburne and "The Garden of Proserpine" — more false assurances,
more mellifluous play-acting, another tinkling make-believe —
but how sweet on blue days!

One of the things to remember here (too often it is forgotten, and Prescott deserves favorable mention for stressing it) is
that a man's conscious desires are not always identical with his
subconscious longings; in fact, the two are often directly anti-
thetical. The real man lies in the depths of the subconscious,
like a carp lurking in mud. His conscious personality is largely
a product of his environment — the reaction of his subconscious
to the prevailing notions of what is meet and seemly. Here, of
course, I wander into platitude, for the news that all men are
frauds was already stale in the days of Hammurabi. Freud simply translated the fact into pathological terms, added a bedroom
scene, and so laid the foundations for his psychoanalysis. He
made a curious mistake when he brought sex into the fore-
ground of his new magic. He was, of course, quite right when
he argued that, in civilized societies, sex impulses were more apt

to be suppressed than any other natural impulses, and that the subconscious thus tends to be crowded with their ghosts. But in considering sex impulses, he forgot sex imaginings. Digging out, by painful cross-examination in a darkened room, some startling tale of carnality in his patient's past, he committed the incredible folly of assuming it to be literally true. More often than not, I believe, it was a mere piece of boasting, a materialization of desire — in brief, a poem. He should have psychoanalyzed a few poets instead of wasting all his time upon psychopathic women with sclerotic husbands. He would have dredged amazing things out of their subconsciouses, heroic as well as amorous. Imagine the billions of Boers, Germans, Irishmen and Hindus that Kipling would have confessed to killing!

A man's preferences in poetry constitute an excellent means of estimating his inner cravings and credulities. The music disarms his critical sense, and he confesses to cherishing ideas that he would repudiate with indignation if they were put into plain words. I say he cherishes those ideas. Maybe he simply tolerates them unwillingly; maybe they are no more than inescapable heritages from his barbarous ancestors, like his vermiform appendix. Think of the poems you like, and you will come upon many such intellectual fossils — ideas that you by no means subscribe to openly, but that nevertheless give you a strange joy. I put myself on the block as Exhibit A: there is my delight in Lizette Woodworth Reese's sonnet, "Tears." Nothing could do more violence to my conscious beliefs. Put into prose, the doctrine in the poem would make me laugh. There is no man in Christendom who is less a Christian than I am. But here the dead hand grabs me by the ear. My barbarian ancestors were converted to Christianity in the year 1535, and remained of that faith until near the middle of the Eighteenth Century. Observe, now, the load I carry; more than three hundred years of Christianity, and perhaps a thousand years (maybe even two, or three thousand) of worship of heathen gods before that — at the least, thirteen hundred years of uninterrupted belief in the immortality of the soul. Is it any wonder that, betrayed by the music of Miss Reese's Anglo-Saxon monosyllables, my conscious faith is lulled to sleep, thus giving my subconscious a chance to wallow in its immemorial superstition?

There are days when every one of us experiences this ontogenetic back-firing, and returns to an earlier stage of development. It is on such days that grown men play games, or cheer the flag, or fall in love. And it is then that they are in the mood for poetry, and get comfort out of its asseverations of the obviously not true. A truly civilized man, when he is wholly himself, derives no pleasure from hearing a poet state, as Browning stated, that all is well with the world. Such tosh not only does not please him; it definitely offends him, as he is offended by an idiotic article in a newspaper; it roils him to encounter so much stupidity in Christendom. But he may like it when he is drunk, or suffering from some low toxemia, or staggering beneath some great disaster. Then, as I say, the ontogenetic process reverses itself, and he slides back into infancy. Then he goes to poets, just as he goes to women and to theology. The very highest orders of men, perhaps, never suffer from such malaises of the spirit, or, if they suffer from them, never succumb to them. Charles Darwin was such a man. There was never a moment in his life when he sought religious consolation, and there was never a moment when he turned to poetry; in fact, he regarded it as silly. Other first-rate men, more sensitive to the possible music in it, regard it with less positive aversion, but I have never heard of a truly first-rate man who got any permanent satisfaction out of its content. The Browning Societies of the latter part of the Nineteenth Century (and I choose the Browning Societies because Browning's poetry was often more or less logical in content, and thus above the ordinary intellectually) were not composed of such men as Huxley, Spencer, Lecky, Buckle and Trevelyan, but of third-rate schoolmasters, moony old maids, candidates for theosophy, literary vicars, and other such Philistines. The chief propagandist for Browning in the United States was not Henry Adams, or William Sumner, but an obscure professor of English who was also an ardent spook-chaser. And what is thus true ontogenetically is also true phylogenetically. That is to say, poetry is chiefly produced and esteemed by peoples that have not yet come to maturity. The

Romans had a dozen poets of the first talent before they had a single prose writer of any skill whatsoever. So did the English.

In its character as a sort of music poetry is plainly a good deal more respectable, and makes an appeal to a far higher variety of reader, or, at all events, to a reader in a stage of greater mental clarity. A capacity for music — by which I mean melody, harmony and clang-tint — comes late in the history of every race. The savage can apprehend rhythm, but he is quite incapable of carrying a tune in any intelligible scale. The Negroes of our own South, who are commonly regarded as very musical, are actually only rhythmical; they never invent melodies, but only rhythms. And the whites to whom their barbarous dance-tunes chiefly appeal are in their own stage of culture. When one observes a room full of well-dressed men and women swaying and wriggling to the tune of some villainous mazurka from the Mississippi levees, one may assume very soundly that they are all the sort of folk who play golf and bridge. A great deal of superficial culture is compatible with that pathetic barbarism, and even a high degree of esthetic sophistication in other directions. The Greeks who built the Parthenon knew no more about music than a hog knows of predestination; they were almost as ignorant in that department as the modern Iowans or New Yorkers. It was not, indeed, until the Renaissance that music as we know it appeared in the world, and it was not until less than two centuries ago that it reached a high development. In Shakespeare's day music was just getting upon its legs in England; in Goethe's day it was just coming to full flower in Germany; in France and America it is still in the savage state. It is thus the youngest of the arts, and the most difficult, and hence the noblest. Any sane young man of twenty-two can write an acceptable sonnet, or draw a horse that will not be mistaken for an automobile, but before he may write even a bad string quartet he must go through a long and arduous training, just as he must strive for years before he may write prose that is instantly recognizable as prose, and not as a string of mere words.

The virtue of such great poets as Shakespeare does not lie in the content of their poetry, but in its music. The content of the Shakespearean plays, in fact, is often puerile, and sometimes quite incomprehensible. No scornful essays by George Bernard Shaw and Frank Harris were needed to demonstrate the fact; it lies plain in the text. One snickers sourly over the spectacle of generations of pedants debating the question of Hamlet's mental processes; the simple fact is that Shakespeare gave him no more mental processes than a Fifth avenue rector has, but merely employed him as a convenient spout for some of the finest music ever got into words. As it is intoned on the stage by actors, it commonly loses content altogether. One cannot make out what the poor ham is saying; one can only observe that it is beautiful. There are whole speeches in the Shakespearean plays whose meaning is unknown even to scholars — and yet they remain favorites, and well deserve to. Who knows, again, what the sonnets are about? Is the bard talking about the inn-keeper's wife at Oxford, or about a love affair of a pathological character? Some say one thing, and some another. But all who have ears must agree that the sonnets are extremely beautiful stuff — that the English language reaches in them the topmost heights of conceivable beauty. Shakespeare thus ought to be ranked among the musicians, along with Beethoven. As a philosopher he was a ninth-rater — but so was Ludwig. I wonder what he would have done with prose. I can't make up my mind about it. One day I believe that he would have written it as well as Dryden and the next day I begin to fear that he would have produced something as bad as Swinburne. He had the ear, but he lacked the logical sense. Poetry has done enough when it charms, but prose must also convince.

At the extremes there are indubitable poetry and incurable prose, and the difference is not hard to distinguish. Prose is simply a form of writing in which the author intends that his statements shall be accepted as conceivably true, even when they are about imaginary persons and events; its appeal is to the fully conscious and alertly reasoning man. Poetry is a form of writing in which the author attempts to disarm reason and evoke emotion, partly by presenting images that awaken a powerful response in the subconscious and partly by the mere sough and blubber of words. Poetry is not distinguished from prose, as John Livingston Lowes says in his "Convention and Revolt in Poetry," by an exclusive phraseology, but by a peculiar attitude of mind — an attitude of self-delusion, of fact-denying, of saying what isn't true. It is essentially an effort to elude facts, whereas prose is essentially a means of unearthing and exhibiting them. The gap is bridged by sentimental prose, which is half prose and half poetry. Immediately the thing acquires a literal meaning it ceases to be poetry; immediately it becomes capable of convincing an adult and perfectly sober man during the hours between breakfast and luncheon it is indisputably prose.

Once, after plowing through sixty or seventy volumes of bad verse, I described myself as a poetry-hater. The epithet was and is absurd. The truth is that I enjoy poetry as much as the next man — when the mood is on me. But what mood? The mood, in a few words, of intellectual and spiritual fatigue, the mood of revolt against the insoluble riddle of existence, the mood of disgust and despair. Poetry, then, is a capital medicine. First its sweet music lulls, and then its artful presentation of the beautifully improbable soothes and gives surcease. It is an escape from life, like religion, like alcohol, like a pretty girl. And to the mere sensuous joy in it, to the mere low delight in getting away from the world for a bit, there is added, if the poetry be good, something vastly better, something reaching out into the realm of the intelligent, to wit, appreciation of good workmanship. A sound sonnet is almost as pleasing an object as a well-written fugue. Well, who ever heard of a finer craftsman than William Shakespeare? His music was magnificent, he played superbly upon all the common emotions — and he did it magnificently, he did it with an air. No, I am no poetry-hater. But even Shakespeare I most enjoy, not on brisk mornings when I feel fit for any deviltry, but on dreary evenings when my old war wounds are troubling me, and bills are piled up on my desk, and I am too sad to work. Then I mix a stiff dram — and read poetry.

The New Poetry

From FIVE LITTLE EXCURSIONS, PREJUDICES: SIXTH SERIES,
1927, pp. 176–77

THE TROUBLE with most of the new poets is that they are too cerebral — that they attack the problems of a fine art with the methods of science. That error runs through all their public discussions of the business. Those discussions are full of theories, by the new psychology out of the cant of the studios, that do not work and are not true. The old-time poet did not bother with theories. When the urge to write was upon him, he simply got himself into a lather, tied a towel around his head, and then tried to reduce his feelings to paper. If he had any skill the result was poetry; if he lacked skill it was nonsense. But even his worst failure still had something natural and excusable about it — it was the failure of a man admittedly somewhat feverish, with purple paint on his nose and vine-leaves in his hair. The failure of the new poet is the far more grotesque failure of a scientist who turns out to be a quack — of a mathematician who divides 20 by 4 and gets 6, of a cook who tries to make an omelette of china doorknobs.

Poetry can never be concocted by any purely intellectual process. It has nothing to do with the intellect: it is, in fact, a violent and irreconcilable enemy to the intellect. Its purpose is not to establish facts, but to evade and deny them. What it essays to do is to make life more bearable in an intolerable world by concealing and obliterating all the harsher realities. Its message is that all will be well tomorrow, or, at the latest, next Tuesday; that the grave is not cold and damp but steam-heated and lined with roses; that a girl is not a viviparous mammal, full of pathogenic organisms and enlightened self-interest, but an angel with bobbed wings and a heart of gold. Take this denial of the bald and dreadful facts out of poetry — make it scientific and sensible — and it simply ceases to be what it pretends to be. It may remain good prose; it may even remain beautiful prose. But it cannot stir the blood as true poetry does; it cannot offer that soothing consolation, that escape from reality, that sovereign balm for every spiritual itch and twinge which is the great gift of poetry to man.

On Style

From THE FRINGES OF LOVELY LETTERS, PREJUDICES: FIFTH SERIES, 1926, pp. 196–202

WITH only one or two exceptions, all the books on prose style in English are by writers quite unable to write. The subject, indeed, seems to exercise a special and dreadful fascination over schoolma'ams, bucolic college professors, and other such pseudo-literates. In a thousand texts they set forth their depressing ideas about it, and millions of suffering high-school pupils have to study what they say. Their central aim, of course, is to reduce the whole thing to a series of simple rules — the overmastering passion of their melancholy order, at all times and everywhere. They aspire to teach it as bridge whist, the flag-drill and double-entry bookkeeping are taught. They fail as ignominiously as that Athenian of legend who essayed to train a regiment of grasshoppers in the goose-step.

For the essence of a sound style is that it cannot be reduced to rules — that it is a living and breathing thing, with something of the demoniacal in it — that it fits its proprietor tightly and yet ever so loosely, as his skin fits him. It is, in fact, quite as securely an integral part of him as that skin is. It hardens as his arteries harden. It is gaudy when he is young and gathers decorum when he grows old. On the day after he makes a mash on a new girl it glows and glitters. If he has fed well, it is mellow. If he has gastritis it is bitter. In brief, a style is always the outward and visible symbol of a man, and it cannot be anything else. To attempt to teach it is as silly as to set up courses in making love.

The schoolma'am theory to the contrary is based upon a faulty inference from a sound observation. The sound observation is that the great majority of American high-school pupils, when they attempt to put their thoughts upon paper, produce only a mass of confused and puerile nonsense. The faulty inference is to the effect that what ails them is a defective technical equipment — that they can be trained to write clearly as a dog may be trained to walk on its hind legs. This is all wrong. What ails them is not a defective technical equipment but a defective natural equipment. They write badly simply because they cannot think clearly. They cannot think clearly because they lack the brains. Trying to teach them is as hopeless as trying to teach a dog with only one hind leg. Any human being who can speak English understandably has all the materials necessary to write English clearly, and even beautifully. There is nothing mysterious about the written language; it is precisely the same, in essence, as the spoken language. If a man can think in English at all, he can find words enough to express his ideas. The fact is proved abundantly by the excellent writing that often comes from so-called ignorant men. Such writing commonly arouses little enthusiasm among pedagogues. Its transparency excites their professional disdain, and they are offended by its use of homely words and phrases. They prefer something more ornate and complex — something, as they would probably put it, demanding more thought. But the thought they yearn for is the kind, alas, that they secrete themselves — the muddled, highfalutin, vapid thought that one finds in their own textbooks.

I do not denounce them because they write so badly; I merely record the fact in a sad, scientific spirit. Even in such twilight regions of the intellect the style remains the man. What is in the head infallibly oozes out of the nub of the pen. If it is sparkling Burgundy the writing is full of life and charm. If it is mush the writing is mush too. The late Dr. Harding, twenty-ninth President of the Federal Union, was a highly self-conscious stylist. He practised prose composition assiduously, and was regarded by the pedagogues of Marion, Ohio, and vicinity as a very talented fellow. But when he sent a message to Congress it was so muddled in style that even the late Henry Cabot Lodge, a professional literary man, could not understand it. Why? Simply because Dr. Harding's thoughts, on the high and grave subjects he discussed, were so muddled that he couldn't understand them himself. But on matters within his range of customary meditation he was clear and even charming, as all of us are. I once heard him deliver a brief address upon the ideals of the Elks. It was a topic close to his heart, and he had thought about it at length and *con amore*. The result was an excellent speech — clear, logical, forceful, and with a touch of wild, romantic beauty. His sentences hung together. He employed simple words, and put them together with skill. But when, at a public meeting in Washington, he essayed to deliver an oration on the subject of Dante Alighieri, he quickly became so obscure and absurd that even the Diplomatic Corps began to snicker.

A pedagogue, confronted by Harding in class, would have set him to the business of what is called improving his vocabulary — that is, to the business of making his writing even worse than it was. In point of fact, he had all the vocabulary that he needed, and a great deal more. Any idea that he could formulate clearly he could convey clearly. Any idea that genuinely moved him he could invest with charm. But style cannot go beyond the ideas which lie at the heart of it. If they are clear, it too will be clear. If they are held passionately, it will be eloquent. Trying to teach it to persons who cannot think, especially when the business is attempted by persons who also cannot think, is a great waste of time, and an immoral imposition upon the taxpayers of the nation. It would be far more logical to devote all the energy to teaching, not writing, but logic — and probably just as useless. For I doubt that the art of thinking can be taught at all — at any rate, by school-teachers. It is not acquired, but congenital. Some persons are born with it. Their ideas flow in straight channels; they are capable of lucid reasoning; when they say anything it is instantly understandable; when they write anything it is clear and persuasive. They constitute, I should say, about one-eighth of one per cent. of the human race. The rest of God's children are just as incapable of logical thought as they are incapable of jumping over the moon. Trying to teach them is as vain an enterprise as trying to teach a streptococcus the principle of Americanism. The only thing to do with them is to make Ph.D.'s of them, and set them to writing handbooks on style.

Authorship as a Trade

From the same, pp. 175–80

MOST beginning authors are attracted to the trade of letters, not because they have anything apposite and exigent to say, but simply because it seems easy. Let us imagine an ambitious and somewhat gassy young gal, turned out of the public high-school down the street with good marks in English — that is, in the sort of literary composition practised and admired by school-ma'ams. She is disinclined to follow her mother too precipitately into the jaws of holy monogamy —, or at all events, she shrinks from marrying such a clod as her father is, and as her brothers and male classmates will be tomorrow. What to do? The professions demand technical equipment. Commerce is sordid. The secretary, even of a rich and handsome man, must get up at 7.30 a.m. Most of the fine arts are regarded, by her family, as immoral. So she pays $3 down on a second-hand typewriter, lays in a stock of copy paper, and proceeds to enrich the national literature.

It is such aspirants who keep the pot boiling for the schools of short-story writing and scenario writing that now swarm in the land. Certainly these schools, in so far as I have any acquaintance with them, offer nothing of value to the beginner of genuine talent. They seem to be run, in the main, by persons as completely devoid of esthetic sense as so many street railway curve-greasers. Their text-books are masses of unmitigated rubbish. But no doubt that rubbish seems impressive enough to the customers I have mentioned, for it is both very vague and very cocksure — an almost irresistible combination. So a hundred thousand second-hand Coronas rattle and jingle in ten thousand remote and lonely towns, and the mail of every magazine editor in America is as heavy as the mail of a radio star.

Alas, what he finds in it, day in and day out, is simply the same dull, obvious, shoddy stuff — the same banal and threadbare ideas set forth in the same flabby and unbeautiful words. They all seem to write alike, as, indeed, they all seem to think alike. They react to stimuli with the machine-like uniformity and precision of soldiers in a file. The spectacle of life is to all of them exactly the same spectacle. They bring no more to it, of private, singular vision, than so many photographic lenses. One and all, they lack the primary requisite of the imaginative author: the capacity to see the human comedy afresh, to discover new relations between things, to discover new significances in man's eternal struggle with his fate. What they have to say is simply what any moderately intelligent suburban pastor or country editor would have to say, and so it is not worth hearing.

This disparity between aspiration and equipment runs through the whole of American life; material prosperity and popular education have made it a sort of national disease. Two-thirds of the professors in our colleges are simply cans full of undigested knowledge, mechanically acquired; they cannot utilize it; they cannot think. We are cursed likewise with hordes of lawyers who would be happier and more useful driving trucks, and hordes of doctors who would be strained even as druggists. So in the realm of beautiful letters. Poetry has become a recreation among us for the intellectually unemployed and unemployable: persons who, a few generations ago, would have taken it out on china-painting. The writing of novels is undertaken by thousands who lack the skill to describe a dog-fight. The result is a colossal waste of paper, ink and postage — worse, of binding cloth and gold foil. For a great deal of this drivel, by one dodge or another, gets into print. Many of the correspondence-school students, after hard diligence, learn how to write for the pulp magazines; a few of them eventually appear between covers, and are solemnly reviewed.

Does such stuff sell? Apparently it does, else the publishers would not print so much of it. Its effect upon those who read it must be even worse than that of the newspapers. They come to it with confident expectations. It is pretentiously bound; *ergo*, there must be something in it. That something is simply platitude. What has been said a thousand times is said all over again. This time it must be true! Thus the standardization of the American mind goes on, and against ideas that are genuinely novel there are higher and higher battlements erected. Meanwhile, on the lower levels, where the latest recruits to letters sweat and hope, this rubbish is laboriously imitated. Turn to any of the pulp magazines, and you will find out how bad it can be at its worst. No, not quite at its worst, for the contributors to the pulp magazines have at least broken into print — they have as they say, made the grade. Below them are thousands of aspirants of even slenderer talents — customers of the correspondence schools, patrons of "writers' conferences" and of lectures by itinerant literary pedagogues, patient manufacturers of the dreadful stuff that clogs every magazine editor's mail. Here is the ultimate reservoir of the national literature — and here, unless I err, is only bilge.

The Author at Work

From the same, pp. 186–90

IF authors could work in large, well-ventilated factories, like cigarmakers or garment-workers, with plenty of their mates about and a flow of lively professional gossip to entertain them, their labor would be immensely lighter. But it is essential to their craft that they perform its tedious and vexatious operations *a cappella*, and so the horrors of loneliness are added to stenosis and their other professional infirmities. An author at work is continuously and inescapably in the presence of himself. There is nothing to divert and soothe him. Every time a vagrant regret or sorrow assails him, it has him instantly by the ear, and every time a wandering ache runs down his leg it shakes him like the bite of a tiger. I have yet to meet an author who was not a hypochondriac. Saving only medical men, who are always ill and in fear of death, the literati are perhaps the most lavish consumers of pills and philtres in this world, and the most assiduous customers of surgeons. I can scarcely think of one, known to me personally, who is not constantly dosing himself with medicines, or regularly resorting to the knife.

It must be obvious that other men, even among the intelligentsia, are not beset so cruelly. A judge on the bench, entertaining a ringing in the ears, can do his work quite as well as if he heard only the voluptuous rhetoric of the lawyers. A clergyman, carrying on his mummery, is not appreciably crippled by a sour stomach: what he says has been said before, and only scoundrels question it. And a surgeon, plying his exhilarating art and mystery, suffers no professional damage from the wild thought that the attending nurse is more sightly than his wife. But I defy anyone to write a competent sonnet with a ringing in his ears, or to compose sound criticism with a sour stomach, or to do a plausible love scene with a head full of private amorous fancies. These things are sheer impossibilities. The poor literatus encounters them and their like every time he enters his work-room and spits on his hands. The moment the door bangs he begins a depressing, losing struggle with his body and his mind.

Why then, do rational men and women engage in so barbarous and exhausting a vocation — for there are relatively intelligent and enlightened authors, remember, just as there are relatively honest politicians, and even bishops. What keeps them from deserting it for trades that are less onerous, and, in the eyes of their fellow creatures, more respectable? One reason, I believe, is that an author, like any other so-called artist, is a man in whom the normal vanity of all men is so vastly exaggerated that he finds it a sheer impossibility to hold it in. His overpowering impulse is to gyrate before his fellow men, flapping his wings and emitting defiant yells. This being forbidden by the police of all civilized countries, he takes it out by putting his yells on paper. Such is the thing called self-expression.

In the confidences of the literati, of course, it is always depicted as something much more mellow and virtuous. Either they argue that they are moved by a yearning to spread the enlightenment and save the world, or they allege that what steams them and makes them leap is a passion for beauty. Both theories are quickly disposed of by an appeal to the facts. The stuff written by nine authors out of ten, it must be plain at a glance, has as little to do with spreading the enlightenment as the state papers of the late Chester A. Arthur. And there is no more beauty in it, and no more sign of a feeling of beauty, than you will find in the décor of a night-club. The impulse to create beauty, indeed, is rather rare in literary men, and almost completely absent from the younger ones. If it shows itself at all, it comes as a sort of afterthought. Far ahead of it comes the yearning to make money. And after the yearning to make money comes the yearning to make a noise. The impulse to create beauty lingers far behind. Authors, as a class, are extraordinarily insensitive to it, and the fact reveals itself in their customary (and often incredibly extensive) ignorance of the other arts. I'd have a hard job naming six American novelists who could be depended upon to recognize a fugue without prompting, or six poets who could give a rational account of the difference between a Gothic cathedral and a Standard Oil filling-station.

The thing goes even further. Most novelists, in my experience, know nothing of poetry, and very few poets have any feeling for the beauties of prose. As for the dramatists, three-fourths of them are unaware that such things as prose and poetry exist at all. It pains me to set down such inconvenient and blushful facts. If they ought to be concealed, then blame my babbling upon scientific passion. That passion, today, has me by the ear.

Foreign Poisons

From THE NATIONAL LETTERS, PREJUDICES: SECOND SERIES, 1920, pp. 44–49

WHEN a native author of any genuine force and originality appears in the United States he is almost invariably found to be under strong foreign influence, either English or Continental. It was so in the earliest days. Freneau, the poet of the Revolution, was thoroughly French in blood and traditions. Irving, as H. R. Haweis has said, "took to England as a duck takes to water," and was in exile seventeen years. Cooper, with the great success of "The Last of the Mohicans" behind him, left the country in disgust, and was gone for seven years. Emerson, Bryant, Lowell, Hawthorne and even Longfellow kept their eyes turned across the water; Emerson, in fact, was little more than an importer and popularizer of stale German ideas. Bancroft studied in Germany; Prescott, like Irving, was enchanted by Spain. Poe, unable to follow the fashion, invented mythical travels to save his face — to France, to Germany, to the Greek isles.[1] The Civil War gave the national consciousness some stimulation, but it did not halt the movement of *émigrés*. Henry James, in the 70s, went to England, Bierce and Bret Harte followed him, and even Mark Twain, absolutely American though he was, was forever pulling up stakes and setting out for Vienna, Florence or London. Only poverty tied Whitman to the soil; his audience, for many years, was chiefly beyond the water, and there, too, he often longed to be.

This distaste for the national scene is often based upon a genuine alienness. The more, indeed, one investigates the ancestry of Americans who have won distinction in the fine arts, the more one discovers tempting game for the critical Know Nothings. Whitman was half Dutch, Harte was half Jew, Poe was Irish, James had an Irish grandfather, Howells was Irish and German, and Dreiser was German. Fully a half of the painters discussed in John C. Van Dyke's "American Art and Its Tradition" were of mixed blood, with the Anglo-Saxon plainly recessive. And of the five poets singled out for encomium by Miss Lowell in "Tendencies in Modern American Poetry" one was a Swede, two were partly German, one was educated in the German language, and three of the five exiled themselves to England as soon as they got out of their nonage. The exiles are of all sorts: T. S. Eliot, Ezra Pound, Henry B. Fuller, Ambrose Bierce, Edith Wharton. They have gone to England, France, Germany, Italy — anywhere to escape. Even at home the literatus is perceptibly foreign in his mien. If he lies under the New England tradition he is furiously colonial — more English than the English. If he turns to revolt, he is apt to put on a French hat and a Russian red blouse. *The Little Review*, once the organ of the extreme wing of *révoltés*, was so violently exotic that during the plupatriotic days of 1914–18 some of its readers protested. With characteristic lack of humor it replied with an American number — and two of the stars of that number bore the fine old Anglo-Saxon names of Ben Hecht and Elsa von Freytag-Loringhoven.

This tendency of American literature, the moment it begins

[1] This curious foreignness is dealt with at length in Van Wyck Brooks's The Flowering of New England, 1815–1865; New York, 1936.

to show enterprise, novelty and significance, to radiate an alien smell is not an isolated phenomenon. The same smell accompanies practically all other sorts of intellectual activity in the Republic. Whenever one hears that a new political theory is in circulation, or a scientific heresy, or a movement toward rationalism in religion, it is always safe to guess that some discontented stranger or other has a hand in it. In the newspapers and on the floor of Congress a new heterodoxy is always denounced forthwith as a product of foreign plotting, and here public opinion undoubtedly supports both the press and the politicians, and with good reason. The native culture of the country — that is, the culture of the low caste Anglo-Saxons who preserve the national tradition — is almost completely incapable of producing ideas. All the arts are thoroughly exotic. Music is German or Jewish, painting is French, literature may be anything from English to Russian, architecture (save when it becomes a mere branch of engineering) is a maddening phantasmagoria of borrowings. Even so elemental an art as that of cookery shows no native development, and is greatly disesteemed by Americans of the Anglo-Saxon majority; any decent restaurant that one blunders upon in the land is likely to be French, and if not French, then Italian or German or Chinese.

So with the sciences. Organized scientific research began in the country with the founding of the Johns Hopkins University, a bald imitation of the German universities, and long held suspect by native opinion. Even after its great success there was rancorous hostility to its scheme of things on chauvinistic grounds, and some years ago efforts were begun to Americanize it, with the result that it sank to the level of a glorified highschool, and was dominated by native savants who would have been laughed at in any Continental university. Science, oppressed by such assaults from below, moves out of the academic grove into the freer air of the great foundations, where the pursuit of the shy fact is uncontaminated by football and social pushing. The greatest of these foundations is the Rockefeller Institute. Its salient men have been such investigators as Flexner, Loeb and Carrel — all of them Continental Jews.

The Blue-Nose

From the *Smart Set*, May, 1919, p. 53

ALL the histories of American literature, with perhaps one exception, devote a good deal of space to the lofty idealism of the snuffling pre-Methodists who settled New England. Reading such books, one somehow gets the notion that these bilious theologians were, in some strange way, noble fellows, and that, in particular, they cherished the fruits of the intellect, and so laid the foundations of whatever culture now exists in the United States. But what is the actual fact? The actual fact is that the fruits of the intellect were held in about as much esteem, in Puritan New England, as the fruits of the vines of Burgundy now get at a banquet of Presbyterians. The Puritans not only tried their damndest to shut out every vestige of sound information, of clean reasoning, of ordinary intellectual self-respect and integrity; they absolutely *succeeded* in shutting these things out. The gigantic play of ideas that went on in Europe during the Sixteenth and Seventeenth Centuries had no effect upon them whatsoever; it was not until foreign influences, slowly percolating into the country on the heels of commerce, gave a start to Transcendentalism that New England could show so much as a single third-rate college, a single readable journal or a single genuinely educated man. And even Transcendentalism was moony, hollow and sterile. Its highest product was a puerile confusion of European ideas, as in Emerson and Thoreau. It produced no art that is alive today — only poor schoolboys, abominably forced to the business by idiot pedagogues, read its masterpieces. And it produced no civilization, but only a tawdry pseudo-civilization — a codfish civilization.

Even in politics it has always been stupid and imitative. What! Even in politics? Then what of Abolition? Answer: Abolition was no more a New England invention than the affected broad *a* was a New England invention: both were borrowed from the English middle classes toward the end of the Eighteenth Century. And business? Here we let down the last bar: it requires a racking stretch of the imagination to put a talent for business among the evidences of culture. But even so, New England fails again. Can you think of a conspicuous captain of industry who was born there? Finally, of the twenty-seven general officers who stood at the head of the Army List at the close of the Civil War exactly three were New Englanders.

Folk-Literature

From the *Smart Set*, June, 1921, pp. 143–44.
A review of Poetic Origins and the Ballad, by Louise Pound;
New York, 1921

DR. POUND's book completely disposes of the theory upon which nine-tenths of all the pedagogical discussions of the ballad and its origins are based. This is the theory that the ballads familiar to all of us — for example, "Chevy Chase" and "Lord Bateman" — are the product, not of individual authors, but of whole herds of minnesingers working together, and that most of them came into being during dance ceremonies — in brief, that the primitive balladists first joined in a communal hoofing, then began to moan and hum a tune, and finally fitted words to it. It is difficult to imagine anything more idiotic, and yet this doctrine is cherished as something almost sacred by whole droves of professors and rammed annually into the skulls of innumerable candidates for the Ph.D. Dr. Pound proves by the analogy of the customs observed among existing savages and barbarians, and by ordinary common sense no less, that the ballads really did not originate in that way at all — that they were written, on the contrary, by individual poets with talents as far above those of the populace as the talents of the late J. Gordon Cooglar, say, were above those of the average Carolinian, and that most of them first saw the light, not at vulgar shindigs on the village green, but at fashionable and even intellectual ale-parties in castle halls.

The notion that *any* respectable work of art can have a communal origin is wholly nonsensical. The plain people, taking them together, are quite as incapable of a coherent esthetic impulse as they are of courage, honesty or honor. The cathedrals of the Middle Ages were not planned and built by whole communities, but by individual men; all the communities had to do with the business was to do the hard work, reluctantly and often badly. So with folk-song, folk-myth, folk-balladry. The fable of Adam and Eve in the Garden was not invented by the ancient Jews as a people, bit by bit, slowly and painfully; it was composed *in toto* on some fair morning by some long-forgotten Babylonian O. Henry, just as *Gefüllte Fisch* was invented centuries later by some cook of brilliant gifts; all the Jews did was to adopt both fable and dish — and spoil both. German folk-song, the loveliest in the world, had precisely the same sort of origin. It used to be credited to a mysterious native talent in the German yokelry, but scientific investigation reveals that some of the songs regarded as especially characteristic of the folk-soul were actually written by the director of music at the University of Tübingen, Prof. Dr. Friedrich Silcher, and that he was still alive so recently as 1860.

The English ballads are to be accounted for in the same way. Dr. Pound shows that some of the most famous of them, in their earliest forms, are full of concepts and phrases that would have been as incomprehensible to the English peasantry of Elizabeth's time as the Ehrlich hypothesis of immunity — that it is a sheer impossibility to imagine them being composed by a gang of oafs whooping and galloping around a May pole, or even assembled solemnly in an *Eisteddfod* or *Allgemeinesänger-fest*. More, she shows the process of ballad making in our own time — how a song by a Paul Dresser or a Stephen Foster is borrowed by the folk, and then gradually debased. Her work is extraordinarily learned, and yet the writing is clear and charming. It is a capital example of what scholarship might be in America if there were more scholars and less of the ponderous mummery of sorcerers and corn-doctors.

The Literary Amenities

From the *American Mercury*, May, 1931, pp. 34–35

Now that realtors and used-car dealers, chiropractors and job-
bers in plumbing supplies, keepers of one-arm lunchrooms and
chattel loan brokers all have rigid codes of professional ethics,
some of them enforced by drastic pains and penalties, I suppose
that the authors of the United States will presently experiment
in the same direction. So far all their discussion of right and
wrong has had to do with the acts of the other fellow, to wit,
of the publisher in his various forms: already, indeed, their trade
union, the Authors' League, has drawn up elaborate regulations
for his conduct, not unlike the regulations prevailing in a well-
conducted reformatory. But what authors themselves may do
or not do is still rather vague, and so one encounters a wide
variation in practise. There are authors in America who, in their
transactions with a magazine editor, are as considerate and
punctilious as so many Galahads, but there are others who are
not above trying to rook him out of a few postage stamps.

In the matter of the relations between author and reviewer
there seems to be a great difference of opinion, with English
ideas running one way and American ideas another. Not long
ago an eminent English novelist was protesting bitterly because
one of the American reviewers had printed two reviews of a
book of his, in two different periodicals, both of them unfavorable. He let it be known that this was regarded as immoral in
England, at all events among novelists. But why it should be
considered immoral I can't understand. Certainly the complain-
ant would have entered no caveat if both of the reviews had
been favorable, and certainly the reviewer would have been
open to suspicion if one had been favorable and the other not.
I see no reason why, in such a case, a reviewer should not print
as many reviews as he can induce editors to print. If his opinion
is worth printing at all, then it is worth printing as much as
possible. But it appears that different views prevail in the Motherland, at least among novelists with American hopes.

In another direction the English are far less squeamish. Here

in the Republic it is considered *infra dig* for an author to protest against anything printed about his book; even in case of
gross libel he leaves his publisher to make whatever representa-
tions may be called for. But in England authors are always protesting and complaining, and the letter columns of such journals
as the *Literary Supplement* of the London *Times* are filled with
their murmurs. This is most unusual west of the Atlantic. The
few authors who indulge in the English habit are generally
thought to be bounders, and no one pays any attention to them.
But the English, as an offset, are far more careful than their
American brethren about the use of private communications
from reviewers, and never publish them as advertising blurbs
and without permission, as is common over here.

Some time ago a young author who had just published his
first book asked me if he should send letters of thanks to the
reviewers who had noticed it favorably. I told him that the custom of the trade was against it — that he was estopped by etiquette from taking any cognizance of reviews, save, of course,
those which happened to be written by personal friends. But I
have since been wondering whether I advised him correctly.
The fact is that the matter has never been discussed judicially
by any author with a talent for ethical science, and that in consequence no one knows what is right and what is wrong. I am
also in doubt about another matter. Two or three years ago,
when an American novelist dedicated a novel to me and I reviewed it in due course, I was denounced for logrolling. The
book was of such character that my customers naturally expected me to deal with it, and the review had vinegar in it as
well as goosegrease; nevertheless, I was belabored as a logroller,
and the doctrine was set up that a man to whom a book is dedicated should never notice it. Is this doctrine sound? If so, then
it puts a burden upon reviewers of any experience, for they
naturally meet a good many authors, and not a few books are
dedicated to them. But I am by no means sure that my critics
were wrong. Nor am I sure that it is good professional practise
for an author to dedicate a book to a practising reviewer, even
though the reviewer may be a personal friend.

The whole subject of dedications, indeed, deserves to be considered at length by a committee of elderly and discreet authors,

to the end that sin may be avoided at either end. Personally, I have never dedicated a book to anyone, nor have I ever taken any notice of a review, whether good or bad, save (*a*) when the reviewer happened to be a personal friend, or (*b*) when he sent me his review and solicited my opinion of it. In the latter case I have always replied that it was swell, though not infrequently this was, in the strictest sense, not true. On sleepless nights I often think of such things, and find my conscience in a swollen and feverish state. If the subject were treated in books on moral theology I'd resort to them, but it isn't. Thus I propose that a national *duma* of authors be called, and that the whole subject of professional ethics be pondered officially. Even psychiatrists and movie magnates now have rigid codes; nay, even newspaper editors. But authors continue to wander in a moral wilderness.

The Authors' League

From THE NATIONAL LETTERS, PREJUDICES: SECOND SERIES, 1920, pp. 36–37

I QUOTE from a literary manifesto of 1920:

There are some conspicuous word merchants who deal in the English language, but the general public doesn't clamor for their wares. They write for the "thinking class." The élite, the discriminating. As a rule, they scorn the crass commercialism of the magazines and movies and such catch-penny devices. However, literary masterpieces live because they have been and will be read, not by the few, but by the many. That was true in the time of Homer, and even today the first move made by an editor when he receives a manuscript, or a gentle reader when he buys a book, or a T.B.M. when he sinks into an orchestra chair is to look around for John Henry Plot. If Mr. Plot is too long delayed in arriving or doesn't come at all, the editor usually sends regrets, the reader yawns and the tired business man falls asleep. It's a sad state of affairs and awful tough on art, but it can't be helped.

Observe the lofty scorn of mere literature — the superior irony at the expense of everything beyond the bumping of boobs. Note the sound judgment as to the function and fate of literary masterpieces, *e.g.*, "Endymion," "The Canterbury Tales," "Faust," "Typhoon." Give your eye to the chaste diction — "John Henry Plot," "T.B.M.," and so on. No doubt you will at once assume that this curious counterblast to literature was written by some former bartender promoted to composing scenarios. But it was not. It was written and signed by the president of the Authors' League of America.

XXVI. LITERATI

The Moonstruck Pastor

From the *American Mercury*, Oct., 1930.
A review of Emerson: The Enraptured Yankee, by Régis Michaud;
New York, 1930

IT is one of the mysteries of American life that Rotary has never discovered Emerson. His so-called philosophy, even more than that of Elbert Hubbard, seems to be made precisely for the lunch-table idealists. There is in it an almost incomparable sweep of soothing generalities, a vast marshaling of sugary and not too specific words, a wholesale assurance, a soaring optimism. It sets up a magnificent glow without generating any destructive heat. I can imagine nothing better suited to the spiritual needs of used-car dealers, trust company vice-presidents, bath-fixture magnates, and the like, gathered together in the sight of God to take cheer from one another and shove the Republic along its rocky road. Its effects upon the circulation is as powerful as that of a swig of C_6H_3 $(OH)_2$—$CHOH$—CH_2—$NHCH_3$. And yet the Rotarians neglect this powerful medicine for the feeble philtres of Hubbard, and gulp the even more watery perunas of Roger W. Babson and Bishop Manning as chasers.

M. Michaud is plainly surprised by this blindness. As he points out over and over again, Emerson was always very careful to keep idealism within the bounds of American respectability. He incited to hope, optimism, enterprise, enthusiasm, but never to any downright violation of decorum. Did he preach the sacredness of the individual, the kingship of the lonely soul? Then he always stopped far short of Thoreau's corollary that it was unnecessary to pay taxes. Did he view theologians with a fishy eye, and distrust their mumbo-jumbo of sacraments and ceremonials? Then he still found it discreet and decent to go to

477

church on Sunday. Did he call for frank words, honest exultations, dancing with arms and legs? Then he knew how to be cautious when it came to Walt Whitman. And did he praise the simple life and renounce luxury? Then it was always from the security of an ample income. In this last field, indeed, the student scarcely detects any difference between his philosophy and that of Arthur Brisbane. "One can read between the lines," says Michaud, "that in Emerson's eyes the poor, like the sick, are rogues, that the capitalists are the real 'representative men,' that all compensation which pays in specie is divine, and that Wall Street is the true temple of the Other-Soul."

If this is not a philosophy made for soaring American business men, then I am surely no tailor of the psyche. But, as I say, they pass it over for inferior goods, and so leave it to the New Thoughters and the New Humanists. Both, alas, make a sad hash of it. The New Thoughters force it into a miscegenation with deep breathing, umbilicular contemplation and other borrowings from the heathen Hindus, and the New Humanists try to ram it into the mold of Calvinism. Emerson, if he were alive today, would feel uncomfortable in either camp. He was, for all his ventures into interstellar space, far too realistic a Yankee to believe that reading the Bhagavad-Gita could wake his solar plexus or give him second sight, and he owed far too much to the Romantic movement to countenance the Humanists' saucy denunciations of Rousseau. He was, indeed, the real founder of Romanticism in America, though he took his Rousseau at third hand. It was precisely from Romanticism that he got the ammunition for his polite and pussy-footing revolt against Calvinism.

Aristotelian Obsequies

From PREJUDICES: FIRST SERIES, 1919, pp. 246–47.
First printed in the *Smart Set*, May, 1919, p. 49

I TAKE the following from the Boston *Herald* of May 1, 1882:

A beautiful floral book stood at the left of the pulpit, being spread out on a stand. . . . Its last page was composed of white carnations, white daisies and light-colored immortelles. On the leaf was displayed, in neat letters of purple immortelles, the word "Finis." This device was about two feet square, and its border was composed of different colored tea-roses. The other portion of the book was composed of dark and light-colored flowers. . . . The front of the large pulpit was covered with a mass of white pine boughs laid on loosely. In the center of this mass of boughs appeared a large harp composed of yellow jonquils. . . . Above this harp was a handsome bouquet of dark pansies. On each side appeared large clusters of calla lilies.

Well, what have we here? The funeral of a Grand Exalted Pishposh of the Odd Fellows, of a venerable Tammany leader, of an aged and much respected brothel-keeper? Nay. What we have here is the funeral of Ralph Waldo Emerson. It was thus that the Puritan *Kultur* mourned its philosopher.

Poe

From The National Letters, Prejudices: Second Series, 1920, pp. 59–63

It would certainly seem reasonable for a man of so forceful a habit of mind as Poe, and of such prodigal and arresting originality, to have founded a school in his own country, but a glance at the record shows that he did nothing of the sort. Immediately he was dead, the shadows of the genteel Irving tradition closed around his tomb, and for nearly thirty years thereafter all his chief ideas went disregarded. If, as the literature books argue, Poe was the father of the American short story, then it was a posthumous child, and had step-fathers who did their best to conceal its true parentage. When it actually entered upon the vigorous life that we know today Poe had been dead for a generation. Its father, at the time of its belated adolescence, seemed to be Bret Harte — and Harte's debt to Dickens was vastly more apparent than his debt to Poe. What he got from Poe was probably essential, but he himself seems to have been unaware of it. It remained for foreign criticism, and particularly for French criticism, to lift Poe to the secure place that he now holds.

It is true enough that he enjoyed, during his lifetime, a certain popular reputation, and that he was praised by such men as N. P. Willis and James Russell Lowell, but that reputation was considerably less than the fame of men who were much his inferiors, and that praise, especially in Lowell's case, was much corrupted by reservations. Not many native critics of respectable position, during the 50s and 60s, would have ranked him clearly above, say, Irving or Cooper, or even above Longfellow, his old enemy. A few partisans argued for him, but in the main, as Saintsbury once said, he was the victim of "extreme and almost incomprehensible injustice" at the hands of his countrymen. It is surely not without significance that it took ten years of effort to raise money enough to put a cheap and hideous tombstone upon his neglected grave in Baltimore, that it was not actually set up until he had been dead twenty-six years, that no contemporary American writer took any part in furthering the project, and that the only one who attended the final ceremony was Whitman.

It was Baudelaire's French translation of the prose tales and Mallarmé's translation of the poems that brought Poe to Valhalla. The former, first printed in 1856, founded the Poe cult in France, and during the two decades following it flourished amazingly. It was one of the well-springs, in fact, of the whole so-called decadent movement. If Baudelaire, the father of that movement, "cultivated hysteria with delight and terror," he was simply doing what Poe had done before him. Both, reacting against the false concept of beauty as a mere handmaiden of logical ideas, sought its springs in those deep feelings and inner experiences which lie beyond the range of ideas and are to be interpreted only as intuitions. Emerson started upon the same quest, but was turned off into mazes of contradiction and unintelligibility by his ethical obsession — the unescapable burden of his Puritan heritage. But Poe never wandered from the path. You will find in "The Poetic Principle" what is perhaps the clearest statement of this new and sounder concept of beauty that has ever been made — certainly it is clearer than any ever made by a Frenchman. But it was not until Frenchmen had watered the seed out of grotesque and vari-colored pots that it began to sprout. The tide of Poe's ideas, set in motion in France in the second half of the century, did not wash England until the last decade, and in America, save for a few dashes of spray, it has yet to show itself. There is no American writer who displays the influence of this most potent and original of Americans so clearly as whole groups of Frenchmen display it, and whole groups of Germans, and even a good many Englishmen.

What we have from Poe at first hand is simply a body of obvious yokel-shocking, with the tales of Ambrose Bierce as its finest flower — in brief, an imitation of Poe's externals without any comprehension whatever of his underlying aims and notions. What we have from him at second hand is a somewhat childish Maeterlinckism, a further dilution of Poe-and-water. This Maeterlinckism got itself intermingled with the Whitmanic stream flowing back to America through the channel of French Imagism, with results destructive to the sanity of earnest critics and fatal to the gravity of those less austere. It is significant that the critical writing of Poe, in which there lies most that was best in him, has not come back; no normal American ever thinks of him as a critic, but only as a poet, as a raiser of goose-flesh, or as an immoral fellow. The cause thereof is plain enough. The French, instead of borrowing his critical theory directly, deduced it afresh from his applications of it; it became criticism *of* him rather than *by* him. Thus his own speculations lacked the authority of foreign approval, and consequently made no impression. The weight of native opinion was naturally against them, for they were at odds, not only with its fundamental theories, but also with its practical doctrine that no criticism can be profound and respectable which is not also dull.

"Poe," says Arthur Ransome, in his capital study of the man and the artist, "was like a wolf chained by the leg among a lot of domestic dogs." The simile here is somewhat startling, and Ransome, in a footnote, tries to ameliorate it. The "domestic dogs" it refers to were Longfellow, Whittier, Holmes and Emerson.

Whitman

From the same, pp. 63–65. With additions from THE FRINGES OF
LOVELY LETTERS, PREJUDICES: FIFTH SERIES, 1926, pp. 202–08

NOTHING could be more indecent (or more American) than
the hostility which surrounded Whitman at home until the
end of his long life. True enough, it was broken by certain
feeble mitigations. Emerson, in 1855, praised him — though
later, when he came under active fire, was very eager to forget
it and desert him, as Clemens and Howells, years afterward,
deserted Gorky. Alcott, Thoreau, Lowell and even Bryant, during his brief Bohemian days, were more or less polite to him.
A group of miscellaneous enthusiasts gradually gathered about
him, and out of this group emerged at least one man of some
distinction, John Burroughs. Young adventurers of letters —
for example, Huneker — went to see him and hear him, half
drawn by genuine admiration and half by mere deviltry. But the
general tone of the opinion that beat upon him, the attitude of
domestic criticism, was unbrokenly inimical; he was opposed by
misrepresentation and neglect. "The prevailing range of criticism on my book," he wrote in "A Backward Glance on My
Own Road" in 1884, "has been either mockery or denunciation — and . . . I have been the marked object of two or three
(to me pretty serious) official buffetings." "After thirty years of
trial," he wrote in "My Book and I," three years later, "public
criticism on the book and myself as author of it shows marked
anger and contempt more than anything else."

Down to the time of his death the prevailing American doctrine was that he was a third-rate poet and a dirty fellow. Any
young professor who, in the 70s or even in the early 80s, had
presumed to whoop for him in class would have been cashiered
at once, as both incompetent and immoral. Indeed, if there
was anything definitively established in those days, it was that
old Walt was below the salt. But today he is taught to sophomores everywhere, perhaps even in Tennessee, and everyone
agrees that he is one of the glories of the national letters. Has
that change been brought about by a purely critical process?

Does it represent a triumph of criticism over darkness? It does not. It represents, rather, a triumph of external forces over criticism. Whitman's first partisans were not interested in poetry; they were interested in sex, and perhaps especially in homosexuality. They were presently reënforced by persons interested in politics. They were finally converted into a majority by a tatterdemalion horde of persons interested mainly, and perhaps only, in making a noise.

Literary criticism, properly so-called, had little if anything to do with this transformation. Scarcely a critic of any recognized authority had a hand in it. What started it off, after the first furtive, gingery snuffling over "A Woman Waits for Me" and the "Calamus" cycle, was the rise of political radicalism in the early 80s, in reaction against the swinish materialism that followed the Civil War. I am tempted to say that Terence V. Powderly had more to do with the rehabilitation of Whitman than any American critic, or, indeed, than any American poet. And if you object to Powderly, then I offer you Karl Marx. The radicals made heavy weather of it at the start. To the average respectable citizen they seemed to be mere criminals. What they needed, obviously, was some means of stilling the popular fear of them — some way of tapping the national sentimentality. There stood Whitman, conveniently to hand. In his sonorous strophes to an imaginary and preposterous democracy there was an eloquent statement of their own vague and windy yearnings, and, what is more, a certificate to their virtue as sound Americans. So they adopted him with loud hosannas, and presently he was both their poet and their philosopher. Long before any professor at Harvard dared to mention him (save, perhaps, with lascivious winks), he was being read to tatters by thousands of lonely Socialists in the mining-towns. As radicalism froze into Liberalism, and so began to influence the intelligentsia, his vogue rose, and by the end of the century even school-teachers had begun to hear of him. There followed the free verse poets, *i.e.*, a vast herd of emerging barbarians with an itch to make an uproar in the world, and no capacity for mastering the orthodox rules of prosody. Thus Whitman came to Valhalla, pushed by political propagandists and pulled by literary mountebanks.

Memorial Service

From PREJUDICES: FIRST SERIES, 1919, pp. 249–50.
First printed in the *Smart Set*, June, 1919, p. 45

LET us summon from the shades the immortal soul of James Harlan, born in 1820, entered into rest in 1899. In the year 1865 this Harlan resigned from the United States Senate to enter the Cabinet of Abraham Lincoln as Secretary of the Interior. One of the clerks in that department, at $600 a year, was Walt Whitman, lately emerged from the three years of service as an army nurse during the Civil War. One day, discovering that Whitman was the author of a book called "Leaves of Grass," Harlan ordered him incontinently kicked out, and it was done forthwith. Let us remember this event and this man; he is too precious to die. Let us repair, once a year, to our accustomed houses of worship and there give thanks to God that one day in 1865 brought together the greatest poet that America has ever produced and the damndest ass.[1]

Footnote

From the Baltimore *Evening Sun*, Dec. 9, 1929

THE REAL objection to Whitman is that he was a vulgar and trashy fellow. He wrote "A Woman Waits for Me." A civilized man would have put *the* in place of *a*.

[1] This squib became a fixture in the *Smart Set*, and in some form or other was reprinted at least once a year. It was then taken over into the *American Mercury*, but its first appearance there, in April, 1924, p. 453, seems to have been its last.

Credo

From the *Smart Set*, Feb., 1913, p. 152

I BELIEVE that "Huckleberry Finn" is one of the great master-pieces of the world, that it is the full equal of "Don Quixote" and "Robinson Crusoe," that it is vastly better than "Gil Blas," "Tristram Shandy," "Nicholas Nickleby" or "Tom Jones." I believe that it will be read by human beings of all ages, not as a solemn duty but for the honest love of it, and over and over again, long after every book written in America between the years 1800 and 1860, with perhaps three exceptions, has disappeared entirely save as a classroom fossil. I believe that Mark Twain had a clearer vision of life, that he came nearer to its elementals and was less deceived by its false appearances, than any other American who has ever presumed to manufacture generalizations. I believe that, admitting all his defects, he wrote better English, in the sense of cleaner, straighter, vivider, saner English, than either Irving or Hawthorne. I believe that four of his books — "Huck," "Life on the Mississippi," "Captain Stormfield's Visit to Heaven," and "A Connecticut Yankee" — are alone worth more, as works of art and as criticisms of life, than the whole output of Cooper, Irving, Holmes, Mitchell, Stedman, Whittier and Bryant. I believe that he ranks well above Whitman and certainly not below Poe. I believe that he was the true father of our national literature, the first genuinely American artist of the blood royal.

The Man Within

From the *Smart Set*, Oct., 1919, pp. 139–43

THE BITTER, of course, goes with the sweet. To be an American is, unquestionably, to be the noblest, the grandest, the proudest mammal that ever hoofed the verdure of God's green footstool. Often, in the black abysm of the night, the thought that I am one awakens me with a blast of trumpets, and I am thrown into a cold sweat by contemplation of the fact. I shall cherish it on the scaffold; it will console me in Hell. But there is no perfection under Heaven, so even an American has his small blemishes, his scarcely discernible weaknesses, his minute traces of vice and depravity. Mark, alas, had them: he was as thoroughly American as a Knight of Pythias, a Wheeling stogie, or Prohibition. One might almost exhibit his effigy in a museum as the archetype of the *Homo americanus*. And what were these stigmata that betrayed him? In chief, they were two in number, and both lay at the very foundation of his character. On the one hand, there was his immovable moral certainty, his firm belief that he knew what was right from what was wrong, and that all who differed from him were, in some obscure way, men of an inferior and sinister order. And on the other hand, there was his profound intellectual timorousness, his abiding fear of his own ideas, his incurable cowardice in the face of public disapproval. These two characteristics colored his whole thinking; they showed themselves in his every attitude and gesture. They were the visible signs of his limitation as an Emersonian Man Thinking, and they were the bright symbols of his nationality. He was great in every way that an American could be great, but when he came to the border of his Americanism he came to the end of his greatness.

The true Mark Twain is only partly on view in his actual books — that is, in his printed books. The real *Mensch* was not the somewhat heavy-handed satirist of "A Tramp Abroad" and "Tom Sawyer." He was not even the extraordinarily fine and delicate artist of "Joan of Arc" and "Huckleberry Finn." Nay, he was a different bird altogether — an intensely serious and even lugubrious man, an iconoclast of the most relentless sort, a man not so much amused by the spectacle of life as appalled by it, a pessimist to the last degree. Nothing could be more unsound than the Mark legend — the legend of the lighthearted and kindly old clown. The real Mark was a man haunted to the point of distraction by the endless and meaningless tragedy of existence — a man whose thoughts turned to it constantly, in season and out of season. And to think, with him, was to write; he was, for all his laziness, the most assiduous of scribblers; he piled up notes, sketches of books and articles, even whole books, about it, almost mountain high.

Well, why did these notes, sketches, articles and books get no further? Why do most of them remain unprinted, even to-day? You will find the answer in a prefatory note that Mark appended to "What Is Man?" published privately in 1905. I quote it in full:

> The studies for these papers were begun twenty-five or twenty-seven years ago. The papers were written seven years ago. I have examined them once or twice per year since and found them satisfactory. I have just examined them again, and am still satisfied that they speak the truth. Every thought in them has been thought (and accepted as un-assailable truth) by millions upon millions of men — and concealed, kept private. Why did they not speak out? Be-cause they dreaded (*and could not bear*) the disapproval of the people around them. Why have I not published? The same reason has restrained me, I think. I can find no other.

Imagine a man writing so honest and excellent a book, imag-ine him examining it and re-examining it and always finding it good — and yet holding off the printing of it for twenty-five years, and then issuing it timorously and behind the door, in an edition of 250 copies, none of them for sale. Even his death did not quench his fear. His executors, taking it over as part of his goods, withheld the book for five years more — and then printed it very discreetly, with the betraying preface omitted. Surely it would be impossible in the literature of any other civilized country since the Middle Ages to find anything to match that long hesitation. Here was a man of the highest dignity in the national letters, and here was a book into which he had put the earnest convictions of his lifetime, a book carefully and deliber-ately written, a book representing him more accurately than any other, both as artist and as man — and yet it had to wait thirty-five years before it saw the light of day. An astounding affair, in all conscience — but thoroughly American, Messieurs, thoroughly American. Mark knew his countrymen. He knew their intense suspicion of ideas, their blind hatred of heterodoxy, their bitter way of dealing with dissenters. He knew how, their pruderies outraged, they would turn upon even the gaudiest hero and roll him in the mud. And knowing, he was afraid. He "dreaded the disapproval of the people around him." But part of that dread, I suspect, was peculiarly internal. In brief, Mark himself was also an American, and he shared the national horror of the unorthodox. His own speculations always half appalled him. He was not only afraid to utter what he believed; he was even a bit timorous about *believing* what he believed.

The weakness takes a good deal from his stature. It leaves him radiating a subtle flavor of the second-rate. With more courage, he would have gone a great deal further, and left a far deeper mark upon the intellectual history of his time. Not, perhaps, intrinsically as artist. He got as far in that direction as it is possible for a man of his training to go. "Huckleberry Finn" is a truly stupendous piece of work — perhaps the greatest novel ever written in English. And it would be difficult to surpass the sheer artistry of such things as "A Connecticut Yankee," "Captain Stormfield," "Joan of Arc" and parts of "A Tramp Abroad." But there is more to the making of literature than the mere depiction of human beings at their obscene follies; there is also the play of ideas. Mark had ideas that were clear, that were vigorous, and that had an immediate appositeness. True enough, most of them were not quite original. As Prof. Schoenemann, of Harvard, once demonstrated, he got the notion of "The Mysterious Stranger" from Adolf Wilbrandt's "Der Meister von Palmyra"; much of "What Is Man?" you will find in the forgotten harangues of Ingersoll; in other directions he borrowed right and left. But it is only necessary to read either of the books I have just mentioned to see how thoroughly he recast everything he wrote; how brilliantly it came to be marked by the charm of his own personality; how he got his own peculiar and unmatchable eloquence into the merest statement of it. When, entering these regions of his true faith, he yielded to a puerile timidity — when he sacrificed his conscience and his self-respect to the idiotic popularity that so often more than half dishonored him — then he not only did a cruel disservice to his own permanent fame, but inflicted genuine damage upon the national literature. He was greater than all the others because he was more American, but in this one way, at least, he was less than them for the same reason.

Well, there he stands — a bit concealed, a bit false, but still a colossus. As I have said, I am inclined year by year to rate his achievement higher. In such a work as "Huckleberry Finn" there is something that vastly transcends the merit of all ordinary books. It has a merit that is special and extraordinary; it lifts itself above all hollow standards and criteria; it seems greater every time I read it. The books that gave Mark his first celebrity do not hold up so well. "The Jumping Frog" still wrings snickers, but after all, it is commonplace at bottom; even an Ellis Parker Butler might have conceivably written it. "The Innocents Abroad," re-read today, is largely tedious. Its humors are artificial; its audacities are stale; its eloquence belongs to the fancy journalism of a past generation. Even "Tom Sawyer" and "A Tramp Abroad" have long stretches of flatness. But in "Huckleberry Finn," though he didn't know it at the time and never quite realized it, Mark found himself. There, working against the grain, heartily sick of the book before it was done, always putting it off until tomorrow, he hacked out a masterpiece that expands as year chases year. There, if I am not wrong, he produced the greatest work of the imagination that These States have yet seen.

The Dean

From PREJUDICES: FIRST SERIES, 1919, pp. 52–58.
First printed, in part, in the *Smart Set*, Jan., 1917, pp. 266–68.
Howells died in 1919

WILLIAM DEAN HOWELLS, during his lifetime, was almost the national ideal of a literary character: an urbane, cleanly and highly respectable gentleman, a sitter on committees, an intimate of professors and the prophets of movements, a placid conformist. The result was that in his last twenty years his successive books were not criticized, nor even adequately reviewed, but merely fawned over; the critics of the newspapers, male and female, could no more bring themselves to question them than they could question Lincoln's Gettysburg speech, or Paul Elmer More, or their own virginity. The dean of American letters in point of years, and in point of published quantity, and in point of public prominence and influence, he was gradually enveloped in a web of superstitious reverence, and it still grates somewhat harshly to hear his actual achievement discussed in cold blood.

Nevertheless, all this merited respect for an industrious and inoffensive man is bound, soon or late, to yield to a critical examination of the artist within, and that examination will have its bitter moments for those who naïvely accept the Howells legend. It will show, without doubt, a competent journeyman, a contriver of pretty things, a facile stylist — but it will also show a long row of uninspired and hollow books, with no more ideas in them than so many volumes of the *Ladies' Home Journal*, and no more deep and contagious feeling than so many reports of autopsies, and no more glow and gusto than so many tables of prices. The profound dread and agony of life, the surge of passion and aspiration, the grand crash and glitter of things, the tragedy that runs eternally under the surface — all this the critic will seek in vain in Howells's elegant and shallow volumes. And seeking it in vain, he will probably dismiss all of them together with fewer words than he gives to "Huckleberry Finn."

Already, indeed, the Howells legend tends to become a mere legend, and empty of all genuine significance. Who actually reads the Howells novels? Who even remembers their names? "The Minister's Charge," "An Imperative Duty," "The Unexpected Guests," "Out of the Question," "No Love Lost" — these titles are already as meaningless as a roll of Sumerian kings. Perhaps "The Rise of Silas Lapham" survives, at least in the colleges — but go read it if you would tumble downstairs. The truth about Howells is that he really had nothing to say, for all the charm he got into saying it. His psychology was superficial, amateurish, often nonsensical; his irony was scarcely more than a polite facetiousness; his characters simply refused to live. No figure even remotely comparable to Norris's McTeague or Dreiser's Frank Cowperwood is to be encountered in his novels. He was quite unequal to any such evocation of the race-spirit, of the essential conflict of forces among us, of the peculiar drift and color of American life. The world he moved in was suburban, caged, flabby. He could no more have written the last chapters of "Lord Jim" than he could have written the Book of Mark.

As a critic he belonged to a measurably higher level, if only because of his eager curiosity, his gusto for minor novelty. He dealt valiant licks for E. W. Howe, Frank Norris, Edith Wharton and William Vaughn Moody. He brought forward the Russians diligently and persuasively, albeit they left no mark upon his own manner. In his ingratiating way, back in the 70s and 80s, he made war upon some of the worst of the prevailing sentimentalities. But his history as a critic is full of errors and omissions. One finds him loosing a fanfare for W. B. Trites, the Philadelphia Zola, and praising Frank A. Munsey — and one finds him leaving the discovery of all the Shaws, George Moores, Dreisers, Synges and Galsworthys to the Pollards and Hunekers. Busy in the sideshows, he didn't see the elephants go by. . . . Here temperamental defects handicapped him. Turn to his "My Mark Twain" and you will see what I mean. The Mark that is exhibited in this book is a Mark whose Himalayan outlines are discerned but hazily through a pink fog of Howells. There is a moral note in the tale — an obvious effort to palliate, to touch up, to excuse. Poor Mark, of course, was charming, and there was talent in him, but what a weakness he had for thinking aloud — and such shocking thoughts! What oaths in his speech! What awful cigars he smoked! How barbarous his contempt for the strict sonata form! It seems incredible that two men so unlike should have found common denominators for a friendship lasting forty-four years. The one derived from Rabelais, Chaucer, the Elizabethans and Benvenuto — buccaneers of the literary high seas, loud laughters, law-breakers, giants of a lordlier day; the other came down from Jane Austen, Washington Irving and Hannah More. The one wrote English as Michelangelo hacked marble, broadly, brutally, magnificently; the other was a maker of pretty waxen groups. The one was utterly unconscious of the way he achieved his staggering effects; the other was the most toilsome, fastidious and self-conscious of craftsmen. . . .

What remains of Howells is his style. He invented a new harmony of "the old, old words." He destroyed the Johnsonian periods of the Poe tradition, and erected upon the ruins a complex and savory carelessness, full of soft naïvetés that were sophisticated to the last degree. Like Mark, but in a diametrically different way, he loosened the tightness of English, and let a blast of air into it. He achieved, for all his triviality, for all his narrowness of vision, a pungent and often admirable style.

Ambrose Bierce

From PREJUDICES: SIXTH SERIES, 1927, pp. 259–65. With additions from the *American Mercury*, Sept., 1929, pp. 125–26. Bierce disappeared in Mexico in 1914 and is supposed to have been killed there

THE REPUTATION of Bierce has always radiated an occult, artificial, drug-store scent. He has been hymned in a passionate, voluptuous, inordinate way by a small band of disciples, and he has been passed over altogether by the great majority of American critics, and no less by the great majority of American readers. Certainly it would be absurd to say that he is generally read, even by the *intelligentsia*. Most of his books, in fact, are out of print and almost unobtainable, and there is little evidence that his massive Collected Works, printed in twelve volumes between 1909 and 1912, have gone into anything even remotely approaching a wide circulation.

I have a suspicion, indeed, that Bierce did a serious disservice to himself when he put those twelve volumes together. Already an old man at the time, he permitted his nostalgia for his lost youth to get the better of his critical faculty, never very powerful at best, and the result was a depressing assemblage of worn-out and fly-blown stuff, much of it quite unreadable. If he had boiled the collection down to four volumes, or even to six, it might have got him somewhere, but as it is, his good work is lost in a morass of bad and indifferent work. I doubt that anyone save the Bierce fanatics aforesaid has ever plowed through the whole twelve volumes. They are filled with epigrams against frauds long dead and forgotten, and echoes of old and puerile newspaper controversies, and experiments in fiction that belong to a dark and expired age. But in the midst of all this blather there are some pearls — more accurately, there are two of them. One consists of the series of epigrams called "The Devil's Dictionary"; the other consists of the war stories, commonly called "Tales of Soldiers and Civilians." Among the latter are some of the best war stories ever written — things fully worthy to be ranged beside Zola's "L'Attaque du Moulin," Kipling's "The Taking of Lungtungpen," or Ludwig Thoma's "Ein Bayrischer Soldat." And among the former are some of the most gorgeous witticisms in the English language.

Bierce, I believe, was the first writer of fiction ever to treat war realistically. He antedated even Zola. It is common to say that he came out of the Civil War with a deep and abiding loathing of slaughter — that he wrote his war stories in disillusion, and as a sort of pacifist. But this is certainly not believed by anyone who knew him, as I did in his last years. What he got out of his services in the field was not a sentimental horror of it, but a cynical delight in it. It appeared to him as a sort of magnificent *reductio ad absurdum* of all romance. The world viewed war as something heroic, glorious, idealistic. Very well, he would show how sordid and filthy it was — how stupid, savage and degrading. But to say this is not to say that he disapproved it. On the contrary, he vastly enjoyed the chance its discussion gave him to set forth dramatically what he was always talking about and gloating over: the infinite imbecility of man. There was nothing of the milk of human kindness in old Ambrose; he did not get the nickname of Bitter Bierce for nothing. What delighted him most in this life was the spectacle of human cowardice and folly. He put man, intellectually, somewhere between the sheep and the horned cattle, and as a hero somewhere below the rats. His war stories, even when they deal with the heroic, do not depict soldiers as heroes; they depict them as bewildered fools, doing things without sense, submitting to torture and outrage without resistance, dying at last like hogs in Chicago. So far in this life, indeed, I have encountered no more thorough-going cynic than Bierce was. His disbelief in man went even further than Mark Twain's; he was quite unable to imagine the heroic, in any ordinary sense. Nor, for that matter, the wise. Man to him, was the most stupid and ignoble of animals. But at the same time the most amusing. Out of the spectacle of life about him he got an unflagging and Gargantuan joy. The obscene farce of politics delighted him. He was an almost amorous connoisseur of theology and theologians. He howled with mirth whenever he thought of a professor, a doctor or a husband.

Another character that marked him, perhaps flowing out of this same cynicism, was his curious taste for the macabre. All of his stories show it. He delighted in hangings, autopsies, dissecting-rooms. Death to him was not something repulsive, but a sort of low comedy — the last act of a squalid and rib-rocking buffoonery. When, grown old and weary, he departed for Mexico, and there — if legend is to be believed — marched into the revolution then going on, and had himself shot, there was certainly nothing in the transaction to surprise his acquaintances. The whole thing was typically Biercian. He died happy, one may be sure, if his executioners made a botch of dispatching him — if there was a flash of the grotesque at the end. Once I enjoyed the curious experience of going to a funeral with him. His conversation to and from the crematory was superb — a long series of gruesome but highly amusing witticisms. He had tales to tell of crematories that had caught fire and singed the mourners, of dead bibuli whose mortal remains had exploded, of widows guarding the fires all night to make sure that their dead husbands did not escape. The gentleman whose carcass we were burning had been a literary critic. Bierce suggested that his ashes be molded into bullets and shot at publishers, that they be presented to the library of the New York Lodge of Elks, that they be mailed anonymously to Ella Wheeler Wilcox, then still alive. Later on, when he heard that they had been buried in Iowa, he exploded in colossal mirth. The last time I saw him he predicted that the Christians out there would dig them up and throw them over the State line. On his own writing desk, he once told me, he kept the ashes of his son. I suggested idly that the ceremental urn must be a formidable ornament. "Urn hell!" he answered. "I keep them in a cigar-box!"

Bierce followed Poe in most of his short stories, but it is only a platitude to say that he wrote better than Poe. He had a far firmer grasp upon character; he was less literary and more observant. Unluckily, his stories seemed destined to go the way of Poe's. Their influence upon the modern American short story, at least upon its higher levels, is almost nil. When they are imitated at all, it is by the lowly hacks who manufacture thrillers for the pulp magazines. Meanwhile, it remains astonishing that his wit is so little remembered. In "The Devil's Dictionary" are some of the most devastating epigrams ever written. "Ah, that we could fall into women's arms without falling into their hands": it is hard to find a match for that in Oscar himself. I recall another: "Opportunity: a favorable occasion for grasping a disappointment." Another: "Once: enough." A third: "Husband: one who, having dined, is charged with the care of the plate." A fourth: "Our vocabulary is defective: we give the same name to woman's lack of temptation and man's lack of opportunity." A fifth: "Slang is the speech of him who robs the literary garbage cans on their way to the dump."

Bierce's critical judgments were often silly, as when he put Longfellow above Whitman, and not infrequently they were strongly colored by personal considerations, as when he overpraised George Sterling's poem, "The Wine of Wizardry." He was too little read to be a sound critic of letters, and he lacked the capacity to separate the artist from the man. Even his treatise on the art of writing, "Write it Right," is full of puerilities, for it never seems to have occurred to him that language, like literature, is a living thing, and not a mere set of rules. Writing of the trade he practised all his life, he wrote like a somewhat saucy schoolma'am, and when another schoolma'am lifted his stuff the theft went almost undetected. His own style was extraordinarily tight and unresilient, and his fear of rhetoric often took all the life out of his ideas. His stories, despite their melodramatic effectiveness, begin to seem old-fashioned; they belong to the era before the short story ceased to be a formal intellectual exercise and became a transcript of life. The people in them simply do not live and breathe; Ring Lardner, whose manner Bierce would have detested, did a hundred times better in that direction. They are probably read today, not as literature, but as shockers. Their appalling gruesomeness is what keeps in them such life as they have. Some of them deserve a better kind of immortality.

Bierce's social criticism, like his literary criticism, was often amusing but seldom profound. It had, however, the virtue of being novel in its day, and so it made its mark. He was the first American to lay about him with complete gusto, charging and battering the frauds who ranged the country. The timorousness of Mark Twain was not in him; no head was lofty enough to escape his furious thwack. Such berserk men have been rare in our history; the normal Americano, even when he runs amok, shows a considerable discretion. But there was no more discretion in Bierce than you will find in a runaway locomotive. Had he been a more cautious man, the professors of literature would be politer to him today.

Stephen Crane

From the Baltimore *Evening Sun*, Jan. 19, 1924.
A review of Stephen Crane, by Thomas Beer; New York, 1923

Next to Poe and Walt Whitman, Crane seems destined to go down into history as the most romantic American author of the Nineteenth Century. Even while he lived legend was busy with him. He was, by one story, a young man of mysterious and probably aristocratic origin, the scion of a Junker family in decay. He was, by another, a practitioner of strange, levantine vices — an opium smoker, a devotee of hashish. He was, by a third, the heaviest drinker known to vital statistics since Daniel Webster. He was, by a fourth, a consorter with harlots and the lover of Sarah Bernhardt. He was, by a fifth, sixth, seventh and eighth, the worst dead beat in New York.

All these yarns were fictions. Crane was actually the son of a respectable burgher in New Jersey and his mother was a member of the Methodist Church. If he drank somewhat freely when he was in funds, then so did all the other newspaper reporters of his era. If he borrowed money when he was out of a job, then ditto, ditto. If he took drugs, it was only to relieve his frequent and distressing infirmities, of which the last was the tuberculosis pulmonalis which took him off. As for his offenses against sex hygiene, they were chiefly imaginary. All through his youth he was romantically in love with a lady visibly his senior, and before he was much beyond 25 he married another lady still more his senior. In brief, a somewhat banal life. Even his war adventures were far less thrilling in fact than in his florid accounts of them. When he went to the Greek-Turkish War he came to grief because he could speak no language save English; when he went to the Spanish-American War he came down with severe cramps and had to be nursed by his fellow-correspondents.

But Crane could write, so some of his books have outlived their time. It was his distinction that he had an eye for the cold, glittering fact in an age of romantic illusion. The dignified authors of that time were such shallow, kittenish fellows as Howells, F. Hopkinson Smith and Frank R. Stockton, with Richard Watson Gilder as their high priest. The popular authors revolved around Richard Harding Davis. Crane's first writings alarmed Howells and shocked Gilder, but gradually a gang of younger men gathered around him, and before he died he was a national celebrity — in fact, a sort of American Kipling. He was, indeed, the head and forefront of the Young America movement in the middle nineties. No man of that movement was more vastly admired, and none has survived with less damage. How far would he have got if he had lived? It is useless to speculate. He died, like Schubert, at 30. He left behind him one superlatively excellent book, four or five magnificent short stories, some indifferent poems and a great mass of journalistic trash. The Gilders of his time left only trash.

Hamlin Garland

From SIX MEMBERS OF THE INSTITUTE, PREJUDICES: FIRST SERIES, 1919, pp. 134–38. Garland was born in 1860 and died in 1940. In one of his later books — I think it was My Friendly Contemporaries, 1932 — he got revenge for the following by plastering me violently. It was by no means my first onslaught on him. I began by denouncing his The Shadow World in the *Smart Set* for Feb., 1909, pp. 153–54, only four months after I had set up shop as a reviewer. He was greatly overestimated in his lifetime, mainly because of his energy and effrontery as a literary politician. His actual talents were very meagre, and he was shabby and devious as a man

THE CASE of Garland belonged to pathos in the grand manner, as you will discover on reading his autobiography, "A Son of the Middle Border." What ailed him was a vision of beauty, a seductive strain of bawdy music over the horizon. That vision, in his youth, tore him from his prairie plow and set him to clawing the anthills at the foot of Parnassus. He became an elocutionist. He aspired to write for the *Atlantic Monthly*. He fell under the spell of the Boston *aluminados* of 1885, which is as if one were to take fire from a June-bug. Finally, after embracing the Single Tax, he achieved a couple of depressing story-books, earnest, honest and full of indignation.

American criticism, which always mistakes a poignant document for esthetic form and organization, greeted these moral volumes as works of art, and so Garland found himself an accepted artist. No more grotesque miscasting of a diligent and worthy man is recorded in profane history. He had no more feeling for the intrinsic dignity of beauty, no more comprehension of it as a thing in itself, than a policeman. He was a moralist endeavoring ineptly to translate his messianic passion into esthetic terms, and always failing. "A Son of the Middle Border," undoubtedly the best of all his books, projects his failure brilliantly. It is, in substance, a document of considerable value — a naïve and often highly illuminating contribution to the history of the American peasantry. It is, in form, a thoroughly third-rate piece of writing — amateurish, flat, banal, repellent. Garland got facts into it; he got the relentless sincerity of the rustic Puritan; he got a sort of evangelical passion. But he couldn't get any charm. He couldn't get any beauty.

In such a career, as in such a book, there is something profoundly pathetic. One follows the progress of the man with a constant sense that he was steering by faulty compasses, that fate led him into paths too steep and rocky — nay, too dark and lovely — for him. An awareness of beauty was there, and a wistful desire to embrace it, but the confident gusto of the artist was always lacking. What one encountered in its place was the enthusiasm of the pedagogue, the desire to yank the world up to the soaring Methodist level, the hot yearning to displace old ideas with new ideas, and usually much worse ideas, for example, the Single Tax and spook-chasing. The natural goal of the man was the evangelical stump. He was led astray when those Boston Brahmins, enchanted by his sophomoric platitudes about Shakespeare, set him up as a critic of the arts, and then as an imaginative artist. He should have gone back to the saleratus belt, taken to the chautauquas, preached his foreordained perunas, got himself into Congress, and so helped to save the Republic from the demons that beset it. What a gladiator he would have made against the White Slave Traffic, the Rum Demon, the Kaiser!

His worst work, I daresay, is in some of his fiction, but my own favorite is "The Shadow World," a record of his communings with the gaseous precipitates of the departed. He took great pains at the start to assure us that he was a man of alert intelligence and without prejudices or superstitions. He had no patience, it appeared, with those idiots who swallowed the buffooneries of spiritualist mediums too greedily. For him the scientific method — the method which examines all evidence cynically and keeps on doubting until the accumulated proof, piled mountain-high, sweeps down in an overwhelming avalanche. . . . Thus he proceeded to the haunted chamber and began his dalliance with the banshees. They touched him with clammy, spectral hands; they wrung music for him out of locked pianos; they threw heavy tables about the room; they gave him messages from the golden shore and made him the butt of their coarse, transcendental humor. Through it all he sat tightly and solemnly, his mind open and his verdict up his sleeve. He was belligerently agnostic, and called attention to it proudly. . . . Then, in the end, he gave himself away. One of his fellow "scientists," more frankly credulous, expressed the belief that real scientists would soon prove the existence of spooks. "I hope they will," said the scientific Mr. Garland.

Henry James

From the *Smart Set*, Nov., 1920, pp. 140–41

HENRY JAMES would have been vastly improved as a novelist by a few whiffs from the Chicago stockyards. Finding New England all culture and no soul, he decided to escape, but he made the mistake of going in the wrong direction. In London he was in exactly the same situation as a young Westerner in Boston — that is, he was confronted by a culture more solid and assured than his own. It kept him shaky all his life long; it also kept him fawning, as his letters inconveniently reveal. He died a sort of super-Howells, with a long row of laborious but essentially hollow books behind him. The notion that James was a master mind is confined to the sort of persons who used to regard Browning as the greatest of poets. He was a superb technician, as Joseph Conrad has testified, but his ideas were always timorous; he never overcame his bashfulness in the presence of such superior fauna as the Lord Chancellor, the Master of Pembroke and Mrs. Humphrey Ward. Thus his painful psychologizings, when translated into plain English, turn out to be chiefly mere kittenishness — an arch tickling of the ribs of elderly virgins — the daring of a grandma smoking marijuana. But I believe that the makings of a genuinely first-rate artist were in James, and that Chicago would have developed him. What he needed was intimate contact with the life of his own country. He was unhappy in New England because he was an American, and New England, then as now, was simply a sort of outhouse of old England — a Devil's Island of intellectual poor relations, eternally wearing out the English chemises and pantaloons of season before last. A very defective psychologist, he made the blunder of jumping from the frying pan into the fire. The West would have amused, intrigued and finally conquered him. He would have been a great artist in his own country.

Dreiser

From the *American Mercury*, March, 1926, pp. 379–81. A review of An American Tragedy, by Theodore Dreiser; two volumes; New York, 1926. Dreiser died in 1945

WHATEVER else this vasty double-header may reveal about its author, it at least shows brilliantly that he is wholly devoid of what may be called literary tact. A more artful and ingratiating fellow, facing the situation that confronted him, would have met it with a far less difficult book. It was ten years since he had published his last novel, and all his old customers, it is reasonable to assume, were hungry for another — all his old customers and all his new customers. His publisher, after a long and gallant battle, had at last chased off the comstocks who sought to hamstring him. Rivals, springing up at intervals, had all succumbed. The Dreiser cult, once grown somewhat wobbly, was full of new strength and enthusiasm. The time was thus plainly at hand to make a ten-strike. What was needed was a book full of all the sound and solid Dreiser merits, and agreeably free from the familiar Dreiser defects — a book carefully designed and smoothly written, with no puerile clichés in it and no maudlin moralizing — in brief, a book aimed deliberately at readers of a certain taste, and competent to estimate good workmanship. Well, how did Dreiser meet the challenge? He met it, characteristically, by throwing out the present shapeless and forbidding monster — a heaping cartload of raw materials for a novel, with rubbish of all sorts intermixed — a vast, sloppy, chaotic thing of 385,000 words — at least 250,000 of them unnecessary. Such is scientific salesmanship as Dreiser understands it. Such is his reply to a pleasant invitation to a party.

The plot is extremely simple. Clyde Griffiths, the son of a

street preacher in Kansas City, revolts against the piety of his squalid home, and gets himself a job as bellboy in a gaudy hotel. There he acquires a taste for the luxuries affected by traveling salesmen, and is presently a leader in shop-girl society. An automobile accident, for which he is not to blame, forces him to withdraw discreetly, and he proceeds to Chicago, where he goes to work in a club. One day his father's rich brother, a collar magnate from Lycurgus, N. Y., is put up there by a member, and Clyde resolves to cultivate him. The old boy, taking a shine to the youngster, invites him to Lycurgus, and gives him a job in the factory. There ensues the conflict that makes the story. Clyde has hopes, but very little ready cash; he is thus forced to seek most of his recreation in low life. But as a nephew to old Samuel Griffiths he is also taken up by the Lycurgus *haut ton*. The conflict naturally assumes the form of girls. Roberta Alden, a beautiful female operative in the factory, falls in love with him and yields herself to him. Almost simultaneously Sondra Finchley, an even more beautiful society girl, falls in love with him and promises to marry him. Clyde is ambitious and decides for Sondra. But at that precise moment Roberta tells him that their sin has found her out. His reply is to take her to a lonely lake and drown her. The crime being detected, he is arrested, put on trial, convicted, and electrocuted.

A meagre tale. Hardly more, in fact, than the plot of a three page story in *True Confessions*. But Dreiser rolls it out to such lengths that it becomes, in the end, a sort of sequence of serials. The whole first volume, of 431 pages of small type, brings us only to the lamentable event of Roberta's pregnancy. The home life of the Griffithses in Kansas City is described in detail. We make intimate acquaintance with the street preacher himself, a poor fanatic, always trusting in the God who has fooled him incessantly, and with his pathetic, drab wife, and with his daughter Esta, who runs away with a vaudeville actor and comes home with a baby. There ensues a leisurely and meticulous treatise upon the life of the bellboys in the rococo Green-Davidson Hotel — how they do their work, what they collect in tips, how they spend their evenings, what sort of girls they fancy. The automobile accident is done in the same spacious manner. Finally, we get to Lycurgus, and page after page is devoted to the operations of the Griffiths factory, and to the elegant doings in Lycurgus society, and to the first faint stirrings, the passionate high tide, and the disagreeable ebb of Clyde's affair with Roberta. So much for Volume I: 200,000 words. In Volume II we have the murder, the arrest, the trial and the execution: 185,000 more.

Obviously, there is something wrong here. Somewhere or other, there must be whole chapters that could be spared. I find, in fact, many such chapters — literally dozens of them. They incommode the action, they swamp and conceal the principal personages, and they lead the author steadily into his weakness for banal moralizing and trite, meaningless words. In "The 'Genius'" it was *trig* that rode him; in "An American Tragedy" it is *chic*. Did *chic* go out in 1896? Then so much the better! It is the mark of an unterrified craftsman to use it in 1926 — more, to rub it in mercilessly. Is Freudism stale, even in Greenwich Village? Ahoy, then, let us heave in a couple of bargeloads of complexes — let us explain even judges and district attorneys in terms of suppressions. Is the "chemic" theory of sex somewhat fly-blown? Then let us trot it out, and give it a polishing with the dish-rag. Is there such a thing as sound English, graceful English, charming and beautiful English? Then let us defy a world of scoundrels, half Methodist and half esthetic, with such sentences as this one:

The "death house" in this particular prison was one of those crass erections and maintenances of human insensibility and stupidity principally for which no one primarily was really responsible.

And such as this:

Quite everything of all this was being published in the papers each day.

What is one to say of such dreadful bilge? What is one to say of a novelist who, after a quarter of a century at his trade, still writes it? What one is to say, I feel and fear, had better be engraved on the head of a pin and thrown into the ocean: there is such a thing as critical *politesse*. Here I can only remark that sentences of the kind I have quoted please me very little.

One of them to a page is enough to make me very unhappy. In "An American Tragedy" — or, at all events, in parts of it — they run to much more than that. Is Dreiser actually deaf to their dreadful cacophony? I can't believe it. He can write, on occasion, with great clarity, and even with a certain grace. I point, for example, to Chapter XIII of Book III, and to the chapter following. There is here no idiotic "quite everything of all this," and no piling up of infirm adverbs. There is, instead, straightforward and lucid writing, which is caressing in itself and gets the story along. But elsewhere! . . .

Thus the defects of this gargantuan book. They are the old defects of Dreiser, and he seems to be quite unable to get rid of them. They grow more marked, indeed, as he passes into later life. His writing in "Jennie Gerhardt" was better than his writing in "The 'Genius,'" and so was his sense of form, of structure. But what of the more profound elements? What of his feeling for character, his capacity to imagine situations, his skill at reaching the emotions of the reader? I can only say that I see no falling off in this direction. "An American Tragedy," as a work of art, is a colossal botch, but as a human document it is searching and full of a solemn dignity, and at times it rises to the level of genuine tragedy. Especially the second volume. Once Roberta is killed and Clyde faces his fate, the thing begins to move, and thereafter it roars on, with ever increasing impetus, to the final terrific smash. What other American novelist could have done it? His method, true enough, is the simple, bald one of the reporter — but of *what* a reporter! And who could have handled so magnificently the last scenes in the death-house? Here his very defects come to his aid. What we behold is the gradual, terrible, irresistible approach of doom — the slow slipping away of hopes. The thing somehow has the effect of a tolling of bells. It is clumsy. It lacks all grace. But it is tremendously moving.

In brief, the book improves as it nears its shocking climax — a humane fact, indeed, for the reader. The first volume heaves and pitches, and the second, until the actual murder, is full of psychologizing that usually fails to come off. But once the poor girl is in the water, there is a change, and thereafter "An American Tragedy" is Dreiser at his plodding, booming best.

The means are often bad, but the effects are superb. One gets the same feeling of complete reality that came from "Sister Carrie," and especially from the last days of Hurstwood. The thing ceases to be a story, and becomes a harrowing reality. Dreiser, I suppose, regards himself as an adept at the Freudian necromancy. He frequently uses its terms, and seems to take its fundamental doctrines very seriously. But he is actually a behaviorist of the most advanced wing. What interests him primarily is not what people think, but what they do. He is full of a sense of their helplessness. They are, to him, automata thrown hither and thither by fate — but suffering tragically under every buffet. Their thoughts are muddled and trivial — but they can feel. And Dreiser feels with them, and can make the reader feel with them. It takes skill of a kind that is surely not common. Good writing is far easier.

The Dreiserian ideology does not change. Such notions as he carried out of the experiences of his youth still abide with him. They take somewhat curious forms. The revolt of youth, as he sees it, is primarily a revolt against religious dogmas and forms. He is still engaged in delivering Young America from the imbecilities of a frozen Christianity. And the economic struggle, in his eye, has a bizarre symbol: the modern American hotel. Do you remember Carrie Meeber's first encounter with a hotel beefsteak in "Sister Carrie"? And Jennie Gerhardt's dumb wonder before the splendors of that hotel in which her mother scrubbed the grand staircase? There are hotels, too, and aplenty, in "The Titan" and "The 'Genius'"; toward the end of the latter there is a famous description, pages long, of the lobby of a New York apartment house, by the Waldorf-Astoria out of the Third avenue car-barn. It was a hotel that lured Jennie (like Carrie before her) to ruin, and it is a hotel that starts Clyde Griffiths on his swift journey to the chair. I suggest a more extensive examination of the matter, in the best Dreiser-Freud style. Let some ambitious young *Privat Dozent* tackle it.

So much for "An American Tragedy." Hire your pastor to read the first volume for you. But don't miss the second.

Ring Lardner

FROM FOUR MAKERS OF TALES, PREJUDICES: FIFTH SERIES,
1926, pp. 49–56.
First printed in the *American Mercury*, July, 1924, pp. 376–77.
Lardner was born in 1885 and died in 1933

A FEW years ago a young college professor, eager to make a name for himself, brought out a laborious "critical" edition of "Sam Slick," by Judge Thomas C. Haliburton, eighty-seven years after its first publication. It turned out to be quite unreadable — a dreadful series of archaic jocosities about varieties of *Homo americanus* long perished and forgotten, in a dialect now intelligible only to paleophilologists. Sometimes I have a fear that the same fate awaits Ring Lardner. The professors of his own days, of course, were quite unaware of him, save perhaps as a low zany to be enjoyed behind the door. They would no more have ventured to whoop him up publicly and officially than their predecessors of 1880 would have ventured to whoop up Mark Twain, or their remoter predecessors of 1837 would have dared to say anything for Haliburton. In such matters the academic mind, being chiefly animated by a fear of sneers, works very slowly. So slowly, indeed, does it work that it usually works too late. By the time Mark Twain got into the text-books for sophomores two-thirds of his compositions had already begun to date; by the time Haliburton was served up as a sandwich between introduction and notes he was long dead. As I say, I suspect sadly that Lardner is doomed to go the same route. His stories, it seems to me, are superbly adroit and amusing; no other American of his generation, sober or gay, wrote better. But I doubt that they last: our grandchildren will wonder what they are about. It is not only, or even mainly, that the dialect that fills them will pass, though that fact is obviously a serious handicap in itself. It is principally that the people they depict will pass, that Lardner's incomparable baseball players, pugs, song-writers, Elks, small-town Rotarians, and golf caddies were flittering figures of a transient civilization, and are doomed to be as puzzling and soporific, in the year 2000, as Haliburton's Yankee clock peddler is today.

The fact — if I may assume it to be a fact — is certain not to be set against Lardner's account; on the contrary, it is, in its way, highly complimentary to him. For he deliberately applied himself, not to the anatomizing of the general human soul, but to the meticulous histological study of a few salient individuals of his time and nation, and he did it with such subtle and penetrating skills that one must belong to his time and nation to follow him. I doubt that anyone who is not familiar with professional ball players, intimately and at first hand, will ever comprehend the full merit of the amazing sketches in "You Know Me, Al"; I doubt that anyone who has not given close and deliberate attention to the American vulgate will ever realize how magnificently Lardner handled it. He had more imitators, I suppose, than any other American writer of the first third of the century, but had he any actual rivals? If so, I have yet to hear of them. They all tried to write the speech of the streets as adeptly and as amusingly as he wrote it, and they all fell short of him; the next best was miles and miles behind him. And they were all inferior in observation, in sense of character, in shrewdness and insight. His studies, to be sure, are never very profound; he made no attempt to get at the primary springs of human motive; all his people share the same amiable stupidity, the same transparent vanity, the same shallow swinishness; they are all human Fords in bad repair, and alike at bottom. But if he thus confined himself to the surface, it yet remains a fact that his investigations on that surface were extraordinarily alert, ingenious and brilliant — that the character he finally set before us, however roughly articulated as to bones, was so astoundingly realistic as to epidermis that the effect is indistinguishable from that of life itself. The old man in "The Golden Honeymoon" is not merely well done: he is perfect. And so is the girl in "Some Like Them Cold." And so, even, is the idiotic Frank X. Farrell in "Alibi Ike" — an extravagant grotesque and yet quite real from glabella to calcaneus.

Lardner knew more about the management of the short story than all of its professors. His stories are built very carefully, and yet they seem to be wholly spontaneous, and even formless. He grasped the primary fact that no conceivable ingenuity can save a story that fails to show a recognizable and interesting character; he knew that a good character sketch is always a good story, no matter what its structure. Perhaps he got less attention than he ought to have got, even among the anti-academic critics, because his people were all lowly boors. For your reviewer of books, like every other sort of American, is always vastly impressed by fashionable pretensions. He belongs to the white collar class of labor, and shares its prejudices. He can't rid himself of the feeling that Edith Wharton, whose people have butlers, was a better novelist than Willa Cather, whose people, in the main, dine in their kitchens. He lingers under the spell of Henry James, whose most humble character, at any rate of the later years, was at least an Englishman, and hence superior. Lardner, so to speak, hit such critics under the belt. He not only filled his stories with people who read the tabloids, said "Shake hands with my friend," and bought diamond rings on the instalment plan; he also showed them having a good time in the world, and quite devoid of inferiority complexes. They amused him sardonically, but he did not pity them. A fatal error! The moron, perhaps, has a place in fiction, as in life, but he is not to be treated too easily and casually. It must be shown that he suffers tragically because he cannot abandon the plow to write poetry, or the sample-case to study for opera. Lardner was more realistic. If his typical hero has a secret sorrow it is that he is too old to take up osteopathy and too much in dread of his wife to venture into bookmaking.

In his later years a sharply acrid flavor got into Lardner's buffoonery. His baseball players and fifth-rate pugilists, beginning in his first stories as harmless jackasses, gradually converted themselves into loathsome scoundrels. Turn, for example, to the sketches in the volume called "The Love Nest." The first tells the story of a cinema queen married to a magnate of the films. On the surface she seems to be nothing but a noodle, but underneath there is a sewer; the woman is such a pig that she makes one shudder. Again, he investigated another familiar type: the village practical joker. The fellow, in one form or other, has been laughed at since the days of Aristophanes. But here is a mercilessly realistic examination of his dunghill humor, and of its effects upon decent people. A third figure is a successful theatrical manager: he turns out to have the professional competence of a phrenologist and the honor of a high-jacker. A fourth is a writer of popular songs: stealing other men's ideas has become so fixed a habit with him that he comes to believe that he has an actual right to them. A fourth is a trained nurse — but I spare you this dreadful nurse. The rest are bores of the homicidal type. One gets the effect, communing with the whole gang, of visiting a museum of anatomy. They are as shocking as what one encounters there — but in every detail they are unmistakably real.

Lardner concealed his new savagery, of course, beneath his old humor. It did not flag. No man writing among us had greater skill at the more extravagant varieties of jocosity. He saw startling and revelatory likeness between immensely disparate things, and he was full of pawky observations and bizarre comments. Two baseball players are palavering, and one of them, Young Jake, is boasting of his conquests during Spring practise below the Potomac. "Down South ain't here!" replies the other. "Those dames in some of those swamps, they lose their head when they see a man with shoes on!" The two proceed to the discussion of a third imbecile, guilty of some obscure tort. "Why," inquires Young Jake, "didn't you break his nose or bust him in the chin?" "His nose was already broke," replied the other, "and he didn't have no chin." Such wise cracks seem easy to devise. Broadway diverts itself by manufacturing them. They constitute the substance of half the town shows. But in those made by Lardner there is something far more than mere facile humor: they are all rigidly in character, and they illuminate that character. Few American novelists, great or small, have had character more firmly in hand. Lardner did not see situations; he saw people. And what people! They are all as revolting as so many Methodist bishops, and they are all as thoroughly American.

Huneker: a Memory

FROM PREJUDICES: THIRD SERIES, 1922, pp. 65–83. First printed in the *Century*, June, 1921, pp. 191–97. Huneker died Feb. 9, 1921. My first writing about him was a review of his Egoists, in the *Smart Set*, June, 1909. In Oct., 1913, I gave a long review to The Pathos of Distance, and included a discussion of his work in general. In July, 1914, I reviewed a new edition of Old Fogy, and in July, 1915, I led my *Smart Set* article with New Cosmopolis, under the title of The Prometheus of the Western World. In Dec., 1915, I reviewed Ivory, Apes and Peacocks; in Dec., 1917, Unicorns; in May, 1920, Bedouins; in Dec., 1920, Steeplejack; in Feb., 1922, Variations (published posthumously), and in Jan., 1923, the bowdlerized edition of Huneker's letters brought out by his widow. In 1929 I edited a volume of selections from his writings, entitled Essays by James Huneker

THERE was a stimulating aliveness about him always, an air of living eagerly and a bit recklessly, a sort of defiant resiliency. In his very frame and form something provocative showed itself — an insolent singularity, obvious to even the most careless glance. That Caligulan profile of his was more than simply unusual in a free republic, consecrated to good works; to a respectable American, encountering it in the lobby of the Metropolitan, it must have suggested inevitably the dark enterprises and illicit metaphysics of a Heliogabalus. More, there was always something rakish and defiant about his hat — it was too white, or it curled in the wrong way, or a feather peeped from the band — and a hint of antinomianism in his cravat. Yet more, he ran to exotic tastes in eating and drinking, preferring occult goulashes and risi-bisi to honest American steaks, and great floods of Pilsner to the harsh beverages of God-fearing men. Finally, there was his talk, that cataract of sublime trivialities: gossip lifted to the plane of the gods, the unmentionable bedizened with an astounding importance, and even profundity.

In his early days, when he performed the tonal and carnal prodigies that he liked to talk of afterward, I was at nurse, and too young to have any traffic with him. When I encountered him at last he was in the high flush of the middle years,[1] and had already become a tradition in the little world that critics

[1] I met him in 1914.

inhabit. We sat down to luncheon at one o'clock at Lüchow's, his favorite refuge and rostrum to the end. At six, when I had to go, the waiter was hauling in his tenth (or was it twentieth?) *Seidel* of Pilsner, and he was bringing to a close *prestissimo* the most amazing monologue that these ears (up to that time) had ever funneled into this consciousness. What a stew, indeed! Berlioz and the question of the clang-tint of the viola, the psychopathological causes of the suicide of Tschaikowsky, why Nietzsche had to leave Sils Maria between days in 1887, the echoes of Flaubert in Joseph Conrad (then but newly dawned), the precise topography of the warts of Liszt, how Frau Cosima saved Wagner from the libidinous Swedish baroness, what to drink when playing Chopin, what Cézanne thought of his disciples, the defects in the structure of "Sister Carrie," Anton Seidl and the musical union, the complex love affairs of Gounod, the varying talents and idiosyncrasies of Lillian Russell's earlier husbands, whether a girl educated at Vassar could ever really learn to love, the exact composition of chicken paprika, the correct tempo of the Vienna waltz, the style of William Dean Howells, what George Moore said about German bathrooms, the true inwardness of the affair between D'Annunzio and Duse, the origin of the theory that all oboe players are crazy, Ibsen's loathing of Norwegians, the best remedy for Rhine wine *Katzenjammer*, how to play Brahms, the sheer physical impossibility of getting Dvořák drunk, the genuine last words of Walt Whitman . . .

I left in a sort of fever, and it was a couple of days later before I began to sort out my impressions, and formulate a coherent image. Was the man allusive in his books — so allusive that popular report credited him with the actual manufacture of authorities? Then he was ten times as allusive in his discourse — a veritable geyser of unfamiliar names, shocking epigrams in strange tongues, unearthly philosophies out of the backwaters of Scandinavia, Bulgaria, the Basque country. And did he, in his criticism, pass facilely from the author to the man, and from the man to his wife, and to the wives of his friends? Then at the *Biertisch* he began long beyond the point where the last honest wife gives up the ghost, and so, full tilt, ran into such complexities of adultery that a plain sinner could scarcely fol-

low him. I try to give you, ineptly and grotesquely, some notion
of the talk of the man, but I must fail inevitably. It was, in
brief, chaos, and chaos cannot be described. But it was chaos
drenched in all the colors imaginable, chaos scored for an orchestra which made the great band of Berlioz seem like a fife
and drum corps.

The real Huneker never got himself between covers, if one
forgets "Old Fogy" and parts of "Painted Veils." The volumes
of his regular canon are made up, in the main, of articles written for the more intellectual magazines and newspapers of their
era, and they are full of a conscious striving to qualify for respectable company. Huneker, always curiously modest, never got
over the notion that it was a singular honor for a man such as
he — a mere diurnal scribbler, innocent of academic robes — to
be published by such a publisher as Scribner. More than once,
anchored at the beer-table, we discussed the matter at length, I
always arguing that all the honor was enjoyed by Scribner. But
Huneker, I believe in all sincerity, would not have it so, any
more than he would have it that he was a better music critic
than his two colleagues, the pedantic Krehbiel and the nonsensical Finck. This illogical modesty, of course, had its limits;
it made him cautious about expressing himself, but it seldom
led him into downright assumptions of false personality. Nowhere in all his books will you find him doing the things that
every right-thinking Anglo-Saxon critic is supposed to do —
solemn essays on Coleridge and Addison, abysmal discussions
of the relative merits of Schumann and Mendelssohn, horrible
treatises upon the relations of Goethe to the Romantic Movement, dull scratchings in a hundred such exhausted and sterile
fields. Enterprises of that sort were not for Huneker; he kept
himself out of that black coat. But I am convinced that he always had his own raiment pressed carefully before he left Lüchow's for the temple of Athene — and maybe changed cravats,
and put on a boiled shirt, and took the feather out of his hat.
The simon-pure Huneker, the Huneker who was the true essence and prime motor of the more courtly Huneker — remained behind.

This real Huneker survives in conversations that still haunt
the rafters on the beer-halls of two continents, and in a vast

mass of newspaper impromptus, thrown off too hastily to be
reduced to complete decorum, and in two books that stand outside the official canon, and yet contain the man himself as not
even "Iconoclasts" or the Chopin book contains him, to wit,
the "Old Fogy" aforesaid and the "Painted Veils" of his last
year. Both were published, so to speak, out of the back door —
the former by a music publisher in Philadelphia and the latter
in a small and expensive edition for the admittedly damned.
There is a chapter in "Painted Veils" that is Huneker to every
last hitch of the shoulders and twinkle of the eye — the chapter
in which the hero soliloquizes on art, life, immortality, and
women — especially women. And there are half a dozen chapters in "Old Fogy" — superficially buffoonery, but how penetrating! how gorgeously flavored! how learned! — that come
completely up to the same high specification. If I had to choose
one Huneker book and give up all the others, I'd choose "Old
Fogy" instantly. In it Huneker is utterly himself. In it the last
trace of the pedagogue vanishes. Art is no longer, even by im-
plication, a device for improving the mind. It is wholly a magnificent adventure.

That notion of it is what he brought into American criticism,
and it is for that bringing that he will be remembered. Almost
single-handed he overthrew the esthetic theory that had flourished in the United States since the death of Poe, and set up an
utterly contrary esthetic theory in its place. If the younger men
of today who followed him emancipated themselves from the
Puritan esthetic, if the schoolmaster is now palpably on the
defensive, and no longer the unchallenged assassin of the fine
arts that he once was, then Huneker certainly deserves all the
credit for the change. What he brought back from Paris was
precisely the thing that was most suspected in the America of
those days: the capacity for gusto. He had that capacity in a
degree unmatched by any other critic. When his soul went ad-
venturing among masterpieces it did not go in Sunday broad-
cloth; it went with vine leaves in its hair. The rest of the
appraisers and criers-up could never rid themselves of the professorial manner. When they praised it was always with some
hint of ethical, or, at all events, of cultural purpose; when they
condemned that purpose was even plainer. The arts, to them,

constituted a sort of school for the psyche; their aim was to discipline and mellow the spirit. But to Huneker their one aim was always to make the spirit glad — to set it, in Nietzsche's phrase, to dancing with arms and legs. He had absolutely no feeling for extra-esthetic valuation. If a work of art that stood before him was honest, if it was original, if it was beautiful and thoroughly alive, then he was for it to his last corpuscle. What if it violated all the accepted canons? Then let the accepted canons go hang. What if it lacked all purpose to improve and lift up? Then so much the better. What if it shocked all right-feeling men, and made them blush and tremble? Then damn all men of right feeling forevermore.

With this ethical atheism, so strange in the United States and so abhorrent to most Americans, there went something that was probably also part of the loot of Paris: an insatiable curiosity about the artist as man. This curiosity was responsible for one of Huneker's salient characters: his habit of mixing even the most serious criticism with cynical and often scandalous gossip. I believe that it is almost literally true to say that he could never quite make up his mind about a new symphony until he had seen the composer's mistress, or at all events a good photograph of her. He thought of Wagner, not alone in terms of melody and harmony, but also in terms of the Triebschen idyl and the Bayreuth tragi-comedy. Go through his books and you will see how often he was fascinated by mere eccentricity of personality. I doubt that even Huysmans, had he been a respectable French Huguenot, would have interested him; certainly his enthusiasm for Verlaine, Villiers de l'Isle Adam and other such fantastic fish was centered upon the men quite as much as upon the artists. His air of foreignness, so often urged against him by defenders of the national tradition, was grounded largely on the fact that such eccentric personalities were rare in the Republic — rare, and well watched by the *Polizei*. The rest of the American people he dismissed as a horde of slaves, goose-steppers, cads, Methodists; he could not imagine one of them becoming a first-rate artist, save by a miracle. Even the American executant was under his suspicion, for he knew very well that playing the fiddle was a great deal more than scraping four strings of copper and catgut with a switch from a horse's tail. What he asked himself was how a man could play Bach decently, and then, after playing, go from the hall to a soda-fountain or a lecture at the Harvard Club. Overseas there was a better air for artists, and overseas Huneker looked for them.

These fundamental theories of his, of course, had their defects. They were a bit too simple, and often very much too hospitable. Huneker, clinging to them, certainly did his share of whooping for the sort of revolutionist who is here today and gone tomorrow; he was fugleman, in his time, for more than one cause that was lost almost as soon as it was stated. More, his prejudices made him somewhat anesthetic, at times, to the new men who were not brilliant in color but respectably drab, and who tried to do their work within the law. Particularly in his later years, when the old gusto began to die out and all that remained of it was habit, he was apt to go chasing after strange birds and so miss seeing the elephants go by. I could put together a very pretty list of frauds that he praised. I could concoct another list of genuine *arrivés* that he overlooked. But all that is merely saying that there were human limits to him; the professors, on their side, have sinned far worse, and in both directions. Looking back over the whole of his work, one must needs be amazed by the general soundness of his judgments. He discerned, in the main, what was good and he described it in terms that were seldom bettered afterward. His successive heroes, always under fire when he first championed them, almost invariably moved to secure ground and became solid men, challenged by no one save fools — Ibsen, Nietzsche, Brahms, Cézanne, Stirner, the Russian novelists. He did for this Western world what Georg Brandes was doing for Continental Europe — sorting out the new comers with sharp eyes, and giving mighty lifts to those who deserved it. Brandes did it in terms of the old academic bombast; he was never more the professor than when he was arguing for some hobgoblin of the professors. But Huneker did it with verve and grace; he made it, not schoolmastering, but a glorious deliverance from schoolmastering. The fine arts, at his touch, shed all their Anglo-American lugubriousness, and became provocative and joyous. The spirit of senility got out of them and the spirit of youth got into them.

Though he was an Easterner and a cockney of the cockneys, he picked up some of the Western spaciousness that showed itself in Mark Twain. And all the young men followed him.

A good many of them, I daresay, followed him so ardently that they got a good distance ahead of him, and often, perhaps, embarrassed him by taking his name in vain. For all his enterprise and iconoclasm, indeed, there was not much of the berserk in him, and his floutings of the national esthetic tradition seldom took the form of forthright challenges. Here the strange modesty that I have mentioned always stayed him as a like weakness stayed Mark Twain. He could never quite rid himself of the feeling that he was no more than an amateur among the gaudy doctors who roared in the reviews, and that it would be unseemly for him to forget their authority. I have a notion that this feeling was born in the days when he stood almost alone with the whole faculty grouped in a pained circle around him. He was then too miserable a worm to be noticed at all. Later on, gaining importance, he was lectured somewhat severely for his violation of decorum; in England even Max Beerbohm made an idiotic assault upon him. It was the Germans and the French, in fact, who first praised him intelligently — and these friends were too far away to help a timorous man in a row at home.

This sensation of isolation and littleness, I suppose, explains his fidelity to the newspapers, and the otherwise inexplicable joy that he always took in his forgotten work for the *Musical Courier*, in his day a somewhat dubious journal. In such waters he felt at ease. There he could disport without thought of the dignity of publishers and the eagle eyes of campus reviewers. Some of the connections that he formed were full of an ironical inappropriateness. His discomforts in his *Puck* days showed themselves in the feebleness of his work; when he served the *Times* he was as well placed as a Cabell at a colored ball. Perhaps the *Sun*, in the years before it was munseyized, offered him the best berth that he ever had, save it were his old one on *Mlle. New York*. But whatever the flag, he served it loyally, and got a lot of fun out of the business. He liked the pressure of newspaper work; he liked the associations that it involved, the gabble in the press-room of the Opera House, the exchanges of news and gossip; above all, he liked the relative ease of the intellectual harness. In a newspaper article he could say whatever happened to pop into his mind, and if it looked thin the next day, then there was, after all, no harm done. But when he sat down to write a book — or rather to compile it, for all of his volumes were reworked magazine (and sometimes newspaper) articles — he became self-conscious, and so knew uneasiness. The tightness of his style, its one salient defect, was probably the result of this weakness. The corrected clippings that constituted most of his manuscripts are so beladen with revisions and rerevisions that they are almost indecipherable.

His criticism had the dazzling charm of an ornate and intricate design, a blazing fabric of fine silks. It was no mere pontifical statement of one man's reactions to a set of ideas; it was a sort of essence of the reactions of many men — of all the men, in fact, worth hearing. Huneker discarded their scaffolding, their ifs and whereases, and presented only what was important and arresting in their conclusions. It was never a mere *pastiche*; the selection was made delicately, discreetly, with almost unerring taste and judgment. And in the summing up there was always the clearest possible statement of the whole matter. What finally emerged was a body of doctrine that came, I believe, very close to the truth. Into an assembly of national critics who had long wallowed in dogmatic puerilities, Huneker entered with a taste infinitely surer and more civilized, a learning infinitely greater, and an address infinitely more engaging. No man was less the reformer by inclination, and yet he became a reformer beyond compare. He emancipated criticism in America from its old slavery to stupidity, and with it he emancipated all the arts themselves.

Joseph Conrad

From FOUR MAKERS OF TALES, PREJUDICES: FIFTH SERIES,
1926, pp. 34–41.
First printed in the *Smart Set*, Dec., 1922, pp. 141–44.
Conrad was born in 1857 and died in 1924

SOME time ago I put in a blue afternoon re-reading Joseph Conrad's "Youth." A *blue* afternoon? What nonsense! The touch of the man is like the touch of Schubert. One approaches him in various and unhappy moods: depressed, dubious, despairing; one leaves him in the clear, yellow sunshine that Nietzsche found in Bizet's music. But here again the phrase is inept. Sunshine suggests the imbecile, barnyard joy of the human kohlrabi — the official optimism of a steadily delighted and increasingly insane Republic. What the enigmatical Pole has to offer is something quite different. If its parallel is to be found in music, it is not in Schubert, but in Beethoven — perhaps even more accurately in Johann Sebastian Bach. It is the joy, not of mere satisfaction, but of understanding — the profound but surely not merry delight which goes with the comprehension of a fundamental fact — above all, of a fact that has been coy and elusive. Certainly the order of the world that Conrad sets forth with diabolical eloquence and plausibility is no banal moral order, no childish sequence of virtuous causes and edifying effects. Rather it has an atheistic and even demoniacal smack: to the earnest Bible student it must be more than a little disconcerting. The God he visualizes is no loving papa in a housecoat and carpet-slippers, inculcating the great principles of Christian ethics by applying occasional strokes *a posteriori*. What he sees is something quite different: an extremely ingenious and humorous Improvisatore and Comedian, with a dab of red on His nose and maybe somewhat the worse for drink — a furious and far from amiable banjoist upon the human spine, and rattler of human bones. Kurtz, in "Youth," makes a capital banjo for that exalted and cynical talent. And the music that issues forth — what a superb *Hexentanz* it is.

One of the curiosities of critical stupidity is the doctrine that

Conrad was without humor. No doubt it flows out of a more general error; to wit, the assumption that tragedy is always pathetic, that death itself is inevitably a gloomy business. That error, I suppose, will persist in the world until some extraordinary astute mime conceives the plan of playing "King Lear" as a farce — I mean deliberately. That it *is* a farce seems to me quite as obvious as the fact that "Romeo and Juliet" is another, this time lamentably coarse. To adopt the contrary theory — to view it as a great moral and spiritual spectacle, capable of purging and uplifting the psyche like marriage to a red-haired widow or a month in the trenches — to toy with such notions is to borrow the critical standards of a party of old ladies weeping over the damnation of the heathen.

This, at all events, is the notion that seems to me implicit in every line of Conrad. I give you "Heart of Darkness" as the archetype of his whole work and the keystone of his metaphysical system. Here we have all imaginable human hopes and aspirations reduced to one common denominator of folly and failure, and here we have a play of humor that is infinitely mordant and searching. Turn to pages 136 and 137 of the American edition — the story is in the volume called "Youth" —: the burial of the helmsman. Turn then to 178–184: Marlow's last interview with Kurtz's intended. The farce mounts by slow stages to dizzy and breath-taking heights. One hears harsh roars of cosmic laughter, vast splutterings of transcendental mirth, echoing and reëchoing down the black corridors of empty space. The curtain descends at last upon a wild dance in a dissecting-room. The mutilated dead rise up and jig. . . .

It is curious, re-reading a thrice-familiar story, how often one finds surprises in it. I have been amazed, toward the close of "The End of the Tether," to discover that the *Fair Maid* was wrecked, not by the deliberate act of Captain Whalley, but by the machinations of the unspeakable Massy. How is one to account for so preposterous an error? Certainly I thought I knew "The End of the Tether" as well as I knew anything in this world — and yet there was that incredible misunderstanding of it, lodged firmly in my mind. Perhaps there is criticism of a sort in my blunder: it may be a fact that the old skipper willed the thing himself — that his willing it is visible in all that goes before — that Conrad, in introducing Massy's puerile infamy at the end, made some sacrifice of inner veracity to the exigencies of what, at bottom, is somewhat too neat and well-made a tale. The story, in fact, belongs to the author's earlier manner; my guess is that it was written before "Youth" and surely before "Heart of Darkness." But for all that, its proportions remain truly colossal. It is one of the most magnificent narratives, long or short, old or new, in the English language, and with "Youth" and "Heart of Darkness" it makes up what is probably the best book of imaginative writing that the English literature of the Twentieth Century can yet show.

Conrad learned a great deal after he wrote it, true enough. In "Lord Jim," in "Victory," and, above all, in "A Personal Record," there are momentary illuminations, blinding flashes of brilliance that he was incapable of in those days of experiment; but no other book of his seems to me to hold so steadily to so high a general level — none other, as a whole, is more satisfying and more marvelous. There is in "Heart of Darkness" a perfection of design which one encounters only rarely and miraculously in prose fiction: it belongs rather to music. I can't imagine taking a single sentence out of that stupendous tale without leaving a visible gap; it is as thoroughly *durch componiert* as a fugue. And I can't imagine adding anything to it, even so little as a word, without doing it damage. As it stands it is austerely and beautifully perfect, just as the slow movement of the Unfinished Symphony is perfect.

I observe of late a tendency to examine the English of Conrad rather biliously. This folly is cultivated chiefly in England, where, I suppose, chauvinistic motives enter into the matter. It is the just boast of great empires that they draw in talents from near and far, exhausting the little nations to augment their own puissance; it is their misfortune that these talents often remain defectively assimilated. Conrad remained the Slav to the end. The people of his tales, whatever he calls them, are always as much Slavs as he is,[1] the language in which he describes them retains a sharp, exotic flavor. But to say that this flavor consti-

---

[1] Conrad himself objected to this idea when it was first set forth in the *Smart Set*, Dec., 1919, p. 68, and remonstrated politely. But I stick to my guns.

tutes a blemish is to say something so preposterous that only schoolmasters and their dupes may be thought of as giving it credit. The truly first-rate writer is not one who uses the language as such dolts demand that it be used; he is one who reworks it in spite of their prohibitions. It is his distinction that he thinks in a manner different from the thinking of ordinary men; that he is free from that slavery to embalmed ideas which makes them so respectable and so dull. Obviously, he cannot translate his notions into terms of everyday without doing violence to their inner integrity. What Conrad brought into English literature was a new concept of the relations between fact and fact, idea and idea, and what he contributed to the complex and difficult art of writing English was a new way of putting words together. His style now amazes and irritates pedants because it does not roll along in the old ruts. Well, it is precisely that rolling along in the old ruts that he tried to avoid — and it was precisely that avoidance which made him what he is. No Oxford mincing is in him, despite his curious respect for Henry James. If he cannot find his phrase above the salt, he seeks it below. His English, in a word, is innocent. And if, at times, there gets into it a color that is strange and even bizarre, then the fact is something to rejoice over, for a living language is like a man suffering incessantly from small internal hemorrhages, and what it needs above all else is constant transfusions of new blood from other tongues. The day the gates go up, that day it begins to die.

A very great man, this Mr. Conrad. As yet, I believe, decidedly underestimated, even by many of his post-mortem advocates. Most of his first acclaimers mistook him for a mere romantic — a talented but somewhat uncouth follower of the Stevenson tradition, with the orthodox cutlass exchanged for a Malay *kris*. Later on he began to be heard of as a linguistic and vocational marvel: it was astonishing that any man bred to Polish should write English at all, and more astonishing that a country gentleman from the Ukraine should hold a master's certificate in the British merchant marine. Such banal attitudes are now archaic, but I suspect that they have been largely responsible for the slowness with which his fame has spread in the world. At all events, he is vastly less read and esteemed than he ought to be.

When one reflects that the Nobel Prize was given to such third-raters as Benavente, Heidenstam, Gjellerup and Spitteler, with Conrad passed over, one begins to grasp the depth and density of the ignorance prevailing in the world, even among the relatively enlightened. One "Lord Jim," as human document and as work of art, is worth all the works produced by all the Benaventes and Gjellerups since the time of Rameses II. Nor is "Lord Jim" a chance masterpiece, an isolated peak. On the contrary, it is but one unit in a long series of extraordinary and almost incomparable works — a series sprung suddenly and overwhelmingly into full dignity with "Almayer's Folly." I challenge the nobility and gentry of Christendom to point to another Opus 1 as magnificently planned and turned out as "Almayer's Folly." The more one studies it, the more it seems miraculous. If it is not a work of genius then no work of genius exists on this earth.

XXVII. MUSIC

Beethoven

From PREJUDICES: FIFTH SERIES, 1926, pp. 87–94.
First printed in part in the Baltimore *Evening Sun*, April 24, 1922,
and in part in the *American Mercury*, April, 1926, pp. 509–10

BEETHOVEN was one of those lucky men whose stature, viewed in retrospect, grows steadily. How many movements have there been to put him on the shelf? At least a dozen in the hundred years since his death. There was one in New York in 1917, launched by idiot critics and supported by the war fever: his place, it appeared, was to be taken by such prophets of the new enlightenment as Stravinsky. The net result of that movement was simply that the best orchestra in America went to pot — and Beethoven survived unscathed. Surely the Nineteenth Century was not deficient in master musicians. It produced Schubert, Schumann, Chopin, Wagner and Brahms, to say nothing of a whole horde of Dvořáks, Tschaikowskys, Debussys, Verdis and Puccinis. Yet it gave us nothing better than the first movement of the Eroica. That movement, the first challenge of the new music, remains its last word. It is the noblest piece of absolute music ever written in the sonata form, and it is the noblest piece of programme music. In Beethoven, indeed, the distinction between the two became purely imaginary. Everything he wrote was, in a way, programme music, including even the first two symphonies, and everything was absolute music.

It was a bizarre jest of the gods to pit Beethoven, in his first days in Vienna, against Papa Haydn. Haydn was undeniably a genius of the first water, and, after Mozart's death, had no apparent reason to fear a rival. If he did not actually create the symphony as we know it today, then he at least enriched the form with its first genuine masterpieces — and not with a scant few, but literally with dozens. Tunes of the utmost loveliness gushed from him like oil from a well. More, he knew how to manage them; he was a master of musical architectonics. But when Beethoven stepped in, poor old Papa had to step down. It was like pitting a gazelle against a bull. One colossal bellow, and the combat was over. Musicians are apt to look at it as a mere contest of technicians. They point to the vastly greater skill and ingenuity of Beethoven — his firmer grip upon his materials, his greater daring and resourcefulness, his far better understanding of dynamics, rhythms and clang-tints — in brief, his tremendously superior musicianship. But that was not what made him so much greater than Haydn — for Haydn, too, had his superiorities; for example, his far readier inventiveness, his capacity for making better tunes. What lifted Beethoven above the old master was simply his greater dignity as a man. The feelings that Haydn put into tone were the feelings of a country pastor, a rather civilized stockbroker, a viola player gently mellowed by Kulmbacher. When he wept it was with the tears of a woman who has discovered another wrinkle; when he rejoiced it was with the joy of a child on Christmas morning. But the feelings that Beethoven put into his music were the feelings of a god. There was something olympian in his snarls and rages, and there was a touch of hell-fire in his mirth.

It is almost a literal fact that there is not a trace of cheapness in the whole body of his music. He is never sweet and romantic; he never sheds conventional tears; he never strikes orthodox attitudes. In his lightest moods there is the immense and inescapable dignity of the ancient prophets. He concerns himself, not with the transient agonies of romantic love, but with the eternal tragedy of man. He is a great tragic poet, and like all great tragic poets, he is obsessed by a sense of the inscrutable meaninglessness of life. From the Eroica onward he seldom departs from that theme. It roars through the first movement of the C minor, and it comes to a stupendous final statement in the Ninth. All this, in his day, was new in music, and so it caused murmurs of surprise and even indignation. The step from Mozart's Jupiter to the first movement of the Eroica was uncomfortable; the Viennese began to wriggle in their stalls. But there was one among them who didn't wriggle, and that was Franz Schubert. Turn to the first movement of his Unfinished or to the slow movement of his Tragic, and you will see how quickly the example of Beethoven was followed — and with what genius. There was a long hiatus after that, but eventually the day of November 6, 1876, dawned in Karlsruhe, and with it came the first performance of Brahms' C minor. Once more the gods walked in the concert-hall. They will walk again when another Brahms is born, and not before. For nothing can come out of an artist that is not in the man. What ails the music of all the Tschaikowskys, Mendelssohns — and Chopins? What ails it is that it is the music of shallow men. It is often, in its way, lovely. It bristles with charming musical ideas. It is infinitely ingenious and workmanlike. But it is as hollow, at bottom, as a bull by an archbishop. It is the music of second-rate men.

Beethoven disdained all their artifices: he didn't need them. It would be hard to think of a composer, even of the fourth rate, who worked with thematic material of less intrinsic merit. He borrowed tunes wherever he found them; he made them up out of snatches of country jigs; when he lacked one altogether he contented himself with a simple phrase, a few banal notes. All such things he viewed simply as raw materials; his interest was concentrated upon their use. To that use of them he brought the appalling powers of his unrivaled genius. His ingenuity began where that of other men left off. His most complicated structures retained the overwhelming clarity of the Parthenon. And into them he got a kind of feeling that even the Greeks could not match; he was preëminently a modern man, with all trace of the barbarian vanished. Into his gorgeous music there went all of the high skepticism that was of the essence of the Eighteenth Century, but into it there also went the new enthusiasm, the new determination to challenge and beat the gods, that dawned with the Nineteenth.

The older I grow, the more I am convinced that the most portentous phenomenon in the whole history of music was the first public performance of the Eroica on April 7, 1805. The manufacturers of programme notes have swathed that gigantic work in so many layers of banal legend and speculation that its intrinsic merits have been almost forgotten. Was it dedicated to Napoleon I? If so, was the dedication sincere or ironical?

Who cares — that is, who with ears? It might have been dedicated, just as well, to Louis XIV, Paracelsus or Pontius Pilate. What makes it worth discussing, today and forever, is the fact that on its very first page Beethoven threw his hat into the ring and laid his claim to immortality. Bang! — and he is off. No compromise! No easy bridge from the past! The Second Symphony is already miles behind. A new order of music has been born. The very manner of it is full of challenge. There is no sneaking into the foul business by way of a mellifluous and disarming introduction; no preparatory hemming and hawing to cajole the audience and enable the conductor to find his place in the score. Nay! Out of silence comes the angry crash of the tonic triad, and then at once, with no pause, the first statement of the first subject — grim, domineering, harsh, raucous, and yet curiously lovely — with its astounding collision with that electrical C sharp. The carnage has begun early; we are only in the seventh measure. In the thirteenth and fourteenth comes the incomparable roll down the simple scale of E flat — and what follows is all that has ever been said, perhaps all that ever *will* be said, about music-making in the grand manner. What was afterward done, even by Beethoven, was done in the light of that perfect example. Every line of modern music that is honestly music bears some sort of relation to that epoch-making first movement.

The rest of the Eroica is Beethovenish, but not quintessence. There is a legend that the funeral march was put in simply because it was a time of wholesale butchery, and funeral marches were in fashion. No doubt the first-night audience in Vienna, shocked and addled by the piled-up defiances of the first movement, found the lugubrious strains grateful. But the *scherzo?* Another felonious assault upon poor Papa Haydn! Two giants boxing clumsily, to a crazy piping by an orchestra of dwarfs. No wonder some honest Viennese in the gallery yelled: "I'd give another kreutzer if the thing would stop!" Well, it stopped finally, and then came something reassuring — a theme with variations. Everyone in Vienna knew and esteemed Beethoven's themes with variations. He was, in fact, the rising master of themes with variations in the town. But a joker remained in the pack. The variations grew more and more complex and surprising. Strange novelties got into them. The polite exercises became tempestuous, moody, cacophonous, tragic. At the end a harsh, hammering, exigent row of chords — the C minor Symphony casting its sinister shadow before.

It must have been a great night in Vienna. But perhaps not for the actual Viennese. They went to hear "a new grand symphony in D sharp" (*sic!*). What they found in the Theater-an-der-Wien was a revolution.[1]

Schubert

From the *American Mercury*, Nov., 1928, pp. 284–86

FRANZ SCHUBERT, at least in Anglo-Saxondom, has evaded the indignity of too much popularity. Even his lovely "Serenade," perhaps the most moving love-song ever written, has escaped being mauled at weddings in the manner of Mendelssohn's march from "A Midsummer Night's Dream" and Wagner's from "Lohengrin." It is familiar, but not threadbare: I have listened to it within the past week with new delight in its noble and poignant melody, its rhythmic and harmonic ingenuity, its indescribable Schubertian flavor. Nor is there anything stale about nine-tenths of his piano music, or the songs. The former is played very little — far, far too little. The latter are yowled in all the music studios of the world, but the populace remains unaware of them, and so they manage to hold their dignity and charm. "The Erl King" and "Who is Sylvia?" have become familiar on the air, but surely not many of the remaining six hundred.

Schubert, indeed, was far too fine an artist to write for the mob. When he tried to do it in the theater he failed miserably, and more than once he even failed in the concert-hall. There is the case, for example, of "Heidenröslein," to Goethe's words.

---

[1] The reader with any curiosity about Beethoven's method of planning and writing the stupendous first movement will find plenty to his taste in The Unconscious Beethoven, by Ernest Newman; New York, 1927. It is a story packed with almost incredible marvels.

Goethe wrote them in 1773 and J. F. Reichardt set them in 1793. In 1815, a year after Reichardt's death, Schubert made a new setting. Was it better — that is, considering the homely words? No; it was harder to sing, but not better. Twelve years later the text was reset again by Heinrich Werner, a composer so obscure that even Grove's Dictionary is silent about him, but a man, obviously, with all the gift for simple, transparent melody of a Friedrich Silcher. When "Heidenröslein" is sung today it is to Werner's melody, not Schubert's.

Great stretches of Schubert's music, indeed, remain almost unknown, even to musicians. Perhaps a hundred of his songs are heard regularly in the concert-hall; the rest get upon programmes only rarely. Of his chamber music little is heard at all, not even the two superb piano trios, the octet, and the quintet with the two 'cellos. Of his symphonies the orchestras play the Unfinished incessantly — but never too often! — and the huge C major now and then, but the Tragic only once in a blue moon. Yet the Tragic remains one of Schubert's masterworks, and in its slow movement, at least, it rises to the full height of the Unfinished. There are not six such slow movements in the whole range of music. It has an eloquence that has never been surpassed, not even by Beethoven, but there is no rhetoric in it, no heroics, no exhibitionism. It begins quietly and simply and it passes out in a whisper, but its beauty remains overwhelming. I defy anyone with ears to listen to it without being moved profoundly, as by the spectacle of great grief.

Schubert paid the price that all artists pay for trying to improve upon the world made by the gods. "My compositions," he once wrote in his diary, "spring from my sorrow." Biographers, finding that sorrow in the lives of their victims, search for its sources in objective experience. They hunt, commonly, for the woman. Thus such a colossus as Beethoven is explained in terms of the trashy Giulietta Guicciardi. It is not necessary to resort to these puerilities. The life of an artist is a life of frustrations and disasters. Storms rage endlessly within his own soul. His quest is for the perfect beauty that is always elusive, always just beyond the sky-rim. He tries to contrive what the gods themselves have failed to contrive. When, in some moment of great illumination, he comes within reach of his heart's desire, his happiness is of a kind never experienced by ordinary men, nor even suspected, but that happens only seldom. More often he falls short, and in his falling short there is agony almost beyond endurance.

We know little directly about what Schubert thought of his compositions. He was, for a musician, strangely reserved. But indirectly there is the legend that, in his last days, he thought of taking lessons in counterpoint from Simon Sechter. The story has always appealed pleasantly to the musical biographers; mainly ninth-rate men, they delight in discovering imbecilities in artists. My guess is that Schubert, if he actually proposed to seek the den of Sechter, did it in a sportive spirit. Going to school to a pedant would have appealed charmingly to his sardonic humor. What Sechter had to teach him was precisely what a Hugh Walpole might have taught Joseph Conrad, no less and no more.

It is astonishing how voluptuously criticism cherishes nonsense. This notion that Schubert lacked skill at counterpoint seems destined to go on afflicting his fame forever, despite the plain evidence to the contrary in his most familiar works. How can anyone believe it who has so much as glanced at the score of the Unfinished? That score is quite as remarkable for its adroit and lovely combinations of melodies as it is for its magnificent modulations. It is seldom that one is heard alone. They come in two by two, and they are woven into a fabric that is at once simple and complicated, and always beautiful. Here is contrapuntal writing at its very best, for the means are concealed by a perfect effect. Here is the complete antithesis of the sort of counterpoint that is taught by the Sechters.

No doubt the superstition that Schubert had no skill at polyphony gets some support from the plain fact that he seldom wrote a formal fugue. There is one at the end of his cantata, "Miriams Siegesgesang," and in his last year he wrote another for piano duet. The strict form, however, was out of accord with the natural bent of his invention: he did not think of terse, epigrammatic subjects, as Bach did and Beethoven afterward; he thought of complete melodies, the most ravishing ever heard in this world. It would be hard to imagine his making anything of the four austere notes which Beethoven turned into the first movement of the C minor symphony. He would have gone on to develop them melodically before ever he set himself to manipulating them contrapuntally. But that was not a sign of his inferiority to Beethoven; it was, in its way, a sign of his superiority. He was infinitely below old Ludwig as a technician; he lacked the sheer brain-power that went into such master-pieces as the first movement of the Eroica and the *allegretto* of the Seventh. Such dizzy feats of pure craftsmanship were beyond him. But where he fell short as an artisan he was unsurpassed as an artist. He invented more beautiful musical ideas in his thirty-one years than even Mozart or Haydn, and he proclaimed them with an instinctive skill that was certainly not inferior to any mere virtuosity, however dazzling and however profound.

This instinctive skill is visible quite as clearly in his counterpoint as it is in his harmony. Throwing off the pedantic fetters that bound even Bach, he got into polyphony all the ease and naturalness of simple melody. His subjects and counter-subjects are never tortured to meet the rules; they flow on with a grace like that of wheat rippled by the wind. The defect of prettiness is not in them. They show, at their most trivial, all the fine dignity of Schubert the man. Beautiful always in their simple statement, they take on fresh and even more enchanting beauties when one supports another. There are passages in the Unfinished, especially in the first movement, that are almost unparalleled in music, and there are passages equally fine in compositions that are seldom heard, notably the aforesaid quintet. When Schubert died the art of writing so magnificently seemed to pass out of the world. It was not until the colossal figure of Brahms arose that it found another master.

He was, to music, its great heart, as Beethoven was its great mind. All the rest begin to seem a bit archaic, but he continues to be a contemporary. He was essentially a modern, though he was born in the Eighteenth Century. In his earliest compositions there was something far beyond the naïve idiom of Mozart and Haydn. Already in "The Erl King" there was an echo of Beethoven's fury; later on it was to be transformed into a quieter mood, but one none the less austere. The man lived his inner life upon a high level. Outwardly a simple and unpretentious fellow, and condemned by poverty to an uneventful routine, he yet walked with the gods. His contacts with the world brought him only defeat and dismay. He failed at all the enterprises whereby the musicians of his day got fame and money. But out of every failure there flowed a masterpiece.

In all the history of music there has never been another man of such stupendous natural talents. It would be difficult, indeed, to match him in any of the other fine arts. He was the artist *par excellence*, moved by a powerful instinct to create beauty, and equipped by a prodigal nature with the precise and perfect tools. The gabble about his defective training probably comes down to us from his innocent friends and fellows in Vienna. They never estimated him at his true stature, but they at least saw that there was something extraordinary and even miraculous about him — that what he did could not be accounted for logically, but lay far beyond the common bounds of cause and effect. We know next to nothing about his mental processes. He was surrounded by inferiorities who noted with wonder how savagely he worked, how many hours a day he put in at his writing-table, and what wonders he achieved, but were too dull to be interested in what went on inside his head. Schubert himself was silent on that subject. From him there issued not even the fragmentary revelations that came from Mozart. All we know is that his ideas flowed like a cataract — that he knew nothing of Beethoven's tortured wooing of beauty — that his first thoughts, more often than not, were complete, perfect and incomparable.

No composer of the first rank has failed to surpass him in this way or that, but he stands above all of them as a contriver of sheer beauty, as a maker of music in the purest sense. There is no more smell of the lamp in his work than there is in the lyrics of Shakespeare. It is infinitely artless and spontaneous. But in its artlessness there is no sign of that intellectual poverty which so often shows itself, for example, in Haydn. Few composers, not even Beethoven and Bach, have been so seldom banal. He can be repetitious and even tedious, but it seems a sheer impossibility for him to be obvious or hollow. Such defects get into works of art when the composer's lust to create is unaccompanied by a sufficiency of sound and charming ideas. But Schubert never lacked ideas. Within the limits of his interests and curiosities he hatched more good ideas in his thirty-one years than all the rest of mankind has hatched since the beginning of time.

Music is kind to its disciples. When they bring high talents to its service they are not forgotten. They survive among the durably salient men, the really great men, the remembered men. Schubert belongs in that rare and enviable company. Life used him harshly, but time has made up for it. He is one of the great glories of the human race.

Brahms

FROM FIVE LITTLE EXCURSIONS, PREJUDICES: SIXTH SERIES,
1927, pp. 163–69.
First printed in the Baltimore *Evening Sun*, Aug. 2, 1926

MY excuse for writing of the above gentleman is simply that, at the moment, I can think of nothing else. A week or so ago, on a Baltimore Summer evening of furious heat, I heard his sextet for strings, opus 18, and ever since then it has been sliding and pirouetting through my head. I have gone to bed with it and I have got up with it. Not, of course, with the whole sextet, nor even with any principal tune of it, but with the modest and fragile little episode at the end of the first section of the first movement — a lowly thing of nine measures, thrown off like a perfume, so to speak, from the second subject:

What is the magic in such sublime trivialities? Here is a tune so slight and unassuming that it runs to but nine measures and uses but six of the twelve tones in the octave, and yet it rides an elderly and unromantic man, weighing 180 pounds and with a liver far beyond pills or prayer, as if it were the very queen of the succubi. Is it because I have a delicately sensitive ear? Bosh! I am almost tone-deaf. Or a tender and impressionable heart? Bosh again! Or a beautiful soul? *Dreimal* bosh! No theologian not in his cups would insure me against Hell for cent per cent. No, the answer is to be found in the tune, not in the man. Trivial in seeming, there is yet in it the power of a thousand horses. Modest, it speaks with a clarion voice, and having spoken, it is remembered. Brahms made many another like it. There is one at the beginning of the trio for violin, 'cello and piano, opus 8 — the loveliest tune, perhaps, in the whole range of music. There is another in the slow movement of the quintet for piano and strings, opus 34. There is yet another in the double concerto for violin and 'cello, opus 102 — the first subject of the slow movement. There is one in the coda of the Third Symphony. There is an exquisite one in the Fourth Symphony. But if you know Brahms, you know all of them quite as well as I do. Hearing him is as dangerous as hearing Schubert. One does not go away filled and satisfied, to resume business as usual in the morning. One goes away charged with a something that remains in the blood a long while, like the toxins of love or the pneumococcus. If I had a heavy job of work to do on the morrow, with all hands on deck and the cerebrum thrown into high, I'd certainly not risk hearing any of the Schubert string quartets, or the incomparable quintet with the extra 'cello, or the slow movement of the Tragic Symphony. And I'd hesitate a long time before risking Brahms.

It seems an astounding thing that there was once a war over him, and that certain competent musicians, otherwise sane, argued that he was dull. As well imagine a war over Beauvais Cathedral or the Hundred-and-third Psalm. The contention of these foolish fellows, if I recall it aright, was that Brahms was dull in his development sections — that he flogged his tunes to death. I can think of nothing more magnificently idiotic. Turn to the sextet that I have mentioned, written in the early 60s of the last century, when the composer was barely thirty. The development section of the first movement is not only fluent and workmanlike: it is a downright masterpiece. There is a magnificent battle of moods in it, from the fiercest to the tenderest, and it ends with a coda that is sheer perfection. True enough, Brahms had to learn — and it is in the handling of thematic material, not in its invention, that learning counts. When he wrote his first piano trio, at twenty-five or thereabout, he started off, as I have said, with one of the most entrancing tunes ever put on paper, but when he came to develop it his inexperience threw him, and the result was such that years later he rewrote the whole work.

But by the time he came to his piano concerto in D he was the complete master of his materials, and ever thereafter he showed a quality of workmanship that no other composer has ever surpassed, not even Beethoven. The first movement of the Eroica, I grant you, is *sui generis*: it will never be matched until the time two great geniuses collide again. But what is in the rest of the first eight symphonies, even including the Fifth and Ninth, that is clearly better than what is in the four of Brahms? The first performance of his First, indeed, was as memorable an event in the history of music as the first performance of the Eroica. Both were frantically denounced, and yet both were instantaneous successes. I'd rather have been present at Karlsruhe on November 6, 1876, I think, than at the initiation of General Pershing into the Elks. And I'd rather have been present at Vienna on April 7, 1805, than at the landing of Columbus.

More than any other art, perhaps, music demands brains. It is full of technical complexities. It calls for a capacity to do a dozen things at once. But most of all it is revelatory of what is called character. When a trashy man writes it, it is trashy music. Here is where the immense superiority of such a man as Brahms becomes manifest. There is less trashiness in his music than there is in the music of any other man ever heard of, with the sole exception, perhaps, of Johann Sebastian Bach. It was simply impossible for him, at least after he had learned his trade, to be obvious or banal. He could not write even the baldest tune without getting into it something of his own high dignity and profound seriousness; he could not play with that tune, however light his mood, without putting an austere and noble stateliness into it. Hearing Brahms, one never gets any sense of being entertained by a clever mountebank. One is facing a superior man, and the fact is evident from the first note. I give you his "Deutsches Requiem" as an example. There is no hint of what is commonly regarded as religious feeling in it. Brahms, so far as I know, was not a religious man. Nor is there the slightest sign of the cheap fustian of conventional patriotism. Nevertheless, a superb emotion is there — nay, an overwhelming emotion. The thing is irresistibly moving. It is moving because a man of the highest intellectual dignity, a man of exalted feelings, a man of brains, put into it his love for and pride in his country.

But in music emotion is only half the story. Mendelssohn had it, and yet he belongs to the second table. Nor is it a matter of mere beauty — that is, of mere sensuous loveliness. If it were, then Dvořák would be greater than Beethoven, whose tunes are seldom inspired, and who not infrequently does without them altogether. What makes great music is simply the thing I have mentioned: brains. The greatest musician is a man whose thoughts and feelings are above the common level, and whose language matches them. What he has to say comes out of a wisdom that is not ordinary. Platitude is impossible to him. Above all, he is a master of his craft, as opposed to his art. He gets his effects in new, difficult and ingenious ways — and they convince one instantly that they are inevitable. One can easily imagine improvements in the human eye, and in the Alps, and in the art of love, and even in the Constitution, but one cannot imagine improvement in the first movement of the Eroica. The thing is completely perfect, even at the places where the composer halts to draw breath. Any change in it would damage it. But what is inevitable is never obvious. John Doe would not and could not write thus. The immovable truths that are there — and there are truths in the arts as well as in theology — became truths when Beethoven formulated them. They did not exist before. They cannot perish hereafter.

Wagner

From TOWARD A REALISTIC ÆSTHETIC, PREJUDICES: FOURTH SERIES,
1924, pp. 249–51.
First printed in the *Smart Set*, July, 1922, pp. 41–43

IN contemplating the stupendous achievements of Wagner one often finds one's self wondering how much further he would have gone had he not been harassed by his two dreadful wives. The first, Minna Planer, was implacably opposed to his life-work, and made hard efforts to dissuade him from it. She regarded "Lohengrin" as nonsensical and "Tannhäuser" as downright indecent. It was her constant hope, until Wagner finally kicked her out, that he would give over such stuff, and consecrate himself to the composition of respectable operas in the manner of Rossini. She was a singer, and had the brains of one. It must be plain that the presence of such a woman — and Wagner lived with her for twenty years — must have put a fearful burden upon his creative genius. No man can be absolutely indifferent to the prejudices and opinions of his wife. She has too many opportunities to shove them down his throat. If she can't make him listen to them by howling and bawling, she can make him listen by snuffling. To say that he can carry on his work without paying any heed to her is equal to saying that he can carry on his work without paying any heed to his toothache, his conscience, or the zoo next door. In spite of Minna, Wagner composed a number of very fine music dramas. But if he had poisoned her at the beginning of his career it is very likely that he would have composed more of them, and perhaps better ones.

His second wife, the celebrated Cosima Liszt-von Bülow, had far more intelligence than Minna, and so we may assume that her presence in his music factory was less of a handicap upon the composer. Nevertheless, the chances are that she, too, did him far more harm than good. To begin with, she was extremely plain in face — and nothing is more damaging to the creative faculty than the constant presence of ugliness. Cosima, in fact, looked not unlike a modern woman politician; even

Nietzsche, a very romantic young fellow, had to go crazy before he could fall in love with her. In the second place, there is good reason to believe that Cosima, until after Wagner's death, secretly believed that her father, Papa Liszt, was a far better musician. Men's wives almost invariably make some such mistake; to find one who can separate the man of genius from the mere husband, and then estimate the former accurately and fairly, is surely very rare. A woman usually respects her father, but her view of her husband is mingled with contempt, for she is of course privy to the transparent devices by which she snared him. It is difficult for her, being so acutely aware of the weakness of the man, to give due weight to the dignity of the artist. Moreover, Cosima had shoddy tastes, and they played destructively upon poor Wagner. There are parts of "Parsifal" that suggest her very strongly — far more strongly, in fact, than they suggest the author of "Die Meistersinger."

I do not here decry Wagner; on the contrary, I praise him, and perhaps excessively. It is staggering to think of the work he did, with Minna and Cosima shrilling into his ears. What interests me is the question as to how much further he might have gone had he escaped the passionate affection of the two of them and of their various volunteer assistants. The thought fascinates, and almost alarms. There is a limit beyond which sheer beauty becomes unseemly. In "Tristan und Isolde," in the Ring, and even in parts of "Parsifal," Wagner pushes his music very near that limit. A bit beyond lies the fourth dimension of tone — and madness.

More of the Same

From REFLECTIONS ON HUMAN MONOGAMY, PREJUDICES:
FOURTH SERIES, 1924, p. 107–08.
First printed in the *Smart Set*, March, 1922, p. 44

EVEN Nietzsche was deceived by Wagner's "Parsifal." Like the most maudlin German fat woman at Bayreuth, he mistook the composer's elaborate and outrageous burlesque of Christianity for a tribute to Christianity, and so denounced him as a jackass and refused to speak to him thereafter. To this day "Parsifal" is given with all the trappings of a religious ceremonial, and pious folks go to hear it who would instantly shut their ears if the band began playing "Tristan und Isolde." It has become, in fact, a sort of " 'Way Down East" or "Ben-Hur" of music drama — a bait for luring patrons who are never seen in the opera house otherwise. But try to imagine such a thumping atheist as Wagner writing a religious opera seriously! And if, by any chance, you succeed in imagining it, then turn to the Char-Freitag music, and play it on your phonograph. Here is the central scene of the piece, the moment of most austere solemnity — and to it Wagner fits music that is so luscious and so fleshly — indeed, so downright lascivious and indecent — that even I, who am almost anesthetic to such provocations, blush every time I hear it. The Flower Maidens do not raise my blood-pressure a single ohm; I have actually drowsed through the whole second act of "Tristan." But when I hear that Char-Freitag music all my Freudian suppressions begin groaning and stretching their legs in the dungeons of my unconscious. And what does Char-Freitag mean? Char-Freitag means Good Friday!

Johann Strauss

From FIVE LITTLE EXCURSIONS, PREJUDICES: SIXTH SERIES, 1927, pp. 169–74

THE CENTARY of Johann Strauss the Younger in 1925 passed almost unnoticed in the United States. In Berlin and in Vienna it was celebrated with imposing ceremonies, and all the German radio stations put "Wein, Weib und Gesang" and "Rosen aus dem Süden" on the air. Why wasn't it done in this great country? Was the curse of jazz to blame — or was it due to the current pestilence of Prohibition and the consequent scarcity of sound beer? I incline to Answer No. 2. Any music is difficult on well-water, but the waltz is a sheer impossibility. "Man Lebt Nur Einmal" is as dreadful in a dry country as a Sousa march at a hanging.

For the essence of a Viennese waltz, and especially of a Strauss waltz, is merriment, good humor, happiness. Sad music, to be sure, has been written in Vienna — but chiefly by foreigners: Haydn, who was a Croat; Beethoven, whose pap had been a sour Rhine wine; Brahms, who came from the bleak Baltic coast. I come upon Schubert — but all rules go to pot when he appears. As for Strauss, he was a 100% Viennese, and could no more be sad than he could be indignant. The waltz wandered into the minor keys in Paris, in the hands of the sardonic Alsatian Jew, Waldteufel, but at home old Johann kept it in golden major, and so did young Johann after him. The two, taking it from Schubert and the folk, lifted it to imperial splendor. No other dance-form, not even the minuet, has ever brought forth more lovely music. And none other has preserved so perfectly the divine beeriness of the peasant dance. The best of the Strauss waltzes were written for the most stilted and ceremonious court in Europe, but in every one of them, great and little, there remains the boggy, expansive flavor of the village green. Even the stately "Kaiser" waltz, with its preliminary heel-clicks and saber-rattling, is soon swinging jocosely to the measures of the rustic *Springtanz*.

It is a curious, melancholy and gruesome fact that Johann Strauss II was brought up to the variety of delinquency known as investment banking. His father planned that he should be what in our time is called a bond salesman. What asses fathers are! This one was himself a great master of the waltz, and yet he believed that he could save all three of his sons from its lascivious allurement. Young Johann was dedicated to investment banking, Josef to architecture, and Eduard, the baby, to the law. The old man died on September 25, 1849. On September 26 all three were writing waltzes. Johann, it quickly appeared, was the best of the trio. In fact, he was the best musician who ever wrote waltzes for dancing, and one of the salient composers of all time. He took the waltz as his father left it, and gradually built it up into a form almost symphonic. He developed the introduction, which had been little more than an opening fanfare, into a complex and beautiful thing, almost an overture, and he elaborated the coda until it began to demand every resource of the composer's art, including even counterpoint. And into the waltz itself he threw such melodic riches, so vastly a rhythmic inventiveness and so adept a mastery of instrumentation that the effect was overwhelming. The Strauss waltzes, it seems to me, have never been sufficiently studied. Consider, for example, the astonishing skill with which Johann manages his procession of keys — the inevitable air which he always gets into his choice. And the immense ingenuity with which he puts variety into his bass — so monotonous in Waldteufel, and even in Lanner and Gung'l. And the endless resourcefulness which marks his orchestration — never formal and obvious for an instant, but always with some new quirk in it, some fresh and charming beauty. And his codas — how simple they are, and yet how ravishing.

Johann certainly did not blush unseen. He was an important figure at the Austrian court, and when he passed necks were craned as if at an ambassador. He traveled widely and was received with honor everywhere. His waltzes swept the world. His operettas, following them, offered formidable rivalry to the pieces of Gilbert and Sullivan. He was plastered with orders. He took in, in his time, a great deal of money, and left all his wives well provided for. More, he had the respect and a little of the envy of all his musical contemporaries. Wagner delighted in his waltzes and so did Brahms. Once one of the Strauss wives, encountering Brahms at the annual ball of the Third Assembly District Democratic Association of Vienna, asked him to sign her fan. He wrote upon it the opening theme of "The Beautiful Blue Danube" and added "Leider *nicht* von Johannes Brahms" — Unfortunately, *not* by Johannes Brahms. It was a compliment indeed — perhaps the most tremendous recorded in history — nor was there any mere politeness in it, for Brahms had written plenty of waltzes himself, and knew that it was not as easy as it looked.

The lesser fish followed the whales. There was never any clash of debate over Strauss. It was unanimously agreed that he was first-rate. His field was not wide, but within that field he was unchallenged. He became, in the end, the dean of a sort of college of waltz writers, centering at Vienna. The waltz, as he had brought it up to perfection, became the standard ball-room dance of the civilized world, and though it had to meet rivals constantly, it held its own for two generations, and even now, despite the murrain of jazz, it comes back once more. Disciples of great skill began to appear in the Straussian wake — Ziehrer with the beautiful "Weaner Mad'l," Komchak with "Fidelis Wien," Lincke with "Ach, Frühling, Wie Bist Du So Schön," and many another. But old Johann never lost his primacy. Down to the very day of his death in 1899 he was *primus inter omnes*. Vienna wept oceans of beery tears into his grave. A great Viennese — perhaps the ultimate flower of old Vienna — was gone.

Tempo di Valse

From THE ALLIED ARTS, PREJUDICES: SECOND SERIES, 1920, pp. 204–06. First printed in the *Smart Set*, Sept., 1919, p. 40

THE WALTZ never quite goes out of fashion; it is always just around the corner; every now and then it returns with a bang. And to the sore harassment and corruption, I suspect, of chemical purity. The popular dances that come and go are too gross to be very dangerous to civilized human beings; they suggest drinking beer out of buckets; the most elemental good taste is proof enough against them. But the waltz! Ah, the waltz, indeed! It is sneaking, insidious, disarming, lovely. It does its work, not like a college-yell or an explosion in a munitions plant, but like the rustle of the trees, the murmur of the illimitable sea, the sweet gurgle of a pretty girl. The jazz-band fetches only vulgarians, barbarians, idiots, pigs. But there is a mystical something in "Wiener Blut" or "Künstlerleben" that fetches even philosophers.

The waltz, in fact, is magnificently improper — the art of tone turned lubricious. I venture to say that the compositions of Johann Strauss have lured more fair young creatures to complaisance than all the movie actors and white slave scouts since the fall of the Western Empire. There is something about a waltz that is irresistible. Try it on the fattest and sedatest or even upon the thinnest and most acidulous of women, and she will be ready, in ten minutes, for a stealthy smack behind the door — nay, she will forthwith impart the embarrassing news that her husband misunderstands her, and drinks too much, and is going to Cleveland, O., on business tomorrow.

Richard Strauss

From VIRTUOUS VANDALISM, DAMN! A BOOK OF CALUMNY, 1918, pp. 56–57

IF, after hearing an unfamiliar Strauss work, one turns to the music, one is invariably surprised to find how simple it is. The performance reveals so many purple moments, so staggering an array of lusciousness, that the ear is bemused into detecting scales and chords that never were on land or sea. What the exploratory eye subsequently discovers, perhaps, is no more than our stout and comfortable old friend, the highly well-born *hausfrau*, Mme. C Dur — with a vine leaf or two of C sharp minor or F major in her hair. The trick, of course, lies in the tonecolor — in the flabbergasting magic of the orchestration. There are some moments in "Elektra" when sounds come out of the orchestra that tug at the very roots of the hair, sounds so unearthly that they suggest a caroling of dragons or *bierfisch* — and yet they are made by the same old fiddles that play the Kaiser Quartet, and by the same old trombones that the Valkyrie ride like witch's broomsticks, and by the same old flutes that sob and snuffle in Tit'l's Serenade. And in parts of "Feuersnot" — but Roget must be rewritten before "Feuersnot" is described. There is one place where the harps, taking a running start from the scrolls of the violins, leap slambang through (or is it into?) the firmament of Heaven. Once, when I heard this passage played at a concert, a woman sitting beside me rolled over like a log, and had to be hauled out by the ushers.

Bach at Bethlehem

From the Baltimore *Evening Sun*, May 30, 1923. For many years, after my annual visit to Bethlehem, I wrote an article on it for the *Evening Sun*. This is an early example, much abridged

A DUSTY, bottle-green hillside rising from a river front made harsh and hideous by long lines of blast furnaces; the sunshine blazing down through a haze shot through with wisps of golden orange smoke. Thick woods all the way to the top. In the midst of the solid leafage, rather less than half way up, half a dozen stretches of dingy granite, like outcroppings of the natural rock. Coming closer, one discovers that they are long, bare, stone buildings — the laboratories, dormitories and so on of Lehigh University. Low down the hillside one of them stands up more boldly than the rest. It is Packer Memorial Church, a huge tabernacle in austere, apologetic pseudo-Gothic, with a high square tower — the chapel, in brief, of the university, made wide and deep to hold the whole student body at once, and so save the rev. chaplain the labor of preaching twice.

It is here that the Bach Choir, for years past, has been lifting its hosannas to old Johann Sebastian — a curious scene, in more ways than one, for so solemn and ecstatic a ceremonial. Bethlehem, in the main, surely does not suggest the art of the fugue, nor, indeed, any form of art at all. It is a town founded mainly on steel, and it looks appropriately hard and brisk — a town, one guesses instantly, in which Rotarians are not without honor, and the New York *Times* is read far more than Anatole France. But, as the judicious have observed in all ages, it is hazardous to judge by surfaces. Long before the first steel mill rose by the river, the country all about was peopled by simple Moravians with a zest for praising God by measure, and far back in 1742 they set up a *Singakademie* and began practising German psalm-tunes on Saturday nights. The great-great-grandchild of that *Singakademie* is the Bethlehem Bach Choir of today.

What, indeed, is most astonishing about the whole festival is not that it is given in a Pennsylvania steel town, with the snorting of switching-engines breaking in upon Bach's colossal

"Gloria," but that it is still, after all these years, so thoroughly peasant-like and Moravian, so full of homeliness and rusticity. In all my life I have never attended a public show of any sort, in any country, of a more complete and charming simplicity. With strangers crowding into the little city from all directions, and two takers for every seat, and long columns of gabble in the newspapers, the temptation to throw some hocus-pocus about it, to give it a certain florid gaudiness, to bedeck it with bombast and highfalutin must be very trying, even to Moravians. But I can only say that they resist the temptation utterly and absolutely. There is no affectation about it whatever, not even the affectation of solemn religious purpose. Bach is sung in that smoky valley because the people like to sing him, and for no other reason at all. The singers are business men and their stenographers, schoolmasters and housewives, men who work in the steel mills and girls waiting to be married. If not a soul came in from outside to hear the music, they would keep on making it just the same, and if the Packer Memorial Church began to disturb them with echoes from empty benches they would go back to their bare Moravian church.

I can imagine no great public ceremonial with less fuss to it. No committee swathed in badges buzzes about; there is none of the usual sweating, fuming and chasing of tails. If one has a ticket, one simply goes to one's pew, plainly numbered on a simple plan, and sits down. If one lacks a ticket, one is quite free to lie in the grass outside, and listen to the music through the open doors. No bawling of hawkers is heard; a single small stand suffices for the sale of programs and scores; there is no effort to rook the stranger. The cops have nothing to do save tangle the light traffic; there is no confusion, no parade, no noise save from the railroad yards. The conductor slips into his place unnoticed; when a session is over he slips out the same way. It is indeed not a public performance at all, in the customary sense; it is simply the last of this year's rehearsals — and as soon as it is over next year's begin.

Opera

From The Allied Arts, Prejudices: Second Series, 1920, pp. 197–200.
First printed in the New York *Evening Mail*, Feb. 22, 1918

Opera, to a person genuinely fond of aural beauty, must inevitably appear tawdry and obnoxious, if only because it presents aural beauty in a frame of purely visual gaudiness, with overtones of the grossest sexual provocation. It is chiefly supported in all countries by the same sort of wealthy sensualists who also support musical comedy. One finds in the directors' room the traditional stock company of the stage-door alley. Such vermin, of course, pose in the newspapers as devout and almost fanatical partisans of art. But one has merely to observe the sort of opera they think is good to get the measure of their actual artistic discrimination.

The genuine music-lover may accept the carnal husk of opera to get at the kernel of actual music within, but that is no sign that he approves the carnal husk or enjoys gnawing through it. Most musicians, indeed, prefer to hear operatic music outside the opera house; that is why one so often hears such lowly things, say, as "The Ride of the Valkyrie" in the concert hall. "The Ride of the Valkyrie" has a certain intrinsic value as pure music; played by a competent orchestra it may give civilized pleasure. But as it is commonly performed in an opera house, with a posse of fat beldames throwing themselves about the stage, it can only produce the effect of a dose of ipecacuanha. The sort of person who actually delights in such spectacles is the sort of person who delights in gas-pipe furniture. Such halfwits are in a majority in every opera house west of the Rhine. They go to the opera, not to hear music, not even to hear bad music, but merely to see a more or less obscene circus. A few, perhaps, have a further purpose; they desire to assist in that circus, to show themselves in the capacity of fashionables, to enchant the yokelry with their splendor. But the majority must be content with the more modest aim. What they get for the outrageous prices they pay for seats is a chance to feast their eyes upon glittering members of the superior *demi-monde*, and to abase their groveling souls before magnificoes on their own side of the footlights. They esteem a performance, not in proportion as true music is on tap, but in proportion as the display of notorious characters on the stage is copious, and the exhibition of wealth in the boxes is lavish. A soprano who can gargle her way up to F sharp in alt is more to such simple souls than a whole drove of Johann Sebastian Bachs; her one real rival in the entire domain of art is the contralto who has a pension from a former grand duke and is reported to be *enceinte* by several stockbrokers.

The music that such ignobles applaud is often quite as shoddy as they are themselves. To write a successful opera a knowledge of harmony and counterpoint is not enough; one must also be a sort of Barnum. All the first-rate musicians who have triumphed in the opera house have been skillful mountebanks as well. I need cite only Wagner and Richard Strauss. The business, indeed, has almost nothing to do with music. All the actual music one finds in many a popular opera — for example, "Thaïs" — mounts up to less than one may find in a pair of Gung'l waltzes. It is not this mild flavor of tone that fetches the crowd; it is the tinpot show that goes with it. An opera may have plenty of good music in it and fail, but if it has a good enough show it will succeed.

Such a composer as Wagner, of course, could not write even an opera without getting some music into it. In all of his works, even including "Parsifal," there are magnificent passages, and some of them are very long. Here his natural genius overcame him, and he forgot temporarily what he was about. But these magnificent passages pass unnoticed by the average opera audience. What it esteems in his music dramas is precisely what is cheapest and most mountebankish — for example, the more lascivious parts of "Tristan und Isolde." The sound music it dismisses as tedious. The Wagner it venerates is not the musician, but the showman. That he had a king for a backer and was seduced by Liszt's daughter — these facts, and not the fact of his stupendous talent, are the foundation stones of his fame in the opera house.

Greater men, lacking his touch of the quack, have failed where he succeeded — Beethoven, Schubert, Schumann, Brahms,

Bach, Haydn. Not one of them produced a genuinely successful opera; most of them didn't even try. Imagine Brahms writing for the diamond horseshoe! Or Bach! Or Haydn! Beethoven
attempted it, but made a mess of it; "Fidelio" survives today
chiefly as a set of concert overtures. Schubert wrote more actual
music every morning between 10 o'clock and lunch time than
the average opera composer produces in 250 years, yet he always came a cropper in the opera house.

Music as a Trade

From the *Smart Set*, June, 1922, p. 46

MUSIC is enormously handicapped as an art by the fact that its
technique is so frightfully difficult. I do not refer, of course, to
the technique of the musical executant, but to that of the composer. Any literate man can master the technique of poetry or
the novel in ten days, and that of the drama — despite all the
solemn hocus-pocus of the professors who presume to teach it —
in three weeks, but not even the greatest genius could do a
sound fugue without long and painful preparation. To write
even a string quartet is not merely an act of creation, like
writing a sonnet; it is also an act of applied science, like cutting out a set of tonsils. I know of no other art that demands
so elaborate a professional training. The technique of painting
has its difficulties, particularly in the direction of drawing, but
a hundred men master them for one who masters counterpoint.
So with sculpture. Perhaps the art which comes nearest to music
in technical difficulties is architecture — that is, modern architecture. As the Greeks practised it, it was relatively simple, for
they used simple materials and avoided all delicate problems of
stress and strain; and they were thus able to keep their whole
attention upon pure design. But the modern architect, with his
complex mathematical and mechanical problems, must be an
engineer before he is an artist, and the sort of engineering that
he must master bristles with technical snares and conundrums.
The serious musician is in even worse case. Before he may write

at all he must take in and coördinate a body of technical knowledge that is about as great as the outfit of an astronomer.

I say that all this constitutes a handicap on the art of music.
What I mean is that it scares off many men who have charming
musical ideas and would make good composers, but who have
no natural talent or taste for the technical groundwork. For
one Schubert who overcomes the handicap by sheer genius there
must be dozens who are repelled and discouraged. There is another, and perhaps even worse disadvantage. The potential
Schuberts flee in alarm, but the Professor Jadassohns march in
bravely. That is to say, music is hard for musicians, but easy
for pedants and quacks. Its constant invasion by tinpot revolutionists is the result. It offers an inviting playground to the
jackass whose delight it is to astonish the bourgeoisie with insane feats of virtuosity.

The Music-Lover

From THE ALLIED ARTS, PREJUDICES: SECOND SERIES, 1920, pp. 194–96.
First printed in the *Smart Set*, Dec., 1919, pp. 70–71

OF all forms of the uplift, perhaps the most futile is that
which addresses itself to educating the proletariat in music. The
theory behind it is that a taste for music is an elevating passion, and that if the great masses of the plain people could only
be inoculated with it they would cease to herd into the moving-
picture parlors, or to listen to demagogues, or to beat their
wives and children. The defect in this theory lies in the fact
that such a taste, granting it to be elevating — which, pointing
to professional musicians, I certainly deny — simply cannot be
implanted. Either it is born in a man or it is not born in him.
If it is, then he will get gratification for it at whatever cost —
he will hear music if Hell freezes over. But if it isn't, then no
amount of education will ever change him — he will remain indifferent until the last sad scene on the gallows.

No child who has this congenital taste ever has to be urged or
tempted or taught to love music. It takes to tone inevitably and

irresistibly; nothing can restrain it. What is more, it always tries to *make* music, for the delight in sounds is invariably accompanied by a great desire to produce them. I have never encountered an exception to this rule. All genuine music-lovers try to make music. They may do it badly, and even absurdly, but nevertheless they do it. Any man who pretends to cherish the tone-art and yet has never learned the scale of C major — any and every such man is a fraud. The opera-houses of the world are crowded with such liars. You will even find hundreds of them in the concert-halls, though here the suffering they have to undergo to keep up their pretense is almost too much for them to bear. Many of them, true enough, deceive themselves. They are honest in the sense that they credit their own buncombe. But it is buncombe none the less.

In the United States the number of genuine music-lovers is probably very low. There are whole States, *e.g.*, Alabama, Arkansas and Idaho, in which it would be difficult to muster a hundred. In New York, I venture, not more than one person in every thousand of the population deserves to be counted. The rest are, to all intents and purposes, tone deaf. They can not only sit through the infernal din made by the current jazz-bands; they actually like it. This is precisely as if they preferred the works of The Duchess to those of Thomas Hardy, or the paintings of the men who make covers for the magazines to those of El Greco. Such persons inhabit the sewers of the bozart. No conceivable education could rid them of their native infirmity. They are born incurable.

The Reward of the Artist

From DAMN! A BOOK OF CALUMNY, 1918, p. 97

A MAN labors and fumes for a whole year to write a symphony in G minor. He puts enormous diligence into it, and much talent, and maybe no little downright genius. It draws his blood and wrings his soul. He dies in it that he may live again. Nevertheless, its final value, in the open market of the world, is a great deal less than that of a fur overcoat, or a handful of authentic hair from the whiskers of Henry Wadsworth Longfellow.

Masters of Tone

From the *Smart Set*, May, 1912, p. 158

WAGNER — The rape of the Sabines . . . a *kommers* in Olympus.

Beethoven — The glory that was Greece . . . the grandeur that was Rome . . . a laugh.

Haydn — A seidel on the table . . . a girl on your knee . . . another and different girl in your heart.

Chopin — Two embalmers at work upon a minor poet . . . the scent of tuberoses . . . Autumn rain.

Richard Strauss — Old Home Week in Gomorrah.

Johann Strauss — Forty couples dancing . . . one by one they slip from the hall . . . sounds of kisses . . . the lights go out.

Puccini — Silver macaroni, exquisitely tangled.

Debussy — A pretty girl with one blue eye and one brown one.

Bach — Genesis I, 1.

XXVIII. THE LESSER ARTS

ॐ

Hand-Painted Oil Paintings

From Toward a Realistic Æsthetic, Prejudices: Fourth Series, 1924, pp. 240–48.
First printed in the *Smart Set*, Jan., 1921, pp. 39–40

To me, at all events, painting seems to be half an alien among the fine arts. The trouble with it is that it lacks movement, which is to say, the chief function of life. The best a painter can hope to accomplish is to fix the mood of an instant, the momentary aspect of something. If he suggests actual movement he must do it by palpable tricks, all of which belong to craftsmanship rather than to art. The work that he produces is comparable to a single chord in music, without preparation or resolution. It may be beautiful, but its beauty plainly does not belong to the highest order, and the mind soon tires of it. If a man stands before a given painting for more than five or ten minutes, it is usually a sign of affectation: he is trying to convince himself that he has more delicate perceptions than the general. Or he is a painter himself and thus engrossed by the technical aspects of it, as a plumber might be engrossed by the technical aspects of a bathroom. Or he is enchanted by the story that the picture tells, which is to say, by the literature that it illustrates.

Sculpture is in measurably better case. The spectator, viewing a fine statue, does not see something dead, embalmed and fixed in a frame; he sees something that moves as *he* moves. A fine statue, in other words, is not one statue, but hundreds, perhaps even thousands. The transformation from one to another is infinitely pleasing; one gets out of it the same satisfying stimulation that one gets out of the unrolling of a string quartet. So with architecture. It not only revolves; it also moves vertically, as the spectator approaches it. When one walks up a street past a beautiful building one certainly gets an effect beyond that of a mere chord; it is the effect of a whole procession of beautiful chords, like that at the beginning of the slow movement of the "New World" symphony or that in the well-known and much-battered Chopin prélude. If it were a painting it would soon grow tedious. No one, after a few days, would give it a glance.

This intrinsic hollowness of painting has its effects even upon those who most vigorously defend it as the queen of all the fine arts. One hears of such persons "haunting the galleries," but one always discovers, on inquiry, that it is the show-rooms that they actually haunt. In other words, they get their chief pleasure by looking at an endless succession of *new* paintings: the multitude of chords produces, in the end, a sort of confused satisfaction. The other arts make a far more powerful and permanent appeal. I have heard each of the first eight symphonies of Beethoven more than fifty times, and most of Mozart's, Haydn's, Schubert's and Schumann's quite as often. Yet if Beethoven's C Minor were announced for performance tonight, I'd surely go to hear it. More, I'd enjoy every instant of it. Even second-rate music has this lasting quality. Some time ago I heard Johann Strauss' waltz, "Geschichten aus dem Wiener Wald," for the first time in a long while. I knew it well in my goatish days; every note of it was still familiar. Nevertheless, it gave me immense delight. Imagine a man getting delight out of a painting of corresponding calibre — a painting already so familiar to him that he could reproduce it from memory.

Painters, like barbers and cigarmakers, are able to talk while they are at work, so they commonly gabble about their art a great deal more than other artists, and the world, in consequence, has come to assume that it is very complex, and full of subtleties. This is not true. Most of its so-called subtleties are manufactured by painters who cannot paint. The genuinely first-rate painters of the world have little to say about the technique of their art, and seem to be unaware that it is difficult. Go back to Leonardo's notes and sketches: you will find him a great deal more interested in anatomy than in painting. In fact, painting was a sort of afterthought with him; he was primarily an engineer, and the engineering that fascinated him most was that of the human body. Come down, then, to Cézanne. He painted in the way that seemed most natural to him, and was greatly astonished when a group of bad painters, seeking to imitate him, began crediting him with a long string of more or less mystical theories, by the Boul' Mich' out of the article on optics in the Encyclopædia Britannica.

The earliest Paleolithic men were already accomplished painters. They were so near to the ape that they had not even invented bows and arrows, usury, the gallows or the notion of baptism by total immersion, yet they were excellent draftsmen. Some of their drawings on the walls of their caves, indeed, remain a great deal more competent than the average magazine illustration of today. They also carved in stone and modeled in clay, and no doubt they were adept poets, as are the lowest Zuñi Indians of our own time. Moreover, they soon began to move out of their caves into artificial houses, and the principles of architectural design that they devised at the very dawn of history have been unchanged ever since, and are poll-parroted docilely every time a sky-scraper thrusts its snout among the cherubim. True enough, they could not draw as accurately as a photographic lens, but they could certainly draw as accurately as, say, Matisse or Gauguin. It remains for physicists, *i.e.*, men disdainful of drawing, to improve it. All the progress that has been made in the art during the past fifty or sixty years has been based upon quiet filches from the camera, just as all the progress that has been made in painting has been based upon filches from the spectroscope. When one finds a painter who professes to disdain these scientific aids, one always beholds a painter who is actually unable to draw or paint, and who seeks to conceal his incompetence by clothing it in hocus-pocus. This is the origin of the Modern Art that regales us with legs eight feet long, complexions of olive green, and human heads related to the soap-box rather than to the Edam cheese. This is the origin of all the gabble one hears in ratty and unheated studios about cubism, vortism, futurism and other such childish follies.

I regard any human being who, with proper instruction, cannot learn to draw reasonably well as, to all intents and purposes, a moron. He is in a stage of culture actually anterior to that of the Crô-Magnons. As for a human being incapable of writing passable verse, he simply does not exist. It is done, as everyone knows, by children — and sometimes so well that their poems are printed in books and quite solemnly reviewed. But good music is never written by children — and I am not forgetting Mozart, Schubert and Mendelssohn. Music belongs to the very latest stage of culture; to compose it in the grand manner requires painful training, and the highest sort of natural skill. It is complex, delicate, difficult. A miraculous youth may show talent for it, but he never reaches anything properly describable as mastery of it until he is mature. The music that all of us think of when we think of the best was written by men a bit bent by experience. And so with prose. Prose has no stage scenery to hide behind, as poetry has. It cannot use masks and wigs. It is not spontaneous, but must be fabricated by thought and painstaking. Prose is the ultimate flower of the art of words. Next to music, it is the finest of all the fine arts.

Art Critics

From THE FRINGES OF LOVELY LETTERS, PREJUDICES: FIFTH SERIES, 1926, pp. 208–14.
First printed in the Baltimore *Evening Sun*, Nov., 20, 1925

HAVING emerged lately from a diligent course of reading in so-called art criticism, and especially in that variety of it which is concerned with the painters since Cézanne, I can only report that I find it windy stuff, and sadly lacking in clarity and sense. The new critics, indeed, seem to me to be quite as vague and absurd as some of the new painters they celebrate. The more they explain and expound the thing they profess to admire, the more unintelligible it becomes. Criticism, in their hands, turns into a sort of cabalism. One must prepare for it, as one prepares for the literature of the New Thought, by acquiring a wholly new vocabulary, and a new system of logic.

I do not argue here that the new painting, in itself, is always absurd. On the contrary, it must be manifest to anyone with eyes that some of its inventions are bold and interesting, and that now and then it achieves a sort of beauty. What I argue is simply that the criticism it has bred does not adequately account for it — that no man of ordinary sense, seeking to find out just what it is about, will get any light from what is currently written about it. All he will get will be a bath of metaphysics, heated with indignation. Polemics take the place of exposition. One comes away with a guilty feeling that one is somehow grossly ignorant and bounderish, but unable to make out why. This tendency to degenerate into a mere mouthing of meaningless words seems to be peculiar to art criticism. There has never been, so far as I know, a critic of painting who wrote about it simply and clearly, as Sainte-Beuve, say, wrote about books, or Schumann and Berlioz about music. Even the most orthodox of the brethren, when he finds himself before a canvas that genuinely moves him, takes refuge in esoteric winks and grimaces and mysterious gurgles and belches. He can never put his feelings into plain English.

Painters themselves, when they discuss their art, go the same route. Every time a new revolutionist gives a show he issues a manifesto explaining his aims and achievements, and in every such manifesto there is the same blowsy rodomontadizing that one finds in the texts of the critics. The thing, it appears, is very profound. Something new has been discovered. Rembrandt, poor old boy, lived and died in ignorance of it. Turner, had he heard of it, would have yelled for the police. Even Gauguin barely glimpsed it. One can't make out what this new arcanum is, but one takes it on faith and goes to the show. What one finds there is a series of canvases that appear to have been painted with asphalt and mayonnaise, and by a man afflicted with binocular diplopic strabismus. Is this sound drawing? Is this a new vision of color? Then so is your grandmother left-fielder of the Giants. The exceptions are very few. I have read, I suppose, at least two hundred such manifestoes during the past twenty years; at one time I even started out to collect them, as odd literary delicatessen. I can't recall a single one that embodied a plain statement of an intelligible idea — that is, intelligible to a man of ordinary information and sanity. It always took a special talent to comprehend them, as it took a special talent to paint the fantastic pictures they discussed.

Two reasons, I believe, combine to make the pronunciamentos of painters so bombastic and flatulent. One lies in the plain fact that painting is a relatively simple and transparent art, and that nothing much of consequence is thus to be said about it. All that is remarkable in even the most profound painting may be grasped by an educated spectator in a few minutes. If he lingers longer he is simply seeing again what he has seen before. His essential experience, in other words, is short-lived. It is not like getting shaved, coming down with cholera morbus, or going to the wars; it is like jumping out of the way of a taxicab or getting kissed. Consider, now, the position of a critic condemned to stretch this experience into material for a column article or for a whole chapter in a book. Obviously, he soon finds it insufficient for this purpose. What, then, is he to do? Tell the truth, and then shut up? This, alas, is not the way of critics. When their objective facts run out they always turn to subjective facts, of which the supply is unlimited. Thus the art critic begins to roll his eyes inward. He begins to poetize and philosophize his experience. He indulges himself in dark hints and innuendoes. Putting words together aimlessly, he presently hits upon a combination that tickles him. He has invented a new cliché. He is a made man. The painter, expounding his work, falls into the same bog. The plain fact, nine times out of ten, is that he painted his picture without any rational plan whatever. Like any other artist, he simply experimented with his materials, trying this combination and then that. Finally he struck something that pleased him. Now he faces the dreadful job of telling why. He simply doesn't know. So he conceals his ignorance behind recondite and enigmatical phrases. He soars, insinuates, sputters, coughs behind his hand. If he is lucky, he, too, invents a cliché. Three clichés in a row, and he is a temporary immortal.

The New Architecture

From the *American Mercury*, Feb., 1931, pp. 164–65

THE NEW ARCHITECTURE seems to be making little progress in the United States. The traces of it that are visible in the current hotels, apartment-houses and office buildings are slight, and there are so few signs of it in domestic architecture and ecclesiastical architecture that when they appear they look merely freakish. A new suburb built according to the plans of, say, Le Corbusier would provoke a great deal more mirth than admiration, and the realtor who projected it would probably be badly stuck. The advocates of the new style are full of earnestness, and some of them carry on in the shrill, pedagogical manner of believers in the Single Tax or the New Humanism, but save on the level of factory design they do not seem to be making many converts. In other directions precious few persons seem to have been persuaded that their harsh and melodramatic designs are either logical or beautiful, or that the conventions they denounce are necessarily meaningless and ugly.

Those conventions, in point of fact, are often informed by an indubitable beauty, as even the most frantic Modernist must admit when he contemplates the Lincoln Memorial at Washington or St. Thomas's Church in New York; and there is not the slightest reason for holding that they make war upon anything essential to the modern spirit. We live in a Machine Age, but there are still plenty of us who have but little to do with machines, and find in that little no answer to our aspirations. Why should a man who hates automobiles build a house designed upon the principles which went into the Ford Model T? He may prefer, and quite honestly, the principles which went into the English dwelling-house of the Eighteenth Century, and so borrow them with a clear conscience.

I can sympathize with that man, for in many ways he is I and I am he. If I were building a house tomorrow it would certainly not follow the lines of a dynamo or a steam shovel; it would be, with a few obvious changes, a replica of the houses that were built in the days when human existence, according to my notion, was pleasanter and more spacious than ever before or since. The Eighteenth Century, of course, had its defects, but they were vastly overshadowed by its merits. It got rid of religion. It lifted music to first place among the arts. It introduced urbanity into manners, and made even war relatively gracious and decent. It took eating and drinking out of the stable and put them into the parlor. It found the sciences childish curiosities, and bent them to the service of man, and elevated them above metaphysics for all time. Lastly and best, it invented the first really comfortable human habitations ever seen on earth, and filled them with charming fittings. When it dawned even kings lived like hogs, but as it closed even colonial planters on the banks of the Potomac were housed in a fashion fit for gentlemen.

The Eighteenth Century dwelling-house has countless rivals today, but it is as far superior to any of them as the music of Mozart is superior to Broadway jazz. It is not only, with its red brick and white trim, a pattern of simple beauty; it is also durable, relatively inexpensive, and pleasant to live in. No other sort of house better meets the exigencies of housekeeping, and none other absorbs modern conveniences more naturally and gracefully. Why should a man of today abandon it for a house of harsh masses, hideous outlines, and bald metallic surfaces? And why should he abandon its noble and charming furniture for the ghastly imitations of the electric chair that the Modernists make of gas-pipe? I can find no reason in either faith or morals. The Eighteenth Century house fits a civilized man almost perfectly. He is completely at ease in it. In every detail it accords with his ideas. To say that the florid chicken-coops of Le Corbusier and company are closer to his nature is as absurd as to say that the tar-paper shacks behind the railroad tracks are closer to his nature.

Nor is there any sense in the common contention that Gothic has gone out, and is now falsetto. The truth is that St. Thomas's Church not only represents accurately the Christian mysticism of Ralph Adams Cram, who designed it, but also the uneasy consciences of the rich Babbitts who paid for it. It is a plain and highly intelligible signal to the world that, at least on Sundays, those Babbitts search their hearts and give thought to

Hell. It is, in its sordid surroundings, distinctly otherworldly, just as Bishop Fulbert's cathedral was otherworldly when it began to rise above the medieval squalor of Chartres. The otherworldliness is of the very essence of ecclesiastical architecture. The moment it is lost we have the dreadful "plants" that barbaric Baptists and Methodists erect in the Pellagra and Goitre Belts. Of all forms of visible otherworldiness, it seems to me, the Gothic is at once the most logical and the most beautiful. It reaches up magnificently — and a good half of it is palpably useless. When men really begin to build churches like the Bush Terminal there will be no religion any more, but only Rotary. And when they begin to live in houses as coldly structural as step-ladders they will cease to be men, and become mere rats in cages.

Art Galleries

From the Baltimore *Evening Sun*, Dec. 24, 1923

IT will not surprise the faunal naturalist specializing in *Homo sapiens* to note that the chief argument currently adduced in favor of building a public art gallery in Baltimore is that the works of art now stored in cellars and garrets, beyond the voluptuous gaze of the plain people, are worth millions. No one, it appears, argues that they deserve to be exhumed and displayed on the bald ground that they are beautiful — which, in point of fact, is probably not true in most cases. The contention is simply this: that the money sunk in them by dead and forgotten collectors ought to be put to some productive use — that it is as immoral to keep them locked up as it would be to buy a $1,000 fur overcoat and then let it remain in the icebox. This, I take it, is the 100% American view of the nature and function of the fine arts.

Well, perhaps it is as good as any other. The contrary view that beauty deserves cherishing and display for its own sweet sake would probably blow up, as I hint, if the treasures in question were actually examined. And the correlative view that public exhibitions of art have some occult power to mellow and uplift the human mind, and to fill it with esthetic passion — this notion does not survive analysis, even if it be assumed that every work of art is necessarily beautiful. The two great galleries in Paris probably house more celebrated paintings than are to be found anywhere else in the world, and yet, as everyone knows, the French people, and particularly the Parisians, show very little elevation of spirit and almost no esthetic sense. If you don't believe this last, look into their shop-windows. The sort of beauty that they admire privately — in furniture, in pictures, in hangings and lighting fixtures, even in clothing — is precisely the sort of beauty that is cherished by a retired saloon-keeper.

Is this a fair test? It is not only fair; it is the *only* fair one. For the esthetic tastes of an individual are to be determined, not by his occasional genuflexions before public displays of alleged masterpieces, but by the character of the private environment that he tries to create for himself. What sort of wallpaper has he hung on the walls of his dining-room? To what degree do his neckties match his shorts? What pictures does he put where he must see them every day? The answers to these questions are enormously more important than his record of attendance at art exhibitions, at least half of which offer no more actual beauty than a display of glass eyes.

But only the rich can afford to buy beautiful things for themselves? Is it so, indeed? I deny it. The fact is that, even on the lowest planes, there is always a free choice between what is less ugly and what is more ugly, and that choosing the better costs no more than choosing the worse. Furniture of reasonably decent design and material doesn't cost a cent more than the frightful stuff sold by the instalment houses. Reproductions of good pictures cost no more than the gilt-framed abominations in the department stores. Good wallpaper, simple and sound in color, is actually much cheaper than a bad wallpaper, with its florid designs and intolerable clashes. In sum, the expense of fitting out an ordinary dwelling house in a harmonious and charming manner is not a dollar above fitting it out like the studio of a fortune-teller. Moreover, all persons of even rudimentary taste are well aware of it. Everyone knows dignified and pleasing houses in which there is not the slightest sign of heavy expenditure. And everyone knows expensive houses that are hideous.

It is, indeed, simply impossible to imagine a genuine lover of beautiful things who does not make some attempt to get them into his immediate surroundings, just as it is impossible to imagine a genuine lover of music who does not try to make it. Let a man gabble about art day in and day out and know all the public collections by heart — and if his own home is unmitigatedly ugly, then his frenzy for beauty is fraudulent. Let him subscribe to all public funds for the preservation of bad paintings and worse statuary — and if he wears a green necktie with a blue shirt, then he remains a Philistine.

Two grave defects lie in all public art galleries. The first is the defect that the varieties of beautiful objects which they show — chiefly costly paintings and even more costly antiques of other sorts — lie quite beyond the acquisitive aspiration of the average man, and so send him away with the false notion that beauty is not for him. In other words, they fail at their primary business of inducing him to cherish and increase beauty himself. The other defect is that nine-tenths of the objects they show are actually not beautiful at all, but merely curious and expensive. They are gathered, it would seem, on the principle that if a given artist ever created anything of genuine beauty, then everything else he created is beautiful. This is precisely like admiring Mendelssohn's Reformation symphony on the ground that he also wrote the Scotch.

Suppose orchestras constantly played the former and never the latter? Yet that is the sort of fare that a provincial art gallery in a young country must inevitably offer, principally and often exclusively. The genuine masterpieces of painting and sculpture are beyond its reach. It must content itself with third-rate pictures, a great many of them mere forgeries. Looking at them is not immersing one's self in beauty; it is mere yokelish gaping, like looking at George Washington's false teeth.[1]

---

[1] This was written in 1923. It goes without saying that the art gallery I protested against was duly built, and that it has since cost the taxpayers of Baltimore many millions. Meanwhile, Henry Walters, a rich distiller and railway magnate, had been accumulating a really distinguished collection in the town, and when he died in 1931 not only left it to the municipality

Art and Nature

From The Artists' Model, Prejudices: Fourth Series, 1924, p. 140

The doctrine that art is an imitation of nature is full of folly. Nine-tenths of all the art that one encounters in this world is actually an imitation of other art. Fully a half of it is an imitation twice, thrice or ten times removed. The true artist, in fact, is seldom an accurate observer of nature; he leaves that gross and often revolting exploration to geologists, engineers and anatomists. The last thing he wants to see is a beautiful woman in the bright, pitiless sunlight.

The Artist

From the Baltimore *Evening Sun*, April 7, 1924

It is almost as safe to assume that an artist of any dignity is against his country, *i.e.*, against the environment in which God hath placed him, as it is to assume that his country is against the artist. The special quality which makes an artist of him might almost be defined, indeed, as an extraordinary capacity for irritation, a pathological sensitiveness to environmental pricks and stings. He differs from the rest of us mainly because he reacts sharply and in an uncommon manner to phenomena which leave the rest of us unmoved, or, at most, merely annoy us vaguely. He is, in brief, a more delicate fellow than we are, and hence less fitted to prosper and enjoy himself under the conditions of life which he and we must face alike. Therefore, he takes to artistic endeavor, which is at once a criticism of life and an attempt to escape from life.

So much for the theory of it. The more the facts are studied,

---

but also provided funds for its maintenance in perpetuity. So Baltimore now has two art galleries — the one superb and perhaps incomparable in the United States, and the other a helter-skelter assemblage of left-overs, largely filled with Modernist trash. The former costs the taxpayer nothing; the latter mulcts him for more and more every year.

the more they bear it out. In those fields of art, at all events, which concern themselves with ideas as well as with sensations it is almost impossible to find any trace of an artist who was not actively hostile to his environment, and thus an indifferent patriot. From Dante to Tolstoy and from Shakespeare to Mark Twain the story is ever the same. Names suggest themselves instantly: Goethe, Heine, Shelley, Byron, Thackeray, Balzac, Rabelais, Cervantes, Swift, Dostoevsky, Carlyle, Molière, Pope — all bitter critics of their time and nation, most of them piously hated by the contemporary 100 percenters, some of them actually fugitives from rage and reprisal.

Dante put all of the patriotic Italians of his day into Hell, and showed them boiling, roasting and writhing on hooks. Cervantes drew such a devastating picture of the Spain that he lived in that it ruined the Spaniards. Shakespeare made his heroes foreigners and his clowns Englishmen. Goethe was in favor of Napoleon. Rabelais, a citizen of Christendom rather than of France, raised a cackle against it that Christendom is still trying in vain to suppress. Swift, having finished the Irish and then the English, proceeded to finish the whole human race. The exceptions are few and far between, and not many of them will bear examination. So far as I know, the only eminent writer in English history who was also a 100% Englishman, absolutely beyond suspicion, was Samuel Johnson. The Ku Klux of his day gave him a clean bill of health; he was the Roosevelt of the Eighteenth Century. But was Johnson actually an artist? If he was, then a cornet-player is a musician. He employed the materials of one of the arts, to wit, words, but his use of them was hortatory, not artistic. Johnson was the first Rotarian: living today, he would be a United States Senator, or a university president. He left such wounds upon English prose that it was a century recovering from them.

The Greenwich Village Complex

From the *American Mercury*, June, 1925

A BAD artist almost always tries to conceal his incompetence by whooping up a new formula. Hence Dadaism, Vortism, and all the rest of that sort of buncombe. No really *good* new formula, it must be obvious, has ever come out of a bad artist — which is to say, out of an artist who could not do good work within the old formulæ. Among the so-called "modern" musicians, the only ones worthy of any respect are those who have proved their right to be revolutionaries by writing sound fugues. Among the advanced poets who now bray in every cellar the only genuinely amusing ones are those who have sound sonnets behind them. The rest are frauds — and bores.

Reflection on the Drama

From PREJUDICES: THIRD SERIES, 1922, pp. 299–309.
First printed in the *Smart Set*, Dec., 1920, pp. 47–50

THE DRAMA (counting in the movie and the radio as part of it) is the most democratic of the art forms, and perhaps the only one that may legitimately bear the label. Painting, sculpture, music and literature, so far as they show any genuine esthetic or intellectual content at all, are not for crowds, but for selected individuals, mostly with bad kidneys and worse morals, and th ee of the four are almost always enjoyed in actual solitude. Even architecture and religious ritual, though they are publicly displayed, make their chief appeal to man as individual, not to man as mass animal. One goes into a church as part of a crowd, true enough, but if it be a church that has risen above mere theological disputation to the beauty of ceremonial, one is, even in theory, alone with the Lord God Jehovah. And if, passing up Fifth avenue in the 5 o'clock throng, one pauses before St. Thomas's to drink in the beauty of that archaic façade, one's drinking is almost sure to be done *a cappella*; of the other passers-by, not one in a thousand so much as glances at it.

But the drama, as representation, is inconceivable save as a show for the mob, and so it has to take on protective coloration to survive. It must make its appeal, not to individuals as such, nor even to individuals as units in the mob, but to the mob as mob — a quite different thing, as Gustav Le Bon long ago demonstrated in his "Psychologie des Foules." Thus its intellectual content, like its esthetic form, must be within the mental grasp of the mob, and what is more important, within the scope of its prejudices. *Per corollary*, anything even remotely approaching an original idea, or an unpopular idea, is foreign to it and abhorrent to it. The best a dramatist can hope to do is to give poignant and arresting expression to an idea so simple that the average man will grasp it at once, and so banal that he will approve it in the next instant.

So much for the theory. An appeal to the facts quickly substantiates it. The more one looks into the so-called drama of ideas of the last age — that is, into the acting drama — the more one is astounded by the vacuity of its content. The younger Dumas's "La Dame aux Camélias," the *Stammvater* of all the "problem" and propaganda plays that have raged since 1852, is based upon the sophomoric thesis that a prostitute is a human being like you and me, and suffers the slings and arrows of the same sorrows, and may be potentially quite as worthy of Heaven. Augier's "La Mariage d'Olympe" (1854), another pioneer, is even hollower; its four acts are devoted to rubbing in the revolutionary discovery that it is unwise for a young man of good family to marry an elderly cocotte. Proceed now to Ibsen. Here one finds the same tasteless platitudes — that it is unpleasant for a wife to be treated as a doll; that professional patriots and town boomers are frauds; that success in business is often grounded upon a mere willingness to do what a man of honor is incapable of; that a woman who continues to live with a debauched husband may expect to have unhealthy children; that a joint sorrow tends to bring husband and wife together; that a neurotic woman is apt to prefer death to maternity; that a man of 55 is an ass to fall in love with a flapper of 17. Do I burlesque? If you think so, turn to Ibsen's "Nachgelassene

Schriften" and read his own statements of the ideas in his social dramas — read his own succinct summaries of their theses. Such "ideas" are what one finds in newspaper editorials, speeches before Congress, sermons by fashionable divines — in brief, in the literature expressly addressed to those persons whose distinguishing mark is that ideas never enter their heads.

Ibsen himself, an excellent poet and a reflective man, was under no delusions about his "dramas of ideas." It astounded him greatly when the sentimental German middle-classes hailed "Ein Puppenheim" as a revolutionary document; he protested often and bitterly against being mistaken for a prophet of feminism. His own interest in this play and in those that followed it was chiefly technical; he was trying to displace the well-made play of Scribe and company with something simpler, more elastic and more hospitable to character. He wrote "Ghosts" to raise a laugh against the fools who had seen something novel and horrible in the idea of "A Doll's House"; he wanted to prove to them that that idea was no more than a platitude. Soon afterward he became thoroughly disgusted with the whole "drama of ideas." In "The Wild Duck" he cruelly burlesqued it, and made a low-comedy Ibsenist his chief butt. In "Hedda Gabler" he played a joke on the Ibsen fanatics by fashioning a first-rate drama out of the oldest, shoddiest materials of Sardou, Feuillet, and even Meilhac and Halévy. And beginning with "Little Eyolf" he threw the "drama of ideas" overboard forever, and took to mysticism. What could be more comical than the efforts of critical talmudists to read a thesis into "When We Dead Awaken"? I have put in many a gay hour perusing their commentaries. Ibsen, had he lived, would have roared over them — as he roared over the effort to inject portentous meanings into "The Master Builder," at bottom no more than a sentimental epitaph on a love affair that he himself had suffered at 60.

The notion that there are ideas in the "drama of ideas," in truth, is confined to a special class of illuminati, whose chief visible character is their capacity for ingesting nonsense. The mob rules in the theater, and so the theater remains infantile and trivial — a scene, not of the exposure of ideas, nor even of the exhibition of beauty, but one merely of the parading of mental and physical prettiness and vulgarity. It is at its worst when its dramatists seek to corrupt this function by adding a moral or intellectual purpose. It is at its best when it confines itself to the unrealities that are its essence, and swings amiably from the romance that never was on land or sea to the buffoonery that is at the bottom of all we actually know of human life. Shakespeare was its greatest craftsman: he wasted no tortured ratiocination upon his plays. Instead, he filled them with the gaudy heroes that all of us see ourselves becoming on some bright tomorrow, and the lowly frauds and clowns we are today. No psychopathic problems engaged him; he took love and ambition and revenge and braggadocio as he found them. He held no clinics in dingy Norwegian apartment-houses: his field was Bohemia, glorious Rome, the Egypt of the scene-painter, Arcady. . . . But even Shakespeare, for all the vast potency of his incomparable, his stupefying poetry, could not long hold the talmudists out in front from their search for invisible significances. Think of all the tomes that have been written upon the profound and revolutionary "ideas" in the moony musings of the schizophrenic sophomore, Hamlet of Denmark!

Actors

From DAMN! A BOOK OF CALUMNY, 1918, pp. 40–44.
First printed in the *Smart Set*, Jan., 1917, p. 269

"IN France they call an actor a *m'as-tu-vu*, which, anglicized, means a have-you-seen-me? . . . The average actor holds the mirror up to nature and sees in it only the reflection of himself." I take the words from a late book on the art of the mime by the editor of a magazine devoted to the stage. The learned author evades plumbing the psychological springs of this astounding and almost invariable vanity, this endless bumptiousness of the *cabotin* in all climes and all ages. His one attempt is banal: "a foolish public makes much of him." With all due respect, Nonsense! The larval actor is full of hot and rancid gases long before a foolish public has had a fair chance to make anything of him at all, and he continues to emit them long after it has tried him, condemned him and bidden him be damned. There is, indeed, little choice in the virulence of their self-respect between a Broadway star who is slobbered over by press agents and fat women, and the poor ham who plays thinking parts in a No. 7 road company. The two are alike charged to the limit; one more ohm, or molecule, and they would burst. Actors begin where militia colonels, Fifth avenue rectors and Rotary orators leave off. The most modest of them (barring, perhaps, a few unearthly traitors to the craft) matches the conceit of the solitary pretty girl on a slow ship.

But why are actors, in general, such blatant and obnoxious posturers and wind-bags? Why is it as surprising to find an unassuming and intelligent fellow among them as to find a Greek without fleas? The answer is quite simple. To reach it one needs but consider the type of young man who normally gets stage-struck. Is he, taking averages, the alert, ingenious, ambitious young fellow? Is he the fellow with ideas in him, and a yearning for hard and difficult work? Is he the diligent reader, the hard student, the eager inquirer? No. He is, in the overwhelming main, the neighborhood fop and beau, the human clothes-horse, the nimble squire of dames. He seeks in the world, not a chance to test his mettle by hard and useful work, but an easy chance to shine. He craves the regard, not of men, but of women. He is, in brief, a hollow and incompetent creature, a strutter and poseur, a pretty one.

I thus beg the question, but explain the actor. He is this silly youngster grown older, but otherwise unchanged. An initiate of a profession requiring little more information, culture or capacity for ratiocination than that of the lady of joy, and surrounded in his workshop by men who are as stupid, as vain and as empty as he himself will be in the years to come, he suffers an arrest of development, and the little intelligence that may happen to be in him gets no chance to show itself. The result, in its usual manifestation, is the average bad actor — a man with the cerebrum of a floor-walker and the vanity of a bishop. The result, in its highest and holiest form, is the actor-manager, with his retinue of press-agents, parasites and worshiping wenches — perhaps the most preposterous and awe-inspiring donkey that civilization has yet produced.

The relatively greater intelligence of actresses is easily explained. They are, at their worst, quite as bad as the generality of actors. There are she-stars who are all temperament and balderdash — intellectually speaking, beggars on horseback, servant girls well washed. But no one who knows anything about the stage need be told that it can show a great many more quick-minded women than intelligent men. And why? Simply because its women are recruited, in the main, from a class much above that which furnishes its men. It is, after all, not unnatural for a woman of considerable intelligence to aspire to the stage. It offers her, indeed, one of the most tempting careers that are open to her. She can hardly hope to succeed in business, and in the other professions she is an unwelcome and much-scoffed-at intruder, but on the boards she can meet men on an equal footing. It is, therefore, no wonder that women of a relatively superior class often take to the trade. Once they embrace it, their superiority to their male colleagues is quickly manifest. All movements against puerility and imbecility in the drama have originated, not with actors, but with actresses — that is, in so far as they have originated among stage folks at all. In the days when Ibsen was new in the world, his pioneers were such women as Helena Modjeska, Agnes Sorma and Janet Achurch; the men all hung back. Ibsen, it would appear, was aware of this superior alertness and took shrewd advantage of it. At all events, all his best acting parts are feminine ones.

The Comedian

From the Baltimore *Evening Sun*, Nov. 18, 1929

THE ACTING that one sees upon the stage does not show how human beings actually comport themselves in crises, but simply how actors think they ought to. It is thus, like poetry and religion, a device for gladdening the heart with what is palpably

not true. But it is lower than either of those arts, for it is forced
to make its gaudy not-true absurd by putting it alongside the
true. There stands Richard Cœur de Lion — and there, plainly
enough, also stands a poor ham. Relatively few reflective persons seem to get any pleasure out of acting. They often, to be
sure, delight in comedians — but a comedian is not an actor:
he is a sort of *reductio ad absurdum* of an actor. His work bears
the same relation to acting properly so called as that of a hangman, a midwife or a divorce lawyer bears to poetry, or that of a
bishop to religion.

Arrière-Pensée

From PREJUDICES: FOURTH SERIES, 1924, p. 116.
First printed in the *Smart Set*, April, 1919, pp. 51–52. With
additions from the *Smart Set*, Nov., 1919, pp. 141–43

MEN of all other trades always contemplate the actor with
lifted eyebrow and superior snort; I myself, casting about for
chances to prove my own lofty quality, have had at him many
a time, hissing at him and mocking him. But on blue days it
often occurs to me that nine-tenths of this unanimous masculine scorn may be buncombe — that other men dislike actors,
not because they are intrinsically disgusting, but because
women like them — in brief, because of jealousy. For women
do like them; it would be silly to deny it; not even aviators are
such heroes at tea-parties; a women's club favored with a lecture on Shakespeare by Lionel Balderdash turns out to the last
flapper and grandma.

Well, what is the attraction? An actor is empty of ideas; he is
bombastic; he is ignorant; he is lazy; he is got up absurdly; he
has the manners of a head waiter or a fashionable gynecologist.
And yet the gals indubitably incline toward him. No doubt the
answer, like most answers to human riddles, is very complex;
one cannot hope to put it into a sentence. Part of it, I fancy, is
to be found in this fact: that the actor is free from the smell of
commerce and yet shows none of the social detachment that
goes with the authentic professions. The average American

woman is tired of business men and their ways. Her husband is typically a business man; his friends are business men; most of the men she meets are business men. She knows, by long experience, what oafs they are; she knows that they are as hollow as so many jugs; she revolts against their naïve stupidity and sentimentality. But when she turns to superior classes of men she immediately misses something. These men are quite as intelligent as she is, and hence do not take her seriously; her whole technique thus goes to pieces. Here the actor, like the clergyman, comes to the bat. Putatively a professional man and showing some of the outward signs of a professional man, he is yet as simple-minded at bottom as a cheesemonger. Thus, when he turns his blather upon a woman, he gives her the illusion that she is beset by a man who is at once intellectual and idiotic, her full equal and her abject slave — in brief, by the ideal of her dreams. And to help out this benign hallucination there is the actor's elaborately urgent, creamy, unctuous and flattering manner — a thing as much a part of his stock in trade as his shaven upper lip, his broad *a* or the perfect hang of his pantaloons.

Also, there is something more, and it was once revealed to me in the confidences of a theatrical manager, couched in the following terms: "Let me ask you a question. At what time of the day do men and women begin to meet socially? Is it in the morning? No; all men are too busy. Is it in the early afternoon? No, for the same reason. Social relaxation begins, in Christendom, at about five o'clock. Well, now consider an actor's day. Say there is no matinée. He gets up at 2 p.m., eats breakfast, reads the *Morning Telegraph* for an hour, bathes, shaves, spends half an hour selecting his cravat, and then goes out. Consider, now, his advantage when he encounters women. *He has just shaved.* All other men have been shaved eight or nine hours before. They are beginning to look scrubby and dirty. But the actor is as spick and span as a hard-boiled egg. And that is what fetches women. They like a man who is courageous. They like to be noticed by a man who is prominent. But most of all they like a man who has just come out of a barber-shop. There is your whole story."

Nevertheless, I still seem to detect the faint glare of something else over the horizon. Men may dislike actors because women like them, but they also dislike them on their own account. Perhaps the really fundamental objection to them, stripping the business of all mere sophistry and snobbery, is that they give away the idiotic vanity of the whole male sex. An actor is simply a man who, by word and strut, says aloud of *him*self what all normal men think of *them*selves. Thus he exposes, in a highly indiscreet and disconcerting manner, the full force of masculine vanity. But I doubt that he exaggerates it. No healthy male is ever actually modest. No healthy male ever really thinks or talks of anything save himself. His conversation is one endless boast — often covert, but always undiluted. Even his theology is seldom more than a stealthy comparison of himself and God, to the disadvantage of God. . . . The youngest flapper knows all this. Feminine strategy, in the duel of sex, consists almost wholly of an adroit feeding of this vanity. Man makes love by braggadocio. Woman makes love by pretending to believe.

Oratory

From the *American Mercury*, Dec., 1924

THE THEORY that the ancient Greeks and Romans were men of a vast and ineffable superiority runs aground on the fact that they were great admirers of oratory. No other art was so assiduously practised among them. Today we venerate the architects and dramatists of Greece far more than we venerate its orators, but the Greeks themselves put the orators first, and in consequence much better records of them are preserved today. But oratory, as a matter of fact, is the lowest of all the arts. Where is it most respected? Among savages, in and out of civilization. The yokels of the open spaces flock by the thousand to hear imbeciles yawp and heave; the city proletariat goes to political meetings and glues its ears to the radio every night. But what genuinely civilized man would turn out to hear even the champion orator of the country? Dozens of the most eminent professors of the art show off their tricks every day in the United States Senate. Yet the galleries of the Senate, save when news goes out that some Senator is stewed and about to make an ass of himself, are occupied by Negroes who have come in to get warm and hand-holding bridal couples from rural North Carolina and West Virginia.

The Libido for the Ugly

From FIVE LITTLE EXCURSIONS, PREJUDICES: SIXTH SERIES, 1927, pp. 187-93

ON a Winter day some years ago, coming out of Pittsburgh on one of the expresses of the Pennsylvania Railroad, I rolled eastward for an hour through the coal and steel towns of Westmoreland county. It was familiar ground; boy and man, I had been through it often before. But somehow I had never quite sensed its appalling desolation. Here was the very heart of industrial America, the center of its most lucrative and characteristic activity, the boast and pride of the richest and grandest nation ever seen on earth — and here was a scene so dreadfully hideous, so intolerably bleak and forlorn that it reduced the whole aspiration of man to a macabre and depressing joke. Here was wealth beyond computation, almost beyond imagination — and here were human habitations so abominable that they would have disgraced a race of alley cats.

I am not speaking of mere filth. One expects steel towns to be dirty. What I allude to is the unbroken and agonizing ugliness, the sheer revolting monstrousness, of every house in sight. From East Liberty to Greensburg, a distance of twenty-five miles, there was not one in sight from the train that did not insult and lacerate the eye. Some were so bad, and they were among the most pretentious — churches, stores, warehouses, and the like — that they were downright startling; one blinked before them as one blinks before a man with his face shot away. A few linger in memory, horrible even there: a crazy little church just west of Jeannette, set like a dormer-window on the side of a bare, leprous hill; the headquarters of the Veterans of Foreign Wars at another forlorn town, a steel stadium like a huge rat-trap somewhere further down the line. But most of all

I recall the general effect — of hideousness without a break. There was not a single decent house within eye-range from the Pittsburgh suburbs to the Greensburg yards. There was not one that was not misshapen, and there was not one that was not shabby.

The country itself is not uncomely, despite the grime of the endless mills. It is, in form, a narrow river valley, with deep gullies running up into the hills. It is thickly settled, but not noticeably overcrowded. There is still plenty of room for building, even in the larger towns, and there are very few solid blocks. Nearly every house, big and little, has space on all four sides. Obviously, if there were architects of any professional sense or dignity in the region, they would have perfected a chalet to hug the hillsides — a chalet with a high-pitched roof, to throw off the heavy Winter snows, but still essentially a low and clinging building, wider than it was tall. But what have they done? They have taken as their model a brick set on end. This they have converted into a thing of dingy clapboards, with a narrow, low-pitched roof. And the whole they have set upon thin, preposterous brick piers. By the hundreds and thousands these abominable houses cover the bare hillsides, like gravestones in some gigantic and decaying cemetery. On their deep sides they are three, four and even five stories high; on their low sides they bury themselves swinishly in the mud. Not a fifth of them are perpendicular. They lean this way and that, hanging on to their bases precariously. And one and all they are streaked in grime, with dead and eczematous patches of paint peeping through the streaks.

Now and then there is a house of brick. But what brick! When it is new it is the color of a fried egg. When it has taken on the patina of the mills it is the color of an egg long past all hope or caring. Was it necessary to adopt that shocking color? No more than it was necessary to set all of the houses on end. Red brick, even in a steel town, ages with some dignity. Let it become downright black, and it is still sightly, especially if its trimmings are of white stone, with soot in the depths and the high spots washed by the rain. But in Westmoreland they prefer that uremic yellow, and so they have the most loathsome towns and villages ever seen by mortal eye.

I award this championship only after laborious research and incessant prayer. I have seen, I believe, all of the most unlovely towns of the world; they are all to be found in the United States. I have seen the mill towns of decomposing New England and the desert towns of Utah, Arizona and Texas. I am familiar with the back streets of Newark, Brooklyn and Chicago, and have made scientific explorations to Camden, N. J. and Newport News, Va. Safe in a Pullman, I have whirled through the gloomy, God-forsaken villages of Iowa and Kansas, and the malarious tide-water hamlets of Georgia. I have been to Bridgeport, Conn., and to Los Angeles. But nowhere on this earth, at home or abroad, have I seen anything to compare to the villages that huddle along the line of the Pennsylvania from the Pittsburgh yards to Greensburg. They are incomparable in color, and they are incomparable in design. It is as if some titanic and aberrant genius, uncompromisingly inimical to man, had devoted all the ingenuity of Hell to the making of them. They show grotesqueries of ugliness that, in retrospect, become almost diabolical. One cannot imagine mere human beings concocting such dreadful things, and one can scarcely imagine human beings bearing life in them.

Are they so frightful because the valley is full of foreigners — dull, insensate brutes, with no love of beauty in them? Then why didn't these foreigners set up similar abominations in the countries that they came from? You will, in fact, find nothing of the sort in Europe — save perhaps in the more putrid parts of England. There is scarcely an ugly village on the whole Continent. The peasants, however poor, somehow manage to make themselves graceful and charming habitations, even in Spain. But in the American village and small town the pull is always toward ugliness, and in that Westmoreland valley it has been yielded to with an eagerness bordering upon passion. It is incredible that mere ignorance should have achieved such masterpieces of horror.

On certain levels of the American race, indeed, there seems to be a positive libido for the ugly, as on other and less Christian levels there is a libido for the beautiful. It is impossible to put down the wallpaper that defaces the average American home of the lower middle class to mere inadvertence, or to the obscene humor of the manufacturers. Such ghastly designs, it must be obvious, give a genuine delight to a certain type of mind. They meet, in some unfathomable way, its obscure and unintelligible demands. They caress it as "The Palms" caresses it, or the art of the movie, or jazz. The taste for them is as enigmatical and yet as common as the taste for dogmatic theology and the poetry of Edgar A. Guest.

Thus I suspect (though confessedly without knowing) that the vast majority of the honest folk of Westmoreland county, and especially the 100% Americans among them, actually admire the houses they live in, and are proud of them. For the same money they could get vastly better ones, but they prefer what they have got. Certainly there was no pressure upon the Veterans of Foreign Wars to choose the dreadful edifice that bears their banner, for there are plenty of vacant buildings along the track-side, and some of them are appreciably better. They might, indeed, have built a better one of their own. But they chose that clapboarded horror with their eyes open, and having chosen it, they let it mellow into its present shocking depravity. They like it as it is: beside it, the Parthenon would no doubt offend them. In precisely the same way the authors of the rat-trap stadium that I have mentioned made a deliberate choice. After painfully designing and erecting it, they made it perfect in their own sight by putting a completely impossible pent-house, painted a staring yellow, on top of it. The effect is that of a fat woman with a black eye. It is that of a Presbyterian grinning. But they like it.

Here is something that the psychologists have so far neglected: the love of ugliness for its own sake, the lust to make the world intolerable. Its habitat is the United States. Out of the melting pot emerges a race which hates beauty as it hates truth. The etiology of this madness deserves a great deal more study than it has got. There must be causes behind it; it arises and flourishes in obedience to biological laws, and not as a mere act of God. What, precisely, are the terms of those laws? And why do they run stronger in America than elsewhere? Let some honest *Privat Dozent* in pathological sociology apply himself to the problem.

XXIX. BUFFOONERIES

❦

Death: a Philosophical Discussion

From A BOOK OF BURLESQUES, 1916, pp. 11–23.
First printed in the *Smart Set*, Dec., 1914, pp. 213–16

The back parlor of an American home. A dim suggestion of festivity: strange chairs, the table pushed back, a decanter and glasses. A heavy, suffocating, discordant scent of flowers — roses, carnations, lilies, gardenias. A general stuffiness and mugginess, as if it were raining outside, which it isn't.

A door leads into the front parlor. It is open, and through it the flowers may be seen. They are banked about a long black box with huge nickel handles, resting upon two folding horses. Now and then a man comes into the front room from the street door, his shoes squeaking hideously. Each visitor approaches the long black box, looks into it with ill-concealed repugnance, snuffles softly, and then backs off toward the door. A clock on the mantel-piece ticks loudly.

In the back parlor six pallbearers sit upon chairs, all of them bolt upright, with their hands on their knees. They are in their Sunday clothes, and their hats are on the floor beside their chairs. Each wears upon his lapel the gilt badge of a fraternal order, with a crêpe rosette. In the gloom they are indistinguishable; all of them talk in the same strained, throaty whisper. Between their remarks they pause, clear their throats, blow their noses, and shuffle in their chairs. They are intensely uncomfortable. Tempo: Adagio lamentoso, with occasionally a rise to andante maesto. So:

First Pallbearer
Who woulda thought that *he* woulda been the next?

Second Pallbearer
Yes; you never can tell.

577

Third Pallbearer

(*An oldish voice, oracularly.*) We're here today and gone tomorrow.

Fourth Pallbearer

I seen him no longer ago than Chewsday. He never looked no better. Nobody would have —

Fifth Pallbearer

I seen him Wednesday. We had a glass of beer together in the Huffbrow Kaif. He was laughing and cutting up like he always done.

Sixth Pallbearer

You never know who it's gonna hit next. Him and me was pallbearers together for Hen Jackson no more than a month ago, or say five weeks.

First Pallbearer

Well, a man is lucky if he goes off quick. If I had *my* way I wouldn't want no better way.

Second Pallbearer

My brother John went thataway. He dropped like a stone, settin' there at the supper table. They had to take his knife outen his hand.

Third Pallbearer

I had an uncle to do the same thing, but without the knife. He had what they call appleplexy. It runs in my family.

Fourth Pallbearer

They say it's in *his'n*, too.

Fifth Pallbearer

But he never looked it.

Sixth Pallbearer

No. Nobody woulda thought *he* woulda been the next.

First Pallbearer

Them are the things you never can tell anything about.

Second Pallbearer

Ain't it true!

Third Pallbearer

We're here today and gone tomorrow.
(*A pause. Feet are shuffled. Somewhere a door bangs.*)

Fourth Pallbearer

(*Brightly*). He looks elegant. I hear he never suffered none.

Fifth Pallbearer

No; he went too quick. One minute he was alive and the next minute he was dead.

Sixth Pallbearer

Think of it: dead so quick!

First Pallbearer

Gone!

Second Pallbearer

Passed away!

Third Pallbearer

Well, we all have to go *some* time.

Fourth Pallbearer

Yes; a man never knows but what his turn'll come next.

Fifth Pallbearer

You can't tell nothing by looks. Them sickly fellows generally lives to be old.

Sixth Pallbearer

Yes; the doctors say it's the big stout person that goes off the soonest. They say pneumoney never kills none but the healthy.

First Pallbearer

So I have heered it said. My wife's youngest brother weighed 240 pounds. He was as strong as a mule. He could lift a whiskey-barrel, and then some. Once I seen him drink damn near a whole keg of beer. Yet it finished him in less'n a week — and *he* had it mild.

Second Pallbearer

It seems that there's a lot of it this Winter.

Third Pallbearer

Yes; I hear of people taken with it every day. My brother Sam's oldest is down with it.

Fourth Pallbearer

I had it myself once. I was out of my head for four weeks.

Fifth Pallbearer

That's a good sign.

Sixth Pallbearer

Yes; you don't die as long as you're out of your head.

First Pallbearer

It seems to me that there is a lot of sickness around this year.

Second Pallbearer

I been to five funerals in six weeks.

Third Pallbearer

I beat you. I been to six in five weeks, not counting this one.

Fourth Pallbearer

A body don't hardly know what to think of it scarcely.

Fifth Pallbearer

That's what *I* always say: you can't tell who'll be next.

Sixth Pallbearer

Ain't it true! Just think of *him*.

First Pallbearer

Yes; nobody woulda picked *him* out.

Second Pallbearer

Nor my brother John, neither.

Third Pallbearer

Well, what *must* be *must* be.

Fourth Pallbearer

Yes; it don't do no good to kick. When a man's time comes he's got to go.

Fifth Pallbearer

We're lucky if it ain't us.

Sixth Pallbearer

So I always say. We ought to be thankful.

First Pallbearer

That's the way *I* always feel about it.

Second Pallbearer

It wouldn't do *him* no good, no matter *what* we done.

Third Pallbearer

We're here today and gone tomorrow.

Fourth Pallbearer

But it's hard all the same.

Fifth Pallbearer

It's hard on *her*.

Sixth Pallbearer

Yes, it is. Why should *he* go?

First Pallbearer

It's a question nobody ain't ever answered.

Second Pallbearer

Nor never won't.

Third Pallbearer

You're right there. I talked to a preacher about it once, and even *he* couldn't give no answer to it.

Fourth Pallbearer

The more you think about it the less you can make it out.

Fifth Pallbearer

When I seen him last Wednesday he had no more ideer of it than what you had.

Sixth Pallbearer

Well, if I had *my* choice, that's the way I would always want to die.

First Pallbearer

Yes; that's what *I* say. I am with you there.

Second Pallbearer

Yes; you're right, bœchen you. It don't do no good to lay sick for months, with doctors' bills eatin' you up, and then have to go anyhow.

Third Pallbearer

No; when a thing has to be done, the best thing to do is to get it done and over with.

Fourth Pallbearer

That's just what I said to my wife when I heerd.

Fifth Pallbearer

But nobody hardly thought that *he* woulda been the next.

Sixth Pallbearer

No; but that's one of them things you can't tell.

First Pallbearer

You never know *who'll* be the next.

Second Pallbearer

It's lucky you don't.

Third Pallbearer

I guess you're right.

Fourth Pallbearer

That's what my grandfather used to say: you never know what is coming.

Fifth Pallbearer

Yes; that's the way it goes.

Sixth Pallbearer

First one, and then somebody else.

First Pallbearer

Who it'll be you can't say.

Second Pallbearer

I always say the same: we're here today —

Third Pallbearer

(*Cutting in jealously and humorously*). And tomorrow we ain't here.

(*A subdued and sinister snicker. It is followed by sudden si-lence. There is a shuffling of feet in the front room, and whis-pers. Necks are craned. The pallbearers straighten their backs, and hitch their coat collars. The clergyman has arrived. From above comes the sound of weeping.*)

The Declaration of Independence in American

From The American Language, Third Edition, 1923, pp. 398–402. First printed, as Essay in American, in the Baltimore *Evening Sun*, Nov. 7, 1921. Reprinted in The American Language, Second Edition, 1921, pp. 388–92. From the preface thereof: "It must be obvious that more than one section of the original is now quite unintelligible to the average American of the sort using the Common Speech. What would he make, for example, of such a sentence as this one: 'He has called together bodies at places unusual, uncomfortable, and distant from the depository of their public records, for the sole purpose of fatiguing them into compliance with his measures'? Or of this: 'He has refused for a long time, after such dissolutions, to cause others to be elected, whereby the legislative powers, incapable of annihilation, have returned to the people at large for their exercise.' Such Johnsonian periods are quite beyond his comprehension, and no doubt the fact is at least partly to blame for the neglect upon which the Declaration has fallen in recent years. When, during the Wilson-Palmer saturnalia of oppressions [1918–20], specialists in liberty began protesting that the Declaration plainly gave the people the right to alter the government under which they lived and even to abolish it altogether, they encountered the utmost incredulity. On more than one occasion, in fact, such an exegete was tarred and feathered by shocked members of the American Legion, even after the Declaration had been read to them. What ailed them was simply that they could not understand its Eighteenth Century English." This jocosity was denounced as seditious by various patriotic Americans, and in England it was accepted gravely and deplored sadly as a specimen of current Standard American

When things get so balled up that the people of a country got to cut loose from some other country, and go it on their own hook, without asking no permission from nobody, excepting maybe God Almighty, then they ought to let everybody know why they done it, so that everybody can see they are not trying to put nothing over on nobody.

All we got to say on this proposition is this: first, me and you is as good as anybody else, and maybe a damn sight better; second, nobody ain't got no right to take away none of our rights; third, every man has got a right to live, to come and go as he pleases, and to have a good time whichever way he likes, so long as he don't interfere with nobody else. That any government that don't give a man them rights ain't worth a damn; also, people ought to choose the kind of government they want themselves, and nobody else ought to have no say in the matter. That whenever any government don't do this, then the people have got a right to give it the bum's rush and put in one that will take care of their interests. Of course, that don't mean having a revolution every day like them South American yellow-bellies, or every time some jobholder goes to work and does something he ain't got no business to do. It is better to stand a little graft, etc., than to have revolutions all the time, like them coons, and any man that wasn't a anarchist or one of them I.W.W.'s would say the same. But when things get so bad that a man ain't hardly got no rights at all no more, but you might almost call him a slave, then everybody ought to get together and throw the grafters out, and put in new ones who won't carry on so high and steal so much, and then watch them. This is the proposition the people of these Colonies is up against, and they have got tired of it, and won't stand it no more. The administration of the present King, George III, has been rotten from the start, and when anybody kicked about it he always tried to get away with it by strong-arm work. Here is some of the rough stuff he has pulled:

He vetoed bills in the Legislature that everybody was in favor of, and hardly nobody was against.

He wouldn't allow no law to be passed without it was first put up to him, and then he stuck it in his pocket and let on he forgot about it, and didn't pay no attention to no kicks.

When people went to work and gone to him and asked him to put through a law about this or that, he give them their choice: either they had to shut down the Legislature and let him pass it all by himself, or they couldn't have it at all.

He made the Legislature meet at one-horse tank-towns, so that hardly nobody could get there and most of the leaders would stay home and let him go to work and do things like he wanted.

He give the Legislature the air, and sent the members home every time they stood up to him and give him a call-down or bawled him out.

When a Legislature was busted up he wouldn't allow no new one to be elected, so that there wasn't nobody left to run things, but anybody could walk in and do whatever they pleased.

He tried to scare people outen moving into these States, and made it so hard for a wop or one of these here kikes to get his papers that he would rather stay home and not try it, and then, when he come in, he wouldn't let him have no land, and so he either went home again or never come.

He monkeyed with the courts, and didn't hire enough judges to do the work, and so a person had to wait so long for his case to come up that he got sick of waiting, and went home, and so never got what was coming to him.

He got the judges under his thumb by turning them out when they done anything he didn't like, or by holding up their salaries, so that they had to knuckle down or not get no money.

He made a lot of new jobs, and give them to loafers that nobody knowed nothing about, and the poor people had to pay the bill, whether they could or not.

Without no war going on, he kept an army loafing around the country, no matter how much people kicked about it.

He let the army run things to suit theirself and never paid no attention whatsoever to nobody which didn't wear no uniform.

He let grafters run loose, from God knows where, and give them the say in everything, and let them put over such things as the following:

Making poor people board and lodge a lot of soldiers they ain't got no use for, and don't want to see loafing around.

When the soldiers kill a man, framing it up so that they would get off.

Interfering with business.

Making us pay taxes without asking us whether we thought

the things we had to pay taxes for was something that was worth paying taxes for or not.

When a man was arrested and asked for a jury trial, not letting him have no jury trial.

Chasing men out of the country, without being guilty of nothing, and trying them somewheres else for what they done here.

In countries that border on us, he put in bum governments, and then tried to spread them out, so that by and by they would take in this country too, or make our own government as bum as they was.

He never paid no attention whatever to the Constitution, but he went to work and repealed laws that everybody was satisfied with and hardly nobody was against, and tried to fix the government so that he could do whatever he pleased.

He busted up the Legislatures and let on he could do all the work better by himself.

Now he washes his hands of us and even goes to work and declares war on us, so we don't owe him nothing, and whatever authority he ever had he ain't got no more.

He has burned down towns, shot down people like dogs, and raised hell against us out on the ocean.

He hired whole regiments of Dutch, etc., to fight us, and told them they could have anything they wanted if they could take it away from us, and sicked these Dutch, etc., on us.

He grabbed our own people when he found them in ships on the ocean, and shoved guns into their hands, and made them fight against us, no matter how much they didn't want to.

He stirred up the Indians, and give them arms and ammunition, and told them to go to it, and they have killed men, women and children, and don't care which.

Every time he has went to work and pulled any of these things, we have went to work and put in a kick, but every time we have went to work and put in a kick he has went to work and did it again. When a man keeps on handing out such rough stuff all the time, all you can say is that he ain't got no class and ain't fitten to have no authority over people who have got any rights, and he ought to be kicked out.

When we complained to the English we didn't get no more

satisfaction. Almost every day we give them plenty of warning that the politicians over there was doing things to us that they didn't have no right to do. We kept on reminding them who we was, and what we was doing here, and how we come to come here. We asked them to get us a square deal, and told them that if this thing kept on we'd have to do something about it and maybe they wouldn't like it. But the more we talked, the more they didn't pay no attention to us. Therefore, if they ain't for us they must be agin us, and we are ready to give them the fight of their lives, or to shake hands when it is over.

Therefore be it resolved, That we, the representatives of the people of the United States of America, in Congress assembled, hereby declare as follows: That the United States, which was the United Colonies in former times, is now a free country, and ought to be; that we have throwed out the English King and don't want to have nothing to do with him no more, and are not taking no more English orders no more; and that, being as we are now a free country, we can do anything that free countries can do, especially declare war, make peace, sign treaties, go into business, etc. And we swear on the Bible on this proposition, one and all, and agree to stick to it no matter what happens, whether we win or we lose, and whether we get away with it or get the worst of it, no matter whether we lose all our property by it or even get hung for it.

The Visionary

From A Book of Burlesques, 1916, pp. 71–79.
First printed in the *Smart Set*, Dec., 1914, pp. 276–78

"Yes," said Cheops, helping his guest over a ticklish place, "I daresay this pile of rocks will last. It has cost me a pretty penny, believe me. I made up my mind at the start that it would be built of honest stone, or not at all. No cheap and shoddy brickwork for *me!* Look at Babylon. It's all brick, and it's always tumbling down. My ambassador there tells me that it costs a million a year to keep up the walls alone — mind you, the walls alone! What must it cost to keep up the palace, with all that fancy work!

"Yes, I grant you that brickwork *looks* good. But what of it? So does a cheap cotton nightshirt — you know the gaudy things those Theban peddlers sell to my sand-hogs down on the river bank. But does it *last*? Of course it doesn't. Well, I am putting up this pyramid to *stay* put, and I don't give a damn for its looks. I hear all sorts of funny cracks about it. My barber is a sharp nigger and keeps his ears open: he brings me all the gossip. But I let it go. This is *my* pyramid. I am putting up the money for it, and I have got to be mortared up in it when I die. So I am trying to make a good, substantial job of it, and letting the mere beauty of it go hang.

"Anyhow, there are plenty of uglier things in Egypt. Look at some of those fifth-rate pyramids up the river. When it comes to shape they are pretty much the same as this one, and when it comes to size, they look like warts beside it. And look at the Sphinx. There is something that cost my grandfather four millions if it cost a copper — and what is it now? A burlesque! A caricature! An architectural paralytic! So long as it was *new*, good enough! It was a showy piece of work. People came all the way from Tyre to gape at it. Everybody said it was one of the sights no one could afford to miss. But soon a piece began to peel off here and another piece there, and then the nose cracked, and then an ear dropped off, and then one of the eyes began to get mushy and watery looking, and finally it was a mere smudge, a false-face, a scarecrow. My father spent a lot of money trying to fix it up, but what good did it do? By the time he had the nose cobbled the ears were loose again, and so on. In the end he gave it up as a bad job.

"Yes; this pyramid has kept me on the jump, but I'm going to stick to it if it breaks me. Some say I ought to have built it across the river, where the quarries are. Such gabble makes me sick. Do I look like a man who would go looking around for such *child's-play*? I hope not. A one-legged man could have done *that*. Even a Babylonian could have done it. It would have been as easy as milking a cow. What I wanted was something that would keep me on the jump — something that would put a strain on me. So I decided to haul the whole business *across* the river — six million tons of rock. And when the engineers said that it couldn't be done, I gave them two days to get out of Egypt, and then tackled it myself. It was something new and hard. It was a job I could get my teeth into.

"Well, I suppose you know what a time I had of it at the start. First I tried a pontoon bridge, but the stones for the bottom course were so heavy that they sank the pontoons, and I lost a couple of hundred niggers before I saw that it couldn't be done. Then I tried a big raft, but in order to get her to float with the stones I had to use such big logs that she was unwieldy, and before I knew what had struck me I had lost six big dressed stones and another hundred niggers. I got the laugh, of course. Every numskull in Egypt wagged his beard over it; I could hear the chatter myself. But I kept quiet and stuck to the problem, and by and by I solved it.

"I suppose you know how I did it. In a general way? Well, the details are simple. First I made a new raft, a good deal lighter than the old one, and then I got a thousand water-tight goat-skins and had them blown up until they were as tight as drums. Then I got together a thousand niggers who were good swimmers, and gave each of them one of the blown-up goat-skins. On each goat-skin there was a leather thong, and on the bottom of the raft, spread over it evenly, there were a thousand hooks. Do you get the idea? Yes; that's it exactly. The niggers dived overboard with the goat-skins, swam under the raft, and tied the thongs to the hooks. And when all of them were tied on, the raft floated like a bladder. You simply *couldn't* sink it.

"Naturally enough, the thing took time, and there were accidents and setbacks. For instance, some of the niggers were so light in weight that they couldn't hold their goat-skins under water long enough to get them under the raft. I had to weight those fellows by having rocks tied around their middles. And when they had fastened their goat-skins and tried to swim back, some of them were carried down by the rocks. I never made any exact count, but I suppose that two or three hundred of them were drowned in that way. Besides, a couple of hundred were drowned because they couldn't hold their breaths long enough to swim under the raft and back. But what of it? I wasn't trying to hoard up niggers, but to make a raft that would float. And I *did* it.

"Well, once I showed how it could be done, all the wise-acres caught the idea, and after that I put a big gang to work making more rafts, and by and by I had sixteen of them in operation, and was hauling more stone than the masons could set. But I won't go into all that. Here is the pyramid; it speaks for itself. One year more and I'll have the top course laid and begin on the surfacing. I am going to make it plain marble, with no fancy work. I could bring in a gang of Theban stonecutters and have it carved all over with lions' heads and tiger claws and all that sort of gim-crackery, but why waste time and money? This isn't a menagerie, but a pyramid. My idea was to make it the boss pyramid of the world. The king who tries to beat it will have to get up pretty early in the morning.

"But what troubles I have had! Believe me, there has been nothing but trouble, trouble, trouble from the start. I set aside the engineering difficulties. They were hard for the engineers, but easy for me, once I put my mind on them. But the way these niggers have carried on has been something terrible. At the beginning I had only a thousand or two, and they all came from one tribe; so they got along fairly well. During the whole first year I doubt that more than twenty or thirty were killed in fights. But then I began to get fresh batches from up the river, and after that it was nothing but one rough-house after another. For two weeks running not a stroke of work was done. I really thought, at one time, that I'd have to give up. But finally the army put down the row, and after a couple of hundred of the ringleaders had been thrown into the river peace was restored. But it cost me, first and last, fully three thousand niggers, and set me back at least six months.

"Then came the so-called labor unions, and the strikes, and more trouble. These labor unions were started by a couple of smart, yellow niggers from Chaldea, one of them a sort of lay preacher, a fellow with a lot of gab. Before I got wind of them, they had gone so far it was almost impossible to squelch them. First I tried conciliation, but it didn't work a bit. They made the craziest demands you ever heard of — a holiday every ten days, meat every day, no night work and regular houses to live in. Some of them even had the effrontery to ask for money. Think of it! Niggers asking for money! Finally, I had to order out the army again and let some blood. But every time one was knocked over, I had to get another one to take his place, and that meant sending the army up the river to rope one gang after another, and more expense, and more devilish worry and nuisance.

"In my grandfather's time niggers were honest and faithful workmen. You could take one fresh from the bush, teach him to handle a shovel or pull a rope in a year or so, and after that he was worth almost as much as he could eat. But the nigger of today isn't worth a damn. He never does an honest day's work if he can help it, and he is forever wanting something. Take these fellows I have now — mainly young bucks from around the First Cataract. Here are niggers who never saw baker's bread or butcher's meat until my men grabbed them. They lived there in the bush like so many hyenas. Well, now they get first-class beef or mutton once a week, good bread and all the fish they can catch. They don't have to begin work until broad daylight, and they lay off at dark. There is hardly one of them that hasn't got a psaltery, or a harp, or some other musical instrument. If they want to dress up and make believe they are Egyptians, I give them clothes. If one of them is killed on the work, or by a stray lion, or in a fight, I have him embalmed by my own embalmers and plant him like a man. If one of them breaks a leg or loses an arm or gets too old to work, I turn him loose without complaining, and he is free to go home if he wants to.

"But are they contented? Do they show any gratitude? Not at all. Scarcely a day passes that I don't hear of some fresh soldiering. And, what is worse, they have stirred up some of my own people — the carpenters, stonecutters, gang bosses and so on. Every now and then my inspectors find some rotten libel cut on a stone — something to the effect that I am overworking them, and knocking them about, and holding them against their will, and generally mistreating them. I haven't the slightest doubt that some of these inscriptions have actually gone into the pyramid: it's impossible to watch every stone. Well, in the years to come, they will be dug out and read by strangers, and I will get a black eye. People will think of Cheops as a heartless old rapscallion — *me*, mind you! Can you beat it?"

A Neglected Anniversary

First printed in the New York *Evening Mail*, Dec. 28, 1917. The success of this idle hoax, done in time of war, when more serious writing was impossible, vastly astonished me. It was taken gravely by a great many other newspapers, and presently made its way into medical literature and into standard reference books. It had, of course, no truth in it whatsoever, and I more than once confessed publicly that it was only a jocosity — for example, in Prejudices: Sixth Series, 1927, pp. 194–201. Moreover, it was exposed and denounced by various other men — for example, Vilhjalmur Stefansson, the arctic explorer (and a great connoisseur of human credulity), in his Adventures in Error; New York, 1936, pp. 279–99. But it went on prospering, and in fact is still prospering. Scarcely a month goes by that I do not find the substance of it reprinted, not as foolishness but as fact, and not only in newspapers but in official documents and other works of the highest pretensions

On December 20 there flitted past us, absolutely without public notice, one of the most important profane anniversaries in American history, to wit, the seventy-fifth anniversary of the introduction of the bathtub into These States. Not a plumber fired a salute or hung out a flag. Not a governor proclaimed a day of prayer. Not a newspaper called attention to the day.

True enough, it was not entirely forgotten. Eight or nine months ago one of the younger surgeons connected with the Public Health Service in Washington happened upon the facts while looking into the early history of public hygiene, and at his suggestion a committee was formed to celebrate the anniversary with a banquet. But before the plan was perfected Washington went dry,[1] and so the banquet had to be abandoned. As it was, the day passed wholly unmarked, even in the capital of the nation.

Bathtubs are so common today that it is almost impossible to imagine a world without them. They are familiar to nearly everyone in all incorporated towns; in most of the large cities

---

[1] This was war-time Prohibition, preliminary to the main catastrophe.

it is unlawful to build a dwelling house without putting them in; even on the farm they have begun to come into use. And yet the first American bathtub was installed and dedicated so recently as December 20, 1842, and, for all I know to the contrary, it may be still in existence and in use.

Curiously enough, the scene of its setting up was Cincinnati, then a squalid frontier town, and even today surely no leader in culture. But Cincinnati, in those days as in these, contained many enterprising merchants, and one of them was a man named Adam Thompson, a dealer in cotton and grain. Thompson shipped his grain by steamboat down the Ohio and Mississippi to New Orleans, and from there sent it to England in sailing vessels. This trade frequently took him to England, and in that country, during the '30s, he acquired the habit of bathing.

The bathtub was then still a novelty in England. It had been introduced in 1828 by Lord John Russell and its use was yet confined to a small class of enthusiasts. Moreover, the English bathtub, then as now, was a puny and inconvenient contrivance — little more, in fact, than a glorified dishpan — and filling and emptying it required the attendance of a servant. Taking a bath, indeed, was a rather heavy ceremony, and Lord John in 1835 was said to be the only man in England who had yet come to doing it every day.

Thompson, who was of inventive fancy — he later devised the machine that is still used for bagging hams and bacon — conceived the notion that the English bathtub would be much improved if it were made large enough to admit the whole body of an adult man, and if its supply of water, instead of being hauled to the scene by a maid, were admitted by pipes from a central reservoir and run off by the same means. Accordingly, early in 1842 he set about building the first modern bathroom in his Cincinnati home — a large house with Doric pillars, standing near what is now the corner of Monastery and Orleans streets.

There was then, of course, no city water supply, at least in that part of the city, but Thompson had a large well in his garden, and he installed a pump to lift its water to the house. This pump, which was operated by six Negroes, much like an old-time fire engine, was connected by a pipe with a cypress tank in the garret of the house, and here the water was stored until needed. From the tank two other pipes ran to the bathroom. One, carrying cold water, was a direct line. The other, designed to provide warm water, ran down the great chimney of the kitchen, and was coiled inside it like a giant spring.

The tub itself was of new design, and became the grandfather of all the bathtubs of today. Thompson had it made by James Cullness, the leading Cincinnati cabinetmaker of those days, and its material was Nicaragua mahogany. It was nearly seven feet long and fully four feet wide. To make it water-tight, the interior was lined with sheet lead, carefully soldered at the joints. The whole contraption weighed about 1,750 pounds, and the floor of the room in which it was placed had to be reinforced to support it. The exterior was elaborately polished.

In this luxurious tub Thompson took two baths on December 20, 1842 — a cold one at 8 a.m. and a warm one some time during the afternoon. The warm water, heated by the kitchen fire, reached a temperature of 105 degrees. On Christmas day, having a party of gentlemen to dinner, he exhibited the new marvel to them and gave an exhibition of its use, and four of them, including a French visitor, Col. Duchanel, risked plunges into it. The next day all Cincinnati — then a town of about 100,000 people — had heard of it, and the local newspapers described it at length and opened their columns to violent discussions of it.

The thing, in fact, became a public matter, and before long there was bitter and double-headed opposition to the new invention, which had been promptly imitated by several other wealthy Cincinnatians. On the one hand it was denounced as an epicurean and obnoxious toy from England, designed to corrupt the democratic simplicity of the Republic, and on the other hand it was attacked by the medical faculty as dangerous to health and a certain inviter of "phthisic, rheumatic fevers, inflammation of the lungs and the whole category of zymotic diseases." (I quote from the *Western Medical Repository* of April 23, 1843.)

The noise of the controversy soon reached other cities, and in more than one place medical opposition reached such strength that it was reflected in legislation. Late in 1843, for example, the Philadelphia Common Council considered an ordinance prohibiting bathing between November 1 and March 15, and it failed of passage by but two votes. During the same year the legislature of Virginia laid a tax of $30 a year on all bathtubs that might be set up, and in Hartford, Providence, Charleston and Wilmington (Del.) special and very heavy water rates were levied upon those who had them. Boston, early in 1845, made bathing unlawful except upon medical advice, but the ordinance was never enforced and in 1862 it was repealed.

This legislation, I suspect, had some class feeling in it, for the Thompson bathtub was plainly too expensive to be owned by any save the wealthy; indeed, the common price for installing one in New York in 1845 was $500. Thus the low caste politicians of the time made capital by fulminating against it, and there is even some suspicion of political bias in many of the early medical denunciations. But the invention of the common pine bathtub, lined with zinc, in 1847, cut off this line of attack, and thereafter the bathtub made steady progress.

The zinc tub was devised by John F. Simpson, a Brooklyn plumber, and his efforts to protect it by a patent occupied the courts until 1855. But the decisions were steadily against him, and after 1848 all the plumbers of New York were equipped for putting in bathtubs. According to a writer in the *Christian Register* for July 17, 1857, the first one in New York was opened for traffic on September 12, 1847, and by the beginning of 1850 there were already nearly 1,000 in use in the big town.

After this medical opposition began to collapse, and among other eminent physicians Dr. Oliver Wendell Holmes declared for the bathtub, and vigorously opposed the lingering movement against it in Boston. The American Medical Association held its annual meeting in Boston in 1849, and a poll of the members in attendance showed that nearly 55 per cent. of them now regarded bathing as harmless, and that more than 20 per cent. advocated it as beneficial. At its meeting in 1850 a resolution was formally passed giving the imprimatur of the faculty to the bathtub. The homeopaths followed with a like resolution in 1853.

But it was the example of President Millard Fillmore that, even more than the grudging medical approval, gave the bathtub recognition and respectability in the United States. While he was still Vice-President, in March, 1850, he visited Cincinnati on a stumping tour, and inspected the original Thompson tub. Thompson himself was now dead, but his bathroom was preserved by the gentlemen who had bought his house from the estate. Fillmore was entertained in this house and, according to Chamberlain, his biographer, took a bath in the tub. Experiencing no ill effects, he became an ardent advocate of the new invention, and on succeeding to the Presidency at Taylor's death, July 9, 1850, he instructed his secretary of war, Gen. Charles M. Conrad, to invite tenders for the construction of a bathtub in the White House.

This action, for a moment, revived the old controversy, and its opponents made much of the fact that there was no bathtub at Mount Vernon, or at Monticello, and that all the Presidents and other magnificoes of the past had got along without any such monarchical luxuries. The elder Bennett, in the New York *Herald*, charged that Fillmore really aspired to buy and install in the White House a porphyry and alabaster bath that had been used by Louis Philippe at Versailles. But Conrad, disregarding all this clamor, duly called for bids, and the contract was presently awarded to Harper & Gillespie, a firm of Philadelphia engineers, who proposed to furnish a tub of thin cast iron, capable of floating the largest man.

This was installed early in 1851, and remained in service in the White House until the first Cleveland administration, when the present enameled tub was substituted. The example of the President soon broke down all that remained of the old opposition, and by 1860, according to the newspaper advertisements of the time, every hotel in New York had a bathtub, and some had two and even three. In 1862 bathing was introduced into the Army by Gen. McClellan, and in 1870 the first prison bathtub was set up at Moyamensing Prison, in Philadelphia.

So much for the history of the bathtub in America. One is astonished, on looking into it, to find that so little of it has been recorded. The literature, in fact, is almost nil. But perhaps this brief sketch will encourage other inquirers and so lay the foundation for an adequate celebration of the centennial in 1942.

Star-Spangled Men

From PREJUDICES: THIRD SERIES, 1922, pp. 133–45. First printed in the *New Republic*, Sept. 29, 1920, pp. 118–20. This piece belongs to my private archeology. It is dated beyond repair, but I print it because it is full of my view of the issues and leaders of World War I. In World War II I took a similar line, but by that time I had ceased to write on public matters and so not much indication of it got on paper. In World War I, as I indicate, there were no gauds for civilians, but that lack was remedied in a wholesale manner in World War II

I OPEN the memoirs of General Grant, Volume II, at the place where he is describing the surrender of General Lee, and find the following:

> I was without a sword, as I usually was when on horseback on the field, and wore a soldier's blouse for a coat, with the shoulder straps of my rank to indicate to the army who I was.

Anno 1865. I look out of my window and observe an officer of the United States Army passing down the street. Anno 1922. Like General Grant, he is without a sword. Like General Grant, he wears a sort of soldier's blouse for a coat. Like General Grant, he employs shoulder straps to indicate to the Army who he is. But there is something more. On the left breast of this officer, apparently a major, there blazes so brilliant a mass of color that, as the sun strikes it and the flash bangs my eyes, I wink, catch my breath and sneeze. There are two long strips, each starting at the sternum and disappearing into the shadows of the axilla — every hue in the rainbow, the spectroscope, the kaleidoscope — imperial purples, *sforzando* reds, wild Irish greens, romantic blues, loud yellows and oranges, rich maroons, sentimental pinks, all the half-tones from ultra-violet to infrared, all the vibrations from the impalpable to the unendurable.

A gallant *Soldat* indeed! How he would shame a circus ticket-wagon if he wore all the medals and badges, the stars and crosses, the pendants and lavallières, that go with those ribbons! . . . I glance at his sleeves. A simple golden stripe on the one — six months beyond the raging main. None on the other — the Kaiser's cannon missed him.

Just what all these ribbons signify I am sure I don't know; probably they belong to campaign medals and tell the tale of butcheries in foreign and domestic parts — mountains of dead Filipinos, Mexicans, Haitians, Dominicans, West Virginia miners, perhaps even Prussians. But in addition to campaign medals and the Distinguished Service Medal there are now certainly enough foreign orders in the United States to give a distinct brilliance to the national scene, viewed, say, from Mars. The Frederician tradition, borrowed by the ragged Continentals and embodied in Article I, Section 9, of the Constitution, lasted until 1918, and then suddenly blew up; to mention it today is a sort of indecorum, and tomorrow, no doubt, will be a species of treason. Down with Frederick; up with John Philip Sousa! Imagine what Sir John Pershing would look like at a state banquet of his favorite American order, the Benevolent and Protective one of Elks, in all the Byzantine splendor of his casket of ribbons, badges, stars, garters, sunbursts and cockades — the lordly Bath of the grateful motherland, with its somewhat disconcerting "Ich dien"; the gorgeous tricolor baldrics, sashes and festoons of the Légion d'Honneur; the grand cross of SS. Maurizio e Lazzaro of Italy; the Danilo of Montenegro, with its cabalistic monogram of Danilo I and its sinister hieroglyphics; the breastplate of the Paulownia of Japan, with its rising sun of thirty-two white rays, its blood-red heart, its background of green leaves and its white ribbon edged with red; the mystical St. Saviour of Greece, with its Greek motto and its brilliantly enameled figure of Christ; above all, the Croix de Guerre of Czecho-Slovakia, a new one and hence not listed in the books, but surely no shrinking violet.

Alas, Pershing was on the wrong side — that is, for one with a fancy for gauds of that sort. The most blinding of all known orders is the Medijie of Turkey, which not only entitles the holder to four wives, but also requires him to wear a red fez and a frozen star covering his whole façade. I was offered this order by Turkish spies during the war, and it wobbled me a good deal. The Alexander of Bulgaria is almost as seductive. The badge consists of an eight-pointed white cross, with crossed swords between the arms and a red Bulgarian lion over the swords. The motto is "Za Chrabrost!" Then there are the Prussian orders — the Red and Black Eagles, the Pour le Mérite, the Prussian Crown, the Hohenzollern and the rest. And the Golden Fleece of Austria — the noblest of them all. Think of the Golden Fleece on a man born in Linn County, Missouri. . . . I begin to doubt that the General would have got it, even supposing him to have taken the other side. The Japs, I note, gave him only the grand cordon of the Paulownia, and the Belgians and Montenegrins were similarly cautious. There are higher classes. The highest of the Paulownia is only for princes, which is to say, only for non-Missourians.

Pershing is the champion, with General March a bad second. March is a K.C.M.G., and entitled to wear a large cross of white enamel bearing a lithograph of the Archangel Michael and the motto, "Auspicium Melioris Aevi," but he is not a K.C.B.[1] Admirals Benson and Sims are also grand crosses of Michael and George, and like most other respectable Americans, members of the Legion of Honor, but they seem to have been forgotten by the Greeks and Montenegrins.[2] British-born and extremely Anglomaniacal Sims[3] refused the Distinguished Service Medal of his adopted country, but is careful to mention

[1] March went to the Philippines as commander of the forgotten Astor Battery and saw long and hard service here. He was a commander of the artillery in the A.E.F. and later its chief of staff. He retired from the Army in 1921. He had many decorations besides the grand cross of the order of St. Michael and St. George, including the grand cordon of the Chia Ho of China and that of Polonia Restituta.

[2] Benson was chief of naval operations in World War I. He had the order of the Rising Sun of Japan, the order of St. Gregory the Great, conferred by the Pope, and a gold medal struck in his honor by New Mexico. He died in 1932.

[3] Sims was born in Canada. He was commander of the naval forces in European waters throughout World War I. He had Japanese, Belgian and Italian orders, and was a LL.D. of Yale, Harvard, Tufts, Pennsylvania, Columbia, Williams, Juniata, Stevens, McGill, Queen's, California, Union, Wesleyan, and Cambridge (England). He died in 1936.

in "Who's Who in America" that his grand cross of Michael and George was conferred upon him, not by some servile gold-stick, but by "King George of England"; [4] Benson omits mention of His Majesty, as do Pershing and March. It would be hard to think of any other American officers, real or bogus, who would refuse the D.S.M., or, failing it, the grand decoration of chivalry of the Independent Order of Odd Fellows. I once saw the latter hung, with ceremonies of the utmost magnificence, upon a bald-headed tinner who had served the fraternity long and faithfully; as he marched down the hall toward the throne of the Supreme Exalted Pishposh a score of scared little girls, the issue of other tinners, strewed his pathway with roses, and around the stem of each rose was a piece of glittering tinfoil. The band meanwhile played "The Rosary," and, at the conclusion of the spectacle, as fried oysters were served, "Wien Bleibt Wien."

It was, I suspect, by way of the Odd Fellows and other such gaudy heirs to the Deutsche Ritter and the Rosicrucians that the lust to gleam and jingle got into the arteries of the American people. For years the austere tradition of Washington's day served to keep the military bosom bare of spangles, but all the while a weakness for them was growing in the civil population. Rank by rank, they became Knights of Pythias, Odd Fellows, Red Men, Nobles of the Mystic Shrine, Knights Templar, Patriarchs Militant, Elks, Moose, Woodmen of the World, Foresters, Hoo-Hoos, Ku Kluxers — and in every new order there were thirty-two degrees, and for every degree there was a badge, and for every badge there was a yard of ribbon. The Nobles of the Mystic Shrine, chiefly paunchy wholesalers of the Rotary Club species, are not content with swords, baldrics, stars, garters, jewels; they also wear red fezzes. The Elks run to rubies. The Red Men array themselves like Sitting Bull. The patriotic ice-wagon drivers and Methodist deacons of the Ku Klux Klan carry crosses set with incandescent lights. An American who is forced by his profession to belong to many such orders — say a life insurance solicitor, an undertaker or a dealer in oil stock — accumulates a trunk full of decorations, many of them weighing a pound. There is a mortician in Hagerstown,

---

[4] From 1922 onward he struck this out.

Md., who has been initiated eighteen times. When he robes himself to plant a fellow joiner he weighs three hundred pounds and sparkles and flashes like the mouth of Hell itself. He is entitled to bear seven swords, all jeweled, and to hang his watch chain with the golden busts of nine wild animals, all with precious stones for eyes. Put beside this lowly washer of the dead, Pershing newly polished would seem almost like a Trappist.

But even so the civil arm is robbed of its just dues in the department of gauds and radioactivity, no doubt by the direct operation of military vanity and jealousy. Despite a million proofs (and perhaps a billion eloquent arguments) to the contrary, it is still the theory at the official ribbon counter that the only man who serves in a war is the man who serves in uniform. This is soft for the Bevo officer,[5] who at least has his service stripes and the spurs that gnawed into his desk, but it is hard upon his brother Elmer, the dollar-a-year man, who worked twenty hours a day for fourteen months buying soap-powder, canned asparagus and raincoats for the army of God. Elmer not only labored with inconceivable diligence; he also faced hazards of no mean order, for on the one hand was his natural prejudice in favor of a very liberal rewarding of commercial enterprise, and on the other hand were his patriotism and his fear of Atlanta Penitentiary. I daresay that many and many a time, after working his twenty hours, he found it difficult to sleep the remaining four hours. I know, in fact, survivors of that obscure service who are far worse wrecks today than Pershing is. Their reward is — what? Winks, sniffs, innuendoes. If they would indulge themselves in the now almost universal American yearning to go adorned, they must join the Knights of Pythias. Even the American Legion fails them, for though it certainly does not bar non-combatants, it insists that they shall have done their non-combating in uniform.

What I propose is a variety of the Distinguished Service Medal for civilians — perhaps, better still, a distinct order for civilians, closed to the military and with badges of different colors and areas, to mark off varying services to democracy. Let

[5] A Bevo officer was one who fought the wicked Hun from a desk in Washington. The name derived from that of a near-beer of the time.

it run, like the Japanese Paulownia, from high to low — the lowest class for the patriot who sacrificed only time, money and a few nights' sleep; the highest for the great martyr who hung his country's altar with his dignity, his decency and his sacred honor. For Elmer and his nervous insomnia, a simple rosette, with an iron badge bearing the national motto, "Safety First"; for the university president who prohibited the teaching of the enemy language in his learned grove, heaved the works of Goethe out of the university library, cashiered every professor unwilling to support Woodrow for the first vacancy in the Trinity, took to the stump for the National Security League,[6] and made two hundred speeches in moving picture theaters — for this giant of loyal endeavor let no 100 per cent. American speak of anything less than the grand cross of the order, with a gold badge in stained glass, a baldric of the national colors, a violet plug hat with a sunburst on the side, the privilege of the floor of Congress, and a pension of $10,000 a year. After all, the cost would not be excessive; there are not many of them. Such prodigies of patriotism are possible only to rare and gifted men. For the grand cordons of the order, *e.g.*, college professors who spied upon and reported the seditions of their associates, state presidents of the American Protective League,[7] alien property custodians, judges whose sentences of conscientious objectors mounted to more than 50,000 years, members of George Creel's herd of 2,000 American historians, the authors of the Sisson documents,[8] etc. — pensions of $10 a day would be

[6] A band of patriots which made a deafening uproar in the 1914–1918 era. Its fronts were Elihu Root and Alton B. Parker.

[7] An organization of amateur detectives working under the ægis of the Department of Justice. In 1917 its operatives reported that I was an intimate associate and agent of "the German monster, Nietzsky," and I was solemnly investigated. But I was a cunning fellow in those days and full of a malicious humor, so I not only managed to throw off the charge but even to write the report upon myself. I need not say that it gave me a clean bill of health — and I still have a carbon to prove it. As a general rule the American Protective League confined itself to easier victims. Its specialty was harassing German waiters.

[8] Creel served as chairman of what was called the Committee on Public Information from 1917 to 1919. Its chief business was to propagate the official doctrine as to the causes and issues of the war. To that end Creel recruited his horde of college historians and they solemnly certified to the

enough, with silver badges and no plug hats. For the lower ranks, bronze badges and the legal right to the title of "The Hon.," already every true American's by courtesy.

Not, of course, that I am insensitive to the services of the gentlemen of those lower ranks, but in such matters one must go by rarity rather than by intrinsic value. If the grand cordon or even the nickel-plated eagle of the third class were given to every patriot who bored a hole through the floor of his flat to get evidence against his neighbors, the Krausmeyers, and to every one who visited the Hofbräuhaus nightly, dénounced the Kaiser in searing terms, and demanded assent from Emil and Otto, the waiters, and to every one who notified the catchpolls of the Department of Justice when the wireless plant was open in the garret of the Arion Liedertafel, and to all who took a brave and forward part in slacker raids, and to all who lent their stenographers funds at 6 per cent. to buy Liberty bonds at 4¼ per cent., and to all who sold out at 99 and then bought in again at 83.56, and to all who served as jurors or perjurers in cases against members and ex-members of the I.W.W., and to the German-American members of the League for German Democracy, and to all the Irish who snitched upon the Irish — if decorations were thrown about with any such lavishness, then there would be no nickel left for our bathrooms. On the civilian side as on the military side the great rewards of war go, not to mere dogged industry and fidelity, but to originality — to the unprecedented, the arresting, the bizarre. The New York *Tribune* liar who invented the story about the German plant for converting the corpses of the slain into soap did more for democracy and the Wilsonian idealism, and hence deserves a more brilliant recognition, than a thousand uninspired hawkers of atrocity stories supplied by Viscount Bryce and his associates. For that great servant of righteousness the grand cordon, with two silver badges and the chair of history at Columbia, would be scarcely enough; for the ordinary hawkers any precious metal would be too much.

truth of everything that emanated from Washington and London. The Sisson documents were supposed to show a sinister conspiracy of the Russian Communists, but what the specifications were I forget. Creel's committee was also in charge of newspaper censorship during the war.

Whether or not the Y.M.C.A. has decorated its chocolate peddlers and soul-snatchers I do not know; since the chief Y.M.C.A. lamasery in my town of Baltimore became the scene of a homosexual scandal I have ceased to frequent evangelical society. If not, then there should be some governmental recognition of these highly characteristic heroes of the war for democracy. The veterans of the line, true enough, dislike them excessively, and have a habit of denouncing them obscenely when the corn-juice flows. They charged too much for cigarettes; they tried to discourage the amiability of the ladies of France; they had a habit of being absent when the shells burst in air. Well, some say this and some say that. A few, at least, of the pale and oleaginous brethren must have gone into the Master's work because they thirsted to save souls, and not simply because they desired to escape the trenches. And a few, I am told, were anything but unpleasantly righteous, as a round of Wassermanns would show. If, as may be plausibly argued, these Soldiers of the Double Cross deserve to live at all, then they surely deserve to be hung with white enameled stars of the third class, with gilt dollar marks superimposed. Motto: "Glory, glory, hallelujah!"

But what of the vaudeville actors, the cheer leaders, the doughnut fryers, the camp librarians, the press agents? I am not forgetting them. Let them be distributed among all the classes from the seventh to the eighth, according to their sufferings for the holy cause. And the agitators against Beethoven, Bach, Brahms, Wagner, Richard Strauss, all the rest of the cacophonous Huns? And the specialists in the crimes of the German professors? And the collectors for the Belgians, with their generous renunciation of all commissions above 80 per cent? And the pathologists who denounced Johannes Müller as a fraud, Karl Ludwig as an imbecile, and Paul Ehrlich as a thief? And the patriotic chemists who discovered arsenic in dill pickles, ground glass in pumpernickel, bichloride tablets in Bismarck herring, pathogenic organisms in aniline dyes? And the inspired editorial writers of the New York *Times* and *Tribune*, the Boston *Transcript*, the Philadelphia *Ledger*, the Mobile *Register*, the Jones Corners *Eagle*? And the headline writers? And the Columbia, Yale and Princeton professors? And the authors of books describing how the Kaiser told them the whole plot in 1913, while they were pulling his teeth or shining his shoes? And the ex-ambassadors? And the *Nietzschefresser*? And the chautauqua orators? And the four-minute men? [9] And the Methodist pulpit pornographers who switched so facilely from vice-crusading to German atrocities? And Dr. Newell Dwight Hillis? And Dr. Henry van Dyke? [10] And the Vigilantes? [11] Let no grateful heart forget them!

Palmer and Burleson I leave for special legislation.[12] If mere university presidents, such as Nicholas Murray Butler, are to have the grand cross, then Palmer deserves to be rolled in malleable gold from head to foot, and polished until he blinds the cosmos — then Burleson must be hung with diamonds like Mrs. Warren and bathed in spotlights like Gaby Deslys. . . . Finally, I reserve a special decoration, to be conferred *in camera* and worn only in secret chapter, for husbands who took chances

[9] These were bores who visited the movie parlors of the time and broke in upon The Perils of Pauline with brief but rousing speeches. How many were in practise first and last I do not know, but there must have been hundreds of thousands. They were chiefly recruited from the ranks of Rotarians, Kiwanians, chautauquans, evangelical clergymen, and minor political aspirants.

[10] Hillis was a Presbyterian clergyman, but went over to the Congregationalists and spent most of his life in the old pulpit of Henry Ward Beecher in Brooklyn. He brought out a book called German Atrocities in 1918, in which all of the most fantastic inventions of the English propaganda bureau were treated gravely. Such horrors apparently fascinated him, and he wallowed in them in a really obscene manner. He died in 1929. Van Dyke, another Presbyterian, took the same line, though less violently. He had been pastor of the Brick Presbyterian Church in New York, but in the war era was professor of English literature at Princeton. He was taken gravely as a poet and essayist in his day, and rose to be president of the National Institute of Arts and Letters, but his writings were hollow and he is now pretty well forgotten. He died in 1933.

[11] An organization of professional patriots analogous to the American Protective League, but even worse. Its heroic members specialized in daubing yellow paint on the houses of persons suspected of having doubts about the Wilson idealism. In some regions they also resorted to assault, always at odds of at least 10 to 1.

[12] A. Mitchell Palmer, a Quaker, was Attorney-General under Wilson. He was the superintendent of many ferocious spy-hunts. He died in 1936. Albert Sidney Burleson was Wilson's Postmaster General. He specialized in the censorship of the mails. He died in 1937.

and refused to read anonymous letters from Paris: the somber
badge of the Ordre de la Cuculus Canorus, first and only class.

The Incomparable Physician

From A BOOK OF BURLESQUES, 1916, pp. 184–88. First printed in the
Smart Set, Nov., 1915, pp. 241–42. This piece has attracted the opera-
tors of private presses, and there have been half a dozen arty prints of it

THE EMINENT physician, Yen Li-Shen, being called in the middle of the night to the bedside of the rich tax-gatherer, Chu
Yi-Foy, found his distinguished patient suffering from a spasm
of the liver. An examination of the pulse, tongue, toe-nails, and
hair-roots revealing the fact that the malady was caused by the
presence of a multitude of small worms in the blood, the
learned doctor forthwith dispatched his servant to his surgery
for a vial of gnats' eyes dissolved in the saliva of men executed
by strangling, that being the remedy advised by Li Tan-Kien
and other high authorities for the relief of this painful and dangerous condition.

When the servant returned the patient was so far gone that
Cheyne-Stokes breathing had already set in, so the doctor decided to administer the whole contents of the vial — a heroic
dose, truly, for it has been immemorially held that even so little
as the amount that will cling to the end of a horsehair is sufficient to cure. Alas, in his professional zeal and excitement, the
celebrated pathologist permitted his hand to shake like a myrtle
leaf in a Spring gale, and so he dropped not only the contents
of the vial, but also the vial itself down the esophagus of his
moribund patient.

The accident, however, did not impede the powerful effects
of this famous remedy. In ten minutes Chu Yi-Foy was so far
recovered that he asked for a plate of rice stewed with plums,
and by morning he was able to leave his bed and receive the reports of his spies, informers and extortioners. That day he sent
for Dr. Yen and in token of his gratitude, for he was a just and
righteous man, settled upon him in due form of law, and upon
his heirs and assigns in perpetuity, the whole rents, rates,

imposts and taxes, amounting to no less than ten thousand Hang-kow taels a year, of two of the streets occupied by money-chang-ers, bird-cage makers and public women in the town of Szu-Loon, and of the related alleys, courts and lanes. And Dr. Yen, with his old age and the old age of his seven sons and thirty-one grandsons now safely provided for, retired from the practise of his art, and devoted himself to a tedious scientific inquiry (long the object of his passionate aspiration) into the precise physio-logical relation between gravel in the lower lobe of the heart and the bursting of arteries in the arms and legs.

So passed many years, while Dr. Yen pursued his researches and sent his annual reports of progress to the Academy of Med-icine at Chan-Si, and Chu Yi-Foy increased his riches and his influence, so that his arm reached out from the mountains to the sea. One day, in his eightieth year, Chu Yi-Foy fell ill again, and, having no confidence in any other physician, sent once more for the learned and now venerable Dr. Yen.

"I have a pain," he said, "in my left hip, where the stomach dips down over the spleen. A large knob has formed there. A lizard, perhaps, has got into me. Or perhaps a small hedge-hog."

Dr. Yen thereupon made use of the test for lizards and hedge-hogs — to wit, the application of madder dye to the Adam's apple, turning it lemon yellow if any sort of reptile is within, and violet if there is a mammal — but it failed to oper-ate as the books describe. Being thus led to suspect a mis-placed and wild-growing bone, perhaps from the vertebral col-umn, the doctor decided to have recourse to surgery, and so, after the proper propitiation of the gods, he administered to his eminent patient a draught of opium water, and having ex-cluded the wailing women of the household from the sick chamber, he cut into the protuberance with a small, sharp knife, and soon had the mysterious object in his hand. . . . It was the vial of dissolved gnats' eyes — *still full and tightly corked!* Worse, it was *not* the vial of dissolved gnats' eyes, but a vial of common burdock juice — the remedy *for infants griped by their mothers' milk.* . . .

But when the eminent Chu Yi-Foy, emerging from his be-nign stupor, made a sign that he would gaze upon the cause of his distress, it was a bone that Dr. Yen Li-Shen showed him —

an authentic bone, ovid and evil-looking — and lately the knee-cap of one Ho Kwang, brass maker in the street of Szchen-Kiang. Dr. Yen carried this bone in his girdle to keep off the black, blue and yellow plagues. Chu Yi-Foy, looking upon it, wept the soft, grateful tears of an old man.

"This is twice," he said, "that you, my learned friend, have saved my life. I have hitherto given you, in token of my gratitude, the rents, rates, imposts and taxes, of two streets, and of the related alleys, courts and lanes. I now give you the weight of that bone in diamonds, in rubies, in pearls or in emeralds, as you will. And whichever of the four you choose, I give you the other three also. For is it not said by K'ung Fu-tsze, 'The good physician bestows what the gods merely promise'?"

And Dr. Yen Li-Shen lowered his eyes and bowed. But he was too old in the healing art to blush.

A *Smart Set* Circular

From Suggestions to Our Visitors, a four-page leaflet distributed in the 1921–22 era. Nathan and I, in those days, took our editorial duties very lightly, and sought to relieve them with various buffooneries. The following circular was one of several that I wrote

1. The editorial chambers are open daily, except Saturdays, Sundays and Bank Holidays, from 10.30 a.m. to 11.15 a.m.

2. Carriage calls at 11.15 a.m. precisely.

3. The Editors sincerely trust that guests will abstain from offering fees or gratuities to their servants.

4. Visitors expecting telephone calls while in audience will kindly notify the Portier before passing into the consulting rooms.

5. Dogs accompanying visitors must be left at the *garderobe* in charge of the Portier.

6. Visitors are kindly requested to refrain from expectorating out of the windows.

7. The Editors regret that it will be impossible for them, under any circumstances, to engage in conversations by telephone.

8. The Editors assume no responsibility for hats, overcoats, walking sticks or hand luggage not checked with the Portier.

9. Solicitors for illicit wine merchants are received only on Thursday, from 12 o'clock noon until 4.30 p.m.

10. Interpreters speaking all modern European languages are in daily attendance, and at the disposal of visitors, without fee.

11. Officers of the military and naval forces of the United States, in full uniform, will be received without presenting the usual letters of introduction.

12. The House Surgeon is forbidden to accept fees for the treatment of injuries received on the premises.

13. Smoking is permitted.

14. Visitors whose boots are equipped with rubber heels are requested to avoid stepping from the rugs to the parquetry.

15. A woman Secretary is in attendance at all interviews between the Editors, or either of them, and lady authors. Hence it will be unnecessary for such visitors to provide themselves with either duennas or police whistles.

16. Choose your emergency exit when you come in; don't wait until the firemen arrive.

17. Visiting English authors are always welcome, but in view of the severe demands upon the time of the Editors, they are compelled to limit the number received to 50 head a week.

18. The objects of art on display in the editorial galleries are not for sale.

19. The Editors regret that they will be unable to receive visitors who present themselves in a visibly inebriated condition.

20. Cuspidors are provided for the convenience of our Southern and Western friends.

21. The Editors beg to make it known that they find it impossible to accept invitations to public dinners, memorial services or other functions at which speeches are made, or at which persons are present who ever make speeches elsewhere.

22. The Editors assume that visitors who have had the honor of interviews with them in the editorial chambers will not subsequently embarrass them in public places by pointing them out with walking sticks.

23. Photographs of the Editors are on sale at the Portier's desk.

24. Members of the hierarchy and other rev. clergy are received only on Thursdays, from 12 o'clock noon to 4.30 p.m.

25. The Editors cannot undertake to acknowledge the receipt of flowers, cigars, autographed books, picture postcards, signed photographs, loving cups or other gratuities. All such objects are sent at once to the free wards of the public hospitals.

26. Positively no cheques cashed.

Suite Américaine

From PREJUDICES: THIRD SERIES, 1922, pp. 320–24. Aspiration was first printed in the *Smart Set*, Nov., 1921, pp. 34–35, and Eminence in the same magazine, July, 1922, p. 41

1

Aspiration

POLICE sergeants praying humbly to God that Jews will start poker-rooms on their posts, and so enable them to educate their eldest sons for holy orders. . . . Newspaper reporters resolving firmly to work hard, keep sober and be polite to the city editor, and so be rewarded with jobs as copy-readers. . . . College professors in one-building universities on the prairie, still hoping, at the age of sixty, to get their whimsical essays into the *Atlantic Monthly*. . . . Pastors of one-horse little churches in decadent villages, who, whenever they drink two cups of coffee at supper, dream all night that they have been elected bishops. . . . Delicatessen dealers who spend their lives searching for a cheap substitute for the embalmed veal used in chicken-salad. . . . Italians who wish that they were Irish. . . . Mulatto girls in Georgia and Alabama who send away greasy dollar bills for bottles of Mme. Celestine's Infallible Hair-Straightener. . . . Ashmen who pull wires to be appointed superintendents of city dumps. . . . Mothers who dream that the babies in their cradles will reach, in the mysterious after years, the highest chairs in the Red Men and the Maccabees.

. . . Contestants for the standing broad-jump champion-ship of the Altoona, Pa., Y.M.C.A. . . .

2

Diligence

Pale druggists in remote towns of the Epworth League and flannel nightgown belts, endlessly wrapping up bottles of Pe-runa. . . . Women hidden away in the damp kitchens of un-painted houses along the railroad tracks, frying tough beef-steaks. . . . Lime and cement dealers being initiated into the Knights of Pythias, the Red Men or the Woodmen of the World. . . . Watchmen at lonely railroad crossings in Iowa, hoping that they'll be able to get off to hear the United Breth-ren evangelist preach. . . . Ticket-sellers in the subway, breath-ing sweat in its gaseous form. . . . Farmers plowing sterile fields behind sad meditative horses, both suffering from the bites of insects. . . . Grocery-clerks trying to make assignations with soapy servant-girls. . . . Women confined for the ninth or tenth time, wondering helplessly what it is all about. . . . Methodist preachers retired after forty years of service in the trenches of God, upon pensions of $600 a year. . . . Wives and daughters of Middle Western country bankers, marooned in Los Angeles, going tremblingly to swami séances in dark, smelly rooms. . . . Decayed and hopeless men writing editorials at midnight for leading papers in Mississippi, Arkansas and Ala-bama. . . . Owners of the principal candy-stores in Green River, Neb., and Tyrone, Pa. . . . Presidents of one-building universities in the rural fastnesses of Kentucky and Tennessee. . . . Babies just born to the wives of milk-wagon drivers. . . . Judges on the benches of petty county courts in Vermont and Idaho. . . . Conductors of accommodation trains running be-tween Kokomo, Ind., and Logansport. . . .

3

Eminence

The leading Methodist layman of Pottawattamie county, Iowa. . . . The man who won the limerick contest conducted

by the Toomsboro, Ga., *Banner*. . . . The secretary of the
Little Rock, Ark., Kiwanis Club. . . . The man who owns the
best bull in Coosa county, Ala. . . . The tallest man in Coving-
ton, Ky. . . . The oldest subscriber to the Raleigh, N. C.,
News and Observer. . . . The most fashionable milliner in Bu-
cyrus, O. . . . The business agent of the Plasterers' Union of
Somerville, Mass. . . . The author of the ode read at the un-
veiling of the monument to General Robert E. Lee at Valdosta,
Ga. . . . The owner of the champion Airedale of Buffalo, N. Y.
. . . The first child named after Warren Gamaliel Harding.
. . . The old lady in Wahoo, Neb., who has read the Bible 38
times. . . . The youngest murderer awaiting execution in Chicago. . . . The leading dramatic critic of Des Moines. . . .
The night watchman in Penn Yan, N. Y., who once shook
hands with Admiral Dewey. . . . The Lithuanian woman in
Bluefield, W. Va., who has had five sets of triplets. . . . The
best horse doctor in Montana. . . . The highest-paid church-
choir soprano in Knoxville, Tenn. . . . The most eligible bachelor in Cheyenne, Wyo. . . . The girl who got the most votes
in the popularity contest at Egg Harbor, N. J. . . .

People and Things

From PREJUDICES: FOURTH SERIES, 1924, pp. 294–301. The Capital of
a Great Republic first appeared in the *Smart Set*, Sept., 1922, p. 46; The
High Seas in Dec., 1922, pp. 49–50, and The Shrine of Mnemosyne in
Dec., 1920, p. 41

1

The Capital of a Great Republic

THE FOURTH secretary of the Paraguayan legation. . . . The
secretary to the secretary to the Secretary of Labor. . . . The
brother to the former Congressman from the third Nebraska
district. . . . The messenger to the chief of the Senate folding-
room. . . . The door-keeper outside the committee-room of the
House committee on the disposition of useless executive papers.
. . . The stenographer to the assistant chief entomologist of

the Bureau of Animal Industry. . . . The third assistant chief computer in the office of the Naval Almanac. . . . The assistant Attorney-General in charge of the investigation of postal frauds in the South Central States. . . . The former wife of the former secretary to the former member of the Interstate Commerce Commission. . . . The brother to the wife of the *chargé d'affaires* of Czecho-Slovakia. . . . The press-agent to the chaplain of the House. . . . The acting substitute elevator-man in the Washington monument. . . . The aunt of the sister of the wife of the officer in charge of ceremonials, State Department. . . . The neighbor of the cousin of the step-father of the sister-in-law of the President's pastor. . . . The superintendent of charwomen in Temporary Storehouse B7, Bureau of Navy Yards and Docks. . . . The assistant confidential clerk to the chief clerk to the acting chief examiner of the Patent Office. . . . The valet to the Chief Justice.

2

Ambassadors of Christ

Fifth avenue rectors with shining morning faces, preaching on Easter to pews packed with stockbrokers, defendants in divorce suits, members of the Sulgrave Foundation and former Zionists. . . . Evangelists of strange, incomprehensible cults whooping and bawling at two or three half-witted old women and half a dozen scared little girls in corrugated iron tabernacles down near the railroad yards. . . . Mormon missionaries pulling doorbells in Wheeling, W. Va., and Little Rock, Ark., and handing naughty-looking tracts to giggling colored slaveys. . . . Methodist candidates for the sacred frock, sent out to preach trial sermons to backward churches in the Mail-order Belt, proving magnificently in one hour that Darwin was an ignoramus and Huxley a scoundrel. . . . Missionaries in smelly gospel-shops along the waterfront, expounding the doctrine of the Atonement to boozy Norwegian sailors, half of them sound asleep. . . . Little fat Lutherans with the air of prosperous cheesemongers. . . . Dunkards with celluloid collars and no neckties. . . . Former plumbers, threshing-machine engineers and horse-doctors turned into United Brethren bishops. . . . Missionaries collecting money from the mill children in Raleigh, N. C., to convert the Spaniards and Italians to Calvinism. . . . Episcopal archdeacons cultivating the broad English *a*. . . . Swedenborgians trying to explain the "Arcana Cœlestia" to flabbergasted newspaper reporters. . . . Polish clergymen leaping out of the windows at Polish weddings in Johnstown, Pa., hoping that the next half-dozen beer-bottles won't hit them. . . . Quakers foreclosing mortgages. . . . Baptists busy among the women.

3

The High Seas

The boy who sits in the bucket of tar. . . . The buxom stewardess who comes in and inquires archly if one rang. . . . The humorous piano-tuner who tunes the grand piano in the music-room in the 15-16ths-tone scale. . . . The electric fan which, when a stray zephyr blows in through the porthole, makes a noise like a dentist's drill. . . . The alien ship's printer who, in the daily wireless paper, reports a baseball score of 165 to 3. . . . The free Christian Science literature in the reading-room. . . . The pens in the writing-room. . . . The red-haired girl in the green sweater. . . . The boy who climbs into the lifeboat. . . . The chief steward wearing the No. 18¾ collar. . . . The mysterious pipes that run along the stateroom ceilings. . . . The discovery that one forgot to pack enough undershirts. . . . The night watchman who raps on the door at 3.30 a.m. to deliver a wireless message reading "Sorry missed you. Bon voyage." . . . The bartender who adds a dash of witch-hazel to cocktails. . . . The wilting flowers standing in ice-pitchers and spittoons in the hallway. . . . The fight in the steerage. . . . The old lady who gets stewed and sends for the doctor. . . . The news that the ship is in Long. 43°, 41', 16" W, Lat. 40°, 23', 39" N. . . . The report that the starboard propeller has lost a blade.

4

The Shrine of Mnemosyne

The little town of Kirkwall, in the Orkney Islands, in a mid-Winter mist, flat and charming like a Japanese print. . . . San

Francisco and the Golden Gate from the top of Twin Peaks.
. . . Gibraltar on a Spring day, all in pastel shades, like the
back-drop for a musical comedy. . . . My first view of the trop-
ics, the palm-trees suddenly bulging out of the darkness of
dawn, the tremendous stillness the sweetly acid smell, the im-
measurable strangeness. . . . he Trentino on a glorious morning, up from Verona to the Brenner Pass. . . . Central Germany from Bremen to Munich, all in one day, with the apple
trees in bloom. . . . Copenhagen on a wild night, with the *Polizei* combing the town for the American who upset the piano.
. . . Christiania [1] in January, with the snow-clad statue of Ibsen looming through the gloom like a ghost in a cellar. . . .
The beach at Tybee Island, with the faint, blood-curdling rattle
of the land-crabs. . . . A child playing in the yard of a God-
forsaken town in the Wyoming desert. . . . The little pile of
stones on the beach of Watling's Island, marking the place
where Columbus landed. . . . A dull night in a Buffalo hotel,
reading the American Revised Version of the New Testament.
. . . The day I received the proofs of my first book.

[1] Now Osle.

XXX. SENTENTIÆ

These maxims, epigrams and apothegms cover a long range in time. The earliest were first printed in the *Smart Set* in 1912; the latest come from note-books never printed at all. In 1916 I published a collection under the title of A Little Book in C Major. Four years later it was taken, in part, into a revised edition of A Book of Burlesques, and there survived until that book went out of print in the late 30s

The Mind of Man

WHEN a man laughs at his troubles he loses a good many friends. They never forgive the loss of their prerogative.

In any combat between a rogue and a fool the sympathy of mankind is always with the rogue.

Friendship is a common belief in the same fallacies, mountebanks and hobgoblins.

The chief value of money lies in the fact that one lives in a world in which it is overestimated.

Never let your inferiors do you a favor. It will be extremely costly.

Nature abhors a moron.

The New Logic — It would be nice if it worked. *Ergo*, it will work.

The most costly of all follies is to believe passionately in the palpably not true. It is the chief occupation of mankind.

A metaphysician is one who believes it when toxins from a dilapidated liver makes his brain whisper that mind is the boss of liver.

First stanza: Millions now living will never die. Second stanza: No more war.

I am against slavery simply because I dislike slaves.

Living with a dog is messy — like living with an idealist.

Philosophy, as the modern world knows it, is only intellectual club-swinging.

Whenever you hear a man speak of his love for his country it is a sign that he expects to be paid for it.

Conscience is the inner voice which warns us that someone may be looking.

Evil is that which one believes of others. It is a sin to believe evil of others, but it is seldom a mistake.

Men are the only animals that devote themselves, day in and day out, to making one another unhappy. It is an art like any other. Its virtuosi are called altruists.

Every failure teaches a man something, to wit, that he will probably fail again next time.

Fame — An embalmer trembling with stagefright.

Hope is a pathological belief in the occurrence of the impossible.

Immorality is the morality of those who are having a better time. You will never convince the average farmer's mare that the late Maud S. was not dreadfully immoral.

An idealist is one who, on noticing that a rose smells better than a cabbage, concludes that it will also make better soup.

Every man is his own hell.

What makes philosophy so tedious is not the profundity of philosophers, but their lack of art; they are like physicians who sought to cure a slight hyperacidity by prescribing a carload of burned oyster-shells.

Immortality is the condition of a dead man who doesn't believe that he is dead.

As I stoop to lace my shoe you clout me over the coccyx with a length of hickory (*Carya laciniosa*). I conclude instantly that you are a jackass. This is a whole process of human thought in little. This also is free will.

A celebrity is one who is known to many persons he is glad he doesn't know.

Morality is the theory that every human act must be either right or wrong, and that 99% of them are wrong.

Platitude — An idea (*a*) that is admitted to be true by everyone, and (*b*) that is not true.

Progress is the process whereby the human race is getting rid of whiskers, the vermiform appendix and God.

The difference between a moral man and a man of honor is that the latter regrets a discreditable act, even when it has worked and he has not been caught.

Remorse — Regret that one waited so long to do it.

Self-Respect — The secure feeling that no one, as yet, is suspicious.

Suicide is a belated acquiescence in the opinion of one's wife's relatives.

Temptation is an irresistible force at work on a movable body.

Tombstone — An ugly reminder of one who has been forgotten.

Truth — Something somehow discreditable to someone.

Popularity — The capacity for listening sympathetically when men boast of their wives and women complain of their husbands.

Pensioner — A kept patriot.

There are men so philosophical that they can see humor in their own toothaches. But there has never lived a man so philosophical that he could see the toothache in his own humor.

We are here and it is now: further than that all human knowledge is moonshine.

The life of man in this world is like the life of a fly in a room filled with 100 boys, each armed with a fly-swatter.

Nevertheless, it is even harder for the average ape to believe that he has descended from man.

Thanksgiving Day — A day devoted by persons with inflammatory rheumatism to thanking a loving Father that it is not hydrophobia.

As the arteries grow hard, the heart grows soft.

A sob is a sound made by women, babies, tenors, clergymen, actors and drunken men.

A bad man is the sort who weeps every time he speaks of a good woman.

Liar — (*a*) One who pretends to be very good; (*b*) one who pretends to be very bad.

It costs more to maintain ten vices than one virtue.

Before a man speaks it is always safe to assume that he is a fool. After he speaks, it is seldom necessary to assume it.

Do I let the *chandala* suffer, and consign them, as old Friedrich used to say, to statistics and the devil? Well, so does God.

A gentleman is one who never strikes a woman without provocation.

Historian — An unsuccessful novelist.

Life is a dead-end street.

Of all escape mechanisms death is the most efficient.

Masculum et Feminam Creavit Eos.

Love is the delusion that one woman differs from another.

At the end of one millennium and nine centuries of Christianity, it remains an unshakable assumption of the law in all Christian countries and of the moral judgment of Christians everywhere that if a man and a woman, entering a room together, close the door behind them, the man will come out sadder and the woman wiser.

When a woman says she won't, it is a good sign that she will. And when she says she will it is an even better sign.

Happiness is peace after strife, the overcoming of difficulties, the feeling of security and well-being. The only really happy folk are married women and single men.

When women kiss it always reminds one of prize-fighters shaking hands.

No matter how much a woman loved a man, it would still give her a glow to see him commit suicide for her.

The honeymoon is the time during which the bride believes the bridegroom's word of honor.

Every bachelor is a hero to some married woman.

At the Altar — The Bride: "At last! At last!" The Bridegroom: "Too late! Too late!"

Jealousy is the theory that some other fellow has just as little taste.

The first kiss is stolen by the man; the last is begged by the woman.

Wealth — Any income that is at least $100 more a year than the income of one's wife's sister's husband.

If women believed in their husbands they would be a good deal happier. And also a good deal more foolish.

In the duel of sex woman fights from a dreadnaught and man from an open raft.

Alimony — The ransom that the happy pay to the devil.

Temptation is woman's weapon and man's excuse.

Optimist — The sort of man who marries his sister's best friend.

When you sympathize with a married woman you either make two enemies or gain one wife and one friend.

Women do not like timid men. Cats do not like prudent rats.

He marries best who puts it off until it is too late.

In every woman's life there is one real and consuming love. But very few women guess which one it is.

A bachelor is one who wants a wife, but is glad he hasn't got her.

Women usually enjoy annoying their husbands, but not when they annoy them by growing fat.

A man always remembers his first love with special tenderness. But after that he begins to bunch them.

Dispatch from Reno — The rich leap from the bed to the altar; the poor leap from the altar to the bed.

Husband — One who played safe and is now played safely. A No. 16 neck in a No. 15½ collar.

Misogynist — A man who hates women as much as women hate one another.

Man's objection to love is that it dies hard: women's, that when it is dead it stays dead.

Women have simple tastes. They can get pleasure out of the conversation of children in arms and men in love.

Men have a much better time of it than women. For one thing, they marry later. For another thing, they die earlier.

The man who marries for love alone is at least honest. But so was Czolgosz.

When a husband's story is believed, he begins to suspect his wife.

A man always blames the woman who fools him. In the same way he blames the door he walks into in the dark.

Love begins like a triolet and ends like a college yell.

Whenever a husband and wife begin to discuss their marriage they are giving evidence at a coroner's inquest.

How little it takes to make life unbearable. . . . A pebble in the shoe, a cockroach in the spaghetti, a woman's laugh.

Man weeps to think that he will die so soon; woman, that she was born so long ago.

Whenever a woman begins to talk of anything, she is talking to, of, or at a man.

No matter how happily a woman may be married, it always pleases her to discover that there is a nice man who wishes that she were not.

Women always excel men in that sort of wisdom which comes from experience. To be a woman is in itself a terrible experience.

The worst man hesitates when choosing a mother for his children. And hesitating, he is lost.

Adultery is the application of democracy to love.

Husbands never become good; they merely become proficient.

The worst of marriage is that it makes a woman believe that all other men are just as easy to fool.

The great secret of happiness in love is to be glad that the other fellow married her.

A man may be a fool and not know it — but not if he is married.

No man is ever too old to look at a woman, and no woman is ever too fat to hope that he will look.

Bachelors have consciences. Married men have wives.

Bachelors know more about women than married men. If they didn't they'd be married, too.

Man is a natural polygamist. He always has one woman leading him by the nose and another hanging on to his coat-tails.

All women, soon or late, are jealous of their daughters; all men, soon or late, are envious of their sons.

The Citizen and the State

Every decent man is ashamed of the government he lives under.

If x is the population of the United States and y is the degree of imbecility of the average American, then democracy is the theory that $x \times y$ is less than y.

Syllogisms à la Mode — If you are against labor racketeers, then you are against the working man. If you are against demagogues, then you are against democracy. If you are against

Christianity, then you are against God. If you are against trying a can of Old Dr. Quack's Cancer Salve, then you are in favor of letting Uncle Julius die.

The New Deal began, like the Salvation Army, by promising to save humanity. It ended, again like the Salvation Army, by running flop-houses and disturbing the peace.

It takes only one Communist to ruin a labor union. It takes only one drop of *Oleum tiglii* to turn a respectable glass of rye into a Mickey Finn.

Nothing is so abject and pathetic as a politician who has lost his job, save only a retired stud-horse.

Democracy is the theory that the common people know what they want, and deserve to get it good and hard.

The war on privilege will never end. Its next great campaign will be against the special privileges of the underprivileged.

Politician — Any man with influence enough to get his old mother a job as charwoman in the City Hall.

Democracy tries an endless succession of arcana as a movie gal tries an endless series of husbands, hoping against hope for one who is sober, self-supporting, faithful, and not too watchful.

Congress consists of one-third, more or less, scoundrels; two-thirds, more or less, idiots; and three-thirds, more or less, poltroons.

If Wall Street really wants to dispose of John L. Lewis, let it invite him to a swell feed, hand him a fifty-cent cigar with a torpedo in it, and so burn off his eyebrows.

There are no institutions in America: there are only fashions.

The lunatic fringe wags the underdog.

There are now only two classes of men in the United States: those who work for their livings, and those who vote for them.

The believing mind reaches its perihelion in the so-called Liberals. They believe in each and every quack who sets up his booth on the fair-grounds, including the Communists. The Communists have some talents too, but they always fall short of believing in the Liberals.

A demagogue's mind is a beautiful mechanism. It can think anything he asks it to think.

Democracy is the art and science of running the circus from the monkey-cage.

Any defeat, however trivial, may be fatal to a savior of the plain people. They never admire a messiah with a bloody nose.

Unquestionably, there is progress. The average American now pays out twice as much in taxes as he formerly got in wages.

The real charm of the United States is that it is the only comic country ever heard of.

Chorus of Socialists: "To hell with capital!" Antiphon of anti-Socialists: "To hell with 'Das Kapital'!"

Democracy is that system of government under which the people, having 60,000,000 native-born adult whites to choose from, including thousands who are handsome and many who are wise, pick out a Coolidge to be head of the state. It is as if a hungry man, set before a banquet prepared by master cooks and covering a table an acre in area, should turn his back upon the feast and stay his stomach by catching and eating flies.

The smarter the politician, the more things he believes and the less he believes any of them.

The aim of New Deals is to exterminate the class of creditors and thrust all men into that of debtors. It is like trying to breed cattle with all cows and no bulls.

The theory seems to be that so long as a man is a failure he is one of God's chillun, but that as soon as he has any luck he owes it to the Devil.

The kind of man who demands that government enforce his ideas is always the kind whose ideas are idiotic.

Judge — A law student who marks his own examination-papers.

Jury — A group of twelve men who, having lied to the judge about their hearing, health and business engagements, have failed to fool him.

Courtroom — A place where Jesus Christ and Judas Iscariot would be equals, with the betting odds in favor of Judas.

Fine — A bribe paid by a rich man to escape the lawful penalty of his crime. In China such bribes are paid to the judge personally; in America they are paid to him as agent for the public. But it makes no difference to the men who pay them — nor to the men who can't pay them.

Lawyer — One who protects us against robbers by taking away the temptation.

In this world of sin and sorrow there is always something to be thankful for. As for me, I rejoice that I am not a Republican.

Arcana Cœlestia

Theology — An effort to explain the unknowable by putting it into terms of the not worth knowing.

Clergyman — A ticket speculator outside the gates of Heaven.

Archbishop — A Christian ecclesiastic of a rank superior to that attained by Christ.

The delusion of immortality is what ruined Egypt.

Hymn of Hate, with Coda — If I hate any class of men in this world, it is evangelical Christians, with their bellicose stupidity, their childish belief in devils, their barbarous hoofing of all beauty, dignity and decency. But even evangelical Christians I do not hate when I see their wives.

The Christian always swears a bloody oath that he will never do it again. The civilized man simply resolves to be a bit more careful next time.

Creator — A comedian whose audience is afraid to laugh.

In every unbeliever's heart there is an uneasy feeling that, after all, he *may* awake after death and find himself immortal. This is his punishment for his unbelief. This is the agnostic's Hell.

Puritanism — The haunting fear that someone, somewhere, may be happy.

Sunday — A day given over by Americans to wishing that they themselves were dead and in Heaven, and that their neighbors were dead and in Hell.

Christian — One who is willing to serve three Gods, but draws the line at one wife.

To be a successful clergyman a man must be buttered on both sides.

I read the other day a book defending the Ten Commandments. The best of all arguments for them, however, was omitted. It is that there are not forty of them.

Christian Science — The theory that, since the skyrockets following a wallop in the eye are optical delusions, the wallop itself is a delusion and the eye another.

Christian Science and the Coroner: the initiative and referendum.

A devotee on her knees in some abysmal and mysterious cathedral, the while solemn music sounds, and clouds of incense come down the wind, and priests in luxurious, operatic costumes busy themselves with stately ceremonials in a dead and not too respectable language — this is unquestionably beautiful, particularly if the devotee herself be sightly. But the same devotee aroused to hysterical protestations of faith by the shrieks and contortions of a Methodist dervish in the costume of a Southern member of Congress, her knees trembling with the fear of God, her hands clenched as if to do combat with Beelzebub, her lips discharging hosannas and hallelujahs — this is merely obscene.

The seasick passenger on an ocean liner detests the good sailor who stalks past him 265 times a day grandly smoking a large, greasy cigar. In precisely the same way the democrat hates the man who is having a better time in the world. This is the origin of democracy. It is also the origin of Puritanism.

Pastor — One employed by the wicked to prove to them by his example that virtue doesn't pay.

The Atheist Confesses — Let us thank God that there is no God.

Christendom may be defined briefly as that part of the world in which, if a man stands up in public and swears with any show of earnestness that he is a Christian, all his auditors will laugh.

God must love the poor, said Lincoln, or he wouldn't have made so many of them. He must love the rich, or he wouldn't divide so much *mazuma* among so few of them.

Show me a Puritan and I'll show you a son-of-a-bitch.

This and That

In the long run all battles are lost, and so are all wars.

Osteopath — One who argues that all human ills are caused by the pressure of hard bone upon soft tissue. The proof of his theory is to be found in the heads of those who believe it.

A newspaper is a device for making the ignorant more ignorant and the crazy crazier.

Pathology would remain a lovely science, even if there were

no therapeutics, just as seismology is a lovely science, though no one knows how to stop earthquakes.

American Proverbs of Tomorrow — Set a *ganov* to catch a *ganov*. There's many a slip 'twixt the *shidduchin* and the *chuppa*. Many a true word is spoken by a *marshallik*. No man was ever as *fromm* as a *bachur* looks. The *goy* is not afraid of the *cherem*.

Conscience is a mother-in-law whose visit never ends.

What the South really needs is fewer scrub bulls — on the human level.

The Americans are the illegitimate children of the English.

To believe that Russia has got rid of the evils of capitalism takes a special kind of mind. It is the same kind that believes that a Holy Roller has got rid of sin.

Anyhow, the hole in the doughnut is at least digestible.

Anti-Vivisectionist — One who gags at a guinea-pig and swallows a baby.

Psychotherapy — The theory that the patient will probably get well anyhow, and is certainly a damned ijjit.

Is it hot in the rolling-mill? Are the hours long? Is $15 a day not enough? Then escape is very easy. Simply throw up your job, spit on your hands, and write another "Rosenkavalier."

Eugenics is the theory that charm in a woman is the same as charm in a prize-fighter.

It is only in countries where there is no wine, *e.g.*, England, that the answer to Genesis IV, 9 is yes.

XXXI. APPENDIX

Catechism

From Miscellaneous Notes, Prejudices: Fifth Series,
1926, p. 304.
First printed in the *American Mercury*, Sept., 1924, p. 63

Q. If you find so much that is unworthy of reverence in the United States, then why do you live here?
A. Why do men go to zoos?

Epitaph

From the *Smart Set*, Dec., 1921, p. 33

IF, after I depart this vale, you ever remember me and have thought to please my ghost, forgive some sinner and wink your eye at some homely girl.

HENRY LOUIS MENCKEN was born in Baltimore, Maryland, on September 12, 1880, and died there during the night of January 28–9, 1956. A son of August and Anna (Abhau) Mencken, he was educated privately and at the Baltimore Polytechnic. He married (August 27, 1930) Sara Powell Haardt, who died on May 31, 1935.

Mencken became a reporter for the Baltimore *Morning Herald* in 1899, its city editor in 1903, and editor of the *Evening Herald* in 1905. He served on the staff of the Baltimore *Sun* from 1906 to 1910 and on that of the *Evening Sun* from 1910 to 1917 and again from 1920 to 1935. But he never ceased to be associated with the *Sun* papers, and was for many years a director of their publishers, the A. S. Abell Company. He became literary critic of the *Smart Set* in 1908, and was its co-editor (with George Jean Nathan) from 1914 to 1923. With George Jean Nathan he founded *The American Mercury* and was its sole editor from 1924 to 1933.